Joseph Grigely

My Two Birthplaces

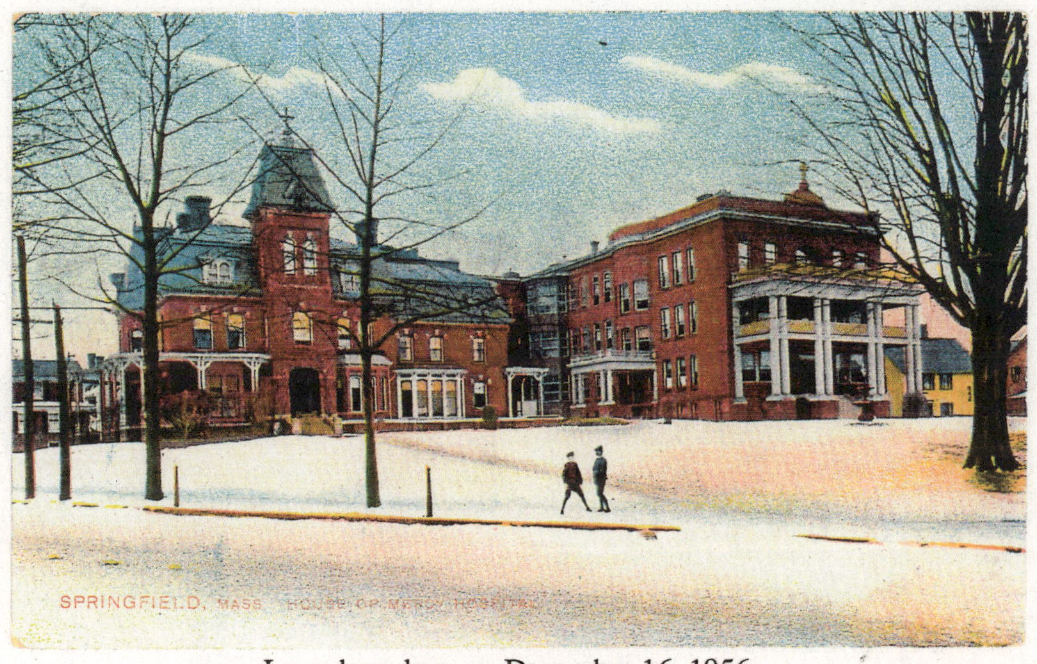

I was born here on December 16, 1956

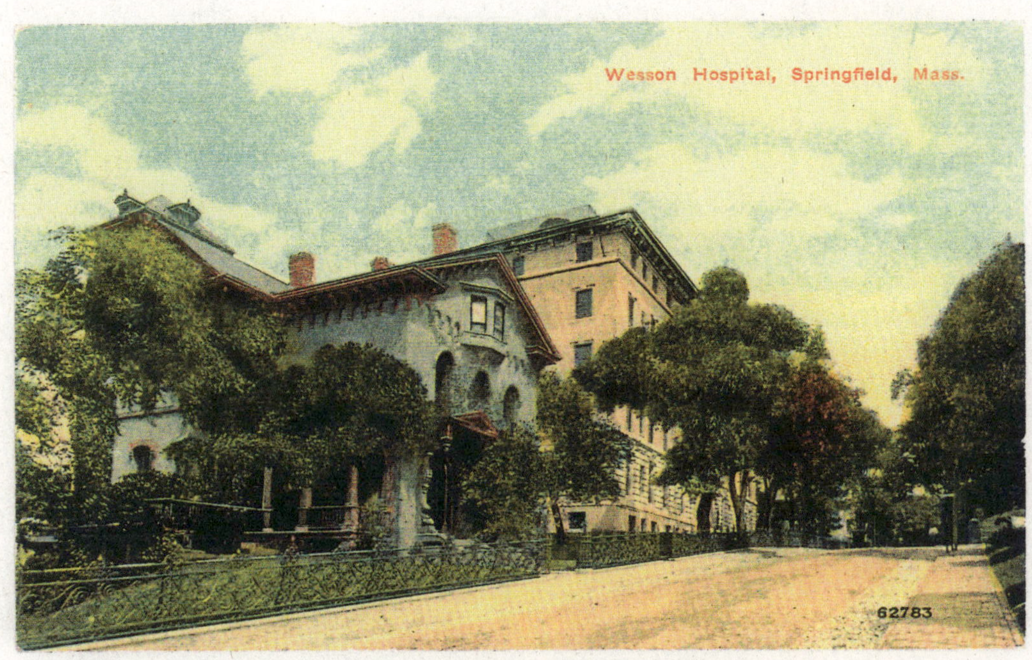

I was born here on June 9, 1967

Frontispiece: Joseph Grigely, *My Two Birthplaces*, 1991. Color Xerox

Otherhow

Essays and Documents on Art and Disability 1985–2024

Joseph Grigely

Letters, Statements, Proposals, Incidents: Part 2, Access

Advocacy

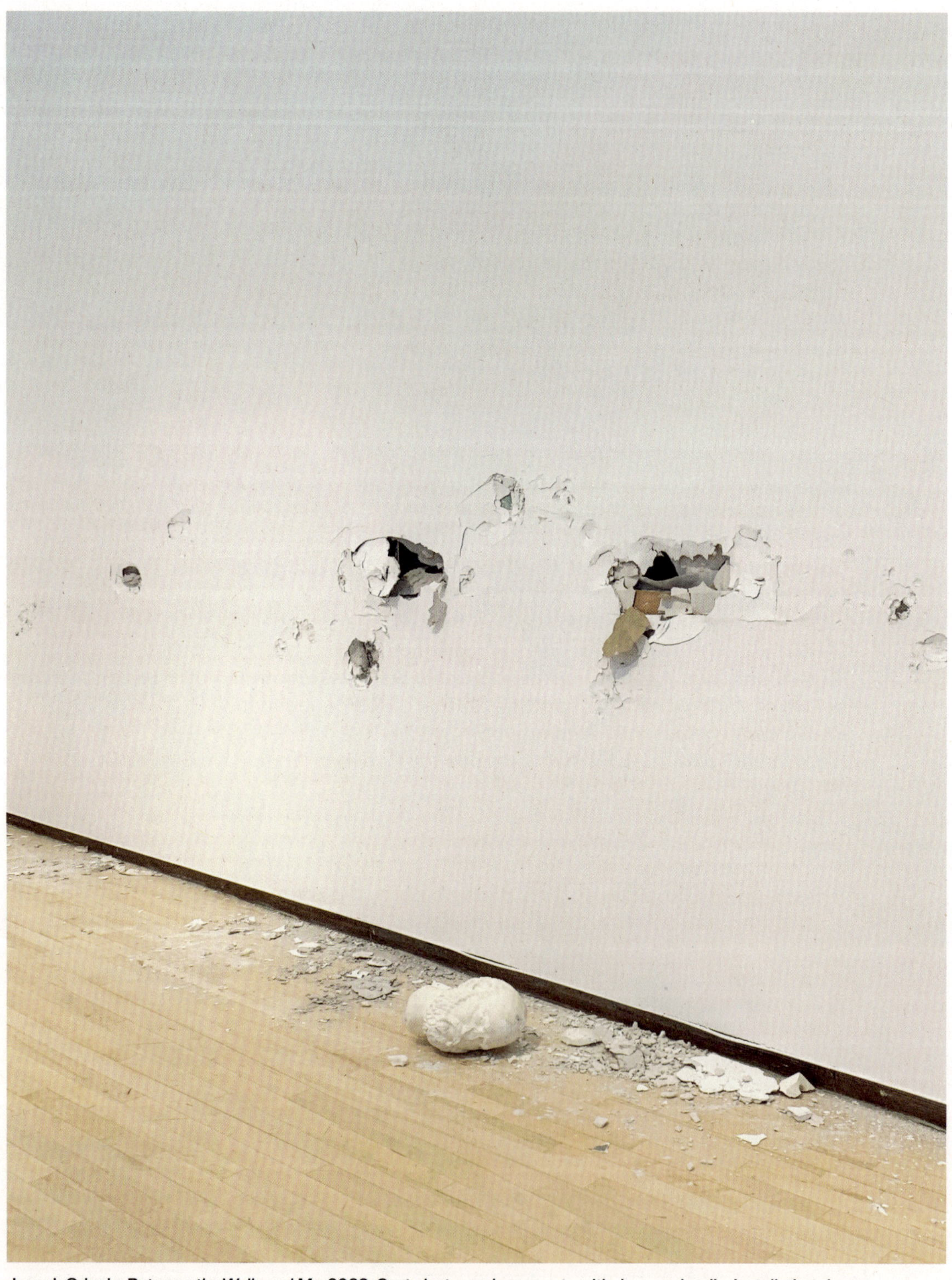

Joseph Grigely, *Between the Walls and Me*, 2023. Cast plaster and aggregate with damaged walls. Installation view, Massachusetts Museum of Contemporary Art, 2023. Photo: Jon Verney

> One writes out of one thing only—one's own experience. Everything depends on how relentlessly one forces from this experience the last drop, sweet or bitter, it can possibly give. This is the only real concern of the artist, to recreate out of the disorder of life that order which is art.
> —James Baldwin

I do not remember which incident was the first one to leave a mark. It might have been when, at the age of ten, I had a hearing test, and the audiological report, handwritten by Dr. Harold Schuknecht at the Massachusetts Eye and Ear Infirmary, said quite plainly: "Audiometry reveals profound hearing loss—so advised patient and parents." Or maybe it was later, when I asked the dean during my senior year of college if I could take a class in sign language instead of Latin, and he said no, because Latin would be better for me if I wanted to go to graduate school. Or maybe it was the time in the 1990s when a bank denied me a credit card because I did not have a "verifiable" telephone number. Or maybe it was during the lead-in to my participation in the 2000 Whitney Biennial, when I asked for a sign language interpreter for the opening and was told no by both the exhibition manager and the museum director. Or maybe it was one of the many dozens of incidents that took place over the years while working professionally as an artist and educator, where my deafness caused an impasse of some kind—usually regarding access. Almost mechanically, I saved relevant documentation—faxes, letters, emails, photos, and related evidence—not because I anticipated a story they might someday tell, but because they held within them my state of being—a state of unresolved conflict. Some of these documents later served as the basis of an essay, or a lecture, or an artwork, or even an access lawsuit, and these in turn—the drafts, the proposals, the legal briefs—became additional layers of documentation. A life with a disability fills a lot of archive boxes.

Otherhow: Essays and Documents on Art and Disability, 1985–2024 is, as the title suggests, a critical miscellany that collects essays and related material I wrote and gathered over the past forty years, working primarily as an artist and educator, and doing both as a deaf person. Being deaf touched everything I did: how I imagined and made my work; how I communicated about it; how I developed around it a practice and a career. While the Americans with Disabilities Act (ADA) was passed in 1990, it would be many years—arguably decades—before it became part of the operational consciousness of educational and arts institutions. Prior to this, in the 1980s, I was teaching literary and cultural studies, both at Gallaudet University (where my students were deaf) and Stanford (where they were hearing), and trying at the same time to make sense out of things. There was then no "disability studies" as we know the discipline today; it largely emerged after 2000. There was no genre of "disability art" either. The transition from the 1980s to the 1990s was a time of uncertainty and ambiguity, and it wasn't clear to me how to place or otherwise locate disability within the space of my work as an artist and literary scholar. My first exhibitions that folded together art and disability included *Body Signs* at Washington Project for the Arts in 1993, and *Conversations with the Hearing* at White Columns in New York in 1994. These two exhibitions were based on different bodies of work: At WPA, I presented a series of dispersion paintings and conceptual sculptures that addressed the ways eugenic thinking sought to maintain a medical model of disability by repairing and rehabilitating the disabled body. It was a very political show. The show at White Columns did something different by using my conversation notes with hearing people and making from a disabling condition an enabling form of art—where, rather than making art *about* disability, I was making art *with* my disability. Over subsequent years, I continued to make art that explored these extremes between political and abstract thought and aesthetics—not just in galleries, or in publications, but in the space of legal filings.

The documents in this book have as their subject either art or disability, and often both at the same time. Some were composed with the intention of having a public audience; some are more incidental. The materials include essays, letters and emails, public statements, exhibition proposals, and a genre of writing which, for lack of a better term, can be called complaints. Together, they constitute a historiography of art and disability during the post-ADA period. Chapter 1 begins with an essay in the form of postcards, "Postcards to Sophie Calle," a meditative critique of Calle's installation *The Blind* that was first published in 1993 in the Swiss art journal *Parkett*. It was my first formal effort to write about art and disability, and I approached the topic with a mixture of intrigue and bewilderment. Calle's show rubbed me the wrong way, but I wasn't sure how or why this was so—was it me? was it her?—and this essay, like others that followed, was largely about trying to understand how disability is simultaneously represented and misrepresented in society and culture. Chapter 2 focuses on lectures that I gave as a visiting artist at various institutions, and these present many of the same topics, reshaped into a verbal and visual narrative, where art gets to tell some of the story. Chapter 3 consists of interviews with curators and critics. Chapters 4 and 5 include letters, statements, and exhibition proposals. These chapters expose the largely private underside of the art world, and how it is not so much about the art itself as it is about human interactions that are part of the process of realizing exhibitions. Chapter 6 documents advocacy efforts in the shape of formal disability-discrimination filings with the Department of Justice, as well as lawsuit filings and consent decrees, to the extent they can be shared. "Discrimination" as a concept is very abstract, and when it comes to formal complaints, it is interpreted in very precise and objective quantification. These details, which are almost dizzying, are documented in the suit and consent decree for *United States of America v. GPH Management, LLC*. I hesitated to include these documents in this collection, but they make concrete a story about how what was originally perceived by the hotel's attorneys as a "consumer complaint" was, when all the details were considered, a civil rights complaint.

The documents in this book are not just about the relationship between me as an artist and my disability, but are, perhaps more important, about the art world and its relationship to disability more generally—particularly in the years following the passage of the ADA. By this time the art world had begun to understand better its relationship with diverse states of being, and how making art is synonymous with making identity. Between Linda Nochlin's essay "Why Have There Been No Great Women Artists?" (1971) and Thelma Golden's *Black Male* show at the Whitney Museum of American Art (1994–95), museum programming started to acknowledge a shift toward increasing diversity. But disability remained on the fringes—not so much disparaged as neglected, as if it was a subject too awkward and unresolved to address. When I wrote most of this material, I was in many instances working without precedent—there were no direct models to lean on for guidance, although I did benefit from the indirect influence of the civil rights movement—legally in the writings of Thurgood Marshall, and culturally in the work of James Baldwin. Both were models of temperate equanimity, which I repeatedly failed to emulate. It was Baldwin more than anyone who taught me that disability is largely about an imbalance of power between the body and society. He teases from binary conditions the sense in which it is more about conflicts, conundrums, and invisible riddles couched in the guise of white and Black. "Progress" is presented as a form of suspended balance—a form of give-and-take, where advocacy, legislation, and lawsuits all play out. Baldwin's strength was in being outspoken and plainspoken in the same breath of the same sentence—a remarkable achievement. Like Baldwin, I wanted moral justice, and I reacted with appreciable anger when institutions looked down on disability as not being their problem, much less their responsibility—such as when the Modern Language Association refused to provide interpreters for a conference I was presenting at, saying that since they received no federal funding, they were not obligated to provide interpreting. I didn't want excuses. Working alone on these issues for the most part, and finding my own employers unwilling to support and facilitate access requests, created a skewed and imbalanced approach to institutional access. Advocacy became a second job—or maybe it was really my first job, and teaching and making art my second and third jobs. They were all inextricable.

Chapters 4, 5, and 6 present a range of access complaints and statements I wrote over the years. Complaints are an awkward genre. They have a legitimate place in the history of advocacy in civil rights, something discussed in detail in Sara Ahmed's book *Complaint!* Complaints are a form of institutional critique: They put to the test policies and procedures, because the institutional mechanisms that relate to disability and access are largely experimental and unproven administrative designs. Sometimes they work; sometimes they don't. Sometimes having a great access policy means little when the human agency required to implement it fails to do so. Complaints are simply part of the process, a sort of feedback loop. But complaints, for the lack of a better way of putting it, are not pretty: They often divert attention from the substance of the complaint to the person making the complaint. Reviewing the dozens of complaints I have made over the years with art museums, colleges, airlines, banks, and hospitals, it is an onerous task to compose a sequence that holds meaning and relevance for the reader—and does not simply come across as a diatribe by an offended person. Sometimes this can't be avoided—you can't hide in a complaint: You own it, it's yours, so it's an obligation to see it as part of your being. And when you are your own voice of complaint, it is hard to find the calm and collected thought to cultivate anger into something that is both eloquent and productive. But for all their messiness, complaints and institutional responses to them document a particular transitional moment in history that *should* be messy. In hindsight, as I look back at many of the documents in this volume, I want to think they are probably as good as I could have written them at the time—that perhaps a few sentences might be changed here and there, but the fundamental arguments were as I wished them to be.

Most of the documents printed here are presented as originally written; minor corrections have been made to spelling and punctuation. To avoid repetition, I have also deleted some redundant material where it is presented in another text. Most of the texts are preceded by editorial notes to provide history about the incident or incidents that precipitated the work, and their eventual resolution. Others are self-explanatory.

I am grateful to the team at Primary Information for their thoughtful consideration of the intricacies of taking thirty years of unwieldy documentation and reshaping it into a book. In particular, I want to thank my editor James Hoff and my designer Siiri Tännler for their fastidious attention to detail.

I would like to thank the institutions that previously published some of the essays and other documents in this book. These include *Parkett*; *Michigan Quarterly Review*; *Gagarin*; *VoCA, Voices in Contemporary Art*; Kunstmuseum Bern; *Journal of Visual Culture*; The Douglas Hyde Gallery, Dublin; *Artforum*; *The Chronicle of Higher Education*; *Ursula*; and the Bowdoin College Museum of Art. I am also grateful to the institutions that invited me to give lectures that are printed here for the first time: the University of California, Berkeley; the College Art Association; Architectural Association, London; the Society for Contemporary Art at the Art Institute of Chicago; Studium Generale Rietveld Academie; and CalArts.

I am grateful for the many people who have taken a principled position in supporting disability access as it relates to the art world. This usually begins with mutual support among disabled artists and critics, and among those whose conversations have been meaningful to me I want to thank Aaron Williamson and the late Katherine Araniello (who together formed the group the Disabled Avant-Garde), Katherine Sherwood, Ryan Gander, Ana García Jácombe, Andy Slater, Cai Steele, Kristin Johnson, Stephen Brathwaite, Thomas Rapai, Georgina Kleege, Stephen Lapthisophon, Alexandra Trencséni, and Emily Barker.

I would like to thank gallerists, curators, and colleagues whose support and care, in one way or another, made a difference to my practice: Andrew Heyward, Florence Bonnefous, Nadine Gandy, Francesca Pia, Ralf Beil, Anthony Elms, Pierre Von-Ow, Tess Davey, Gordon Hall,

Forrest Nash, Paula Hayes, Ellen Cantor, Ben Kinmont, Marcia Tucker, Emily Watlington, Andrew Witkin, Ian Berry, Irene Hofmann, Julie Rodrigues Widholm, Paul Longmore, Cathy Kudlick, Lennard Davis, Denise Markonish, Debra Singer, Bess Williamson, Danny Floyd, Kristi McGuire, Susan Holt, Lisa Bessette, Amanda Cachia, Ine Gevers, John M. Hull, Ellen Tani, Don Russell, Daniel Birnbaum, Diane Brentari, Molly Nesbit, and Hans Ulrich Obrist. I am also grateful for the support and insights of a number of my former students, especially those who have taken my class Theorizing Disability, as well as others who have said and done things that have stayed with me: Dizzy Ransmeier, Seth Stolbun, Juan Herrera, Karen Archey, Kate Korroch, Evan Fusco, Dove ER, Doug Montalbano, and Jenny Schmid.

Many of my assistants wrangled with my thinking about art and disability over the years, sometimes in ways we didn't plan for or expect, but with results that were regularly surprising. Among them I'd like to thank Paige Sarlin, Emma Cole, Jeremy Pellington, Katy Niner, Jesse Choy-Gong, Chance Roberts, Ahnali Tran, Rachel Wang, and, especially, Tess Davey. When we filed a large DOJ complaint, it was Tess who suggested that we needed more than just the law on our side: We needed God too, and maybe we should also seek a papal indulgence to bolster our case? We didn't. We should have.

I'd never thought in my lifetime I'd be thanking lawyers, but here I am thanking lawyers, among them the New York District Attorney Brian Feldman, who worked in Preet Bharara's office and oversaw *United States of America v. GPH Management, LLC.* I also want to acknowledge the ADA Archive at the Department of Justice, which has made crucial legal documentation—including my own—publicly accessible. I'm especially grateful to Doug Parker, Laura Rovner, and the staff of Georgetown University's Institute for Public Representation, which oversaw *Grigely v. Union Station Redevelopment Corp., et al.* The late William Van Wyke has always played a role in my thinking about disability—in law, in language, and in life. The afternoons we spent discussing these topics, while drinking Rolling Rock and eating pistachios on the porch of our house at 810 Silver Spring Avenue in Maryland are greatly missed. There are other lawyers and firms I would like to thank, but cannot do so in a public forum because of nondisclosure agreements.

In the process of interacting with others professionally I have had the satisfaction of working with a number of especially skilled and savvy sign language interpreters. But they didn't just interpret: When the occasion required it, they made it their challenge to explain to individuals and to institutions what needed to be done to create effective communication for everyone. They were, without exception, the most critical cogs of my professional practice. Among them I'd like to thank Josh Garrett, Amy Kisner, Kacie Hall, Shelly Liuzza, Elisabeth Treger, Diana Thorpe, Michael Albert, Rivka Hozinsky, Kevin Cikatricis, Mary Higgins, and Lissa Zeviar.

My most important acknowledgements are to Amy Vogel, who was always there when I needed her. To Girma Grigely, for perspective. And to the family dogs, Kunya, Bonnie, and Ollie, who shared with me the sounds they heard.

Essays on Art, Culture, and Disability

Postcards to Sophie Calle, 1991

Originally published in *Parkett*, vol. 36, June 1993.

The "Postcards to Sophie Calle" were written during the spring of 1991 when I stumbled onto Sophie Calle's installation *The Blind* at Luhring Augustine Gallery in New York City. At that time I was living in Washington, DC, and teaching literary studies at Gallaudet University, America's first and only liberal arts college for deaf students; I also had a studio in Baltimore and made regular trips to New York to see exhibitions. It was only a year earlier, in 1990, that the Americans with Disabilities Act had become a federal law, and disability was slowly being reconceptualized as a social rather than physiological construction—it was emerging as a new paradigm that was also gradually becoming part of the public consciousness.

Driving back to Washington that evening, I started to write out some thoughts on the scraps of paper I regularly carry with me. Phrases, sentences, paragraphs. At this point, there was not a lot of critical scholarship related to what would eventually become known as disability studies.

A week later, I was back in New York. And the next week. And the next week.

While driving back to Washington each week, my brief handwritten notes started to take shape as a narrative. Without quite realizing it, I was working with a structure that had no beginning and no end; it was all middle—random, reactive thoughts that addressed, individually, a single topic or idea that emerged from repeated contact with the exhibition. After five weeks, there were about forty postcards, and some unfinished ones too. It was one of those things that seemed unfinishable. Yet they were personally satisfying in a way my scholarly writing was not. This is because they were the first piece of writing I produced as an academic that I didn't feel obligated to write. On the last day of the exhibition, I took photocopies of the postcards with me to New York, and with the gallery's permission handed out copies to visitors. I also brought a Braille copy of the text with me, on the off chance the gallery might have a blind visitor that day. Finally, I gave to the gallery a set of postcards and asked that they be forwarded to Calle.

My first attempts to publish the "Postcards" with mainstream cultural publications did not get far. Was it me? Was it them? I sent the "Postcards" to Mary Johnson, who was then editor of *The Disability Rag*, a journal focused on disability activism, asking her for feedback. I explained that my goal in the "Postcards" was to question the discourse with which we discuss representations of difference in contemporary society. Calle's art and its relation to the disabled provided a convenient framework for this discussion. Sophie Calle may very well have been a fiction; it's merely fortuitous that she created herself, thereby saving me the trouble of having to invent her.

I could have published the "Postcards" in *The Disability Rag*, but that is not who my audience was—it was the art world I wanted to reach. When Calle came to New York some months later, we met at Bubby's in Tribeca for pie and coffee and a long conversation. It was at her behest that a selection of sixteen of the "Postcards" was published in *Parkett* in 1993. The complete set of postcards was later printed in *Michigan Quarterly Review* (Spring 1998), and subsequently reprinted in the book *The Body Aesthetic: From Fine Art to Body Modification* in 2000. Twenty-five years after its initial publication, I reprinted the full sequence of postcards for Ellen Tani's 2018 exhibition *Second Sight: The Paradox of Vision in Contemporary Art* at the Bowdoin College Museum of Art. That same year, a Spanish version was prepared by Maite Barrera Villarías for the ONCE Foundation Biennial in Madrid.

Dear Sophie,

I am writing to you about your New York show at Luhring Augustine in the spring of 1991, particularly one installation: *Les Aveugles*. My curiosity—or is it my concern?—is a reflection of anomalies and ambiguities: New York, with its unforgiving inaccessibility, is not a city of patience, nor is Luhring Augustine an art space where one expects the voice of an oppressed minority; and you, Sophie Calle, a professed voyeur of private lives, what is this installation you present to us?

On a small pedestal in the center of the room is a lectern on which is placed the conceptual locus of *Les Aveugles*: "*I met people who were born blind. Who had never seen. I asked them what their image of beauty was*."

Around the room framed texts record the responses of these people: brief, printed declarations of beauty. I—like others around me—am easily taken in by these voices and their resonance:

> What pleases me aesthetically is a man's body, strong and muscular.
>
> Hair is magnificent. Especially African hair. I curl up in women's long hair. I pretend I'm a cat and meow.
>
> In the Rodin Museum, there is a naked woman with very erotic breasts and a terrific ass. She is sweet, she is beautiful.

I am—how shall I say it?—entranced. No other word will do.

Yours,
Joseph

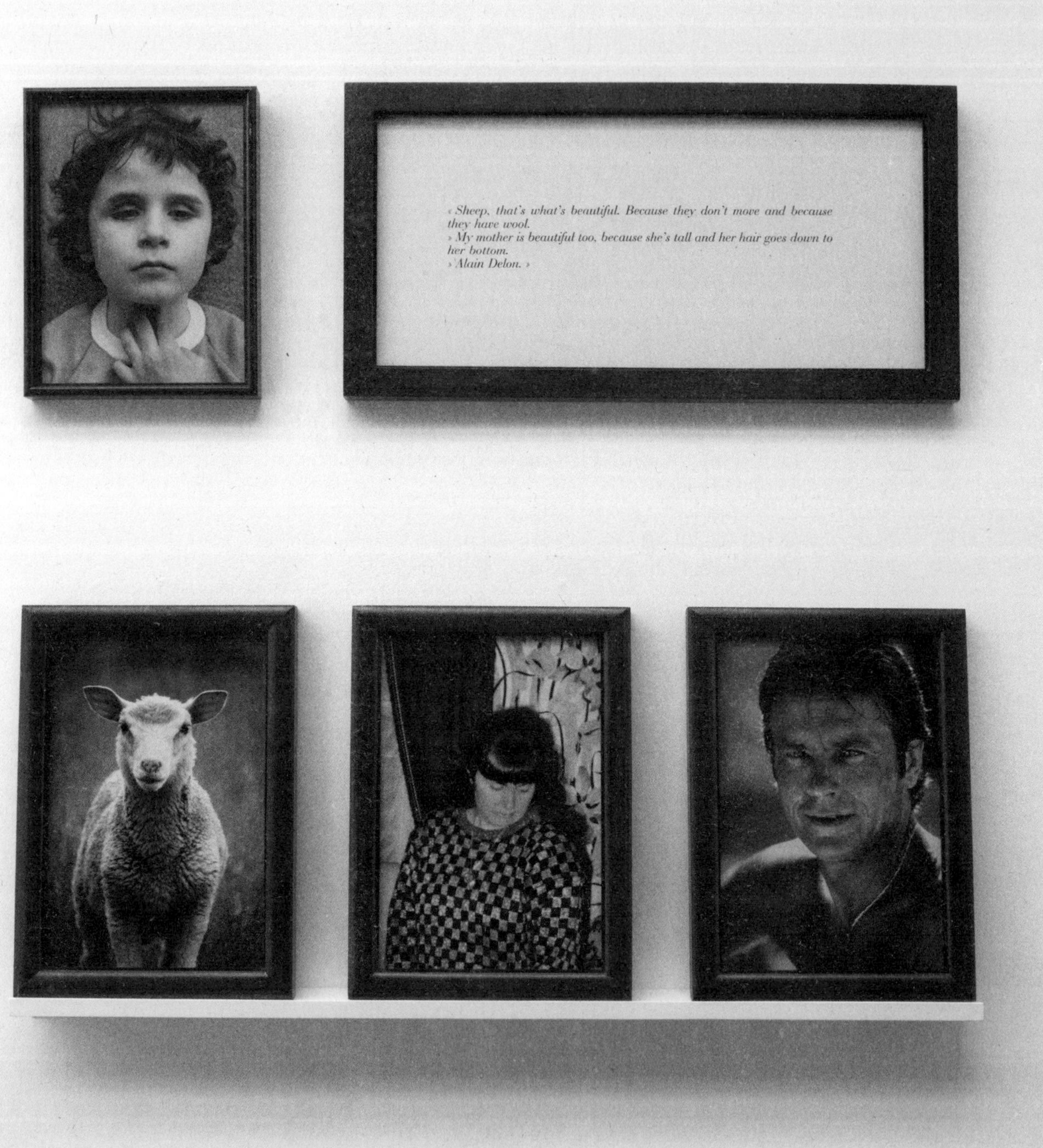

Sophie Calle, *The Blind*, 1986/89. Luhring Augustine Gallery, New York, 1991

Dear Sophie,

My entrancement is mitigated by something troubling about these words, and what is troubling is that they are, shall we say, *forthright*. They do not apologize for the fact that it is the body, the engendered body particularly, that must be touched to be seen. This is the tactile gaze of the blind. It is a gaze unconditioned by whatever feminism and sexual politics have taught us about touching. The terms and conditions by which this tactile gaze exists thus cannot be judged by our own standard, where the actions of the blind become rendered—I use that word advisedly—into our vocabulary of tactile violence. This touching is not about feeling, not about touching even, but about seeing. Touching itself is elided; it is a semantic projection of our own physiology, not that of the blind. If everyone in the world were blind, perhaps touching would be called seeing.

Am I being too romantic? Quite possibly. But inasmuch as the deaf do not see sign language as a pretty way of communicating—it's language, language pure and simple—I think the same can be said about this tactile gaze: It's about seeing, not about touching. This is the inevitable effect of an imposed transmodality: It reconfigures our physiological conventions and the language with which we describe those conventions. This room and the voices of the people within it require much patience, Sophie. I need to slow down here, we all need to slow down and begin to try to understand what is behind this tactile gaze—we need to rediscover the act of seeing, and should we freeze up at the sight—*our* sight—of this seeing-as-touching, it is our preconceptions that freeze us and our unwillingness—not inability, but unwillingness—to see what we are seeing.

And what are we seeing, Sophie?

Yours,
Joseph

Dear Sophie,

Beguiled now, I am almost afraid to face the photographs that supplement these texts, almost afraid to go past the honest audacity of this language to that which lies beyond: images that presume to be of the objects, people, places, and passions described. But here they are: the Rodin, her erotic breasts and terrific ass flattened by Ektachrome into two dimensions; a woman's head covered with blond hair; a man's body tangled in sheets. Yet, the most troubling part remains: your photographs of the faces of these blind people: their signatures. I am arrested by the fact that these images do not, because of their visual modality, return themselves to the blind. *Since your face is not available to me, why should my face be available to you?* An echo from somewhere, but I cannot pin it down. Something seems wrong to me: I am able to gaze, look, stare into the faces, into the eyes, of faces and eyes that cannot stare back. "Subjects," they are called. I feel I am in the presence of a social experiment. I feel I am being watched, feel as if I am a part of this experiment. Alone and not alone, I am uncomfortable.

Yours,
Joseph

Dear Sophie,

I hate myself here, yet I am taken in, seduced, drawn closer to this cultural keyhole. I struggle with my ambivalences—don't we all, don't you?—and I struggle with these images: hypostatization, the inscribed voice, and Sophie Calle's photographic interpretation of that voice. I look closer at the voices, try to listen, try to expunge the images that intervene—the faces, the photographs, the presence of Sophie Calle. It isn't easy. The photographs of the voices, your photographs, your interpretations, are resolutely hermeneutic: They crowd around me, crowd around the texts, impose themselves, and in the end reveal not so much the voices of the blind as the voice of Sophie Calle. I turn from the keyhole; I feel guilty, angry. Pushing away, I push myself closer.

Yours,
Joseph

Dear Sophie,

One thing becoming clear just now is that recent cultural representations of the disabled are often, it seems, mediated by those who are from outside the experience: Nicholas Nixon's photographs of blind children, Frederick Wiseman's documentary films on schools for the Deaf and the Blind, and Nancy Burson's photographs of children with craniofacial disorders. All of these works have, I must admit, brilliant, sensitive, and (in)sightful moments, but they simultaneously evince a certain awkwardness in the fact that they remain "documentary" works. They are, that is, representations that are at best interpretations, like your own photographs. Looking at this art, people remain on the outside looking in, looking in through the camera's eye, looking in through the double turn of culture and aesthetics—looking in, that is, at the inextricable tangle of truth and fiction, at a tangle that will never, can never, untangle itself. Nor, I suppose, can we.

Yours,
Joseph

Dear Sophie,

I'm stepping back now, stepping outside of this room, stepping into the register of contemporary critical discourse and thoughts about how issues concerning the disabled fit into paradigms of this discourse. Perhaps you are aware that one acknowledgment of postcolonial criticism is how our predecessors engaged in cultural voyeurism and aesthetic appropriation. Both in art and literature, modernism arguably owes much of its existence to the confluence of "primitive" aesthetics and discourse. By reifying aspects of the colonized other into a Western white male ethos, our cultural practices evolved as a mode of "refined" (and hence permissible, even desirable) barbarism. Perhaps unconsciously, this barbarism remains within us, remains—dare I say it?—within your work: The other is not a colonized other living elsewhere, but a native other, a physiological other living in our midst. Why have you transcribed the voices of the blind into a medium to which they do not have access? What difference is there between gazing at the eyes of the blind or the labia of the Hottentot Venus? It is a discomfiting analogy, and I realize some people will not like it. They will be angry. Perhaps then they will begin to understand the anger of the disabled—how the gaze that acts under the guise of curiosity, like colonialist curiosity, is actually a gaze of violence. We are at a stage in cultural history where our conceptions of "otherness," to be truly other, must move beyond representations of the canonized Other. The colonized no longer necessarily live abroad; they live next door to us, and within our own homes.

Yours,
Joseph

Dear Sophie,

Despite my initial resistance to your work, I sense that there is something uniquely engaging about *Les Aveugles*. Part of my ambivalence is in realizing that what strikes me in a negative way is striking others quite differently. Is this because I am disabled and others are not? Is this because I see, as others perhaps do not, a convoluted relationship between the studied history of colonization and the (largely) unstudied history of the disabled? Is this because I see emerging from these texts the horror of domestic colonization? "Colonization" is of course a strong word, because it suggests subjection through the use of physical force. But frightful too—perhaps more frightful when one realizes how subtle and psychologically tortuous it is—is the use of language as a colonizing agent. The oppression of native languages and attempts to control the genesis of a language by other means (what is most often termed "language planning") is an undeniable aspect of the history of many oppressed people. More difficult to acknowledge as oppression is when the language one social group uses to discuss another social group marks itself in negative terms: The identity is branded—"marked"—by language. Metaphor, particularly, is a form of latent violence that becomes manifest in the use of blindness and deafness as pejorative metaphors to imply ignorance, witlessness, and stupidity.

The phenomenon is ingrained, a reflection of how easily the disabled are stereotyped, and, in its ongoing pervasiveness, a reflection of how the changes related to racism and sexism in language have not yet been felt by the disabled. The English language has yet to respond to the vast semantic space between not being able to see and not being willing to see, between being unable to hear and being unwilling to hear. This, for example, is Elaine Showalter, writing in *Raritan* (Fall 1983):

> We can hardly fail to welcome male feminist criticism when we have so long lamented the blindness, the deafness, and indifference of the male critical establishment towards our work.

This is Kwame Anthony Appiah, writing in *Critical Inquiry* (Winter 1991):

> All aspects of contemporary African cultural life—including music and some sculpture and painting, even some writings with which the West is largely not familiar—have been influenced, often powerfully, by the transition of African societies *through* colonialism, but they are not all in the relevant sense *post*colonial. For the *post-* in postcolonial, like the *post-* in postmodernism, is the *post-* of the space-clearing gesture I characterized earlier, and many areas of contemporary African cultural life—what has come to be theorized as popular culture, in particular—are not in this way concerned with transcending, with going beyond, coloniality. Indeed, it might be said to be a mark of popular culture that its borrowings from international cultural forms are remarkably insensitive to, not so much dismissive of as blind to, the issue of neocolonialism or "cultural imperialism."

And this—it's a long quotation but needs a full citation—is from an artists' statement by Houston Conwill, Joseph De Pace, and Estella Conwill Majozo that accompanied their 1992 installation at the Brooklyn Museum:

> We create maps of language that present cultural pilgrimages and metaphorical journeys of transformation that can be experienced as rites of passage through life and death to rebirth and resurrection, fostering greater cultural awareness and understanding. They are composed of collaged and edited quotations from world music including spirituals, blues, gospel, soul, jazz, funk, samba, merengue, reggae, rap music, and freedom songs in dialect, and critical voicings from speeches of heroic models of African American culture. Their prophetic and humanistic words reflect the values and aspirations of the culture—hope, wisdom, temperance, justice, and love—and function as both a critique and a healing, addressing issues of world peace, social justice, human rights, civil rights, rights of the physically challenged, freedom, equality, democracy, history, memory, cultural identity, loss, cultural diversity, multicultural education, pro-choice, public support for the arts, ecology, and caring. They also address the universal enemies of war, hatred, racism, oppression, classism, violence, bigotry, censorship, sickness, drug addiction, sexism, ageism, apartheid, homelessness, AIDS, greed, imperialism, colonialism, militarism, historical and cultural amnesia, cross-cultural blindness, and fear of the Other.

Cross-cultural blindness? It is almost ironic, Sophie, that the people who continue to use these pejorative metaphors are also the people who have done the most to open our cultural consciousness to the diversity of the human condition. *Almost* ironic; what else, Sophie, can it mean?

Yours,
Joseph

Dear Sophie,

I have a hypothesis about the English language and how our sensitivity toward human differences is aligned with certain linguistic factors: Terms like "racism" and "sexism" work successfully in English because they use a monosyllable in an easily engaged disyllabic form, and this adds to their ubiquitous presence in everyday discourse. Hence, it is easy to see how such terms and their concomitant ideologies are more readily assimilated by the American population: "Race" and "sex" are quick draws. "Disabled"—already an inadequate term—is trisyllabic, burdened with awkwardness. "Differently abled"; "physically challenged"; "handicapped": None of these terms work, nor have we a term to describe conscious and unconscious oppression of the disabled ("paternalism" comes close, but as a metaphor it does its own share of unjust damage). Defeated by the aporia of language and the strictures of etymology, we crawl back into our present: We are we to ourselves alone. You remain you. The gulf widens.

Yours,
Joseph

Dear Sophie,

I have a little more to say about language today, about semantics particularly—that is, about meanings and connotations.

My concern just now is about why the disabled as a social group have made little progress in becoming a central part of our social consciousness. I mean, Sophie, when people talk about "multiculturalism," they seem to mean everyone except the disabled—we're something else. *Something else.* I'm sure there are many reasons why this categorizing occurs—some are political, some demographic, some educational—but the most important reason, I think, is linguistic.

A large part of the problem is that the word "disabled" is not exclusively applied to humans or human culture. When we speak of "African Americans" or "Asians," or adjectival variations ("African American history," "Asian culture," and so on), we identify a human nexus from which consequent human activity originates. We are thus constantly reminded of the human center, that it is a people, even a diverse people, not an ideology, that is at the root of signification. But this is not so for the disabled: The word "disabled" does not automatically engage a human context because it is part of an independent matrix for that which is dysfunctional or otherwise adjudicated by prefixes: *dis*abled, *ab*normal, *mal*functional. On the New Jersey Turnpike between Delaware and New York are a great number of signs that, as social texts, reiterate this matrix: "Please park disabled cars behind cones"; "Please wait with disabled vehicles." What the matrix continually communicates is that a disabling condition is a deviant condition, one which subverts an illusory normalcy and needs assistance of some kind to restore ("rehabilitate") it to a more socially accepted condition.

This is important, because the matrix assures us that society will continue to see the disabled in the same way that it sees its automobiles: in need of new fan belts, patched tires, and overhauled engines. It is not a people at the center of being, but a dysfunction. And we cannot easily undo this matrix: We cannot say "Please park broken cars behind cones," because, though semantically honest, it does not have the psychological imperative that the word "disabled" conveys. Our world is a world made of metaphors: They make language, they make ideas, and they even make poetry, but they also unmake people.

Yours,
Joseph

Dear Sophie,

Every time I get a bit of space to relax, that echo keeps coming back to me: *Since your face is not available to me, why should my face be available to you?* There is something about this utterance that is both searching and defiant, something about it that stops short of absolute resistance. Perhaps it is the curl of the question mark that dares us, hanging on to the final word: *you*.

Today it came back to me. The voice I mean; its origin. It's from John Hull's *Touching the Rock: An Experience of Blindness* (1990):

> Another aspect ... is the horror of being faceless, of forgetting one's own appearance, of having no face. The face is the mirror image of the self.
>
> Is this linked with the desire which I sometimes feel quite strongly to hide my face from others? I find I want to hold my chin and to cover my mouth with one hand, pressing my hand against my nose, as if I were wearing a mask. Is this a primitive desire to find some kind of equality? Since your face is not available to me, why should my face be available to you? Or does it spring from a sense that the face has been lost? Am I somehow mourning over the loss of the face? Am I trying to regain the assurance that I have got a face by feeling it with my own hands? I want to touch my very lips as I am speaking. Other people's voices come from nowhere. Does my own voice also come from nowhere?

I can't say more.

Yours,
Joseph

Dear Sophie,

Friday, March 22. I have returned to your show and purchased a catalogue. It is a catalogue from your 1989 exhibition at the Fred Hoffman Gallery in Santa Monica, but it is all that the gallery here has. In the introduction, Deborah Irmas—she curated your show there, yes?—writes:

> What is so compelling about this project is its didactic function. We measure our notions of beauty (which most of us seldom think about) against the simplistic but often heartfelt responses of the subjects.

I look again at the inscribed voices:

> Flowers bother me, I'm afraid to step on them.
>
> My mother stopped me from touching things. She would say: "Don't touch, it makes you look like a blind person."
>
> I don't need beauty, I don't need images in my brain.
>
> I've never come across absolute perfection.
>
> I believe what I want to believe.

... "simplistic"?

Yours,
Joseph

Dear Sophie,

The New Yorker has printed a brief description of your show in the gallery listings for April 8. In part, it goes like this:

> Calle interviewed a number of people who were born blind, asking them to describe their images of beauty, then illustrating these definitions by taking pictures of the subjects and what they described. Some of these people look blind, some of them don't.

I stop at that last sentence, reread it: *Some of these people look blind, some of them don't.* I am not sure what exactly this means, how it is intended to mean; yet it somehow means much in an unbearably unpredictable way. The very idea of looking blind, of bearing visible signs of identity, is somehow striking: One thinks of Paul Strand's photograph of a blind woman, a string with a sign card placed around her neck: "BLIND." Look at the Xerox copy I've enclosed. To what extent should otherness be a visible attribute? Would *The New Yorker* say of Robert Mapplethorpe's photographs: "Some of these people look homosexual, some of them don't"?

I look into a mirror at myself, search for my deafness, yet fail to find it. For some reason we have been conditioned to presume difference to be a visual phenomenon, the body as the locus of race and gender. Perhaps I need a hearing aid, not a flesh-colored one but a red one: a signifier that leaves little room for discursiveness, a signifier that ceremoniously announces itself. But I know too that the moment I open my mouth my nasal sibilants will give me away; I know that the moment you speak to me behind my back you will think I am ignoring you. It is a scenario that is a cliché, yet a cliché that is at times unbearably real. Once, at the Metropolitan Museum of Art, while sitting on the floor as I spent time with David's *Marat*, a museum guard struck me on the shoulder and berated me for not getting up on my feet the first time he warned me.

Some of these people look blind, some of them don't.

Yours,
Joseph

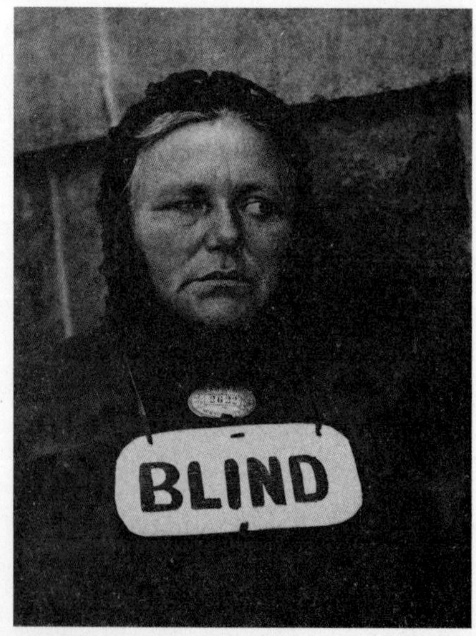

Paul Strand, *Blind Woman*, New York, 1916. Platinum print

Dear Sophie,

Can I tell you a story? It is not the sort of story that we describe as a tale with a moral, but a real story that is itself a moral.

One evening an acquaintance of mine, visiting New Orleans, went straight to the French Quarter for the sort of reasons people go to New Orleans: for the vibrations of jazz, the rhythms of blues, and the carnivalesque atmosphere that makes the French Quarter what it is. For her it was an inviting thing to do, and for a while at least it was inviting indeed. But then, early in the evening, something happened. A policeman had noticed her unsteady gait and stopped her to ask a few questions. She could not, however, understand him very well, nor did he understand her responses. He was a smart policeman and knew intoxication when he saw it.

She was arrested for public drunkenness. Her arrest record cites her "slurred speech," her "uncomprehending behavior," and her "erratic movement." She spent a very long night alone in jail trying to understand why she was arrested for being everything she was, everything she could possibly be: a young deaf woman with cerebral palsy.

Some of these people look blind, some of them don't.

Yours,
Joseph

Dear Sophie,

You might think that Joseph's story is a lie, a fiction. But when I first heard it—I—along with fourteen students who shared a room with this woman—recognized at once not the verisimilitude of the story (for there is almost none), but its raw truth: For us, all sixteen of us deaf, it was familiar, too familiar, a familiar surrealism that makes our lives inexplicable and unbelievable to everyone except ourselves.

And that is why, when we read books and see movies about the lives of disabled people, we recognize that these are not real lives, but lives filtered through the ideologies of able-bodied people, lives that are made believable so that they can be marketed to a believing audience.

Like *Les Aveugles*.

Yours,
Joseph

Dear Sophie,

My last postcard was perhaps a bit strong. I'm sorry for that. Truth is rarely polite.

You must be wondering: What is Joseph's agenda, what is the agenda of this person who questions and vilifies Sophie Calle for her aesthetics and her parsimonious gesture of magnanimity?

I will try to explain.

Part of the problem is (as I suggested in an earlier postcard) related to representations of the disabled, and what are more generally discussed as "authentic" and "inauthentic" representations of racial and sexual difference. These are really difficult terms to qualify and they substantiate themselves only by virtue of the fact that they provide the grounds for an ongoing cultural debate, the tension by which culture necessarily sustains, perpetuates, and remakes itself. I may chastise you, Sophie, but I cannot correct you. In the realm of cultural exchanges everything that is right for somebody is wrong for somebody else.

It is not an ideology I am sending you in these postcards; there is no theoretical locus here, but only a theoretical tangle, a tangle of frayed perceptions about the disabled as a part of the network of human differences. How, Sophie, can we measure and quantify something so abstract as difference? Why should we? We are all tangled in each other: Joseph, Sophie, *Les Aveugles*. All of us different, all of us equal in our differences.

A contradiction, yes. There are many of them, and that is my purpose here: to peel back the contradictions of ideology, not to create an ideology that represses contradictions. I would not be honest to you or to myself if what I said did not also reflect the chaos of who and what we are.

Yours,
Joseph

Dear Sophie,

Among the reviews and observations of your earlier exhibition of *Les Aveugles* at the Fred Hoffman Gallery in Santa Monica are the following (generous) comments:

> What is so compelling about this project is its didactic function.
> (D. Irmas in the Hoffman catalogue)
>
> All of these cerebral landscapes are emotionally piercing.
> (B. Weissman in *Artforum*, November 1989)
>
> In contrast to more theatrically inclined artists, Calle's involvement with the social yields a celebration of the individual.
> (B. Butler in the *New Art Examiner*, October 1989)
>
> In short, *The Blind*, with its open empathy for her subjects, seems symptomatic of Calle's growing self-confidence as an artist.
> (R. Pincus in *Art in America*, October 1989)

The question that necessarily follows is this: Why is it that when deaf artists use sign language in their art or blind artists engage in the tactile or auditory, their work is seen as a cliché; but when sighted, hearing artists appropriate the bodies and thoughts of the disabled their work is applauded as a magnanimous gesture?

Yours,
Joseph

Dear Sophie,

Language, which seems to be the locus here, keeps coming back to me: yours, mine, that of the blind. We mingle our selves, our voices; this room doesn't know passiveness. Perhaps unintentionally, language keeps intruding, asserting itself, taking control. It was Rousseau and Condillac who explained with a sense of irresolvable resolve the humanizing role of language in our lives, how it both makes and unmakes us, defines and de-defines what is around us—even, it seems, what one cannot see, what one cannot hear. It strikes me with a certain acuteness how a number of textual "images" of beauty began as language and remain as language, projected by the seeing on the unseeing:

> *I'm told* white is beautiful.
>
> Green is beautiful. Because every time I like something, *I'm told* it's green.
>
> The sea must be beautiful too. *They tell me* it is blue and green and that when the sun reflects in it, it hurts your eyes.

It is easy to tell disabled people what they are missing; much more difficult to listen to, and understand, what they have. Deafness, as Victor Hugo said, is an illness of the mind, not the ears.

Yours,
Joseph

Dear Sophie,

Essentially the matter at hand is difference, or, more precisely, alterity. History is filled with examples of desire to relate to the other in some configuration: to experience the other, possess it, control it. It is, almost ironically, a way of learning more about ourselves, of seeing how we fit into the grand scheme of being—the endless taxonomy of differences that we are forever trying to map, order, and organize into convenient compartments of knowledge. If it were only so simple, Sophie! But of course it isn't. And it is not always quite the gesture of disinterested benevolence that it seems to be. Difference implies a degree of dispossession; it implies that someone else is simultaneously what we want to be and what we fear to be. We want to touch this experience of difference, but we also want to do this from the safe distance of our own identity. We cannot quite forsake who we are to become someone else. We presume that to close our eyes is to experience blindness, or to sleep is to experience death—yet we know that we do not, can not, abandon the sense of self in these endeavors; we cannot "unknow" ourselves as individuals. The imagination, or as Keats might have it, the *inmagination*, cannot wholly enter into the consciousness of the other, cannot actually become the other. Empathy is an illusion, not a truth: The chameleon may change colors to blend in with its surroundings, but it does not become those surroundings.

Yours,
Joseph

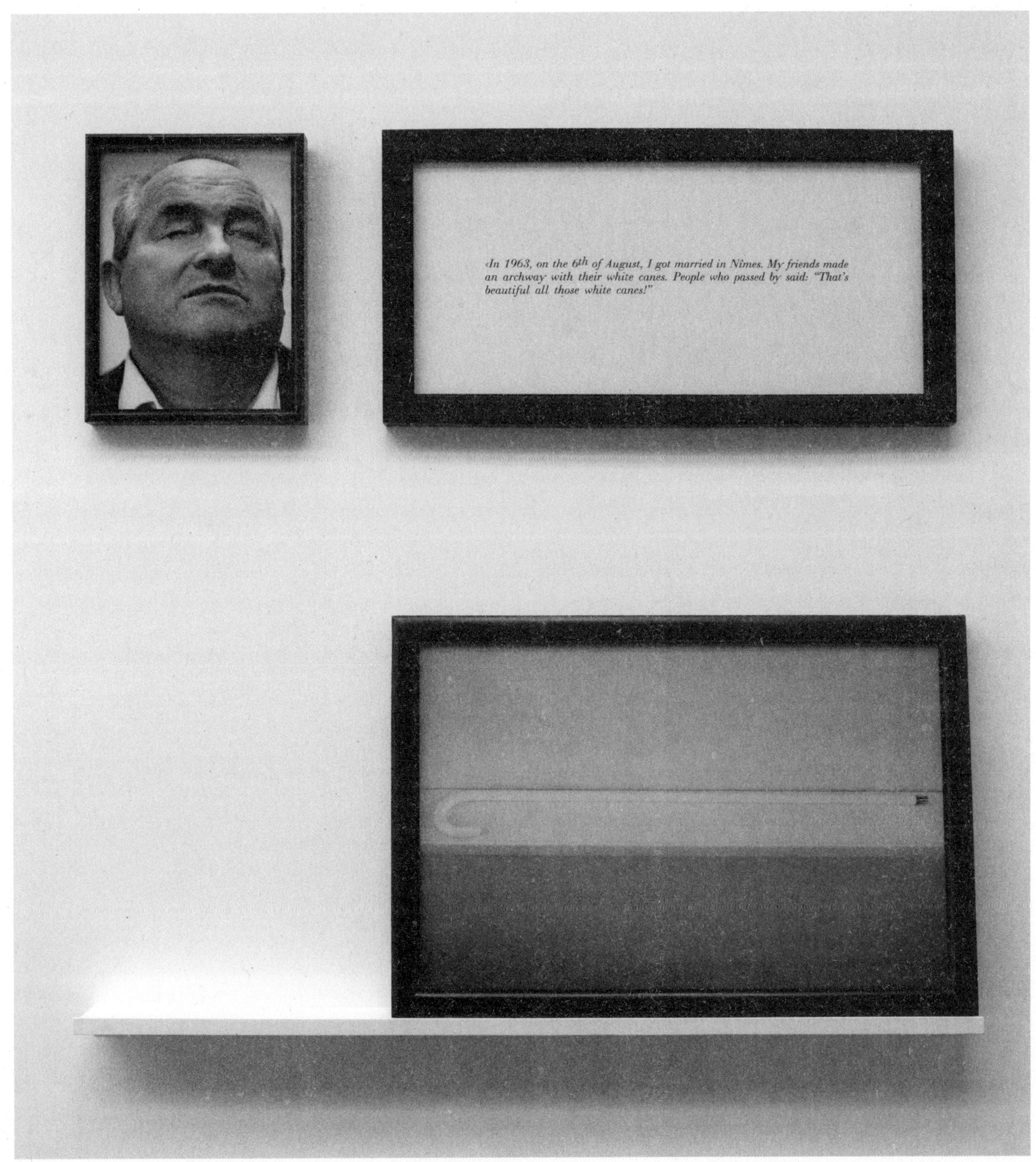

Sophie Calle, *The Blind*, 1986/89. Luhring Augustine Gallery, New York, 1991

Dear Sophie,

Have you ever seen Eadweard Muybridge's nineteenth-century photographs of humans and animals in motion? If you look closely at the serial photographs of people walking, particularly those of disabled people, you might notice among all of them that the idea of "walking" is a generalization for human locomotion—of moving one's body from point A to point B using nothing more than one's own physiological reality. Whether the person is a young child or a young man, a woman with multiple cerebrospinal sclerosis or a young boy with double amputation of the thighs (Muybridge photographed all of these people), there is no way to define normalcy except through the abstract idea of locomotion: Everyone gets from A to B, and that is what is supremely important—not the fact that they get there in different ways.

What one discovers from this is a general idea about difference. As Paul Souriau observed in *The Aesthetics of Movement* (first published in 1889), movement is a product of physiology (or "organic structure"): There is no "normal" body and concomitant movement, but rather an array of differences that reflect themselves in different movements. What is normal is the fact that locomotion is generally possible and that the body will adapt itself to its available resources, exhaust them if necessary, to ensure this possibility—most remarkably—or I should say *un*remarkably—in the case of the double amputee. It is for the same reason that one can argue that speech is not normal to humans, but the basis of speech is—language—and the brain will find another means to produce language in those for whom speech is not possible. Even Rousseau thought of this in his *Essay on the Origin of Language*, struggled with it, but did not have the sort of proof that sign languages of the Deaf offer us today. Thus what is normal is not defined by references to static physiology, but by a dynamic physiology, by the presence of difference. Like atoms spinning off and repelling each other, the marks of difference are ironic formants: At once threatening the collapse of order, they also sustain order. It is only by virtue of differences that we are able to discriminate, it is only by virtue of otherness that language itself is possible: For what is language but the compounding of a finite set of phonological differences into an infinite set of utterances?

Yours,
Joseph

Dear Sophie,

A short, recommended reading list in physiological otherness:

Harlan Lane, *The Mask of Benevolence*
John Hull, *Touching the Rock*
Georges Canguilhem, *The Normal and the Pathological*

Happy reading.

Yours,
Joseph

Dear Sophie,

Saturday, March 23; I am here again in this room, here again among the blind and Sophie Calle. I am surrounded by your signature, yet I do not know who Sophie Calle really is, or who, for that matter, the author of this work really is. The advertisements read "Sophie Calle," but I am inclined to feel that the real artist in this room is not Sophie Calle but the blind themselves, for it is they who do what the artist must necessarily do: find beauty where others do not presume it to be. It is something not unique to the blind with whom Sophie Calle met and talked, but with all blind people, all disabled people, all of us, everyone—even, perhaps, Sophie Calle.

Art historians and contemporary critics are fond of saying that we now live in an age when the ontological distinctions between art and life are necessarily blurred; yet, at the same time, we seem unwilling to acknowledge art that makes no claim to itself as art, but modestly assumes the position of being whatever it finds itself being. Duchamp, it has been claimed, changed the rules by making the everyday object an object of art. The challenge today is to turn this around: to admire the everyday object or the ordinary person precisely because they are not art, and don't care to be.

I'm afraid of my own voice. What, Sophie, have I said?

Yours,
Joseph

Dear Sophie,

There's something more than just a little bit engaging about how the idea of living can itself take on an aesthetic identity, how the *act* of living can supplant the mere object as an aesthetic ideal. At the present moment in cultural history we are facing the end of a century of objecthood, the end of a period in which (particularly during the 1980s) the art object became an object of physically and economically aggrandized proportions. To dismiss this art is not a sign of mere disaffection or residual Marxism; it is instead an act of turning, a gesture toward a certain kind of heretofore unacknowledged unpretentiousness where art is defined by a sincere sense of purpose, by a desire to be everything except this fiction we call art itself. It is, surely, not the only kind of art there is or will be, but it is an art germane, not ancillary, to our contemporary cultural consciousness. Perhaps this is what you yourself are trying to say in *Les Aveugles*. If so, it is a beautiful failure.

Yours,
Joseph

Dear Sophie,

April 17. I am back, again. The faces, the voices now familiar, a family almost. I give the texts more time now, more space, and as I walked into the gallery today I found myself attracted at once to the blue Braille text of Claude Jaunière. Of all the photographs of objects, reliefs, places, and people which constitute your hermeneutic exercise, it is the Braille text that most belongs here, yet flattened as a photograph it somehow contradicts itself, an oxymoron even. Looking closer—and I must look closer because this text, made to be touched, to be read, is sealed behind glass—I find that this icon of the blind alphabet has been mounted upside down.

Yours,
Joseph

Dear Sophie,

I have double-checked, triple-checked, quadruple-checked the placement of Jaunière's Braille text: Upside down, upside down, it keeps echoing in my eyes. As I walk up to it, look closely, and step back again, again and again, the visitors to the gallery stare at me, try to comprehend my incomprehension. Surely this is unintentional; yet to call it a "mistake" does not redeem it from my consciousness, where I carry it to a café for coffee.

A year ago an acquaintance sent me a postcard, one of a series of *Traffic Signs for the Hearing Impaired* by the painter Martin Wong. In areas frequented by deaf people, particularly near schools for the deaf, America has a tradition of putting up street signs to alert motorists. The signs, normally black lettering on a yellow background, are straightforward and succinct: "Deaf Pedestrians"; "Deaf Child"; "Deaf Children." Wong's postcard showed an attempt to present bilingual texts by spelling "School for Deaf" in both English and the Deaf fingerspelling alphabet. I'm sending you a copy. My acquaintance, an artist herself, thought I would be pleased by this small act of cultural sharing, and at first I was. But when I looked closely at the postcard I noticed that both *f*'s had been made wrongly: Rather than the thumb and index finger making contact, as they would in a properly configured *f*, Wong depicted the thumb in contact with the pinky—the number 6. Instead of saying "School for Deaf" the sign thus said "School 6or Dea6."

The coffee consoles me. Jaunière's Braille text upside down. This *f* that is not an *f*. Not mere mistakes, but misplaced desire.

Yours,
Joseph

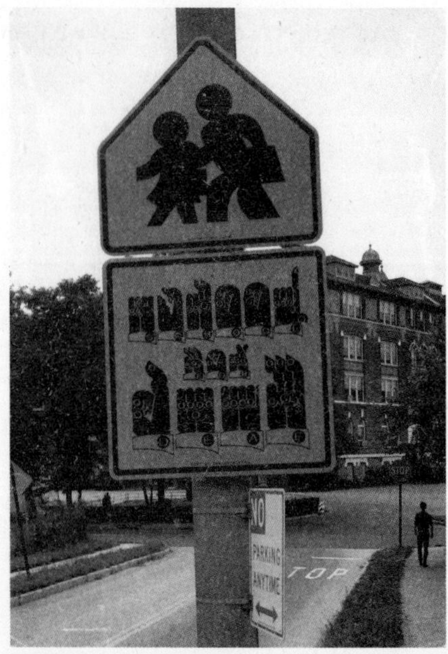

Martin Wong, *Traffic Signs for the Hearing Impaired*, 1990. DOT aluminum street sign

Dear Sophie,

April 30. According to the *New York Gallery Guide*, *Les Aveugles* has closed, but according to the artworks on the walls of the gallery it continues. The sixth week now. I do not stay long today: The comfort of familiar faces and familiar voices betrays my discomfort.

In the galleries I am genuinely surprised by the presence of traces of the lives of disabled people: enlarged Braille texts, paintings that incorporate codified messages in the Deaf fingerspelling alphabet, sign language tattoos. The disabled seem to be everywhere in the galleries today, but only as subjects, the ordinariness of their lives framed and mounted for those who find it unordinary, "aesthetic," perhaps even strange.

To describe this activity as "appropriation" does not say enough. Couched within this quintessentially postmodern term is a desire to make something one's own, an audacity to assume that we can transpose ourselves to another state of being, or to some identity unique to another. The idea of theft is natural when it is unconsciously done within an intertextual matrix—every utterance necessarily steals something—but conscious theft is measured by its consequences, by those who are violated. The question is how far we can take the idea of appropriation, how willfully—or ruefully—we can make it serve our own needs at the expense of others'. There is an unspoken line at which appropriation becomes a form of human violence, a point at which theft is transgressed by assault on the human psyche: the point at which appropriation becomes expropriation.

Yours,
Joseph

Dear Sophie,

I am beginning to think of you as a social archaeologist, as one who excavates the shards of human existence, makes notes, photographs, and so on. No scruples, no pettish qualms—truth only.

But whose truth?

Yours,
Joseph

Dear Sophie,

Why is it that I absolutely fail to see any charm or redeeming value in Sam Messer's use of fingerspelling in his paintings? A friend argued that I should at least feel grateful that he brings attention to sign language, and perhaps I should. But what kind of attention is brought to bear here—what perception about sign language, what insights does it offer? The texts are ambiguous, as perhaps they should be; one enters, decodes, and confronts a transcription: "Stop. Listen. Look. Hell Hurts."

Perhaps my problem is with the painting's lifeless two-dimensionality—a travesty of the three-dimensional dynamics of sign language. When fingerspelling is printed as a code, it becomes, like other writing, inescapably linear: It must be chased by the eye. It is not the mere unnaturalness of this format that is troublesome, but the implication that, by decoding the message, people might be led to think that they are using sign language, when in fact they are doing no more than exercising a simple transcription code: There is no morphology here, no syntax, no movement; the dynamic aspect, the "movement envelope," is lost altogether.

No language, then, but merely the residue of language, a trace of its existence. Like Martin Wong's street signs, Messer's paintings become mere clichés, tokens of familiarity. I do not think, however, that this is the consequence of the artists being able to hear, but because they are outsiders, attracted more to the ostensibly sequined surface of deafness than the raw undercurrents of the deaf psyche. Even deaf artists are themselves subject to this failure, as is Morris Broderson, who, like Wong and Messer, has a predilection for using fingerspelled texts. One Los Angeles reviewer (Kristine McKenna in the *LA Times*, December 5, 1986) described Broderson's work as "the kind of stuff you might find adorning the walls of a 12-year-old girl with very bad taste." Frightful criticism, but justified.

From this lesson we might extract two morals: one, that physiology is not the sole criterion for cultural consciousness; and two, a sign cannot exist, cannot mean in a socially meaningful way, apart from the body.

Yours,
Joseph

Dear Sophie,

The paintings by Messer, like your own *Les Aveugles*, lead to a question about the privilege of voices: Who "owns" Braille, who "owns" sign language, who has a right to the insights, the mindsights, of the deaf and the blind?

The question itself, though outwardly simple, does not easily engage an answer. Revisionist views of modernism's appropriation of African and Asian mythologies tend to chastise the condescension inherent in the activity (the notion of "primitivism," for example) while acknowledging the aesthetic objects that resulted from this cultural interaction—say, Picasso's *Les Demoiselles*—and the new directions they made possible. This revisionist paradigm can also be found in critical artworks like those of Fred Wilson, where there is an overt, almost unforgiving critique of Western expropriation of foreign cultures, the museum being seen as a kind of cultural keyhole. The desire to gaze also embraces mass-produced objects for Western consumption. If you browse through the ubiquitous flea markets in Europe, you can find in shoeboxes old postcards of the people of North Africa entitled *Scènes et Types*, the Tunisian and Moroccan women's uniqueness being measured by their jewelry and their exposed breasts. These cards are not of the tradition of the risqué (although in contemporary postcard catalogues and auction lists they are grouped with the risqué), but instead attempt to proclaim their innocence, exploring and marketing cultural differences. Even Fred Wilson cannot undo the history of museology without himself becoming a part of that museological context, or without engaging in the use of the same cultural objects that, as a critique, look manifestly more uncomfortable in a commercial gallery like Gracie Mansion or Metro Pictures than they do in a museum.

Thus it would probably be wrong to say that the deaf "own" sign languages or that the blind "own" Braille. Yet it would not be wrong to say that the deaf and the blind deserve the autonomy of self-determination, and each excursion made into their cultural territory is subject to critical veracity—it will be looked at, scrutinized even, by those for whom it is a part of their everyday lives. Transgressions are severely challenged because they evoke myths that disability communities have strived for a long time to eradicate. Most of these myths focus on the illusion of normalcy, the desire of able-bodied people to make the disabled appear normal so that they are less different, less visible in social and educational domains. Both sign language and Braille, being arbitrary semiotic codes (one a natural language; the other an alphabet surrogate), tend to mark their difference in such a way that it is either aggrandized for the sake of this difference (as in the work of Messer), or it is repressed because the difference offends the sense of normalcy in the human community—the same sort of repressive activity that contributes to the fact that most schools for the deaf and blind, like mental institutions, have been located in rural environments.

Yours,
Joseph

Dear Sophie,

A troubling thought strikes me: Who am I to adjudicate the possession of cultural identity? I am embarrassed to think that the postcards I write might be seen as an accretion of warnings from the ubiquitous Culture Police. Am I doing something so low? Who is this Joseph Grigely anyhow? Why does he pronounce so many sentences (both utterances and judgments) upon the work of Sophie Calle? Why is he so obsessed with one solitary installation—*Les Aveugles*?

Perhaps if the history of the disabled were not so static, repetitive, and maligned with stereotypes, this would not be necessary; one always feels less comfortable having to react to others than to act on one's own inner impulses. But all art, like all writing, is essentially a conflation of action and reaction, and *Les Aveugles* occupies a very distinct intertextual place among two histories: that of the disabled and that of postmodernism. I am reading these histories, reading into them, and misreading them, as one inevitably will do. But I will not be cajoled by them, and perhaps here we find the source of my resistançe and skepticism: I am searching, in a very undeconstructive fashion, for some kind of truth. I do not know what this truth is exactly, so perhaps it is actually truthfulness that I am looking for.

Think of Joseph Grigely not as a person writing these lines but as your conscience coming out of a back room.

Hello, hello!

Yours,
Joseph

Dear Sophie,

Perhaps mere truthfulness is not enough; perhaps what we need here is a hard truth, an upsetting truth, one that can at best be disconcerting and at worst will ultimately be proven wrong. Let me try, anyhow. Listen, Sophie: The presumptuous error of colonialism and the perpetuating error of postcolonialism is a belief that the majority and the minority are static forms. The truth is this: As historically conceived minorities achieve the status of power, they take on the very same qualities as the social institutions they once sought to retract. They become, so to speak, "certified" or "canonized" minorities, perpetuating a myth that is no myth but reality itself: the separation between those who control and those who are controlled. The oppressed become the oppressors.

Nobody, Sophie Calle, can be more "other" than another person. Not you, not I.

Yours,
Joseph

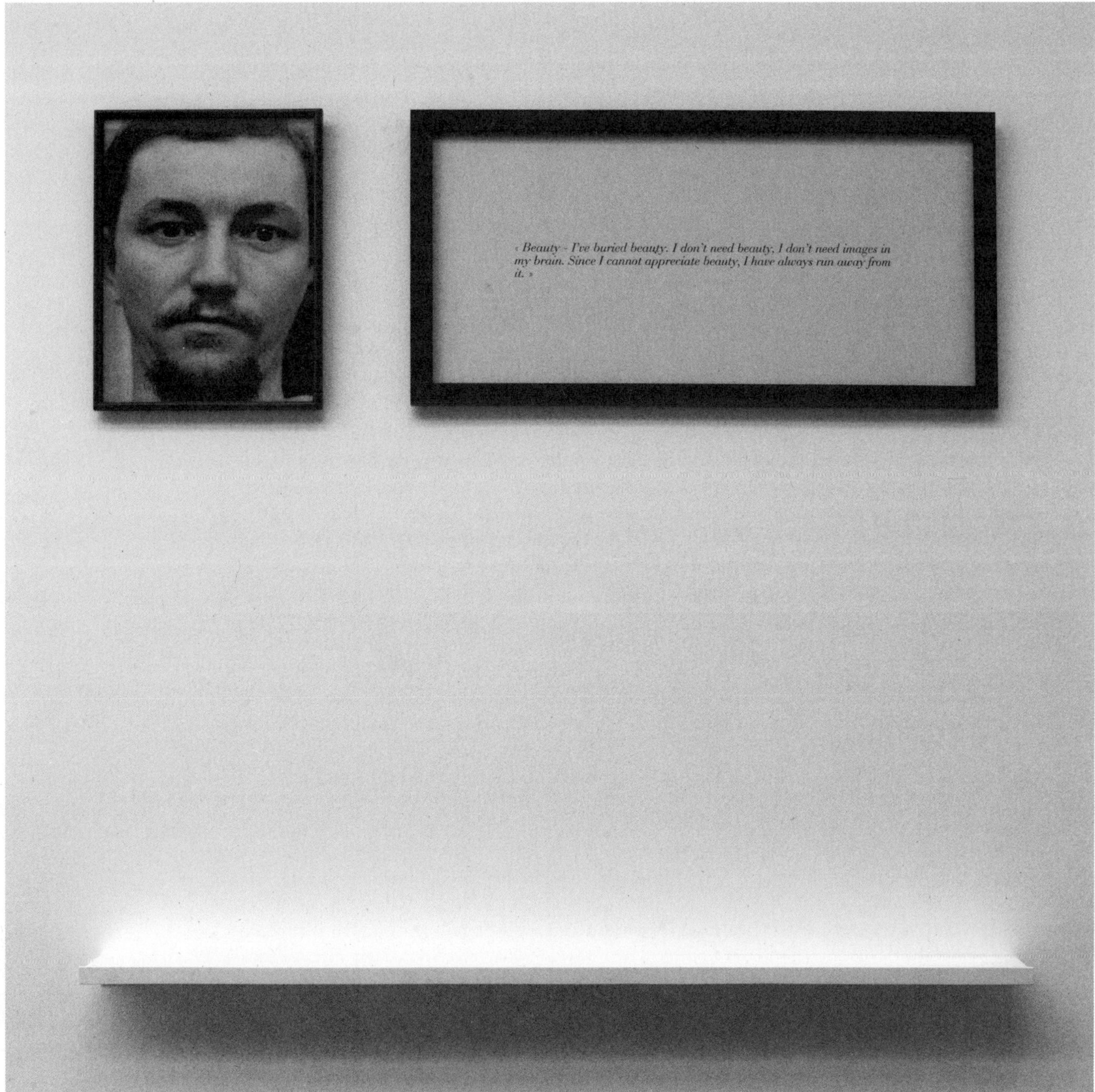

Sophie Calle, *The Blind*, 1986/89. Luhring Augustine Gallery, New York, 1991

Dear Sophie,

I am getting closer to a theme now. Maybe I was wrong when I first wrote to you and said I had no theoretical locus here. Perhaps there really is. I think it has to do with a topic that hasn't received serious critical discussion: the canonization of difference. The phrase must sound a little bit odd, perhaps even contradictory, but I think that this is a proper moment to bring it up and ask ourselves if in fact it is possible that there are marginalized people beyond the margins of the marginalized. Already you can sense that I believe there are. It is not, however, easy to write about the relationship between, say, disability theory and cultural theory, between the disabled as a minority and other canonized minorities and the means by which we define them: race, gender, religion, and national origin. These are familiar phrases because, in America at least, they are used to define difference politically, legislatively, and (in critical discourse) theoretically. But when was the last time a critical journal like *Representations* or *Critical Inquiry* or *Cultural Critique* published an essay about the disabled other—even in special issues devoted to "identity"? Is it because the disabled continue to be patronized as inferiors—that is, as people incapable of participating in contemporary critical discourse? Is it because our signs of difference are just too different to fit into mainstream critical theory? Is it because our presence provokes discomfort that is best kept out of sight—as, historically, has often been the case? Remember those schools for the deaf and the blind located in rural environments? The very fact that we remain largely absent from mainstream debates about identity and difference, or from the art canon itself, seems to echo the earlier absences felt by now-canonized minorities, who, perhaps understandably, have their territory to protect, their claims of empowerment to guard. Part of the problem, I think, is that we tend to define too much, categorize too much, and find ourselves trapped by our definitions and categories. If we really think about it, it's hard to define what a "mother" is: In Washington, DC, a series of posters promoting foster parenthood have recently appeared. They picture a middle-aged African American man surrounded by three children, with the caption: "We need more mothers like him." The poster is an eloquent testimony to the fragility of our preconceptions about stereotyped social roles. What it does so well is get alterity out of theories, onto the streets, and into the public consciousness. We need more posters like that. More critical discourse. And more art.

Yours,
Joseph

Dear Sophie,

Never enough time, is there? Or space…

After eight visits to *Les Aveugles*, after thirty-two postcards, perhaps it is time to come to an end of my monospondence.

I do not mean to imply that I have exhausted possibilities for continuing. No, not that. An ending is a mere formality, the point at which writing stops, the point at which the writer, as a character, exits from his text.

A friend encourages me to be blunt, straightforward, precise.

Since your face is not available to me, why should my face be available to you?

Perhaps, Sophie, you might someday return what you have taken, might someday undress your psyche in a room frequented by the blind, and let them run their fingers over your body as you have run your eyes over theirs.

Yours,
Joseph

23 Footnotes on Sound in Kunstmuseum Bern, 2002

Originally published as "23 Anmerkungen zu Klängen und Geräuschen im Kunstmuseum Bern," in *Zeitmaschine*, ed. Ralf Beil (Kunstmuseum Bern, 2002).

"23 Footnotes on Sound in Kunstmuseum Bern" was written for the catalogue for the exhibition *Zeitmaschine* [Time Machine] at Kunstmuseum Bern in 2002. My installation for the exhibition involved selecting from the museum's permanent collection works that presented a visual embodiment of sound. These were arranged as a show-within-a-show in the main space of the museum. The works included an array of media: Paintings, sculptures, conceptual works, public programming activities (concerts, performances), and even the telephone number of the museum's café were presented under the umbrella of auditory activities. The most significant part of the project involved reconstructing a long-lost audio component of James Lee Byars's sculpture *The Golden Box for Speaking*.

The catalogue publication of "23 Footnotes on Sound in Kunstmuseum Bern" was presented in German; this is the first time the essay has been published in English.

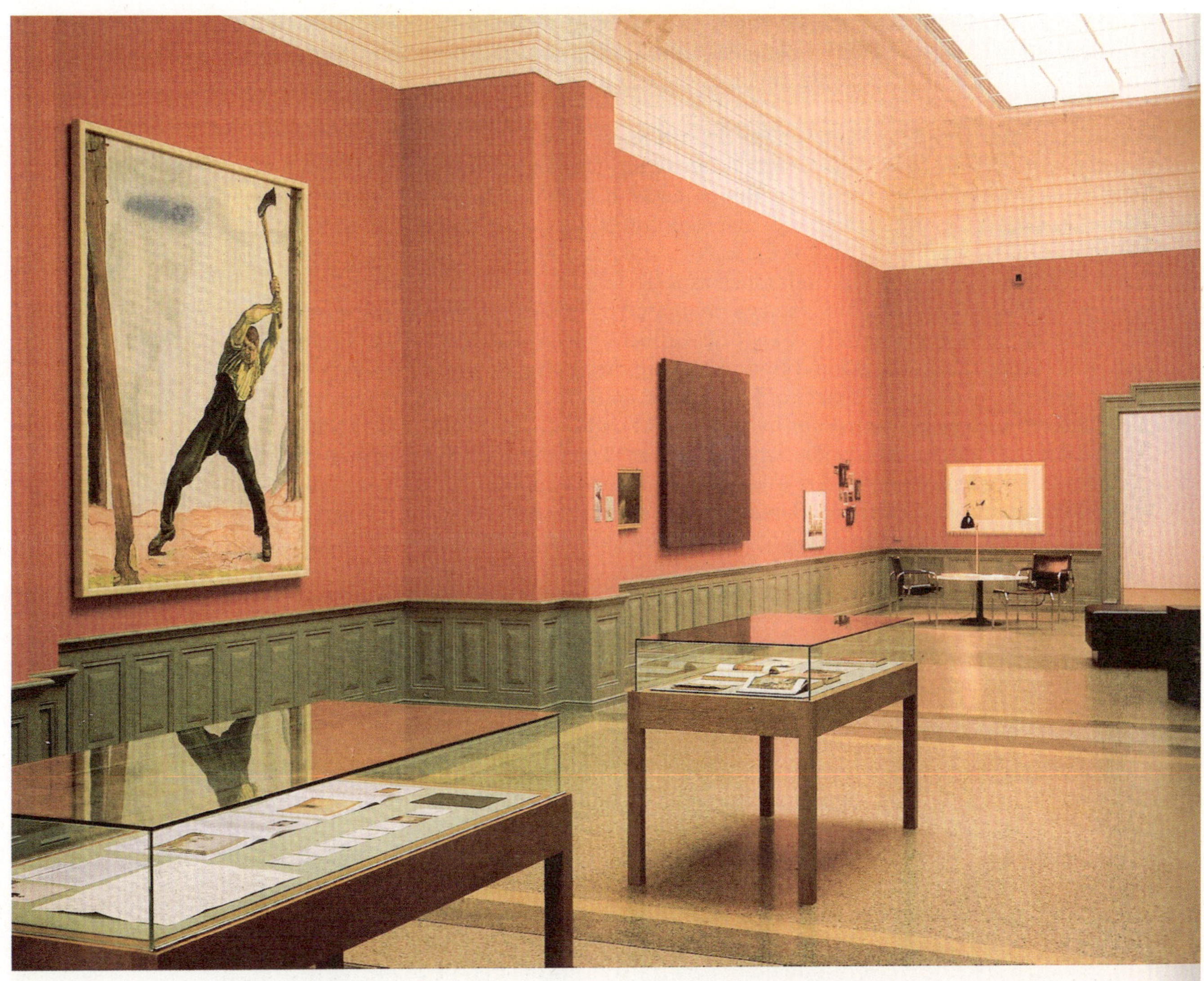

Obergeschoss Stettlerbau, Teilansicht der Künstlerintervention von Joseph Grigely mit Ferdinand Hodlers *Der Holzfäller*, 1910, Karten und Folder mit Abbildungen von Goya und Hodler, das Gemälde *Giessbachfall*, o. J., von Heinrich Rieter, Suzan Frecons *Tractor trailor adagio ma non troppo e molto espressivo*, 1990, Thomas Struths Schwarzweißfotografie *Tokyo*, 1988, eine Accrochage mit Miniaturen von Joseph Werner, Detailaufnahmen von Elisabeth Vigée-Lebrun und Franz Niklaus König sowie Vernissage-Fotos von 1976 und 2001, eine Zeichnung *Reihe Duo*, 1966, von Sigmar Polke, ein Tisch mit Literatur zum Thema Konversation und Kunst sowie zwei Vitrinen, Ausstellung *Zeitmaschine*, Kunstmuseum Bern, 2002

From the catalogue *Zeitmaschine*, edited by Ralf Beil. Kunstmuseum Bern, 2002, p. 112

1. The dilemma is as follows: We generally know what a conversation sounds like, but what does a conversation *look* like? This is not an easy question to answer. Research into auditory phenomena by art historians frequently involves the representation of hearing as a sense organ, or as a metaphor for perception, as in Elizabeth Sears's essay "The Iconography of Auditory Perception in the Early Middle Ages," in *The Second Sense: Studies in Hearing and Musical Judgement from Antiquity to the Seventeenth Century*, ed. Charles Burnett, Michael Fend, and Penelope Gouk (Warburg Institute, 1991). But perception—or "listening" in a broader sense—is only part of our concern: Among paintings and sculpture alike can be found stylized imagery representing both the production and reception of aural phenomena. This is an expansive topic and includes environmental sounds (such as waterfalls) and social discourse as well. Such discourse is not simply language, but language mediated by bodies, and by the visual representation of those bodies across a variety of historical epochs and aesthetic practices. In the present study my goal consists of collecting and commenting upon examples of aural imagery in the permanent collection and public spaces of Kunstmuseum Bern. I have not confined myself to any particular period, genre, or medium; instead, I have chosen to assemble a variety of auditory experiences, even when those experiences are unrealized and constitute silences that hold sound. For assistance in research and related matters, I am very grateful to the following individuals: Daniel Baumann, Ralf Beil, Lisa Bessette, Therese Bhattacharya, Celeste Brusati, Wendy Dunaway, Johannes Gachnang, Josef Helfenstein, Francesca Pia, Markus Raetz, George Roeder, Elizabeth Sears, Kenneth Soehner, Amy Vogel, and the staff of Kunstmuseum Bern.

2. The conversation piece is an eighteenth- and nineteenth-century genre of painting typically practiced in England and the Netherlands. Hogarth, Gainsborough, and to some extent Rowlandson all painted conversation pieces. The genre is distinguished by the fact that people are present and a conversation of some kind is taking place, as suggested by the proximity of bodies in relation to each other, or the presence of a gesture signifying conversation or communication of some kind. The irony is that the conversations themselves are never disclosed to the viewer: We cannot see, much less hear, the content of the exchanges taking place before us. As the art historian Norman Bryson said of Watteau's paintings, imagery like this involves a kind of "semantic vacuum" that insists on meaning, but at the same time withholds it (*Word and Image: French Painting of the Ancien Régime*, Cambridge University Press, 1981).

Most critical interest in the conversation piece occurred during the middle of the twentieth century: Sacheverell Sitwell's *Conversation Pieces* was published in 1936; in 1946, the Arts Council of Great Britain hosted a touring show of English conversation pieces of the eighteenth century; and in 1948 the Detroit Institute of Arts also organized a show on eighteenth-century English conversation pieces. This was an expansive exhibition and included not only paintings reflecting the genre, but also period furniture that evinced the genre: It was an exhibition both of and about its subject. In this sense, conversation was essentially a domestic activity: It took place—and was represented as taking place—in a setting defined by family life. For further study related to the conversation piece and the representation of conversational exchange, see Mario Praz, *Conversation Pieces: A Survey of the Informal Group Portrait in Europe and America* (Pennsylvania State University Press, 1971); Sacheverell Sitwell, *Conversation Pieces: A Survey of English Domestic Portraits and Their Painters* (B. T. Batsford, 1936); and Mary Vidal, *Watteau's Painted Conversations: Art, Literature, and Talk in Seventeenth- and Eighteenth-Century France* (Yale University Press, 1992).

3. A group of three small paintings by Joseph Werner (Bern, 1637–1710), and one by an anonymous member of the school of Joseph Werner (chosen from a group of four). See the catalogue of the collection of Kunstmuseum Bern, *Die Gemälde* (1983), cat. nos. 124, 128,

130, 132. Werner's figures are distinguished by how they are positioned within an iconographic setting: They illustrate not only historical narratives in a literal (or "wörtlich") way, but also the dynamic exchanges that constitute these narratives. His figures touch, lean, whisper, cajole, shirk, accede. Even the dog in *Das Urteil des Paris* (ca. 1670) (cat. no. 124) has turned its head to listen to the words that fall from the lips and hand of Venus. This is also common in Canaletto, whose dogs similarly turn their heads and ears to locate the source of a sound within the expanse of a painting (see note 13).

4. James Lee Byars, *The Golden Box for Speaking* (1977/78). See *Kunstmuseum Bern: Die Skulpturen und Objekte* (1986), cat. no. 536. This work has a curious history. When it was shown at Kunsthalle Bern in 1978, it was titled somewhat differently: *I hum when I think (Golden Voice Box)*, and it was materially different as well: It included inside it a loudspeaker connected to the office of the Kunsthalle's director, Johannes Gachnang. Gachnang had a predilection for humming while he made a decision about something—a unique trait that earned him a place in Byars's collection of anecdotes entitled *One Hundred Secrets of Bern* (date unknown). For the exhibition at the Kunsthalle, Byars materialized this "secret" by placing a microphone in the director's office, and when Gachnang made decisions in the course of his daily activities, he would turn on the microphone and hum—and this humming sound was transmitted to the speaker and gilt box in the exhibition space nearby. Afterward, the microphone was shut off; no other sounds were transmitted. This process continued throughout the exhibition. The work in this regard was an ongoing performance; without Gachnang, what remains is the object of the performance, not the performance itself.

Later exhibitions that included the gilt box (for example, at the Stedelijk Van Abbemuseum Eindhoven and the Musée d'Art Moderne de la Ville de Paris, both in 1983) apparently used the current title (*The Golden Box for Speaking*) and omitted the audio component. The earlier title, *I hum when I think (Golden Voice Box),* is documented in the catalogue *Die Sammlung Toni Gerber im Kunstmuseum Bern* (1986), cat. no. 105, vol. 1, p. 98; however, the history of the audio component is rather more obscure. According to Gachnang, Byars's original plan was to exhibit two golden boxes, one on each side of the entrance to the Kunsthalle, and to close the museum for the entire six-week period of the exhibition. Visitors would still be able to hear the director hum as he made his decisions. Gachnang supported this proposal, but for various complex political reasons, it was not enacted in the end, and the piece that was ultimately exhibited was the less radical version, consisting of one gilt box inside the museum. Given this history, Byars's *Golden Box for Speaking* can be said to have transpired through three versions: (1) the unrealized original version with two boxes placed outside the closed museum; (2) the 1978 version, *I hum when I think (Golden Voice Box)*, which included Gachnang's humming performance; and (3) the retitled version, *The Golden Box for Speaking*, which, lacking the audio component, is currently in the collection of Kunstmuseum Bern.

5. What words do people utter and what sounds do they exclaim when they fall off a cliff or down the stairs? Such events are marked by instantaneous and diametrically opposed extremes: At one moment there is the fracture of the fall—at the next, the utter stillness at its conclusion, when the slightest interruption can be heard. The sound in the paintings of mountaineering accidents by Ferdinand Hodler (*Absturz II/III/IV*, *Die Gemälde*, cat. nos. 755, 756, 757, all painted in 1894) is muffled by the falling snow; but in a 1797–98 drawing by Goya of a boy falling down a flight of stairs (held in the collection of the Staatliche Museum in Berlin), the boy's mouth is open, his arms broadly extended, his back in full contact with the stairs. It's a harder sound, a painfulness made ironic by the implied humor in the title: *Valentías? Cuenta con los años* (Showing off? Remember your age). Do Hodler's

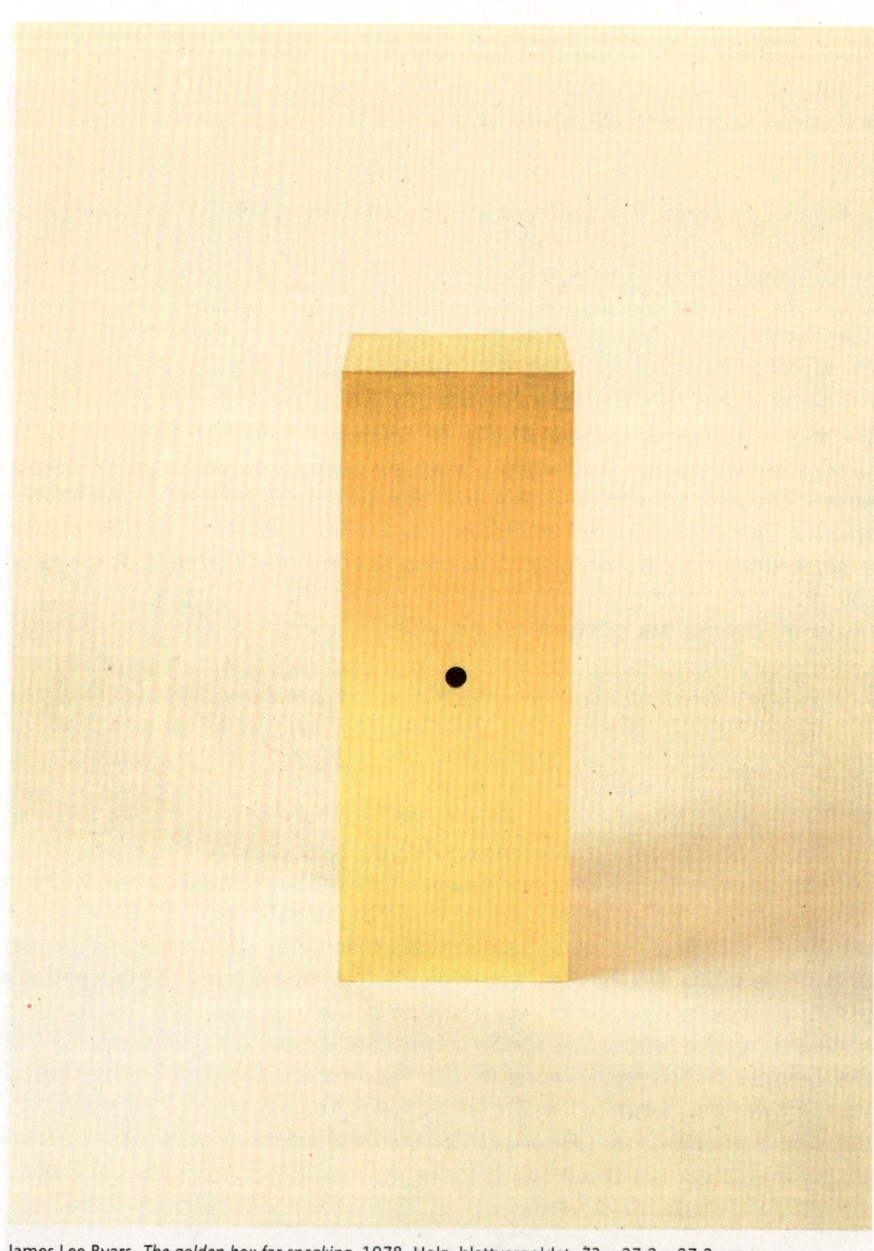

James Lee Byars, *The golden box for speaking*, 1978, Holz, blattvergoldet, 73 x 27,2 x 27,2 cm, Kunstmuseum Bern, Hermann und Margrit Rupf-Stiftung, Ankauf aus der Sammlung Toni Gerber

From the catalogue *Zeitmaschine*, edited by Ralf Beil. Kunstmuseum Bern, 2002, p. 115

mountaineers live or not? Is Goya's boy hurt or not? The outcome of the fall—the fate of the people who fall, and the silence at the end of their fall—is always outside the frame of the painting, and hence denied to the viewer. Compare Norman Bryson's remark on Watteau's paintings and how they communicate a narrative that "insists on meaning," but at the same time withholds it.

6. One excellent study on the subject of the visual representation of auditory phenomena is Richard Leppert's *The Sight of Sound: Music, Representation, and the History of the Body* (University of California Press, 1993). Leppert is primarily interested in the visual representation of domestically produced music in early modern Europe, but he is also good at getting inside the very idea of an aural body in an aural landscape. He writes: "The body, simultaneously site, sight, and possessing sight, is an object of tactile sensation and an aural phenomenon. The body *sounds*: it is audible; it hears" (p. xix). Leppert also reminds us that the body is not alone in the landscape of sounds, and that it encompasses both real and imagined voices within the context of social and environmental sonority. In Franz Niklaus König's paintings, the waterfalls, the wind in the trees, and the birds contribute to this sonority; in Canaletto, the commingling of voices and noises on the Venetian waterfront does the same—these are sounds that seem very abstract from a distance, very particular when listened to up close. By definition the rhetorical strategies by which we examine visual art are ocular. It is idiomatic to say "OK, let's take a close look at this painting"—but somehow it seems a little odd to say "OK, let's listen carefully to this painting." Even when we do listen, we remain distant from the specificity of these noises because they are by necessity imagined noises. In English, the term "picture window" is used to describe a large glass window typically placed in the front of a domestic living room, whereby one can see, though not necessarily hear, what goes on through and beyond it. In a similar way, landscapes and street scenes provide visual access while simultaneously denying aural access.

7. Regarding water: Markus Raetz's installation *Ohne Titel* (1980–83, *Die Skulpturen und Objekte*, cat. no. 583) is composed of twenty-four interrelated elements, several of them triangular-shaped paintings of breaking ocean waves, each of which could be called, or considered, a slice of noise. In general, there are so many varieties of sounds of water—both those engaged by musicians on the one hand, and by Fluxus artists like Dick Higgins on the other—that it would be a study in itself to construct a comprehensive taxonomy of such sounds. Our more immediate question concerns the visual representation of water within a distinct geographical context, and how human communication is affected—and represented—by this context. The Swiss alpine landscape seems to have furnished painters like Franz Niklaus König with a particularly unusual sort of Romantic landscape, one defined by waterfalls and a vertical, rather than horizontal, composition. These are loud paintings—so loud that the figures beside the waterfalls have to gesture and point as they speak. In one of these vertical landscapes, *Der Reichenbachfall im Oberhasli*, which König painted in 1807, the visual narrative of the painting is articulated through gestures: Two figures in the lower left of the painting point to three figures in the upper right of the painting, and the three figures in the right corner point to the heart of the falls. In this regard the painting can be said to exhibit two kinds of auditory fields: that of nature, and that of human commentary on that nature.

8. "bababadalgharaghtakammminarronnkonnbronntonnerronnthunntrovarrhounawnskawntoohoohoordenenthurnik," although there is a question as to whether or not the word should be capitalized.

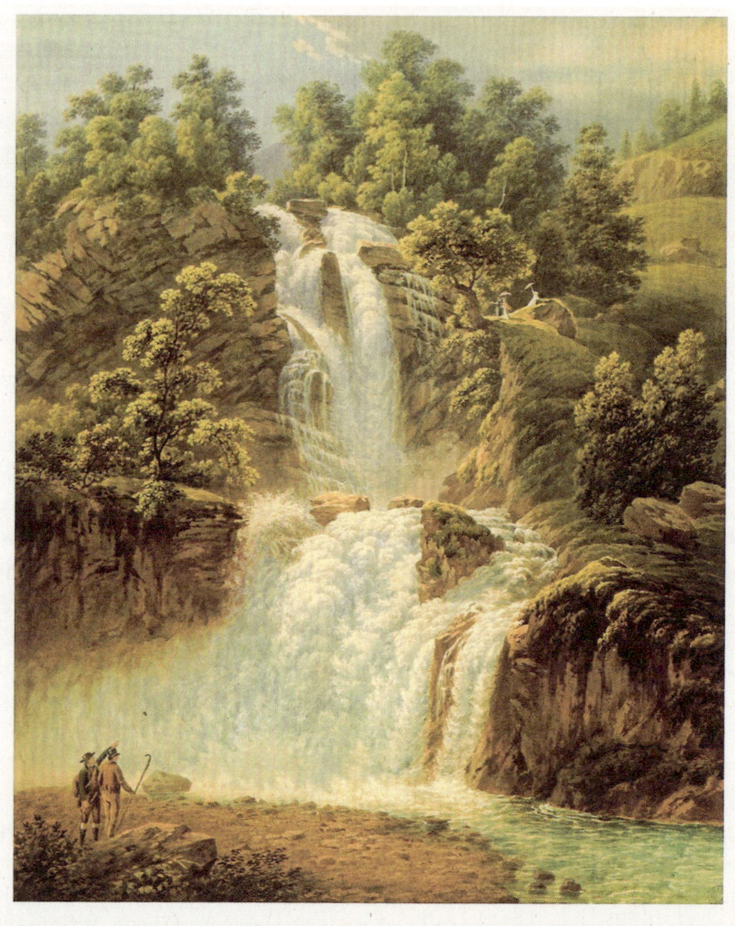

Franz Niklaus König, *Unterer Reichenbachfall*, um 1800,
kolorierte Radierung und Aquatinta, 50,4 x 40 cm, Kunstmuseum Bern

From the catalogue *Zeitmaschine*, edited by Ralf Beil. Kunstmuseum Bern, 2002, p. 118

9. Mark Twain's account of his time spent with "Tintoretto's three-acre picture in the Great Council Chamber" in Venice is as follows:

> The movement of this great work is very fine. There are ten thousand figures and they are all doing something. There is a wonderful "go" to the whole composition. Some of the figures are diving headlong downward with clasped hands, others are swimming through the cloud-shoals—some on their faces, some on their backs—great processions of bishops, martyrs and angels are pouring swiftly centerward from various outlying directions—everywhere is enthusiastic joy, there is rushing movement everywhere. There are fifteen or twenty figures scattered here and there with books but they cannot keep their attention on their reading—they offer the books to others but no one wishes to read now. The Lion of St. Mark is there with his book. St. Mark is there with his pen uplifted. He and the Lion are looking each other earnestly in the face, disputing about the way to spell a word—the Lion looks up in rapt admiration while St. Mark spells. This is wonderfully interpreted by the artist. It is the master-stroke of this incomparable painting.
>
> I visited the place daily, and never grew tired of looking at that grand picture. As I have intimated, the movement is almost unimaginably vigorous. The figures are singing, hosannahing, and many are blowing trumpets. So vividly is noise suggested, that spectators who become absorbed in the picture almost always fall to shouting comments in each other's ears, making ear-trumpets of their curved hands, fearing they may not otherwise be heard. One often sees a tourist, with the eloquent tears pouring down his cheeks, funnel his hands at his wife's ear, and hears him roar through them, "OH, TO BE THERE AND AT REST!"
>
> None but the supremely great in art can produce effects like these with the silent brush. (*A Tramp Abroad*, ed. Charles Neider, 1977, pp. 302–3).

10. In the space between the raised and outstretched hand of Socrates in David's *The Death of Socrates* (1787) and the hands clutching the head in Munch's *The Scream* (1893), the range of possible gestures in painting seems limited only by the range of possible human emotions. Such gestures both speak and are spoken for; they possess latent paralinguistic function, and might in certain situations be indicative of speech, conversation, nonverbal communication, or even the act of listening (on this latter subject, see Vidal, *Watteau's Painted Conversations*, pp. 18–19). In traditional studies of rhetoric, gesture is seen as a supplement to speech, but there are occasions where it supplants speech (as in certain dismissive gestures). This subject has been studied in exploratory ways from the perspectives of cultural history (see Jan Bremmer and Harold Roodenburg, *A Cultural History of Gesture*, Cornell University Press, 1992), comparative psychology (Wilhelm Wundt's *Die Gebärdensprache*, published in 1900, is a pioneering work in this discipline), and linguistics (since it was founded in 1972, the journal *Sign Language Studies* has covered the subjects of gesticulation, facial expression, kinesics, and proxemics)—however, much more work remains to be done in relation to comparative and metaphorical gesture. For example, it might be a useful exercise to compare a subtle abstract painting like Bethan Huws's *Ohne Titel (A Gesture)* (1991) with more literal examples of gesturing, such as studies of hands by Franz Niklaus König (*Studiensammlung von Figuren aus dem gewöhnlichen Leben...*) and Adolf von Stürler (*Elf diverse Handstudien in Bewegung*). Equally interesting is how fugitive figures in landscape paintings are frequently represented in pairs, one person gesturing in a way that is both indexical (in relation to the subject of the gesture) and symbolic (in relation to their implied conversational exchange). Franz Niklaus König, Cornelis Huysmans, and Élisabeth Louise Vigée Le Brun all painted such pictures. This technique of representing paired figures is also common in works by the Hudson River School of landscape painting in America—Thomas

Cole, Frederic Church, Asher Durand, and John Kensett painted works like this, many of which can be found in the collection of the Wadsworth Atheneum in Hartford, Connecticut.

11. Despite some misgivings, I have not included the work of Albert Anker (1831–1910) in the exhibition installation. This is not because Anker's work does not reference conversation—it does, and it does so more directly than most of the works I have selected. Anker's characters are very distinctive in this regard: They whisper, they tell stories, they lecture, they narrate monologues, they even seem to talk baby-talk—and they listen both passively and impassively (in one painting, *Die Gemeindeversammlung*, which Anker painted in 1857, a man cups his hand behind his ear in order to hear a little better). Social and domestic conversation, in fact, seems to have been one of Anker's most prominent concerns. He seems inexplicably compelled to tell stories about the importance of conversational hierarchies: His is a milieu of responsibilities and obligations commensurate with our roles as members of a community or family. The trouble with this is that Anker often pushes it too far—like the American painter Norman Rockwell sometimes does, he starts with a theme and illustrates that theme in an overly didactic and sentimental manner, leaving the viewer little room to explore the ambiguities and absences that characterize daily life.

12. In both the collection of Kunstmuseum Bern and the archive of the history of the museum are photographs of openings, receptions, and related events. Typically, these photographs constitute a visual record of social exchanges, but sometimes they are seen as extensions of the art of the photographer—which is the case with a series of photographs that Sigmar Polke took of James Lee Byars and others at Gerechtigkeitsgasse 40 in Bern in 1978 (inv. F.1984.2503, F.1984.2510, F.1984.2508). These might be compared with a series of photographs taken by Gerhard Howald during the opening of the exhibition of the work of Adolf Wölfli in 1976: In both, people are sitting, drinking, talking, gesturing, listening. Regardless of their status as part of the museum's collection, these photographs are important by virtue of their incidental retention of aural phenomena—a process that can be likened to the unintended retention of significance in Antonioni's film *Blow-Up*.

13. Canaletto painted one of his Schiavoni paintings—*Riva degli Schiavoni, Looking West*—in 1735. The painting is now in the Sir John Soane's Museum, London. It's a very conventional Canaletto, of the sort he painted for the English tourist crowd. Whether he was painting a palazzo or a lido, Canaletto typically filled his canvases with small groups of people who seem to be chatting, people who seem to yell, and people whose gestures bespeak directions. It's usually the dogs that give away the paintings' intimate secret: It is not just a visual scene being represented—a visual experience—but the human occupation of that expanse, and the fact that this occupation is characterized not by things seen, but by the subtlety of things heard. Canaletto is a noisy painter, and he is noisy in a way that does not require histrionics. You can hear it in the foreground of his *Schiavoni* painting, where a dog's head is cocked to the conversation of a cluster of people a few steps away; nearby, a bargeman gestures and shouts loudly enough to capture the attention of a woman walking by. Canaletto's dogs have none of the grace of Gainsborough's, nor the sleek eloquence of the Berner Nelkenmeister's; they're street-smart stragglers that both make noise and, with a turn of their head and ear, point it out to us.

14. Synesthesia is usually described as the intermingling of senses, such as when sound evokes color, or color evokes sound. In this regard, Markus Raetz's *Music in Color* and *Musik in Farbe* (1974) could be regarded as straightforward experiments in synesthesia; and his aquatint

Sinne I (1987) is an exquisite meditation on the subject. For an early effort to construct an apparatus that would translate organ music to color, see A. Wallace Rimington's *Colour-Music: The Art of Mobile Colour* (Hutchinson, 1912). Also relevant are Klee's ideas about "polyphonic painting," which he regarded as being "superior" to music and which he briefly comments upon in his *Diaries* in July 1917. Vowel-color relations are discussed in Wendy Steiner's *Colors of Rhetoric: Problems in the Relation Between Modern Literature and Painting* (University of Chicago Press, 1982).

15. The photograph *Kassetten* and a related work, *Optische und akustische Aufnahme*, were made in 1970 by Markus Raetz and Balthasar Burkhard. On January 10, 1970, they placed a cassette recorder on the floor, to which was connected a handheld microphone. A Super 8 camera containing Tri-X reversal film was mounted on a tripod and positioned above the microphone and the recorder. For three minutes, between 2:38 p.m. and 2:41 p.m., the camera and the recorder were turned on, so that the noise of the running camera was recorded by the tape player, while the recorder's movement was filmed by the camera. Responding to a query about the project, Raetz explained in a fax dated February 21, 2002: "Then, without being played, the two cassettes were vacuum-packed together in transparent plastic. From this moment on I just used them as models for photographs, paintings and drawings."

16. See Johann Jakob Sulzer's *Wasserfrosch* (inv. A9551) as an example of latent environmental sound. It's hard to imagine a visual image devoid of sound—even implied silences make a certain kind of noise.

17. One of the most enigmatically engaging paintings in Kunstmuseum Bern is Joseph Plepp's still life *Austern, Kirschen, Käse und Wein* (1632) (*Die Gemälde*, cat. no. 71, although it is worth noting that there are no oysters in the painting). In many ways the painting is a typical example of its genre: It consists of a table on which are spread a knife and an assortment of fresh foods—cherries, cheese, bread, and apricots. Like most still-life paintings, there is a sense of ordinariness about the work: It is neither grand nor heroic, but rather sublimates itself within the realm of the ephemeral—what the Greeks, in their own recognition of the transience of life, called "rhopography."

But what sets the painting apart—and also distinguishes it from another Plepp still life in the collection of Kunstmuseum Bern (*Melone, Quitten und Trauben*, ca. 1632, cat. no. 72)—is the fact that the painting is bisected by that ubiquitous winged emblem of death, a fly. The fly rests not on the food, but on the table itself, among the food, and thus is also the axis of the passing life it represents. It is not an accident that such a seemingly innocuous painting should be so didactic: Plepp's fly, like the fly in Emily Dickinson's poem "I heard a Fly buzz – when I died," is a harbinger, one typically heard before it is seen. Dickinson describes this sound as a "Blue – uncertain stumbling Buzz" (*The Complete Poems of Emily Dickinson*, ed. Thomas H. Jackson, no. 465).

18. When people get up from their table and leave a café, the residue of their conversational exchange usually remains in the form of physical detritus: coffee on the bottom of the cup, grains of sugar and crumbs on the table, stained napkins. This residue evokes the ineloquent rubbish of rhopography. In the traditional still life—Caravaggio's, for example, where the fruit is blemished and bruised—we are confronted with a sense that the imperfections of ordinary life are somehow sacred, unique, and deserving of the status of a higher order. Similarly,

the omnipresence of everyday conversation—what we sometimes call "small talk"—defines our sense of the quotidian. Imagine how different it would be if every word we spoke took on a material presence and occupied space and place within a café: There would be scraps of language lying on the counter, sentences would be piled on tables, and words would litter the floor. Cf. Luc Tuymans's watercolor *Der Tisch* (1986).

19. The telephone number for the café at the Kunstmuseum is 328 09 90.

20. On the subject of auditory stimulation, see Sigmar Polke's *Telefonzeichnung* (1975), of which there are several examples in the collection of Kunstmuseum Bern (e.g., inv. A.1984.2490, A.1984.2470, and A.1984.2474). For a comprehensive anthology of filmic quotations exploring the duality of speaking and listening, see Christian Marclay's two-channel video *Telephones* (1995). For a discursive meditation on the psychosocial history of the telephone in relation to contemporary life, see Avital Ronell's *The Telephone Book: Technology, Schizophrenia, Electric Speech* (University of Nebraska Press, 1989).

21. There are numerous ways in which aural speech might be represented visually. These include writing (whether printed or orthographic) and syllabic and alphabetic phonetic transcriptions. See James Joyce, *Finnegans Wake* (1939), and Alexander Graham Bell's somewhat arcane notion of "visible speech" in *The Mechanism of Speech* (Funk & Wagnalls, 1911). The distinction between speech (as a linguistic system) and writing (as a semiotic system) is extremely important; as Saussure wrote in his *Course in General Linguistics*, writing exists "for the sole purpose of representing language" and is thus not language itself, but a visual representation of it (*Course in General Linguistics*, ed. Charles Bally and Albert Sechehaye, McGraw-Hill, 1959, pp. 23–24).

22. A turn to quietness is evoked by a small untitled and unattributed "shushing" miniature from the permanent collection (*Die Gemälde*, cat. no. 2076). Like James Lee Byars's *Golden Box for Speaking*, this work has a complex and compelling history. It came into the collection of the Kunstmuseum in 1902 as part of the Adolf von Stürler bequest. The work is signed "Marcqfoy," but whether this Marcqfoy is the artist (most likely) or the sitter has not yet been ascertained; the name is not to be found in standard reference dictionaries. Sandor Kuthy, who was curator at Kunstmuseum Bern from 1968 to 1999, has dated the work to the period of the late nineteenth century—which would make the artist a contemporary of Stürler. The miniature itself is a slightly irregular tondo, 72 × 72 mm, tempera on parchment. In the hundred years since it came into the collection of the Kunstmuseum it has been exhibited only once, in a show entitled *1. to 4. Storage (Depot) – Presentation*, which took place between 1970 and 1971.

"Shushing" pictures like this one are so named because of the evident nature of the gesture involved: an index finger placed to the lips, usually in combination with the implied utterance "shhhhhh." While this gesture-genre is generally uncommon, works of this nature make occasional, if not frequent, appearances in seventeenth-century Dutch art, such as Nicolaes Maes's *Eavesdropper with a Scolding Woman* (1655). The theme grew out of Reformation ideas that gave prominence to the spoken word, particularly in relation to the counterpoint of silence.

23. The text is from James Lee Byars's performance at Kunstmuseum Bern on July 8, 1978: "The perfect whisper continues indefinitely and may be heard in the museum at any time."

Right at Home: James Castle and the Slow Life of Drawing, 2010

Originally published in *James Castle*, ed. John Hutchinson (Douglas Hyde Gallery, 2010).

Over the years I presented two exhibitions that were organized by the curator John Hutchinson at the Douglas Hyde Gallery at Trinity College Dublin: *Conversations and Portraits* in 1998 and *The Paradise [32]* in 2009. We also published two catalogues, both quite unconventional in form and content. When Hutchinson was organizing a show on the deaf artist James Castle (1899–1977), he invited me to contribute an essay to the catalogue. I had first encountered Castle's work at a show at the Drawing Center in New York in 2000 and felt an instant connection to the way his work involved interactions with his immediate environment. The essay was later reprinted as a leporello by Peter Freeman Inc. in New York in 2014.

It was a doorknob that first caught my attention. Two of them, actually—one doorknob facing right, one doorknob facing left, with the edge of the door in the middle. This was in 2000. It was the first time I saw James Castle's drawings, in a decidedly modest show at the Drawing Center in New York. I wasn't looking for the show—I just walked into it while I was making my usual gallery rounds in SoHo. And there were the doorknobs. The angle of perspective was an unusual one; not one knob or the other, but both, sideways, in between the edge of the frame of the door.

What is it that makes the edge of a door and two doorknobs so compelling despite also being so banal? His is not a world of small things made big—the word "masterpiece" feels awkward in Castle's critical lexicon. Instead, his is a world of objects, people, and places that penetrate our consciousness through their understatement. He presents us with fragile moments of human existence, a narrative compendium of daily life, magnified and multiplied by decades of nuanced variations of infinite experience—outside there were landscapes and farmscapes, barns and buildings, outbuildings and outhouses, buggies and wheelbarrows, silos and silage piles, and birds of all kinds, ducks and geese and turkeys and roosters; and inside there were doorknobs and doorjambs, screen doors and bedroom doors, blue doors and tan doors, walls and wallpaper, beds and bookshelves, the Morton Salt Girl and Royal Baking Powder. We can add to this the word and phrase drawings derived from newspapers and matchboxes and toilet paper packaging. Gauguin had to go halfway around the world to Tahiti to find his subject; Castle found it right at home.

Not that this is a new observation. Commenting on the exhibition at the Drawing Center, John Russell said of Castle: "His lifelong subject matter was his own surroundings." One is inclined to think of Vermeer in this regard—and the Dutch still life more generally—as part of the process of coming to terms with the reality of Castle's surroundings. In his eloquent book *Looking at the Overlooked*, Norman Bryson made a case for how the still life is best characterized by a certain kind of ordinariness that he (like his predecessor Charles Sterling) called "rhopography":

> Rhopography works against the idea of greatness: while human beings may be capable of extraordinary heroism, passions, ambitions, it leaves the exploration of these things to others, and against megalography it asserts another view of human life, one that attends to the ordinary business of daily living, the life of houses and tables, of individuals on a plane of material existence where the ideas of heroism, passion and ambition have no place.

"Rhopography" is derived from the Greek *rhopos*, meaning "trivial or petty objects"—the sort of mundane things that, in composing a still-life painting, compose our lives as human beings: tables, shelves, closets, doors and doorknobs. Castle's realities are unadorned—they exist, like Caravaggio's basket of fruit, with a characteristic feeling of coarseness, blemishes, and imperfections. The still life stops time to reveal time: Flowers are withered, overripened fruit shrivels, flies pause from their monotonic droning. What distinguishes the still life from the slow life is how the slow life involves continuous peregrinations through a physical place: inside and outside, front side and back side, on top and underneath. The slow life is quiet, as if the wind and the clouds and the people have all taken a break from their diurnal duties. The still life is microcosmic; the slow life is macrocosmic. The still life is a metaphor for what happens outside it; the slow life is a simile for what happens alongside it.

Castle's field of vision is peopled not with voices or with conversations, but with subtle traces of human habitation. When people are present, their presence is part of the perspective of a scene, as familiar and as static as furniture or trees. The inhabitants of his work are nouns, not verbs; yet as nouns they remind one of Ezra Pound's short poem "In a Station of the Metro":

> The apparition of these faces in the crowd:
> Petals on a wet, black bough.

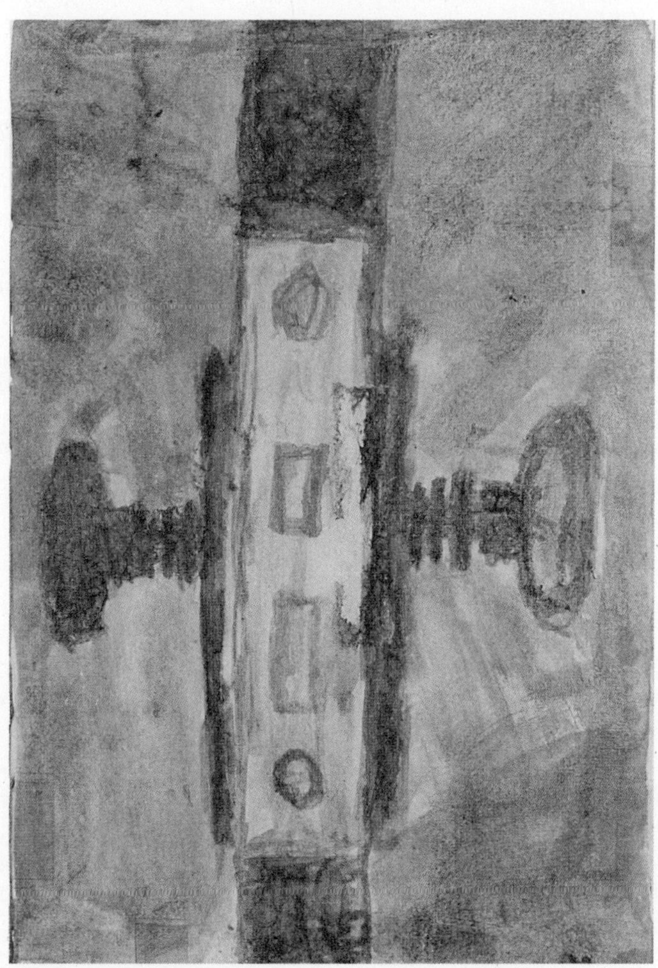

James Castle, *Untitled (Doorknobs)*, n.d. Soot on found paper

Castle's individuals have this quality of being petals; their edges are soft, their brightness slightly washed out, their individuality overlapping each other. They are typically called "figures" in checklists of Castle's work—but what is a figure? A form or a shape or an outline, what is more fundamentally a presence lacking clear definition. This is also true for the portrait, which is distinguished not by what it includes, but by what it leaves out—and Castle's portraits leave out a lot. They are perhaps less portrayals of their subjects than they are betrayals. Sometimes the portraits leave out their subjects entirely—we have only their clothes to see, as in Castle's very singular portraits of purple, gray, and red coats.

Keats once said in a letter that poems should explain themselves without commentary—and in many ways, Castle's oeuvre forces us to address this dilemma. So many of the works come down to us untitled, undated, unannotated—the specificity of their origins so much like James Castle himself, blurred by time and distance and the absence of language, leaving us with the commentary-less image. Sometimes we do not even know the source of the materials that make up the color of the work—many of Castle's works are described as having "color of unknown origin." What adds to the intrigue of Castle's work is the way it withholds from the viewer the sort of ordinary details that would otherwise locate the work in time and space. All art has a way of withholding information from the viewer; this is what gives art a distinct place in the realm of visual information theory—its very incompleteness creates a vacuum for the imagination of the viewer. This is especially true with Castle's titleless titles. Jackson Pollock, for example, numbered his paintings so as to free them from the semantic weight of the title. Likewise, Lessing wrote in his *Hamburg Dramaturgy* that "the less [a title] betrays of the contents, the better it is," and somehow this is befitting in Castle's case. His works have titles now—placeholders that taxonomize an enormous and expansive body of work—but it is important to remind ourselves that these titles are not Castle's.

Yet, there remains much we know about James Castle the person and James Castle the artist. The most salient and inescapable fact is that he was deaf, although the extent to which he was deaf is not very clear—to be "deaf" covers a very broad range of hearing impairments. If Castle's deafness was disabling, it was enabling as well—it took him to a place of human experience that is privileged by being an unchosen place—one goes there because one has to.

This is the point when the myth of James Castle emerges. As one curator wrote: "A deaf nonspeaking man in a hearing, speaking world, Castle created, against all odds, a moving, complex and intelligent body of work, with almost no benefit of instruction, travel, or interaction with the professional art world." For a lot of people Castle is the King of Overcoming. For others, it was his deafness that enabled and enlarged his visual world, and his lack of interaction with the professional art world likewise freed him from the pressure of expectations. In his autobiography, which was published in 1969, the deaf poet David Wright ends his narrative by pointing out that the trials of being deaf are not really much different than the trials anyone faces as a human being:

> There is a story about Sigmund Freud that bears on this. Somebody was telling him about the fate that had befallen one of his old friends, a Swedish professor I think it was. This professor was in the middle of writing a book when he had a stroke that left him paralyzed, able only to move his eyes. However he went on with his work, dictating the book to a secretary by the laborious expedient of directing his glance from one letter to another of an alphabet painted on the wall opposite his bed. The man who told this story asked Freud,
>
> "Don't you think that's a supreme example of courage?"
> "Of course I don't," said the psychologist. "What else could he have done?"

All things considered, Castle's deafness commands our attention because it is inerasable as a biographical fact, and irresolvable as a creative influence. He reminds me of the deaf photographer Maggie Lee Sayre, who is rather less well known, but whose story is also compelling. Sayre was born in Kentucky in 1920, and for fifty-one years lived on a riverboat with her family. Her father was a commercial fisherman—using nets and trotlines he caught catfish and bream—and from 1930 onward, when she received her first camera, she photographed her surroundings: the houseboat and the fishing boats, the fish and the fishermen, the landscape and the waterscape. The thing about Sayre's photographs, like Castle's drawings, is that both artists were predisposed to live a life that involved observing and managing visual information. The visual faculty is not by default heightened or more sensitive among deaf people, as a common cliché about deafness suggests. It's merely a default mode—an available option that, in the case of Sayre and Castle, they turned into an available opportunity. Sayre's work is never quite so transformative or singular as Castle's is—Sayre is more of a domestic anthropologist, recording and registering, but not quite remaking, the boats and people and fish that moved through her life. Yet she takes us to a place that is otherwise inaccessible to those of us living outside it. Hers is a tour of the inside as much as David Wright's book *Algarve* is a tour of the outside. *Algarve* is a mid-century British travel book of a conventional genre; Wright wrote it with the painter Patrick Swift, each of them writing alternate chapters. Wright's chapters are a subtle experience because he never lets on to his reader that he is deaf—but slowly, as you read through Wright's prose, you realize that you have entered the realm of seeing and blinking and glancing and noticing.

In the end, Castle found his place within his perceptions of his surroundings. He looked with equal care at the overlooked and the underlooked. The surroundings may have as easily been the Lower East Side as Idaho—what mattered most is the way Castle unmade and remade these surroundings into something other than what they were. It looks easy; it isn't. The irony of work like this is that it has the effect of taking us to a place to which we have never been, and yet it is a place that surrounds us all the time. The kind of intelligence that goes into the making of art like Castle's is not a rational intelligence. It is not a logical intelligence. It is not even what some might call "creative" intelligence. This is because art occupies a space of human activity that involves rearranging the physical universe as part of the process of making the hitherto unmade. This is why the diction of rational humanistic thought fails us in the case of someone like Castle, whose life and art largely occupy the realm of the ineffable. In one of his letters, Keats described the uniqueness of this ineffable thinking as "Negative Capability":

> I had not a dispute but a disquisition with [Charles] Dilke, on various subjects; several things dovetailed in my mind, & at once it struck me, what quality went to form a Man of Achievement especially in Literature & which Shakespeare possessed so enormously—I mean *Negative Capability*, that is when man is capable of being in uncertainties, Mysteries, doubts, without any irritable reaching after fact & reason—Coleridge, for instance, would let go by a fine isolated verisimilitude caught from the Penetralium of mystery, from being incapable of remaining content with half knowledge. This pursued through Volumes would perhaps take us no further than this, that with a great poet the sense of Beauty overcomes every other consideration, or rather obliterates all consideration.

In so many ways, Castle was a quintessential negative capabilitist: Feeling his way through the mysteries of his surroundings and his materials, he left us with even greater mysteries for which language, inevitably, will fail us.

Sanford Friedman's *Conversations with Beethoven*, 2015

Originally published as "On Deaf Ears: Joseph Grigely on Sanford Friedman's *Conversations with Beethoven*," *Artforum*, May 2015.

In 2015, Don McMahon, then the executive editor of *Artforum*, invited me to contribute an essay to the magazine about Sanford Friedman's novel *Conversations with Beethoven*, which had recently been published by NYRB Classics. As McMahon explained: "Given the striking parallel with your artistic practice, we are wondering if you might be interested in writing a consideration of this novel for *Artforum*." I had always wanted to write about Beethoven's conversations, as they struck me as being like so many I had—not heroic or grand, but rather ordinary and inherently uninteresting. While Friedman's novel was essentially a fictionalized portrait of Beethoven and his daily life, the conversations were exceptionally well conceived, and reading them gave me the opportunity to delve into the contents of the 139 original conversation books that Beethoven left behind, which were at that time mostly unpublished in English.

There's an ironic moment in J. D. Salinger's *The Catcher in the Rye* when the solipsistic Holden has a scheme for eliminating from his life the bother of people and conversations. It occurs at the end of the novel, just before Holden meets up with his kid sister, Phoebe, to say goodbye. He's fed up with phonies, and he's fed up with everyone and everything. So he sits on a park bench and concocts this plan to get away: He'll go down to the Holland Tunnel and hitchhike far out West where it's sunny and nobody knows him. He figures he'll get a job at a gas station. And this is what he says he'll do:

> I thought what I'd do was, I'd pretend I was one of those deaf-mutes. That way I wouldn't have to have any goddam stupid useless conversations with anybody. If anybody wanted to tell me something, they'd have to write it on a piece of paper and shove it over to me. They'd get bored as hell doing that after a while, and then I'd be through with having conversations for the rest of my life. Everybody'd think I was just a poor deaf-mute bastard and they'd leave me alone.[1]

It was a great plan, and it might have worked except for one pesky detail: People love to write. If forty-eight years of being deaf has taught me anything, it's that people will write on any scrap of paper in order to be heard: They'll write on envelopes and Post-its, they'll write in notebooks and book margins, on newspapers and dollar bills, they'll even write with Magic Markers on advertising panels outside the Grand Central Oyster Bar. And they'll write with unmitigated fervor in blank notebooks dedicated to the purpose, as Beethoven discovered. His collected conversations, reimagined, retranscribed, and edited into a narrative about the last year of his life, are the basis of Sanford Friedman's brilliant posthumous novel, *Conversations with Beethoven*.

On June 1, 1801, when Beethoven was thirty years old, he wrote in a letter to his friend Karl Amenda:

> How often I wish that you were with me, for your Beethoven lives most unhappily, in discord with nature and the Creator... You must be told the finest part of me, my hearing, has greatly deteriorated. Already then, at the time you were still with me, I felt traces of this and kept quiet about it: now it has grown progressively worse. Whether it can ever be cured, remains to be seen. They say that it is occasioned by the condition of my bowels: but as far as these are concerned, I have almost entirely recovered. Whether my hearing too, will improve—I sincerely hope so, but it is unlikely: illnesses of this kind are the most incurable.[2]

It was a prescient diagnosis: Over the next twenty-six years, Beethoven's hearing got progressively worse. For the last nine years of his life, starting in February 1818, most of his conversations were conducted on paper, usually in the form of bound octavo commonplace books roughly eight inches high and five inches wide. His interlocutors would write down their side of the conversation in pencil, and Beethoven would speak his side of the conversation aloud (in a few instances, when he wanted privacy, he also wrote). It is not known with certainty how many conversation books he filled during the nine years he communicated by this means, but Beethoven scholars today agree that 139 of the books survive. All of this material has been transcribed and published in German by an editorial team under the direction of Karl-Heinz Köhler, and this monumental eleven-volume edition[3] is presently undergoing translation into

1 J. D. Salinger, *The Catcher in the Rye* (1951; Bantam Books, 1964), 198–99.

2 Michael Hamburger, trans. and ed., *Beethoven: Letters, Journals and Conversations* (Pantheon Books, 1952), 37–38.

3 Karl-Heinz Köhler et al., eds., *Ludwig van Beethovens Konversationshefte*, 11 vols. (Deutscher Verlag für Musik, 1968–2001).

English by Theodore Albrecht at Kent State University in Ohio.[4] But to this day, only snippets of the conversations have been published in English, most notably in Michael Hamburger's concise compilation *Beethoven: Letters, Journals and Conversations* (1952), an edition that Friedman relied on for some of his material.

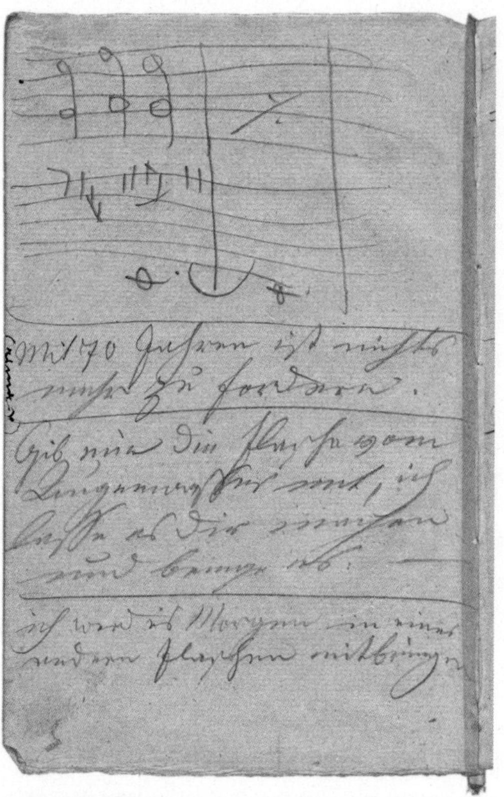

Page from one of Ludwig van Beethoven's conversation books, January 1825

Beethoven asked friends to write their conversations for the same reason many deaf people, including me, ask friends to write: It's practical, it's accessible, and it saves one from the grief that comes from misunderstandings when trying to lipread. The problem with lipreading is that spoken language has too many visual homonyms—words that sound differently but look alike on the lips. It's embarrassingly easy to get things wrong. For example, the word "vacuum" looks like the phrase "fuck you." The phrase "she plays the guitar" looks like "she pees in a jar." "Lipreading" is something of a misnomer; it should be called "lipmisreading."

Except for a few conversations adapted from Hamburger's book, all of the conversations in Friedman's novel are fictionalized—and it's a tricky narrative genre to work with. The challenge is that writing on paper and talking on paper are very different kinds of communicative engagement. The words may seem familiar, but the way they are put down on paper is not: Inscribed conversations backtrack, take sudden turns, and stop abruptly. Sometimes there is punctuation; sometimes not. Sometimes there are lines, arrows, and drawings—gestures of the pencil. Sometimes the words are lopsided (it's really hard to walk and write at the same time).

4 As of 2024, four volumes of Albrecht's translations, comprising Beethoven's first forty-three conversation books, have been published. Theodore Albrecht, trans. and ed., *Beethoven's Conversation Books*, 4 vols. (Boydell & Brewer, 2018–22).

Sometimes there are words on top of words. What makes inscribed conversations particularly important as linguistic artifacts is the way they present both the site and the sight of sound: the site, inasmuch as an otherwise evanescent moment of exchange becomes a material record of that exchange, and the sight, inasmuch as the personality, inflection, and tone of the speaker are revealed by the way the words are written on the page. Human communication is so much more complex than language alone: It also involves the body we put into it.

In an interview with Hans Ulrich Obrist, the philosopher Hans-Georg Gadamer remarked that writing cannot convey all the nuances of human speech: "Writing can never express as many emotions as the voice," he said.[5] Although the inscribed word can be described as a form of embodied speech—one's handwriting is a form of personality—much of this is lost when the written word is transcribed into the printed word. The warbling lines, the spatial pauses, even the paper itself—it all matters. But even a disembodied conversation has considerable intrigue for us, for it registers content that would otherwise seem so unexceptional that one could not imagine writing it down—as exemplified in an exchange between Beethoven and Gerhard von Breuning, the son of his friend Stephan von Breuning, in which Beethoven attempts to tease out from Gerhard an aside that he spoke, and that Beethoven missed. The young man writes:

> I said a dirty word.
>
> I'd rather not repeat it.
>
> Heavens no! It was not as dirty as that.
>
> Please don't insist.
>
> Please, I beg of you.
>
> shit

Ein Fetzen Gemeinschaft—"a scrap of commonness"—is how the late literary critic John Bayley would have described this exchange: a mix of the everyday and the vulgar. Such conversations provide the primary trajectory of Friedman's novel, which in so many ways focuses on Beethoven's domestic life—his health, his financial troubles, his relationships with family members, and, in particular, his relationship with his nephew Karl. The novel is not a narration of these mundane details as much as an activation of them. It provides a valuable reflection on the genre of art known as the conversation piece, which evolved primarily among Dutch, French, and English painters in the seventeenth and eighteenth centuries. Conversation pieces typically represent individuals engaged in a dynamic exchange. They are marked not by any stylistic idiom but by their detail of incident—how they capture the paralinguistic traces of conversation in gestures and poses. In many of his Venetian paintings, Canaletto typically portrayed small groups of people who seem to be chatting, people who seem to be yelling, and people whose gestures define their presence. In work like this, it's not just a visual scene being represented but the human occupation of that expanse—and the fact that this occupation is characterized by things that can be heard. Canaletto is a noisy painter. You hear it in his painting *Riva degli Schiavoni, Looking West* (ca. 1735), for instance. In the foreground, a dog's head is cocked to the conversation of a cluster of people a few steps away; nearby, a boatswain gestures and shouts loudly enough to capture the attention of a woman walking by; beyond them, heads are turned and bodies are positioned in a way that says only one thing: Words are being exchanged.

5 Hans Ulrich Obrist, "Interview with Hans-Georg Gadamer, Heidelberg, May 2000," in *Dynamic Memory: Highway 101*, no. 5 (February 2001): 12.

In Friedman's novel, the words that are exchanged are exceptional by virtue of being totally unexceptional. The utterances in Beethoven's actual conversation books are generally brief; Friedman engages in some poetic license to embellish them with eloquence, though his subject matter is completely in line with the originals. *Conversations with Beethoven* is, in many ways, an antiheroic novel, in which the great composer comes off as someone whose travails are like those of any other artist who lives a life of too much stress and too much alcohol. The details of this sort of existence are the very stuff of "rhopography," as Norman Bryson has termed the depiction of the bits and pieces of ordinariness normally trampled underfoot or otherwise neglected for having no great import. These bits and pieces are what make a still-life painting, and they are what make Friedman's book a still-life novel. As a reader of these conversations, we become more properly voyeurs, not so much listening *to* as listening *in on* the exchanges. We hear things like this conversation, between Beethoven and Gerhard von Breuning, which Friedman borrowed from Hamburger's text, and which reveals only Breuning's side of the exchange:

> Has your appetite improved?
>
> By now you should be eating meat.
>
> Have you been given an enema?
>
> You should be given more of them.
>
> Have you finished reading Walter Scott?
>
> Would you like to read Schiller?

Anyone looking in the novel for grand insights about art and life and music will be disappointed—there are none. Like Gauguin's final years, so well documented in his letters to Georges Daniel de Monfreid, Beethoven's conversations are dominated by concerns about money, suspicions and jealousies, and the imprudence of the wrong things said to the wrong people. (He spites one of his doctors, for example, and many years later, the doctor reminds him of it: "Is it possible to forget such a filthy epithet?") For the three months leading up to his death in March 1827, Beethoven was confined to bed and could not compose—and his penury pained him as badly as his liver did. Nothing makes an artist so wretched as feeling unappreciated, and Beethoven masterfully fulfills our expectations of being a complete crank. It's not for nothing that Goethe charitably described him as "an utterly untamed personality."[6] He lashes out at everyone and everything—his nephew, his nephew's mother, his brother, his doctors, and his amanuensis, who is dismissed at one moment and hired back the next. There's hardly a page without family recriminations of one kind or another. If *Conversations with Beethoven* were to be made into a movie, one could only expect Woody Allen to direct it.

Friedman's reader is treated to the experience of overhearing inspired responses to Beethoven's outbursts:

> I am concealing *nothing*. If your nephew has a mistress, I know nothing of it.
>
> Whether the man fucked her three times or four is beside the point—
>
> Why do your eyes bore into me so?

6 Johann Wolfgang von Goethe to Carl Zelter, September 2, 1812, in *Beethoven: Impressions by His Contemporaries*, ed. O. G. Sonneck (G. Schirmer Inc., 1926; repr., Dover, 1967), 88.

> If I had a kronen for every time you called me a whore—But never mind, that isn't why you sent for me.
>
> Spare me that shit—I won't hear another word!
>
> Calm yourself lest you have a stroke like our worthy grandfather—
>
> Please, you'll have an apoplexy if you don't stop shouting.
>
> It does no good to keep calling him Cain.
>
> But speaking of drinking, may I ask how many glasses of punch you have had?
>
> Why do you look for ulterior motives where none exist?
>
> I've known some pigheaded men, Brother, but you surely take the cake.
>
> Have you taken leave of your senses!
>
> Can you not be civil even in parting!
>
> It would seem that he has some of your hot blood—one might even say that it runs in the Beethoven family.

The only person who seems to escape Beethoven's wrath is Michael Krenn, the semiliterate servant provided to him during an extended stay at his brother's estate in Gneixendorf, whom Beethoven surreptitiously deploys to overhear the dinnertime conversations he himself can't lipread and to relay to him the content of what his family members are saying. It's a familiar scenario: As the painter Paul Bloodgood once wrote to me at a dinner in the mid-1990s, "We are talking about you in front of your front." Being deaf may have been an ideal condition for composing, as Ned Rorem once implied, but for following dinnertime conversations it just plain sucks. Krenn—who was a real person and appears briefly in the German edition of Beethoven's conversation books—comes across, like Beethoven, as an underdog in social relations, and this fact (as well as the wine he regularly sneaked to Beethoven) endeared him to the cantankerous composer.

Conversations with Beethoven is not an easy book. Friedman finished the novel in the late 1980s and spent the next twenty years trying to publish it. In 2010 he died of a heart attack, and it was then that his friend David Alexander brought the manuscript to New York Review Books, a publishing house unintimidated by experimental fiction. The narrative structure of *Conversations with Beethoven* is radically inventive, and so too are the various prosodic tools that Friedman uses to identify the individual speakers: The work could be a play if it weren't also a novel, and it could be a film script if it weren't also a play. In the end, its extraordinariness owes everything to the ordinariness of everyday conversation. Smallness is rarely so big.

Another Story, 2004

Originally published in *Gagarin*, vol. 4, no. 2, 2004.

"Another Story" describes an incident that took place in Boston in the mid-1990s, when I was installing an exhibition at the MIT List Visual Arts Center. Everything went smoothly, until one evening, when something went impossibly wrong at the bed-and-breakfast where I was staying. Like many stories about being deaf, it involved a series of miscommunications and misunderstandings—but in this case, mis-communications and misunderstandings that involved people on the other side of a closed door, people in a copy shop, and both Brookline and university police, all of which eventually landed me on a cot in a dining room at MIT. It was an epic night.

As an artist, there are incidents and events that circle back into your creative production, and for me this was one of those events. This piece was originally written as an email to a friend; in 2004, it was published in *Gagarin*, a Belgian journal devoted to writings by artists and edited by Wilfried Huet. In 2023, *Viseu* published an audio version of the story, which was read aloud by me.

I have a story I've been wanting to tell for years. It's a story about being deaf. Which is never really simple. Just when you think you have it all figured out, something new happens.

The story takes place in the mid-1990s. In Boston. I was installing an exhibition at MIT. My hotel was across the river in Brookline—a big old Victorian mansion that had been converted into a bed-and-breakfast. It was funky but comfortable and suited me well.

One evening I had dinner with an old friend. Rob picked me up in Brookline and drove me out to his home in the suburbs, where we had a pleasant evening—and later Rob drove me back again, waved goodbye, and left me on the steps of the mansion. It was about 11:00 p.m., maybe 11:30. I walked up to the front door, opened it with my key, closed it—and then something strange happened. I walked upstairs to my room, put the key in the lock, turned it, turned the door handle—and the door swung open a few inches before the safety chain suddenly stopped it from swinging more. In a swift moment, the door slammed shut.

I do not remember my initial thoughts just then—maybe I looked at my keys, maybe I looked at the number on the door. I was certain that this was my room, as it had been for the past week. So I tried to open the door again. This time the door slammed shut even quicker.

I had been pretty tired when Rob dropped me off, but now I was wide awake. Someone or something was in my room. A burglar? A ghost? I had no idea. It's hard to talk with someone on the other side of a door when you're deaf. But I tried anyway.

"Hellooooo," I said. "My name is Joe. I'm sorry, I'm deaf, I can't hear whatever you might say, but I want to say that something's wrong here—this is my room, or it was my room for the past week. When I left it this morning my belongings were in it. I'd really like them back, if it's not too much trouble." I tried to open the door again, but it wouldn't open much—I could see through a crack that it looked like a credenza had been pushed up against it.

I tried to explain the situation again: "I really don't know what's going on here, maybe if you could step out for a minute we could figure it out together. Like I said, I'm deaf, and I can't lip-read through doors, I really wish I could."

There was no response.

I tried my key once more, but the door wouldn't move. "I'm really sorry about this situation," I said, "but please—I'm not a burglar, I'm not a bad guy, I'm just a guy who has been sleeping in this room for the past week. I mean, how would I have this key to open the door if I wasn't?"

Again: no response.

I went downstairs to the lobby. There was no night attendant—it was a Saturday night—but there was a nightstand with a telephone and a number to call in case of emergencies. In a situation like this, when you are deaf, and a telephone sits in front of you so innocently, it's really hard to measure your emotions—something so close that's also so far away.

I picked up the phone anyhow and dialed the number. "Hello," I said, "I'm Joe, I'm deaf, there's a problem at the B&B, please come. Hello, I'm Joe, I'm deaf, there's a problem at the B&B, please come. Hello, I'm Joe, I'm deaf, there's a problem at the B&B, please come." I said it three times just to make sure one message got through.

There wasn't too much to do at that point except wait—so I sat on the steps outside and waited.

Five minutes. Ten. Twenty. A half hour. A car swung by; two people got out and walked up the steps.

I tried to explain my situation. "I'm Joe. I'm deaf. I'm a guest here, see, these are my keys. Except there's a problem, there's some people in my room and I can't get in, and the people won't come out so I can talk with them, and there's no night staff, but there's a phone—could you please call the emergency number for me so someone can come and help me?"

They looked at each other, then they looked at me, then we went inside and the man picked up the phone and dialed the number. His brows went up, folded together into an arch, and then he shook his head—no answer. No answering machine. He hung up. "Could you call the police?" I said. "Maybe they can help?" But the woman tugged at the hand of the man, and before I could plead my case further, they were on their way up the stairs.

By now it was getting late—well after midnight. The people in my room probably had every piece of furniture at their disposal piled up against the door, so I didn't see the point in trying them again.

I went outside, walked down the stairs to the street, turned, and started walking.

At this point I could have used a drink—and it occurred to me that going to a bar might not be a bad idea. I could ask the bartender to call the police, and the police could come, and everything would get sorted out.

Except that in the neighborhood I was in, I couldn't find a bar. I did, however, find a twenty-four-hour copy shop, so I went inside and explained to the guy working there that I was locked out of my B&B, and there were people in my room who wouldn't let me in. Would he please call the police for me? He said no. I asked him why, and he said, simply, that he wasn't allowed to make calls for people. I said I'd be happy to make the call myself if my ears worked, but because they didn't, it would help a lot if he could make the call for me. He said no again. Then he said something else, I'm not sure what exactly, and turned away from me. I got a little ornery at that point—I think I said something bad, I don't remember what—and he came back and said that if I didn't get off the property he'd call the police and have me arrested for trespassing.

"Please," I said.

The police took their sweet time arriving. They pulled up at the curb, rolled down their window, and I told my story yet again. "I'm deaf," I said. "I'm staying at this B&B three blocks away. I'm working on an art exhibition at MIT. I've been here for a week. Tonight I came home after a dinner with a friend, and when I tried to get into my room, there were people there already, and they slammed the door on me. Even when I explained to them what I'm explaining to you now. And they wouldn't come out. All I know is I've been sleeping in that room the past week, and my stuff should still be there. And I have a key to the room too—see?"

And the first thing the police guy says to me is: "How much have you been drinking tonight?"

I was taken aback a little—it was bad enough that the couple who showed up at the B&B didn't take me seriously, or the guy at the copy shop, but the cops too? So I said I'd had two glasses of Château Langoa Barton with dinner, and a glass of Lagavulin whisky with two ice cubes after dinner, and that this was three hours ago, and did it matter?

The cop said no, as long as I could really remember which room was mine. I don't think he was trying to be funny, but I had this very distinct impression that they didn't believe me. But they agreed to go with me to the B&B anyhow.

Joseph Grigely, *Untitled Conversations*, 1996. Ink and felt tip pen on paper

When we got to the mansion they seemed genuinely surprised when my key opened the front door. And they seemed even more surprised when I led them upstairs to room 3, put my key in the door, and turned the deadbolt open.

They took over at that point. I'm not sure exactly what transpired, only that they said something back and forth with the people in the room, and it went on for about ten minutes before the door finally opened a bit, and I could see the visage of a woman. She looked a little scared, and I suppose she was. The cops asked her to look around for my stuff, but she couldn't find anything except a couple of conversation papers of mine that had slipped behind a dresser onto the floor. "See?" I said to the police. "My stuff."

We decided to let the lady and her husband keep the room and get some sleep—and try to find, if we could, my clothes and other stuff, and maybe even a room with a bed where I could sleep. The first thing we did was go down to the nightstand phone and call the emergency number. Again, there was no answer. Then we did a little looking around for my stuff—they tried a bunch of doors, the kitchen, the basement—then they tried all the guest room doors, but they were all locked tight. Every door was—and my key only opened room 3.

By now it was getting really late. One cop said he'd tear the place apart if they did something like that to him. I asked him if he would tear the place apart on my behalf, but he said no, because he was in uniform. I felt a little triumphant that he finally believed my story, even if I didn't have my stuff or my room. One of the really frustrating things about being deaf is getting people to believe you. It doesn't matter what the issue is. The fact that you're deaf makes you suspect.

By now the cops themselves were getting a little tired. It was probably way past their 2:00 a.m. coffee break, so I couldn't blame them. In the end they called MIT security and asked around a bit—the plan was for the Brookline police to deliver me to the MIT police, and the MIT police would deliver me to the MIT housing people, and the MIT housing people would deliver me to a cot somewhere.

The handover happened on a bridge above the Charles River separating Boston from Cambridge: One police car met another, and I was traded off at 3:30 in the morning. I said thank you to the Brookline police, who seemed as pleased with my gratitude as they were to get rid of me.

I flew back to Michigan later that day. I think I told the MIT people I wasn't feeling too well, or something—it seemed the easiest way out of an uneasy situation.

A few weeks later, I received at my office at the University of Michigan a letter whose return address I didn't recognize. It was from the lady who had been in the room with her husband. She was apologetic and explained how scared she had been—not sure what was happening, and not sure what to do. It was only later, she said, after returning to her home, that this deafness thing started to make sense to her. She explained how her daughter had told her she actually had a deaf professor who taught art history, and how the professor was cut off from communicating with the students when the room was darkened while he showed slides—he'd be talking and the students would be laughing and there was this tangle of miscommunication. The lady said it was like the door that separated us that night. And she said again that she was sorry, because after she told the story to her daughter, her daughter thought about it for a while, then told her mom that the deaf guy on the other side of the door that night in Brookline was actually her professor from Michigan.

There might be a moral here. But if there is, I'm not sure what it is.

MIT Police
Will be calling their Housing
Dept to see if there
is a place for you Tonight
They Will get back to
us.

I was telling the other
officer I would tear
this place apart if they
Did this to me!

The MIT Police will
meet us at the BU
Bridge.

Joseph Grigely, *Untitled Conversations*, 1996. Ink on paper

Blindness and Deafness as Metaphors: An Anthological Essay, 2006

For William Van Wyke

Originally published in *Journal of Visual Culture*, vol. 5, no. 2, 2006.

For an extended period starting in the 1990s, I collected and inventoried an archive of quotations in which writers had used blindness and deafness as disparaging metaphors for ignorance and indifference. Typically, these quotations involved a pejorative reference, like this comment by the distinguished scholar Elaine Showalter: "We can hardly fail to welcome male feminist criticism when we have so long lamented the blindness, the deafness, and indifference of the male critical establishment towards our work."[1]

As George Lakoff and Mark Johnson write in *Metaphors We Live By*, metaphors like these are most telling for what they reveal about underlying social thought and permissiveness: They express values that are embedded in culture.[2] A metaphor is not just a figure of speech; it is a figure of thinking. The use of such metaphors in social discourse tells us a little about our collective cultural consciousness—and about how, as a community of authors and readers, we express biases, whether those biases are intentional or not.

I continue to inventory the use of metaphors of disablement and re-present these metaphors as a way of mirroring them back to the people who write them. This project is ongoing.

A key defect of most accounts of handicap is their blind disregard for the accretions of history. Insofar as such elements do enter into accounts of handicap, they generally consist of a ragbag of examples from Leviticus via Richard III to Frankenstein, all serving to indicate the supposed perennial, "natural" character of discrimination against the handicapped. Such "histories" serve paradoxically to produce an understanding of handicap which is... an ahistorical one.
—Paul Abberley[3]

I spent part of one afternoon with Evelyn Patterson Burrell, a black poet. She is the author of "Weep No More," a moving narrative poem of black history in America. From her I began to learn how "the two Baltimores" have kept separate chronicles of the city for centuries, something most whites in the city have been too blind to understand.
—Tony Hiss[4]

The nomination of Judge Clarence Thomas to the Supreme Court is expected to become the topic of a difficult and potentially divisive debate when the annual convention of the National Association for the Advancement of Colored People is held here this week.

"It has indeed become a major priority," said Dr. Benjamin L. Hooks, the executive director of the association, which considers itself the oldest and largest civil rights organization in the country....

That Judge Thomas is black by no means assures him of the support of the N.A.A.C.P., Dr. Hooks said. "We are not going to let race blind us to the totality of the situation," he said.
—*The New York Times*[5]

The anti-Semitic outrages of Crown Heights are aimed at the Jews of only one neighborhood in one city—for the moment.

But American Jews who do not understand that the same kind of political thugs will try now to lead the same kind of street thugs to burn Jewish property and break Jewish bones in other cities are blind to reality, deaf to history—and suicidal.
—A. M. Rosenthal, *The New York Times*[6]

More than 200 years of democracy have taught Americans—more than most other people in the world—to see issues with fairness and objectivity. Except when it comes to ethnicity. The subject is so sensitive that people who are otherwise full of common sense lose control of themselves. They become absolutely deaf to any reasoning but the one dictated by their own fears.
—Roger Hernandez, *The Jersey Journal*[7]

Visual elegance and technical refinement are common attributes of the works of David T. Hanson and the collaborative team of Leone & Macdonald. All three artists create deceptively accessible works to reveal human foibles and folly, from destruction of the environment to the blindness, insensitivity, and prejudices in personal relationships.
—Advertisement in *Art New England* for the exhibition *Critical Adjustments* at the David Winton Bell Gallery, Brown University, February 3–March 10, 1996

We create maps of language that present cultural pilgrimages and metaphorical journeys of transformation that can be experienced as rites of passage through life and death to rebirth and resurrection, fostering greater cultural awareness and understanding. They are composed of collaged and edited quotations from world music including spirituals, blues, gospel, soul, jazz, funk, samba, merengue, reggae, rap music, and freedom songs in dialect, and critical voicings from speeches of heroic models of African American culture. Their prophetic and humanistic words reflect the values and aspirations of the culture—hope, wisdom, temperance, justice, and love—and function as both a critique and a healing, addressing issues of world peace, social justice, human rights, civil rights, rights of the physically challenged, freedom, equality, democracy, history, memory, cultural identity, loss, cultural diversity, multicultural education, pro-choice, public support for the arts, ecology, and caring. They also address the universal enemies of war, hatred, racism, oppression, classism, violence, bigotry, censorship, sickness, drug addiction, sexism, ageism, apartheid, homelessness, AIDS, greed, imperialism, colonialism, militarism, historical and cultural amnesia, cross-cultural blindness, and fear of the Other.
—Houston Conwill, Joseph De Pace, and Estella Conwill Majozo[8]

Some artists make us rethink the very foundations of our relationship to art. All of a sudden we may find ourself wondering what it is that links us to a particular set of objects, or an environment, or a project, and, in response, altering the way we used to look at all the others. This is the case with Pierre Joseph's work.... In a word, his work clearly shows why it is henceforth unacceptable to conceive of art as an "inspired" individual expression, or as a self-referential system for justifying all manner of cynicism, not to say blindness.
—Nicolas Bourriaud[9]

The world of Maasai art is a world of bones. Choosing not to work with pigments when making paintings or decorative art, the Maasai use bones from hunting animals in their art to give expression to their relationship with nature and with their ancestors. Maasai artists believe that bones speak—tell all the necessary cultural information, take the place of history books. Bones become the repository of personal and political history. Maasai art survives as a living memory of the distinctiveness of black culture that flourished most vigorously when it was undiscovered by the white man. It is this privacy that white imperialism violates and destroys. Turle [in *The Art of the Maasai*] emphasizes that while the bones are "intense focus points to prime minds into a deeper receptive state," this communicative power is lost on those who are unable to hear bones speak.
—bell hooks[10]

Whites sometimes ask why we continue to find it necessary to invoke the past. They do not want to be blamed for the sins of their fathers, and they exhort us to move on. But this is a story that has not ended. Cultural exclusion continues today—and in some ways it is getting worse. Our entire society is paying a price for this cultural blindness.
—Peggy Cooper Cafritz, *The Washington Post*[11]

Her tires have been slashed, she said. Trash was dumped on her bed. A mousetrap was placed in her boots, and the boots were slashed. And the words of abuse have never let up since Katrina Cannon joined the New York City Fire Department nine years ago, she charged yesterday—all because she is a woman and black.

"Sometimes they say it's sex," Firefighter Cannon said at a news conference yesterday. "I believe it is color as well. It's vindictive, malicious, and cowardly."

Flanked by ministers and politicians on the steps of City Hall, the veteran firefighter said she had complained to the Fire Department and other city officials on many occasions, to no avail. The only official satisfaction came in 1986, when a Federal judge in Brooklyn issued a restraining order barring her male colleagues from "subjecting her to unequal, unfair and discriminatory conditions on account of her sex."

The restraining order has provided little relief, the 37-year-old firefighter said yesterday. "My complaints have fallen on deaf ears."
—*The New York Times*[12]

If the Supreme Court rules in favor of the Boy Scouts, it would be agreeing with the blind and tragic view that gays by their very nature are incapable of being good citizens; it would be sending the message that they shouldn't even bother to try.
—Luke Wyatt[13]

Thomas Jefferson embodied the most powerful contradiction of the American legacy. His declarations on individual liberty, which remain a moral and political compass, showed the brilliance of a transcendent mind. But he also believed in the inferiority of black people, demonstrating how even a great thinker can remain captive of the racist stereotypes of his time. That one man could simultaneously possess such vision and such blindness is intriguing: that his attitudes on race should persist in the culture at large, as they have, tells a troubling story about American society.
—David K. Shipler, *The New York Times*[14]

Quick. What do Linda Pugach, Mary Jo Buttafuoco, and Hillary Clinton all have in common? If you guessed that they are all natural blonds, you lose, but if you guessed that they are all blind, you win. In the love game, you may have noticed, you don't have to be legally blind to be in serious need of a big cane. The three blind mice in this case stood by their men, despite public humiliation and/or physical disfigurement, proving beyond a shadow of a doubt that the women's movement never actually happened.
—Linda Stasi[15]

...this is demonstrated by example, by the problem of the example and the reflective judgment. Now what does the *Critique of Pure Reason* tell us? That examples are the wheelchairs [*roulettes*] of judgment. The French translators sometimes say the "crutches" of judgment: but it really is wheelchairs (*Gängelwagen*), not skateboards [*planches-à-roulettes*] but the little wheeled cars in which children, the old, or the sick are pushed, those who have not enough judgment, enough good sense, that faculty of natural judgment, the best-shared thing (this is not the *sensus communis* of the third *Critique*) that is called—this is Kant's word—*Mutterwitz*. Those who do not have enough of this maternal *Witz*, the sick, imbeciles, need wheelchairs, examples. "Examples are thus the wheelchairs of the faculty of judging (*Gängelwagen der Urteilskraft*) and those who lack (*mangelt*) this natural talent will not be able to do without them." The wheelchairs, however, do not replace judgment: nothing can replace the *Mutterwitz*, the lack of which cannot be supplied by any school (*dessen Mangel keine Schule ersetzen kann*). The exemplary wheelchairs are thus prostheses which replace nothing. But like all examples

(*Beispielen*), as Hegel will have pointed out, they play, there is play in them, they give room to play. To the essence, beside the essence (*beiher*), Hegel goes on to make clear. Thus they can invert, unbalance, incline the natural movement into a parergonal movement, divert the energy of the *ergon*, introduce chance and the abyss into the necessity of the *Mutterwitz*: not a contrary order but an aleatory sidestep which can make one lose one's head suddenly, a Russian roulette if one puts into play pleasure without enjoyment, the deathdrive and the mourning of labor in the experience of the beautiful.
—Jacques Derrida[16]

We can hardly fail to welcome male feminist criticism when we have so long lamented the blindness, the deafness, and indifference of the male critical establishment towards our work.
—Elaine Showalter[17]

The world's largest law firm and one of its former partners turned a blind eye to complaints of sexual harassment, a Superior Court jury decided here today, ending the first stage of a monthlong trial that has put the nation's legal community on notice that it must practice what it preaches.
—*The New York Times*[18]

All aspects of contemporary African cultural life—including music and some sculpture and painting, even some writings with which the West is largely not familiar—have been influenced, often powerfully, by the transition of African societies *through* colonialism, but they are not all in the relevant sense *post*colonial. For the *post-* in postcolonial, like the *post-* in postmodernism, is the *post-* of the space-clearing gesture I characterized earlier, and many areas of contemporary African cultural life—what has come to be theorized as popular culture, in particular—are not in this way concerned with transcending, with going beyond, coloniality. Indeed, it might be said to be a mark of popular culture that its borrowings from international cultural forms are remarkably insensitive to, not so much dismissive of as blind to, the issue of neocolonialism or "cultural imperialism."
—Kwame Anthony Appiah[19]

"Emergency Medicine Found Blind to Needs of Child"
—News headline, *The New York Times*, July 8, 1993

"China and America: Friends in Need of Hearing Aids"
—Op-Ed headline, *The New York Times*, June 28, 1998

"Tone Deaf on Africa"
—Op-Ed headline, *The New York Times*, July 3, 2005

"Ethical Blindness in the Kremlin"
—Editorial headline, *The New York Times*, November 19, 1997

"Din Over Koreas Deafens Reason"
—Letters headline, *The New York Times*, April 3, 1994

"How Good Intelligence Falls on Deaf Ears: A Short History of Leaders Who Ignored Bad News"
—Op-Ed headline, *The New York Times*, March 27, 2004

"The Environment: A Policy of Myopia"
—Letters headline, *The New York Times*, March 2, 2003

"Panel: U.S. Spy Agencies Are 'Disturbingly' Blind"
—News headline, *The Chicago Tribune*, April 2, 2005

"Disability Claims Cripple Newark Housing Agency"
—News headline, *The Star-Ledger* (Newark, NJ), July 30, 1995

The Dalai Lama, the exiled leader of Tibet, today renewed his efforts to visit his homeland by appealing to the world to put pressure on China to allow his return for a fact-finding mission.

In remarks at Yale University, the Tibetan leader expressed frustration with the protracted negotiations between his representatives and China, stating that he was ready to go "as soon as possible."...

The Dalai Lama said that the negotiations led nowhere. Pointing to his ears, he said of the Chinese: "It seemed that one of their organs, their listening organ, was missing."
—*The New York Times*[20]

God of grace and God of glory
Grant us wisdom, grant us courage,
Ears to hear and eyes to see
Ears to hear and eyes to see
—Unitarian hymn[21]

One problem in setting fares is that Aeroflot has no idea what its costs for individual flights are. It has always flown blind, without the discipline considered basic in the West—cost accounting, cost benefit analysis or capital budgeting.
—*The New York Times*[22]

The media, I prefer to speak of television, has become a site of fascination, which is watched but not seen. TV is an industry that manufactures blind eyes.
—Barbara Kruger[23]

Cocaine can make you blind. That's the drug talking. Cocaine really does make you blind to reality. And with what's known about it today, you probably have to be something else to start using coke in the first place. Dumb.
—Advertisement, Partnership for a Drug-Free America[24]

Mr. Hammons fashions art in his Harlem studio mostly from neighborhood detritus—Thunderbird and Night Train bottles, greasy paper bags, bottle caps, inner tubes, even human hair swept off a barber's floor, objects he has described as having a "history." He then transforms them into art, creating fetishlike pyramids from hair or making social puns like "Coke Cane," a wall sculpture in which an empty Coke bottle tied to a blind man's cane suggests the blind waste of addiction.
—Patrick Pacheco, *The New York Times*[25]

Culture is always a process of getting away from stasis, from a pre-established identity, from a closed cultural anthropology, from a geography which is deaf and blocked and stuck to itself.
—Andrea Fraser[26]

To the Editor:

Nothing more painfully demonstrates Martha C. Nussbaum's argument in "Love's Knowledge" that large parts of philosophy are deaf to some of life's most important questions than Jenny Teichman's review of that book. Not a mention at all in the review of the central Aristotelian argument that informs the book, and not a hint either that philosophical ethics has been radically transformed in the last 15 years by recognition of that argument. Nor would the general reader of the review be aware that Ms. Nussbaum is considered one of the most pivotal and eloquent defenders of that argument in philosophy today.

Ms. Teichman's review is blind and hostile. To my mind, it is mainly snake venom.
—Haskel Levi[27]

Writers who do believe in religious realities and propose to get them across in fiction, have to cope with a deaf, dumb, and blind reader; and the grotesque may be one of our desperate answers.
—Flannery O'Connor[28]

Question: This year most of my established daffodils came up blind. No blooms! While the ones planted last fall were fabulous. Can you explain this? When do daffodils set buds for the following year?

Answer: Under favorable conditions, daffodil leaves gradually wither, yellow, die down and eventually fall off. The weeks following are erroneously referred to by some as the dormant period. Actually growth continues at this time underground. The bulbs multiply, increase in weight and size, and set flower buds for next spring. You must have had an early hot and fairly dry spell last spring which caused the leaves of your just-bloomed daffodils to die prematurely. You might have been able to minimize the problem if you had given your bulbs deep waterings and fertilized. Although the dry spell didn't kill them, they weren't able to increase their size or set bulbs for this season. For success next year, provide the necessary water and

fertilizer and the flowers should be back in droves. The daffodils you planted this fall had developed flower buds before they were sold which is why they were able to bloom this spring. To bloom as well next year they, too, will need sufficient watering and fertilizing to thrive.
—C. Z. Guest, *The New York Post*[29]

Recently while riding a train from Washington, D.C., to New York, I found myself along the part of New York Harbor's shoreline that some people unkindly call "the chemical coast." Many New Yorkers forget that this is part of their harbor because it is "out of town" in New Jersey. Usually when I'm returning to New York, at this point I would look homeward to Manhattan at the never-disappointing skyline of the island where I live. Otherwise I would look out at smokestacks and pipes and flames from refineries. But for some reason, this one time, I looked instead right in front of me and realized that I was in a grassy wetland—a magnificent grassy wetland where egrets and herons could live. As the grass rolled in waves and the sun reflected on narrow waterways, I saw that this could have been a northern Everglades. By what act of blind insanity did people decide to build chemical plants, oil refineries, and heavy industry in a beautiful wetland that belonged to one of the world's great waterways? Blind madness? It occurred to me that they had probably never really looked at it either.
—Mark Kurlansky[30]

This work is in response to the recent boom in racism in America and its backlash. Leaving in its wake a mix of blind rage, defiance, and utter despair.
—Wall label at the 1993 Whitney Biennial for Alison Saar's *Man/Club* (1993)

For centuries, women artists have struggled against opposition from family, blind prejudice from society, and even public scorn. They've been forbidden proper training by the art schools of their day... prevented from exhibiting at the best galleries... and overshadowed by better-known fathers, husbands, and brothers.
—Rebecca Phillips Abbott[31]

We keep making excuses for Pollock—he was, after all, a tormented genius, and so needful; and he had that "Pollock charm." Hoping that the next therapist, the next friendship or the next art dealer will bring about a miracle, we watch with horror the drunken binges after which Pollock ends up in the gutter, in Bellevue, or in jail. The self-destruction is tedious, ugly and repetitive, but we are engaged; we keep hoping that each drunken brawl will be the last, until, blind drunk in 1956, Pollock drives his car into a clump of trees.
—Hayden Herrera[32]

The Constitution is not honored by blind worship. The more open-eyed we become, as a nation, to its defects... the nearer we will approach to the sound sense and practical genius of the great and honorable statesmen of 1787.
—Woodrow Wilson, text from a mural on the J. Edgar Hoover FBI Building, 935 Pennsylvania Avenue NW, Washington, DC

The refugees attempting to escape from Haiti do not claim a right of admission to this country. They do not even argue that the Government has no right to intercept their boats. They demand only that the United States, land of refugees and guardian of freedom, cease forcibly

driving them back to detention, abuse and death. That is a modest plea, vindicated by the Treaty [the UN Protocol Relating to the Status of Refugees] and the statute [the US Refugee Act of 1980]. We should not close our ears to it.
—Justice Harry A. Blackmun[33]

Alas, when I installed the sheet-fed Easy Photo Smart Page Pro (about $150 after manufacturer's rebate) from Storm Technology Inc., my Hewlett-Packard ink-jet printer went deaf to software commands. Storm's spokesmen insisted that the scanner and printer should have had no problems together, but the technical help line recommended a fix that disabled the printer's two-way communication. It works, but it will cause much unnecessary grief before users figure it out, and it keeps the printer from reporting things like being out of paper.
—Stephen Manes, *The New York Times*[34]

But the music, oh dear. It's a disaster on a par with the piece of scenery that fell on Philip Casnoff's head and delayed the show's opening night. The score is least dismaying where the composer Paul Chihara has had to supply background music for martial arts pantomimes; where he has had to set John Driver's witless lyrics, it reaches the status of mortal sin. If ever a musical asked to be signed for the deaf, it's *Shogun*.
—Thomas M. Disch[35]

And for those who wonder how Owens, who loved his daughters and talked about them constantly, could leave them so abruptly, a partial answer may be found in Andrew Solomon's prize-winning book, "The Noonday Demon: An Atlas of Depression" (2001), which supplies an unforgettable portrait of severe depression: "Becoming depressed is like going blind, the darkness at first gradual, then encompassing; it is like going deaf, hearing less and less until a terrible silence is all around you."
—Julia Keller, *The Chicago Tribune*[36]

That "Messiah" has stood the test of time in the more conventional sense is beyond question: indeed, it was so popular in its original incarnation as an Easter work that in the 19th century it took on a second life as a Christmas evergreen. But in music, familiarity does not breed contempt but something equally dangerous: a numbing of the senses, a blindness to detail.
—Allan Kozinn, *The New York Times*[37]

What Brillat-Savarin said in 1825 about frying is still true, because it is based on nature's laws, and the same holds for a master like Escoffier on sauces and roasting, for any thoughtful cook, derivative or not, who bows to law and does not wildly say "Twice as much butter, or garlic, or zubzubzub *must* be twice as good... If a pinch of nutmeg picks up this dish of spinach, *two* pinches..." and so on.

We who must eat such well-meant messes can do no better than refuse them and then beseech all such misguided cooks to stop and consider, to ponder on the *reasons* as well as the results, and to decide for themselves and also for our stomachs' sakes to follow the rules based on common sense and experience, the rules set down by great chefs, whatever their sex and in whichever of these last two centuries they have worked.

We must hold out the torch to these taste-deafened friends of ours and promise them that they too can throw away a few, if not all, of their gastronomical hearing aids; they too, once they have learned how to walk among the pots and pipkins, can add saffron where Escoffier said thyme, or put kirsch instead of maraschino into a soufflé—once they have rightly learned what saffron tastes like, and what a soufflé is.
—M. F. K. Fisher[38]

To the Editor:

Sue Halpern ("The Wildlife Next Door," Op-Ed, June 14) has it right: By getting people to accept the nature we find around us—the everyday ant, the familiar butterfly—as the same "nature" we are told we should protect and revere, we can turn appreciation into action....

However, if we do not teach our children to recognize this fact, they will continue to be alienated from the environment, and thus hold themselves unaccountable for its fate. Until we teach that the environment we are trying to save is not just some distant rain forest, but our own Hudson River and Long Island Sound, the environmental lessons will fall on deaf, uneducated ears.
—Adelle Caravanos[39]

The history of New York oysters is a history of New York itself—its wealth, its strength, its excitement, its greed, its thoughtlessness, its destructiveness, its blindness and—as any New Yorker will tell you—its filth. This is the history of the trashing of New York, the killing of its great estuary.
—Mark Kurlansky[40]

I think that one of the saddest aspects of our time is the total destruction in people's awareness of all that goes with a conscious sense of the beautiful. Modern mass culture, aimed at the "consumer," the civilisation of prosthetics, is crippling people's souls, setting up barriers between man and the crucial questions of his existence, his consciousness of himself as a spiritual being. But the artist cannot be deaf to the call of truth; it alone defines his creative will, organises it, thus enabling him to pass on his faith to others. An artist who has no faith is like a painter who was born blind.
—Andrey Tarkovsky[41]

Geology tells us that there have been "greenhouse worlds" in the distant past. These have been times when seas flooded over continents. Even modest sea-level rises would spell the end of densely populated areas of the world like Bangladesh. In such a case, invoking the deity to look after us for the best is just pie in the sky. These are not "acts of God" but acts of man. We can grieve for the human consequences of plate tectonics, but we should be ashamed of the consequences of our own willing blindness.
—Richard Fortey, *The New York Times*[42]

1 Elaine Showalter, "Critical Cross-Dressing: Male Feminists and the Woman of the Year," *Raritan* 3, no. 2 (1983).

2 George Lakoff and Mark Johnson, *Metaphors We Live By* (University of Chicago Press, 1980), 22.

3 Paul Abberley, "Policing Cripples: Social Theory and Physical Handicap," unpublished paper, 1985, quoted in Brendan Gleeson, *Geographies of Disability* (Routledge, 1999), 23.

4 Tony Hiss, "Reinventing Baltimore," Annals of Place, *New Yorker*, April 29, 1991, 69.

5 Robert Suro, "Court Nominee at Focus of Debate as N.A.A.C.P. Meets in Houston," *New York Times*, July 8, 1991.

6 A. M. Rosenthal, "Pogrom in Brooklyn," On My Mind, *New York Times*, September 3, 1991.

7 Roger Hernandez, "On Ethnicity: Some People Are Deaf to All Reasoning," *Jersey Journal*, January 24, 1992.

8 Houston Conwill, Joseph De Pace, and Estella Conwill Majozo, "Artists' Statement," published in conjunction with the exhibition *The New Merengue*, Brooklyn Museum, January 31–May 3, 1992.

9 Nicolas Bourriaud, *Pierre Joseph: Personnages à réactiver* (FRAC Languedoc-Roussillon, 1995).

10 bell hooks, "Altars of Sacrifice: Re-membering Basquiat," *Art in America*, June 1993, 72.

11 Peggy Cooper Cafritz, "Culture in Black and White: Why Don't Washington's Arts Institutions Reflect Our Diversity?," *Washington Post*, January 20, 1991.

12 Dennis Hevesi, "Firefighter Again Makes Her Harassment Charge," *New York Times*, October 18, 1991.

13 Luke Wyatt, letter to the editor, *New York Times*, April 29, 2000.

14 David K. Shipler, "Jefferson Is America—And America Is Jefferson," *New York Times*, April 12, 1993.

15 Linda Stasi, "From the Hip," *Village Voice*, May 13, 1997.

16 Jacques Derrida, *The Truth in Painting*, trans. Geoff Bennington and Ian McLeod (University of Chicago Press, 1987), 79.

17 Elaine Showalter, "Critical Cross-Dressing: Male Feminists and the Woman of the Year," *Raritan* 3, no. 2 (1983).

18 Jane Gross, "Jury Faults Law Firm on Harassment," *New York Times*, August 27, 1994.

19 Kwame Anthony Appiah, "Is the Post- in Postmodernism the Post- in Postcolonial?," *Critical Inquiry* 17, no. 2 (1991): 348.

20 Ari L. Goldman, "Dalai Lama Appeals for Help in Going Home," *New York Times*, October 10, 1991.

21 Harry Emerson Fosdick, "God of Grace and God of Glory," *Singing the Living Tradition: Hymnbook of the Unitarian Universalist Association* (Beacon Press, 1992).

22 G. Bruce Knecht, "Aeroflot Takes Aim at the Post-Communist World," *New York Times*, January 12, 1992.

23 Barbara Kruger, interview by Jeanne Siegel, in *Art Talk: The Early 80s*, ed. Jeanne Siegel (Da Capo, 1988), 304.

24 DDB Needham Worldwide Inc., advertisement in the New Jersey Bell Yellow Pages, n.d.

25 Patrick Pacheco, "Art Gets Serious with a New Set of Stars," *New York Times*, March 3, 1991.

26 Andrea Fraser, *Austrian Contributions to the 45th Biennale of Venice*, 1993, 190.

27 Haskel Levi, letter to the editor, *New York Times Book Review*, March 17, 1991.

28 Flannery O'Connor, unsigned typed letter addressed to Mr. O'Connor, January 19, 1957.

29 C. Z. Guest, "Can't See Why Daffodils Blind [*sic*]," Around the Garden, *New York Post*, June 18, 1994.

30 Mark Kurlansky, *The Big Oyster: History on the Half Shell* (Ballantine Books, 2006), xvi.

31 Rebecca Phillips Abbott, mail solicitation on behalf of the National Museum of Women in the Arts, July 1992.

32 Hayden Herrera, "Artist's Life," *Art in America*, April 1991, 41.

33 Harry A. Blackmun, dissenting opinion, Sale v. Haitian Centers Council, US Supreme Court, 1993. Reported in "Excerpts from High Court Decision Upholding Policy on Haitian Refugees," *New York Times*, June 22, 1993.

34 Stephen Manes, "Color Scans, Now at Bargain Prices," Personal Computers, *New York Times*, October 14, 1997.

35 Thomas M. Disch, "Theater," *The Nation*, January 7/14, 1991, 26.

36 Julia Keller, "The Life He Left Behind," *Chicago Tribune*, October 11, 2002.

37 Allan Kozinn, "Listening to 'Messiah,' Listening to 'Messiah' and Listening Again," *New York Times*, December 24, 1991.

38 M. F. K. Fisher, "An Alphabet for Gourmets," in *The Art of Eating* (World Publishing, 1954), 673–4.

39 Adelle Caravanos, letter to the editor, *New York Times*, June 19, 2001.

40 Kurlansky, *The Big Oyster*, xvi.

41 Andrey Tarkovsky, *Sculpting in Time: Reflections on the Cinema*, trans. Kitty Hunter-Blair (Knopf, 1987), 42–43.

42 Richard Fortey, "Blind to the End," *New York Times*, December 26, 2005.

The Neglected Demographic: Faculty Members with Disabilities, 2017

Originally published in *The Chronicle of Higher Education*, July 21, 2017.

In recent years, one of the challenges of higher education has involved a generational shift in how we understand the ways disability populates postsecondary institutions. A great deal of focus and funding has been devoted to the learning side of the community—the students—in part because the legal obligations are very clearly defined and support services have evolved over many decades of implementation. However, little attention has been paid to the teaching side of the community: how disabled faculty are considered in relation to larger DEI initiatives, and how the Americans with Disabilities Act functions in an educational environment. Every school I've taught at has handled the needs of disabled faculty members with what feels like a DIY approach, and there has been little consistency from school to school. In 2017, after teaching in higher education for thirty-five years, I decided to write an op-ed on the subject of faculty members with disabilities. The original draft was five times longer than the space I was ultimately given—there's so much to say about the topic.

More than twenty-five years after the passage of the Americans with Disabilities Act, the situation for students with disabilities has vastly improved. Most colleges now have offices for disability-related accommodations, and students are using these services in exponential numbers: At the School of the Art Institute of Chicago (SAIC), where I teach, the cumulative demand for services offered by the Disability and Learning Resource Center grew by more than 800 percent between 2002 and 2015.[1] Data gathered by the National Center for Education Statistics shows that about 11 percent of the undergraduates in postsecondary education in the United States have a disability.[2] Faculty members are now required to include in their syllabi statements about disability-related accommodations, and many college websites now advertise their services for disabled students.

One has to look harder to find information on disabled faculty members. What percentage of higher-education faculty members are disabled? How are their requests for reasonable accommodation managed by colleges? How do disability and accommodation figure into tenure and promotion reviews? There's startlingly little published on this subject. At the University of California, Berkeley, a recent Freedom of Information Act request revealed that out of a total of 1,522 full-time faculty members, 24—roughly 1.5 percent—are disabled.[3] The National Center for College Students with Disabilities estimates that 4 percent of all faculty members have disabilities.[4] These numbers are discouraging, given that 22 percent of the general population has disabilities.[5]

One of the biggest challenges for faculty members with disabilities is the process of making requests for accommodations. Few colleges have an accommodations officer who is trained to serve faculty members. At my college, for example, a faculty request for accommodations must first be made to the department chair, which means revealing confidential medical information to someone who probably has no training in how to interpret it—and who, as chair, will contribute to evaluating that person for tenure and promotion.[6] This approach compromises the integrity of the evaluation process, and might dissuade some faculty members who need, and deserve, reasonable accommodations from making such requests.

In contrast, most schools have trained accommodations officers on staff to assess students' requests on a case-by-case basis, and decisions are communicated to teachers without revealing a student's underlying medical condition, which is protected by confidentiality laws. So why should faculty have to reveal their medical conditions—which can range from physical disabilities to psychological conditions—to their department chairs? Or to a hiring committee? As disability studies scholars Jay Dolmage and Stephanie Kerschbaum have recently argued, "The system in place should not require a candidate to open a conversation with a search committee member or department chair that reveals personal health information or specifics about their disability."[7]

1 Valerie St. Germain, director of the Disability and Learning Resource Center at SAIC, personal communication, December 2, 2016.

2 "Fast Facts: Students with Disabilities," US Department of Education, Institute of Education Sciences, National Center for Education Statistics, archived July 2, 2017, at https://web.archive.org/web/20170702130041/https://nces.ed.gov/fastfacts/display.asp?id=60.

3 "Number of Disabled Faculty and Staff at UC Berkeley," Faculty Coalition for Disability Rights at UC Berkeley, accessed July 30, 2024, https://ucbdisabilityrights.org/2017/02/26/number-of-disabled-faculty/.

4 Wendy Harbour, director, National Center for College Students with Disabilities, personal communication, February 27, 2017.

5 As of 2015. See: "Disability Impacts All of Us: A Snapshot of Disability in the United States," Centers for Disease Control and Prevention, archived July 11, 2017, at https://web.archive.org/web/20170711011016/https://www.cdc.gov/ncbddd/disabilityandhealth/infographic-disability-impacts-all.html.

6 "Workplace Accommodation Policy for Faculty," Art Institute of Chicago, archived June 18, 2017, at https://web.archive.org/web/20170618125457/http://www.saic.edu/media/saic/pdfs/faculty/Workplace-Accommodation-Faculty-Policy2-10-17.pdf.

For these reasons it should be a priority to rethink the ways institutions process faculty requests for disability accommodations. For starters, faculty members need a dedicated administrator with appropriate professional training to facilitate on-campus access and to advocate for access when they travel as part of their professional research and work. Ideally, all access requests from faculty, staff, students, and visitors should be managed within a single office staffed by people with requisite training and experience; preferably, these would be people who are themselves disabled, or who grew up with a family member with a disability, which would instill in the accommodations process an often-missing sense of empathy. Colleges that want the best-qualified faculty members have to realize that these professors need access support that is commensurate with their professional status.

Of course, accommodations cost money, but by fostering the inclusion of faculty members with disabilities and providing the resources they need to focus on their academic work, the college benefits in at least three ways:

First, accommodations are not simply for the disabled person; they are for the community. The usual (legal) way of thinking is that ramps are for wheelchair users, sign language interpreters are for deaf people, and readers are for the blind, but these examples of access are monodirectional. Access needs to be bidirectional. If access is only "for" the disabled, it serves no social purpose; and by condescending to meet what is seen as an individual need, we limit our perception of the disabled person to that of a passive agent, a receptacle for experience. Many times I have had an interpreter arrive for an event and say something like "I am here to interpret for Joseph Grigely," when the interpreter is there to facilitate communication for everyone. Access is a *shared* resource: When an institution considers whether a request for accommodation is an "undue hardship," it needs to apportion the cost in relation to all who benefit from it—not just the disabled person.

Second, disability is an affirming identity: People with disabilities contribute to diversity, just as other minorities do. Disability cannot be represented by token conferences and guest speakers during Disability Awareness Month; it must be a daily presence in classrooms, at faculty meetings, in student unions and dorms, in gyms and art galleries. The disability community is a cross section of American society, and the layered identities of people with disabilities offer an important lesson in intersectionality. Legal debates about disability-related accommodations tend to divert our attention from the importance of disability as a powerful, yet consistently marginalized, cultural force and identity. At a roundtable discussion at SAIC, students with disabilities lamented the lack of awareness about artists with disabilities when the subject turns to diversity in their art history classes. "They talk about women artists, and queer artists, and minority artists, but they hardly ever talk about disabled artists," one student said.[8]

Third, students with disabilities need role models with disabilities. Professors who have spent years lobbying for their own access can be proud of what they've accomplished, but it comes at a cost. As William J. Peace, a disability studies scholar and paraplegic, told *The Chronicle of Higher Education* in 2014, "I spend a lot of time—hours and hours—advocating for myself."[9] This may help explain why so few graduate students with disabilities pursue professional careers in academe: The task of having to advocate for yourself is a thankless professional

7 Jay Dolmage and Stephanie Kerschbaum, "Wanted: Disabled Faculty Members," *Inside Higher Ed*, October 30, 2016, https://www.insidehighered.com/advice/2016/10/31/advice-hiring-faculty-members-disabilities-essay.

8 Round Table Discussion on Disability Awareness, School of the Art Institute of Chicago, March 15, 2017.

9 Audrey Williams June, "Indifference Toward Disabled Scholars, Especially at Conferences, Troubles a Disabilities Scholar," *Chronicle of Higher Education*, June 16, 2014, https://www.chronicle.com/article/indifference-toward-disabled-scholars-especially-at-conferences-troubles-a-disabilities-scholar/.

obligation. When I give talks at schools, conferences, and museums, I often spend more time trying to arrange for adequate sign language interpreting than I spend preparing my talk. Not until disabled faculty can teach and research unencumbered by a need to advocate for access will students be able to see the possibilities of a career that extends beyond their disability.

Colleges need to be proactive in their approach to this issue. Ideally, they would establish committees to investigate the needs and experiences of faculty members with disabilities, and from this discussion create policies and procedures that reflect those needs. Guidance must come from the bottom up. According to a 2011 study, only 65 percent of postsecondary institutions offer students, faculty, and staff the opportunity to provide input on accessibility during project planning, and only 64 percent conduct needs-assessment surveys pertaining to disability.[10] These numbers show just how little institutions value the input of the people who know disability issues best—their own faculty members.

10 Kimberley Raue and Laurie Lewis, *Students with Disabilities at Degree-Granting Postsecondary Institutions* (US Department of Education, National Center for Education Statistics, June 2011), http://oeraccess.merlot.org/_media/documents/Students%20with%20Disabilities.pdf.

Stonework: Travels in the Art of Transience, 2019

Originally published in *Ursula*, no. 4, Fall 2019.

In 2019, Randy Kennedy wrote to me after seeing some of my posts on Instagram related to sculptures I made in abandoned quarries in the south of France in 1989. This was a time when I was working with different media and exploring the possibilities of both material and immaterial conceptual practices. Kennedy asked if I might write an essay about the sculptures for Hauser & Wirth's magazine *Ursula*, and this evolved into a longer piece about how I transitioned from making grids of quarried stone to grids of conversation papers between the late 1980s and early 1990s.

If things had gone a bit differently, I might have become a bricklayer instead of an artist. As it turned out, bricklaying led me to stonework, and stonework led me to making art, and in the process I learned about the pleasure of making. I also learned that, as an artist, a lot of what you make is simply for the meaning that comes from the making.

My father was a stonemason, and throughout high school and college I spent my summers doing masonry. We mainly built fireplaces and chimneys and block-walled buildings. The traditional New England house was built up around a massive chimney system with multiple fireplaces, and this was one of my father's specialties. It was hard work, first as a mason's tender, which involves mixing cement, carrying it up scaffolding in a hod, and moving around heavy concrete blocks. We didn't have mechanical lifts back in the 1970s; everything that went into a chimney we carried up a ladder on our shoulders. A hod full of eighteen bricks weighs eighty pounds. A single sixteen-inch concrete block weighs fifty-five pounds. Handling the materials of masonry made a mess of our hands—fingertips and knuckles often got skinned and bloodied. Our most important tool was a box of good Band-Aids.

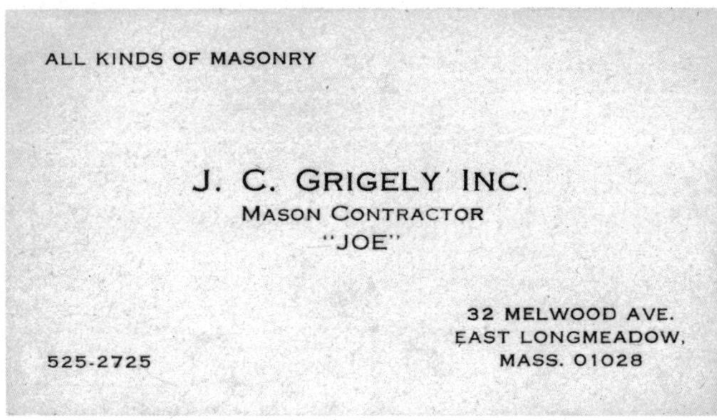

Business card, J. C. Grigely Inc., early 1970s

For various reasons, bricklaying never worked out as a profession for me. Most contractors on our job sites, the plumbers and electricians and framers, also had their sons working alongside them. Their truck doors said things like "William Creighton & Sons, Plumbers," or "Anthony Serafin & Sons, Electricians." But my dad's copper-brown dump truck said simply: "J. C. Grigely Inc., Mason Contractor." The other contractors asked him why he left his sons out, and his reply was always the same: He wanted his sons to do something different. So he was very supportive when I later decided to study English literature as an undergraduate, even if I had no idea what I would do with an English degree. The idea, for a while anyway, was that I liked reading, and if I was going to read a lot of literature, why not get a degree for it? After I had become deaf at the age of ten—I fell down a hill during a game of King on the Mountain—reading was my one, essentially singular, way of learning. But to get to the point of studying literature I had to graduate from high school, and this wasn't easy for a deaf person in the 1970s. There were no sign language interpreters in my school, so I took mostly "see-and-do" classes like woodshop and metal shop. Like bricklaying, these involved working with my hands. In other classes, I learned to feign understanding. To keep my sanity, I would often skip school altogether and go fishing.

My parents, thankfully, understood. To assuage their guilt, they bought me outdoor magazines like *Field & Stream*, *Fly Fisherman*, and *Outdoor Life*. From their perspective, I was reading, and that's what mattered. They wrote absentee notes that said, "Joey wasn't feeling well on Thursday, so he stayed home," when, in fact, I had been drifting muskrat nymphs on the Farmington River all day long. At least by tying flies and fishing, I was learning, which was

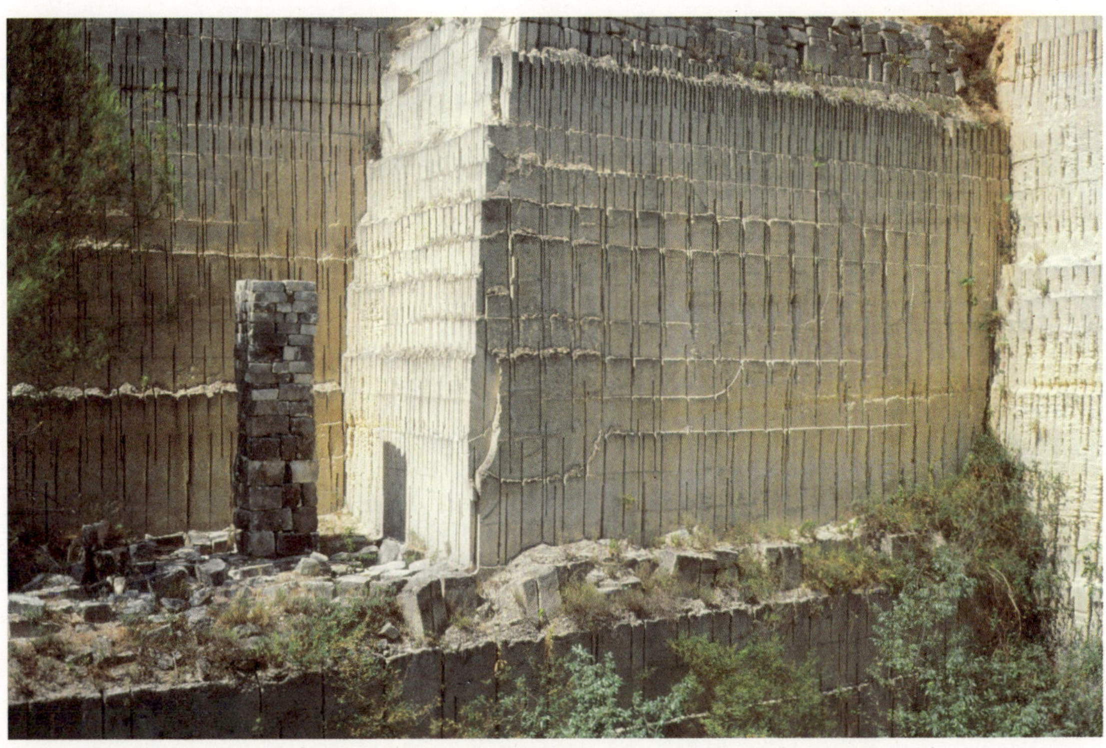

Joseph Grigely, *Re: Quarrying*, 1989. Limestone. Castries, France

more than I could say occurred in English class, where I struggled to lipread the mouths discussing *The Scarlet Letter* and other required texts. I flunked a lot of courses in high school. But somehow I graduated, and got into college, and even made it into Oxford for graduate school. All those fishing stories I had read paid off. There would be rewards for the masonry, too, but they came later.

It was at Oxford that I met the artist Rob Evans, who is largely to blame for my interest in art. One day we were both on a train from London to Oxford. Rob was reading Delacroix's *Journal*, and he gave me an emotional spiel about *The Shipwreck of Don Juan* and Delacroix's handling of paint and scale. He gestured expansively, spelling out words in big letters with his index finger. From Delacroix, he went on to Géricault. This was the beginning of my art education. For a while, when I was commuting to the Keats House in Hampstead, I'd spend mornings researching Keats's manuscripts and afternoons in the galleries with Rob. London was intense in the early 1980s—dungeon masters like Bacon and Freud and Auerbach ruled the Cork Street corridor, Schnabel's plate paintings were making a scene at the Royal Academy and Tate, and Tarkovsky was visiting Riverside Studios. We would sometimes hold all-night life-drawing sessions in the common room of a classmate's house, where we'd take turns being the model, with the model required to read poetry aloud. I got my first serious art lesson during one of these sessions, when I had a large sheet of paper in front of me and had no idea what to do with it. Rob saw the situation and commanded: "Stop staring at that paper. Attack it!"

A few years later, in the summer of 1986, when I was in Chicago and should have been writing on Keats as part of my Mellon Fellowship obligations, I chanced upon an empty lot in Hyde Park that was littered with stone rubble from a demolished building. That rubble seemed to sing a siren's song that said: *Touch me, lift me, pile me up.* And so, for a week, I gathered the rubble and piled it up. I didn't have any equipment to help move the stone, like a wheelbarrow, so it was a bit slow. I had no mason's level, either, so I had to do it all by eye. And I had no

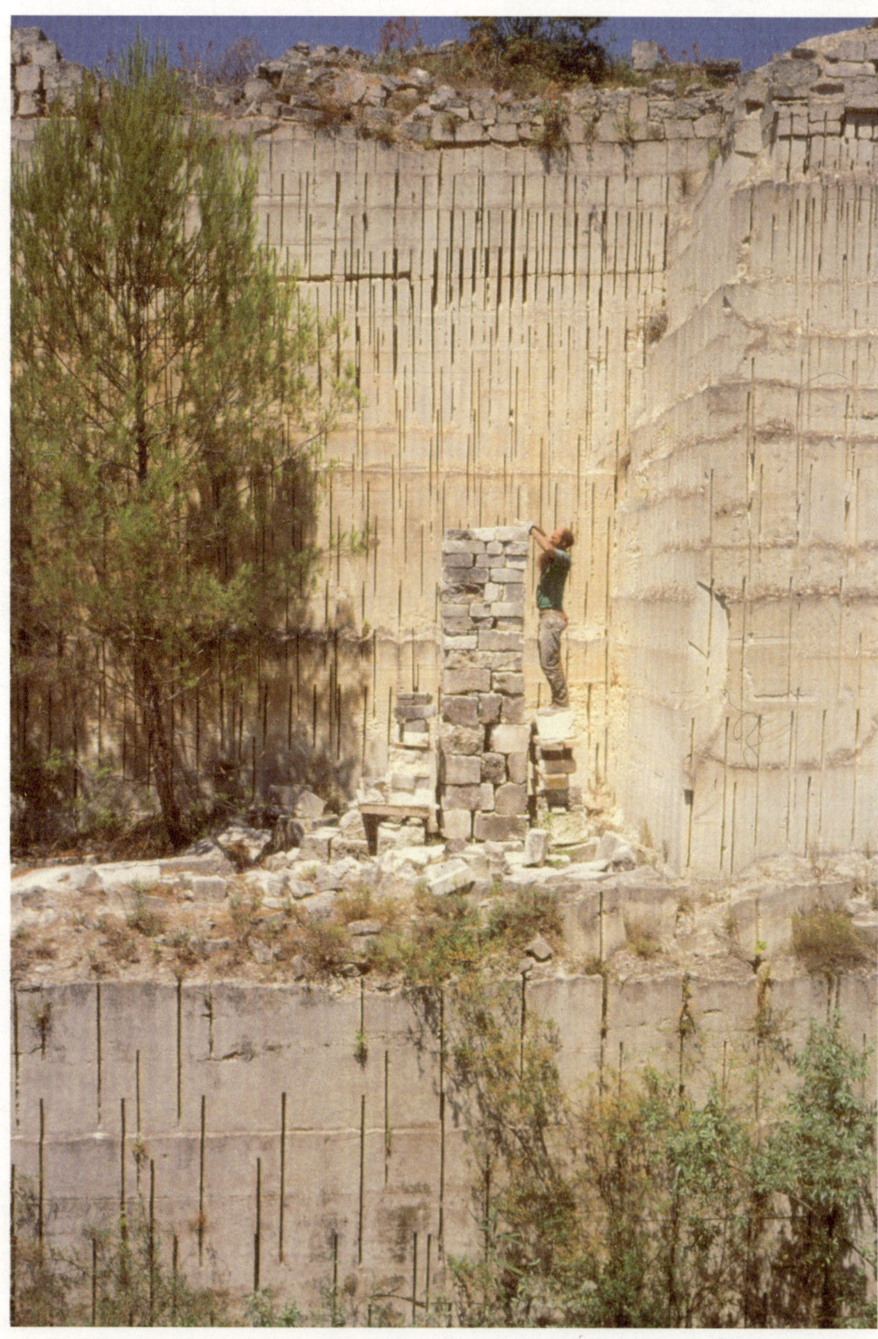

Joseph Grigely, *Re: Quarrying* (in progress), 1989. Limestone. Castries, France. Photo: Diane Brentari

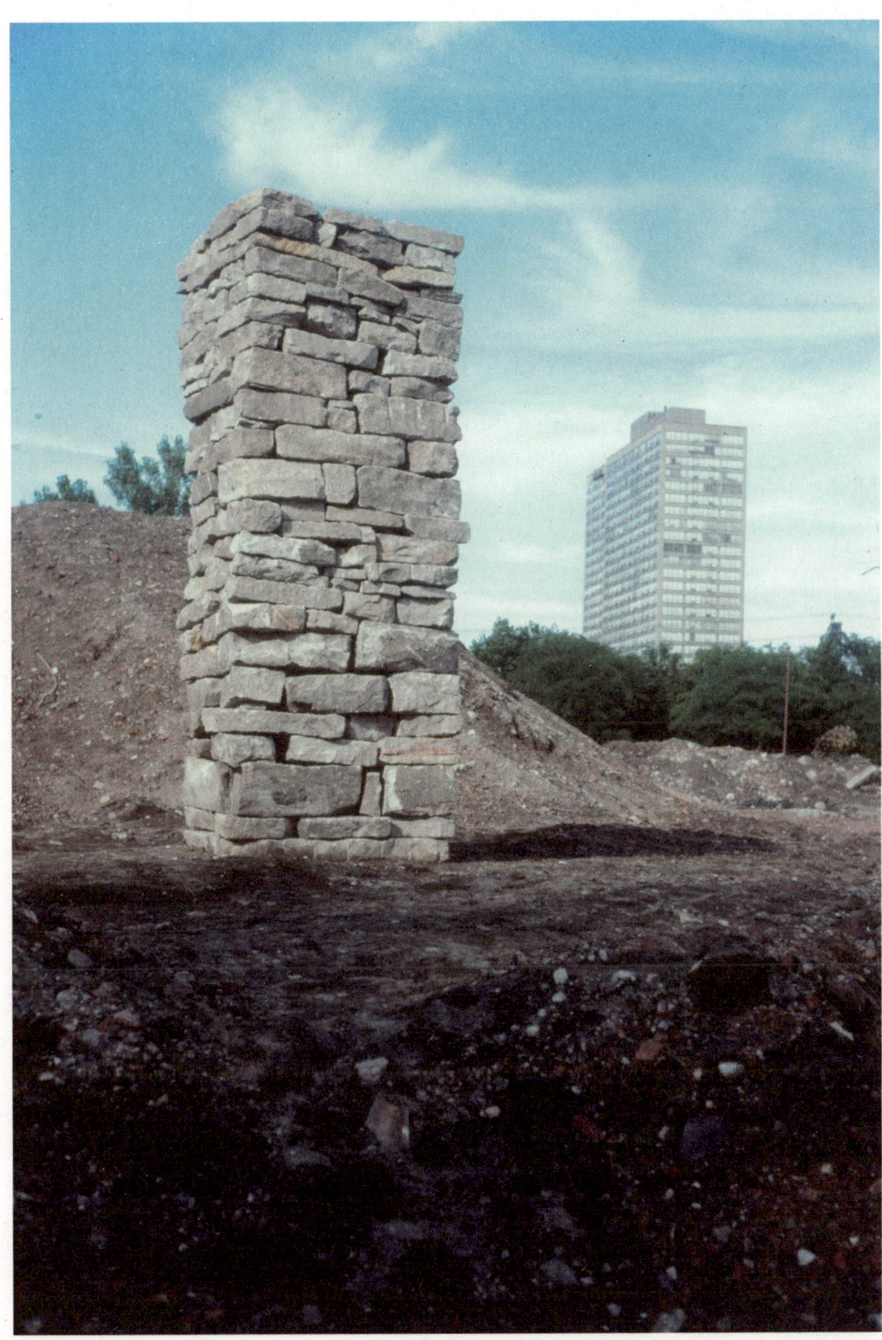

Joseph Grigely, *Re: Construction*, 1988. Limestone. Hyde Park, Chicago, Illinois

scaffolding. As the stack rose higher and higher, I made narrow, tottering shelves of stone and timber to get each stone up to the next level. It took three levels of shelves and four lifts to get the last row of stones in place, one by one. I also learned by mistake a very important rule that every builder of stone walls knows: When you pick up a stone, you want to know where it is going in the wall, because you don't want to have to put it back into the pile of loose stone and pick it up a second time.

In the summer of 1989, I spent two months in France—first in Bordeaux and later in Montpellier. While in Montpellier I spent a lot of time at the workshop of ABRP, a small masonry atelier on the outskirts of the city, near the village of Saint-Geniès-des-Mourgues. ABRP was run by Antoine Bekker and Reginald Pineau. I had previously met Bekker in Chicago, where, during the opening of a show of Ulrich Rückriem's work at the Donald Young Gallery in 1987, he explained, with a series of gestures that only a stoneworker would understand, how Rückriem's minimal monoliths of Normandy blue granite were cut and assembled. At the time, Bekker invited me to visit his workshop should I come to France, and, two years later, I took him up on the offer.

ABRP specialized in *maçonnerie traditionnelle* and restoration using soft limestone from the nearby quarries in Castries and Beaulieu. The atelier was only a short walk from the abandoned part of the quarries. For several weeks, I walked to the quarry daily. I'd proceed along the shoulder of the road for a half kilometer, turn left at the first vineyard, then take another left at a two-track into the quarry. At this point the landscape became a maze of paths among shrubs, small trees, and limestone pits. The walls were scarred with deep cuts from the huge carbide-and-diamond saw wheels that had carved slabs from the quarry decades ago.

In one area containing three large pits, I gathered and piled stones as I had done three years earlier in Chicago. The sculptures were bigger and harder to make this time: The taller one was fourteen feet high, on the edge of a pit, so I could only work from three sides. The second one was longer and wider, less a tower than a blocky edifice. The stones that went into the second one were big, some of them almost eighteen inches square, and weighed more than two hundred pounds each. They were too heavy to lift. Instead, I tumbled them to the site from different locations nearby, using a simple lever apparatus to help prod them along. When they reached the rim of the pit, I'd push them over the edge. It was immensely satisfying to watch them fall thirty feet and thud into the limestone sand, to see the small puff of dust rise into the hot Mediterranean air. Sometimes, when you are making things, small moments like these are their own reward.

The second sculpture was not quite right—a fact my father pointed out to me the moment he saw pictures of it. When building with dry stone, without using mortar, gravity and friction are what hold things together—so the more contact between the stones, the better. When there are long seams, as there are in the second sculpture, it becomes less stable. I'd needed half stones to avoid this problem, but wasn't able to find any, and cutting stones was out of the question. Sometimes you have to overrule your knowledge as a way of getting something done. It was hot, dry, exhausting work, but I had two important tools at my disposal at the time: a broad-rimmed straw hat and a pair of heavy gloves. By the time I was done, the gloves had holes worn clean through the fingers. Over the years, photos of the sculptures have served as a reminder that sometimes, when making art, you are doing it solely for the satisfaction of making it.

I had imagined that the sculptures wouldn't last long. But a little while ago, on a whim, I went looking for them via Google Earth. I started by finding the atelier of ABRP, and then retraced my walk into the quarry. The two-track that led into the quarry was amazingly clear, and before long I had located the three pits where I worked. The tall sculpture was gone, probably pushed into the pit beside it, though it was hard to tell for sure because the site was overgrown with

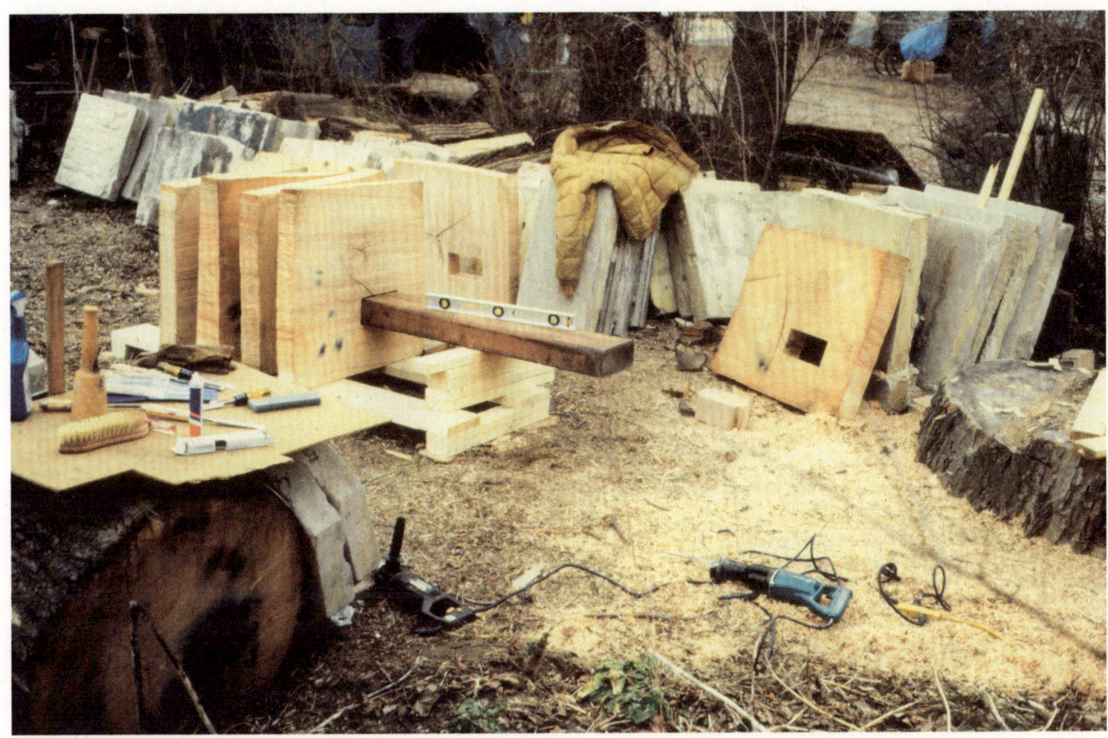

Joseph Grigely, *Perforated Tympanum No. 11* (in progress), 1989. Oak and steel. Silver Spring, Maryland

trees. But the large, blocky sculpture was still there; a corner had been knocked out of it, but it was mostly intact. With Google Earth in 3-D, I could swivel around the piece and see it from different angles. Trees, which had had thirty years to grow, obscured some views. But as I sat in front of my computer, it felt like a small miracle to see the sculpture again at all.

In the mid-'80s I was trying to develop some kind of creative pathway as an artist—experimenting with various media forms in particular. My initial attraction was to the outdoors, in part because it was a defining place for me, especially hiking in the White Mountains in New Hampshire. One of the forms I developed at this time was a genre I call "site-reflexive sculpture." Like site-specific sculpture, the work is made for a specific location; but, crucially, all the materials used to make the work must also come from the site itself. The stone piles I made in Chicago and in the quarries near Castries were site-reflexive sculptures.

I also made sculptures from fallen trees. One such project took place in the woods of northwest New Jersey, on a slope below the Appalachian Trail, near the town of Branchville. At the time, I was working as an assistant for the sculptor Robert Lobe, whose hammered-aluminum rocks and trees were produced in the same area. One day I saw a tree that had been struck by lightning and had fallen atop two rocks. It was about forty feet long, and the way its horizontality intersected the verticality of the trees around it intrigued me. For a couple of weeks I worked on the log, hewing it into a four-sided beam. I made shallow crosscuts with a chain saw, then used a small axe to hack through the sapwood. Cleaving the underside of the log was the hardest part—it was like working in a crawl space. When I began, the nearby trees were just budding, but by the time I finished, they had fully leafed out. The beam curved slowly, then reverted back to a section of tree; a small knob of beam marked the end. When you finish a project like this, it's hard to describe your feelings, knowing the work will have no audience except maybe for some juncos and squirrels.

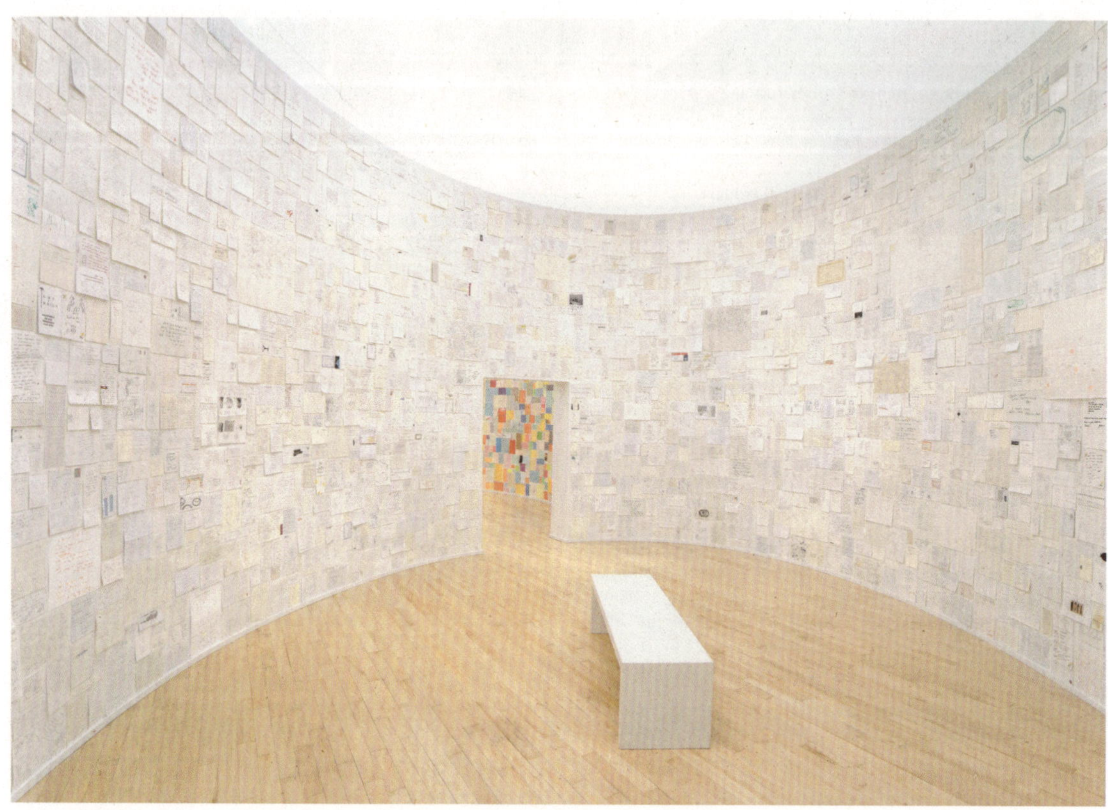

Joseph Grigely, *White Noise (monochrome)*, 2000. Oval-shaped room, conversations on white paper, pins. Installation view, Massachusetts Museum of Contemporary Art, 2023. Photo: Jon Verney

Not all of the log projects were made in the woods. For five years, when I was teaching in Washington, DC, and had a studio in Baltimore, I made a series of sculptures I called *Morphemes* and *Perforated Tympani*. The logs, carcasses of trees felled by storms, mostly came from the log lot maintained by Montgomery County, Maryland. The wood was beautiful: cherry, red oak, ash, and walnut. The *Morphemes* were about two feet thick, cut with a chain saw, then planed with a drawknife to taper at the ends—they looked like an elemental shape in the morphology of visual form. The *Perforated Tympani* were named for the way I became deaf: I fell down a hill and a tree branch perforated my eardrum, totally destroying the ear. The sculptures represented a reversal of this event. They consisted of slabs of tree trunks I cut and shaped with a chain saw, then perforated with steel beams so the wood dried and shrank around each beam. The *Perforated Tympani* combined identity and abstraction, without privileging one over the other.

When I moved my studio to the New Jersey waterfront in 1991, I began to develop more conceptual work that eventually became the basis for my first New York show at White Columns, *Conversations with the Hearing* (1994). These conversations consisted of scraps of paper on which people had written notes to me in the process of communicating. The notes were arranged in formal grids; the handwriting, the shape and color of the paper, and the narrative content all played a role in the work. In my stoneworks, I had employed a similar process of organizing material into an irregular grid—that is, minimizing the length of the seams so constituent elements appeared to be more integrated with one another: more of a piece, or a whole.

As an artist, you learn a lot directly from your materials, and you don't always learn it consciously—it becomes an ineffably intuitive operation. Years later, this became evident while working on my installations of *White Noise* at the Musée d'Art Moderne de Paris (formerly the ARC) (2000), the Whitney Museum of American Art (2001), and the Centre Pompidou-Metz (2009). *White Noise* consists of an oval-shaped room, about thirty feet long, twenty feet wide, and fourteen feet high, filled floor to ceiling with conversations written on white paper. Unlike my smaller wall works, this installation has no template to guide it—it is done largely by intuition, until all 2,300 notes have been affixed to the wall, a process that takes a team of five people ten days to accomplish.

The opportunity to turn from puttering in quarry pits and the studio to showing my work in a public setting arose in 1994, when the curator Bill Arning came to my studio and offered me a show at White Columns, saying I could do what I wanted—show *Perforated Tympani* and *Morphemes*, or show *Conversations with the Hearing*. In the end, I decided to show the work that I had developed in the time since I arrived in New York: the conversations. The stoneworks had done their job in cultivating the grid as a narrative form, and the *Tympani*, especially, had led me in a new direction, personalizing abstraction without letting it become too didactic. It was, in a sense, time to move on.

It's a given for every artist that you have to make bad stuff in order to make good stuff: work that doesn't get seen by others; work that you do because you have to get past it. The trick is to know when to let go. Warhol said to save everything—as if it were easy to lug around sculptures for ten or twenty or thirty years. Sometimes you just need to destroy the work, like Baldessari did with his paintings—making the act of kicking in the canvas a performative turning point in his career. Yet works of art are not easily destroyed unless they can also be destroyed from memory—even in their material absence, they linger. The stonework I built in Hyde Park is long gone, but the photographs I still have keep it alive. The Montpellier work remains, though as a ruin. If the Branchville beam is still there, shrouded under a canopy of green, I can't find it on Google Earth. The *Morphemes* and *Tympani* were ultimately destroyed, starting in 1999. Of course, I wish I had saved one, or even the parts of one—but experience and evanescence are as meaningful as materiality. Sometimes that's all you can hope for as an artist: to make meaning.

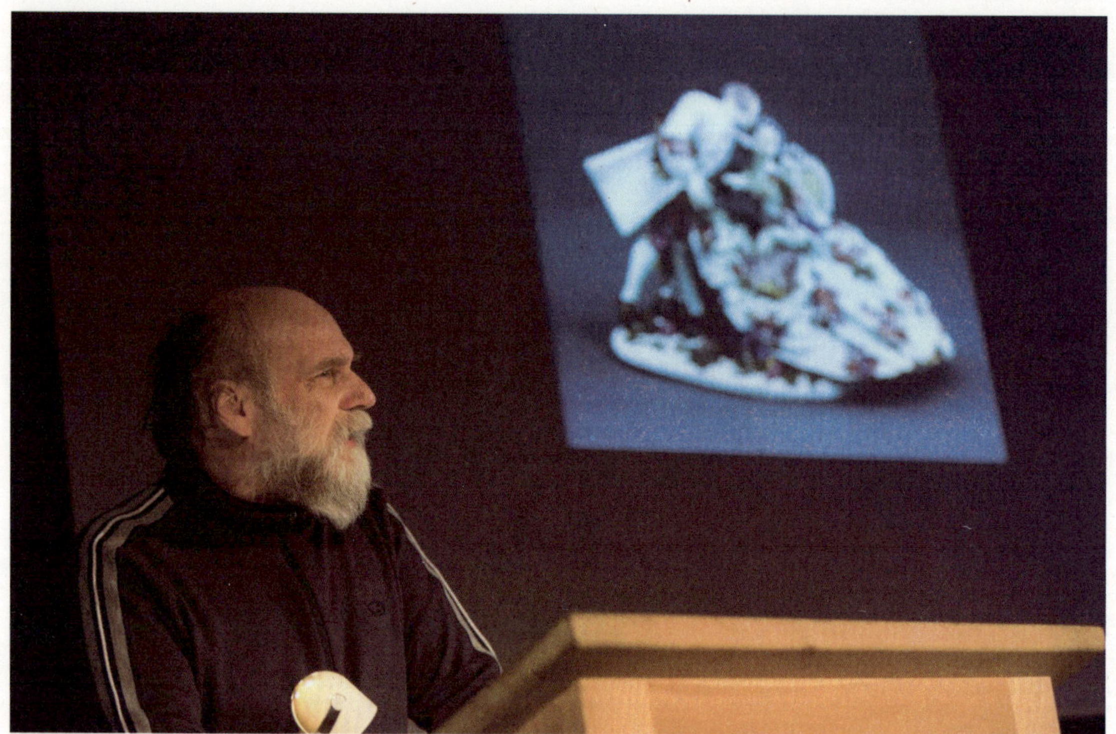

Joseph Grigely delivering "Nothing but Quotations" at Engadin Art Talks, Zuoz, Switzerland, 2016. Photo: Josh Garrett

Lectures

As an artist, one of the routines of my practice involves participating in arts education, not just as a teacher, but as a visiting artist and lecturer. Such talks have as their audience young artists and other art educators—makers, critics, curators, historians—so the focus is very much based on a shared sense of being disciplinary insiders. When the talks printed here were originally presented, they were paired with projected images. The images commented on the words, and the words on the images—neither was inherently privileged over the other.

Usually, my lectures have been a combination of prepared narrative and extemporaneous elaboration on some particular work or exhibition or incident. There's only so much you can say and do in the usual forty-five-minute format, and often my intent takes the audience into consideration. My talks typically involve a lot of storytelling, in part because I tend to use stories as a basis for theory, and theory as a basis for artmaking—and also because storytelling is a means by which people can grasp and hold on to the concrete particulars of a narrative.

A lecture can involve considerable labor and is not especially rewarding from a financial perspective. Typically, a visiting artist might be paid $500 to $1,500 for a two-day engagement that includes studio visits. But the time invested includes preparation and travel, and it all adds up. In my case, I often rehearse pronunciations—it's not easy to get English stresses and accents right when you are deaf. For this reason, I often develop my lectures using templates that are re-edited for various institutional contexts. I have included several actual lecture manuscripts here, which contain additions, deletions, and pronunciation notations. The lectures are a cross sample: Some address my practice as an artist. Some focus on larger questions about disability and artmaking, and disability and society. Some do all these things. To a certain extent, many have an activist subtext—a desire to articulate a need for change, and a means by which this change can be accomplished.

Blah Blah Blah, 2002

University of California, Berkeley, April 2002.

I gave my first lectures on my art shortly after I started showing *Conversations with the Hearing*, between 1994 and 1996. They took place at the University of Michigan; Tyler School of Art and Architecture; University of Colorado Boulder; Hochschule der Künste, Berlin (now Universität der Künste Berlin); Arnolfini, Bristol; Center for Contemporary Art Kitakyushu, Japan; Rutgers University; Cranbrook Art Museum; University of California, Berkeley; and Mills College (now Mills College at Northeastern University). The general theme of these talks was the core of my practice, *Conversations with the Hearing*. As a result, the lectures were generally repetitive: I worked with one basic lecture and adjusted it for different audiences. Often I would use slides as an outline, adding new work as it was made and exhibited, and say what came to my mind as I showed the images. In the margins of my notes I would write "elab," which was my cue to elaborate. For this reason, my lecture notes appear fragmentary in places.

I typically used two slide projectors at each talk, and images were presented side by side. The entire process was largely a show-and-tell event.

For the talk printed here, I have included most of the original images, which are laid out roughly as they were shown on the projector screens. These are presented on the left-hand page, while the right-hand page shows the text I prepared for the lecture. In one instance, a blank screen was shown while I told a story, and the blank screen is presented here as a blank page.

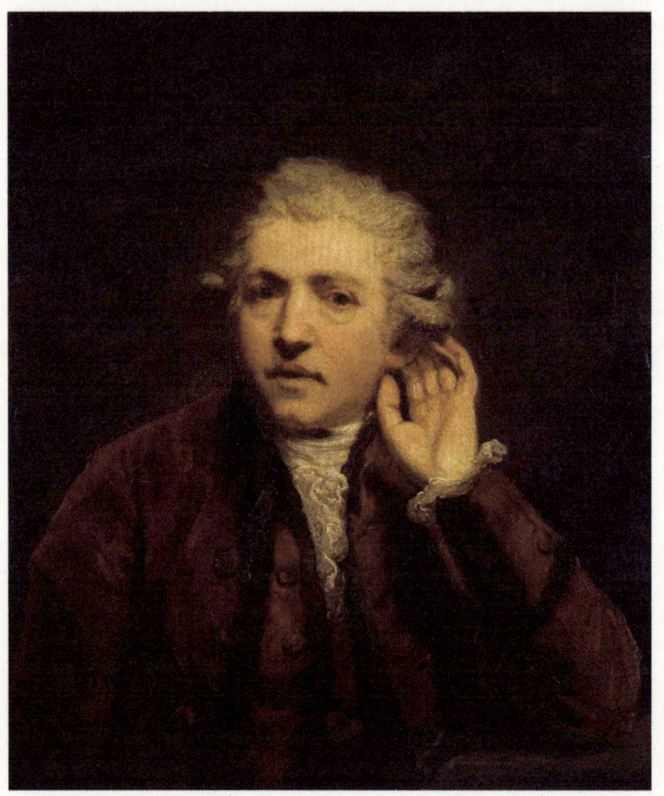

Joseph Grigely
"Blah blah blah"
Berkeley
April 2002

[L Joshua Reynolds, Self Portrait as a Deaf Man]

Prologue:

I would like to begin with a few prefatory words about my approach to my subject. My lecture is not a formal one, but an informal one, and I intend to touch upon critical issues that I think might be of interest to both artists and art historians. There are two parts to my talk. In the first part I intend to explore the relationship between sound and vision as a historical practice—and look at how auditory phenomena might be represented as visual imagery. It's a very broad topic, so I am focusing on a subset of examples about looking at language, and more specifically, about looking at conversation My essential question is this: We all know what a conversation sounds like, but what does a conversation *look* like? My examples are primarily drawn from historical representations of conversational exchange—I favor Canaletto in this regard, but I also spend some time discussing what is generally known as the 'Conversation Piece'.

In the second part of my talk I intend to share with you some recent projects as another way of getting inside what I do, and how my work involves a conflation of creative and critical practices--what Gregory Ulmer calls 'heuretic criticism'. Heuretic criticism is a way of writing that is 'other'—not other than writing, but simply *other than*. Some of you are already familiar with my work, and for others it will be a new experience—so I intend to provide a survey of selected projects from the past five years.

Introduction:

Since the 1960s, many artists have worked with language, and I am one of them. But unlike, say, Lawrence Weiner or Joseph Kosuth, my focus is not so much on language as a mode of representation, but as a practical means of communication. I am interested in how people converse. I am interested in what they do with their hands when they talk, and how they position their bodies, and what they do with their eyebrows. And I am also interested in the history of representing conversational exchanges. Take for example Venice in the early 18th century, and Venice's version of Norman Rockwell, Canaletto.

[L&R]

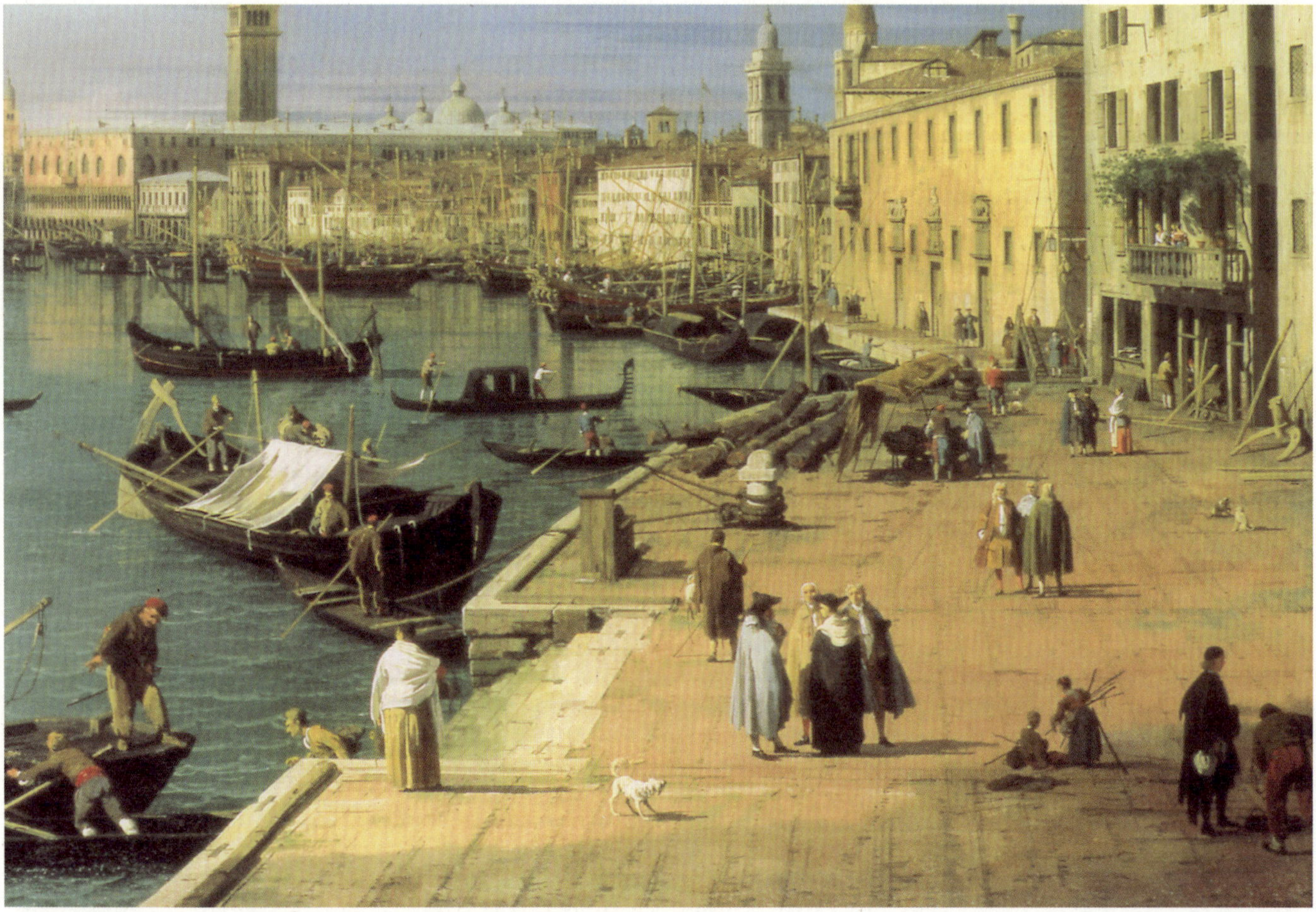

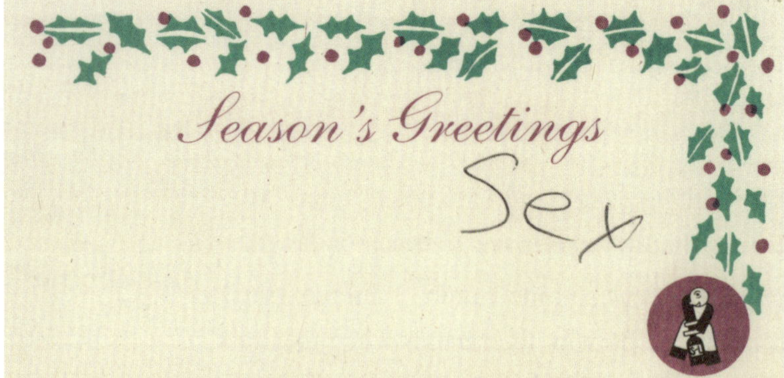

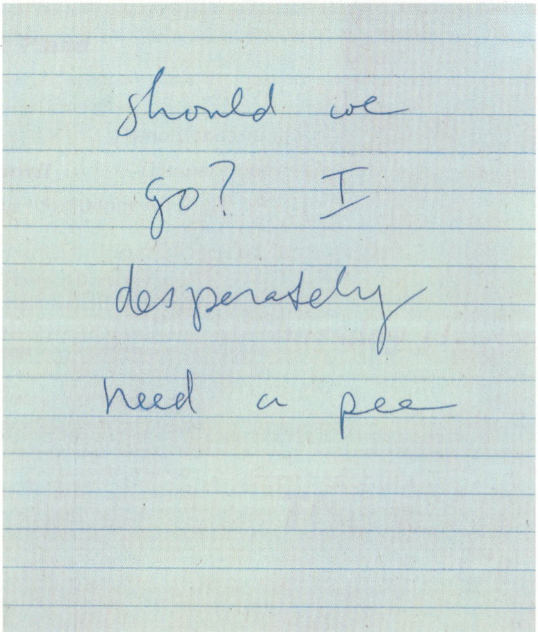

should we go? I desperately need a pee

Canaletto painted one of his Schiavoni paintings—"a view of Venice Looking West"-- in 1736. It's a very conventional Canaletto of the sort he painted for the English tourist crowd. Whether he was painting a palazzo or a lido, Canaletto typically filled his canvases with small groups of people who seem to be chatting, people who seem to yell, and people whose gestures bespeak directions. It's usually the dogs that give away the paintings' intimate secret: it is not just a visual scene being represented—a visual experience—but the human occupation of that expanse, and the fact that this occupation is characterized not by things seen, but by things heard. Canaletto is a noisy painter. You can hear it in the foreground, where a dog's head is cocked to the conversation of a cluster of people a few steps away; nearby, a bargeman gestures and yells loudly enough to capture the attention of a woman walking by; beyond them heads are turned and bodies are position in a way that says only one thing: words are moving. **[L&R Dogs]**

Think of the situation this way:

~~The rhetorical strategies by which we examine visual art are, by definition, oracular. Whether we look at, or we gaze at, or we read a painting, we engage strategies that involve the visual organization of compositional space.~~ It's so easy to say "OK, let's take a close look at this painting"—but somehow it seems a little odd to say "OK, let's listen carefully to this painting." Odd maybe, but not insignificant: it is important to remember that even in 'representational' paintings, it is not just vision being represented, but other senses as well. ~~The trick is that all of these senses must be transfigured—translated even—to a visual experience. This is not simply a form of synaethesia, but rather a form of interpretation: we cannot go from one modality to another without invoking some kind of transitional reading.~~

I'm going to make a turn now from Canaletto. ~~I'll come back to him again later.~~ My turn is to the questions posed by the groups of people in his paintings—we know they are talking, but what are they talking about?

I also want to ask you to shift your frame of reference from the 18th century to the 21st century for the purpose of providing some background material about what I do and how I do it.

(L sex R should we go)

A few facts now:

~~As some of you know~~, I am totally deaf. I can't lipread. Most people I talk with do not know sign language. And so I ask people with whom I am having conversations to write down for me the things they are saying. This happened once about 10 years ago at a dinner with a friend—after the dinner, hundreds of sheets of paper—being as it was a long dinner.

elab. For several months I saved the conversation notepapers I had—hundreds of them—then laid them out on the floor of my studio. The papers made up so many grids; the words made up so many stories and conversations. I started to play with them, not sure really where I was going with it. And continued to engage in written conversations with people—who, for their part, were mostly very happy to communicate this way. Which surprised me—. It was a form of reduced writing—pithy, essential, and a curious exploration of the potential of the situation.

In *The Catcher in the Rye*, Holden Caulfield had imagined it would be different. There's a point in the novel where he imagines himself escaping the miasma of New York City and trading it for the inconspicuous Midwest, where he planned to get a job at a gas station and live quietly ever after. He said:

> I thought what I'd do was, I'd pretend I was one of those deaf-mutes. That way I wouldn't have to have any goddam stupid useless conversations with anybody. If anybody wanted to tell me something, they'd have to write it on a piece of paper and shove it over to me. They'd get bored as hell doing that after a while, and then I'd be through with having conversations for the rest of my life. Everybody'd think I was just a poor deaf-mute bastard and they'd leave me alone.
>
> *The Catcher in the Rye*

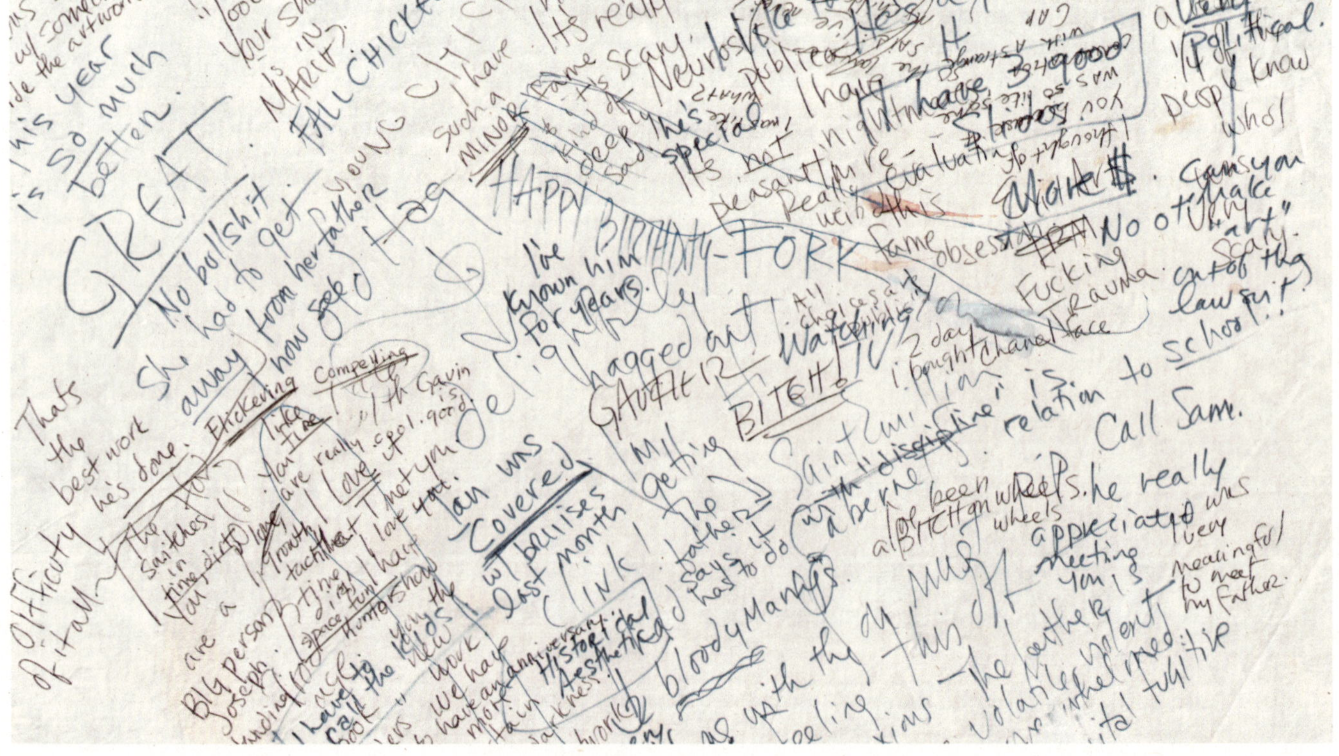

(describe process in the studio—attempt to take people places to which they haven't been to before)
Irony: people loved it—shared communication.

This pleasure has a counterpoint in The Catcher in the Rye.

(L Xmas tree, detail R Paula's Birthday Party)
In the end, though, there are the papers—. Looking at them held a certain discovery: that people did not so much write on paper, as talk on paper. There is a huge difference between writing on paper and talking on paper. The words may be familiar, but the way that they go onto paper is not: they backtrack, they take sudden turns, and they stop abruptly.

Which returns me to the question I asked earlier: what does a conversation look like?

I like this question because of how it directs attention to a range of traditional genres. I often converse with artists who express disdain for these genres. They say things like "The Portrait is dead." Or "Landscape painting sucks." And it's all so ironic to me, because that which is supposedly dead, and supposedly sucks, is fundamental to the process of framing contemporary art and ideas. It is not simply a matter of the omnipresence of such genres. It is not simply a matter of their staying power. It is rather a matter of their ability to remake themselves, and to sustain themselves through their remaking. This is a sign of the inescapability of the continuum of historical practices: genres don't simply 'die away'; they evolve.

[CP (tp) + CP (tp)]
One genre that I'd like to talk about today is the genre of paintings and drawings known as "Conversation Pieces." The Conversation Piece is a seriously neglected genre, simultaneously archaic in temperament, yet fascinating in implication--. The genre is an 18th and 19th century tradition typically practiced in England and the lowlands. Hogarth, Gainsborough, and Rowlandson all painted Conversation Pieces. The genre also has Eastern counterparts—not strictly speaking "Conversation Pieces" as much as they are representations of conversational exchange. Both of these images I am showing here are title pages from a book I published with the Center for Contemporary Art in Kitakyushu, Japan. The Conversation Piece is distinguished by the fact that people are present, but their words are not. There is a sense that a conversation of

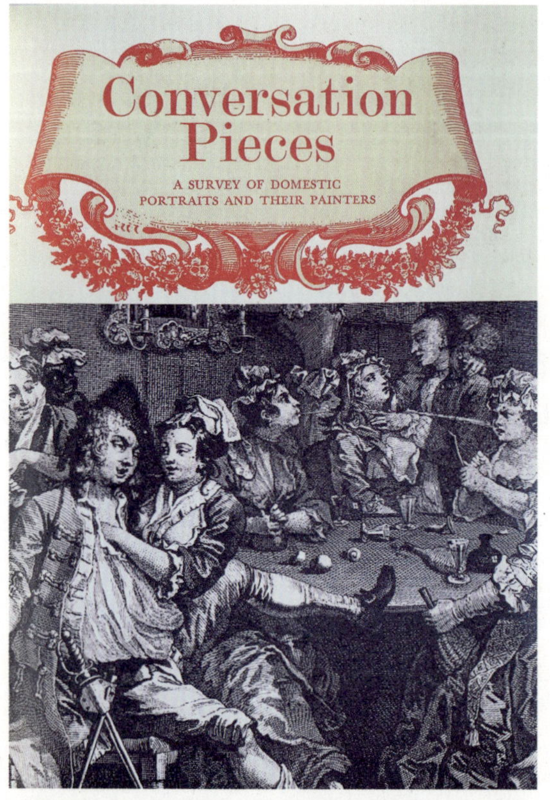

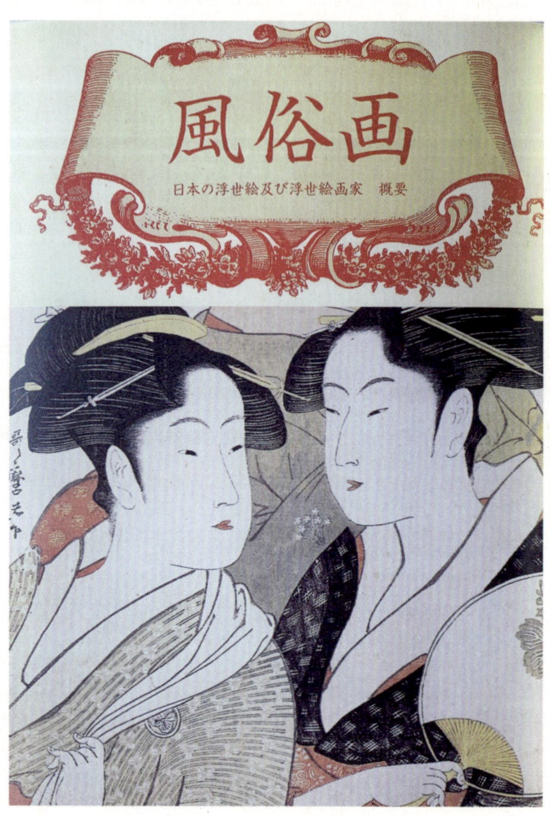

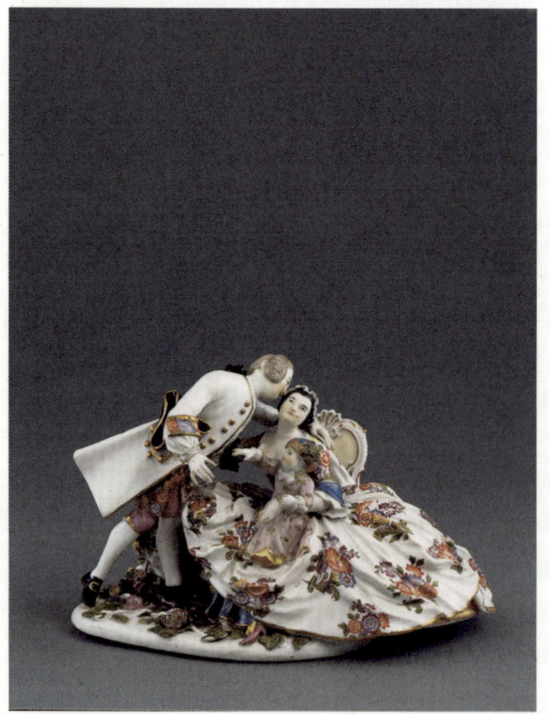

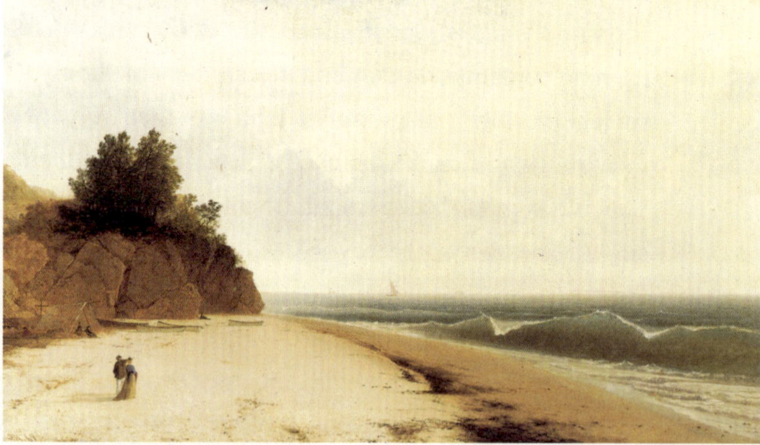

elab. The Kaendler on the left is a Meissen ware sculpture in the Wadsworth Atheneum Museum of Art in Hartford. It's a perfect exponent of the conversation piece—something is clearly being said—whispered, actually—but we're not privileged to the content. On the right is a coastal scene painted by John Kensett, which is also in the Wadsworth. There's a lot going on here—a conversation between the two people on the shore, marked by the gesture of the out-turned hand—and the unmistakable sound of the ocean. What Canaletto accomplished in Venice, Kensett accomplished on the beach.

some kind is taking place. The Italian critic Mario Praz emphasized that a crucial element of Conversation Pieces was the presence of a gesture signifying conversation or communication of some kind. Another critic--Ralph Edwards--expanded this a little bit wider to emphasize how the Conversation Piece involves the representation of two or more persons in a state of dramatic or psychological relation to each other. This is a very liberal definition, but a useful one. **[CP + CP]** Conversation Pieces are marked not by any stylistic idiom, but by their detail of incident--how they capture the paralinguistic traces of conversation in gestures and poses. The irony is that their conversations are never disclosed to us--we cannot see, much less hear, the content of the exchanges that take place before us. As Norman Bryson said of Watteau's paintings, they communicate a narrative that insists on meaning, but at the same time withholds it."

(L fighting couple; R 'discovery')

These exchanges do not always involve language in the most literal sense

> Leppert and the 'sonoric landscape'—can be broadly described as a visual representation of auditory activity. Many forms these take in science: the musical score; the speech spectrogram; and even writing itself, which is a representation not of meaning, not of articulation.

(L Kaendler; R Kensett)

Typically transcends medium, and also conflations of genres—eg Kensett, a landscape with two kinds of auditory fields: that of nature, of the ocean breaking, and that of human commentary on that nature.

Most critical interest in the "Conversation Piece" happened during the middle of the 20th century: Sitwell's book "Conversation Pieces" appeared in 1936; in 1946, the Arts Council of Great Britain hosted a touring show of English Conversation Pieces of the Eighteenth Century; two years later in 1948, the Detroit Institute of the Arts also organized a show on 18th century English Conversation Pieces. It was an expansive exhibition and included not only paintings reflecting the genre, but also interior furnishings and period furniture that evinced the genre: it was an exhibition both of and about its subject. In this sense, "Conversation" was essentially a domestic activity: it took place—and was represented as taking place—in a setting defined by family life.

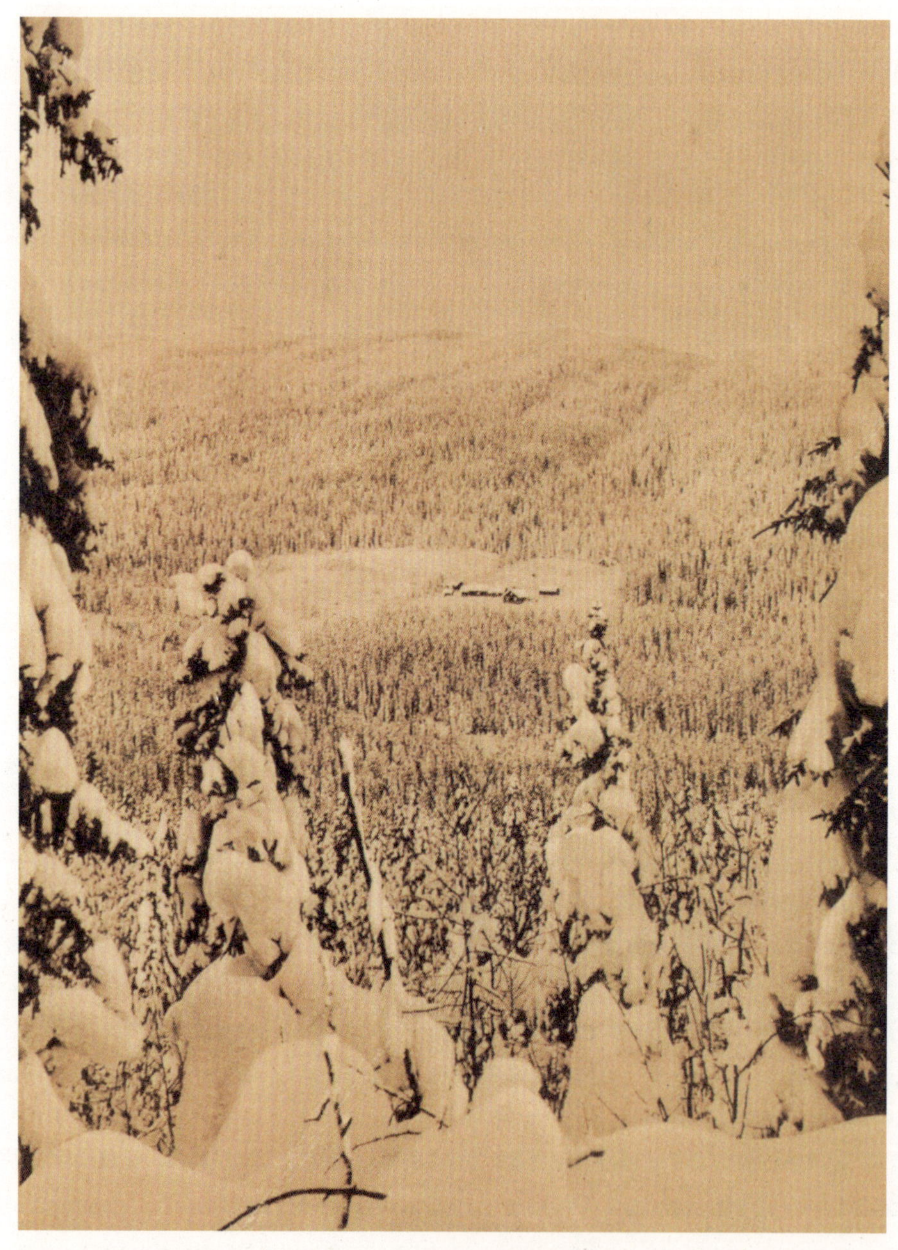

Very important to this subject is Richard Leppert's controversial book, *The Sight of Sound,* which I mentioned earlier. Leppert's book was published in 1993. His focus is on the visual representation of domestically-produced music. He doesn't really get into the issue of representing conversation—but what he does do, and does well, is remind us just how enormously broad the sonoric landscape is, and how it encompasses both real and imagined voices. This is why I began with Canaletto: there's a banal ordinariness about this paintings that reminds me a little of Norman Rockwell. When Rockwell moved out to Stockbridge Massachusetts, he had installed in his studio a huge picture window that overlooked the main street running through the town. It's a very telling architectural phrase: the 'picture window,' which permits one to see, though not necessarily to hear, what goes on through and beyond it. When asked why he installed the window in his studio, Rockwell replied that he wanted to sit and watch the world go by. Watching the world go by is the subject of Canaletto as well--. The essence is in the fact we are watching the world—not listening to it—translating, as it were, its various senses into a purely visual form.

(L walking couple; R house in the woods).

Which now leads us now to storytelling time. I have three stories to tell you. They all have something to do with the relationship between seeing and hearing

<u>This is the first story:</u>

On December 31, 1999, my friend Amy and I were watching the millennium celebrations on Television. We were surfing channels and countries and paused for a while at something a little close to home: a choir singing at the National Cathedral in Washington. The camerawork was very elaborate: fade-ins, fadeouts, and close-ups of the choir members as the sang. After watching this for a while, Amy turned to me and said in sign language, "The world must look really silly without sound."

<u>This is the second story:</u>

A few weeks ago I was working in my studio in New York and had to go take a pee down the hallway and saw one of the building maintenance workers. I said Hi. He said Hi too, or at least I think he did. Then he went on to say something that looked like this: (gestures & c.). I then said thank you, took my pee, and went back to my studio.

p6 (leave blank)

Back at the studio I told Amy that I saw one of the maintenance workers, and he seemed to have something to say. She asked me what he had to say, and I replied: (gestures &c) And she said—oh, he was saying that the heater was making a lot of noise and that the rubber mounting washers needed to be thicker than the ones we have now, and that he'd do what he could to find us some new ones.

Now, the third story:

I was driving cross-country, from Massachusetts to California in the mid-1980s. In Montana I took a detour to Wharton-Glacier National Park, which sits on the border between Canada and the US in the Rocky Mountains. It's quite an amazing park, and my friend Diane and I planned to spend a few days there fishing and hiking.

When we entered the Park's camping grounds, a Forest Ranger warned us that bears were causing trouble and that if we planned to hike into the back country we should attach bells to our packs. These bells are known as 'bear bells' or 'dinner bells.' The idea is that bears don't like being surprised along trails; and if you attach bells to your pack, they jingle and jangle as you walk along the trail, giving bears the opportunity to hear you and saunter off. This avoids unpleasant surprises for both hikers and bears.

This gave me an idea, I had never seen a bear before. ~~This was an unusual~~ But I wanted to. ~~opportunity~~--. I described my plan to Diane: we would hike up above timberline in search of bears. We would not attach bells to our packs. In fact, we would hike as quietly as possible, ostensibly to improve our chances of seeing a bear. Diane said she wasn't too crazy about bears, but that she would come along nonetheless.

We started out together on a gorgeous morning of bright sun and puffy clouds. Our hike took us through meadows of blooming wildflowers, up through forested foothills, and higher still onto the slopes of the Rockies. With each step, I was conscious of the possibility I was making unnecessary noise, and took extra precautions to be quiet as I walked. Before long we reached timberline, and soon we were walking across freshly-fallen snow. This I knew would make us even more quiet, as the snow would muffle our footsteps. We had not gone far before we stumbled on a surprise in our pathway: beartracks! They crossed the trail and descended down the slope somewhat, and as we followed them I whispered to Diane, "Shhhhhh," we want to be careful here. We followed the tracks like a bloodhound on the trail of an escapee, but our search was not successful—the tracks led down the slope and out of the snow and into the woods.

We kept hiking through the afternoon, but found no bears. I was disappointed, of course, and as Diane and I lay together in a meadow near our campsite watching the sun

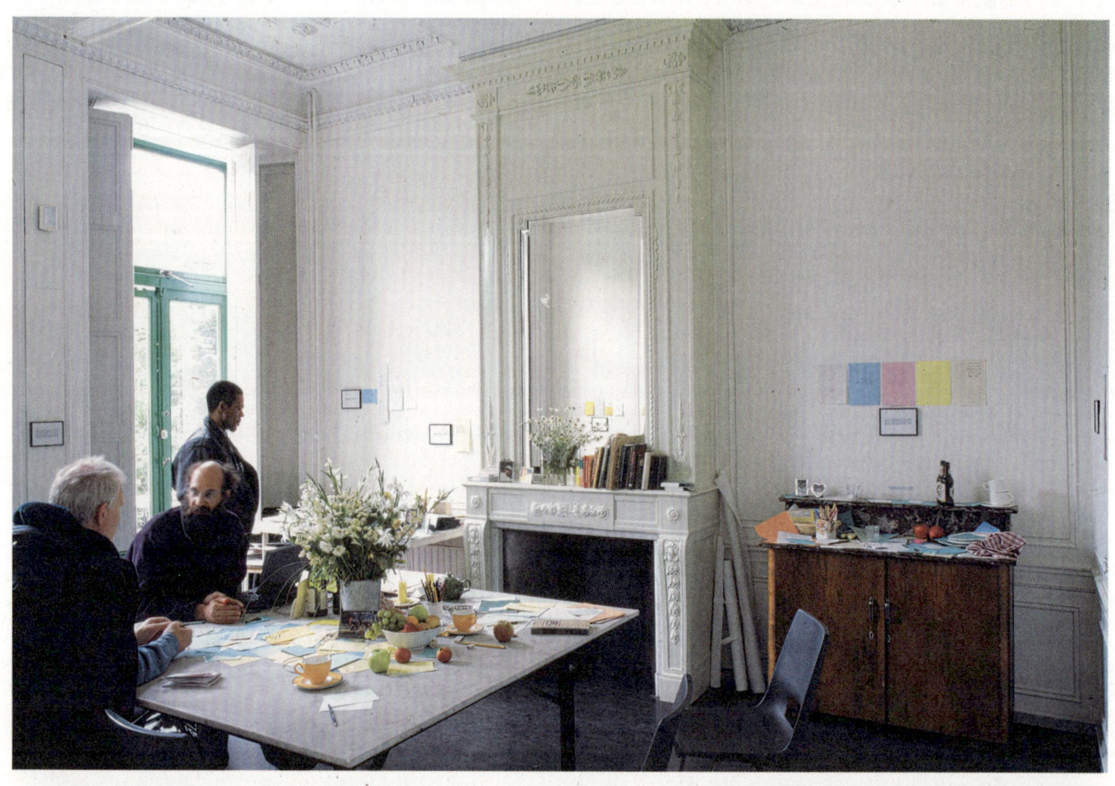

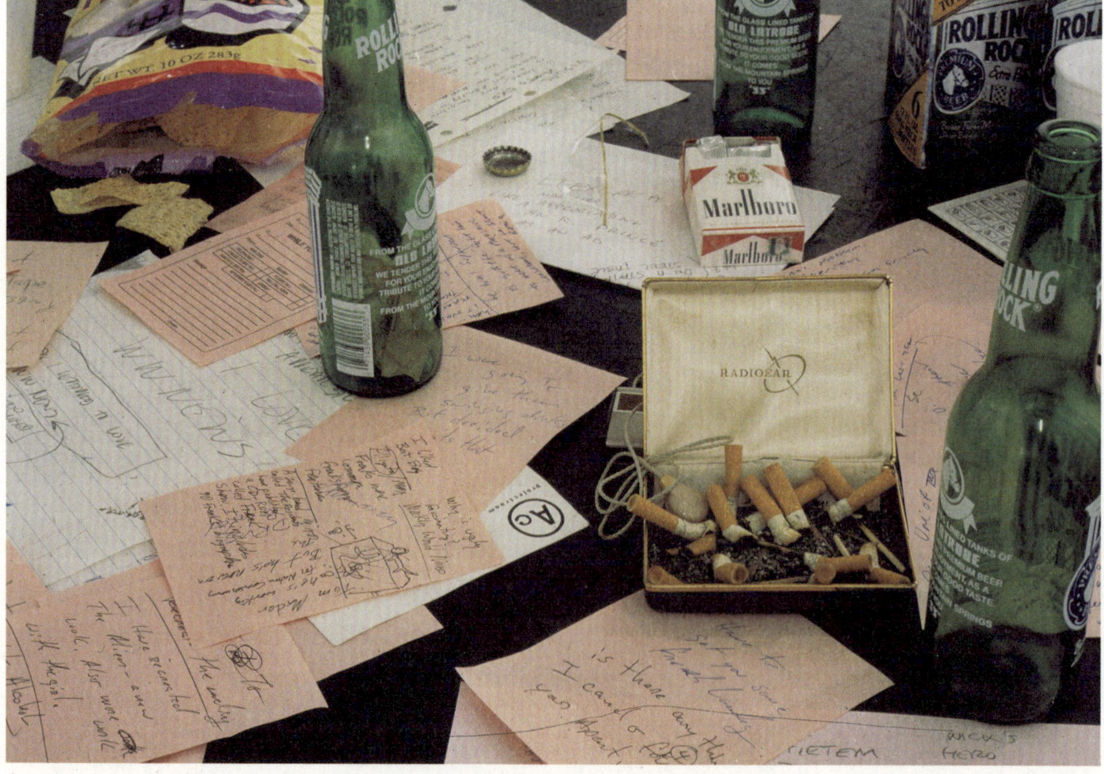
ROLLING ROCK
OLD LATROBE
Marlboro
RADIOEAR

set, I shared with her my perplexity: we were so close, I said, and I tried to be so quiet—I just don't understand it.

Diane turned to me and said: I have a confession

A confession, I asked?

Yes, she said. I know you really wanted to see a bear. I think I can understand this too. Only, you see, as much as you wanted to see a bear, I didn't—the very idea scares me out of my wits—and so all day long, while you walked so quietly, I've been singing at the top of my voice--.

Pause

The point, of course—the point of all of these stories--is that the visual experience does not directly reference the auditory experience. The absence of certitude is what precisely captures our intrigue. The sounds that we imagine—in life or in art—are not always what we think them to be. Which is part of the beauty of it all.

At this point you are probably thinking: but what do you do? –where is your art in all of this? Where are my sharks in formaldehyde? Where are my 2o-ton slabs of Cor-ten steel?

I'm sorry to say: I don't do sharks.
I don't do Cor-ten steel

The thing is: I am a kitchen table artist.
I also do bars.
I especially like tables.

(L Rotterdam R White Columns)

The table is the perfect setting for the exchange of words. We usually merely sit at chairs, but we **do** things at tables--at them, on them, around them, and sometimes under them. Tables function as a site of social activity, and for me the most essential of those activities involves the exchange of words. Words that are perfectly ordinary, yet not quite ordinary in their manifestation as inscriptions--words that reveal, like Caravaggio's basket of fruit, coarseness, blemishes, imperfections--. I am suggesting then that the ordinariness of everyday speech is a form of still life drawing, or rhopography. Rhopography is a word that Norman Bryson recently resurrected. It is derived from the Greek *rhopos*, r-h-o-p-o-s, meaning trivial objects. Odds and ends—the sort of mundane things that, in composing a still-life painting, compose our lives as human beings.

I'm a little drunk now.

because you can't

So - in the movie I saw - the victim is an asshole of a cab driver.

elab. The guards were especially attracted to my large black telescoping suitcase, and asked me what was inside it. I said, "Art." They replied, "Art?" with raised eyebrows, as if they had stumbled onto a smuggling operation of modernist masters. "Show us," they replied, smiling. So in the train's passageway I opened the case—it was more of a plastic crate than it was a suitcase—an elaborate process—straps, packing foam, archival boxes—and took out some of the archival folders that held the conversation papers. They opened them—then with dismay held the conversation papers in the air and looked at the back side of them—. "Art," I said. "Art?" they asked back ... "This is art?" They seemed really disappointed. They opened another folder. Same thing. They handed it back to me, stamped my passport, and told me to enjoy Bern, and sorry for the interruption.

(L I'm a little drunk now R So in the movie I saw)

Implicit to this is the notion that the mundane has a subversive ontology—it doesn't readily draw attention to itself as art.

Once, I was on a train from Paris to Bern to do a show when the Swiss border guards came onto the train and asked to see my passport.
This is art?
Yes. It is an art that involves drawing conversations—an art that explores markmaking as the simultaneous engagement of writing and drawing.

I can imagine some of you are thinking: why not just learn to lipread?

Most people assume that lipreading is something deaf people learn at schools--sort of like learning how to do long division or conjugate Lartin verbs. Some people may disagree with me, but I think lipreading is actually a myth. Not sleight-of-hand, but sleight-of-eye. Cognitive dexterity. Linguistic prestidigitation. It's embarrassingly easy to get things all wrong when lipreading.
When you say "vacuum" it looks like you're saying "fuck you." The subtlety has to do with certain visemes: identical lip formations that produce dissimilar sounds. You can't see voicing. You can't see nasality. There simply aren't enough contrasting features to constitute an efficient representation of linguistic codes, and so lipreading is really less about reading than it is about the inevitability of misreading. What I call Lipmisreading.

[L panhandler R sex]

1995-1996: conversations and storylines. Read panhandler storyline.

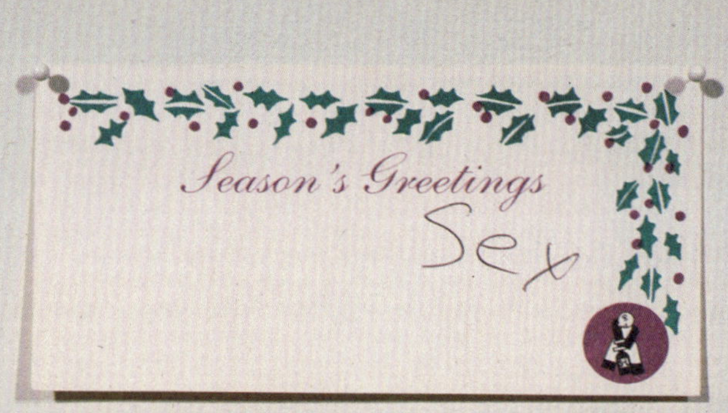

One day not too long ago, I found myself on the upper reaches of Madison Avenue in New York City. It was a cold and slightly snowy afternoon in December at the beginning of the holiday season, and as I walked downtown, I passed by the Sherry-Lehmann wine store. Sherry-Lehmann is not like most wine stores--there is only one bottle of each wine on display, and when you find something you want, a clerk will take your order and descend to the cellar to fetch it for you. It's a service-oriented store, where contact between the staff and the customer is esteemed. Maybe that's why, when I entered, the store was festive, even bustling, full of conversation of different kinds--queries, advice, comments and questions. Or so I thought. When people are talking, you never really know what they're talking about unless you hear them or ask them. Normally I'm intimidated by a store like this, but for some reason I stayed, and looked and gazed at the bottles of wine that stood on the shelves. After a while, I found a couple of bottles of Bordeaux that I wanted to buy, and a very polite clerk took my order, disappeared to the cellar to fetch it, and returned rather shortly--and then a strange thing happened.

She took, so it seemed, at least ten minutes to wrap the four bottles she had brought up from the cellar. Part of the reason it took her so long was because she got involved in a very engaging exchange with one of the other clerks. They stood together at the counter, the two of them--she slowly wrapping the bottles, he slowly adding up numbers of an account--and while she wrapped and he added, they were talking, smiling, laughing, and really enjoying themselves.

I was perplexed, of course, and tried, as well as I could try, to imagine what they were talking about. The wine? The holidays? It *had* to be something about the holidays--it was written all over their faces. When the clerk finally handed me my package, I thanked her politely, and, pardoning myself, I explained to both of the clerks that I was deaf and a little curious as to what they had been discussing. It seemed, so I said, such a pleasurable conversation--would they mind telling me what it was all about? I don't suppose they had to believe me, or even tell me what they were talking about--but they did.

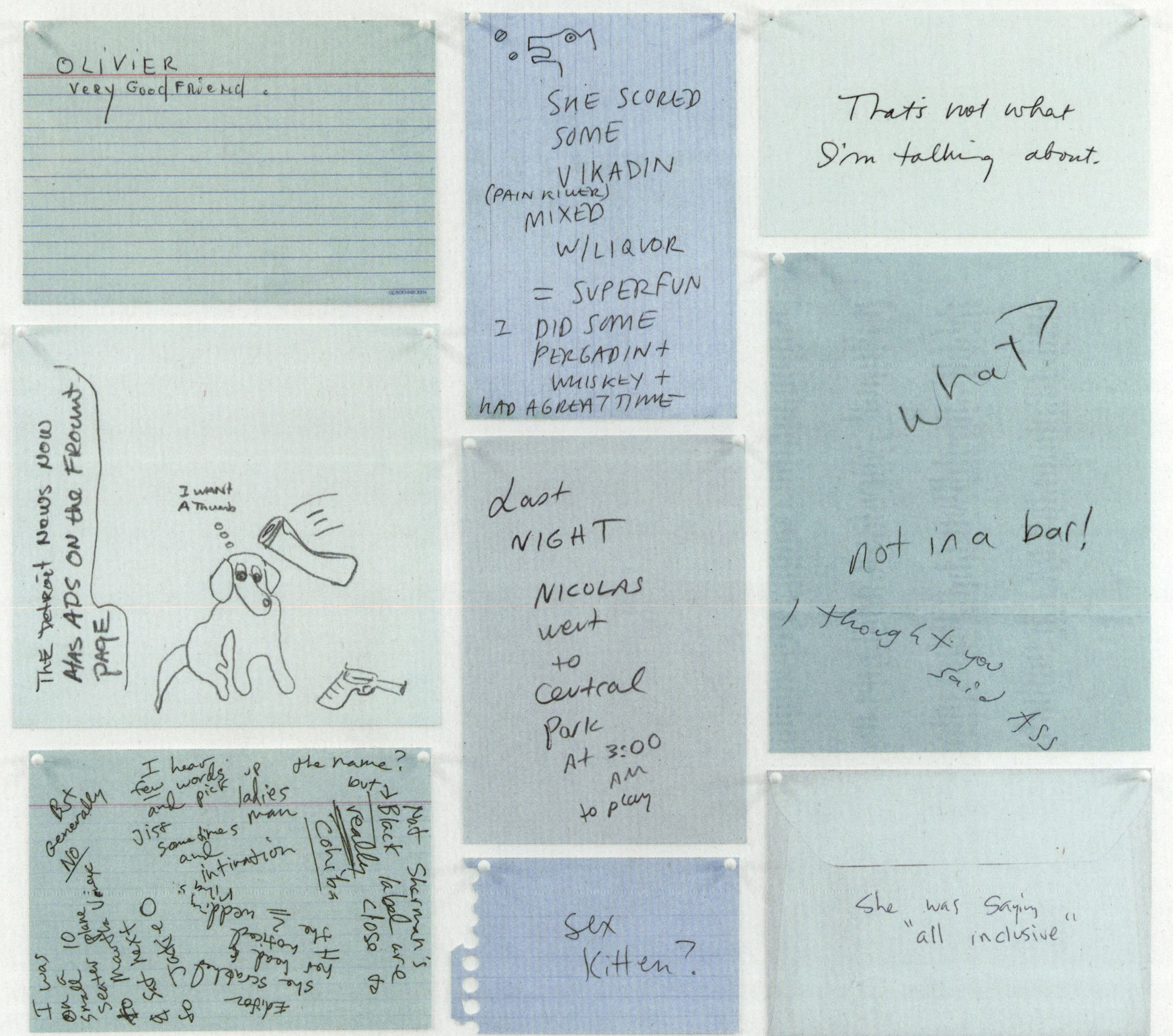
OLIVIER
Very Good Friend.
SHE SCORED
SOME
VIKADIN
(PAIN KILLER)
MIXED
W/LIQUOR
= SUPERFUN
I DID SOME
PERGADIN +
WHISKEY +
HAD A GREAT TIME
That's not what
I'm talking about.
THE Detroit NEWS NOW
HAS ADS ON the FRONT
PAGE
I WANT
A Thumb
What?
not in a bar!
I thought you
said ASS
Last
NIGHT
NICOLAS
went
to
Central
Park
At 3:00
AM
to play
Sex
Kitten?
She was saying
"all inclusive"

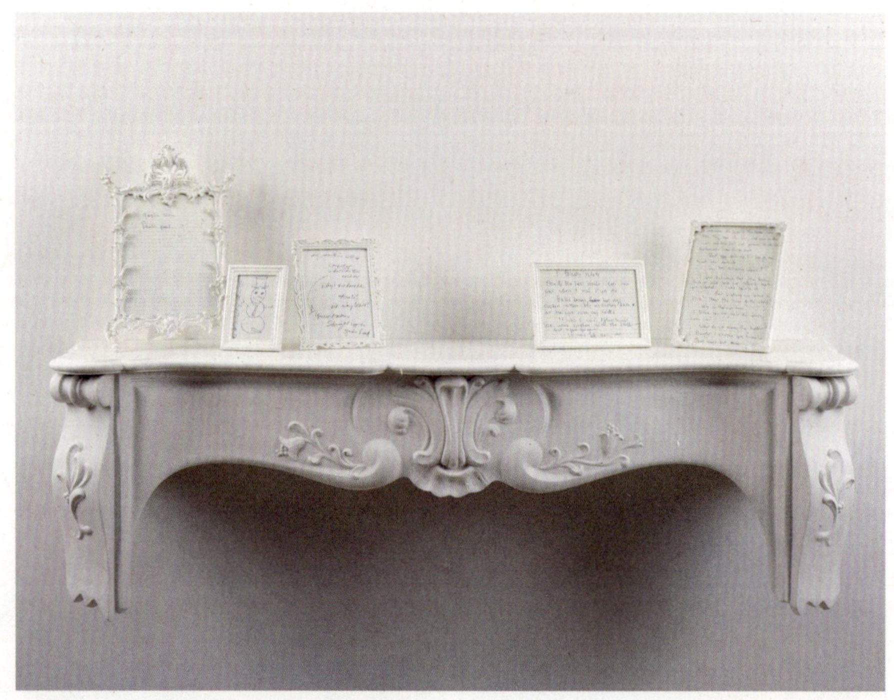

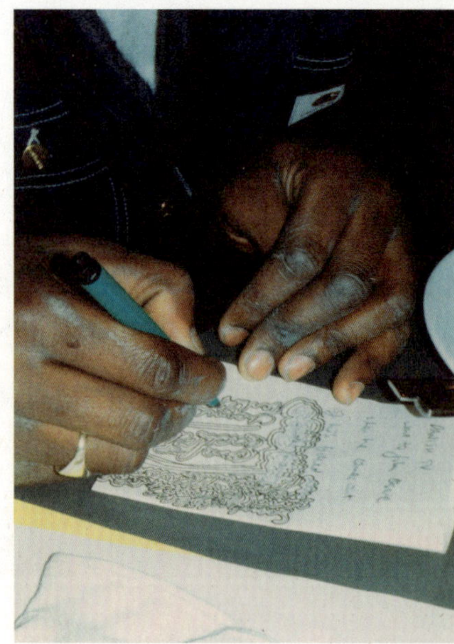

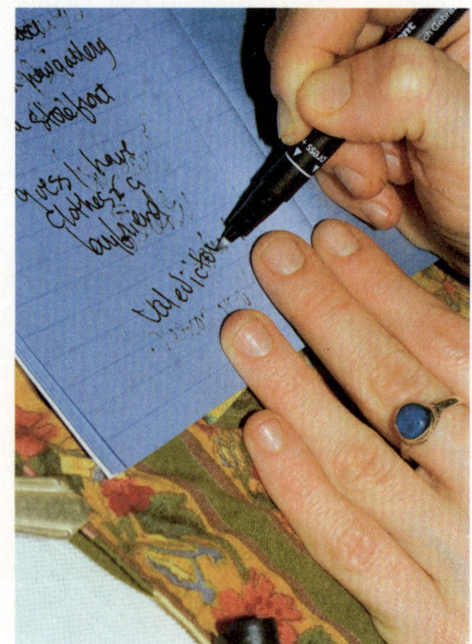

[L R Monochromes 2000-2001]

Now working on as pigment prints—. Very focused narratives but without the storylines of earlier work—and effort to be more formal—think of Albers' Homage to the Square'—.

[L 2000 Whitney Biennial R blank]

Biennial piece "What else are we alive for" last work with storylines--. Intended to show a new video, but the Whitney insisted on a wall piece—very paradoxical curatorial practice that emphasizes the specificity of the work, not the artist.

[L R "White Noise" Musee d'art modern Paris, also as a solo show at the Whitney in 2001]

White Noise: oval room, 2,500-4,000 sheets of paper (depending on size of constructed room--. A sort of peripity with the genre, but plan to do a double installation with separate yet adjoining rooms, one filled entirely with conversations on white paper, the other with conversations on colored papers. Material shape of language: Ken Goldsmith. Postscript to his book "Soliloquy" (suh-lil-uh-kwee): "If every word spoken in New York City were somehow to materialize as a snowflake, each day there would be a blizzard."

[L R: Mantel, fireside talk]

Tableaux, spaces of conversation exchange: Treetrimming party, fireside talk.
Mantels as fictions, 1999-2000. Process of making them.
Reviewers called them 'shelves'

Portraits. L+R
L+R : } portrait is not just a visual construction - but overheard are too -
portrait as portrayal is eclectic -
& therefore also a betrayal.

[L Venice 1995 R Manifesta 1, Rotterdam, 1996]

Notion of the 'performative'—uses material, ideas produced as part of social interaction—sometimes performance as well, as in Rotterdam.

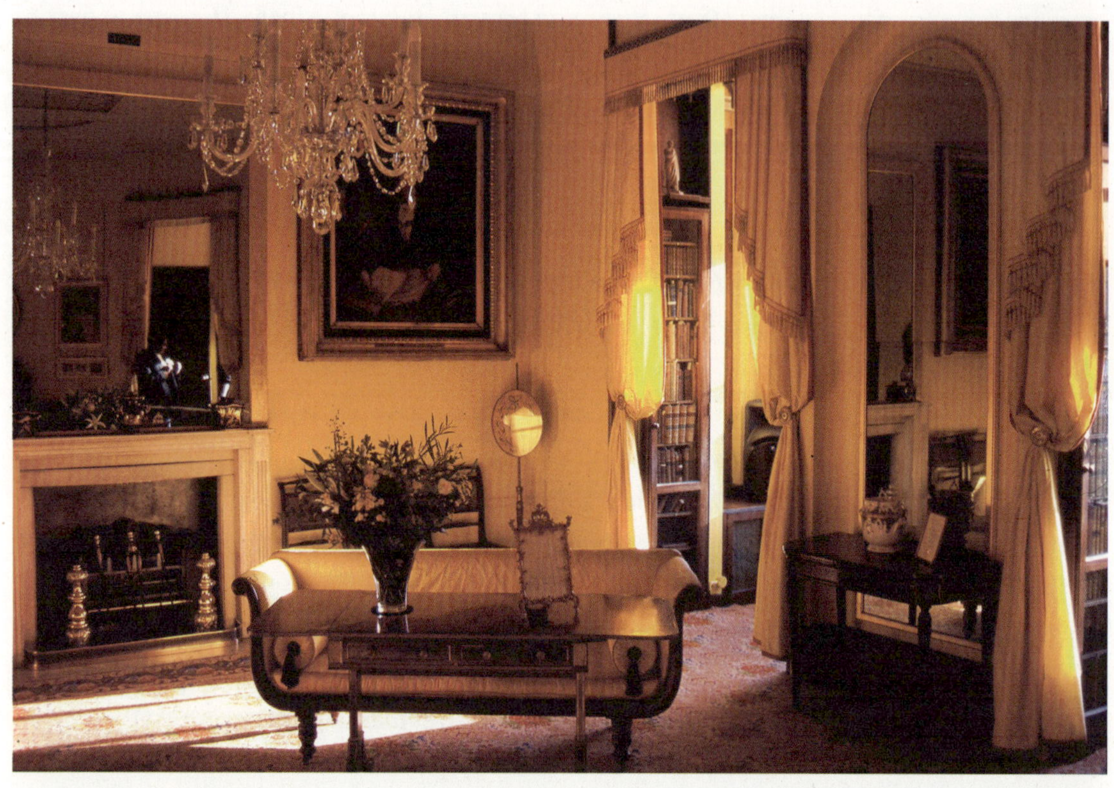

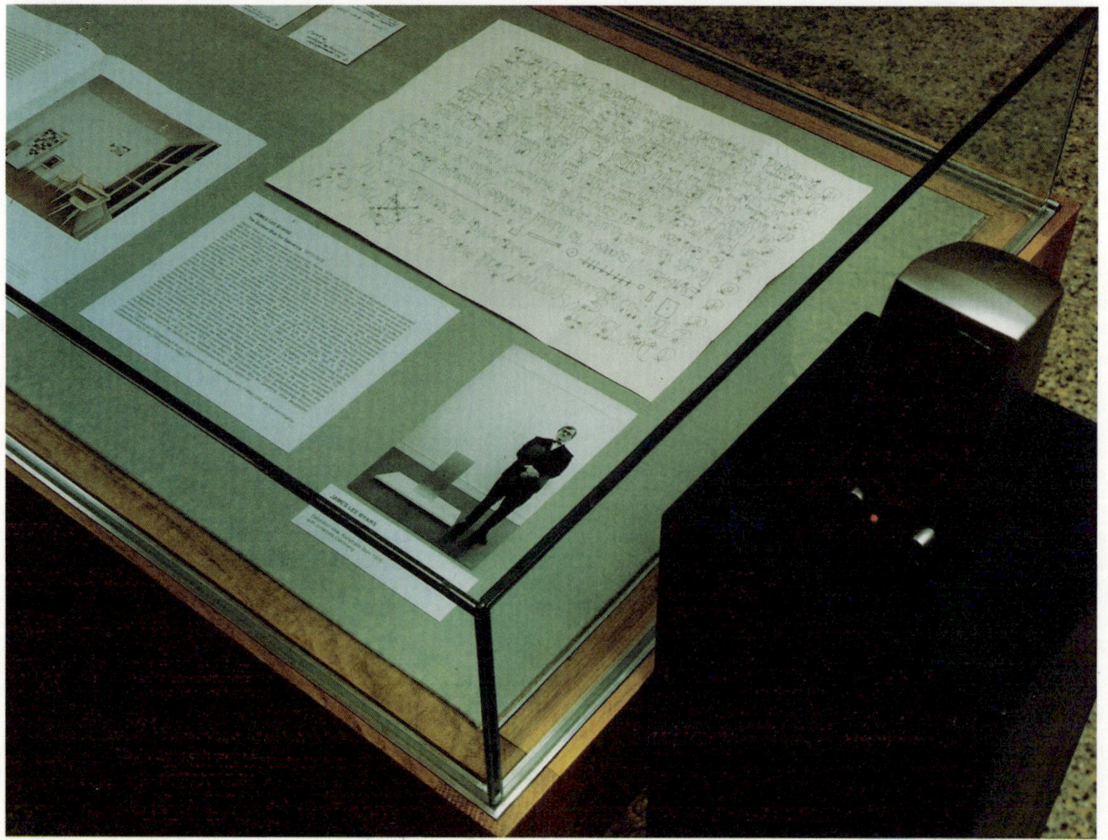

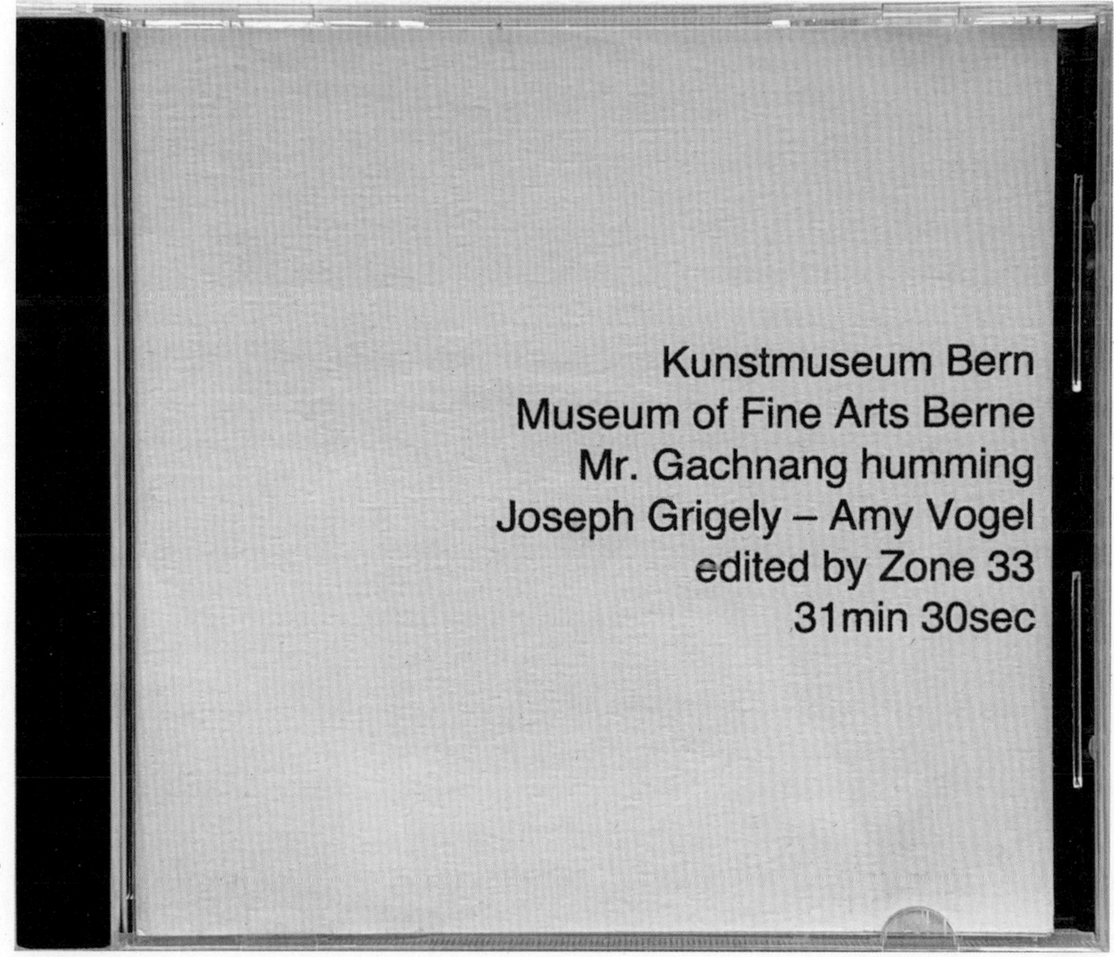
Kunstmuseum Bern
Museum of Fine Arts Berne
Mr. Gachnang humming
Joseph Grigely – Amy Vogel
edited by Zone 33
31min 30sec

[L Soanes Museum, 1999 ~~R Louisiana Museum~~, 1996]

Intervention that involves engagement to establish a 'dialogic' environment. Louisiana: "I don't really know why, but maybe it's more abstract that way (with five untitled paintings by Per Kirkeby"

Soanes: HUO project, first contemp. exhibition in Soanes . Soane as collector of architectural ruins—his is a collection of fragments—and I added to this conversational fragments. Soane's house is also the location of the Schiavoni Canaletto I showed earlier.

[L ~~Wadsworth Atheneum 1999~~ R Barbican Center 1998]

Wadsworth: another intervention, but of work related to "Conversation" and conversational exchange: painting—including another Canaletto, Watteau, Kensett, and also a range of work from other media—glass, porcelain, even mannequins.

Barbican: a social intervention in public spaces—series of broadsheets and brochures of "conversations" distributed in public spaces—and audio in loos.

[L R Kunstmuseum Bern, 2002, Byars' "Golden Box for Speaking"]

Recent show in Bern Switzerland at Kunstmuseum engaged the museum's collection and public spaces—bringing together into one large room works that evinced and represented sound. (no slides) This involved a wide variety—traditional conversation pieces, landscapes with waterfalls, and several works by Byars. Byars is an enigmatic and legendary figure—born in Detroit, lived many years in Bern. One piece—on the right—"The Golden Box for Speaking"--. When researching work for the show, the registrar indicated that it originally had a sound component—she wrote on a piece of paper that when the work was first shown at Kunsthalle Bern in 1978 that it included an audio of Harald Szeemann whistling in his office. She then crossed out 'whistling' and wrote 'huffing'. And then she said not huffing but humming. And then she said maybe it wasn't Harald Szeemann after all. This required a little research. I wrote letters to Byars' widow—I wrote to his friends—and slowly the answers arrived and the situation came together. When it was shown at Kunsthalle Bern in 1978, the work was titled somewhat differently: *I hum when I think* (Golden Voice Box), and it was materially different as well: it included inside it a loudspeaker connected to the office of the director of Kunsthalle, Johannes Gachnang. Gachnang had a predilection for humming when he made a decision about something—a unique trait which earned the director a place in Byars' collection of anecdotes entitled *One Hundred Secrets of Bern.* For the exhibition at the Kunsthalle, Byars materialized this 'secret' by placing a microphone in the directors office, and when Gachnang made decisions in the course of his daily activities, he would turn on the microphone and hum—and this humming sound was transmitted to the speaker and gilt box in the exhibition space nearby. Afterwards, the microphone was shut off; no other sounds were transmitted. This process continued throughout the exhibition. Later exhibitions omitted the audio component, and for the show in Bern my goal was to restore in some way this history—not reconstruct the piece, but rather construct the history so that people could experience its various elements. Gachnang—still alive and still humming as a publisher—agreed to do so. The exhibition shows a photograph of Gachnang standing beside the box and a CD with a single speaker of Gachnang humming his distinctive and unmistably idiosyncratic grumbling hums: I will play a segment—there are long silences in between:

Audio

(Gachnang humming while video on pause).

Pizza, Disability, and Difference, 2004

Mid-America College Art Association Conference, Minneapolis, October 2004.

Untitled Conversation (Salerno's Pizza) is a short video I originally made for *Utopia Station*, a curated show within the 2003 Venice Biennale. The underlying premise involves civic issues in contemporary social life, with a focus on disability, access, and care. How might individuals demonstrate care for others when they are not legally obligated to do so—especially when it means going out of their way to do things differently? After making the film, I later wrote a lecture that was anchored by the various issues the film intended to address.

Good morning, everyone. My talk today is about pizza. In particular, a medium cheese pizza with pepperoni, artichoke hearts, and onions. I know I came here to talk about the subject of expanded forms in art, not expanded waistlines. But trust me: This pizza I shall talk about is a very special one. And it does have something to do with art. It's actually part of a project I did for the Venice Biennale last year. This project explored ways we can engage certain civic issues in contemporary social life. What little things can we do to make the world a better place? It's not about bringing politics to art. It's about bringing art to politics.

As some of you perhaps know, I am totally deaf. Normally, I try to keep the political complexities of deafness and disability out of my art, but today is different. Today this is my entire subject. Along with the pizza. So let me say right now that my talk is about disability in relation to difference, and difference in relation to pizza. It's a full circle—pizza, disability, and difference.

There is a brief version of my story about the medium cheese pizza, and it goes like this: One day during the Christmas holidays, I was working at home, it was cold outside, and for lunch I wanted a pizza. My desire was intensified by the fact that I had just moved to Chicago from Jersey City, New Jersey. Jersey is widely known for a lot of bad things, and in my case it's a distinct and not very endearing memory of the worst pizza I ever ate. Moving to Chicago meant it was time for a Chicago pizza. The trouble was, I was alone at home: I could easily fax in my order for the pizza, but I live in a condo that has an intercom system, so there's no way I would know the pizza man had arrived. I need a doorbell with a flashing light. I actually took up the matter with my condo board, which was in the process of replacing the intercom system anyway. They were nice, they explored options, but in the end they said that there was nothing they could do. Which is a euphemism for saying there is nothing they *would* do. Not for me alone, and not for other apartments in our building. I mean, it's not like I'm the only deaf person in Chicago. So I visited the coordinator for architectural access at Chicago City Hall, and he was quite sympathetic; but he also pointed out that there was nothing in the Americans with Disabilities Act that required my condo to be accessible. He said that had the condo been financed with federal funds, I would have a case; but because it was not, I had no claim to access, and if I wanted my pizza delivered to me, I had two choices: I could sit outside and wait for the pizza to come, even if it means sitting outside in the cold—or I could pay for and install my own doorbell with a flashing light. Installing my own system would not be cheap—but the law does say I have this right, and the condo association cannot stop me from doing so. But the law also says that if I move out of my home, I would be required to restore the system to its "original state"—that is, I would have to uninstall whatever I installed to make my condo accessible.

Does this perplex you? It should.

You may think I am neglecting more serious dilemmas in the world, and to some extent this is true. We've got a postcolonial war of colonial aggression taking place in the Middle East. There's an overwhelming number of people in the world who do not have access to clean water. There's a health crisis of unimaginable proportions imploding in the heart of Africa. The way my late colleague George Roeder put it: Ours is a generation mired in an ever-expanding pool of quickshit.

So why should I care about my pizza?

In many ways, it's not really about the pizza. It's instead about what the French writer Marc Augé calls "the anthropology of the near." This anthropology of the near is about our immediate physical and social environment—and the ways we might get outside of the inside in order to understand it a little better. An anthropology of disability is concerned with how bodies move through spaces, and how information moves through bodies. Most notions of urban and domestic utopia depend on abstract, homogeneous bodies, bodies that move alike, bodies that think alike, bodies that feel alike. This partly explains the impetus behind post-modern biology, and our love affair with recombinant DNA: It is a desire for bodies that are predictable, a desire for bodies that move and age as we desire them to move and age. As much as people want to be different, they are also afraid to be different. There's something terribly ironic about all of this. Julia Kristeva summarized this point very nicely when she recently wrote in an essay about disability: "Will the advanced democracies know how to find the ways to accompany life all the way to its limits and limitations while including and encouraging the subject within?"

It's a good question: How can we support and encourage people who are exploring the limits of what it means to live? We won't understand what this all means without carefully observing the complex and nuanced ways that difference manifests itself in the human body. We move differently through space—we see, we touch, we hear differently because our bodies are different—and the fact our bodies are different is what makes us so special in relation to each other. It's a rare situation where a utopian environment is built up around the notion of difference, as opposed to the notion of similitude.

A house that Rem Koolhaas designed in Bordeaux is a splendid example of this kind of thinking. I don't have a picture to show you—I want you to imagine the house. Rem designed this house for a person who used a wheelchair. Conventional design approaches this situation by seeing the wheelchair as a prosthesis of the body and making elevators a prosthesis of a building. Rem instead saw the wheelchair as integral to the body, and the elevator as integral to the house, and so designed the house with an entire book-lined room that moves vertically through the center of the space. *Time* magazine anointed the house with "Best Design of the Year" in 1998. Somehow in the process of praising the house for its innovative use of glass, *Time* neglected to mention the most compelling aspect of the house: that for the man in the wheelchair, it became a home. This ontological shift was possible because of how Rem redefined the house as a verb. It is the house that moves. It's not a technological gimmick; it's very simple pragmatism. But it is also, while simple, a brilliant and prescient way of thinking about disability, unimaginably rare in society today, and one reason why Rem is the person he is.

That such thinking is so rare also explains why the Americans with Disabilities Act exists: If there is not enough social inertia to acknowledge the values and attributes of disability in our culture, it is necessary to create enforced conditions toward this end. The results have not been good. I have colleagues and friends who sincerely believe that the Americans with Disabilities Act has effectively ended discrimination against the disabled. Few realize this is not the case. As the legal philosopher Martha Minow has written, "Law has failed to resolve the meaning of equality for people defined as different by the society." Not that law hasn't tried: The Civil Rights Act of 1964 defined difference and equalized difference, but it did so only by creating exclusionary categories of difference. The wording of the Civil Rights Act intentionally omits reference to the disabled. The Civil Rights Act only addresses race, gender, religion, and national origin—it does not address disability. This was occasioned by what was then perceived as fiscal fear: that the expense of "accommodating" disabled people would undermine America's economic infrastructure. The ADA is not a civil rights statute, but an "accommodations" statute. In fact, the ADA is so different, so exclusionary, that it creates and abets, rather than eliminates, conditions by which discrimination against the disabled is condoned by the Constitution.

Let me explain this further. One particular problem with the ADA is how it burdens disabled people with proving that a physical impairment is also a disability. As Justice Sandra Day

O'Connor wrote in a recent Supreme Court opinion: "Merely having an impairment does not make one disabled for purposes of the ADA." The ADA defines "disability" as an impairment that "substantially limits someone from engaging in one or more major life activities." But what is a "major" life activity? In the Supreme Court case of *Toyota v. Williams*, a woman with carpal tunnel syndrome sued Toyota for not accommodating her disability. She wished to be transferred to a job that would not involve repetitive motions relating to wiping and sponging cars as they came off the assembly line. Ms. Williams lost her case. It was actually a blowout: The court voted 9–0 against her. Justice O'Connor wrote that Ms. Williams's inability to do her job did not constitute an inability to participate in what the law calls "a major life activity." O'Connor explained that since brushing our teeth constitutes a major life activity, and since Ms. Williams could brush her own teeth, she was not disabled by definition of the law. By this logic, the court affirmed that having a job was not a "major" life activity, but that brushing one's teeth, or performing household chores, is. This dramatically narrows the definition of disability. Issues of race or gender are not put to such a test in quite the same way, where the burden of proving one's difference is part of the process of proving discrimination. In the time since the ADA was passed, 94 percent of the discrimination lawsuits have been decided against disabled people. Ninety-four percent. If that number seems bad, consider the number of disabled people who can't even sue because lawyers won't take their cases with odds like these.

What is so troubling to me is the extent to which people rely on empirical observation to judge someone else's disability. Let me explain this with a story. In the early 1990s, when New York City introduced its disability ID program, there was public concern that the system was being abused. To get the ID you must have a doctor examine you and certify your disability. Despite this process, there was a fear that malingerers were obtaining and using the IDs. The Metropolitan Transportation Authority attempted to investigate this concern by stationing observers near the subway turnstiles to monitor people using disability ID cards. *The New York Times* reported that of the people using them, only 13 percent had what the *Times* called "an obvious disability." The *Times* elaborated by stating: "The audit noted several flagrant abuses, including a young mother who used a disabled half-fare pass to enter the subway and then carried her infant and a stroller up a flight of stairs. Another person ran to catch a train after using a half-fare pass." These observations may be realistic, but the conclusion drawn from them is not. Not all disabilities are visible or obvious—that's why applicants for the IDs are required to have their disability validated by a doctor. One person wrote to the *Times* about the article: "My wife, whose hands, arms and upper body are crippled by fibromyositis is quite capable of running for a train. She is not capable of dressing herself, cutting her food, turning a doorknob, dialing a phone, opening a soda can or bottle, writing, typing, or turning her head more than a few degrees. Her physical therapy bills are $350 a month, but the *Times* feels that even this modest help a half-fare pass gives her is a 'flagrant abuse' because her legs and feet still function normally and she is capable of running for a train."

There is something terribly wrong with how our culture is fixated on the relationship between seeing and believing.

I'd like to tell you a story that illustrates this even more. In 1990, shortly after the ADA became a law, I obtained in Washington, DC, a Metro Transit Identity Card. Up to this point there was no way I could identify myself as a deaf or disabled person should the need arise. Such as when having a tête-à-tête with police officers—you know, when pulled over for speeding, or when looking a little too vagrant-like in train stations, it would help to have something official that said I'm deaf. This is because deafness cannot be seen: It is a difference that cannot be verified by empirical observation. To get my Metro ID I had to visit the downtown transit office, get an application form, and then visit my doctor—actually an audiologist—who filled out the papers verifying my total deafness. Then I had to go back to the downtown office, submit my papers, pay a fee, have my picture taken, and in return for all this trouble I received a plastic ID card that was stamped on the back of it: "Person with Disability."

In New York, when I tried to use my ID on the subway, I was frequently rebuffed by the transit clerks. When this happened, I would sign to them in sign language "Why won't you accept it?"—at which point, because they could then see and validate my disability, they would relent. Once, however, a transit clerk steadfastly refused; I asked him why, and he wrote on a piece of paper: "Washington, DC, this is New York." I then asked him if this meant that I was deaf in Washington but not in New York, and he replied I should go to city hall.

I went to city hall.

At city hall I was told that every city could decide for itself what constitutes a disability. For this reason, my Washington, DC identification card was not valid in New York City. However, if I wished to apply for a New York City disability ID, I was welcome to do so. All I needed to do was go to another office, get an application form, have a doctor certify my disability, submit the paperwork and a fee, have my picture taken, and...

They said something like this to me in Boston, too.

I later wrote a letter to city hall. I explained that each state of the United States has its own specific requirements for what constitutes minimum driving skills to obtain a driver's license, but that individuals were not required to obtain separate driver's licenses in each state in which they wished to drive. So why was I being forced to prove my disability in each state in which I wished to use my Washington, DC transit ID?

City hall never replied.

The thing is, each time my ID was challenged, it was because the transit clerks could not literally see my difference and needed to have it empirically confirmed. Signing did this. But each time I had to sign to prove my difference, there was an implication that perhaps I was cheating the system—that the ID, obtained at considerable expense of time and money and certified by both a doctor and a transit agency, was not in and of itself "proof," but only implied proof: that each instance of its use would require another kind of proof, the seeing-is-believing syllogism. It's hard to explain just how demeaning this is, just how difficult it was to even take out my ID, knowing it would be questioned—that I am assumed guilty until a material manifestation of my deafness should prove otherwise. After a while I stopped using the ID—the daily challenges undercut the notion that even a formal document could define me. There is no national disability identity card; even my driver's license does not state I am deaf.

If seeing is believing, and if what we see matters, then we need to recognize that what we don't see matters even more.

And the stories you don't hear matter, too.

Consider the case of *Tennessee v. Lane*, which was decided by the Supreme Court this past spring. The case involves a paraplegic who received a summons to traffic court. The courtroom was located up two flights of stairs in a county courthouse where there was no elevator. Leaving his wheelchair behind him, he crawled up the stairs, arrived late, and had his case postponed—to be held in the same inaccessible courtroom. At the next hearing he refused to crawl or be carried up the stairs and was arrested and jailed for nonappearance, even though he was present at the foot of the courthouse stairs. Mr. Lane then sued under Title II of the ADA.

Mr. Lane actually won—he won by a 5–4 vote. But the decision was so narrow in its interpretation, it's hard to tell what in fact was won. Initially the case tested whether states were required to make public programs and services accessible to the disabled under Title II of the ADA: places like libraries and museums, for example. The outcome was much more restrained: It simply determined that the disabled have "the fundamental right of access to the courts" and due process granted by the Constitution. The issue of state-funded libraries and museums and related places of "public accommodation" was not addressed. The minority opinion was begrudging. During oral arguments, Mr. Lane's attorneys stated that inaccessible polling places and courtrooms denied access not just to buildings, but to the rights of citizenship. Justice Antonin Scalia replied: "Inaccessible voting place proves nothing at all. It just proves that the state did not go out of its way to make it easy for the handicapped to vote." Scalia added that the courthouse could be deemed inaccessible only if the plaintiff had been denied access; a lack of an elevator did not constitute such a condition. For the four justices who voted against Mr. Lane, the state could have met the requirement for access by carrying Mr. Lane up the stairs to the courtroom. If this is accommodation, it is not "reasonable" accommodation any more than it is reasonable to ask an African American citizen to enter the courtroom through the back door.

Part of the problem—and this is often forgotten by legislators, lawyers, and disabled people themselves—is that the ADA is not a civil rights statute. The ADA is an "accommodations" statute. This is the dirty little secret about the ADA. Unlike the Civil Rights Act of 1964, the ADA requires that disabled people need to be accommodated only when the accommodation is deemed "reasonable" and "rational." Consequently, many instances of overt discrimination lack judicial remedies under the ADA. Chief Justice William H. Rehnquist stated in his *Board of Trustees of the University of Alabama v. Garrett* decision in 2001 that, in passing the ADA, Congress had not proven that states regularly and repeatedly engaged in "irrational" employment discrimination against the disabled. Rehnquist explained that "it would be entirely rational (and therefore constitutional) for a state employer to conserve scarce financial resources by hiring employees who are able to use existing facilities." The problem here is that the term "rational" discrimination euphemizes discrimination by implying that discrimination may be bad, but not so bad as to be unjustifiable. No other American group is subject to such a contingency clause, where one's equality is based on arbitrary fiscal factors. As Rehnquist further stated in his dissenting opinion in *Tennessee v. Lane*: "Financial considerations almost always furnish a rational basis for a State to decline to make those alterations [for access]." "Almost always" is a phrase that reveals that the loopholes of the ADA are almost as big as the law itself.

This abdication of responsibility is known as "rational basis review": It derives from the premise that while discrimination is bad for the individual, it can be justified for the sake of the greater good of others. Imagine if this kind of ideology was written into the Civil Rights Act of 1964: It would have broadly legitimized racial and sexual discrimination for financial reasons. If this seems a preposterous assumption, it is a preposterous reality for disabled people on an everyday basis. In his dissent in the *Garrett* case, Justice Stephen Breyer presented 561 testimonies of disabled individuals who had experienced discrimination by agencies of state governments. For Chief Justice Rehnquist, this is all constitutionally permissible in the name of economic resourcefulness. We are fast reverting to being a nation of unequal citizenship. When the justices voted 9–0 in *Brown v. Board of Education* in 1954, they sent a clear signal that in America, separate was "inherently unequal." The 5–4 vote in *Tennessee v. Lane* fifty years later was only one vote away from symbolically overturning this decision. It's not *Brown* itself that is threatened, but the premises upon which *Brown* was based.

In practical terms, what this all means is that the Americans with Disabilities Act creates a different kind of difference, a category of difference that is very unlike the parameters defined

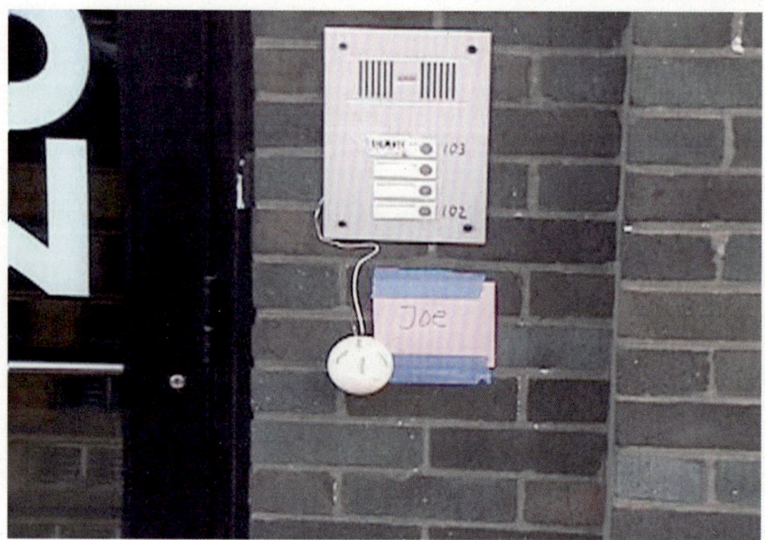

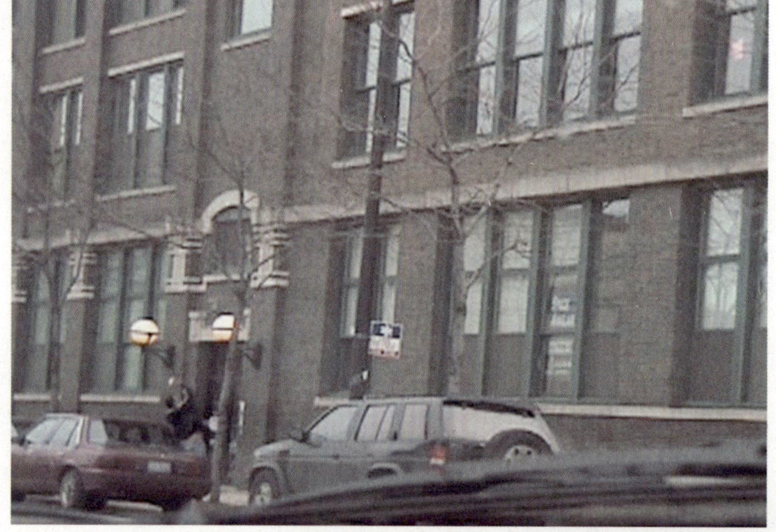

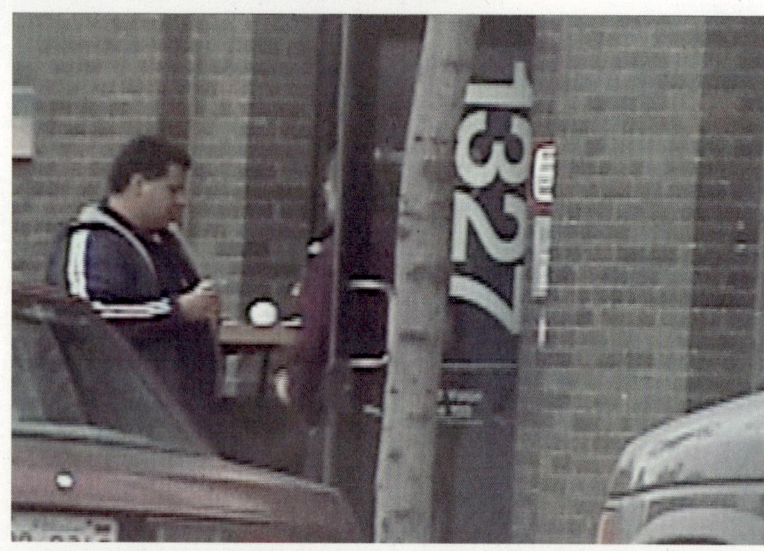

Stills from Joseph Grigely, *Untitled Conversation (Salerno's Pizza)*, 2004. Single-channel video

by the Civil Rights Act of 1964. Chief Justice Rehnquist pointed out quite bluntly that disabled people are not protected by the Fourteenth Amendment's equal protection clause—so their rights as individuals to seek remedial justice are severely curtailed. If I am discriminated against by a state-funded entity, I cannot file my own lawsuit for damages the way others can under the Civil Rights Act; instead, I have to go to the EEOC (Equal Employment Opportunity Commission) and ask them to file a suit. What this process does is extend the paternalistic principle of the ADA—you have to ask others to help you. Individual independence, and by extension true equality, is far, far away.

It's not easy to summarize a situation like this. The history of social change in America has not been predicated by legislative dictates, but by the critical mass of a populace determined to make change real. The workers' movements, the suffrage movement, the civil rights movement: These movements moved because of a certain will, where the actions of one person on the street meant as much as the actions of one person in Congress. As Bill Moyers once said in a talk about democracy: "Ideas need legs." But today our attention is divided by the malfeasance of a presidency that has dragged the world into a war and created the largest national debt in the history of America. The cares of the disabled would not seem to rate very highly against this kind of backdrop. But let me say that the cares of the disabled are not theirs alone: If civil rights are for anyone, they are for everyone, and it is hypocritical of us, if not also immoral, to create for the disabled a condition of equality that is, in the end, separate and unequal. What we need today are artists of the old school, artists unafraid to challenge intransigence. Artists who know what it means to forsake the security of a known aesthetic for the uncertainty and ambiguity of desire. God forbid, I'm not thinking of people like Picasso, or even Matthew Barney. I'm thinking about people like Gandhi and Thurgood Marshall. There is in their art more originality and innovation than there is in many of our museums. Theirs is an art that expanded the possibilities of what it means to be human. It's not an easy art, though; it comes from persistence and faith.

Now, a conclusion of sorts, and, also, a confession.

My confession is that I've always wanted to talk about these issues with an audience gathered together for some other purpose than to discuss disability. As a discipline, "disability studies" is a conflation of law, medicine, sociology, and cultural studies, yet it is often seen as being marginal in the hierarchy of canonized differences—as if its difference is simply too different to have a place in mainstream theories of difference. Not everyone in this room is disabled, but everyone in this room is potentially disabled. We don't usually speak of other canonized groups in quite the same way. One is not so much "born" disabled, though some are; rather, one is "placed," or situated, as disabled within the architecture of built-up environments and information systems. But if this is disabling, I can imagine ways that it is also enabling: I imagine a practice, a modus operandi, where it is blind people who tell us what it means to see, deaf people who tell us what it means to hear, and wheelchair users telling us what it means to navigate the physical world. I don't want euphemisms like "hearing impaired" or "physically challenged." I want honest realities addressed in an honest way. I'm not so cynical to believe that small gestures cannot mean big things. They can.

A final few words: It may interest you to know that I finally got my medium cheese pizza from Salerno's. I faxed in my order to Salerno's Pizza and provided instructions for the delivery person. The instructions said: "I am deaf. To call me, please use the whiffle ball. It is located on a hook beside the intercom. Remove the ball from the hook, step back a few paces, and locate the window that has a pink paper in it. I will be sitting at a desk in front of the window. Throw the ball up at the window a few times, and I will see it and come downstairs."

When the pizza delivery guy arrived, he got out of his car, and, holding the pizza in one hand, he took hold of the ball in the other and threw it up at the window. He was nonplussed, as if he was asked to do this every other day. He threw the ball a few times, and hit the wrong window, but it was close enough. A few minutes later, I was downstairs, paid him, and he handed me my pizza with the whiffle ball on top of the box.

Exhibition Prosthetics, 2009

Architectural Association, London, February 2009.

I began writing on the subject of exhibition prosthetics in the mid-1990s, when I was teaching art history at the University of Michigan, Ann Arbor. My focus was on the infrastructure of exhibitions, and in particular the role played by what was traditionally regarded as ephemera. Is an exhibition solely about the materialization of specific works of art? Or is it also—and if so, in what ways—about the various conventions that go into the making of exhibitions—which include press releases, announcement cards, checklists, wall labels, catalogues, and digital-based media?

Conventions like these are representations. In the process of making an exhibition we engage in different kinds of representations both because of the implausibility of re-presenting, and also because representation is a means by which we further, through the use of language and images, and through a process that is both otherwise and otherhow, the reach of the real. In this respect, moving closer to the artwork involves moving away from the artwork—to look closer at fringes and margins and representations, and ask what seems to me a very fundamental question: To what extent are these various exhibition conventions part of the art and not merely an extension of it?

My first public discussion on the topic was a public lecture I gave at a conference on "Show and Tell" at the University of Michigan in March 1998. Shortly afterward I presented a lecture and seminar on exhibition prosthetics at Cranbrook Academy of Art in November 1999, as part of an exhibition I presented on my art publications and publication projects. For a decade after this, I regularly taught a course on exhibition prosthetics at the School of the Art Institute of Chicago. In the winter of 2009, Zak Kyes, in his role as art director of publications at the Architectural Association in London, invited me to give a public talk on exhibition prosthetics. This talk—reproduced below from my lecture notes—along with a conversation that followed between Kyes, Hans Ulrich Obrist, and myself, was published the following year by Sternberg (Berlin) and the Bedford Press (London).

Architectural Association
School of Architecture

Bedford Press
Excursus Lecture Series
6PM AA Lecture Hall

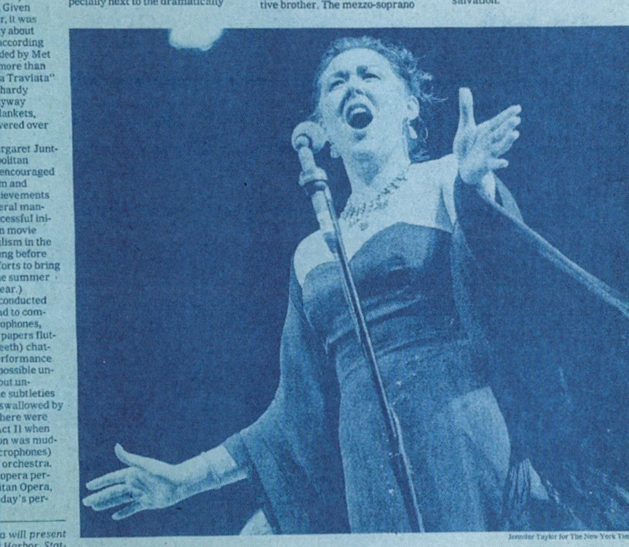

d the Cold Night Air the Devil Dares to Tread

formance featured a young cast alongside the veteran bass James Morris, who portrayed Méphistophélès with chilling conviction and naughty menace.

In the title role, David Pomeroy sang with a powerful, agile tenor and commendable French diction, although his voice sometimes sounded forced in the upper register. His "Salut demeure" was heartfelt, but his portrayal was often rather bland, especially next to the dramatically

Faust
Central Park

convincing Marguerite of Katie Van Kooten whose warm, gracefully expressive soprano was lively in the "Jewel" song and vulnerable in "Anges Purs! Anges Radieux!"

The able baritone Hung Yun was admirable as Valentin, her protective brother. The mezzo-soprano Kate Lindsey sang with an attractive voice and was effective as Siébel. Keith Miller as Wagner and Jane Bunnell as Marthe were also strong.

The musicians and singers must have been almost as frozen as the audience, which predictably, given the plummeting temperature, appeared to have thinned significantly by the end. But a sprinkling of determined listeners braved Faustian frostbite and stayed around for Marguerite's salvation.

Jennifer Taylor for The New York Times

Image from the exhibition Joseph Grigely: St. Cecilia, MCA Chicago, 2008
Printed at Bedford Press, London / bedfordpress.org

Joseph Grigely
Exhibition Prosthetics
18.2.09

In conversation with
Hans Ulrich Obrist and
Zak Kyes

Exhibition Prosthetics is a term used to describe a loosely ordered array of exhibition conventions including labels, titles, checklists, exhibition announcements, press releases and catalogues. Moving closer to the artwork may involve moving away from it, to look more closely at fringes and margins and representations, and ask to what extent these various exhibition conventions are part of the art and not merely an extension of it.

How might it be that 'art' is subsumed by the various representations that we make for it? This talk will focus on situations in which the representations are art, not merely re-presentations of art.

Artist Joseph Grigely's lecture is the first in the Excursus lecture and publication series initiated by Bedford Press, a small-scale private press and publisher operating under the auspices of the AA.

Poster for the lecture "Exhibition Prosthetics," 2009. Bedford Press and the Architectural Association, London

Joseph Grigely

Exhibition Prosthetics

Architectural Association, London, February 2009

Can everyone hear me all right?

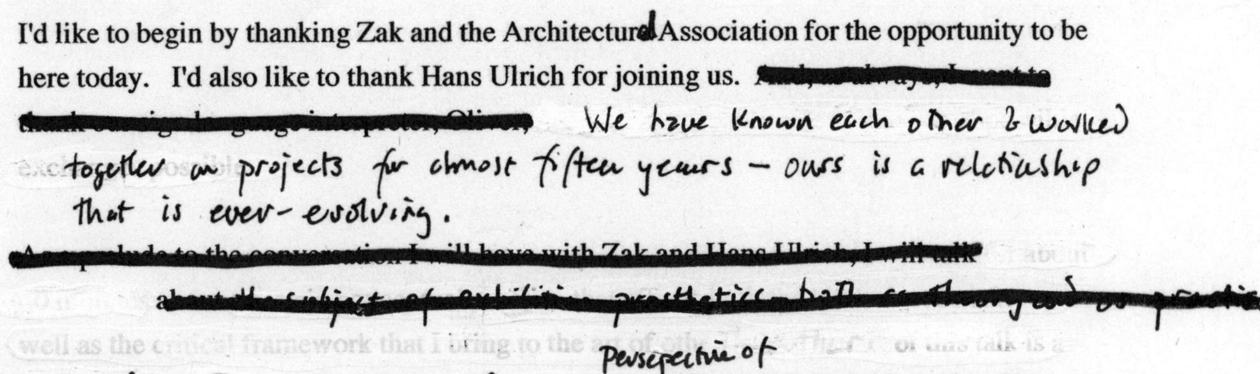

I'd like to begin by thanking Zak and the Architectural Association for the opportunity to be here today. I'd also like to thank Hans Ulrich for joining us. We have known each other & worked together on projects for almost fifteen years—ours is a relationship that is ever-evolving.

My talk today has two perspectives. One is the perspective of Joseph Grigely the artist. He mostly works with conversations and conversational exchanges, and the ways sound is represented visual phenomena.

The other perspective is more academic: it is the perspective of textual criticism and bibliography, which I studied at Oxford in the early 1980s. Textual Criticism & bibliography are disciplinary practices that explore how texts are disseminated in culture. The discipline especially tries to define the parameters of what constitutes textual boundaries—where does a poem begin & end—and by extension, where does an artwork begin & end? Where does an exhibition begin & end? These questions were discussed in a book I wrote which is entitled :*Textualterity: Art, Theory & Textual Criticism*--. My discussion today will focus on one aspect of that research—what I call exhibition prosthetics—

I have used the term 'exhibition prosthetics' for several years to describe an array of exhibition conventions. These conventions include labels, titles, checklists, exhibition announcements, press releases, catalogues, and to some extent even flowers. Flowers are the first thing you see when you enter some of the world's great museums—the Met or the

Art Institute of Chicago—but do we notice them? In what ways do flowers and press releases and checklists affect the ways we 'read' an exhibition? Perhaps out of habit, we are decidedly inured to the experience of these conventions. They are a part of the machinery of exhibiting--we read titles, labels, and catalogues because their authority establishes for the artwork a sense of place. In this respect, moving closer to the artwork involves moving away from the artwork--to look closer at fringes and margins and representations, and ask what seems to me a very fundamental question: to what extent are these various exhibition conventions actually part of the art--and not merely an extension of it?

[Prosthetic arm]

I want to start with an example of a human prosthesis: an arm. A prosthesis is an attachment, an extension.

The first modern usage of the prosthesis as a medical term dates to 1706—it is described as "that which fills up what is wanting." That is, a prosthesis remediates—it fills, it extends, it supplements. But it does not do this without also becoming a part of, not apart from, the body that it fills, extends, and supplements. As the literary critic David Wills has written the "prosthesis is inevitably about belonging." (*Prostheses*, 15).

In theory, this kind of seamlessness is ideal. But it is much harder to accomplish in practice.

Racine St. Building

Consider as an example this wheelchair lift on a building near my home in Chicago. The building is a mixed use building—part business, part residence. On the left is the front of the building; on the right is the side of the building, where the wheelchair lift is situated in a car park abutting the building. It is in situations like this that the prosthesis is an attachment, and the point of attachment becomes pronounced, awkward, and never quite so belonging as we would like it to be.

Deaf Child sign

If buildings are bodies—and I think they are—so too is our social topography. This is a roadside sign from Lake Placid, New York. Like a caption, a sign like this makes evident through language that which is otherwise not present. This is usual for the prosthesis—to simulstaneously stand and stand in for that which is absent.

It could be said that by definition the prosthesis aspires for seamlessness. Aspires to incorporate itself into a whole, so that it is indivisible from the whole. Human prostheses are today incredibly elaborate—they work both as a visual and functional surrogate to the original. They weren't always like this though, in the past their role was primarily visual—to incorporate the body's corporeality. About 30 years ago I had a deaf classmate named Roger who had one arm, and the other was a passive or 'cosmetic' prosthesis. This was my first year of college, and I was learning sign language, and Roger was in my class. On the first day, the teacher tried to teach us to sign "Good morning." So we all said "Good morning" back to her—except Roger, who signed "good morning" with his right hand only. The teacher was nice, she didn't realize Roger had only one arm—so she said "it's important to follow my signs carefully, and if I use two hands you must also use two hands." So she does it again, she signs "Good morning"—and Roger, he's perplexed, but compelled to make people happy, responded in the only way he could: with his right hand he removed his prosthesis, and then, with one hand holding the other hand, signed back—with a smile—"Good morning."

All three of these examples—the wheelchair lift, the deaf child sign, and Roger—involve disability because the prosthesis is historically and etymologically discussed as an extension of the human body. [illegible] The body is both a reality and a metaphor—a metaphor for other bodies. Books are bodies, exhibitions are bodies, buildings are bodies—what is it that makes a body 'complete'? What makes a body of an exhibition 'whole'?

[Edison's Last Breath]

In Mieke Bal's book, *Double Exposures*, she explains that "The discourse around which museums exist, and which defines their primary function, is exposition" (*Double Exposures* , 2). Exposition involves the doubling of both showing and telling. Which is what I am doing right now: showing and telling about the practice of showing and telling. Historically, one role of museums iinvolves authenticating: to vouch for the historical truth of the objects being displayed. This is where much of the 'telling' comes into play. One of my favorite installations is a small vitrine that can be found in the Henry Ford Museum in Dearborn, Michigan. The installation is titled *Edison's Last Breath?* Not *Edison's Last Breath*, stop, but *Edison's Last Breath*, question mark. Here, the truth about history is uncertainty itself.

And so it would seem that the relationship between a body and its prosthesis is a dialogic relationship, each 'informing' the other, each supplementing the other. The French critic Gerard Genette has spoken of verbal appendages such as titles and captions as *paratexts*: that which is alongside the main text. But alongside is not enough—there is movement between the body and its extensions, a movement that is peritextual in design, a movement that involves the peregrinations of a shifting ground.

What I find particularly engaging about *Edison's Last Breath?* is how the label is contained within the vitrine, neatly positioned beside the test tube containing Edison's maybe last breath. Like Piero Manzoni's famous cans shit, it is not the contents of the test tube or the can that matter as much as how they are labeled, and we construct meaning on the basis of our beliefs about those labels.

Soane Poster Cover

This is turn makes a museum like Sir John Soane's museum so compelling: Soane's museum has no labels on the walls. Which is precisely as Soane intended. Instead of labels, Soane prepared three guidebooks for the Museum, and the guidebooks modulated the movement of visitors to the museum.

Soane Layout

This modus operandi continued in the exhibition Hans Ulrich curated at Soane's Museum in 1999. The exhibition consisted of work by a number of contemporary artists, among them Cerith Wynn Evans, Steve McQueen, and Douglas Gordon. Rather than labeling the art, Cerith initiated the design of a fold-out brochure that operated like Soane's guidebooks—as a supplement to the exhibition that was also part of the exhibition.

Among archivists, checklists and similar printed materials are described as 'ephemera.' Ephemera consists of the incarnation of the ephemeral-- it is the sort of unexceptional everyday stuff that typically gets thrown away. Exhibition announcements and press releases and checklists rarely get saved. At times, I wonder why. These various conventions have a profound influence on how we read art--how we work our way to it and through it. Sometimes I think artists realise this better than critics + historians do. Starting in the early 1990s, a body of work has developed around the prosthesis. For a show at the Louisiana Museum in Denmark Neil Cummings and Marysia Lewandowska composed and published an 'errata' to the exhibition catalogue that explores the relationship between everyday objects and art objects-
During the same period of time, Felix Gonzalez-Torres created his singular and well-known poster-projects.

It was at this time that Hans Ulrich Obrist started organizing projects that redefined the parameters of place, by taking the exhibition outside the gallery and the museum. His first exhibition, entitled "The Kitchen Show," took place in 1991 in the kitchen of his apartment in St. Gallen. In the catalogue, Hans Ulrich explained: "[The] starting point is the idea to present an exhibition in an unspectacular space." **Der Standard** As his curatorial oeuvre grew, so too did the definition of what constituted an unspectacular space. In projects he did with the Museum in Progress in Vienna, he turned the Austrian daily newspaper *Der Standard* into a museum with a series of interventions—artists were invited to create projects that were published as part of the regular editorial content of the paper. **Boetti** With Algherio Boetti he curated a project of Boetti's paintings of airplanes that appeared in the in-flight magazine of Austrian Airlines, and the images were also made into jigsaw puzzles that were given to children. A related project is *Point d'ironie*--. *Point d'ironie* is a hybrid poster/exhibition, which began in 1997 with the support of agnes b.: an artist is given a free reign to design each project, and 100,000 copies are produced—and distributed free in museums, cafes, schools, cinemas, and related venues. Projects like *Point d'ironie* work in a way that realigns the conventions by which art is disseminated. **Migrateurs** Such realignment was the modus operandi of the "Migrateurs" exhibitions Hans-Ulrich curated at the Musee d'art Moderne in Paris—where artists were invited to use a variety of public locations in the museum for installations—the bookshop and the café among them—and each exhibition was accompanied by a low-cost catalogue that, rather than reiterating or quoting the exhibition, functioned to inflect the exhibition. **Nanomuseum** It was with Hans Ulrich's Nano Museum, that the migratory museum became pocket-sized—the Nano Museum was precisely 66mm x 97mm, and hosted more than a dozen exhibitions before—this is a rumor—before Douglas Gordon lost in a bar. It is perhaps the first museum ever displaced in such a way.

Yes, you heard me right: Douglas lost the museum in a bar.

It is important to put this in the context of the early 1990s. The stock market crash of 1987 ended the megalomania of the 1980s and redirected aesthetic practices towards something much more modest in scale. At this same time, artists working in a way that could be described as Institutional Critique emerged: Andrea Fraser, for example, who turned the gallery docent into a reflexively criticalperformance. In a similar way that Hans Ulrich made exhibitions happen in the space of the newspaper, the magazine, and the catalogue, Fraser likewise used a conventional institutional prosthesis—the gallery tour—as an exhibition space. Hans-Ulrich's contribution was to render curatorial practice as a form of institutional criticism.—

At this point I am going to make a turn in my discussion. I want to talk about art I have made that reflects on the idea of the exhibition prosthesis—and how it fits into the paradigms I outlined. There are two basic examples here: the first involves unmaking the prosthesis—and the second involves engaging the prosthesis.

NYT 1

The first of these involves the removal of an existing prosthesis—that is, instead of operating in a way where more information is provided by way of labels, titles, captions, the work divests itself of this information. It is a process of making that involves unmaking.

For fifteen years my work as explored the disjunction between the visual experience and the auditory experience—. This body of work is inflected by my deafness—I am totally deaf, and have been deaf since I was ten years old. It's not that the deafness is important, but the implications of it, and the way it realigns the sensory world. What does the world look like with the sound turned off? How might it be that language can be said to caption human experience? Painters like Hogarth and Gainsborough and Canaletto frequently painted people engaged in some kind of conversational discourse—but the inhabitants of those paintings, for all that they say, say nothing at all.

THE NEW YORK TIMES, WEDNE

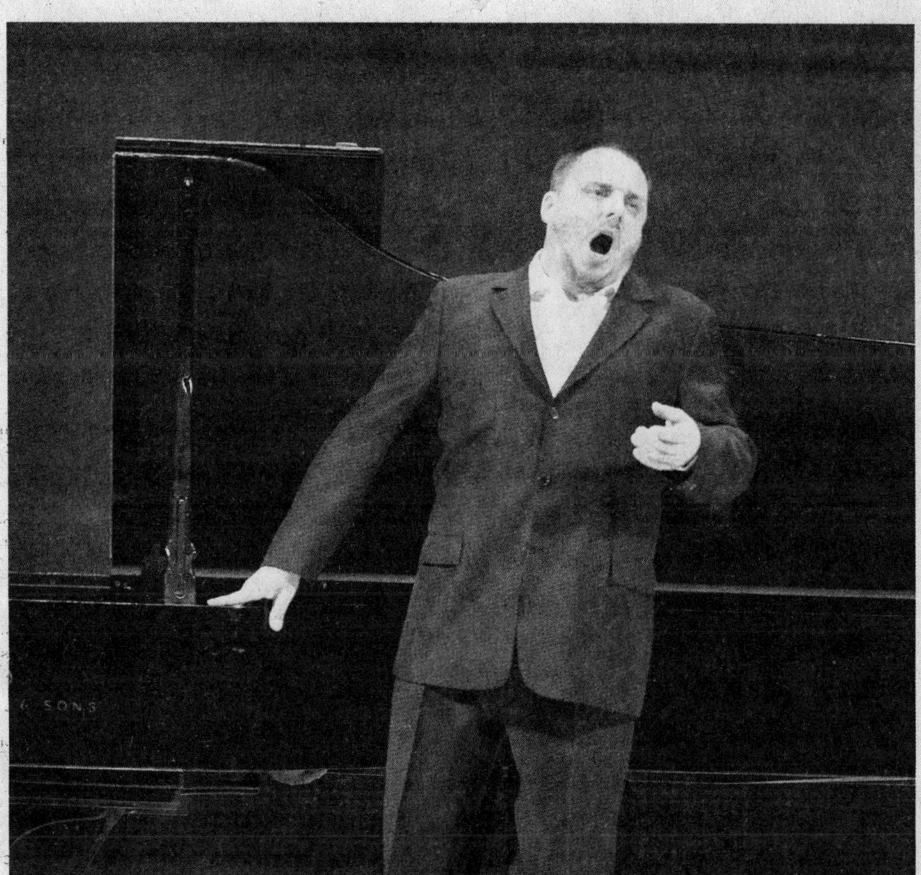

G. Paul Burnett/The New York Times

A Master of Song, Operating at Full Power

If there is one quality that distinguishes Matthias Goerne's singing — apart from the rich, large sound of his baritone — it is his ability both to create and to inhabit the emotional world a song describes. In his recital at Carnegie Hall on Monday evening, Mr. Goerne worked his magic quickly: within a bar or two, he sounded fully at

ALLAN KOZINN

MUSIC REVIEW

Matthias Goerne
Carnegie Hall

Goerne divided his program between Schumann and Brahms, with the Schumann part devoted to settings of poetry by Heinrich Heine. In his opening group, Mr. Goerne capitalized on the fanciful imagery of

filled Carnegie easily and comfortably, but even in gentler, quieter moments, his diction remained remarkably clear and precise.

After the intermission Mr. Goerne and Mr. Eschenbach collaborated on a fluid, gracefully drawn traversal of Brahms's "Lieder und Gesänge" (Op. 32), and a sober and often haunting account of the "Four Serious Songs" (Op. 121).

Joseph Grigely, *Songs Without Words (A Master of Song)*, 2008. Pigment print

A recent project, involving photographs of people singing from the *New York Times*, is called "Songs Without Words". I've removed the captions because they seem too reductive. It was Sontag who told us that every photograph wants a caption, and while the caption labels an image, it also imprisons the image.

NYT2.

There's another way of removing captions from images. All you have to do is turn off the sound on your TV. Watch the news without sound. Watch a concert without sound. Watch a sitcom without sound. At first it seems contrived and awkward—and after a while, the contrivance and awkwardness start to get interesting—because these things remind us just how ambiguous the body is when it doesn't have words to sustain it. This ambiguity is semantically liberating--. The photographs of people singing in the *Times* also have this way of reminding us that visual representations are not just about the visual field, but about the auditory field as well.

So in the Movie

Many of my conversations with hearing people are inscribed on paper, and it is by using papers like the two illustrated here that I construct wall pieces and installations. This has been an ongoing subject of my work for the past 15 years.

We're Bantering Drunkening About What's Important in Life (horizontal)

This piece is a recent work, titled " We're Bantering Drunkening About What's Important in Life." A work like this takes me 3 or 4 months to do, I generally make only two a year—the colored papers are hard to work with because placements are decided by so many factors—the shape and size of the paper, the color of the paper, the actual words, and the way they are written--. As Josef Albers said about color relations: you cannot put one color beside another without also changing both. This is also true for verbal narratives: you cannot put one word beside another without also changing both. This is how relational grammar operates, and how relational practices involve not just the semantics of language, but formal relations more generally.

Barbican Conversations

During the 1990s I did several projects in which a publication served as the exhibition. Some of these I did with Hans Ulrich—*Point d'ironie*, for example. One project I did here in London was called 'Barbican Conversations.' This was organized by the Public Art Development Trust in 1998. The basis of the project was to utilize the Barbican Center as both a source of conversational discourse, and a place of dissemination. If you've been in the Barbican before, you'll know just how complex it is as a center for the arts—there's a cinema, performing stages for both theatre and concerts, and numerous bars for intermissions. The bars are like coffee breaks, they function to enable critical conversational discourse that alternates between being relevant and irrelevant, between being reverent and irreverent.

Another Bottle?

Partly because there is so much public programming at the Barbican, there is throughout the Centre printed information about this programming in the form of brochures, broadsheets, and handbills. The exhibition of Barbican Conversations consisted primarily of redistributing conversations collected in bars in the form of information brochures—which were mingled with information brochures in the Centre. So people did not go to the exhibition—more often, they simply stumbled upon the exhibition.

Susan's Story

We printed three separate brochures—one was a two page spread, a simple design. A second one involved what designers call a roll fold. A roll-fold rolls open, and at each turn a new set of relations is made present—and the third involved a combination roll fold and accordion fold, so that the last story ~~which consists of a two-page spread originally written on a napkin~~ — which I am showing here — opened with the final fold.

Over the years there have been many other publication projects, the goal of these being to take art to people rather than make people go to the art. This kind of thinking is quite antithetical to American curatorial and exhibition practices, where going to a museum is like going to Church. A project like Barbican Conversations could not have been done in America. The few times that I have done publications projects for American museums, the experience was always tempered by various administrative challenges in the process of realizing the publication.

One exception was a project at the Parrish Museum of Art in Southampton, New York, curated by Ingrid Schaffner and Melissa Friedman in 2001. The exhibition involved inviting the artists to interact with the museum and its archives. Among the archives were several cyanotypes that were made at the turn of the century by Alice Chase, the wife of the painter William Merrit Chase. Many of her images showed small groups of people, whose relationships and activities were hard to pin down—which is a perfect captionless quotation of everyday life. My project involved enlarging one of the cyanotypes from approximately 3 x 5 inches to 23 x 33 inches—these were displayed, and distributed, through the museum's gift shop.

Wadsworth project

Another prosthetic convention I find engaging is the exhibition announcement. I don't have the time today to talk about this as extensively as I'd like—but I will mention one project I did for the Wadsworth Atheneum in Hartford. The basic idea here was to do a postcard-sized image of a well-known painting by the Hudson River School painter, John Kensett. The image shows to people talking on the shoreline, gesturing at large breaking waves—the auditory field of nature, and of human commentary on that nature. On the verso I printed a conversation with a friend in NY—something disjunctive in relation to the image. What happened is this—after the cards were sent out, several of them were returned to the museum. Most had a small note enclosed, saying "there are notes on the card, perhaps someone sent it out by mistake?"

The idea of a card like this is not to represent the art, but simply to present it. Announcement cards, like catalogues and posters, have this possible way of taking an exhibition places the exhibition itself does not go.

Berlin Biennial piece.

My favorite publication project was produced for the Berlin Biennale in 2001. Instead of creating work within the traditional exhibition space, my goal was to disperse it throughout the city of Berlin. To do this I printed 4 conversation papers, replicating not just the "conversation" but also the same color and texture paper as the original—including inscriptions on the verso. These papers were then placed in unincidental locations—sometimes one or two, sometimes two or three, they were left on counters in bars, at tales in restaurants, dropped in the street, placed on seats on buses— This was perhaps the most unincidental exhibition project I have ever done—so unincidental, I'm not sure the curators even noticed—they ever commented on it.

My conclusion now is brief.

The narratives of exhibitions are inherently discursive. They are not like the narratives of books where we move from word to word and line to line and page to page. In the space of the museum or the gallery, our movements are more unpredictable: from one painting to another, from one room to another, our path or course is usually determined not by conventions, but by peregrinations. An exhibition is unstable by definition, unstable, incomplete, uncontained and uncontainable. Like film trailers that offer clips and previews of upcoming films, contemporary exhibitions involve the fragmentation of an entity and its dispersion into a variety of representations. Ours is an age of fragmented narratives, a culture of bits and pieces that in themselves become--like the ruins and fragments in Sir John Soane's Museum--a synecdoche for the whole. As the global economy implodes and exhibition practices reinvent themselves to take into account radical shifts in our aesthetic economy, we can assure ourselves that we have not seen the end of this fragmentation.

On Failure, 2012

Society for Contemporary Art, Art Institute of Chicago, January 2012.

This lecture is one of the few times I have given a talk to a broad audience—in this case, a mixture of museum supporters, collectors, art students, and faculty. There was an implied expectation that I would talk about the *Conversations with the Hearing* that formed the core of my art practice at the time; but I decided instead to talk about the thinking that underlies this practice—how the disabled body is essentially a failed body in relation to evolutionary design—and how it paradoxically creates, through failure, the reflexive conditions by which art can be, and often is, created.

Thank you.

As a preface I want to explain that I have been totally deaf for forty-five years, and this makes it a little hard for me to give a public talk. I have prepared a text, into which I am going to bury my nose—and I'll be reading it aloud to myself in a way that you can overhear, and hopefully what you hear will be close to what I hear in my head.

I want to begin now by talking about the things I am not going to talk about.

I will not be talking about the *Conversations* that for a long time were the basis of much of the art that I make. This work started early in my career as an artist, in the early 1990s, when I was struggling with a question every artist struggles with: how to defamiliarize the familiar, how to make art out of something that is essentially artless. The narratives I constructed on the walls were formal fictions; grids filled with conversational exchanges that I have with hearing people, deliberately arranged to tell stories about the most banal moments of our everyday lives. Up to this point in art history the grid offered a way of escaping from language: think of Agnes Martin and Sol LeWitt, and Josef Albers. But for me the grid is also a narrative structure—an opportunity to combine the evanescence of everyday speech with the tradition of the still-life painting. It's an odd mixture to imagine: the still life as a grid painting, and the grid painting as a still life. But there is historical relevance in this—from the eighteenth century onward there is a genre of art that depicts conversational exchanges, such as in paintings by Constable and Canaletto, or in Meissen ware by Johann Kändler.

But all of this is the material for a different talk. Tonight, I am going to talk about something else. My ideas derive from concrete experience that is less focused on finalized outcomes—the finished poem, the finished painting, the finished exhibition—than on the process of working toward the point where a work of art or literature is brought before the public. A work of art is never static; it often exists in a state of becoming, where it aspires to move toward some indefinite and Platonic state of perfection.

At the other end of perfection is failure, and failure—in art, in design, in literature, in everyday life—is a big topic. We live surrounded by the wreckage of businesses, banks, and empires. Even at a much smaller scale of everyday life, failure is omnipresent: Zippers break, buttons pop, toast gets burned. But I won't be talking about that tonight. Even in the matter of cultural failure, I am not, just now, interested in discussing failure as a thematic construction—such as Sean Landers's self-deprecating work from the 1990s, or Peter Santino's *Failure Institute*, or Martin Kippenberger's sublime dumpsters. I love Peter Land's films in which he falls down stairs, falls off ladders, and shoots a hole in the boat in which he's been rowing. He sinks, of course. Eloquently, to the sound of birds chirping in the background. It's such a poetic sort of failure. But I won't talk about that today.

Nor will I talk about the history of unrealized and unfinished projects, which is a monumental history, especially in the case of my favorite genre of failure: the unfinished Romantic fragment poem. I'm also mum for the moment on the Shakespearean kind of moral failure that one finds in *Hamlet* and *King Lear* that is defined by mistakes, errors, and flaws in judgment. And I'd really love to talk about the Tacoma Narrows Bridge. In my first year of engineering school, they showed us a film of the bridge collapsing in a gale, ostensibly suggesting that failure should take place discreetly, in the design studio, and not out in public places. But this, too, is not my subject.

I guess that's a lot of stuff I'm not going to talk about.

Instead, I am primarily interested in the ways failure manifests itself in the process of making art. In one of his essays, the great Russian filmmaker Andrey Tarkovsky wrote: "I don't know a single masterpiece that does not have its weaknesses or is completely free of imperfections." I agree with this. Our general notion of a body of work is defined primarily by the way the body evolves and succeeds. Every January, *Artforum* surveys artists and critics to talk about "The Best of Last Year." In the checkout lane of Home Depot you can find home repair magazines a little like *Artforum*, with articles titled "The Best Tools of Last Year." It's a ubiquitous human desire to want to know about the best. It is, however, rare to find an article about failure in *Artforum*, or magazines about bad tools at Home Depot. For the same reason we don't see exhibitions here at the Art Institute of Chicago with titles like *Mistakes & Boo-Boos of the Old Masters*. But perhaps we should, because the way the body fails and is flawed is inextricably part of the uncontainable totality that defines the creative output of an individual, if not also the individual as well.

An example: Some years ago, I was sitting in the New York apartment of a friend, having tea and a conversation. A large part of our conversation had to do with the senses, and how communication involves a wide array of possibilities outside the norm of what it means to be human. Deep into the conversation, my friend told me a story about a blind baby who had learned to imitate, perfectly, the sound of a refrigerator and the sound of a car going over gravel as it approached the house. After a long pause in which we considered the implications of this, my friend turned to me and said: "Beauty is difficult. Never forget that."

"Beauty Is Difficult"—that is probably a better title for my talk. My intention is to present series of examples from which we might extrapolate an understanding of some of the ways failure has both a certain and uncertain sense of beauty. As Jack Halberstam said in his recent book entitled *The Queer Art of Failure*: "Under certain circumstances failing, losing, forgetting, unmaking, undoing, unbecoming, not knowing may in fact offer more creative, more cooperative, more surprising ways of being in the world." I like that a lot: "surprising ways of being in the world."

My first story takes place at a restaurant on West Broadway in New York. It was the mid-1990s. Jeff Koons had organized a benefit exhibition at the Nicole Klagsbrun Gallery, and after the opening we all went out for dinner. Jeffrey Deitch was there, along with Nicole Klagsbrun, and a diamond dealer named Bill Goldberg and his wife, Lili.

The conversation took a lot of turns, and at a certain point it turned to diamonds. Bill—who was one of the most respected diamond dealers in the world—reached into his coat pocket and pulled out a small black box that looked a little like a box fly fishermen use to carry trout flies—but inside of it, instead of little bits of fur and feathers, were radiant bits of compressed carbon. Bill was beaming. The diamonds sparkled. "Look at these," Bill said to a speechless table of people to whom beauty was something decidedly idiosyncratic. "These are perfect diamonds. If you can find more perfect diamonds than these anywhere on the planet, you'll make a humble man of me."

As if any of us could.

The little box of big diamonds got passed around the table, and the table got rather quiet as they were passed around. "Bill," I said. "These are beautiful. The problem is that their perfection seems sacrosanct. Aren't there diamonds that have flaws, but flaws that are beautiful? A beauty that is perfectly imperfect, shall we say?" I was thinking of art like Robert Smithson's, and how so much beauty could be found where it wasn't expected—often as the result of an entropic force. Beauty that is, in a word, difficult.

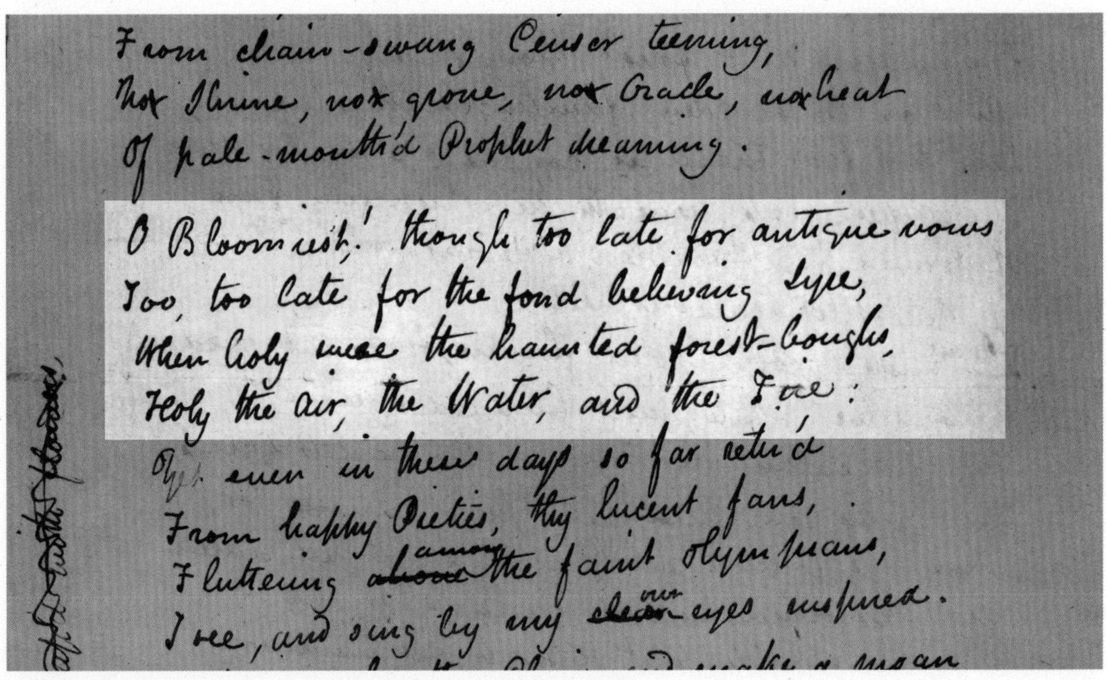

From chain-swung Censer teeming,
Nor Shrine, nor grove, nor Oracle, nor heat
Of pale-mouth'd Prophet dreaming.

O Bloomiest! though too late for antique vows
Too, too late for the fond believing Lyre,
When holy were the haunted forest-boughs,
Holy the air, the Water, and the Fire:
Yet even in these days so far retir'd
From happy Pieties, thy lucent fans,
Fluttering ~~above~~ among the faint Olympians,
I see, and sing by my ~~clear~~ own eyes inspired.

Highlighted holograph manuscript for John Keats's "Ode to Psyche," 1819

Bill was unruffled. "Yes," he said, "there are diamonds like that. But there's no market for them, so they aren't cut and polished and sold—they get used for industrial purposes."

So I asked Bill why.

"Simple," he replied. "Take your average bride-to-be in Kansas City, or any other city in America. She's been dreaming of her wedding since as long as she can remember. It's going to be the most important day of her life. That diamond engagement ring symbolizes her—and she doesn't want to be thought of as being anything less than perfect. The diamond doesn't have to be big, but it has to be as flawless as possible—because no woman in America wants to be thought of as being flawed."

I first got interested in flaws and failure when writing about Keats's poetry more than thirty years ago. At this time, I was doing research on Keats's manuscripts and his marked-up copy of Shakespeare. Keats would mark passages he liked and disliked, and his own manuscripts reveal many revisions—and for me this was an important revelation: The poems we see published in a book, the art we see in galleries and museums, and the music we listen to on iPhones—all of this constitutes a state of resolution that belies the compositional chaos that was part of the process of arriving at the point where the work meets the public.

Keats's poetic oeuvre is rich in what I call "microarchives." A microarchive is a document that both captures and reveals a history of compositional changes to a work of art, regardless of the medium. Manuscripts, drawings, annotated texts of various kinds—these are all micro-archives. Keats died young—he was only twenty-five when he told his friend Joseph Severn, "I am beginning to feel the flowers growing over me." His friends so loved him and his work, they saved every scrap of his writing, and those scraps reveal an agonizing effort to find in his vocabulary what William Butler Yeats called "the right word that is the surprising word."

Keats's poetry is filled with surprising words, and one of the most impossibly awkward words occurs in the holograph of his famous "Ode to Psyche," where he addresses Psyche, the Greek goddess of unremitting beauty. He says—he exclaims:

"O Bloomiest!"

"O Bloomiest"? It's an awkward phrase, for sure; but it's also a deliberate phrase, and I often find myself returning to this phrase—it's for me a talisman, a touchstone, the essence of art. From Keats's manuscripts we know he wrote it twice, and it also appears in two transcripts made by friends. But this wasn't the phrase that was printed when the poem was first published in 1820. Keats's publisher discreetly changed it to "O Brightest!" There's a long story about how this might have happened, as Keats was ill and did not complete the task of proofreading the volume—all we know is that the phrase "O Bloomiest" was published as "O Brightest," and "O Brightest" has been the phrase printed and reprinted in the poem for the past 191 years. The famous repository of lexicography, the *Oxford English Dictionary*, doesn't include "bloomiest" as a legitimate word—it's got "bloom" and "bloomage" and even "bloomy"—but no "bloomiest."

Some years ago, the literary critic Paul de Man wrote: "There always is a strange fascination about the bad verse that great poets write in their youth." But even more fascinating is the unmisgiving verse great poets write when they are at their best. I often imagine Keats being stuck in an end-of-the-semester writing crit at the School of the Art Institute of Chicago, and being told: "So—the panel feels that this phrase 'O Bloomiest' is awkward and not quite syntactic—so why did you leave it? We think 'O Brightest' might be simpler and more straightforward." And how does one respond to this? The logic of art is not the logic of human rationality. It's unfortunate that "O Bloomiest" is confined to the footnotes of editions of Keats's poems, and is very rarely mentioned by Keatsian scholars. This might be because the critical value of the compositional process is not altogether appreciated in Anglo-American criticism as much as it is elsewhere. In France, there is a genre of criticism known as "genetic criticism," which is concerned with the genesis of a text, and considers all available material that might have an interpretative bearing on it. Keats is an ideal subject for genetic criticism because so much of his archive survives. But it is important to remember that not all writers left archives like Keats did. Some, like Mikhail Bulgakov's, were burned. Some, like Walter Benjamin's, were lost. Some, like Mandelstam's, were composed orally because a written document was too incriminating in the age of Stalin. And there were writers like Robert Walser, who wrote without revising. In fact, Benjamin said of Walser that he never corrected a single line of his writing. And there are some writers, like Shakespeare, for whom the disappearance of all traces of their actual manuscripts leaves us with the beautiful and infuriating emptiness of not knowing what they actually wrote or how they wrote it.

Not long ago, at an auction of fly-fishing tackle, I purchased a note card and salmon flies that were in various stages of being tied. The flies were made by Helen Shaw, who is often called the "First Lady of Fly Tying" in America—she had in the mid-1900s a reputation for tying patterns with exceptional clarity, proportion, and efficiency. She also published several books on fly tying. I'm showing here the card and the in-progress salmon flies that came with it, a pattern known as the Popham. Like a Keats manuscript, the card reveals significant compositional changes. "Retie," says the note. "Retie wing & throat," it says.

Fly tiers generally work the way a theater director does: The script for a fly is called a "dressing," and there's a certain allowance that tiers have in the matter of interpreting the dressing. Some materials, because of their rarity, might be changed; but in the end, what matters is the individual eloquence of the fly, and how each interpretation by a tier is a singular reflection of the tier. Shaw struggled to get this right in a way that reflects Shaw's own standards,

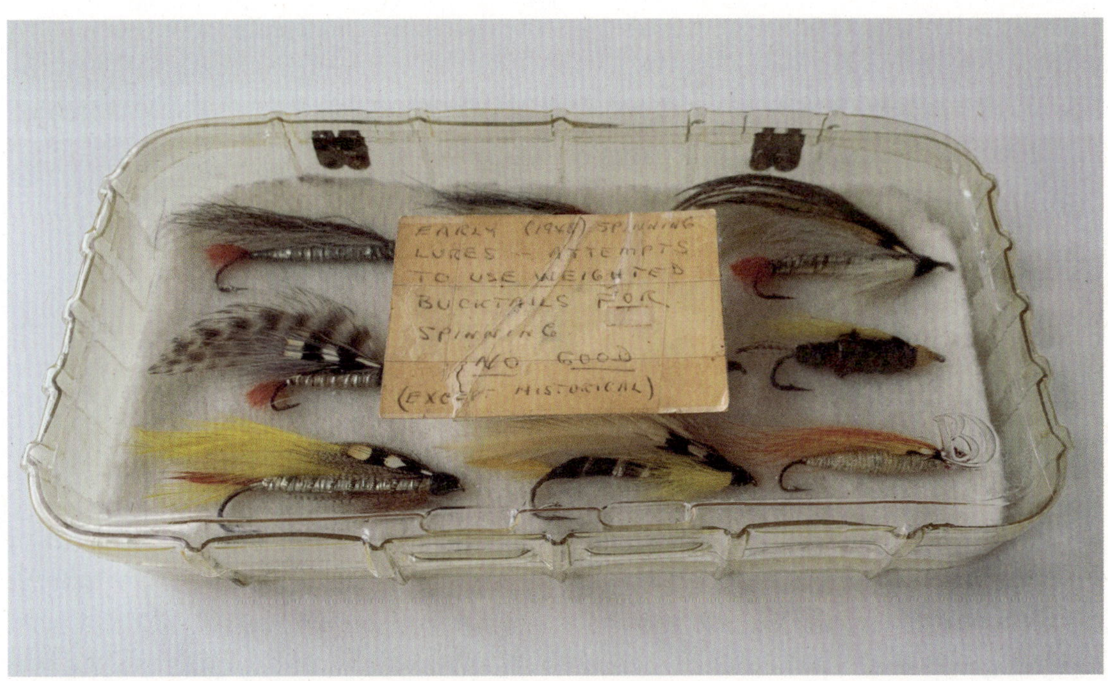

Joseph Bates, weighted spinning lures, 1945. Silk, fur, feathers, steel, and lead

acknowledging in her notes her own failures—the blue was too pale, she observed. The ribbing should be oval gold on the yellow, and oval silver on the blue, she wrote. She had forgotten the Indian Crow feather on the body—and made a pencil note to remember it. Things go wrong. But the fly in the bottom right somehow gets it all right.

Success through failure: This formulation of failure is a traditional formulation in the field of design, where errors are documented and studied so as not to repeat them. The design critic Henry Petroski specializes in this topic; for him, failure is a necessary condition for all design. But this way of thinking extends to art as well, where repetition is rarely without revision, and revision is an acknowledgment of mitigated failure. In a recent review of a Cézanne exhibition at the Metropolitan Museum of Art, Carol Armstrong wrote: "I see repetition, because [Cézanne] was trying to get it right."

Getting it right is one thing. Getting it wrong and recognizing it's wrong in a meaningful way is another thing. Let's look at another example: a selection of streamers and bucktails tied by Joseph Bates in 1945. Streamers and bucktails are a genre of trout flies designed to represent baitfish upon which larger fish feed, and Bates is a legendary figure in this area. He published in 1966 a book on streamers and bucktails that has yet to be superseded. These look like ordinary streamers, but they're not. Hidden beneath the fur and feathers of each fly is a mass of lead weight—ordinary streamers are nearly weightless; a size 2 weighs three-tenths of a gram—but these lead-wrapped streamers weigh up to 6.5 grams—more than twenty times as much. These are not so much weighted flies as they are feathered lures.

What was unique about the Bates streamers is the fact they came to me with a note taped to the fly box, which said: "Early (1945) spinning lures—attempts to use weighted bucktails for spinning NO GOOD (except historical)."

Bates does not explain to us why the streamers were no good. He doesn't have to—that is for us to determine. That he thought enough of them to save them for historical consideration is revealing, because an archive by definition does not express a value judgment about its contents—it aspires for a disinterested kind of comprehensiveness that includes the good alongside the no good.

If Helen Shaw and Joseph Bates were professionals, Carl Bruennig was an amateur. During the winters he lived in New York City, where he worked as a hairdresser, and every summer he drove six hours north to the Adirondacks, where, beside the Ausable River, he kept a small cabin with a fieldstone fireplace. When Carl died in 1987, his cabin and his flies passed on to his neighbor, and in the cabin today can be found a photograph of Carl and his dog from 1962. It's a photograph that tells us much about Carl. He is wearing stiff waders of rubberized canvas, and in his right hand he's holding a homemade wading staff made from a tree branch. In his left hand he has folded over his shoulder a fiberglass rod with an automatic reel. His creel is a modest mesh creel. This is not the kit of a purist; it's the kit of someone who does things his own way and does them with passion.

Neither an outsider nor an insider, Carl was singular. The flies that he tied himself were also singular—among the dried and brittle flies that he left behind are several stonefly nymphs, disproportionately round, dark green with light-green collars, and the body crisscrossed with gold tinsel. They are terrible ties; but an enigma about flies is that even terrible ties catch fish—their functionality is not measured by their visual appearance, but by how they behave as a hydrodynamic form. In Carl's fly boxes I found four flies called the Ausable Wulff that had been tied by the legendary tier Fran Betters, who lived a mile up the road from Carl—you can tell Fran tied them because they are tied with Fran's signature hot-orange thread. They look ratty and faded from years of use, and three of them have the hook points broken off. They are no longer usable to catch fish—no good, shall we say—yet decidedly too precious to throw away.

The latent possibility of failure is rarely explored so well as it is in Tarkovsky's film *Andrey Rublev*. The film is a fifteenth-century parable about artistic faith. The protagonist is Rublev, an icon painter of exceptional talent, whose will to paint is challenged at every turn—by society, by the church, by himself—until the presence of a bell caster named Boriska brings back his faith. Boriska's story goes like this: The prince wants to build a new bell, a bell so large and strong that it would symbolize his own power over others. But there is a problem: The plague has killed so many people, and among them the most skilled bell casters. He sends his men far in search of someone able to manage the casting operation, but his men turn up empty-handed. At one village, where they inquire after a certain bell caster, they are told he too is among the dead—but as they ride off, a young man runs out after them, crying that he is the son of the bell caster and that he knows the secret and only he alone has the knowledge to cast the bell that will make the prince proud. The prince's men are skeptical, of course, but they don't have options—so they bring Boriska back with them.

Boriska plays his part well. In the search for the right clay to make the mold, Boriska sends the prince's men far and wide—he rejects everything they find, and relishes his authority. At every step of the way—finding the clay, making the mold, building the furnaces to melt the alloy—he is difficult and demanding. When the prince's men deliver a load of silver to make the bronze stronger, Boriska is unmoved and asks for more: "Tell the prince not to be so stingy," he says. One is never too sure of Boriska's assuredness. He commands what seems like a hundred men at a task where one small error in judgment could ruin the bell—but from the end of one task to another, to the final moment when the bell is hoisted, hung, and rung, Boriska delivers.

When all is said and done, when the prince's men have departed, when the workers have all dispersed, when nothing is left but smoke and mud and empty scaffolding, Rublev emerges from the shadows to comfort Boriska, who by now has broken out of character and returned to

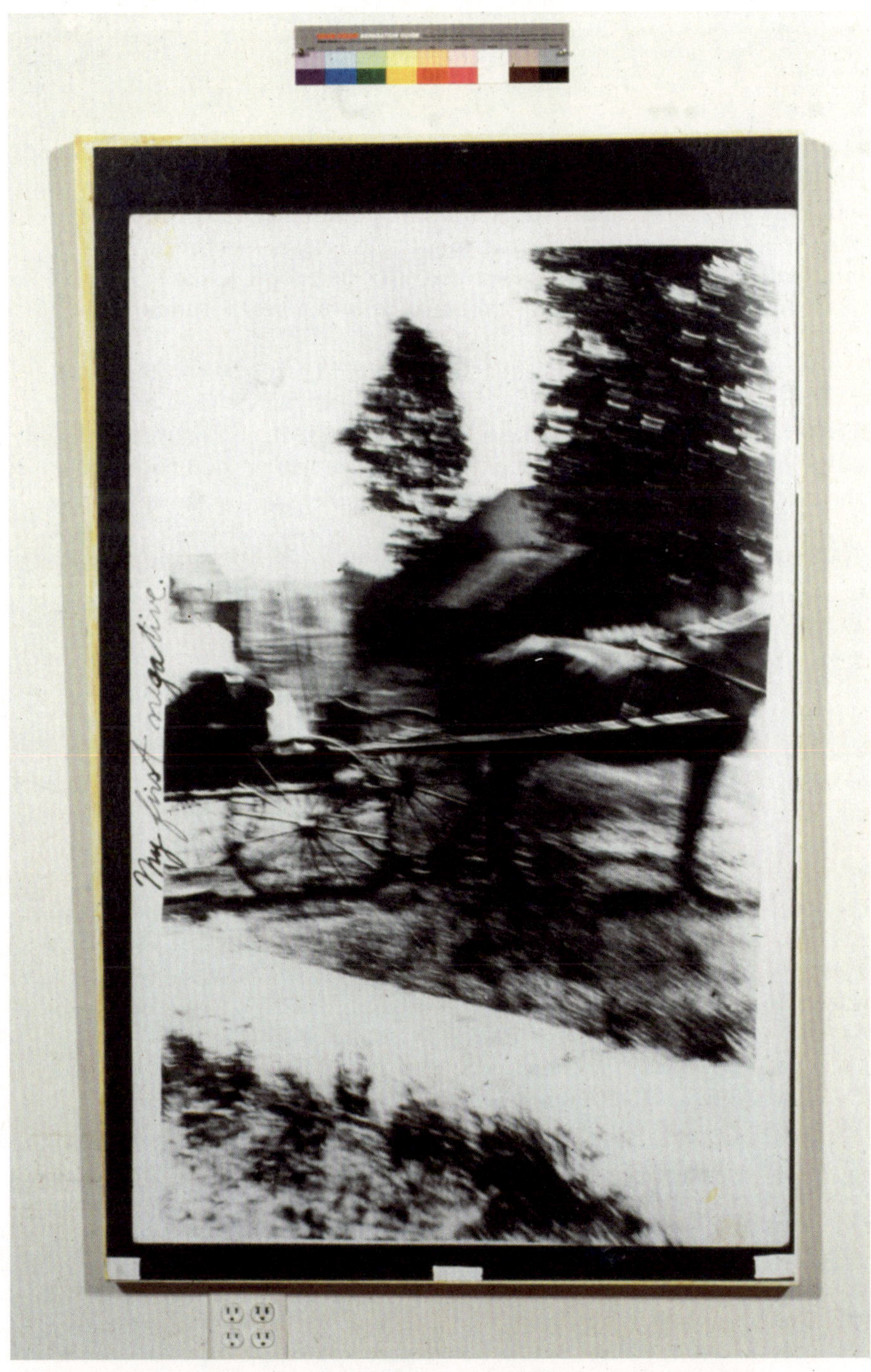

Joseph Grigely, *My First Negative*, 1991. Dispersion on photograph, mounted on canvas

being a boy: "I didn't know," he cries to Rublev with tears streaming down his muddied, tired face. "My father never told me the secret. He took it to the grave with him."

Boriska's ruse turns out to be one of the biggest bluffs in the history of Western art.

***

But suppose it had turned out otherwise? It was Boriska's first bell, after all. He was anything but indifferent to the task before him, perhaps because he had nothing to lose—had he stayed in the village, the plague may have killed him; had the bell turned out bad, the prince himself may have killed him. It has never been easy being an artist in Russia—as the poet Osip Mandelstam once said, "Only in Russia is poetry respected—it gets people killed." But Boriska persevered, and it was—what? his faith? his luck?—that made his first bell a stunning one.

This all reminds me of a postcard I found one day at a flea market in the 1980s. At the time I was making art that was based on early twentieth-century postcards, which I reworked with dispersions, rephotographed, enlarged to about six feet by four feet, and then mounted on canvas. This particular image struck me because of the acknowledgment that had been written on it by the photographer. It said: "My first negative." It looked it, too: It was blurry, the camera was moving, the composition all wrong, and the horse's head was cropped off. *Poor horse*, I thought when I saw it. When I printed and mounted the image, I left the photograph untrimmed and made the stretcher lopsided, and spilled adhesive on the face of the image. It is as if everything that is wrong about the photograph is everything that is right about it. It provides a grounding for a variety of issues revealed by the image: the lack of a pose in an age of the pose, the lack of foresight while using a medium requiring foresight. It is unpremeditated, almost flippant (like Keats's "Bloomiest"), and by breaking so many rules all at once takes us closer to the genre of photography by making us ask: Just what does a photograph do? For a photograph is not just about what's inside the frame; it's about what's outside the frame as well, and how it is in this space outside the frame that the imagination of the reader is most free to move.

In other words: Failure sometimes tells us more—a lot more—about the subject being represented. It is not always, as Petroski puts it, a matter of success "through" failure; it's sometimes a matter of failure as success. And it does this by taking us someplace in the realm of experience that we might not willfully choose.

I want to reiterate that point—how failure takes us close to a situation we would not willfully choose—and how rich and revealing is the potential of such a situation.

This happened to me one night when I was in New York many years ago—it was close to midnight—and I was heading back to my car in SoHo, when a man gestured to me. I couldn't understand what he was saying, so I asked him to write.

The man seemed a little surprised by my request, but he took it seriously and started to write. The letters came slowly: M-O-N and then he stopped. He seemed confused, as if he wasn't sure what came next. There was a long pause, and then he crossed out the unfinished word and tried to start again. He wrote an *M*, but stopped and didn't continue. He paused again. And then he crossed out the *M*.

He then moved over to a railing, leaned on it, and tried a third time: another *M*. By now I sensed anxiety on his part. He stole pained glances at passersby, perhaps hoping that someone would help him in his effort to communicate. He looked back down at the *M* he had made

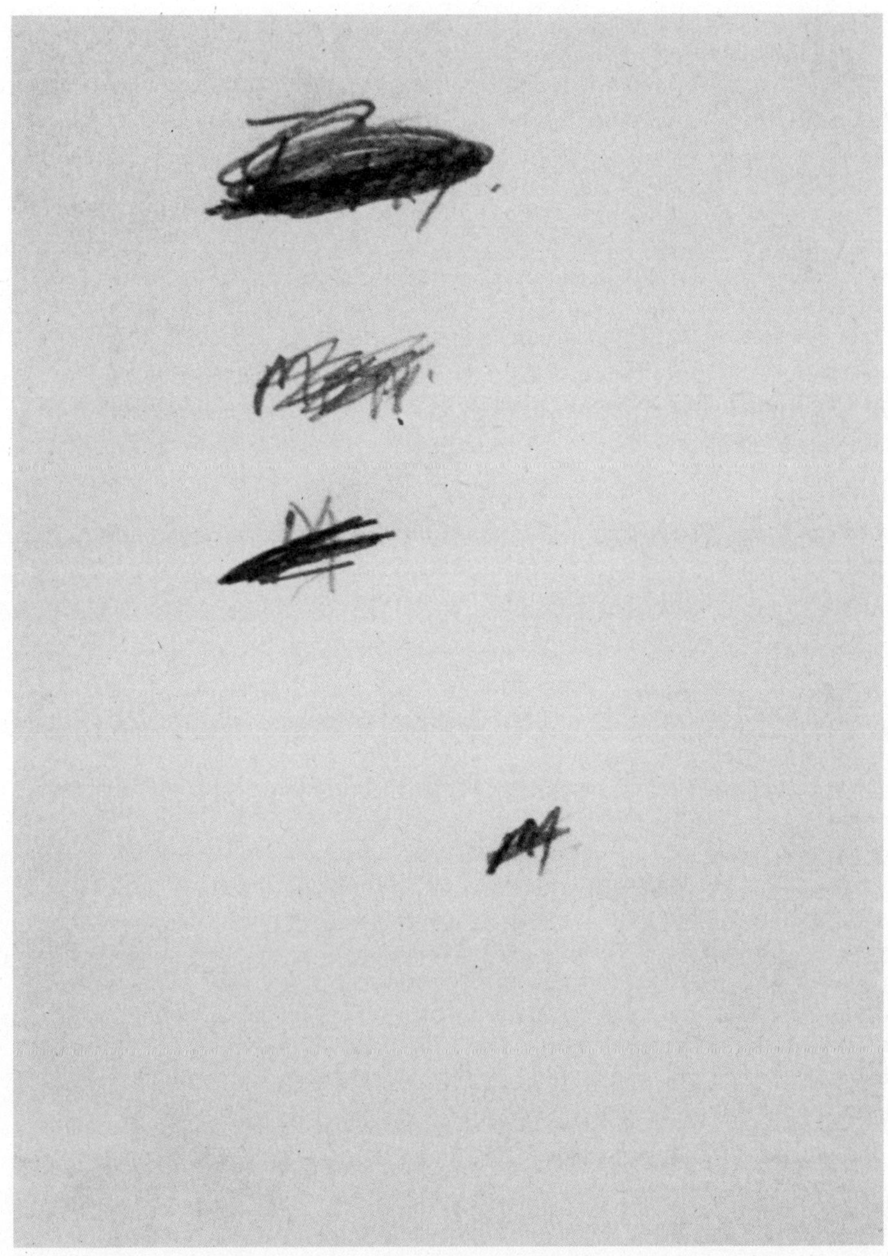

Joseph Grigely, *Untitled Conversation (The Panhandler)* (detail), 1994. Pencil on paper with framed text

and tried to erase it—but my pencil didn't have an eraser, and so he did with this *M* what he did with the previous *M*: He crossed it out.

At this point he could have given up; people were walking by, time was being lost, and this word that begins with an *M* would not write itself.

He tried again. It was his fourth effort now to give words to his gesture, but this time he tried a new direction, one that shifted from object to subject: *I*. A pause. Then: *MY*. And then: another pause. And finally: He crossed it all out.

This was the end, and, in a sense, it said more than enough, more, perhaps, than mere words themselves could have said. Of the tens of thousands of written conversations I have had with people over the past twenty years, this particular one has the fewest words, yet says by far the most.

I'll close now with an example of failure that occurred early in my career as an artist. In some ways, it's a very ordinary situation, but one that I think tells us something about art's relationship with its audience. The occasion was an exhibition I did at the Anthony d'Offay Gallery in London in 1996. At the center of one room, I had one of the messy table pieces that I was making at this time: the detritus of a garden party, the table covered with conversations, beer cans, cherry pits, and so on. It was all carefully and deliberately arranged. There was another messy piece beside the office—a wastepaper basket filled with conversations—so we were a little wary about how the cleaning staff would relate to the work. After installing the work, we put up a sign that said: "Do not clean the gallery."

As it turned out, everything went smoothly at the opening on Friday—and on Sunday I flew home.

On Monday morning I received a fax from the gallery. My girlfriend handed it to me with a big "uh-oh" look on her face.

"Dear Joseph," the fax began. "I really do not know how to begin this letter. We have returned to the gallery this morning to make the most terrible discovery. Despite the repeated warnings, both written and verbal, which we gave our cleaning company last week—I am sure you remember this—they have taken it upon themselves to remove particular objects from *Conversations at Sutton Pond*. They have taken: all the Budweiser cans, the paper plates, the cherry pits, the grape stems, the strawberry hulls, the fruit punnet, the box from the twelve-pack case, the plastic bag with the stuff in it, and the cigarette butts. It appears that all the conversations remain. Inexplicably, they have left the insect repellent cannister."

And so on and so on.

The show was closed for a few days until I could fly back to London and remake the installation. Sometimes it's like this, and the second time around it actually looked a little better than the first.

I also received a contrite apology from the owner of the cleaning company, who shared with me that the cleaner who threw out the work was quite distraught by what had happened. I can imagine the cleaning lady's conversation with her boss: "But it didn't look like art, it looked like they had a party in the gallery, there were crisps and cherry pits and empty beer cans, and I only threw out the garbage, I mean, who in their right mind would pay money for cigarette butts? I left all the note cards; I even made a neat little pile of them."

Telephone/Fax: 071-254 2701 Proprietor: Mrs C. A. Crawford

THE BUSINESS & OFFICE CLEANING SERVICES

14A GREEN LANES, NEWINGTON GREEN, LONDON N16 9ND

19th March 1996

Mr.Joseph Grigely,
c/o Anthony d'Offay Gallery,
23 Dering Street,
London W1

Dear Sir,

Please accept my sincere apologies for the removal of certain crucial elements of your sculpture at the d'Offay Gallery.

The cleaner responsible for work at the gallery was unaware of the importance of these pieces. She is quite distraught at her action and wishes to offer her apology for any distress she may have caused you.

Yours faithfully,

C. Crawford

CAROLE CRAWFORD

Letter from Carole Crawford, March 1996

I felt really bad for her.

A lot of artists have had their work thrown out by mistake—Joseph Beuys, Gustav Metzger, Damien Hirst. But all the same, it helps bring us closer to realizing that the fine line that Duchamp drew between the ordinary object and the art object is a line that is forever in motion. We can never be too sure where the real object ends and the art object begins. Even when the object of concern is situated in the middle of a gallery. It's beautiful to think that art can keep subverting the will of critical human thought. As my friend said when discussing the blind baby who learned to imitate the sound of the refrigerator: "Beauty is difficult. Never forget that."

Why I Am an Asshole, 2021

CalArts, April 2021.

This talk was the product of multiple converging movements and moments. It took place in April 2021, as part of an online lecture series at CalArts during the Covid pandemic, and helped to consolidate as a process many logistical issues related to providing remote access for people with disabilities: how to plan it, arrange it, fund it, make it work—and how, inevitably, the best intentions in this regard will often fail. It also addresses one of the key problems about disability access: Engaging in self-advocacy often puts the individual at the center of a conflict between the desired form of access and the institution's interpretation of "reasonable" access.

Thank you, Juan [Herrera], for your introduction, and for your invitation to be here today. As a personal introduction, let me describe myself. I'm in my sixties, a white man. I'm bald with a white beard. I've been totally deaf for fifty-four years, so my voice is inflected by these years. I'm sitting in a loft, and behind me is a stack of books that reaches from the floor to the ceiling—and there's a large painting of a pair of robins beside the books.

Also important: I have three computer screens in front of me. One is for the sign language interpreter; one is for my PowerPoint; and the third is for captions and the host. My eyes will be in a lot of different places. I'm going to switch into screen-sharing mode now. There will be a few moments when I might lose you, or the interpreter, or maybe both. Let's see how this goes. Zoom was not built with access considerations in mind, and Zoom admits this—saying, as it does here, that it is compliant with access laws "with exceptions." You don't see that often—institutions that admit they follow the law, with exceptions. LOL.

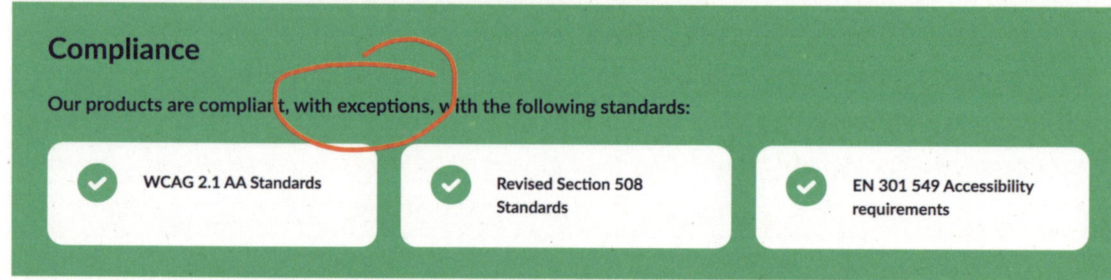

Screenshot, Zoom compliance standards, February 2021

***

So—let me begin with a simple fact: I'm an asshole. It's nothing my best friends don't know already. Sometimes I can be an asshole without even trying, that's how good I am at it.

For example, this happens when people say "Excuse me" and I don't hear them—and they assume I am ignoring them. One incident of this kind happened to me in the late 1980s. I was visiting LA with my girlfriend, and we were staying in a small motel in Marina del Ray. At one point I was riding the elevator alone when a man in a wheelchair came in. We said hello, then we rode a few floors together before I got out.

Later in the afternoon, when my girlfriend and I were waiting for the elevator, the man in the wheelchair joined us. Then, after a few moments when she had been signing to me, the man exclaimed, "Oh shit!"

We paused from talking, turned to the man, and said, "Is something wrong?" He explained that when we had been in the elevator earlier, he saw the T-shirt I was wearing said on it "City Lights Bookstore"—and exclaimed aloud, "City Lights! That's my bookseller!" When I didn't respond, as I didn't know he had said anything, he tried again: "Uh, City Lights! That's my bookseller! Cool T-shirt!" I stood nonplussed and unmoved. The elevator stopped, and I got off. The man continued: "I thought, *What an asshole! I need to call Lawrence Ferlinghetti and tell him to stop selling T-shirts to assholes!* I had no idea you were deaf. I'm sorry. I must have called you an asshole a million times."

The man was Ron Kovic; we got to know each other over coffee the next day. He had written about the Vietnam War in a book called *Born on the Fourth of July*—which was about joining the Marines and coming home in a wheelchair, and all the shit that followed. When we said goodbye, he gave me a letter of introduction to meet Ferlinghetti, which he wrote in the back of his book, and called me "a good friend." It's nice to think that there is elasticity in the space between being an asshole and being a good friend.

Anyway, my point is I get called an asshole a lot, and for a lot of reasons.

It makes sense. Here is a picture of my deafness: It's an audiogram that was taken in July 1967, about a month after I fell down a hill and a twig punctured my one good ear. At the lower left is evidence of just how bad my hearing is: It's off-the-chart bad, over 100 decibels. I had another audiogram made some years later where the sensors registered up to 120 decibels, and I was off the chart of that one, too. I'm as deaf as a doorpost.

So my plan for this talk is to tell you stories that emanate from this state of being. I've been in academia and the art world for over thirty years, and I still don't have answers for anything, no grand theory to impart about art and disability or disability and life. I only have stories, and I think there's a lot to be said for stories—because they are an archive of how people respond to disability, and this process reveals more about them than it does about those who are disabled. So my goal is to tell stories about how disability constitutes what I call a "disruptive ontology"—how it complicates everything for everyone—and how the real goal of my work is not so much to resolve these complications, but to better understand their resistance to being resolved.

Another story now.

Several years ago, the postman attempted to deliver to me a letter that required my signature. Being deaf, I could not hear him knock at the door. He did, however, leave a note, indicating that I should contact the post office. The next day I went to the post office, where I explained that although I was deaf, my doorbell was connected to a flashing light, and if the postman would push the button rather than knock, I would see the light flash. It's a very simple apparatus. The clerk said she would write a note about this and give it to the postman.

The next day the postman arrived, pressed the doorbell button, the light flashed, and I went to the door. The postman handed me my letter. Attached to the letter was the note the clerk at the post office had written for the postman. It was written on a piece of yellow paper that I'm showing here.

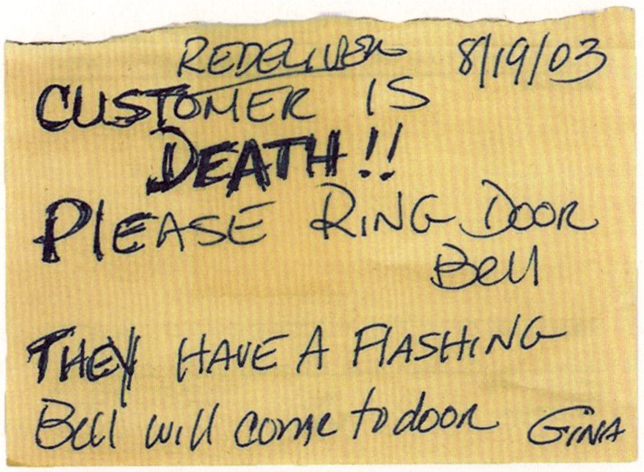

Mail delivery note to my postman from Gina, 2003. Ink on Post-it

The note said: "This customer is DEATH!!" It did not say "deaf." It said "DEATH." In block capitals. This customer is D-E-A-T-H, exclamation point, exclamation point.

It is a revealing mistake. In *The Psychopathology of Everyday Life*, Freud calls slips like these "a means of self-betrayal." The private self, the one that speaks for all, betrays the public self, the one afraid to speak at all. One day, when I explained the situation to my therapist, he was unsurprised by the error, or even by the emphatic nature with which the word "DEATH" is inscribed, and reinscribed, and capitalized, and exclaimed. "But of course," he tells me, "you are death to them—you force them to change their ways in the process of addressing your needs—they must go out of their way, alter their path, push a button instead of knock on your door. You cause trouble."

Sometimes the trouble just lands in your lap. This often happens when I read *The New York Times*—a paper I've been reading every day for about the past thirty-five years, and which has repaid my loyalty by misspelling my name and calling me a death artist like here. However, my problem with the *Times* lies elsewhere.

It started decades ago when I noticed the *Times* was using blindness and deafness as pejorative metaphors—as a synonym for ignorance. There would be articles with titles that said things such as I am showing here—titles like "Blind to Slavery" or "Tone-Deaf in D.C." These are linguistic microaggressions. A metaphor is not just a figure of speech; it is a figure of thinking. Moreover, the ways these metaphors are regularly used and abused, unchallenged by copy editors or editorial standards, is indicative of a larger problem of ableist prejudice in journalism. Whenever the *Times* prints one of these metaphors, the editors can expect to get a letter from me—I've written over twenty in the past few years. Some are nice. Some are not—I think my last one told the editors to go fuck themselves. I mean, they've had dozens of opportunities to address the situation politely. I also published in the *Journal of Visual Culture* an article addressing the subject more generally. A lot of writers use metaphors of disablement without serious consideration to what they are saying. The most surprising and ironic example I have ever read is a blurb for the book *Disability and Art History*. It's on the back cover, which I am showing here. It says: "This original book offers fresh insights as it examines art history's blindness to the burgeoning scholarship in disability studies." I'm like, what? I realize no one is perfect—I, myself, screw up sometimes—but I think art history and disability studies can do a lot better than this.

I'm not especially sanguine about professional academic fields and their organizational bodies. In the fall of 1985, I began a Mellon Postdoctoral Fellowship in the English department at Stanford. Every winter the Modern Language Association—we call it the MLA—hosted a convention that English professors like myself were expected to attend and participate in. I wrote to the MLA to request sign language interpreters. I pointed out how the previous year, when the MLA convention had been in Washington, DC—which was home to Gallaudet College, where I had then been teaching—the MLA refused to provide interpreters. I was more optimistic the second time around. The MLA replied:

> In the interest of being as helpful to you as we can, we have looked into various options and their consequences. I would like to propose two alternatives for your consideration. If someone is accompanying you, we can supply the person with a complimentary badge. Or, if you think it would be useful, we can have a convention aide meet you at the entrance to any meeting room in order to make certain you have a front row seat. [...] Unfortunately, it is not possible for us to provide American Sign Language interpreting services for convention sessions.

I wasn't prepared for this kind of response. Despite [my having invoked] the support of a number of distinguished colleagues, the MLA never sorted out access issues in a satisfactory way. Disability in the 1980s was neither an identity nor an ideology, the way it is today. It was a largely uncharted legal and cultural space. Within my own profession it was a constant battle, year after year, to gain access not just to interpreting, but to qualified, competent interpreting. After five years of fighting the MLA I finally resigned, telling the executive director: "My academic career is beginning to take on the apparition of a defense of my right to equality in the profession." I told the MLA that they needed to organize a commission on the disabled in the profession if there was to be any meaningful progress. Two years later, the executive director of the MLA wrote to say that it was finally happening: "I'm sorry it took us so long to implement your suggestion, but I thought you would like to know we have finally done it." By my math, it took almost seven years, and totally burned me out on the MLA and the field of literary studies. On the bright side, it led to changes in the profession. The MLA was recently described as being "a model of accessibility for organizations across the world." I have to laugh at that—they have done a good job of burying from public view their unbecoming past.

It's a common institutional strategy—acting as if they've been caring and thoughtful and understanding from the beginning, when in fact it often takes enormous effort, if not also lawsuits, to turn the tide at the beginning.

It's hard deciding which stories to tell you today. My friend Doug said, "Tell them about the time you found other people in your motel room and how hard it was to have a conversation with a closed door between you, and how the police had to come, and how it devolved into a shit show." My wife, Amy, said, "Tell them about the spelling bee you had to take in sixth grade, and how they made you lipread words, and if you lipread the word wrong, they marked it wrong even when you spelled it right." Another friend said, "Tell them about the time Cornell wanted to interview you for the chair's job, then after you asked for an interpreter, they canceled the interview."

Sigh. My friends are an index to a lot of shit that has happened to me—they often remember the stuff I've been trying really hard to forget. Repression is a mechanism of survival. Otherwise, that stuff transforms you into something else, though it's not entirely clear to me just what. As my therapist said to me one day, "Probably not PTSD, exactly; just a chronic, justified fury over unending, incompetent, lazy, obstructive people."

***

Sometimes, when things get bad, it's not change that you want—it's something more Shakespearean, like revenge. You don't always think logically, or rationally, or with consideration of the consequences—only that you want something to fucking happen.
Let me describe an example.

When I taught in the School of Art at the University of Michigan, the dean had a curious habit of "forgetting" to get interpreters for things like graduation and some department meetings and visiting artist talks. Once, when I was waiting for an interpreter for a department meeting, the dean decided to start the meeting anyway. I said, "Fine, in that case I'm going back to my office to work. If the interpreter comes, let me know and I'll come back." It's a really rotten feeling to sit in the middle of colleagues talking about things important to you and having no interpreter. But it also says: "You don't matter—you're unimportant. We will proceed without you." In the end the interpreter didn't come. But the dean then did something interesting: In the minutes for the meeting he had me marked as being absent. I truly despised him, and at that point I started plotting revenge—in the form of institutional critique.

At Michigan, one of the rituals of the art school was for the professors to introduce the MFA students when they were delivering their graduate lectures—a brief, two-minute introduction to preface a fifteen-minute talk. It so happened that the timing of the talk overlapped with an exhibition I had to do in Europe, so one of my students and I planned to pre-record the introduction to his work. We filmed my introduction at the home of another grad student in the middle of a raucous party of artists and musicians in downtown Detroit. It was a loud party, and there was a lot of wine and beer, but we succeeded in making the film. You couldn't hear me much, though. It was mostly all just the music and the crowd mixing into some kind of sonic sludge as I sat at a table and gestured and explained for two minutes the virtues of the art of Gregory Steele. This was shown in the lecture hall as part of the graduate symposium. The dean was furious, which was just the response I hoped for. I am glad that for once he got to feel how I felt when there were no interpreters around.

I'm going to show you the video now. I'll show the first minute, then pause and skip ahead to the conclusion. It's a bit painful, which was the whole point, so I'll spare you some of that pain in jumping to the conclusion.

It's not easy doing things like this: Usually you are too angry to channel that anger into a calculated response—especially when you are working alone. It helped to have Gregory and a couple of other students alongside me, organizing the party and making the film. They shared some risk—as does anyone who takes this role, because it comes with the risk of retaliation.

While I still teach, I have largely left academia as a professional practice. Experiences with the MLA convinced me that the field, while it promoted itself as liberal and just, and while it could at times be liberal and just, was also deeply prejudiced. The art world isn't perfect either—far from it. Back in the 1970s, the critic Gregory Battcock, who I am showing here, wrote a novel about the art world. In his outline to the novel, he explained how the art world is essentially corrupt, and his first two points, shown in the slide here, explain: "a) It's managed completely by the rich as a plaything," and "b) It likes to appear concerned with the poor, social problems, etc., but is not and usually acts against social interests." Does that sound familiar?

An important difference between academia and the art world is that academia was governed largely by committee; the art world, at least the gallery system, was managed primarily by individuals. Big difference. If I could convince individuals of my worth—not just as an artist, but also as a human being—I stood a much better chance of finding a platform for sharing my work. There was no Instagram in those days—getting attention for your artwork meant a lot of legwork: seeing shows, talking with other artists and gallerists, and trying to get a gallerist or a curator to go out for a cup of coffee as a prelude to a studio visit. It was, shall we say, a world of interpersonal interactions.

But individuals could, and did, make a difference. When museums and colleges refused to provide interpreters, friends like Paula Hayes, Ellen Cantor, and Amy Vogel would scribble for me notes about what they were hearing. Sometimes it was about the music in the room where we were. Or the audio component of work we saw in the galleries, like this one describing a Kristin Oppenheim installation. Or sometimes an art-world story retold, like this one about Karen Kilimnik. Sometimes it was bits and pieces of a public lecture, like this one the late Ellen Cantor wrote for me at a talk by the Nigerian photographer Iké Udé (I-Kuh Oo-day). And sometimes at the after-parties, friends would share with me casual observations.

I can't thank these people enough—and there are so many to thank, especially the people who have stood with me for twenty-five years, mostly in the shadows, but always ready to help in their own way: friends, assistants, gallerists, curators. And, especially, the sign language interpreters who were willing to work under the table and interpret in bars at 3:00 a.m.—despite being underpaid, no matter how much they are paid. I'd be nowhere, really nowhere, without these people, which is also to say that as a person with a disability, you are just a tiny little node in a network of so many other nodes—and they all matter.

***

If the Covid pandemic relieved the burden of traveling, it introduced problems of its own. As we all know, the pandemic forced many arts institutions to shift public programs to digital platforms. In the process, many neglected to consider access issues. Of the fifty or so online events I attended during the first six months of the pandemic, only two of them provided captions without asking, and without hassles. It was very frustrating to write back and forth with institutions and get an array of excuses and apologies. Some of the apologies I received were very sincere—and some institutions made a good-faith effort to change things for the better. Some apologized and did nothing. And some didn't even apologize. Three weeks ago, I filed a DOJ complaint against a dozen institutions. I hated every moment of the process: collecting the documentation and writing out details of each incident. It took several days to compile everything. There's no relief, no elation to the process. But you do it because no one is going to do it for you, and every institution is going to remember you as the pain in the ass who complained about the lack of captions. You become "the problem." And it hurts your career in more ways than I can count—this is the risk you take in speaking out.

For decades, institutions have perceived disabled people as generally passive and nonthreatening. In one important research report, disabled people were described as "warm but incompetent." Here's a quotation from the study:

> Consider the group often described by our research participants as "the elderly." In virtually all of our studies, older people are stereotyped as warm but incompetent. Their perceived warmth elicits affection and support, while their perceived incompetence elicits disrespect and neglect. People feel a sort of condescending compassion and pity toward them. This leads to paternalistic and patronizing treatment, such as speaking unnecessarily slowly and in an overly endearing manner. (Another group commonly stereotyped as warm but incompetent are people with disabilities.)

So if you're a disabled person and you're competent and a badass, you are breaking all the rules. But sometimes you have to break the rules, pound your fist on the table, and do whatever you need to do on your own terms in order to upend the ableist stereotypes. There's definitely a place for rage in all of this.

This reminds me of Larry Kramer, the indefatigable AIDS activist who died a year ago. In one interview, he said: "I was known as the angriest man in the world, mainly because I discovered that anger got you further than being nice. And when we started to break through in the media, I was better TV than someone who was nice."

Thank you, Larry Kramer, for setting a high standard of achievement. You remind me that I need to up my game, I really do.

Sometimes you do this by suing someone. It's lawsuits that change things, and lawsuits are not easy. In the process the defense lawyers will try to destroy your credibility, your integrity, your sense of self. They will rip into your health history, your tax history, your employment history, trying to find any cause to trip you up. And they will lie their way through all of this, because that is what they are paid to do. A lawsuit is expensive, too—it takes years, if not decades—and

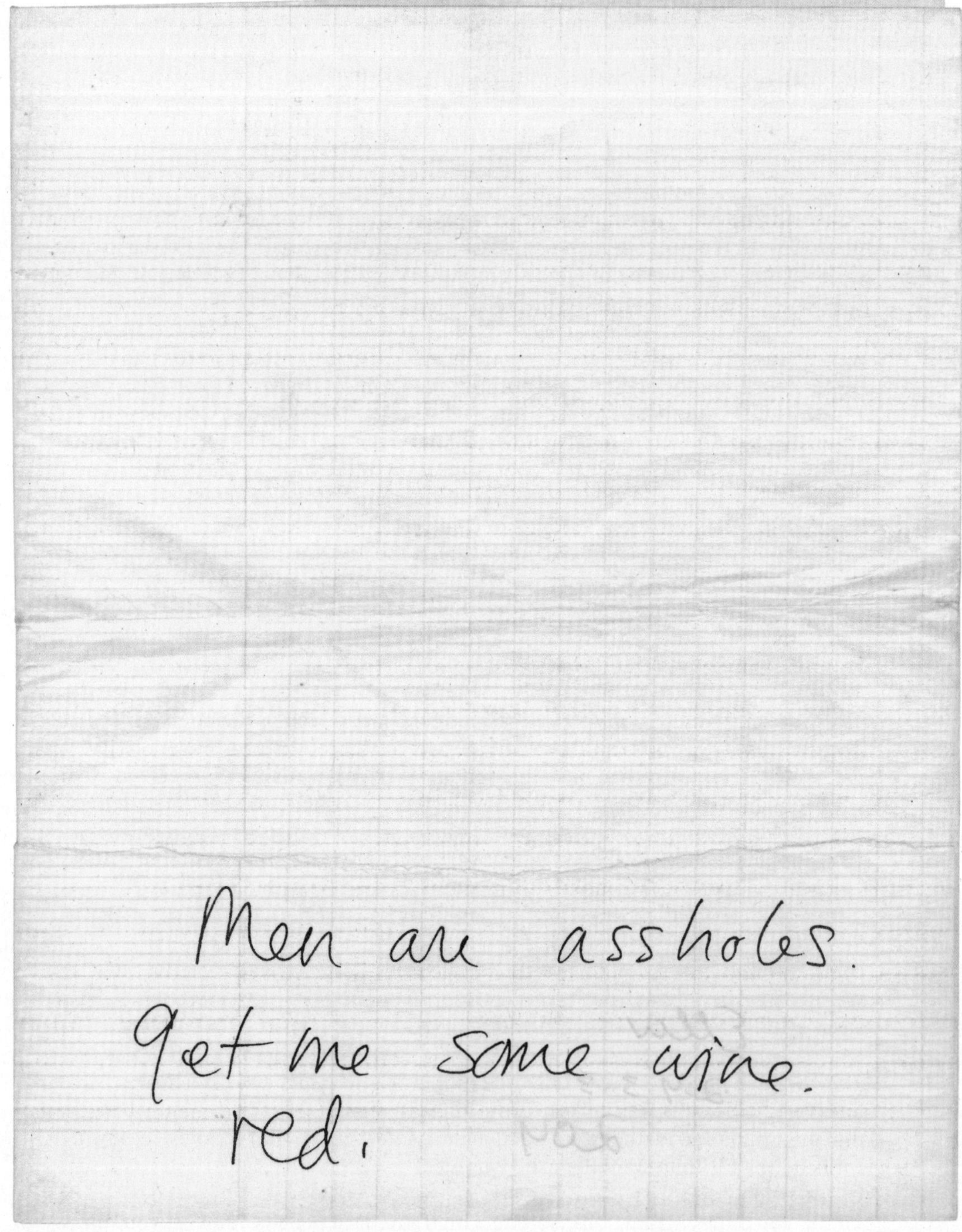

Joseph Grigely, *Untitled Conversation (Men Are Assholes)*, 2005. Archival pigment print and lithography. Printed with Michael Krueger at the University of Kansas, Lawrence

the rewards are small. And even when you win, sometimes you have to go back to court again and again to compel institutions to do the things they promised to do when they signed the agreement. Often their goal is to use massive institutional resources against the individual—just trying to wear you down into nothingness. I wish there were more public clinics to support lawsuits as a way of making them a public record. Looking back at it all, being angry and righteous and impassioned and having a great legal team isn't always enough. Sometimes it just comes down to luck and divine intervention.

I like to think that art and law are not really that different, if they are different at all: With both, you are trying to undo and redo historical conventions and beliefs, and get people to imagine the world in other ways. My favorite artist was actually a lawyer: Thurgood Marshall.

Marshall was originally a civil rights activist who became a lawyer and was later appointed to the Supreme Court by Lyndon B. Johnson. He was the lead lawyer in the case of *Brown v. Board of Education*, the cornerstone case that began the desegregation of education in America. *Brown* is the starting point for any notion of creative access: It's a masterpiece. But getting to the point where he could write *Brown* required unstinting resilience: Marshall was arrested on trumped-up charges, he got worked over by the Feds, and he endured some of the most unimaginable shit in order to make our world a better place.

This has been pretty much a one-sided talk, and I've left out all the nice and good things about being disabled, like the ways it has brought into my life people and experiences for whom I am both grateful and thankful: my family, friends, students, fellow artists, fishing buddies, gallerists, curators, exhibition installers, and strangers on airplanes who were unflustered when I asked them to write down for me what the pilot was saying on the intercom. But sometimes, in the space of being patient, your patience gives out. You yell and write angry letters and make an unpleasant mess of your own state of being. It's like the end of *King Lear*, when Edgar says, "The weight of this sad time we must obey, / Speak what we feel, not what we ought to say." It leaves you tired, cracked, and, in some ways, broken. I just hope, in the end, the cosmic math somehow evens out the disparity between being good and being an asshole.

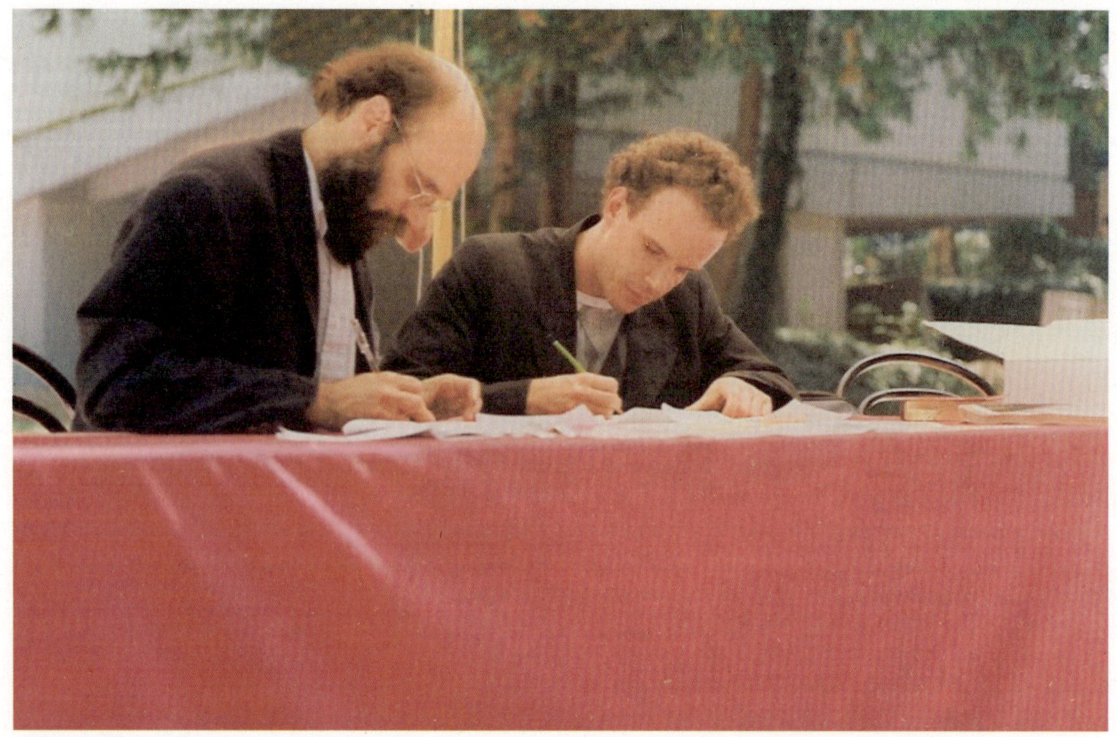

Joseph Grigely and Hans Ulrich Obrist during the release of *Point d'ironie*, no. 1, Venice, 1997. Photo: Amy Vogel

Interviews

This chapter consists of fragments of exchanges and interviews from the past twenty-five years. Most took place between 1997 and 2003, which was an especially hurried period for me, when I was regularly traveling back and forth between Europe and the US. The exchanges are mostly with curators and artists. Some were formal interviews; others were questions posed to me while preparing for an exhibition. Because many of the questions and answers overlapped, I have edited the various interviews together into one long interview, removing redundancies in the process.

One exception is an email exchange I had with the blind theologian John Hull in the process of preparing for the first installation of *White Noise* at the Musée d'Art Moderne de la Ville de Paris in 2000. I had read Hull's book *Touching the Rock: An Experience of Blindness* (1990) a few years earlier and was quite moved by how he described his evolving blindness. I asked him if we might have an exchange about sensory experiences as part of the catalogue for the exhibition. To his credit, Hull said yes, and I am very grateful to him for this. I have reprinted our exchange in full. Hull died in 2015.

A Combined Interview with Ian Berry, Jan Estep, Andreas Gedin and Mats Stjernstedt, Greg Hilty, Hans Ulrich Obrist, Caroline Picard, Debra Singer, and Margaret Sundell, 1997–2011

The text of this interview has been assembled from the following sources: Joseph Grigely, "Playing Footsie on Top of the Table: A Conversation with Joseph Grigely," interview by Jan Estep, *New Art Examiner*, June 2000; Caroline Picard, fragment of an unpublished interview with the author, 2011; Joseph Grigely, interview by Hans Ulrich Obrist (excerpts), in *EVN Sammlung: Ankäufe 1997–1999*, ed. Jeanette Pacher (EVN AG, 1999); Joseph Grigely, "Joseph Grigely im Gespräch mit Hans Ulrich Obrist: Dazwischen entsteht das Wissen," interview by Hans Ulrich Obrist, in *Weltwissen Wissenswelt: Das globale Netz von Text und Bild*, ed. Christa Maar, Ernst Pöppel, and Hans Ulrich Obrist (DuMont Verlag, 2000); Joseph Grigely, interview by Margaret Sundell, *Artforum*, 2001; Joseph Grigely, "Nudist Plays: A Dialogue with Joseph Grigely," interview by Ian Berry, in *Joseph Grigely: St. Cecilia*, ed. Ian Berry and Irene Hofmann (Frances Young Tang Teaching Museum and Art Gallery at Skidmore College and the Contemporary Museum, Baltimore, 2007); Debra Singer, email exchange with the author for the catalogue *White Noise* (published on the occasion of the exhibition of the same name at the Whitney Museum of American Art, June 28–September 9, 2001), April 2001; Joseph Grigely, "Joseph Grigely in a Conversation with Andreas Gedin and Mats Stjernstedt," interview by Andreas Gedin and Mats Stjernstedt, conducted on the occasion of the exhibition *Joseph Grigely*, Index – The Swedish Contemporary Art Foundation, October 7–November 12, 2000, and published as "Conversation avec Joseph Grigely" in the French journal *Trouble*, no. 2 (2002); Greg Hilty, email exchange with the author, 1998.

Jan Estep: How did you lose your hearing? Do you want to tell the story of how you became deaf? How old were you?

Joseph Grigely: It's funny you ask, because this is something people often want to know but are generally timid about asking. My story is marked by two events: The first was when I was about one year old—I had a fever and it left me deaf in my right ear. My doctors couldn't quite figure it out since by all accounts a fever like the one I had should have made me deaf in both ears. So I had one good ear until I was ten, when the second event occurred: I was playing a game of King on the Mountain with some friends and fell about fifteen feet down a small hill. Somewhere on the way down I fell against a tree branch lying on the ground, and a small twig on that branch found its way into my good ear. By the time I stopped rolling at the bottom of the hill, I was totally deaf. It all happened so quickly.

Jan Estep: Do you have memory of sounds?

Lots of them, actually—the sounds of June 1967, which was when I became deaf: lawn mowers, barking dogs, and rhythmic voices on television. I particularly remember the voices in Marlboro cigarette commercials and the song in the Schlitz beer commercial, the one that goes: "Schlitz is a light beer, a mellow beer, a hardy beer, blended into one beer, a light bright fun beer..." I even remember the theme song from *Gilligan's Island*. This is pretty pathetic stuff, but the interesting thing is that the words, the inflections, and the music can stay with one for so long.

Jan Estep: You have developed a way to speak with people who do not know sign language, basically by a system of exchanging notes. How do you think the act of writing and reading affects what gets said? Does it make people more self-conscious? Does it give them certain liberties?

Well, it's complicated. When someone says something to me, I usually reply, "I'm sorry, I'm deaf, would you write that down?" For years it was a habit to say "I'm sorry," because I was inconveniencing people—disrupting their preconceptions about normalcy. For most people, writing instead of talking in a social context is a new experience. Some find it mildly disconcerting; others find it engaging. Ultimately, it's less about writing than it is about finding another way to talk, finding another way of shaping the spoken word into a material form. Sometimes the words stay on the lines of the paper, sometimes they run off the lines. Sometimes there are gaps, sometimes there are drawings, sometimes there is the unmistakable oddness of ordinariness, as when someone might write "Bye" or "Sorry, I have to go and pee." This, to me, marks the difference between writing and talking.

Caroline Picard: How do you think about handwriting? (I'm asking because it seems like such a central part of your work, yet also you've spent hours with Keats's [manuscripts], for instance—and I feel like the particular result of a piece—its mood, and even aesthetic, would vary according to differences in handwriting. Then, too, it seems like a recognizable structure that humanity works within.)

This sort of question is easy to romanticize, since there's a long history of "reading" psychic personality in the handwriting of the writer—but I'm not convinced there's any logical relation between the two. I'm also not sure what to think about the aesthetics of handwriting and whether this has any effect on how we read content. There is, however, something very idiosyncratic about how individuals write—the same way we identify and remember a voice through inflection and intonation, we can identify and remember a person through their handwriting.

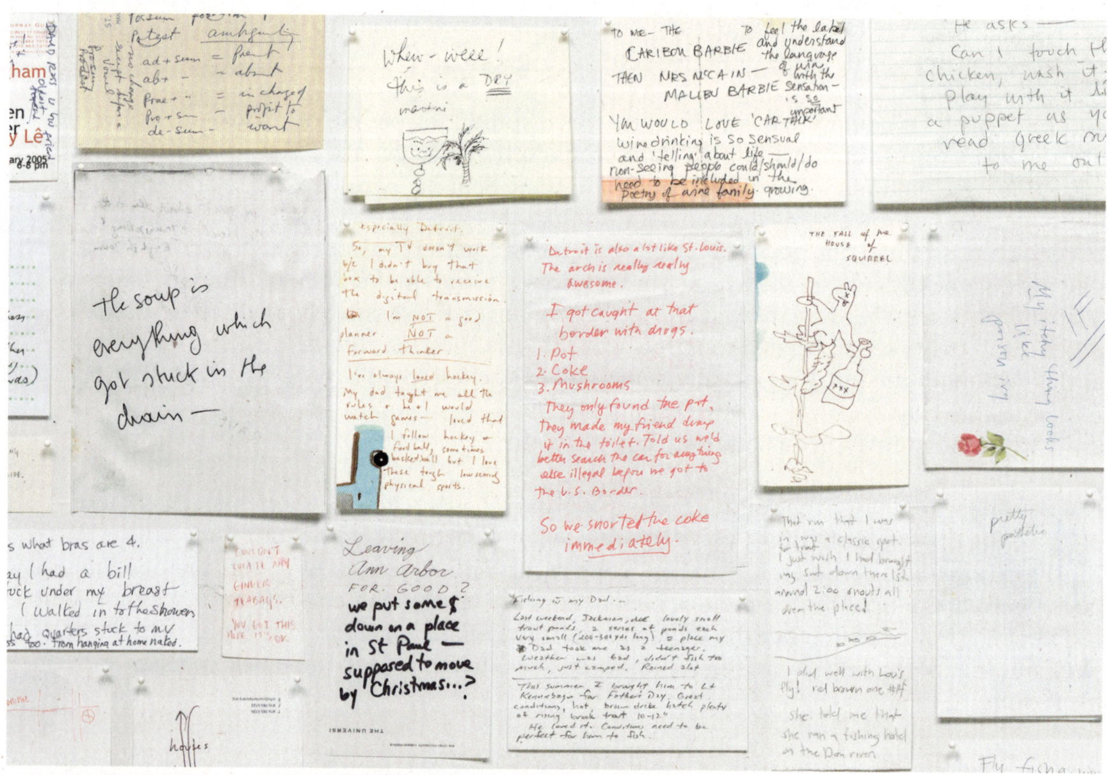

Joseph Grigely, *What Happened After I Left?* (detail), 2007. Pigment print

What's interesting to me is how different it is when people sit down to "write" in a formal sense—a postal letter, for example—and when they write out of immediacy and necessity when asked to do so by a deaf person like me—when standing, or sitting on a bus, or sitting at a bar covered with glasses and spilled beer. This is when handwriting becomes something else, and ventures into a space that is unconstrained by conventions. Instead of being writing, it's a kind of mark-making that occupies a space between speech and writing. This is especially interesting when there are no lines on paper—where the words cross each other, where they run off the page, where words become lines and lines become pictures. "Handwriting" in this regard is a misnomer—it's really drawing.

> Jan Estep: And what do you generally talk about in these notes? Do you steer the conversation in any way (in a way that would make "more interesting" art)?

No, no, not at all—really, they're just conversations. Sometimes they whisper, sometimes they lie, sometimes they get sexy, sometimes they get ugly—as conversations typically do. Sometimes they go to places spoken conversations don't typically go—and you never really know in advance where this may be—which is part of the beauty of it all.

> Hans Ulrich Obrist: When did you install for the first time text fragments in an exhibition?

I started working with the *Conversations with the Hearing* in the early 1990s, and the first exhibition of them was at White Columns in New York in 1994. The paradox, however, is that it took so long. When I became deaf at the age of ten, there was this social expectation that I would learn to lipread. I was really terrible at it, though. I still am. But when I could, I'd ask people to write things down for me. Most people were really happy to do this. It was efficient and simple, and even if it went against the grain of social expectations, it worked for both me and the person with whom I was talking. Then there was a day in the early 1990s when I had dinner with a friend, and afterward there were scraps of paper all over the table with fragments of our conversation. They were all disconnected, quite lacking continuity, and somehow more engaging that way—as if they told a story without telling too much. After that dinner I started saving the papers on which people had written until I had a good-sized archive, and one day I spread them on the floor of my studio. I had expected to see a lot of writing, but what I saw instead was a lot of talking. The words simply went all over the pages. Sometimes there was only one word. Sometimes there were words on top of words. What was so crucial as part of this discovery was to find a way to share the experience of communicating, rather than simply narrate that experience. This is part of an ongoing process for me. The most recent installation of the *Conversations* was a project at the Whitney Museum in New York called *White Noise*: an oval room filled floor to ceiling with over 2,500 sheets of white paper on which people have conversed.

> Margaret Sundell: That's huge. How big is the total archive, and how do you organize it?

The *White Noise* archive consists of about 8,000 sheets of paper. Some are only a few inches square; some are paper tablecloths a few feet square. There's also a different version of *White Noise* where all the conversations are on colored papers, which hasn't been exhibited yet. That one's a little smaller—about 6,500 papers. These are both evolving archives—I can't quite imagine them ever being "complete." There's another part of the overall archive of the *Conversations with the Hearing*—about 4,000 additional papers—which is more specifically organized in terms of certain distinctive features of the paper or the writing or the writer—or even the occasion when the exchange took place. Many of these papers eventually find their way into smaller works.

> Ian Berry: Tell me more about the idea of "language as material object"?

I could talk for hours about this subject—I love it. The Saussurean tradition holds that language is what we speak, whether we speak with our mouths or our hands—it's immaterial—and most linguists today would agree with this. Writing isn't language—it's a material representation of language. But imagine if this materialization happened in a different way—imagine if every word we spoke became palpable and dropped from our lips as we spoke. Think of what would happen, and the places we would find the residue of our words: Imagine scraps of language lying on countertops. Drawers full of sentences. Imagine the dashboards of our cars covered with everyday conversations. This is one reason I find the written conversations so compelling—they're not so much writing as they are talking on paper, and could be described as drawings of speech.

> Debra Singer: What about the fragility of the paper and the inevitable deterioration of certain qualities of the work? How, for you, does this potential decay fit into your intentions in making the work?

Have you ever read David Leatherbarrow and Mohsen Mostafavi's book *On Weathering*? They talk a bit about this—how architectural entropy might be seen not as a pejorative force, but as something that marks time in a positive way, like a patina. We have this strange human desire for stability and permanence, but I find myself attracted to various kinds of transience and change, because of how they create a temporal narrative. Think of architectural ruins like Tintern Abbey: It's not the same abbey it would be if it was intact, yet as a ruin its beauty is partly a product of what is missing and what is changed.

Debra Singer: Although you've worked in an installation format before, *White Noise* is your first work that is somewhat architectural. Could you explain a bit about the environment you are attempting to create? For me (and I am projecting here since I have only seen reproductions), it seems paradoxically both chaotic and serene, almost ecclesiastic…

I wanted to create a space that did not have a beginning or an end. Something that combined a sense of both the continuous and discontinuous. Something that is, in a sense, all middle.

And I also wanted to create some kind of quiet—a room detached from the museum's passageways—which was really a practical consideration. I realize it might seem ironic that I wished to make a "quiet" room only to fill it with "white noise"—but the sense in which "quiet" is a figure of speech is what I'm getting at. It's a deaf kind of quiet, which involves minimal movement.

Margaret Sundell: Another thing that interests me about *White Noise* is the use of installation; you've created environmental works before, but they functioned more as contextualizing mise-en-scènes.

That's right. In the past, many of my installations with the *Conversations* worked around conventional places for conversational exchanges: dinner tables (table talk); fireplaces (fireside chats); Christmas trees (tree-trimming parties). With *White Noise* I wanted to try something much more formal. The oval room evolved out of the nature of the conversations themselves—they are fragments, they have no beginning, no end. In this sense, you could look at the room as a big grid painting.

Margaret Sundell: That's definitely how I saw it—as an extension of your grid pieces, like the one in the last Whitney Biennial. In addition to being a grid, *White Noise* is also a monochrome.

Good point. Sometimes the monochrome and the grid come together in a compelling way. I'm thinking of Josef Albers's *Homage to the Square* series, which in so many ways is quintessentially modernist. Albers's grids, like those of Agnes Martin and Sol LeWitt, work by repressing language: They take a certain familiar form, twist it, tweak it, defamiliarize it—in a way, you could say they take us inside it. Between Malevich's *White on White* and Reinhardt's *Black on Black* there's a long history of explorations like these. A few years ago, I started working on a series of monochromes that use papers of different shades of a single color—blue, say, or green—there might be eight or nine papers arranged into a larger rectangle. It seems pretty simple, but it's usually a very complicated arrangement, because two distinct narratives have to work together: a formal narrative measured by optical experience and a verbal narrative measured by linguistic experience.

Ian Berry: How does your work most often begin? Do you start with a written idea and then figure out how to realize that with a project? Or do you move things around in the studio and find your way to a work's form? Has a work begun as a sculpture and maybe ended as a video?

With the wall works, I start with the papers and conversations, and just go at it, and let the work take shape as it grows. With the films it's very different and not—I'll try to get as much raw footage together as possible, and then sort my way through this material. We once carried an artificial palm tree and forty pounds of film equipment across two miles of sand dunes to film a segment for *Remembering is a difficult job, but somebody has to do it*—and in the end didn't use any of the material for the film, but one of the production shots was used for the

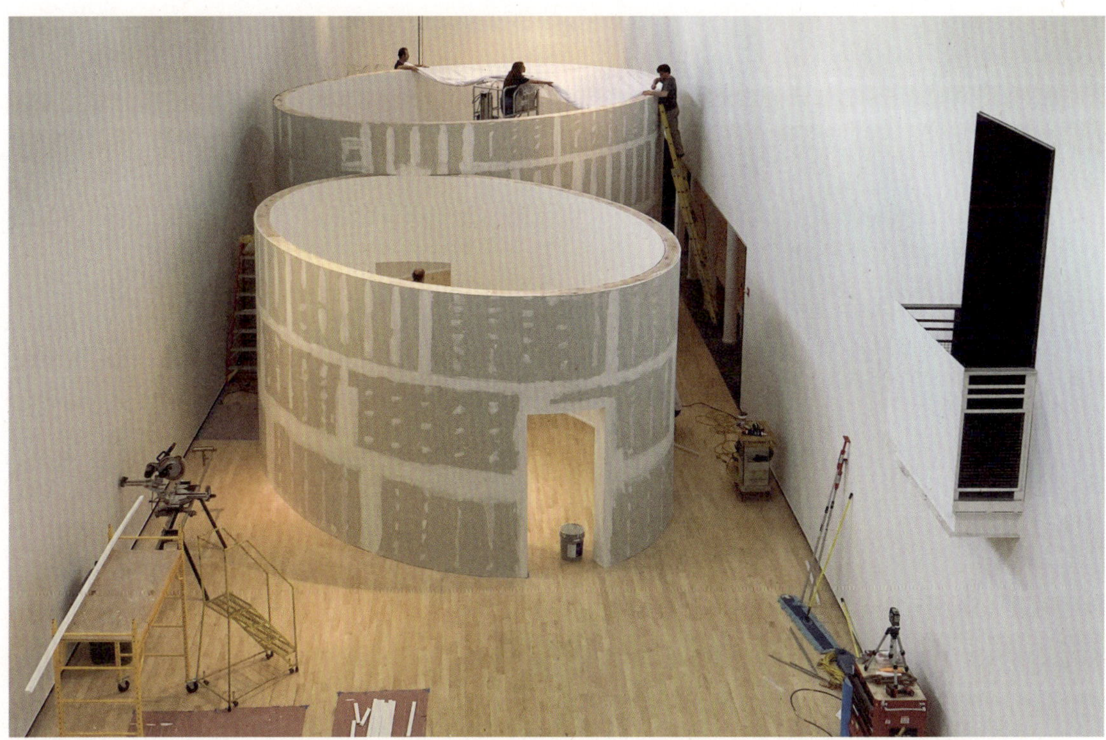

Construction of *White Noise (monochrome)*, 2000, and *White Noise (polychrome)*, 2023. Massachusetts Museum of Contemporary Art, 2023

announcement card. So basically, my process of working involves collecting, often slowly, an archive of raw material, and then editing my way through it. I rarely know where the end will be.

> Ian Berry: In making a wall installation of conversations, what determines the choice of papers? Do you have a drawn shape on the wall that you need to fill regardless of the words, or do you have a set of conversations that you want to group together that then determines the size and shape?

Neither, actually. I usually work on the floor, where I lay down a large piece of linen bonded to paper and on this I might start with a formal question of size or shape. It might be a small work, maybe 14 by 18 inches, but I won't know it's going to be 14 by 18 inches—I'll just start working with an archive of papers and conversations, and simultaneously develop a formal and verbal narrative. Sometimes I have a formal paradigm dominate, like in the monochrome wall works—all the papers might be various shades and hues of a single color, sort of like Albers's *Homage to the Square* series.

The verbal narrative is never quite so arbitrary as it seems—the works often progress from the upper left to the lower right—or through what I call "domino narratives," where one conversation somehow flows into another. Remember how Albers said you can't put one color beside another without affecting both? It's like that with words too—one comment affects the next comment—and so the narrative flow from one paper to the next is usually quite considered rather than arbitrary. And there are other things to consider with each paper—the color of the writing, the density of the writing, the angle of the writing. Even a small work with fifteen papers in it takes weeks to make—because the possible combinations of the arrangement are mathematically astonishing.

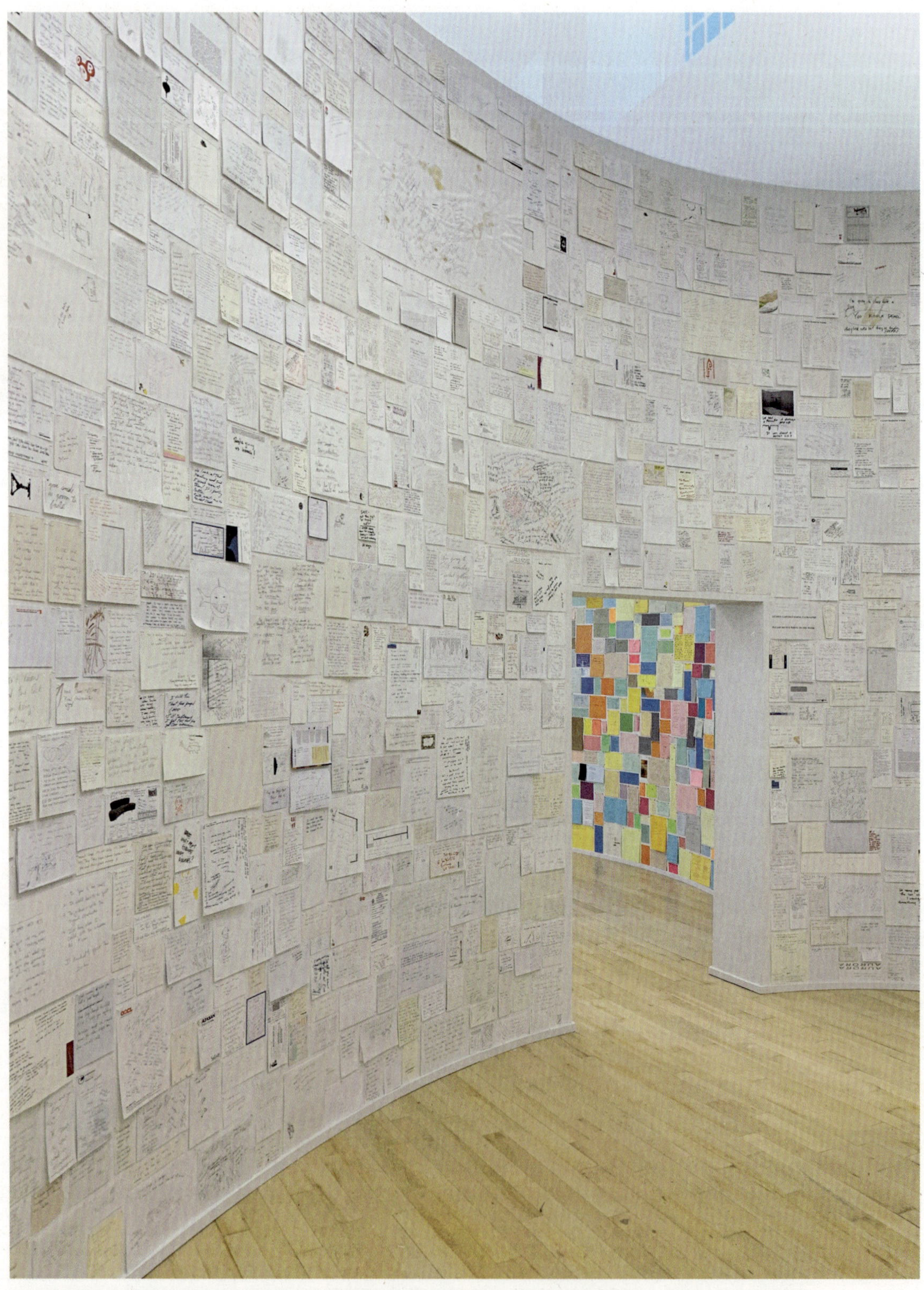

Joseph Grigely, *White Noise (monochrome)*, 2000, and *White Noise (polychrome)*, 2023. Installation view (detail), Massachusetts Museum of Contemporary Art, 2023

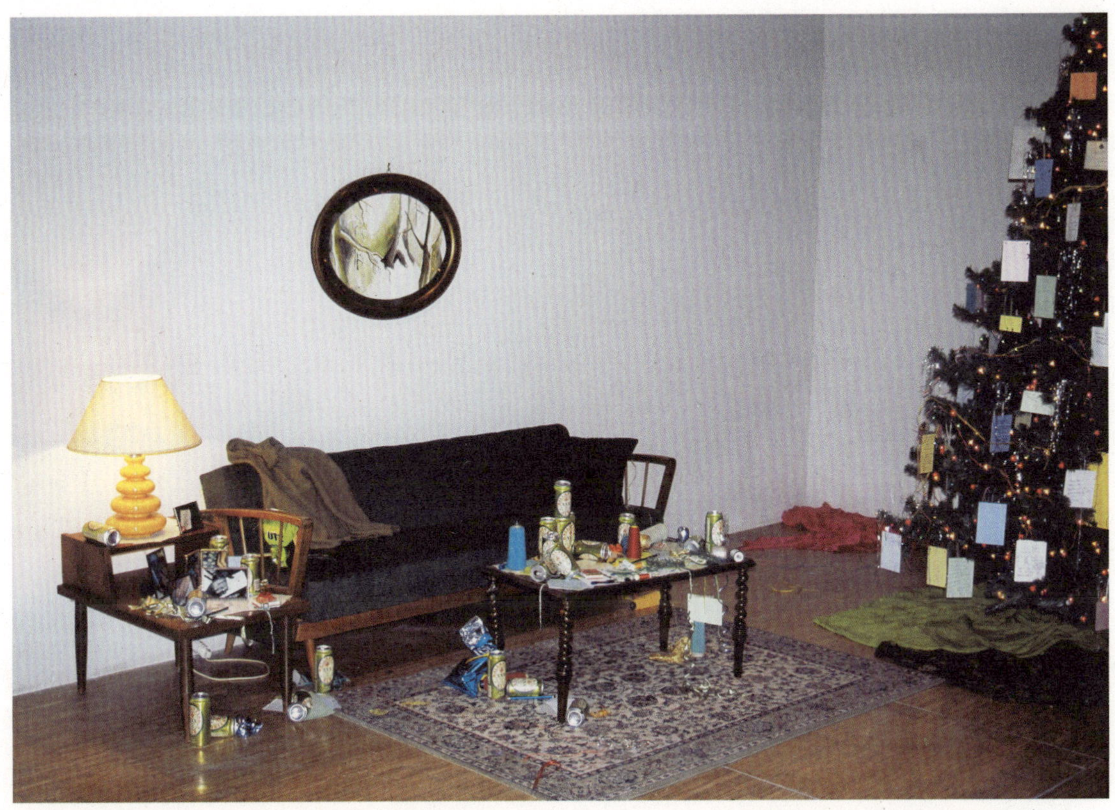

Joseph Grigely, *The Tree-Trimming Party*, 1998. Mixed media. Installation view in the exhibition *Azerty*, Centre Pompidou, Paris, 2001

> Margaret Sundell: By bringing in a verbal narrative, you're introducing language—precisely the thing that, as you just mentioned, modernism works to repress. Do you think of your work as a critique of modernism?

Oh, I don't know—I'd rather like to think I'm expanding the mechanisms of modernism, rather than simply criticizing their ostensible limitations. It's hard to keep growing as an artist without simultaneously unmaking and remaking prior conventions. And because so many conventions are involved—not just that of modernism—this remaking process is a conflation of many genres. One involves still life, in particular what Norman Bryson calls "rhopography"—the throwaway bits of everyday life. The notion of rhopography is derived from the Greek *rhopos*, meaning "trivial objects." Odds and ends—the sort of mundane things that, in composing a still-life painting, compose our lives as human beings. Everyday language is about as mundane as we can get.

> Hans Ulrich Obrist: Could you tell me about how your work refers to the tradition of the conversation piece—especially in the context of the Soane's Museum in London?

The conversation piece is an eighteenth- and nineteenth-century genre of painting and drawing typically practiced in England and the Lowlands. The genre is distinguished by the fact that people are present and seem to be talking, but their words are absent. Their bodies and gestures are positioned in a way as to suggest paralinguistic traces of the conversation. Watteau, Gainsborough, and Rowlandson all painted conversation pieces. Soane's collection of works by Hogarth and Canaletto could be included in this genre. Take, for example, Soane's copy of the *Riva degli Schiavoni, Venice*—a very conventional Canaletto of the sort he painted for the English tourist crowd. Whether he was painting a palazzo or a lido, Canaletto typically filled

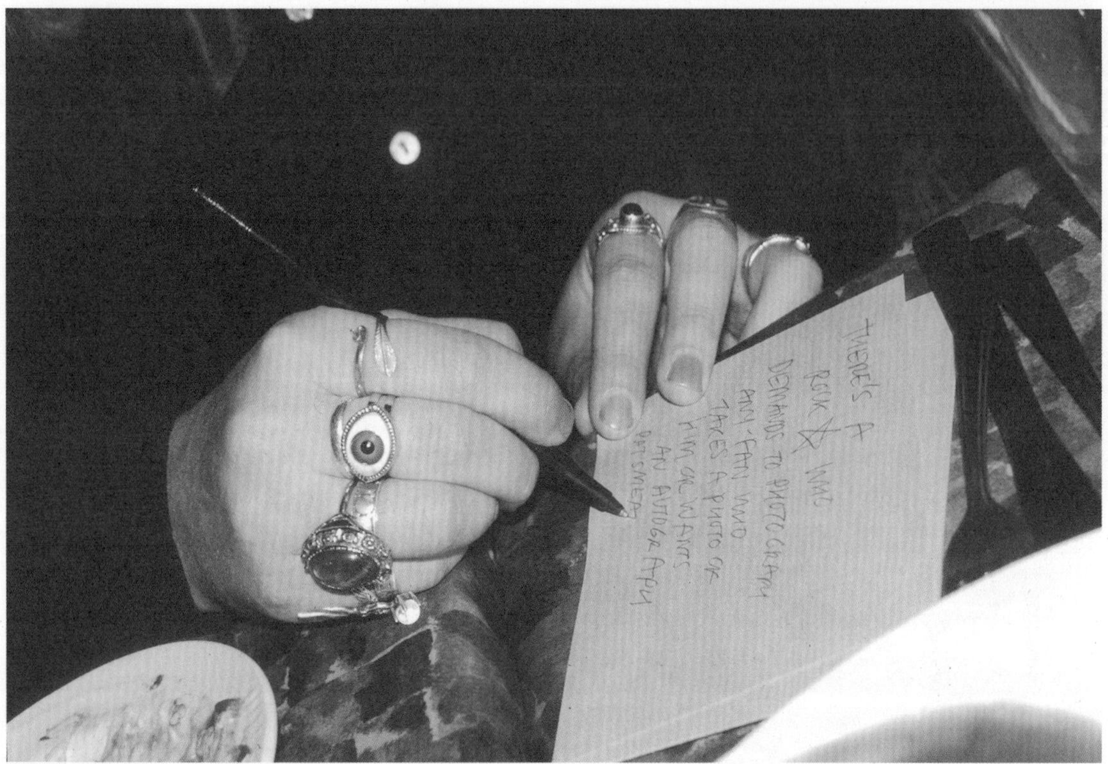

Joseph Grigely, *Jenny S. Detroit, 19 January 1996*, 1996. R-print

his canvases with small groups of people who seem to be chatting, people who seem to yell, and people whose gestures bespeak directions. In the *Riva degli Schiavoni* a dog's head is cocked to the conversation of a cluster of people a few steps away; nearby, a bargeman gestures and yells loudly enough to capture the attention of a woman walking by; beyond them, heads are turned and bodies are positioned in a way that says only one thing: Words are moving. This is the secret of the conversation piece as a genre: It is not just a visual scene being represented—a visual experience—but the human occupation of that expanse, and the fact that this occupation is characterized not by things seen, but by things heard. In this respect I consider Canaletto a noisy painter. Strictly speaking, most art historians would not consider Canaletto or even Watteau as being painters of conversation pieces, but their work is nonetheless about the auditory field.

> Hans Ulrich Obrist: About conversations, one of the interesting things is silence. Hans-Georg Gadamer pointed out to me that the problem with conversations—particularly in interviews—is that language contains many nonverbal utterances and silences that cannot be transcribed or written down. How do you see this issue?

I agree wholeheartedly with Gadamer's point that speech is so nuanced that writing cannot convey its emotional complexity. This is one reason why computer-based speech-to-text recognition programs are so fallible: As humans, we inflect our speech in an incessant variety of changing ways. Silence, to a speech recognition program, is represented as a gap in the speech stream. But silence is never really "empty" or "redundant," even for a deaf person: It's always filled with visual information of some kind—the gestures we make when the voice pauses, for example. Or the weight of one's eyes, or the turn of the brows. Only we don't have a critical or scientific discourse that explores the richness of silence in a way that goes beyond kinesics and the overworn notion of "body language"—so silence has some of its greatest moments in spoken arts, especially theater and cinema.

Jan Estep: Do you think there is a difference, conceptually, between the acts of writing and speaking?

A huge difference. A conversation is fundamentally discursive, not linear; there are breaks, sudden turns, lapses. When you read a novel, for example, or a letter—things that are written—you know where the beginning is, you know where the middle is, you know where the end is. But with an inscribed conversation—when someone talks on paper—it's hard to find a beginning or an end. Instead, there's an endless layering of words, marks, and lines.

Andreas Gedin: Using your very specific situation—being deaf—in an art context distinguishes you from most other artists. Do you find it problematic in any way that your handicap is in focus and that it could take over other aspects of your art?

Good question. I suppose it is problematic that people attach themselves to the matter of my deafness, but it is also perfectly understandable—it's a salient and inescapable reality. It bothers me only when people aggrandize the deafness and invoke platitudes about it. Over time, the emphasis on deafness tends to dissipate as people discover the work that I make is much less about me than it is about the people with whom I have conversations. For me, the whole process of conversing on paper is "normal"—an ordinary daily activity that actually inverts the idea of disability. When I ask people to write things down, their normal process of conversing is changed; they have to converse in a way that disables their normal mode of communication—so they become disabled somewhat—finding that everything they want to say must depend on the words coming from the tip of their pencil.

Jan Estep: There's a feeling of chumminess in these notes, like we're sharing a secret, passing notes back and forth in the back of the classroom. The literal exchange of words (made literal by the writing) feels intimate, like a gift from me to you and from you to me. Have you experienced this in your meetings with people?

Sometimes. What's funny is how other people around us become curious about what we are saying, and how the inability to overhear an inscribed conversation has a certain attraction to it. I have one friend who loves to take advantage of this sort of situation when we are among other people. Once, at a highbrow academic dinner, when we were seated at a table with a dozen other people, she was talking, on paper, about a wild sexual fantasy—which is sort of like playing footsie on top of the table instead of under it.

Jan Estep: There's also a sense that the language shared takes on a material, physical presence: For example, one night at dinner we were talking and advanced the conversation by writing on a paper tablecloth spread out around us. You could see the path of the conversation traced out along the sheet of paper: arcs, interjections, scribbled-out bits. The conversation made a very fine drawing. There seem to be three ways to go here: Do you look at the collected ephemera in *formal* terms? Does their significance lie mainly in the *content* of what gets said? Or is the import primarily in the *act* of recording these everyday exchanges?

Fundamentally, I'd say my priority in the middle of a conversation is the conversation itself—what people are saying—simply because all I want to do is "hear" them talk and participate in a social exchange. Often, too, when someone writes something on a piece of paper and passes it to me, I like to catch a glimpse of their eyes as the paper is passed on to me. It's a very special moment, for some reason, because of how it privileges the difference in our approach to communicating—plays with it—and tries to find a certain pleasure in it. In this respect, I think my deafness is not so much a disabling condition as it is an enabling condition.

As for the papers themselves, it's hard to generalize what I value in them, and how in the process of editing them they come together as art. Sometimes it's the content of the conversation, or the way it's written, or the color and density of the pen or pencil it's written with, or how the content and papers are recombined. Sometimes the words don't matter at all—I've done a few works with blank papers that were anything but silent.

> Jan Estep: Have you always been interested in language per se? What is so interesting about it to you?

Well, I'm not sure I can explain where my interest in language comes from. When I was in fifth grade—just before I became deaf—I had this teacher named Miss Corbett who was, perhaps because of her experience as a WAC [Women's Army Corps member] in World War II, a real disciplinarian. She liked quiet classrooms. I liked to talk. So I got in trouble a lot. She'd make me write, five hundred times in longhand, "I will not talk in class unless spoken to." Then, to make things interesting, she'd take up the pile of papers, count them, say thank you, and tear them up right in front of me. She was actually my teacher at the time when I became deaf. At that time, I lost all interest in television and turned to reading—mostly outdoor and fishing magazines like *Field & Stream* and *Outdoor Life*. I mean, what else could I have done? TV didn't have captions back then. So reading was a default mode for me as a deaf person.

The thing about language I find particularly engaging now is how meaningful it is when inflected by the presence of the person with whom I am talking: how the eyes move, the eyebrows, the hands. This is all part of the experience of a conversation. It's a very different experience than when communicating by email, for example. Or even letters.

> Jan Estep: You have shown quite a lot in Europe and Japan, among other places. Do you think people in other countries respond differently to your exhibitions than Americans?

Yes, though it's hard to explain. I think it's partly because America is fundamentally a monolingual country; people here don't regularly experience the necessary importance of having to construct linguistic bridges. In Europe you're constantly communicating from one language to another. You can go fifty miles, and all of a sudden you're listening to Flemish instead of French, or German instead of Flemish, and so I think that in Europe there's a more considered understanding of the vicissitudes of communicating from one language to another, or from one modality to another. I also think that in Europe the contemporary art scene is fundamentally different than that in the United States. I find this distinction borne out both by the art some artists make and the curatorial vision. And I also find it in art schools, with their emphasis in the US on taxonomizing work—and the curriculum—on the basis of genres and media. It's generally not like this in Europe, at least not in schools like Goldsmiths in London. I think the break began with Beuys: Like Duchamp, he drew attention to ontological issues, and ways in which art involves the exploration of the relationship between material and immaterial values. Here in the States, though, there is more emphasis on the exclusive experience of the material object. Think of American artists who have gone against the grain of this emphasis on objecthood: Lawrence Weiner, James Lee Byars, and Ben Kinmont. They're better known in Europe than the United States. Alternately, the work of many good European artists isn't appreciated in the US as much as it probably should be: Anri Sala, Maria Eichhorn, Liam Gillick, and even Douglas Gordon. Sure, a lot of people know who Douglas is, but how many have seen his work in the US? Or how many get to see shows curated by people like Nicolas Bourriaud, Hans Ulrich Obrist, or Jérôme Sans? All three are unafraid of art that has no precedence as art—something with which few American curators probably feel comfortable. But I do like the

ONCE upon a time
I spent the night
at a friends — on a
mattress on the floor.
I don't know WHAT
happened, but in the
middle of the night
he slept-walked over +
PISSED on my
head! I was —
uh — jeezus, it was
too weird. So I got
up + showered (and found another bed)
In the morning
he saw the wet !!

mattress +
blamed the dog!
I didn't have the
heart to tell
him it was...
his dark side.

Joseph Grigely, *Untitled Conversation (At Home with Susan)*, 1996. Ink on napkin

idea of importing these curatorial visions, and seeing how they will affect the development of American aesthetics.

> Jan Estep: I know you have an academic background in English literature and have taught as an English professor. How do you teach in the classroom? Could you explain how that is possible?

Well, all of my students at the School of the Art Institute of Chicago are hearing—so I always have a sign language interpreter in my classes. It was also like this when I taught at Stanford and the University of Michigan. I speak for myself, and the interpreters translate to sign language questions, comments, and interjections posed by my students. It works really well—whether for undergraduate lectures or graduate seminars. The difficult part is finding interpreters who can handle PhD-level critical discourse. With a great interpreter, though—and I've been very fortunate to have some great ones recently—people forget there's an interpreter in the classroom. When I do studio visits, I usually do these one-on-one: The dynamics involve a very different psychology, and a very different approach.

> Jan Estep: Given this academic background, how and when did you decide to become an artist?

It's not really something I decided self-consciously. I just sort of fell into it. It started when I was in graduate school. Late one night, when taking the train from London to Oxford, I ran into a friend who played on the ice hockey team with me—Rob Evans—and he was reading a book which seemed pretty interesting: Delacroix's *Journal*. So I asked him who Delacroix was; a lot of literature students are naive about visual art, and at that time I was one of them. Rob was then at the Ruskin, which at that time was a pretty staid art school, but most of the time he was living in a squat beside Riverside Studios—which, as a quasi-alternative space, had some of London's most engaging shows in the early 1980s. Even Tarkovsky went there to lecture. So I started hanging out with Rob, seeing shows with him, partying in studios set up in abandoned churches, and having all-night drawing sessions laced with Allen Ginsberg's poetry and indecent British claret. As art educations go, this was a pretty good one.

> Ian Berry: Do you have a studio? Do you have a daily art routine that involves going to the studio? I ask partly because your artwork seems to happen in unexpected ways and places.

I've had a lot of studios over the years—sometimes the lofts I've been living in, sometimes separate places—right now my studio is in my loft: It's got a big desk, a lot of bookshelves, and a lot of floor space to spread things down. It's a "clean" studio where I work on wall pieces, writing projects, and films—but because many of my recent projects have involved specialized production skills, like the audio and film editing of *St. Cecilia* and several sculpture projects involving urethane and fiberglass, I've had to work in facilities with the requisite equipment and technical experience. The hard part about being an artist today, when working with such varied media, is simply a matter of getting the results you want and finding the resources and skills to get those results. In this respect, the studio is really a space inside my head.

> Andreas Gedin: What did your early art look like, before you started working with the *Conversations with the Hearing*?

Well, it looked like art—in the sense that it was trying to be art, trying to be canonical. During the late 1980s I was working with old European postcards—I'd paint on them with ink and dispersion, make an 8-by-10 black-and-white negative, blow it up to 4 by 6 feet, mount it on

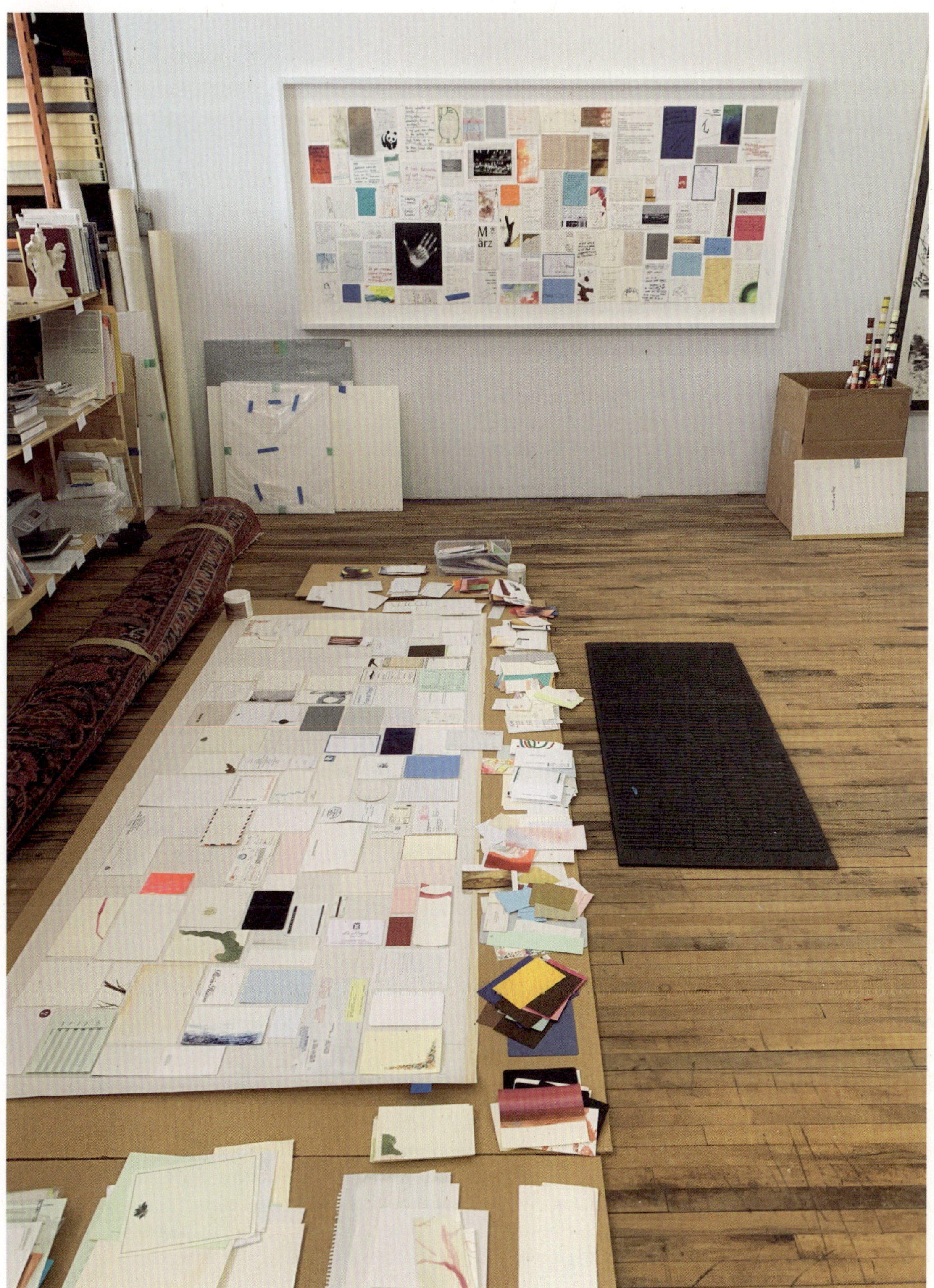

Studio view, 2024. Work in progress (foreground) and *Come to Amsterdam*, 2023 (background)

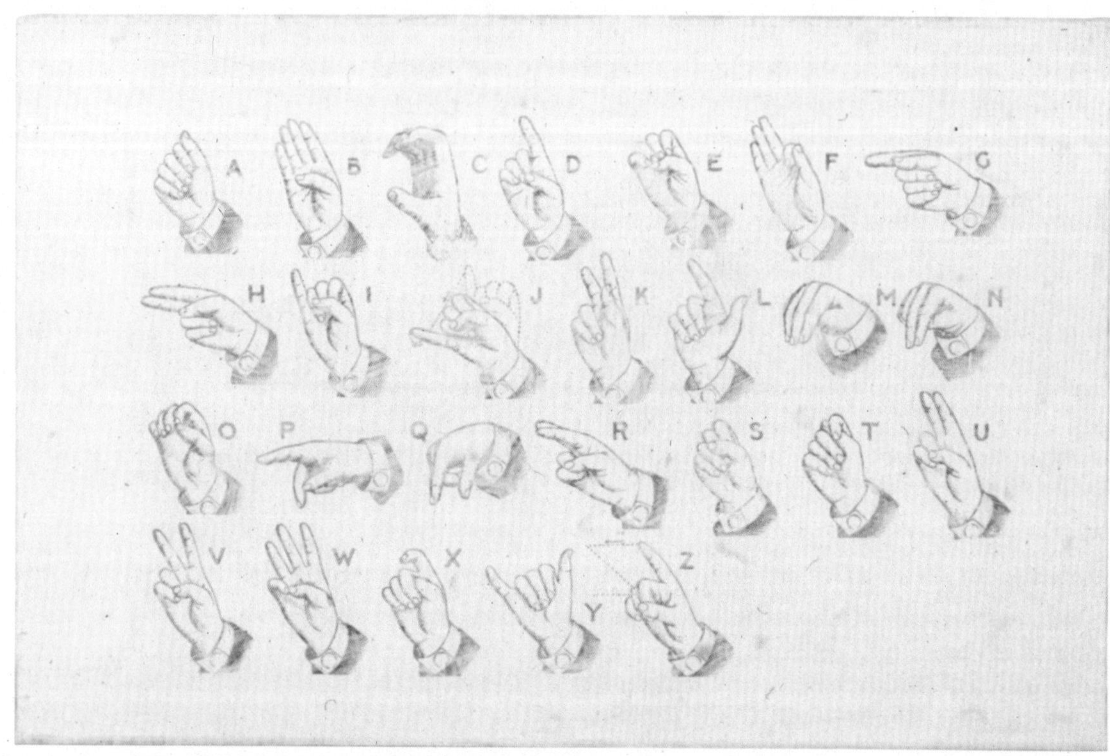

Joseph Grigely, *The Unextravagant Desire*, 1992. Dispersion on photograph, mounted on canvas

canvas, and then rework the surface with another dispersion made from asphaltum and shellac. There was something histrionic about the process, and the results as well. Not that I feel the work was bad—only that it was trying too hard to be something other than I could make it be. The *Conversations with the Hearing* changed all this—they came together not out of desire, but out of necessity. They initially had the effect of taking me someplace within my own life that I had not been to before. It's a strange and ironically ineffable experience, but something that came together with its own inertia and sense of direction. The first time I showed the *Conversations* to people, I'd get this blank stare—people would say "Huh?"—and they said "Huh?" for a few years before they finally caught on.

> Jan Estep: Do you still work in both art and academia? Does art give you something that other fields don't? In other words, why make art?

Hmm. I think it has a lot to do with academic protocol and preconceptions about critical discourse. After my time at Oxford, I taught nineteenth-century English literature at Gallaudet University and Stanford University, where I was a Mellon Postdoctoral Fellow. I loved teaching literature, but my approach to writing criticism involved problematizing a situation rather than trying to resolve it. Criticism generally operates under the assumption that you have a point of view, and an obligation to communicate that view in a way that is convincing. I didn't care much about convincing people. I'd rather take them into a labyrinth where they might learn something from the experience of being entangled with the inherent complexity of literature. I'm still writing about this sort of stuff. My book *Textualterity* was an effort to explore how art and literature are fundamentally transient as part of the process of being disseminated in culture. It is precisely because of this transience that I am attracted to art: It does not depend on maintaining a certain state or form to communicate—and it continues to communicate in ways both intended and unintended by its makers.

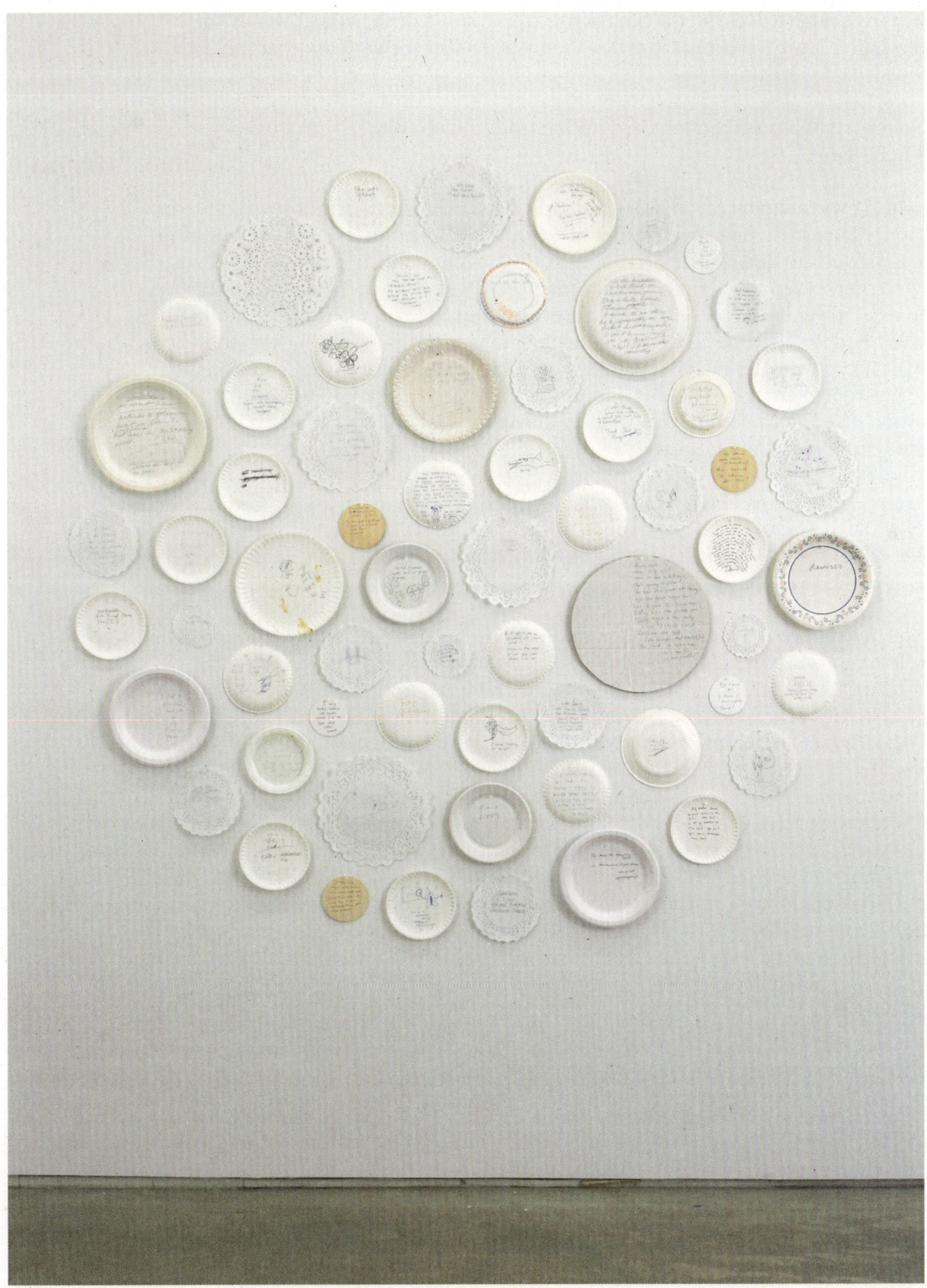

Joseph Grigely, *62 Round Conversations*, 2006. Ink and pencil on paper, pins

So you might say that art gives me the liberty to explore some of the same theoretical enigmas that I have always explored, but does so by providing me with another means with which to construct my arguments.

Jan Estep: What are those means? What tradition are you in? I'm thinking Fluxus here?

No, not Fluxus. It was actually certain kinds of radical literary criticism that revealed to me that all art and criticism involve the creation of some kind of narrative—and the question we all face as artists is to find a voice for that narrative, a uniquely idiomatic way of constructing it. The first time I read Ihab Hassan's *Paracriticisms* I was struck by its unmisgiving tendency to be what it wanted to be—not what others wanted or expected criticism to be. Ditto Derrida, who I find totally comical at times: Reading him is like overhearing someone have a long-drawn-out conversation with himself. And I'd say that Gregory Ulmer's notion of "heuretics" has been very influential too. Heuretics is basically about invention—trying to find a new way of saying something in a visually engaging way. Imagine having a little voice screaming at you: "Invent! Invent! Invent!"

Hans Ulrich Obrist: I want to return to a question I was once asking you in a diner in New York where there was so much noise that I never could understand the recording. What general thoughts do you have about bringing art and science together in a comprehensive context?

This is a huge question, but a good one. One of the more manageable approaches concerns ideas related to reproduction and replication. This was the subject of *Textualterity*. The dissemination of art, like the dissemination of humanity, depends upon how both textual bodies and biological bodies distribute themselves through reproduction. This brings together two seemingly disparate fields: textual criticism and biology. Walter Benjamin's idea of "mechanical reproduction" is important too. But Benjamin seems to have missed how the production of "types" and "copies" also involves the production of unpredictable variations, so a copy is never wholly identical to its original model or form. The same poem printed in a different context ultimately inflects how the poem is read—just as the display of one painting in different sites affects how it, too, is read. Thus, the sequence of exhibition spaces allows for infinite variation—repetition and difference. That's why contemporary culture is so obsessed with cloning. So obsessed with control. Not that this is new: Diderot, in the *Encyclopédie*, remarked how the graft is a triumph of art over nature. Only now, with recent advances in biological engineering, the graft as a paradigm is much more complex in how it addresses the very idea of "reproduction technology."

Hans Ulrich Obrist: In a previous conversation, you mentioned your idea of a new kind of "interdisciplinary institute." I recall you had once referred to it in terms of "posthumanities." Can you tell me about it?

The term "posthumanities" comes out of the book *Posthuman Bodies*, which Ira Livingston and Judith Halberstam edited in 1995—though the term had been talked about for years prior to this. Historically, the typical institute for the humanities explores the various arts—including literature and music—as being part of the continuum of the "natural" human body. But what is a "natural" human body? There is an immense space between Darwin's "natural" world and the "natural" world of creatures that appear in the tabloid *Weekly World News*: bat boy, frog boy, and the horse born with a human face; jackalopes, wolpertingers, professors of interdisciplinary studies. Mutation is most interesting not as a biological fact, but as an etymological construct that emphasizes changed and changing states. Absurd as it may seem, it is the world of

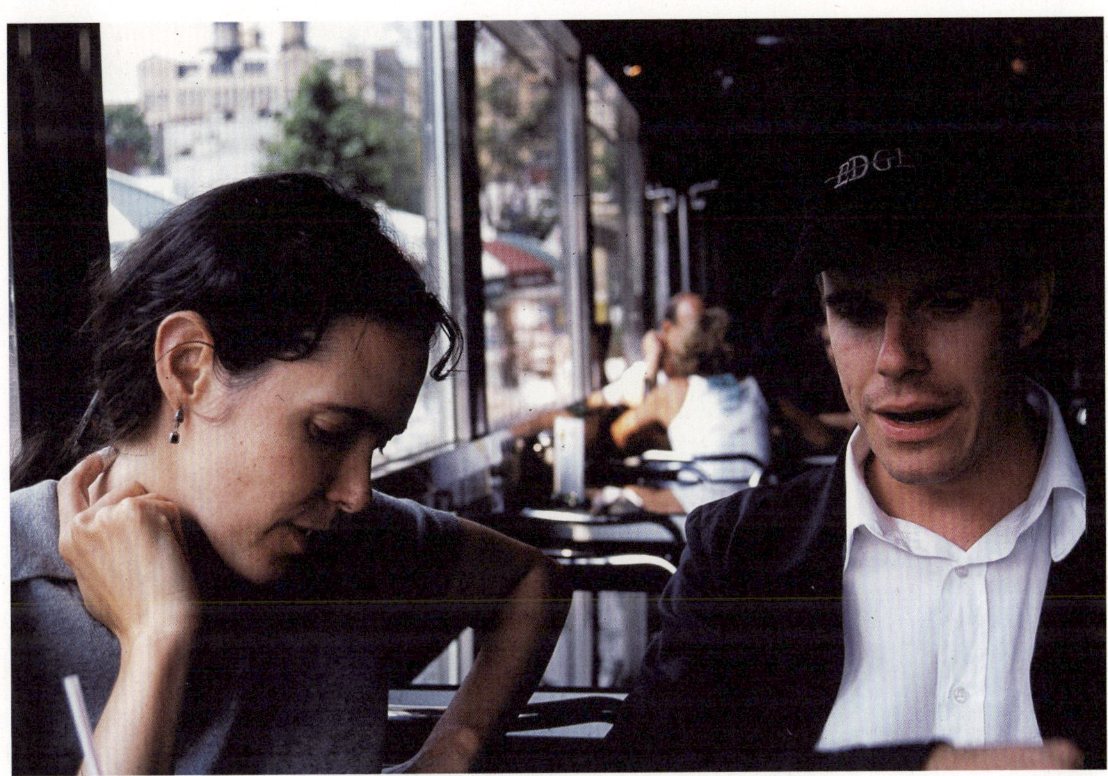

Amy Vogel and Hans Ulrich Obrist, Empire Diner, New York, 1997

the constructed body that is most natural now. Grafting, splicing, eclecticism, conflation—these things happen, not arbitrarily, but because of a certain human will and desire.

> Hans Ulrich Obrist: What about Donna Haraway? Is her work an example of "post-human" criticism?

Haraway's an excellent example. Starting with *Primate Visions* and later in *Modest Witness*, Haraway's work has focused on how the posthuman body is fundamentally a constructed body. One of the characteristics of postmodern bodies is that their filiation is nonlinear. Their genealogies do not have straight lines. Our natural world is a world we had once called "artificial." It is the word "natural" that now wears the scare quotes: "Natural," with its Eden-like mystique and untainted purity, represents a perpetual nostalgia for something that is and is not present. Haraway's universe is a terribly complex universe of transgenic foods, mice with patented cancer-bearing genes, and related fabrications. Frankenstein was relatively simple in comparison: The Monster was the product of edited phenotypes. OncoMouse™, as it is known, is the product of edited genotypes. There's a world of difference between the two. What we need is more critical discourse like Haraway's to address the comparative importance of this difference. The traditional American institute for the humanities rarely addresses these issues—which is why we need, in some form, an institute for the posthumanities.

> Hans Ulrich Obrist: Can such an interdisciplinary institute happen within the existing structures of the academy, where one can sense some kind of omnipresent anxiety of interdisciplinarity?

Well, this is complex—being as it is an administrative sort of question. Many institutional think tanks are already doing engaging interdisciplinary work, both in the US and Europe, as well as in Asia and Latin America. But only to a certain extent. What you describe as the "omnipresent anxiety of interdisciplinarity" is a very real anxiety, since it goes against the grain of institutional history: The Western university is traditionally devoted to the process of taxonomizing knowledge, of breaking it down into discrete categories of disciplinary thought and discourse. The anxiety comes from being in a realm that lacks the precepts of historical continuity. People are, for the most part, reticent to embrace any school of thought whose fundamental superstructure lacks a positivist impulse. Look at deconstruction as an example. In a very broad sense, deconstruction is "interdisciplinary" in the ways that it explores the practice of reading: reading poems, reading novels, reading paintings, reading virtually any act of human communication. Like the philosopher Nelson Goodman, Derrida created a vocabulary to suit his own disciplinary needs: His is a vocabulary of linguistics without being linguistic; a vocabulary of anthropology without being anthropological. Which is precisely why his work is troubling for some people: His notion of *différance* takes pleasure in the very idea of difference, and the peregrinations of the mind.

> Hans Ulrich Obrist: What are the advantages and the dangers of interdisciplinarity?

The ostensible danger is that because people like to label other people—and their work—they tend to ignore or disparage those they can't easily compartmentalize. On the other hand, the most compelling attraction of interdisciplinary work is how it invokes the constant flux of humanist and posthumanist inquiry. It's not inherently better than monotheological forms of inquiry—there's some pretty bad interdisciplinary stuff out there—but when it's good, as it is in Donna Haraway's work, it's engaging, enlightening, intelligent, and accessible.

> Hans Ulrich Obrist: In interdisciplinary projects there is sometimes a disappearance of differences between the disciplines and an adjustment of vocabularies. How is it possible to have an interdisciplinary situation and at the same time allow very complex discourses to develop?

This is difficult, and I have a relevant anecdote that illustrates the dilemma. A little while ago I asked several colleagues of mine who were participating in a yearlong seminar at the University of Michigan's Institute for the Humanities to read a chapter of Richard Leppert's book *The Sight of Sound*. The book is a historical study of visual representations of domestically produced music in the eighteenth century. It covers various fields: history, musicology, art history, and social anthropology. What intrigued me was the way the book explored how ubiquitous sonoric experiences—music and conversation, for example—are represented in painting and drawing. Deep down, it's really an amazing topic: How do we take an auditory experience and translate it into a visual experience? How do we take the discourse of speech and translate it into a discourse of visual representation? How do conversations draw themselves in two-dimensional space? My colleagues seemed unimpressed, if not also unchallenged: One historian was concerned about Leppert's definition of "medieval." A composer was troubled by Leppert's description of a composition. The key thing is that they ultimately read Leppert through the template of their own disciplinary discourse. Cultural criticism is very much a territorial sort of business.

> Hans Ulrich Obrist: You earlier mentioned to me the Library of Alexandria as a model…

It was at the Library of Alexandria that some of the first efforts were made to explore issues related to textual dissemination and reproduction. The efforts centered around Homer's lost texts, and attempts were made to reconstruct them by examining fragments and secondary texts. Ultimately, the Homer we read today is a Homer that has been unmade, remade, and made over—a Homer whose texts live not because they depend upon maintaining a specific form, but because of their malleability, and their ability to sustain themselves through these inevitable remakings.

Hans Ulrich Obrist: Is this exploration of the transmission of cultural texts what you defined as "textualterity" in your book *Textualterity: Art, Theory, and Textual Criticism*?

Yes, exactly. Literally, textualterity is textual alterity: an understanding that a specific text will have many different forms, all of which express a degree or variation. The variation is rarely merely arbitrary, but rather reflects the possibilities of human intention. One of my favorite examples is Thomas Bowdler's 1807 family edition of Shakespeare's plays. History regards Bowdler as a miscreant: He edited Shakespeare's plays in such a way as to omit, as he said, "words and expressions... which cannot with propriety be read aloud in a family." A man of considerable moral probity, Bowdler saw himself performing a public service. Most editors do. Even censors do. The issue for me isn't whether he was "right" or "wrong" to do what he did, but how it reflected his own moral interests, and how he was perfectly honest about it all. His text is not Shakespeare's text, but Shakespeare's as inflected by Bowdler: It is a text of culturally motivated difference. The key idea behind *Textualterity* is that it looks at variation and change not as being "good" or "bad" but as something that is inevitably part of the expression of the vicissitudes of our human nature.

Hans Ulrich Obrist: Can one use notions such as "complex dynamic system," "nonlinearity," and "in-betweenness" to describe this ever-growing text?

Yes, so much so that it's hard to think of an existence that is otherwise. I'm momentarily reminded of Marc Augé's book on supermodernity called *Non-Places*—and how our everyday lives now consist of constant spatial displacement. So-called "transit lounges" or "waiting rooms," which once had the apparition of being points of stasis, are now points of motion. People used to take vacations; they now take "working vacations." We are constantly developing a technological architecture to support this dynamic: Wireless communications, in particular, have freed us from the anchorage of a physical place. In another sense, it seems to me that the entire notion of interactive dynamics is fundamental to our human existence. At almost every level of human evolution, a certain kind of dynamic friction had the effect of challenging the mind, forcing it to push itself a little further and a little harder. And what's especially wonderful is not knowing where the twists and turns of these peregrinations will take us.

Hans Ulrich Obrist: What's your opinion on the current debate on the origins of language, where a structuralist approach is more and more contradicted by a contextual and evolutional approach of dynamic parameters in which language develops? What do you think of the argument between Noam Chomsky and Luc Steels or Brian MacWhinney, who attempt to propose an alternative theory?

This is difficult for me to assess as I don't really know enough about MacWhinney's work to comment on it. But Chomsky and Steels present an intriguing dilemma: How can one decide between a primarily innate theory of language—Chomsky's position—and one in which a minimal innate capacity is developed through a highly interactive environment—which is Steels's position? For me, Steels is putting to test some very interesting Enlightenment philosophy. Rousseau and Condillac both argued that deaf people were incapable of acquiring language. They reasoned that deaf people, lacking auditory input, could not participate in the crucial sort of "language game" that Steels—and others—have found to be fundamental to linguistic development. But the problem is that Rousseau and Condillac equated speech with language and neglected to explore the significance of visual languages such as sign language. It took another Enlightenment thinker—the Abbé de L'Epée—to discover how two deaf siblings were using, and developing, a sign language with each other—and then go on to establish the first school for the deaf to use sign. This was in Paris in the middle of the eighteenth century. L'Epée's experience with the siblings parallels Steels's recent experiments: A human brain, when provided with meaningful linguistic input, will play with it, develop it, and make something out of it. The modality is not important: speech, signing, or colored squares. The amazing thing about the brain is its adaptability. It will make a communication system, if not a language, when provided with appropriate stimuli. In this respect, Chomsky and Steels aren't necessarily counterpoints: Oddly enough, I find them complementary in fundamental ways.

> Mats Stjernstedt: I would like to refer to the situation we are in right now, using internet and email as tools for communication. Has or will this technological development change your way of working?

Yes, and very much so. I first started using email back in the days of BITNET: 1987. I loved it, though not because it replaced or because it replaces other modes of communication—letters, faxes, or even postcards—but because of how it creates and fosters the exigencies of our everyday communication needs. But what's odd about email is how disembodied it is: It lacks the presence of a person. Everything is reduced to certain electronic protocols and font styles. Missing is the intonation of the voice; the gesture of the hands; or, in a letter or fax, the idiosyncrasies of handwriting—all of which constitute for me a kind of presence. But that which is missing creates opportunities for ambiguities—which is, for art anyway, a privileged position. In the conversations that I have with hearing people, my voice is missing, the nods and gestures are missing, the little lipread bits are missing. What's left is just this mass of fragments—like in *White Noise*—and the discontinuity somehow creates a sense of desire. I think this desire is fundamental for all art—it gives the viewer only so much. I haven't used email in art projects yet. Presently, though, I'm interested in exploring speech recognition technologies. Mark Acosta and I recently did a project together, reading Borges's story about [Pierre] Menard's *Quixote* into a speech recognition program and printing the output, which reads like gibberish—which has the effect of showing just how different language and communication can be.

> Mats Stjernstedt: Looking at your installations I might start thinking of graffiti of sorts, of messages remaining from an anonymous city, or rather the citizens of this city. How do you want your work to be perceived by a viewer who did not take part in the situation when it came about, since it seems to deal so much with direct communication?

I don't think there is any ideal condition for viewing the work. I certainly have no preconceptions about how people approach it—because they are always going to find things I did not intend them to find. But the sense in which the *Conversations* might mirror the voices of the viewer is something I think is important—that the *Conversations* are, in a very broad sense—us—all of us—everybody at once and nobody in particular; and that to read them is to discover a little more about the peregrinations of our own humanity—what the brain will do with a pencil and a piece of paper and a need to communicate in a way other than speech or sign language. Reading one of the wall pieces is a voyeuristic activity, like overhearing a conversation. I know this sounds a little grandiose—but it's funny in a way, how language constantly defies our ability to contain it or to predict its evolutionary shifts—it evolves out of the necessity of our need to communicate under constantly changing physical and social conditions.

> Mats Stjernstedt: Have you been commissioned to work on public art projects, and if yes, how did you go about that?

It varies, depending on the place and the situation. For Manifesta 1 in Rotterdam, I tried to engage the public in conversations in a restored villa—we had a comfortable room with a balcony, a large table, and a small kitchen, so the setting was fundamentally domestic rather than institutional. For two months I spent time simply talking with people about language and communication and everyday things—we'd have coffee or beer, and let our words go wherever the words chose to go. I recently did a commission for the Flemish Ministry of Education which was a little more complicated and involved creating works for an office environment of desks and cubicles. For this I mounted inscribed *Conversations* in fabricated white polyurethane frames—they look a little like the sort of frames people use to display photographs of their family and friends—only instead of photographs, the frames contained brief and for the most part banal conversations. The workers at the ministry could place one or two of the frames on their desks and move them around as they wished.

Andreas Gedin: Apart from all the notes you have used in your work, you also study the history of being deaf. Tell us more about it!

Back around 1981–82, I started doing research into sign language poetry. This was a very early period of sign language research, and I was trying to approach it through paradigms of formalist literary criticism. Some very prescient minds made possible such research: people like Bill Stokoe (in the US), Brita Bergman (in Sweden), and Robbin Battison (an American who moved to Sweden) all did pioneering work in sign language linguistics, and this helped legitimize the discipline. In recent years, the discipline has advanced considerably—people like Lars Wallin, Diane Brentari, and Bob Johnson have helped carry sign language research from its initial secular status as a minority discipline into mainstream linguistics. I'm not really working in linguistics or literary criticism now; my interest has shifted to the question of how deafness is a condition of difference, and how difference might best be explored—culturally—through conceptions of alterity. In America, there exists a tendency to understand difference in terms of a majority/minority dichotomy, but this tends to maintain an inclusionary/exclusionary status quo, creating what I call "canonized" minorities—those that are validated by federal and institutional statutes.

Greg Hilty: In what sense are your works intended to be heard?

Oh, I don't know. I suppose someone might hear my stuff by forgetting what it's like to hear. Most of us are pretty much inured to our senses. This experience could be described as one of increasing familiarity—day after day, year after year—we get so used to what it means to hear, or even what it means to see, that it's hard to break away. What's nice is being able to get lost in the tangle of our senses—pausing long enough to let go of those preconceptions about listening and looking that we carry around with us—and spend a little time experiencing little nothings. The Australian director Jocelyn Moorhouse has this astute and engaging film—it's called *Proof*—about a blind photographer who questions the validity of alternative perception. And I like that immensely, because it takes a position that the truth of our perceptions has so little to do with the truth of our imagination. The film sort of says: Who cares what it means to have eyes or have ears? What matters is what we do with them. So the idea of getting lost in our senses—and taking pleasure in the process—is very compelling for me. The fact that I'm deaf is pretty much an inescapable fact, but only as much as it is an enabling rather than disabling condition. I think it was like this for Beethoven too. A lot of people think it was unfortunate that he became deaf, but I don't. I think he was lucky—his deafness gave him another way of listening to the world.

Ian Berry: Music has played a part in many of your works and is central to *St. Cecilia*, the new work in this exhibition. How does music function for you now, as a deaf person?

Between the ages of five and ten, the only art I knew half well was music: I played the clarinet in the school orchestra, and music of various kinds was omnipresent in our distinctly suburban household. A large, credenza-sized stereo was the main piece of furniture in our living room, and on it my mother played an array of her favorite selections. It was an eclectic mix, from classical music to Bing Crosby to traditional Christmas carols. Without us quite realizing it at the time, music marked itself as being a necessary component of our everyday life.

All of this changed for me in 1967, when I became deaf. I stopped playing the clarinet, but the music did not stop playing in my head. The absolute silence of the external world permitted me the freedom to play and replay the various performances I had heard over the years. Sometimes these performances were recorded, sometimes they were live concerts, and sometimes they were from television—background music, commercials, and even, as embarrassing as this may seem, the theme song from *Gilligan's Island*. When you become deaf suddenly, you don't have a choice about what you are privileged to remember. Even now, after forty years of being deaf, I constantly replay and remake these compositions and songs.

One of the more unusual discoveries about being deaf is the fact that I have continued to be intrigued by the process of watching music performances. Even in the absence of actually hearing an orchestra or a choir or a rock band, the visual nature of the performance permits one to "hear" the sound as a fiction: When you watch the bows of the violins, or the conductor, or the faces of a choir, or the wrenched-up faces of rockers, implied sounds come together in an ineffable way. This difference between how sound looks and how sound sounds is in many ways both the theme of my life as a deaf person and the theme of my work as an artist.

> Ian Berry: One way you explore this theme is in your catalogue insert, which features a carefully orchestrated series of clippings from *The New York Times*. How did that project begin and what happens to those images when the captions are removed?

This project—like the *St. Cecilia* video—more or less began on December 31, 1999, when Amy Vogel and I were watching the millennium celebrations on television. We were surfing channels and countries and paused for a while to watch a choir singing at the National Cathedral in Washington. The camerawork was very elaborate: fade-ins, fade-outs, and close-ups of the choir members as they sang. After watching this for a while, Amy turned to me and said in sign language, "The world must look really silly without sound."

She was right, of course—but the silliness of a silent world doesn't mean it's without interest or meaning. It's hard for hearing people to imagine this because you can't close your ears the way you can close your eyes. You can, however, watch TV with the sound turned off—that's one way of understanding this. After five minutes or so, this can be pretty frustrating—you find yourself wanting the words. But if you do it for an hour, you start to notice some interesting things going on. Try watching a couple of episodes of *Everybody Loves Raymond* with the sound turned off—you realize that a lot of basic communicative emotion doesn't really require words at all. And somehow this kind of communicative emotion seems to be one of the distinguishing qualities of photographs of musicians—I mean, when we go to a music performance, do we really go to watch? And if we do, what in fact are we seeing?

I've removed the captions because they seem too reductive—as if the caption made the photograph itself a caption to the performance. There's a lot of emotion in photographs of musicians performing, and I simply want to release the emotion from the burden of rationalization.

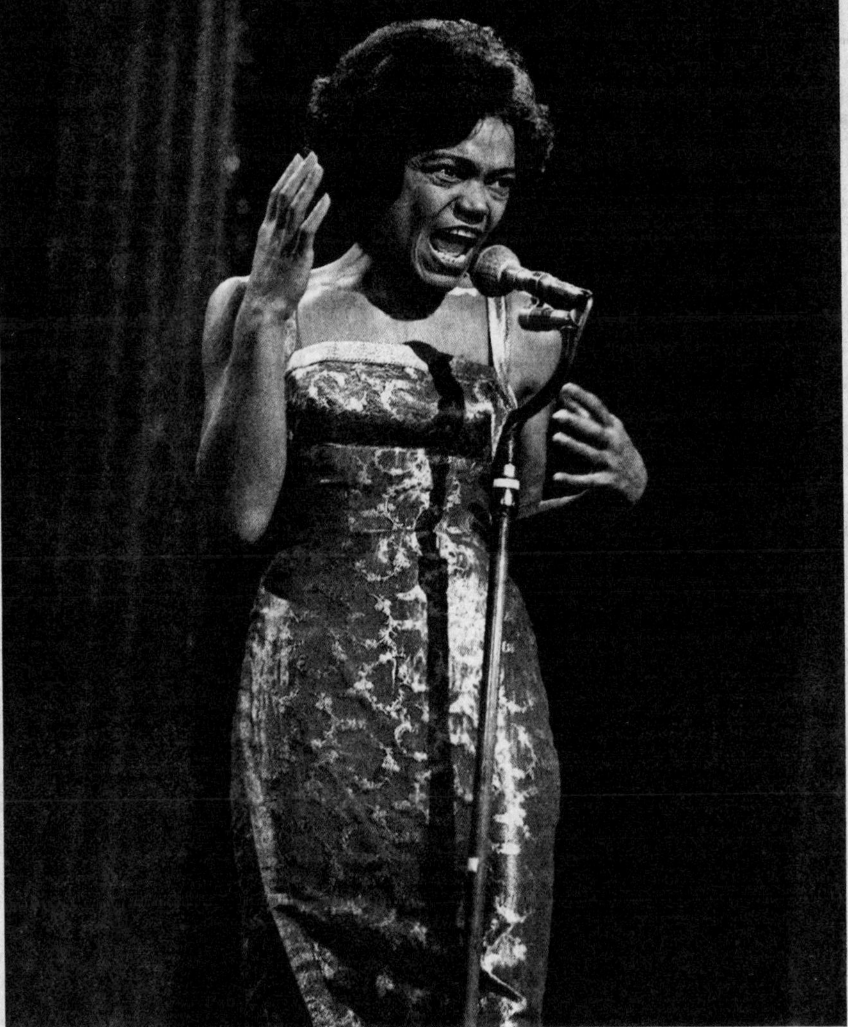

THE NEW YORK TIMES **OBITUARIES** FRIDAY, DECEMBER 26, 2008

rtha Kitt, a Performer Who Seduced Audiences, Di

OB HOERBURGER

Kitt, who purred and ıer way across Broad-ɛes, recording studios ɛ and television screens v-business career that ɔre than six decades, ıursday. She was 81 and ɔnnecticut.

use was colon cancer, longtime publicist, An-reedman.

t, who began perform-late '40s as a dancer in ɛ, went on to achieve ıd acclaim in a variety ıs long before other en-ıt multitaskers like Ju-ws, Barbra Streisand Midler.

er curvaceous frame ashed vocal come-ons, also, along with Lena ıong the first widely African-American sex Orson Welles famously d her "the most excit-ın alive" in the early ırently just after that t prompted him to bite ge during a perform-Time Runs," an adapta-ıust" in which Ms. Kitt len of Troy.

's career-long persona, ıe seen-it-all sybarite, vhen she performed in arets in her early 20s, ɔngs that became her ɛ, like "C'est Si Bon" for Sale."

ng to New York, she on Broadway in "New 952" and added another ɛr vocal crown, "Monot-Traffic has been known r me/Prices even rise for me/Harry S. Tru-ɛ bop for me/Monoto-ınotone-ous"). Brooks wrote in The New York May 1952, "Eartha Kitt oks incendiary, but she ɛ a song burst into

after that run, Ms. Kitt rst best-selling albums rded her biggest hit, aby," whose precise, ɛr diction and vaguely lections (Ms. Kitt, a na-th Carolina, spoke four

POPPERFOTO/GETTY IMAGES

ter, Kitt Shapiro, survives her, as do two grandchildren.

From practically the beginning of her career, as critics gushed over Ms. Kitt, they also began to

sleeping in subways and on the roofs of unlocked buildings. (She would later become an advocate, through Unicef, on behalf of homeless children.)

best of this country off to be shot and maimed. No wonder the kids rebel and take pot." The remark reportedly caused Mrs. Johnson to burst into tears and led to a de-

ONL

nytir

1984 rour Sout cally said ence for t

Tl rapl sion lishe Gra Bus song

A deca acti secc feat "Th into won this stan

A wi the

ed sch Yzn Sch

A fixt hav sha ous dail Eve that um ren Yor Hol saic full

B see

Joseph Grigely, *Songs Without Words (Eartha Kitt)*, 2012. Pigment print

Ian Berry: Has access to many different media changed how you imagine new work?

Oh, definitely. Deep down inside, I'm fundamentally a bricoleur—I like puttering and tinkering around. In high school I flunked a lot of courses—English, biology, civics, local history—mostly because I didn't have sign language interpreters in my classes, so I never knew what people were talking about. I took a lot of what I called "see-and-do" courses: woodshop, metal shop, mechanical drawing, small-engine repair, basic electronics, that sort of stuff. Plus, my father was a bricklayer and a stonemason, and in high school and college I spent my summers building fireplaces and chimneys and stuff like that. So it's almost like a homecoming for me to work on sculpture—the mantelpieces fit in with my past just perfectly. And the film and audio projects are in part about a certain longing—not letting go of the fact I can't hear my own work—and somehow I like that. We live in the age of post-media anyhow—to me, more important are the questions the work asks. Generally speaking, the art world likes to see a signature style in terms of the media of the work—but my signature style is a conceptual practice rather than a material one.

Ian Berry: Can you talk about collaboration and your work? I am thinking of your specific collaborations with Amy Vogel, and whether you describe your conversations in their various forms as collaborations.

The idea of "collaboration" is very general—artists have always had work done "for" them, and they do work "for" others—but it's rare for people to actually work with each other. Sometimes when I am working with Amy on a project, we will pass the work back and forth. But sometimes I will ask her to do something specific which I just don't have the ability to do—listen to audio edits, for example, or do certain modeling work, as she's a much better figurative sculptor than me—though in both cases we'll go back and forth in an effort to get a result we are both happy with. With the conversation pieces, it's very different. If collaboration is involved, if performance is involved, it's the interactive performance of everyday life. When I'm having a conversation with someone, it's the content of the conversation that's important to me—I simply want to "hear" what people are saying—and I'm not really thinking about the conversations as "art." I'll ask people if I can have the papers sometimes, and they get filed away—and later, often many years later, when I pull them out to work on a wall piece, maybe one out of fifty papers, one out of one hundred gets used. It's all just raw material at that point, and has to make an ontological shift between being a historical document and being something entirely different. Like any "found" object, the conversations bear the burden of their past, and it's not an easy thing to unmake and remake that past as a fiction.

Ian Berry: Who were your teachers, either literally, in the classroom, or by example? I am thinking mostly about art lessons here, but would also like to know about important life lessons.

Well, I never really took an art class in college—no studio art, no art history—though I did spend a lot of time reading and going to galleries. I think this was a natural part of my education, since I didn't have sign language interpreters in classes in college in the late 1970s—this was before interpreters were legally required—so I never knew what people were talking about in discussions. I studied English because I figured if I was going to read stuff, I might as well get some college credit for it. I was lucky my senior year when my thesis adviser, Johann Moser, realized I was wasting my time coming to classes—so he proposed to meet with me for an hour a week, and we'd talk about literature and literary theory—or rather I'd talk, and he'd type back to me on this old manual typewriter of his that only typed capital letters. Johann was a formalist, one of the New Critics, and we had great discussions about language as a material object. I also owe a lot to various people who I've never met, but whose work has marked me in certain ways—the poet Keats (especially in his letters), the composer Ned Rorem, Miles Davis, and Thurgood Marshall.

> Ian Berry: How does activism fit into your artwork? Do you see all your work as a form of activism? Or do you see your political ideas taking other forms?

This is a difficult question. In the past I was not fond of the word "activism" in relation to my art—it felt too specialized, too dogmatic. Yet the impulse to change the ways individuals relate to the world around them is important to me. Not as something that might be regarded as a necessary outcome, but rather as a constant possibility. Even when my work is especially formal, like the piece of the two overturned buckets, it tries to invoke the possibilities of human relations by posing questions about those relations. But sometimes I find that understatement and subtlety only go so far, and it takes another approach, another medium, and another audience to effect a certain change. This might be an op-ed in the newspaper, or even a lawsuit. Lawsuits are mediated by some of the same creative impulses that go into art—since you are trying to reframe the conventions by which the status quo of law and life are lived.

> Ian Berry: Do you think we (any "we" you want to imagine) should speak out more? Do artists have a special role or responsibility in this kind of cultural and political criticism?

No more than anyone else, I suppose—we all bear some responsibility for making the world a better place. Ezra Pound called poets "the antennae of the race," but if this suggested poets—artists more generally—are especially prescient, they're also as lacking in worldly care as the worst of us, and Pound was his own best example. I'm always intrigued at the significance of the accomplishments of people working diligently for decades at something quietly meaningful—only to learn about them later in an obituary in *The New York Times*. People like Kathleen Lukens, who started a summer camp for kids with developmental disabilities because none of the summer camps would accept her own kid; or Oseola McCarty, a washerwoman with a singularly benevolent disposition; or Robert McGill Thomas Jr., who wrote wonderful obituaries about others until his own obituary marked the end of his art. There are a lot of great things being done in the world by very humble people we'll probably never hear a word about—and in the best of all possible ways, they are artists too.

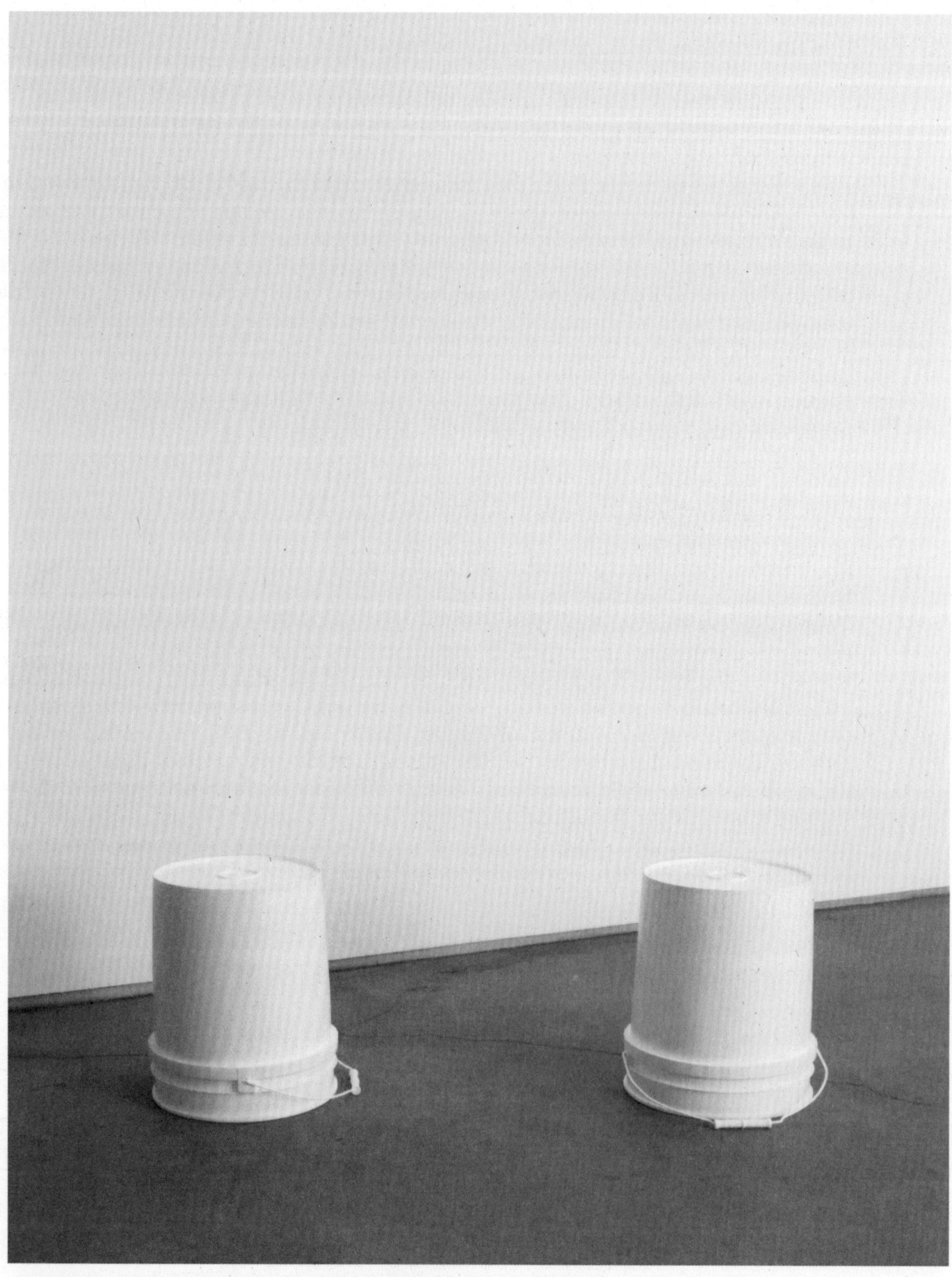

Joseph Grigely, *That's What We Live For*, 2006. White urethane

Email Exchange with John M. Hull, 2000

Originally published, in French, as "John Hull/Joseph Grigely," trans. Rémy Goavec, in *Voilà: le monde dans la tête: du 15 juin au 29 octobre 2000, Musée d'art moderne de la ville de Paris*, exh. cat., ed. Suzanne Pagé and Béatrice Parent (Paris-Musées, 2000), and issued as a supplement to *Les Inrockuptibles*.

April 14, 2000

Dear Joseph Grigely,

I recently received a telephone call from Paris. The caller was a woman with a charming French accent so entrancing that it aroused my fading visual memories of the female face and induced me to respond. How could I help it?

It was all about some exhibition which the gallery is putting on under the [working] title *Memory as Inventory, Archives, Enumeration, and as Personal Experience*. At first, I imagined that the delightful creature was going to invite me to the exhibition, and possibly take me out to dinner, but she refused to discuss her business indicating that she would send me an email.

This message has now arrived, and although she does not invite me to Paris to have a drink with me, she does invite me to conduct a conversation through email with you, with the idea of publishing it or part of it in their catalogue.

I am very happy to have a go at this, and she provided me with your address, telling me at the same time that she had contacted you, and that you would be expecting my own message.

I understand from Julia [Garimorth] that you are an artist who lost auditory sensation, and that we are to exchange views about our respective situations—myself with the visual only in memory, since I have no light sensation, and you with only memories of sound.

I look forward to your response, and to our conversation.

Yours sincerely,
John M. Hull

April 22

Dear John (if I may call you so)—

I was elated to get your message today. Thank you!

I should say at first that I had meant to write to you approximately ten years ago, when I first chanced upon your book *Touching the Rock*. It entranced me by virtue of its familiarity—which may seem an odd thing to say, given that I am not blind. Rather, I am deaf. I think the feeling of familiarity has a lot to do with the fact that we both became what we are—and how our lives, it seems to me, have thereon involved a constant state of becoming.

But having read your story, I know something about you; so let me tell you a little about myself.

I lost my hearing in one ear when I was one year old—a fever. And then, when I was ten, I was playing a game called King on the Mountain—boys play this often where I grew up in New England—and consequently I was pushed from the top of a small hill. Somewhere on the way down I tumbled against a small tree branch, and an even smaller twig on the branch found its way into my good ear.

That was thirty-two years ago.

My deafness is total: I can hear nothing at all. If someone is playing music on a stereo and the volume is turned as high as possible, my body will feel the vibrations—but my ears will not hear it. I suppose it is safe to say that I am as deaf as a doorknob—a cliché, of course, but a cliché that is real.

As the woman from Paris with the pleasant voice explained to you, I am an artist. Usually my art deals with communication in one form or another. Most people with whom I converse do not know sign language, and so to communicate I often ask them to write down what they are saying. Most people love this—they will write and write and write, and after a long conversation there might be dozens of pieces of paper scattered around us. Over the years I began saving those papers, building an archive—and on occasion I exhibit small groups of papers by tacking them up to the wall—they seem so insignificant and unimportant—sometimes utterly banal, as when someone might write down "bye" or "I have to go take a pee"—but such ordinary words, when written down, are special, though it is hard to explain just why.

Does this make sense at all?

When the exhibition organizers invited me to consider an interview with someone as part of my contribution to the catalogue, I immediately thought of you.

Not that it was simply an opportunity—but rather because I have long wanted to find someone with whom I could discuss the experience of losing a primary sense—and how our memory of that sense is inflected by the vicissitudes of time. I remember how you described puzzlement about the number 3 one day—did it face the right or the left?—and how complex these things actually are.

Oliver Sacks, when reviewing your book, spoke about this as a form of "cortical blindness"—and it made me wonder: Is there such a thing as cortical deafness?

I am, for example, aware of my own voice as I speak. Even though I have no auditory feedback—somehow there seems to be a kind of kinesthetic memory in my throat muscles and tongue—a memory that responds to messages from my brain. I can regulate loudness and intonation still—but I am never sure of the effect it might be having.

Perhaps because I am using language—which is really nothing more than a conventionalized code—that it is easy for me to remember and keep using. But what is it like to "remember" the visual field—something that is as expansive and broad as the world itself?

I must at this point apologize for writing in a visual medium—I'm assuming you have a text-to-voice synthesizer on your computer—which makes me wonder what my voice sounds like for you. If you'd like, I could call you on the telephone by using a teledevice for the deaf and a relay operator. By this means, you would hear me speak—and the relay operator would type down for me what you are saying. It is a little slow and cumbersome, but at some point perhaps it might be a worthwhile experiment for both of us.

Thank you again for your kind reply. I very much look forward to talking with you more.

With best wishes for a happy Easter,
Joseph

April 27

Dear Joseph,

I was delighted to have your letter of 22 April. It arrived, of course, in the middle of the Easter weekend, when the university where I work was closed. I could have come in, since I have my own key to the building, but what with a busy time with the family and so on, I did not come in until yesterday, [the] 26th. Then I found not only your original message of [the] 22nd but your second attempt of the 25th. Sorry you had to try a second time.

I was moved to read about the way you lost your hearing. On the one hand, it almost seems as if that tiny twig sought out your good ear, as if it knew. On the other hand, I suppose there must have been thousands of boys playing King of the Castle who also rolled down the hill and the twig seemed to avoid their eyes and ears. We personify nature in an attempt to discover intelligible purpose, even if malevolent.

Well, let me go on to the specific points you raise.

First, you ask about cortical blindness and if there is a corresponding cortical deafness. I do not think that these are the correct terms, at any rate to describe my own experience. I think that cortical blindness takes place when damage occurs to that part of the brain which is concerned with visual stimuli whilst the eye itself remains intact. Thus the loss of sight is cortical rather than optical. The thing I experienced was optical blindness which however I realized in two stages. First, there was the fading of the light sensation, something which took place very slowly, over several years. However, even when all light was gone, I was not a blind person but a sighted person who had become unable to see. In other words, I continued to think of the world as a sighted place and to feel excluded from it. Loss of sight had closed a world. Gradually as the memory of the sighted world began to fade, I began to live in a world which was beyond light and darkness. I no longer wondered about what the world looked like. I wondered at the beauty of the sound of the wind in the trees. It is that experience of deep blindness, of being a person dwelling within a lightless world, which Oliver Sacks described as being cortical. The condition is, however, a matter of psychology not neurology. I cannot imagine if there is a corresponding experience in the case of loss of hearing. It would take place, I suppose, when the memory of sound faded and one no longer wondered about sounds. Only the slightest vibrations remind one of a world of sound. One constructs a different world, one of colour, shadow, brightness, expressions on faces, smiles and so on. You pass into a distinct human world.

This is the curious thing we have in common: To me, your world is but a memory. To you, my world is but a memory. We can, perhaps, only compare notes through memorial construction. But you were much younger when you lost your hearing. You were a boy of twelve; I already a man in middle life. So the slab of memory upon which you draw must be narrower than it is with me. Next, you ask what this experience of losing the visual world is like. You describe this visual world as being as expansive and broad as the world itself.

It is true that the world of the aural and tactile life is lacking in width. For me, there is no horizon, no sky, nothing to mark the place where the earth ends and the heavens begin, no stars to form a ceiling above me, no outspread roads and fields to form a surface in front of me. This is why I love high places, like being on the top of a tall building, or standing on a hilltop—the sounds are now spread out before me and again there is an expansive world—there is the distant sound of the motorway, over there a train passes into the distance, below me the birds sing in the treetops.

Then you ask me about communicating in a visual medium. But this is not so! Behind my keyboard there are two small speakers from which a synthetic voice comes, saying your words but not of course using your voice. So I have the power to restore your speech patterns, except you do not cough or breathe, and although you show surprise, you have no great range of emotion in your voice, which is actually the electronic voice of the computer. My computer is programmed to suppress the visuals. So when a picture appears on the nearby screen, which means nothing to me, the speaker says "Graphic." If, by accident, an erotic location should appear, as they say, on the screen, my speaker says "graphic! graphic! graphic!" and I make it shut up by touching the control key. But what was there? What was the image? This is when memory comes for a moment surging back.

Now, you ask if we should have a telephone call. I do not know what to think about this. Perhaps later.

My message has posed some questions for you. Do you recall the world of sound? What is music to you? Do you lipread, and thus access the human mind? Is your world wide but flat, like looking at a screen?

Do not your thoughts become troublesome when there is no sustaining blanket of sound to absorb your inner words? Joseph, already I feel as if I might know you but there are so many questions to ask.

I wait for your reply.

Yours sincerely,
John

April 28

Dear John,

Thanks so much for your long and thoughtful letter.

One thing you said struck me in a strange and compelling way, and I cannot get it out of my head. It has to do with how old we both were when our [senses] failed us. I was actually ten when I became deaf. You were what?—in your late thirties? Your early forties? Ten is actually a nice age to become deaf. By then I had learned some basics about the sounds of the world—the sounds of voices, of music, of television commercials—the sounds of sputtering lawn mowers, of barking dogs—very ordinary stuff—but I had not constructed a life that depended on these sounds. I was as free to forget them as easily as I had learnt them.

It is true that the slab of memory upon which I must draw is very thin—so thin that it evaporates into the air at times. I do not worry about this as much as many people think—instead, I construct for myself a memory that is by necessity a fiction—a memory where all the sounds sound wrong, where all the pronunciations are mispronounced—but I am comfortable here, and somehow everything sounds just right—eloquent even—though it may all be wrong.

I have always considered this a certain right, a certain privilege—and also, in an unusual way, a certain pleasure.

I presume I still remember the sound of my mother's voice—which somehow remains intact in the presence of her moving lips when she speaks to me. But it is somehow harder to remember the voice of my father, who died in an accident two years ago. Perhaps I remember nothing at all. A few days ago it struck me—with a sudden surprise—that I have forgotten the sound of my own voice. I remember when you had written in your book *Touching the Rock* how startling it was to confront the horror of being faceless and forgetting your appearance—and now I sit here, unaware of the voice with which I talk to others every day. If I put my hand on my throat I can feel a certain low tone entirely lacking in eloquence whatsoever, as if I was some kind of animate log that knew how to utter fundamental human speech.

You ask about lipreading—alas, it is an art about which I know nothing. Had I a little hearing, perhaps, I might become sufficiently adept to lipread more than a few well-placed phrases. But being as deaf as I am, lipreading has never worked for me. I have often thought it is really a myth, and not real. A sort of linguistic prestidigitation. Not sleight of hand, but sleight of eye. The problem is that language is full of homophones—words that sound alike—as well as a visual equivalent for which I know of no proper word—words that look alike on the lips. Should someone say "vacuum" to me, it looks like they are saying "fuck you." I have had many embarrassing misunderstandings thanks to the pleasures of lipreading. Whoever coined the word lipreading got it wrong—it should be called lipmisreading.

For about twenty years this is what I did—or rather tried to do. But at a certain point in my life I wanted to know what people were really saying—and at this point I made it a habit to ask people to write things down for me. I would apologize at first and say: "I'm sorry, I'm deaf—would you please write that down." The apology seems a little odd in retrospect. Why should I apologize for being deaf? But I realize now that the apology is for the inconvenience I am causing people—it is like saying to someone "I'm sorry" when you might wish to have a phrase or a word repeated.

For some reason, I still say "I'm sorry, I'm deaf"—but someday I will break this habit. I must find another way of saying this.

John, do you remember the part in Mary Shelley's novel *Frankenstein* when the Monster ventures inside the house and meets the blind man, De Lacey? I have often thought about that passage, and I would like to ask you if it holds any special importance to you?

With best wishes,
Joseph

April 28

Dear Joseph,

I read your message received Friday [the] 28th several times. Of course, as you know, I read with my ears. I call it aural reading. There is also tactile reading and visual reading. First, about our respective ages. I was aged forty-five when I finally registered as a blind person and forty-eight when I turned the final corner away from the light. I have just had my sixty-fifth birthday. So I was sighted for twice as long as I have been unsighted. Thus the memory slab is huge although sometimes I feel that I have been blind for eternity. I am thinking about your lipreading comment. As you say, it is a bit of a myth and perhaps facial speech might be a better name. I find, for example, that I do not hear people as well as I did when there was facial speech as well as aural speech. Without body language and facial expression, you have to read everything into the sounds. You spoke about reconstructing sound memories. About visual memories, I will make a few remarks for comparison with you.

First, there is a huge difference between someone born blind and someone blinded later. My body carries the visual image of a three-dimensional world, set out in space, in which I move. That is a big advantage to me, and I think that more or less unconsciously I must be depending upon that visual structure a lot. For example, at the railway station, when I am waiting on the platform, I have an image of the line of the platform, the tracks and then the rows of further platforms, and once my cane touches the edge of the platform I am on, I can imagine the layout. Of course, I could be wrong—the platform might curve and I would not know. Nevertheless, the memory helps me to feel less disorientated. When the whole place shakes with the sound of the engine rushing in, I know that provided I am well back from that vital edge, it cannot come where I am, but trucks can go up on the footpath!

A second kind of memory is the kind that comes suddenly back and jabs me with pain. When I hear them at the football match shouting "Well tackled, Joshua!" and I know they are referring to my eleven-year-old son, a picture of him in action floods into my mind and for a moment I feel terribly blind.

Generally, however, I look upon memory as little more than a nostalgic dream upon which I have turned my back so as to live in the concrete world of my present life. The memories disturb me sometimes, like a forgotten music or a fragrance from a dimly suggested past. Then I shrug them off and confront the tactile and acoustic world, which is the real world and not a bit of tempting irrelevance.

I look forward to your next.

John

May 2

Dear John,

I'm very sorry to have lapsed in my communication—not my desire but rather a situation of circumstances—which might otherwise be described as unexpected surprises occurring just as I was preparing for an exhibition in San Francisco. I am on an airplane now, so please pardon my brevity—as I am on an airplane that is a miracle of spatial arrangements—there is absolutely no redundant space whatsoever—so as I type on my computer I am jabbing my elbows into the gentlemen seated to my left and my right—very much a situation that might be characterized by the eloquent expression: Oh, dear.

I'll write again soon.

With apologies,
Joseph

May 2

Dear Joseph,

I now see more clearly the advantages of profound loss of hearing. As you jab your elbow into the arm or side of the person beside you, you are unmoved by his little grunts of protest. On the other hand, you have no warning of the moment when he jumps up and hits you with his briefcase.

In the message before this one, you asked me about a passage from the book by Mary Shelley. I have to confess that I have not read this famous book. Maybe the point is that a blind person might fear attack from a strange madman. If this is the point, then I readily confide in you that I do have this recurrent absurd fear.

I hope your exhibition is a great success.

Yours,
John

Letters, Statements, Proposals, Incidents

Part 1, Art

Some of the most important work I have done relates to the process of conceiving, proposing, and negotiating a particular project, or the conditions for presenting a project. This is what makes archives so important: They document how projects come into being and have a bearing on how we might read the work that ultimately gets made and shown. I have written about this topic as it relates to other artists in *Textualterity: Art, Theory, and Textual Criticism* (1995). However, I was probably less fastidious than I should have been in terms of keeping documentation of my own work over the years. In various project files I retained copies of some letters and faxes, but email records up to 1999 are sparse: Almost all my email between 1984 and 2002 has been lost. Had I realized the dilemma posed by competing digital platforms, and the difficulty of archiving email, I would have been more diligent about preserving digital files as printed records.

I have broken down this chapter into two parts—part 1, which addresses issues of art, and part 2, which addresses issues of access.

What follows in part 1 deals with art projects and proposals in which art and disability intermingle. Much of my conceptual work from the early 1990s was not realized simply because there was no mainstream institutional infrastructure to recognize disability as culturally relevant. I would often imagine and design a project for some future installation, well aware that the description of my intentions and plans might be as far as it would go. In other cases, my proposals tested the limits of institutional flexibility, and were realized in limited ways.

Course Description for SWOPSI 193: Deaf Studies, 1987

Précis for a Lecture on ASL Poetry, 1988

My academic background is in literature, and after receiving a DPhil from the University of Oxford in 1984, I taught English at Gallaudet College (now Gallaudet University) for two years before taking up a Mellon Postdoctoral Fellowship at Stanford. At Stanford, my academic foothold was in English Romantic poetry, primarily Keats, but I was also attracted to ASL poetry and linguistics. In 1981 I gave a lecture on ASL as a medium for poetry at the Second International Symposium on Sign Language Research, and three lectures I gave at the MLA convention between 1986 and 1988 were all on ASL. In 1987 I taught an experimental course on Deaf Studies at Stanford, which was offered through the Stanford Workshops on Political and Social Issues (SWOPSI). This was a time when ASL literature and culture were just emerging, and no one really knew how to define the field—we were all learning by talking and writing and sharing ideas. Because ASL was considered a marginalized language, one of my goals was to validate the place of ASL literature in cultural studies—and, by extension, facilitate access to interpreting as part of my academic life.

SWOPSI 193
Deaf Studies
Spring 1987

Joseph Grigely

Office located in Bldg 40, room 42P
Hours: Tuesday 10am-12noon
Wednesday 3:30-4:30pm
& by appointment
Office tel. 723-2635 voice/TDD

Ethnicity, American Sign Language, and the Deaf

"It is language more than anything else that reveals and validates one's existence, and if the language we really speak is denied us, then it is inevitable that the form we are permitted to assume historically will be one of caricature, reflecting someone else's literary and social fantasy."

--Alice Walker

How might the Deaf be identified as an ethnic minority, or even as a "race"? In a recent issue of Critical Inquiry devoted to "'Race', Writing, and Difference", Henry Louis Gates commented that "Race is the ultimate trope of difference because it is so very arbitrary in its application"--a trope precisely because "race" is arguably a biological misnomer, a metaphor for otherness and difference. What Gates and his colleagues Houston Baker Jr. and Alice Walker attempt to affirm is that "race" is a language-bound phenomenon: its manifestation is most readily identified within discourse itself, within the larger framework of language and sociolects.

Our approach to the Deaf as an ethnic and racial culture will thus be based on the socio-linguistic milieu of ASL speakers. We will not, therefore, examine deafness in its pathological/rehabilitative context; our concern is primarily with the Deaf as a diaspora. Selected topics of discussion will include the socio-linguistic history of ASL; the semiotics of culture and cultural enclavements; the politics of mainstreaming and the Deaf Institute; and ASL "literature". Our collective goal will be to derive from these discussions a better understanding of who exactly the Deaf are, and how their cultural structure correlates with ethnic and racial cultural ideology.

Ontological Issues in ASL Poetry

To what extent is American Sign Language poetry poetry? To what extent is it art? Questions like these are, from the philosophical point of view, immensely difficult because the ontological nature of our inquiry (is it poetry? is it art?) assumes that poetry and art are identifiable norms even before the question of linguistic form is called into play. Both Joseph Margolis and Arthur Danto have suggested that a work of art (and for my purposes here, a work of literature) is 'a culturally emergent entity', so that its identity as art is not bound to its semiotic fact (i.e. its material reality as, perhaps, a painting, a brillo box, or a formally-structured linguistic utterance), but its perceptual context. That is to say, as Wendy Steiner similarly claims in The Colors of Rhetoric, 'no theory can explain art by adverting to its materiality, and no art can be art by virtue of its materiality'.

The 'materiality' of ASL poetry--even in its manifestation as an evanescent oral literature--does not, I would like to suggest, give us a rationale for the term 'poetry'. The linguistic and paralinguistic properties that might be used to distinguish Sam Supalla's 'story' Eyeth from Clayton Valli's 'poem' Snowflake do not in themselves create a taxonomy for poetic ontology any more than the differences between, say, Pope and Stevens, or--to be critically adventurous--Charles Bukowski and Joyce Kilmer. Even a discourse-based taxonomy favoured by Tzvestan Todorov (amongst others) is historically questioned by the phonemic play in the verse ohne worte of Hugo Ball and the Zurich Dadaists, as well as in contemporary sound poetry. Given such considerations, my argument is that a linguistically-based framework cannot guide us to a rationale for terms like "ASL poetry" or "Art Sign". We must instead look elsewhere.

But where exactly? ASL poetry--and stories--exist largely because there is a will for them to exist, and the use of the labels "ASL poetry" and "Art Sign" perhaps says less about ontology than the deliberate attempt to give an established identity to an emergent cultural expression. Such usage 'locates', or otherwise places a cultural construct within the nexus of comparative cultural experience--a fact which also explains my own use of the term "ASL poetry". As literary traditions go, that of ASL poetry is frightfully young. This alone delimits our theoretical possibilities and our attempts to deconstruct an ontological paradigm. Perhaps, then, at this stage the very process of 'emergence' might be used to examine typologies for incipient literatures, and--since ASL poetry is an oral literature--the process of textual transmission in oral traditions might also be examined for typological comparisions.

Documentexts, 1991–93

By the early 1990s, I had become disenchanted with teaching literature, in part because the academic world at that time had numerous barriers to access, especially at conferences. The art world at this time was not much better. However, I saw in the art world the possibility of constructing new narrative forms that addressed some evolving issues as they related to disability and access. I was not worried about convincing people of a particular critical vision; I was more concerned with simply creating that vision, giving it shape and form, and, when possible, inserting it into existing disciplinary structures as an intervention. A few examples of such projects are described below. I called them *Documentexts* as a way of describing their content: textual documentation of certain states of being, or certain activities, that were meant to disrupt normative activities—or bring attention to the disruption taking place. They were intended for dissemination as art, or as publication interventions, or both.

The Incarnation of Alterity, 1991

Previously unexhibited.

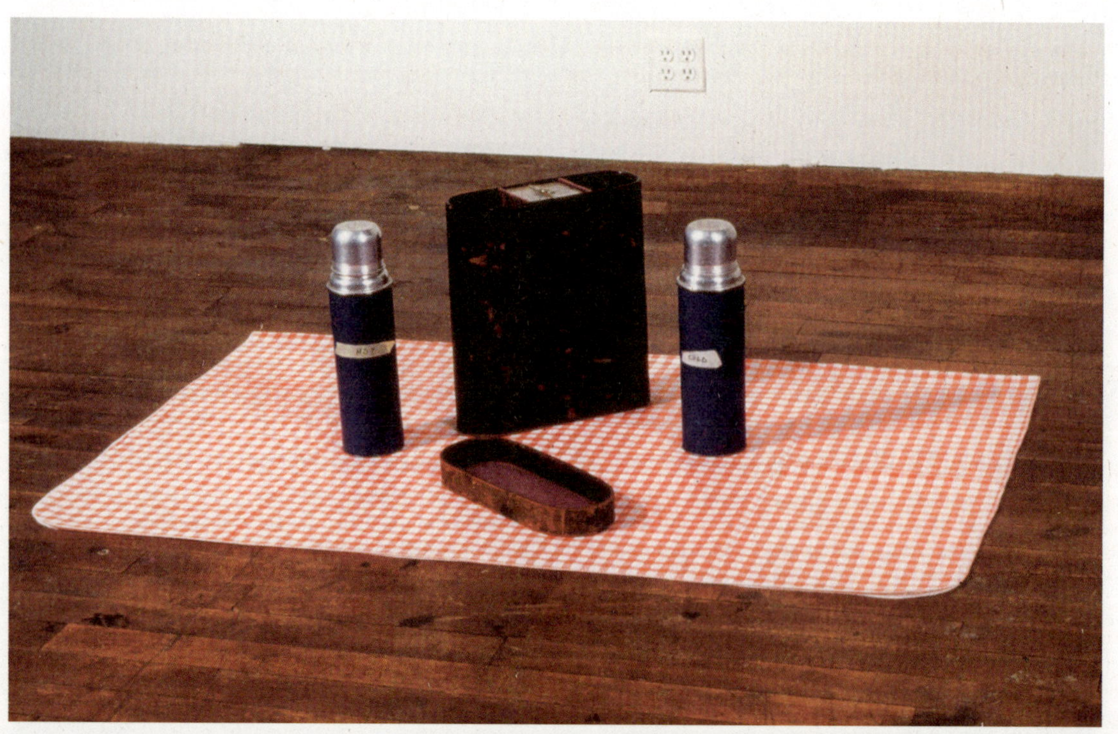

Portraits of the Artist as a Deaf Man, 1967, 1991

Exhibited in *Joseph Grigely: In What Way Wham? (White Noise and Other Works, 1996–2023)*, Massachusetts Museum of Contemporary Art, May 28, 2023–June 30, 2024.

One complicated thing about deafness is the fact you can't see it or measure it, except by way of audiometric assessment. In Sir Joshua Reynolds's famous *Self-Portrait as a Deaf Man*, painted in 1775, one of his hands is cupped behind his ear. It's a simple gesture, and an effective one in terms of making visible something otherwise invisible.

Even when I was teaching at Gallaudet, some of my colleagues wondered if Joseph Grigely was really deaf, or if I was deaf, just how deaf was I? The assumption was if I could speak, I must have some residual hearing. The rumors and prejudice became so troubling I had to put on my office door a copy of my audiogram—several of them in fact—so that they became, as it were, a portrait of who I was. The audiograms showed a scale of hearing, with *X*'s along the bottom of the chart, with arrows indicating my hearing is outside the measurable threshold of 100 decibels. As one audiologist wrote, my deafness was "probably total." I always took pride in that, though I'm not sure why.

OTOLARYNGOLOGY

PRIVATE OFFICES

MASSACHUSETTS EYE AND EAR INFIRMARY

Referred By Sheldon Goldberg, M.D.
120 Maple Street
Springfield, Mass.

DATE July 17, 1967

RATE

NAME Joseph Grigely

ADDRESS 32 Melwood Avenue
East Longmeadow, Massachusetts

TEL. NO.
BUS. HOME 525-2725

HISTORY: Age: 10 Occupation: Father-Joseph Sr.-Mason

1. Rt. hearing loss since early childhood — cause unknown.
2. June 9, 1967 fell on stick, which went into l. ear. No bleeding. Immed. nauseated + unsteady.
3. Hearing diminished during subseq. Could hear 2 wks but progress

M.D.

SUMMARY, DIAGNOSIS AND TREATMENT:

more loss. Now —
4. Complete hearing loss.
5. Regained his balance.

Audiometry reveals profound hearing loss — So advised patient and parents.

[signature] M.D.

Page 1

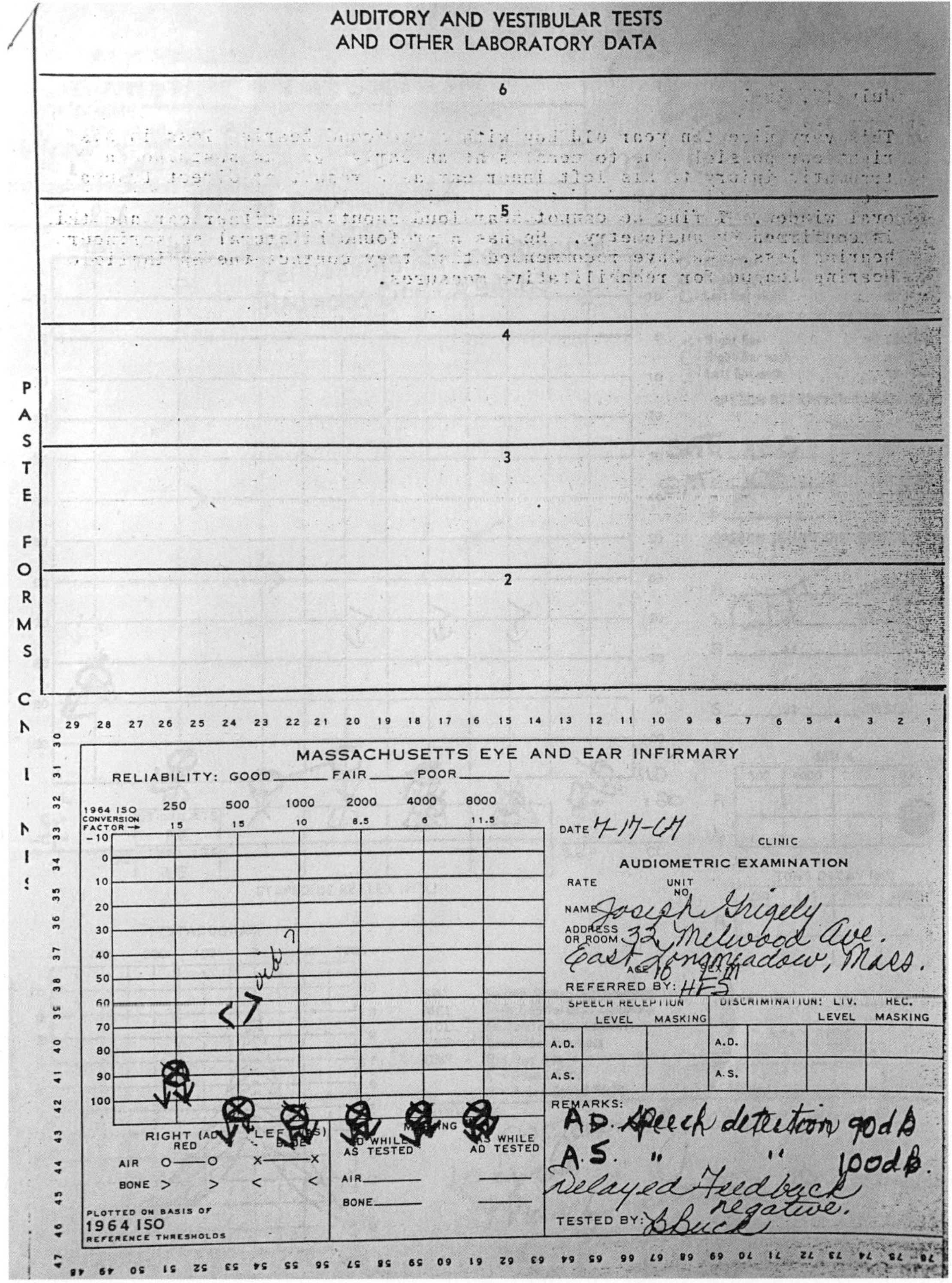

AUDITORY AND VESTIBULAR TESTS
AND OTHER LABORATORY DATA

6

5

4

3

2

PASTE FORMS

MASSACHUSETTS EYE AND EAR INFIRMARY

RELIABILITY: GOOD____ FAIR____ POOR____

1964 ISO CONVERSION FACTOR →	250	500	1000	2000	4000	8000
	15	15	10	8.5	6	11.5

-10, 0, 10, 20, 30, 40, 50, 60, 70, 80, 90, 100

RIGHT (AD) RED — LEFT (AS) BLUE

AIR O—O X—X

BONE > > < <

AD WHILE AS TESTED — MASKING — AS WHILE AD TESTED

AIR____ ____

BONE____ ____

PLOTTED ON BASIS OF
1964 ISO
REFERENCE THRESHOLDS

DATE 7-17-67

CLINIC

AUDIOMETRIC EXAMINATION

RATE UNIT NO.

NAME Joseph Grigely

ADDRESS OR ROOM 32 Melwood Ave. East Longmeadow, Mass.

AGE 10 SEX M

REFERRED BY: HFS

SPEECH RECEPTION	LEVEL	MASKING	DISCRIMINATION: LIV.	LEVEL	REC. MASKING
A.D.			A.D.		
A.S.			A.S.		

REMARKS: A.D. Speech detection 90dB
A.S. " " 100dB.
Delayed Feedback negative.

TESTED BY: B Buck

Doodling, 1991–93

Previously unexhibited.

After the Americans with Disabilities Act was passed in 1990, states were required to implement telephone relay systems. It was an important step in making the phone system, and communications more generally, accessible to those with hearing and speech impairments. But there was another kind of access the process opened up: access to the self. The psychological self. The relay system has a protocol called "voice carryover," where the relay operator types for me what other people say, and I can speak directly to the person I'm having the call with. The first few times I did this, not really paying attention to the process, I found myself doodling. As I talked on the phone, I'd write down the relay operator's number—then unselfconsciously go about doodling. I had not done this since I became deaf thirty-five years earlier, and the relay had, as an unintended consequence, enabled the process. It was a form of gesturing, except the gestures were inscriptions—so ordinary and unexceptional, which is exactly what made them so unusual. I was probably less excited about the fact that the relay enabled me to talk with hearing people than it enabled me to doodle while I talked.

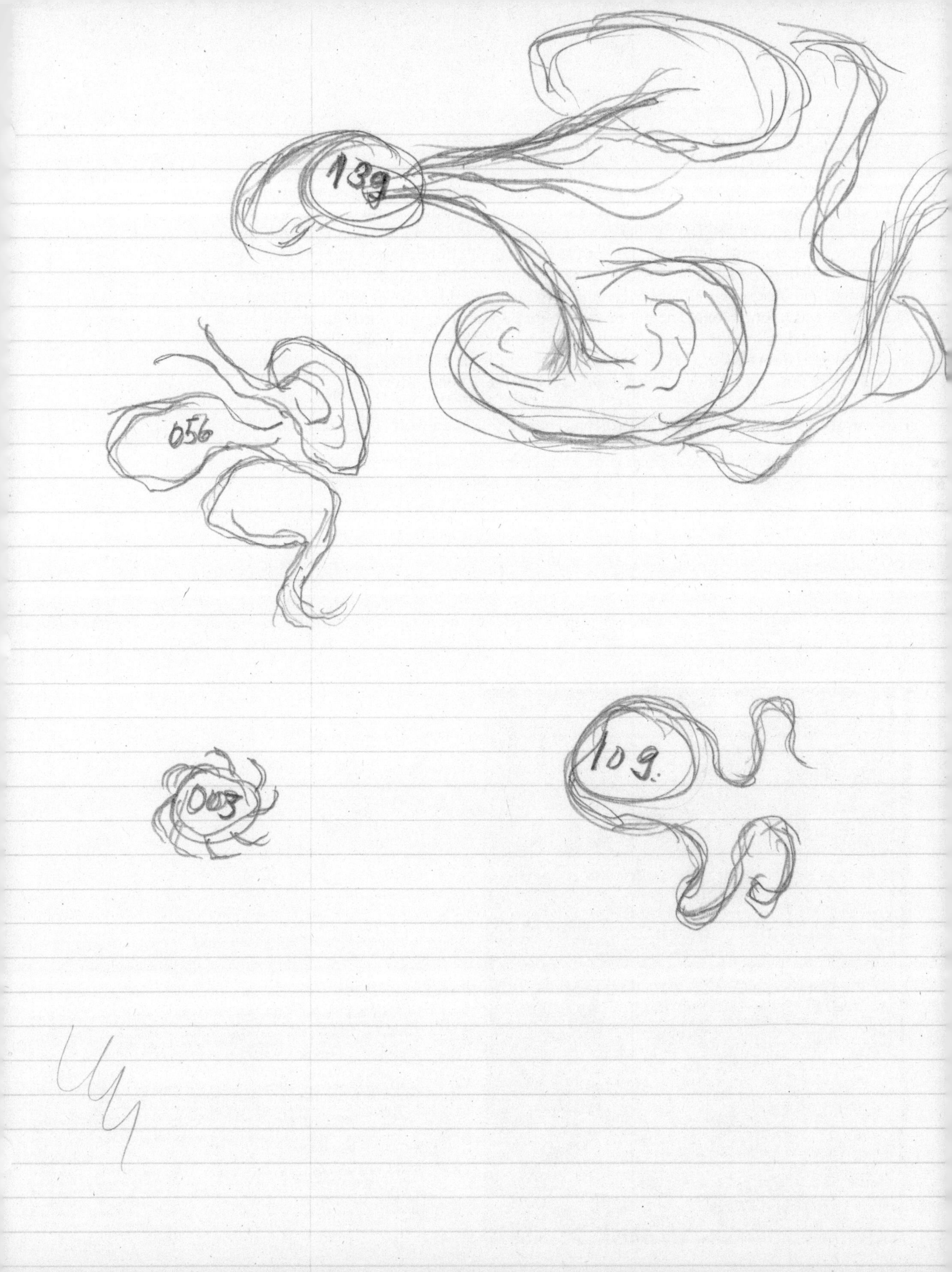
139
056
003
109.

The Reconfigured Self, 1992–93

In 1992 I was invited to be listed in *Who's Who in the East*, a publication devoted to biographical histories of individuals. The publisher sent a standardized form requesting details about my education, achievements, and work. Under the heading of "Publications and Creative Work" I intentionally omitted all of my formal academic publications and cited only one creative work, titled *The Reconfigured Self*. It is dated 1967, the year I fell down a hill and became deaf. The reason was a simple one: The life of a disabled person is an inherently creative act, and for some of us the most important thing we will ever make. *Who's Who* printed my entry exactly as submitted; it didn't occur to their fact-checkers that someone born in 1956 would have been unlikely to author a work titled *The Reconfigured Self* ten years later.

This was the first of my intervention projects. There would be several others later in the 1990s.

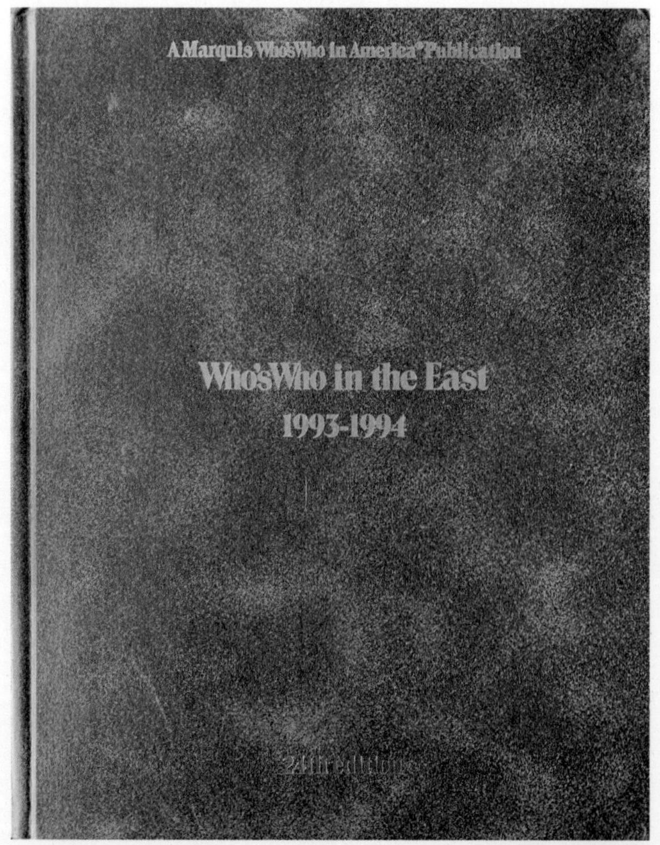

1990-91, East Penn Sch. Dist., 1991—. Vol. ARC, 1985, Am. Cancer Soc., 1986—. Fellow NEA, Pa. State Edn. Assn., Berks County Intermediate Unit Edn. Assn., Kutztown Area Tchrs. Assn., East Penn Area Tchrs. Assn. Republican. Roman Catholic. Home: 332 Welby Dr Schnecksville PA 18078-9500 Office: East Pa Sch Dist 640 Macungie Ave Emmaus PA 18049-2130

GRIGELY, JOSEPH CONSTANTINE, JR., English language educator; b. Springfield, Mass., Dec. 16, 1956; s. Joseph Constantine and Anne Mary (Arlotta) G. AB, St. Anselm's Coll., 1978; DPhil, Oxford U., 1984. Assoc. prof. English Gallaudet U., Washington, 1983—; Mellon postdoctoral fellow in English Stanford (Calif.) U., 1985-87. Author: The Reconfigured Self, 1967. Mem. MLA. Office: Gallaudet U Dept of English 800 Florida Ave NE Washington DC 20002-3660

GRIGGS, SHIRLEY ANN, educator, consultant; b. Detroit, Sept. 15, 1931; d. Cecil W. and Ann (Wynand) G. AB, U. Mich., 1953; MA, Northwestern U., 1956; EdD, Columbia U., 1967. Tchr. South Lake Jr. High Sch., St. Clair Shores, Mich., 1953-55; counselor, asst. prin. Pershing and Eastern High Schs., Detroit, 1956-69; prof. St. John's U., N.Y.C., 1969—; study dir. Human Affairs Rsch. Ctr., N.Y.C., 1970-75; cons. Urban Affairs Ctr., N.Y.C., 1975-78; cons.-evaluator N.Y.C. Pub. Schs., 1975—. Author:

contbr. arti
1956-59. M
Hosp. Phar
Mem. Unit
PA 18901-1

GRIMES,
s. Darrell
July 25, 19
Lee Baldwi
gren, Darir
MA in Bio
assoc. prof
Park, 198
Durham, 1
Jackson es
Washingto
Coordinati
in field.
editor Estu
Microbiolo
(charter, tr

Unrealized Turtles, 1967, 1993, 1997

Originally published in *Unbuilt Roads: 107 Unrealized Projects*, ed. Hans Ulrich Obrist and Guy Tortosa (Hatje Cantz Verlag, 1997).

After I became deaf in 1967, I continued in my regular public school program. There were no provisions for interpreters at that time. I was even expected to take music classes and sing along with everyone in a chorus. It didn't work out very well. I sat beside a classmate and tried to follow his finger as it moved from word to word along each line, but I was either ahead of everyone or behind everyone, and it made a real mess of things for everyone.

Eventually, my teachers let me take an art class instead of music. I liked drawing turtles, and I drew a lot of them, but my teacher wasn't as fond of them as me. One day she said to me, "NO MORE TURTLES!" That was the last time I ever took an art class. After another discussion with my teachers, instead of music and instead of art, they let me go to the library. This was the beginning of my relationship with books and literature.

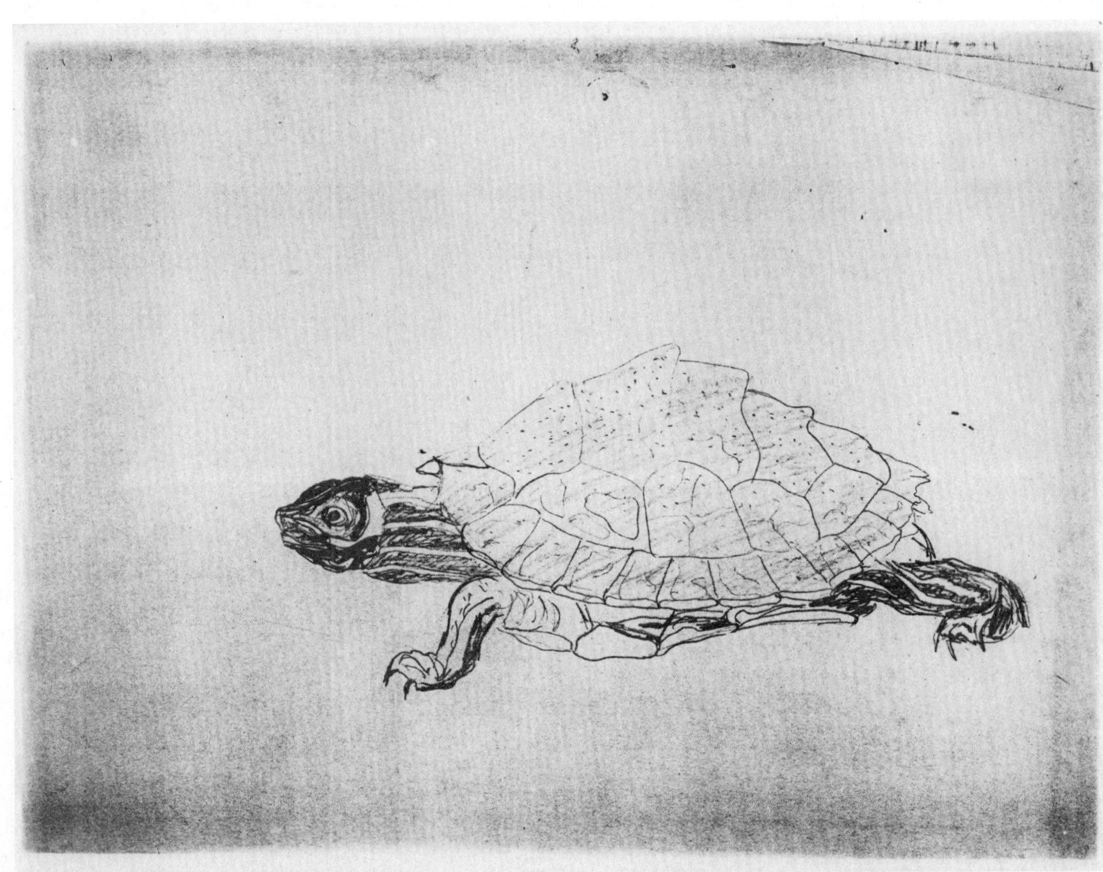

Overhearing, 1991–97

Previously unexhibited.

One of the myths about access is the idea that it only applies to specific situations involving heightened cultural and educational value—like a formal lecture, but not the time before the lecture when people are chatting, or the time after the lecture when everyone is hanging out in a bar. For years I have also been interested in the idea of overhearing: how much of the information economy, as I call it, comes from passive listening to conversations taking place around us.

Generally speaking, if you want an interpreter for the purpose of overhearing conversations in a public or professional setting, there is no way to arrange this unless you are willing to pay for the interpreter yourself. In the early 1990s, I made a grant application with a philanthropic foundation for the cost of a sign language interpreter for one year. The goal was to have an interpreter accompany me through my daily routine—to give me access to the sonic landscape through which I walked and worked. My focus was on ordinariness, and to access an unexceptional and shamelessly ordinary state of everyday life.

My grant request was not funded.

Some years later, I revisited the idea and tried to approach the situation in a different way, by making cassette recordings of walks, events, and incidental encounters. I accumulated dozens of hours of recorded data. But only after doing this for several months did I realize the basic problem of the recordings: They lacked the immediacy of being able to respond to a situation in real time, which was the main point of having an interpreter. The cassettes now have a different kind of meaning: part archive, part unrequited longing.

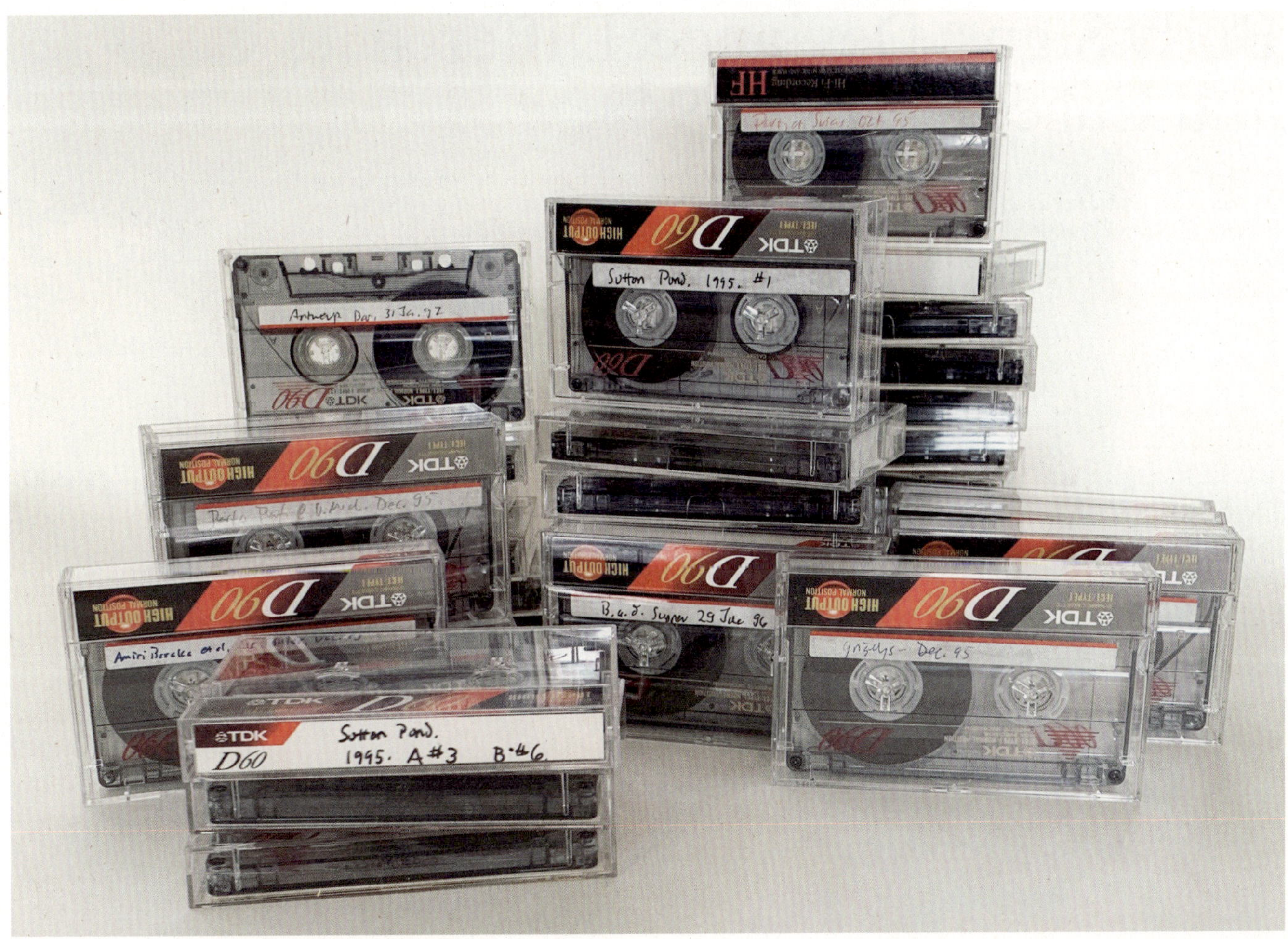
TDK
D60
HIGH OUTPUT
Sutton Pond. 1995. #1
D90
TDK
D60
Sutton Pond.
1995. A#3 B-#6
Grigelys - Dec. 95

Body Signs: Deviance, Difference, and Eugenics, 1993–94

Presented as *Body Signs: Deviance, Difference, and Eugenics*, Washington Project for the Arts, Washington, DC, December 11, 1993–January 29, 1994. A catalogue was also published on the occasion of the exhibition; see Nick Mirzoeff, Ira Livingston, and Joseph Grigely, *Body Signs: Deviance, Difference, and Eugenics* (Washington Project for the Arts, 1993).

Body Signs: Deviance, Difference, and Eugenics, held at the Washington Project for the Arts in 1993–94, was my first solo exhibition. It was organized in the space of a few months and focused on a diverse body of work related to disability—dispersion paintings, sculptures, and an installation/performance. The goal of the installation was to destabilize the idea of the perfect body, or the perfect installation, and imagine them instead as imperfect, fluid, and changing. After the exhibition, the focus of my work shifted to *Conversations with the Hearing*; the dispersion paintings were placed in storage, and the sculptures destroyed. The paintings have not been exhibited since then.

Joseph Grigely
WPA Proposal

Body Signs: Deviance, Difference, and Eugenics

Body Signs: Deviance, Difference, and Eugenics is a multi-media exhibition that simultaneously explores the body as a site of visible and invisible difference, and the implied history of social and scientific efforts to control and contain this difference. Drawing on recent critical theory while also responding to this theory, the subjects of Body Signs include deafness, stigma, social discourse, and twentieth-century eugenic theory.

Eugenics and Difference: A Brief History

The word 'eugenics' (whose Greek root denotes 'good genes') was coined in the late nineteenth century by Francis Galton to describe an evolving science of genetics, whereby the human race might be 'improved' through selective gene management--what Galton called "the cultivation of race:"

> We want a brief word to express the science of improving stock, which is by no means confined to the questions of judicious mating, but which, especially in the case of man, takes cognisance of all influences that tend in however remote a degree to give the more suitable races of strains of blood a chance of prevailing speedily over the less suitable than they otherwise would have had. The word eugenics would sufficiently express the idea; it is at least a neater word and a more generalised one than viriculture, which I once ventured to use.
> (Inquiries into Human Faculty, 1883, p.25n.)

For Galton and his followers (which included, among others, Alexander Graham Bell, Charles Davenport, and Charles William Eliot), certain conditions of difference (categorized by eugenicists to include what they called 'feeblemindedness,' inherited blindness, deafness, and nationalized races) were said to stymie human progress and create a permanently expanding underclass. The fear of a 'dysgenic' society consisting of social and physical deviants was subsequently manifest in a number of treatises, reports, and public lectures. Alexander Graham Bell's Memoir Upon the Formation of a Deaf Variety of the Human Race, published in 1885 under auspices of the National Academy of Sciences, claimed that deaf schools brought together deaf pupils who would, as a consquence, intermarry, and thus foster an alarming spead of deafness through the social fabric. In order to purify society and purge itself of impending disorder, Bell argued, it would be necessary to implement a program of social eugenics consisting of voluntary or imposed segregation (or, as others would later argue, sterilization). By the mid-1930s over 20,000 sterilizations of 'deviants' had been performed in the U.S. (the number would rise to 36,000 by 1941), and Hitler's National Socialist Party, formulating its own eugenics policies, acknowledged a great debt that it owed to the precedence of American eugenics programs (Daniel Kevles, In the Name of Eugenics, 1985, pp. 113-8). While some Americans did in fact complain that the eugenics movement was going too far, some however lamented that it did not go far enough: Dr. Joseph DeJarnette, a proponent of sterilization in Virginia in the 1920s and 1930s, publically remarked in 1934: "The Germans are beating us at our own game" (Kevles, 116).

Xenophobia and the Fear of Difference

Created out of a mixture of post-romantic utopian idealism and images of scientific rationalism, eugenic ideology reconceived the possibilities of Mary Shelley's great novel by suggesting that the Victor Frankensteins of the future would not work with actual physical morphology, but with the genotypes that blueprint this morphology. Our culture is a culture fascinated by, even to the extent that this fascination is a fetish, with possible impossibilities and impossible possibilities: with the monstropomorphic. A recent issue of Weekly World News, a deservedly vaunted example of mass-cultural kitsch available in supermarket checkout lanes, features on its front cover photographs of a horse born with a human head, and--purporting to prove that the visage is a genetic inheritance--a photograph of the child-horse's father is included, their distinctly anthropomorphic features conflated with their equine torsos. The mother, also pictured, connotes the troubling thought that she is simply a horse--that is, merely 'normal.' Bringing the circus out of the circus, 'horse-boy' is a glimpse of a pervasive mass cultural side-show. 'Frog-boy,' which pairs an amphibian with a mammal, and 'bat-boy,' which pairs pre- and post-historical mammals, offer even more intriguing examples of recombinant DNA experiments that can also be read as highly successful applications of recent photo-editing software. Aggrandized like this, gross physiological difference is simultaneously used to evoke pity and fear, thereby doing what circus freak shows and books on monsterism have always sought to do.

Eugenicists do not, of course, use 'horse-boy' as an example of the horrors of genetic mutation and dysgenic lineage. They stress instead conditions like polydactylism (too many fingers), brachydactylism (stub fungers), or diseases like otosclerosis and Huntington's cholera, or even blindness and deafness. Examples like these show that it was not just a fear of the proliferation of difference that disconcerted eugenicists, but difference itself. As a result, 'deviance' acquired pejorative value to designate a social or physical state of abnormality. Those targeted included not just people with physical anomalies, but also those considered socially deviant: alcoholics, homosexuals, even people described as having criminal propensities, and the chronically unemployed: 'pauperism.' Behind the façade of social 'progress' eugenics was actually a symptom of social regression epitomized by an unwillingness (but not inability) on the part of eugenicists themselves to either tolerate difference or account for it in social terms.

The Scope of Difference: Artwork from 'Body Signs'

What is perhaps most disturbing about eugenic ideology is the broad, and often arbitrary categories whereby a certain state of difference is claimed to be dysgenic, and by default pejorative. Under the guise of benevolence a claim like this masks intolerance. The ultimate intention behind this attitude is to convince the public that difference is bad and that we should engage science to protect us from its effects. The artwork chosen for Body Signs works in the opposite direction by revealing the value of difference and the ways in which difference reflects on the human condition. My intention is not just to show that difference is germane to the human organism and social life, but how difference among humans, reflecting biology's dictum that variety is essential to life, is a necessary precondition for our existence, necessary by virtue of the fact that it is difference that configures our understanding of the flux of normalcy. As Georges Canguilhem wrote in The Normal and the Pathological (drafted in the 1940s but not published in English until 1989), "the normal is not static or peaceful, but a dynamic and polemical concept" (p. 239).

Difference helps us relocate our own locations by taking us outside our selves and our quotidian or personal conventions (outside our bodies, outside our sexual orientations, outside our social milieu), thereby permitting us the opportunity the evaluate our position vis-à-vis alterity. We learn, in the process, that we are not the center of the world, nor even the center of our own existence, and that there is in fact no center except that which exists as a fiction of our own making.

While the artwork in Body Signs is critical of eugenics, it is relatively discursive and avoids taking an overtly moralizing or didactic tone. This does not, however, mean that it shirks difficult issues, but rather that these issues are examined in such a way as to permit them to collapse under the weight of their own ostentatious claims. To this end some of the work re-presents images and quotations from early twentieth-century eugenic treatises. By reframing the historical context of these images and quotations within a late twentieth-century art space, the prejudices of history will reveal themselves. There will be no need to 'explain' this history, because, like other histories, it is a fiction, and one cannot correct one fiction by means of another fiction. Instead, the artwork in Body Signs will examine the tension between competing fictions and locate this tension within the interface of science, ethics, and art.

The work presented in Body Signs will not, however, constitute an exhibition in the usual sense. Rather than present individual works of one or two media, or do a large installation, my intention is to organize work of different media to create a discursive narrative on the subject of Body Signs. Some of the work will be conscious of itself as 'art' (photographs, dispersion paintings, and conceptual sculpture), some of it (Weekly World News, discretely placed postcards, and magazine clippings strewn about) will not. There will also be a table piece related to previous works I have done of this genre: a table covered with texts, articles, photographs, and paraphernalia related to the subjects of classical genetics and postmodern genetics. I also plan to use the table piece at odd times during the show; it won't just sit there, nor for that matter will the show itself. I want to change things around during the course of the exhibition: add some things, move other things around, and include work that is not in a strict sense 'finished.' And I intend to do this in order to demonstrate how the work, as part of the process of constructing a narrative, must do that in terms of inter- and intratextual relations. It will be a discursive narrative, of course, but my intention here is to get away from the idea of the 'perfect' object/narrative/story, where perfectionism is symbolized as the eugenicists' holy grail.

Relevance of 'Body Signs' to Washington and the WPA

Recoiling from the Holocaust, the eugenics movement was forced to adapt its approach to a society sensitive to the horror of genocide. Euphemism, for example, replaced directness: the Eugenics Education Society did not disbandon, but merely changed its name to the Francis Galton Institute. And while legally enforced sterilizations are no longer typical at state institutions, they have been replaced with genetic screening and 'counseling.' The present state of research in the Human Genome Project--a massive, government assisted attempt to map every gene in the cells of the human organism--is frequently promoted by its advocates as a panacea for deviance and 'birth defects.' The question remains, however, whether this panacea is necessary, or even desirable; and the art in Body Signs implicitly provides some answers for this.

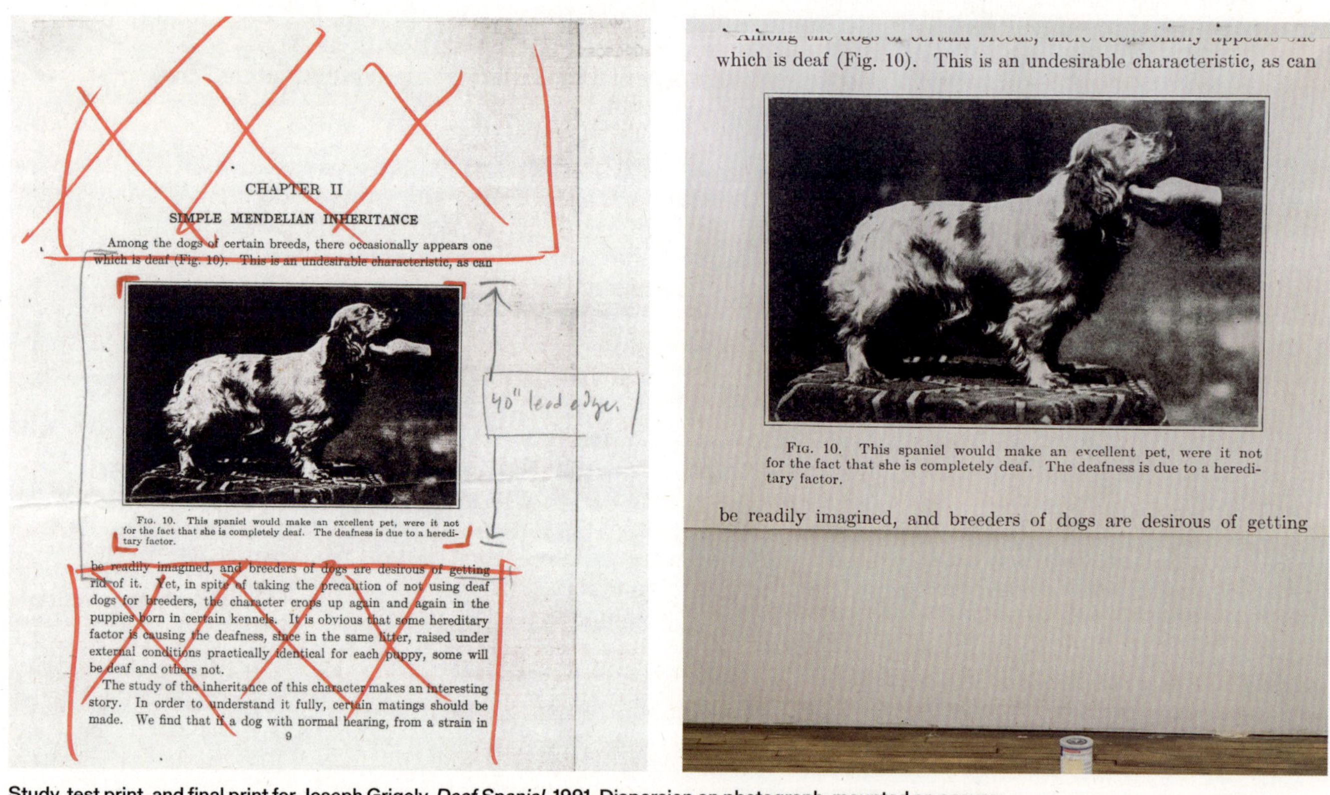

Study, test print, and final print for Joseph Grigely, *Deaf Spaniel*, 1991. Dispersion on photograph, mounted on canvas

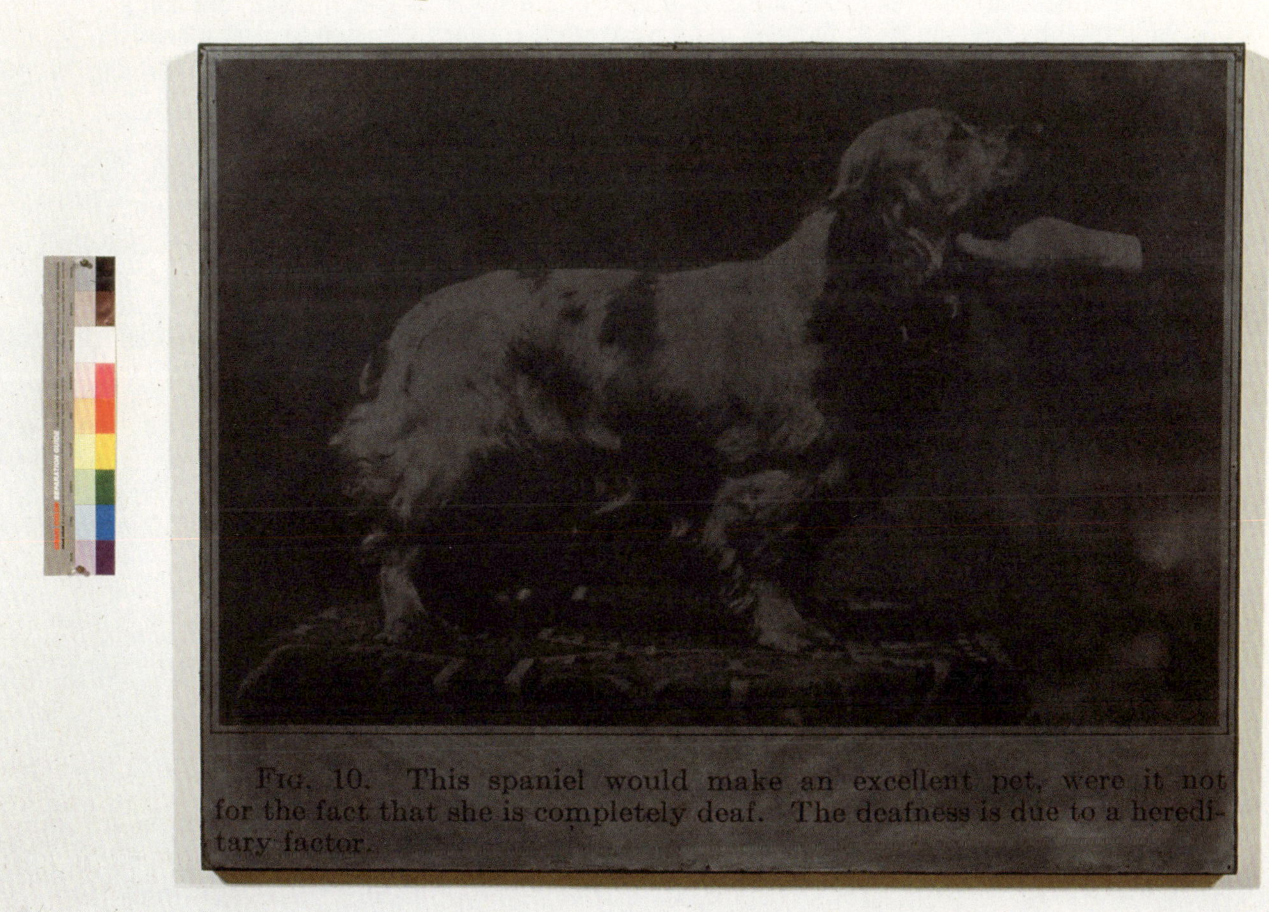
FIG. 10. This spaniel would make an excellent pet, were it not for the fact that she is completely deaf. The deafness is due to a hereditary factor.

Washington, ironically enough, is home to divergent institutions that represent the two primary subjects of Body Signs: deafness and eugenics. The eugenics movement, subsumed by the Human Genome Project, receives extensive funding through the National Institute of Health and the Department of Energy: joint NIH and DOE funding totaled $154 million for 1991 alone. But reminded as we are by the essays in Daniel Kevles' and Leroy Hood's Code of Codes: Scientific and Social Issues in the Human Genome Project (1992), the social and ethical implications of the project are far from being fully understood, and one of the goals of this exhibition is to extend a reminder of this caveat to the Washington research and funding community.

The second conceptual locus of Body Signs--difference as exemplified by deafness --has as its institutional partner Gallaudet University. It is not just that Gallaudet remains the only liberal arts university for the deaf in the world that makes it significant, but that a 1988 revolt by deaf students, faculty, and staff over the trustees' decision to elect a hearing president marked a turn in identity, and the acknowledgement of the validity of deafness as a cultural, not just physiological, condition.

Within this cultural condition is a sense of value, not a sense of loss. It emphasizes how the state of difference is not so much about the status of one's hearing, but about how this status is incorporated by the body, and how, as a consequence, the body is able to thrive under this condition. Is able: isability, not disability. While the eugenics movement is quick to imply that physiological otherness is a state of absence and loss (and therefore to be pitied and ameliorated), the prevailing revisionist attitude in the Deaf community is that the 'loss' is simultaneously a gain: a new way of looking at the world, a new way of looking at language, and, in effect, a new way of looking at what it means to be human.

Body Signs: Deviance, Difference, and Eugenics is designed to bring together a diverse audience of people who do not share the same conceptual paradigms about difference. Both the scientific and legislative communities in Washington will find interest in this exhibition, even though it does not reinforce a neo-Newtonian conception of a mechanistic universe: instead, it suggests that the mechanism of natural order must be examined in relation to the ethical and long-term implications of our manipulation of that order. There is, in this political and scientific community, a potentially large audience. The Deaf community in Washington is also large: there are roughly 2,000 enrolled students at Gallaudet, and a large community of graduates and friends that, like the legislative and science communities, constitute a potentially new audience for the WPA.

Recent & Forthcoming Critical Studies that Offer a Theoretical Orientation for 'Body Signs':

Jenny Terry and Jackie Urla, eds. Deviant Bodies (forthcoming, Indiana UP).

Daniel Kevles and Leroy Hood, eds. The Code of Codes: Scientific and Social Issues in the Human Genome Project (Harvard UP, 1992).

David Hevey, The Creatures Time Forgot: Photography and Disability Imagery (Routledge, 1993).

Harlan Lane, The Mask of Benevolence (Knopf, 1991).

Recent Work by Joseph Grigely Related to the Proposed Exhibition:

'Postcards to Sophie Calle,' Parkett 36 (June 1993), 88-101.

'Textual Eugenics,' in Reimaging Textuality and Reproduction of the Text, ed. Neil Fraistat and Beth Loizeaux (forthcoming, U Michigan P).

Cover Art for Deviant Bodies, ed. Jenny Terry and Jackie Urla (forthcoming, Indiana UP)

Conversations with the Hearing (forthcoming commissioned installation, White Columns, NYC)

Textualterity: Art, Theory, and Textual Criticism (currently under consideration by the U of Michigan P).

Catalogue Essay

Because the work exhibited in Body Signs is part of a theoretical continuum on deviance, difference, and eugenics, and because it will be presented in a discursive format so as not to coerce viewers, it may be useful to contextualize this continuum with a catalogue essay. Two authors committed to the project, both of whom are familiar with my art and my writings, are Nick Mirzoeff and Ira Livingston. Mirzoeff (currently a Getty Fellow) is finishing two books. The first, on representations of the deaf in nineteenth-century art will be published by Princeton UP. The second, on representations of the body, will be published by Routledge. Mirzoeff is also a contributor to the Terry/Urla volume on Deviant Bodies. He will be teaching at U of Wisconsin (Madison) in the autumn of 1993.

Livingston is a critical theorist in the English Department at SUNY-Stony Brook. He writes primarily about the post-humanities' interface of science and art. During 1993-4 he will be in residence at the Humanities Center at Oregon State University.

The essay for this project will focus on the imbrication of identity--how it consists primarily of overlapping and indescrete doublings--and will metonymize this imbrication in the process of being written: Livingston and Mirzoeff will pass a single essay back and forth, rewriting each other's writing, reinscribing each other's inscriptions. Through this process, the 'author' will not be isolable on the basis of the text's phenotype any more than a person is isolable on the basis of the body's phenotype. It will emphasize, that is, the transgenic features of identity. Such an essay will, I think, find a large audience of readers in disciplines that include art, critical theory, and social ethics.

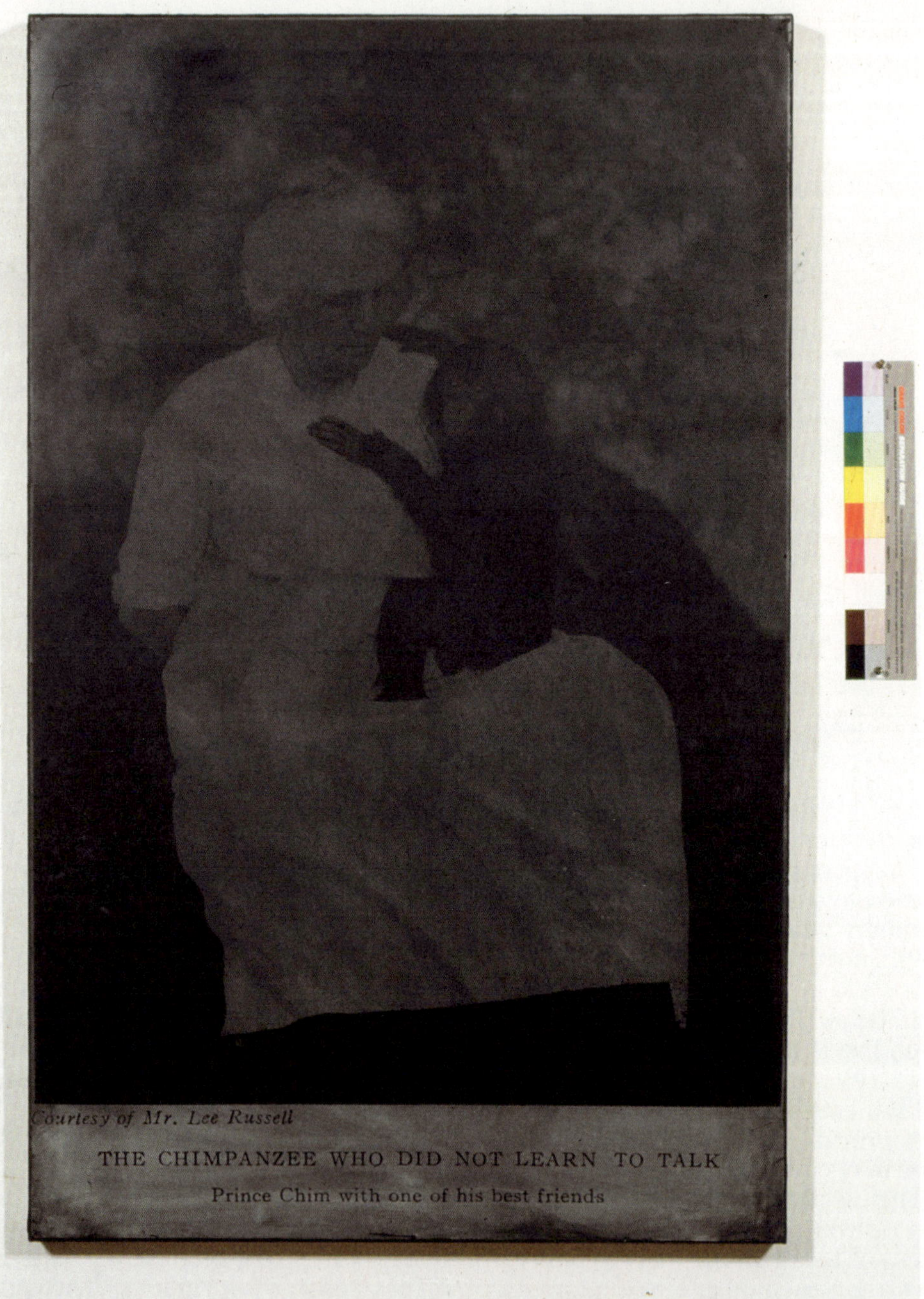

Joseph Grigely, *The Chimpanzee Who Did Not Learn to Talk*, 1991. Dispersion on photograph, mounted on canvas

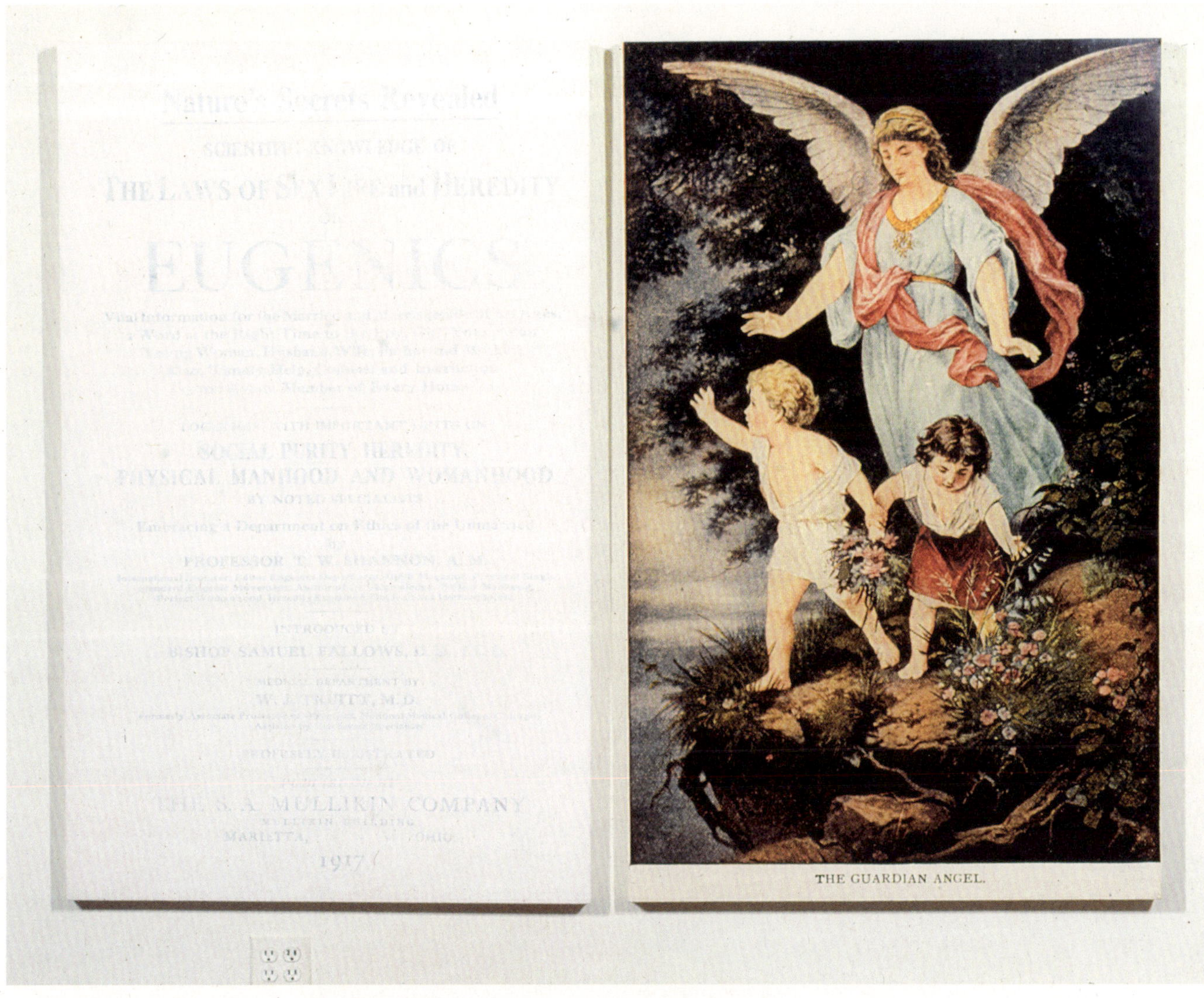

Joseph Grigely, *Nature's Secrets Revealed*, 1992. Dispersion on photographs, mounted on canvas

Disability Resource Center, 1993

Mixed media and public programming, 1993 (unrealized).

The early 1990s were a hopeful time for people with disabilities. The Americans with Disabilities Act had passed in 1990, and it brought with it a promise of change. Little did I realize that the process would be much slower and more complicated than I had imagined.

The art that emerged from the detritus of the 1980s was comparatively modest—especially in the context of the recession that was taking place at the time. A number of artists, such as Felix Gonzalez-Torres, were developing an understated approach to addressing political inequities; and other artists, such as those in the activist group ACT UP, were expanding the canon of political aesthetics, making art that did not necessarily claim to be art. Gregg Bordowitz in particular stands out in this regard.

My own political involvement with the issue of disability and art started with the "Postcards to Sophie Calle," written in 1991–92, and their subsequent publication in *Parkett* in 1993. Until then I had been making work where the topic of disability was folded into a formal aesthetic practice, but Calle's show convinced me of the need to be more direct, more public, and more principled. Some of the dispersion paintings I was developing at this time did exactly that; they would become the basis of my first solo exhibition, *Body Signs: Deviance, Difference, and Eugenics*, held at the Washington Project for the Arts in 1993–94.

At the same time, I was feeling my way through the New York art world. I had a studio in Jersey City and spent four days of the week working there—as well as seeing shows and talking with both artists and gallerists, especially those who had recently relocated to SoHo, such as Colin de Land and Pat Hearn. A lot of the galleries—most of them, actually—were inaccessible to wheelchairs, and their public programming was likewise inaccessible. I imagined doing an exhibition that would address these issues by turning a gallery into a disability resource center for six weeks. I would reconfigure the space to make it accessible, staff it with legal and advocacy teams, develop public programming—performances and readings—that engaged disability in various ways, and create a publication, an anthology/reader, so the "exhibition" would have a life beyond the physical event. It would be an exhibition not about art as a monetized object, but about the political influence of galleries and art on social change. Its title would be *Disability Resource Center*.

I sent a fax to Pat Hearn about this in 1993, and we later met to discuss it. It didn't happen in the end, for various reasons. Shortly later, in the spring of 1994, I had my first solo show in New York at White Columns, and *Disability Resource Center* was shelved—though various parts of the project would go on to appear in my work and writings, such as the anthological essay "Blindness and Deafness as Metaphors," in which I assembled quotations, taken from the work of critics, historians, and journalists, that used blindness and deafness as pejorative metaphors for ignorance and indifference. This piece was published in the *Journal of Visual Culture* in 2006.

111 First Street 6-5N, Jersey City, New Jersey 07302
201.795.9466 Fax/TDD only
March 15, 1993

To: Pat Hearn
Fax 212.941.7046

Dear Pat,

A piece of news: about 8 pages of excerpts from my "Postcards to Sophie Calle" will be published in Parkett in late May. It was more or less Sophie's own idea; she mentioned over coffee that she had showed the texts to you, so I was pleased to hear that. I sent a full set to Peggy Phelan recently--she's out at Irvine just now--but I haven't heard from her yet. I feel good about Sophie's Blind Color installation, so I've continued to add to the "Postcards" with the intention of making a book out of them. Although the "Postcards" are critical texts, they also illuminate some of the things I'm doing in my Conversations with the Hearing and Documentexts. I just finished the copy-editing with Louise Neri and we're working with Sophie on the images and lay-out. The full text version is currently being considered by October. I'll let you know what happens with that in due course.

Anyhow: I'm tinkering with an idea for a working installation entitled Disability Resource Room. It would involve making the gallery completely accessible (lift/ramp, TDDs, braille/cassette texts of statements) and setting up a working resource room on disability issues (access, demographics, and cultural identity) staffed by both disabled people and professionals in the field. I know I can get some very, very good people involved in this project, and I also think I can find enough money to cover the costs and overhead for it. If you're at all interested in this, let me know--maybe even send me a fax. I've been at the gallery quite a bit lately, but I always seem to show up when you're out, alas.

I hope you're well.

Regards,

Joe.

Joseph Grigely

Disability Resource Center

1) Lift/ramp
2) TDD
3) Braille/tape text of statements,
4) terps (?)

- Reconfiguration of gallery to make it completely accessible
- Resource Centre / Clearinghouse on info. related to access & disability identity.
  - legal advice Rep. of ADA
  - Disabled individuals advice
  - Library / resource material
  - telephone / TDD hotline.

[- etymologies]
- metaphors project - paste onto wall quotations of pejorative metaphors.
= 'statistic' releases, - demographics, etc. ~~press releases~~
- performance? - Lilly? -
  reading(s) - taped too.
  panel - (Sophie)? - Houston? - Gates?
- tech, e.g. text reader

→ public interaction / pub. service.
  to disabled in galleries -

⇒ degree of militancy? - to educate rather than provoke - prick the conscience of liberals' - not stab. -

Grant Proposal for a Book on Disability, Difference, and Culture, 1994 (rejected)

General Research Interests

As both a scholar and a conceptual artist my work deals with the relationship between agency and identity. As a scholar I am interested in the ways in which works of art and literature are made, unmade, and remade in the course of their transmission as cultural texts. As an artist I am interested in the enabling, rather than disabling, effect of deafness in relation to language. Essentially, both areas of my work emphasize how identity is the product of the vicissitudes of unstable forces.

In my recently completed book, Textualterity: Art, Theory, and Textual Criticism (U of Michigan Press, 1995), I explore some of the specific ways in which works of art undergo change as part of the process of being disseminated in culture. The underlying premise is that the uniqueness of the unique art object is constantly undergoing continuous and discontinuous transience at it ages, is altered by editors and conservators, and as it is resituated or reterritorialized in different publications and exhibition sites. The emphasis here is not on objects, but on the processes through which the aesthetic object is an outcome. Whether the changes that occur are the result of accidents or human agency complicit with certain intentions, what is important is how the artworks tend to incorporate these events, retain traces of them, and continue to exist as artworks marked by time, marked by the organic environments and social contexts through which they must pass. In this respect, Textualterity introduces the principles of the discipline of textual criticism to a larger field of cultural practices. It also reassesses textual criticism itself by exploring the social value of texts that in the past were rejected or marginalized as being 'flawed,' 'deformed,' or 'corrupt.'

In my most recent work I am extending the question of the relationship between agency and textual difference to agency and human difference. My specific interest here is in understanding how changes to the body ultimately effect how the body constructs itself: how, for example, deafness engages the body in reconfiguring the modality through which language is constructed (speech to signing) or reconstructed (speech to writing). In the following pages I explain in greater detail the path in which I intend this research to take. My project is entitled "Disability, Difference, and Culture."

Project Proposal:
Disability, Difference, and Culture

Introduction

At the present moment in intellectual and cultural history, we live in what might be described as an age of difference: an age in which the narratives of human history are increasingly explored as micro-narratives whose existence depends upon conditions of dissimilarity and difference, both in our human bodies and in the discourse with which we express ourselves. The sense of difference, or alterity, underlying subjects such as gender and race thus functions to affirm the uniqueness of identity and its significance to sustaining human culture: we are all made up of differences that, playing off each other, create the dynamic conditions by which culture itself is created. How then, at this important stage in the evolution of historical studies and critical thought, might the significance of difference be studied in relation to disability and the disabled: what does it mean to be 'disabled,' and how might disability and its manifestations (in the body, in language, and in art) contribute to defining what it means to be human in cultural terms?

Proposal

Expanding on ideas introduced in Textualterity, my intention in Disability, Difference, and Culture is to complete a book-length study that explores the nature of disability as a normative, rather than deviant, condition. Textualterity deals with texts as bodies; Disability, Difference and Culture reverses this paradigm to deal with bodies as texts. My approach to my subject is by necessity transdisciplinary and by choice heuretic. It is transdisciplinary in that it takes into account discipline-anchored studies in disability and difference, including art (Jacques Derrida on blindness), law (Martha Minow on difference), medical hermeneutics (Georges Canguilhem on the pathological), photojournalism (David Hevey on photography and disability imagery), Deaf studies (Harlan Lane, Oliver Sacks, and Carol Padden on American Sign Language and Deaf Culture), and recent critical discussions on race and difference (Henry Louis Gates, Jr. and Cornel West).

Disability, Difference, and Culture is also (to use Gregory Ulmer's phrase) a heuretic study in that it might be described as criticism written in a mode other than critical writing; it is written in a way in which the discourses of art and theory cross and become entangled with each other. None of the chapters are written as continuous critical prose. Instead they are an amalgamation of various genres of writing and speech: postcards, quotations, monologues, and inscriptions. Each chapter is, in this sense, both history and criticism, both an assemblage of historical evidence and a critique of it. The very complexity of disability as a social and cultural phenomenon suggests that a straightforward hermeneutic approach would not adequately convey just how problematic and difficult the subject is. This is one reason few critical theorists have tried to relate disability to other theoretical narratives about identity. A heuretic approach permits me the opportunity to explore the tensions and the contradictions in these hermeneutic narratives, particularly when those tensions and contradictions lack resolution. At present the work is mid-stage: of six projected chapters, two have already been published, a third (consisting of inscribed conversations between a deaf person and several hearing people) has been exhibited as an art installation, and a fourth chapter is scheduled to be published in the spring of 1995. What follows is a brief synopsis of the work done thus far.

Chapter one, "Postcards to Sophie Calle," introduces the book's primary questions about conventional categories of difference--race and gender particularly--and shows how the notion of disability is both imbricated with these categories and is also distinct from them. The purpose of this chapter is to interrogate what I call canonized categories of difference and show how disability is a condition (rather than kind) of difference in the continuum of human differences.

Written as a series of 32 postcards addressed to the French conceptual artist Sophie Calle, the chapter uses as its locus Calle's installation, Les Aveugles ('The Blind'), which was exhibited at Luhring Augustine Gallery in New York in the spring of 1991. The postcards (which vary in length from twenty-five words to almost five hundred) function rhetorically to both organize and sequence the ideas, and to maintain an accessible and interpersonal level of communication. An edited selection of 16 of the postcards was published in the Swiss art quarterly, Parkett 36 (1993): 88-101.

Chapter two, Deaf & Dumb: A Tale, is a brief (36pp) and discursive history of the evolution of the Deaf Community. Exploring sensitive social issues including paternalism and linguistic colonialism, Deaf & Dumb does not so much attempt to provide a corrective to this history as it attempts to expose this history, and show how the history of the Deaf is essentially a series of histories anchored by the voices of (mostly) hearing narrators.

The text of Deaf & Dumb is essentially an assemblage of already-published but little-known writings about the Deaf; each page is a full-page facsimile from works ranging from Johann Conrad Amman's The Talking Deaf Man (1694) to twentieth-century examples of the pathetic sublime, Complete Guide for the Deafened (1940) and How to Help Your Hearing (1940). The pages of Deaf & Dumb are arranged in such a way as to develop a narrative outside the chronology of the texts themselves. By moving from the 17th century to the 20th and back to the 19th in the space of three pages (for example), it becomes possible to witness, in a concrete way, the historical continuity of social attitudes about the Deaf. The chapter concludes with an index that, in repeated cross-references to specific pages, excavates the tensions, the ironies, and the contradictions within them.

Deaf and Dumb: A Tale was originally published as an integral component of my exhibition, Conversations with the Hearing at White Columns, New York, between March 18-April 16, 1994.

Chapter three, Conversations with the Hearing, explores the relationship between speech and writing by way of an exhibition of textual artwork within the context of a book. The Conversations with the Hearing are part of an ongoing project that examines the communication exchanges that occur between the deaf and the hearing. The Conversations themselves consist primarily of pieces of paper that were written upon by hearing people in the course of a conversation with me. Partly because of my total deafness, and partly because of the idiosyncracies of individual speech habits, I frequently find myself in the position of being unable to lipread people. In these situations I simply reconfigure the act of face-to-face communication by asking people to write down what they are saying. My interlocutors vary considerably and include friends, colleagues, and complete strangers; and topics range from a conversation in a bar with a friend, gossip with a neighbor, and questions asked by strangers in the street--in essence, what is a part of ordinary life. Like still-life paintings, the Conversations record ordinariness *in terms of* ordinariness; yet because of the speakability of the inscriptions, they are unordinary as written texts. They reflect both our self-conscious attempts to perfect ourselves and our unself-conscious imperfections--both of which are further examples of what I describe in chapter one as conditions of difference. Their purpose as art, or as social documents, is to frame certain truths about what it means to be human--the means by which we create our own existence, and how the life of every person is, by necessity, a creative act.

The Conversations with the Hearing were first exhibited as an installation at White Columns, New York, in March and April 1994, and again (in an expanded format) at the University Galleries of Eastern Washington University, between July and August 1994.

Chapter four, "Figures of Speech" is a discussion about specific theoretical implications of the Conversations with the Hearing. Despite all that has been written about the difference between speech and writing in formal linguistics (primarily in discourse analysis, such as Herbert Clark's Arenas of Language Use), very little has been written about speech and writing from the point of reversal: speech as writing, writing as speech. This is what the Conversations offer: an archive of speech that, out of a human necessity, has become writing.

In "Figures of Speech" I have selected 24 Conversations that present evidence of how certain discourse strategies related to speech communication (turn taking, overhearing, interruptions, and so on) are both configured and reconfigured when transmodulated to writing. "Figures of Speech" will be published as a catalogue / artist's book in conjunction with a forthcoming exhibition of Conversations at A/C Project Room in New York between March and April 1995.

Chapter five, "The Diction of Difference," explores in contemporary discourse the use of the words 'blind' and 'deaf' as pejorative metaphors. The range is wide. It includes commonplace expressions frequently used as headlines in the New York Times (turning "a blind eye" and "a deaf ear"), complex constructions (MFK Fisher's evocative "taste-deafened" and a gardener's query as to why her daffodils had "come up blind," that is, without blooms), and the irony exposed when the leaders of democratic critical discourse themselves engage blindness and deafness as signs of degenerate behavior (this is Elaine Showalter in Raritan: "We can hardly fail to welcome male feminist criticism when we have so long lamented the blindness, the deafness, and indifference of the male critical establishment towards our work.") Ironies like

Willy + Sign "smell deaf"

"Disability Claims Cripple Newark Housing Agency" "~~Atten~~"

this are important, in part because of how they reveal that the disabled are not only at the margins of critical thought, but at the margins of the discourse of critical thought--at the margins of the margins, so to speak.

"The Diction of Difference" consists of 23 quotations drawn from a wide range of writers and publications, each quotation interspersed with a discussion that writes around the quotations rather than about them. My intention is not so much to implicate the authors as show how the body, as a fundamental site of difference, tends to be the site at which metaphors of difference are anchored. Like chapter two ("Deaf & Dumb: A Tale") and chapter four ("Figures of Speech"), "The Diction of Difference" is both an assemblage of historical evidence and a critique of it.

Chapter six, "The Pose of Difference," is structurally like the previous chapter in that it writes around, not about, its subject: a postcard from the early 1950s of seventeen disabled children posed at the edge of a fence overlooking the Ohio River at Camp Koch for Crippled Children in Troy, Indiana. It is not just the individual poses that are crucial, and the ways the children relate to each other, but the way they are posed as a group: we are behind them; that is, responsible for how they are both socially situated and socially dislocated. The narrative voice of this chapter thus focuses on the relationship between different kinds of bodies (individual, social), their modulating apparatuses (fences, prostheses), and the ways in which absences (of the photographer, of 'normals') create an ambience of artificial normalcy in which everyone is alike in their difference.

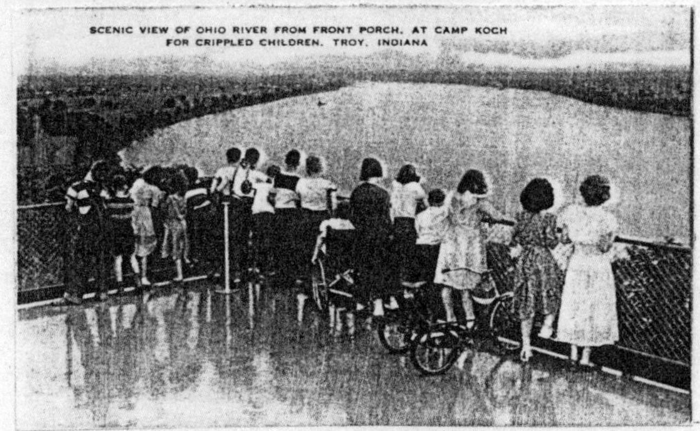

The book's narrative sequence moves from being 'seen' to being 'heard' to the discourse with which we are seen and heard: words and images. Conceptually, my strategy involving raising questions: to pose problems by juxtaposing and transposing history and theory, criticism and art, and thereby engage readers in rethinking their own conceptualization of difference. My intended audience is therefore quite broad. Although my primary audience consists of cultural and critical theorists, the initial response to the publication of chapter one ("Postcards to Sophie Calle") and the exhibition of chapter three (Conversations with the Hearing) suggests that the work will also engage a diverse and general audience.

In conclusion I would like to briefly explain my reasons for writing Disability, Difference, and Culture. This is not a book I want to write as much as it is a book I am compelled to write. Like James Baldwin (who once remarked that he wanted to write about anything but being black, but had to write about being black first), I am in an intractable position of assessing my own identity in relation to extant narratives about this identity. As a disabled person, I have not yet read a book about disability and the disabled that I felt strongly enough about to share with colleagues in academia or with friends more generally. In most studies of the disabled, there is a tendency towards valiance: the Noble Savage Syndrome. This is especially true in the case of work written about the Deaf, almost all of which has been written by (or in the case of films, directed by) hearing people: Oliver Sacks's Seeing Voices (1989), Harlan Lane's When the Mind Hears (1984) and The Mask of Benevolence (1992), and Nicolas Philibert's recent film, In the Land of the Deaf (1992) all fall into this category. As Harlan Lane acknowledged in his preface to The Mask of Benevolence, "I recognize that my pursuit of knowledge about deaf poeple, however intense and prolonged, will never give me the knowledge of a deaf person." It is precisely this "knowledge of a deaf person" that constitutes the basis of Disability, Difference, and Culture. Ultimately, my intention is not to aggrandize this knowledge but to share its subtleties and complexities in a way that my artistic sensibilities find most effective and my scholarly obligations find most compelling.

Representative Bibliography

Canguilhem, Georges. The Normal and the Pathological. Tr. Carolyn Fawcett. 1966. New York: Zone Books, 1989.

Connolly, William. Identity / Difference: Democratic Negotiations of Political Paradox. Ithaca: Cornell UP, 1991.

Clark, Herbert. Arenas of Language Use. Chicago: U of Chicago P, 1992.

Davis, Lennard. "Signing On." Rev. of The Mask of Benovelence: Disabling the Deaf Community. The Nation. July 6, 1992.

Derrida, Jacques. Memoirs of the Blind: The Self-Portrait and Other Ruins. Tr. Pascale-Anne Brault and Michael Naas. Chicago: U of Chicago P, 1993.

Gates, Henry Louis Jr. "Writing 'Race' and the Difference It Makes." Critical Inquiry 12.1 (Autumn 1985): 1-20.

_____. Figures in Black: Words, Signs, and the 'Racial' Self. Oxford: Oxford UP, 1985.

Grigely, Joseph. Body Signs: Deviance, Difference, and Eugenics. Exhibition. Washington, D.C.: Washington Project for the Arts, December 1993-February 1994.

_____. Conversations With the Hearing. Exhibition. New York: White Columns, March-April 1994.

_____. Deaf & Dumb: A Tale. New York: White Columns, 1994.

_____. "Postcards to Sophie Calle." Parkett 36 (1993): 88-101.

_____. Textualterity: Art, Theory, and Textual Criticism. Ann Arbor: U of Michigan P, 1995.

Hevey, David. The Creatures Time Forgot: Photography and Disability Imagery. New York: Routledge, 1992.

Lane, Harlan. The Mask of Benevolence: Disabling the Deaf Community. New York: Knopf, 1992.

_____. When the Mind Hears: A History of the Deaf. New York: Random House, 1984.

Minow, Martha. Making All the Difference: Inclusion, Exclusion and American Law. Cambridge, Ma.: Harvard UP, 1990.

Padden, Carol, and Tom Humpries. Deaf in America: Voices from a Culture. Cambridge, Ma.: Harvard UP, 1988.

Philibert, Nicolas, dir. In the Land of the Deaf. Film, 1992. Dist. International Film Circuit.

Sacks, Oliver. Seeing Voices: A Journey Into the Land of the Deaf. Berkeley: U of California P, 1989.

Ulmer, Gregory. "The Heuretics of Deconstruction." In Deconstruction and the Visual Arts: Art, Media, Architecture. Ed. Peter Brunette and David Wills. Cambridge: Cambridge UP, 1994.

_____. Heuretics: The Logic of Invention. Baltimore: Johns Hopkins UP, 1994.

Statement on *Conversations with the Hearing*, 1994

Joseph Grigely

Conversations with the Hearing

The Conversations with the Hearing are part of an ongoing project that examines the communication exchanges that occur between the deaf and the hearing. The Conversations themselves consist primarily of pieces of paper that were written upon by hearing people in the course of a conversation with me. Partly because of my total deafness, and partly because of the indiosyncracies of individual speech habits, I frequently find myself in the position of being unable to lipread people. In these situations I simply reconfigure the act of face-to-face communication by asking people to write down what they are saying. My interlocutors vary considerably and include friends, colleagues, and complete strangers; and topics range from a conversation in a bar with a friend, gossip with a neighbor, and questions asked by strangers in the street--in essence, what is a part of ordinary life. Like still-life paintings, the Conversations record ordinariness *in terms of* ordinariness; yet because of the speakability of the inscriptions, they are unordinary as written texts. They are written images of things that usually do not get written down--slips, secrets, whispers, spontaneous insights--thereby preserving, in a way that is both compelling and disturbing, the evanescence of speech.

In this sense, the Conversations might be described as linguistic portraits: they are essentially a representational, or figurative art. The portrait of the conversation is 'drawn' in words and visual suprasegmentals: paper, handwriting, spacings, spellings, and so on. Yet, the portrait is one mediated by the exchange taking place, an exchange that is a necessary condition for all portraiture. The features, or words, that are present are selective features whose dichotomies are revealed by the absence of my own words: I am present and I am not present.

In the end the Conversations are not just about being deaf or about being hearing, but about being different in a world of difference. They explore both the ways in which language 'humanizes' us as social beings and--for this is equally important--the ways in which language dehumanizes us as well. Their purpose as art, or as social documents, is to frame certain truths about what it means to be human--the means by which we create our own existence, and how the life of every person is, by necessity, a creative act.

Figures of Speech (Unpublished Notes), 1995

As part of an exhibition of *Conversations with the Hearing* at AC Project Room in New York, I had planned to prepare a catalogue that reproduced many of the conversation notepapers alongside commentary explaining, to the extent it could be explained, what I was doing, why I was doing it, and what I found compelling about handwritten conversations. I made a paste-up version using photocopies of the conversation papers and typed the narrative in the margins between the conversations with a manual typewriter. In the end I decided not to produce this version of the catalogue, as it felt too didactic; another version was printed, using the same conversation papers but without the narrative. The version printed here is a marked-up copy that I later used for a lecture.

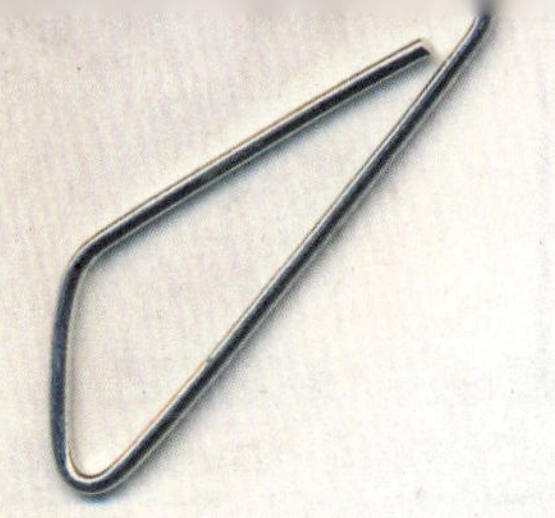

Figures of Speech

For those who are deaf, their history is usually reduced to two extremes: that of pathology on the one hand, and culture on the other. The pathological model conceptualizes deafness as a deviant condition that must be 'rehabilitated' or otherwise restored to an appearance of hearing normalcy, usually by way of speech and speechreading. The cultural model of the Deaf community conceptualizes deafness as a social condition that has as its primary identifying feature an indigenous sign language.

This is about neither. Instead, it is about the space between pathology and culture. This space is not about deafness in any conventional or explicit sense. It is, instead, about the communication that occurs between those who hear and those who do not. It is about the relationship between speech and writing. About the possibility of speech as writing, or as something similar to writing. Similar to writing by virtue of being inscribed. In this respect, the essay that follows constitutes a reversal of usual the paradigms by which the deaf are studied as 'subjects' of deviance and difference. I am not interested in the communication 'disorders' of the deaf, nor am I interested in the enabling capability of sign language. My interest is in something quite different: the ways in which the presence of deafness affects the communication strategies of those who hear. My subject is, therefore, primarily hearing people: how they speak, how they draw what they speak, how they gesture what they speak.

Draw and gesture? Yes. It begins, inevitably, as a body without a voice, a body without a name. It happens all the time, everywhere one goes: the omnipresence of conversation, of social exchanges. You know people are talking. You know they are real. You can see it too. When you cannot hear, language is reduced to what is visible: glances, gestures, movements of the mouth--saying everything and saying nothing. It's a little ironic almost: speech is not present but the speaker is. Language is not present, but its traces are.

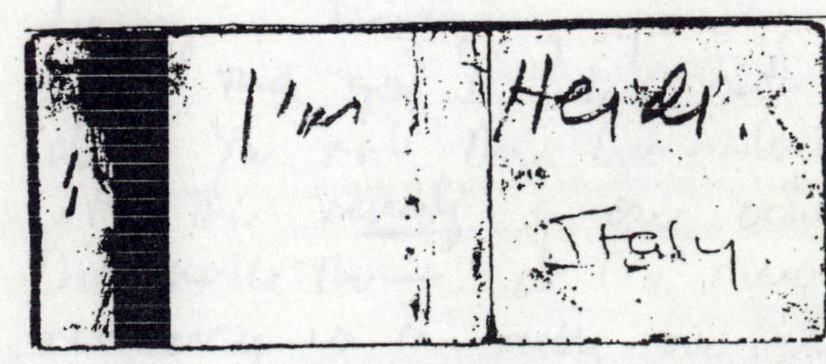

What does one make out of this activity? Except to say: it is an activity. Something mundane is going on, something ordinary. Bodies turn, arms move, heads twist, mouths flap. Ordinary to everyone except those to whom it is not ordinary. Which, in a way, is not a disadvantage but an advantage, because it gives us another way of looking at language. Another way of thinking about communication more generally. It's fascinating to watch how people talk; how, as individuals, they move the movement of speech itself with their entire bodies. They push words with their hands, lean against them with their torso, blink at words with their eyes. These are articulatory gestures. Always legible, but never quite readable. Always telling something, but never telling enough. It does not take more than a gesture to say hello, but it takes more than a gesture to make a conversation.

what kind of
Art do you make.

~~But this~~ ought to say hello,
And then, ~~there~~ is the question, an inevitable
question: — what kind of art do I make? —
~~what kind of art do all of us make?~~

~~Well, you see, it goes a little~~ like
~~this, I mean, — well, this~~ is it.
~~This is the stuff I do. —~~
~~Well, I say, it's pretty straightforward~~
~~Not~~ I ~~just sort of life on life,~~

It's a simple question, really, and the
answer I have is pretty simple too:
this, the paper you write on,
the words you inscribe. I make
drawings. Drawings of speech.
Except that ~~you~~ I don't make them
alone. You make them. We make them.
It's this reality of our ordinariness
that makes them — at this moment
ordinary us is really ourselves —
there is this contact of difference;
~~X makes the~~
happening here. — A certain uncertain spe

This ~~kind of Art,~~ —

one of
the defining gap

One of the defining aspects of human conversation is its extemporaneous possibilities. Introductions, compliments, interjections, asides, and offhand remarks exemplify the ways in which spontaneity is a fundamental part of our social exchanges. The trajectory and consequent path of a conversation is, in part, determined by the way we engage these possibilities--how we respond to them or (for our own part) create them. When one person is deaf and another person is hearing, the movement from gesture to language is initiated by writing. Sometimes I ask people to write. Sometimes they ask if it's OK to write. Sometimes it is not necessary for anyone to ask anyone: the logic of the situation is usually sufficiently compelling to initiate an expression of the desire to communicate. This is crucial. When people are conscious of the necessity of writing things down, the extemporaneous nature of speech is mitigated by an awareness of the effort that writing involves: of finding--at the very moment--paper upon which to write, a pen or a pencil to write with, and a flat surface to press upon. These activities seem perfunctory, but in fact they are not. They require a conscious effort that must answer to more than just natural needs. There are also social considerations--protocols, shall we say--that regulate speaking what cannot be overheard by others. It's just not polite to have private conversations in the public. And so the act of writing among those who are speaking will be read as a subterfuge: like exchanging phone numbers in the presence of others, it is something that is done discreetly. Usually, people prefer that you lipread. It's less conspicuous. Besides, it has a touch of the heroic about it--the deaf person knows tricks. So people tend to begin a conversation by asking "Can you read my lips?" and they often end it--a sentence of waning patience later--with "Oh, it's not important. Forget it." It's a lot easier for hearing people to talk with people who hear.

Not everyone is like this, though. It's surprising how some people are unintimidated by intimidation. And so they write. Some speak first and wait for the failure of lipreading before writing. Others just write. And some do more than just write: you can see, in the way they hold their pencil, and in the way they gesture with their words, that something other than writing is going on. In the end there are fragments, marks on paper. Traces, names. An archive of speech that, out of human necessity, has become writing. But this is not really the end. We are still at the beginning.

My spelling is poor without the help of the typewriter.

Sorry.

Sometimes when I am writing — I expect to hear it. The beep. misspelling.

And I love dictionaries — very fun.

But of what exactly? Lipreading? A myth. It's just not real. Actually, it's magic. Not sleight-of-hand, but sleight-of-eye. Cognitive dexterity. Linguistic prestidigitation. Scholars with scientific propensities who study lipreading would rather explain how lipreading works in terms of statistics, standard deviations, and acoustic prostheses. But it's not that at all. It's magic.

Magic, luck, error. Error especially. When you say "vacuum" it looks like you're saying "fuck you." Or vice-versa. The subtlety has to do with certain visemes: identical lip formations that produce dissimilar sounds. You can't see voicing. You can't see nasality. There simply aren't enough contrasting features to constitute an efficient representation of linguistic codes, and so lipreading is really less about reading than it is about the inevitability of misreading. Lipmisreading.

I mean--what's beautiful is this very inability to communicate. Where would we be without our misunderstandings, our misreadings, our mutual disagreements? Where would we be without memory betraying us, and words evading us? Lipmisreading metonymizes the success of the failure of communication. So instead of reading what cannot be read, I ask people to write while I look around, watch their gestures, watch whatever seems worth watching. It's like being lost, and taking pleasure in being lost--to wander around in this meta-communication, going nowhere in particular and everywhere in general. A strange journey. Misreading lips and misreading gestures, I put together wrong all of my conversations. All of them. All wrong.

My little fictions.

Who am I then? The awkwardness of not hearing myself for 27 years grows on me. Were I to hear again, would I recognize a voice no longer my own? Could anyone recognize a voice no longer their own? Perhaps this doesn't even matter. Perhaps what matters is that we are, for better or worse, the voices that we are. Articulate or inarticulate, nasal or not: this is me. It's not my pronunciations that say so much about me as my mispronunciations. How does one get right what one has never heard? How do we make visible what is

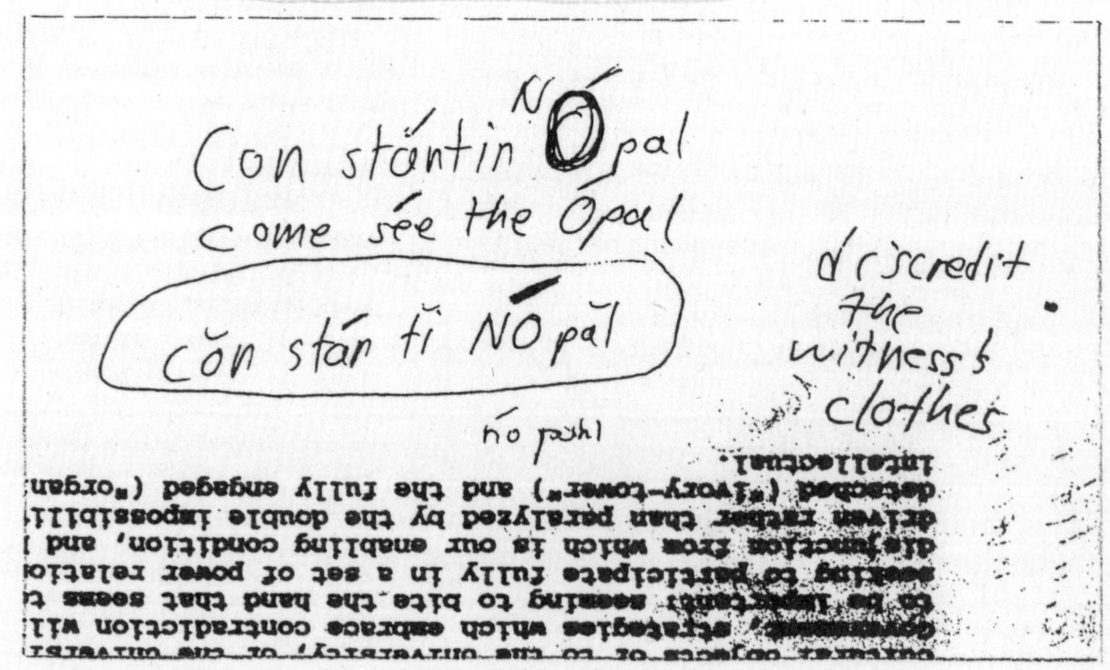

auditory, how do we translate, transmodulate, something so ordinary as speech? Writing is supposed to do that already. If writing can't, what can? (R)

Thats your excuse.

No one can communicate

Not with words anyway.

Maybe smell or hair

or something

Perhaps what we are looking for, what we are looking at, is something that is neither speech nor writing. Something that lies between speech and writing, without being the one or the other.

Something.

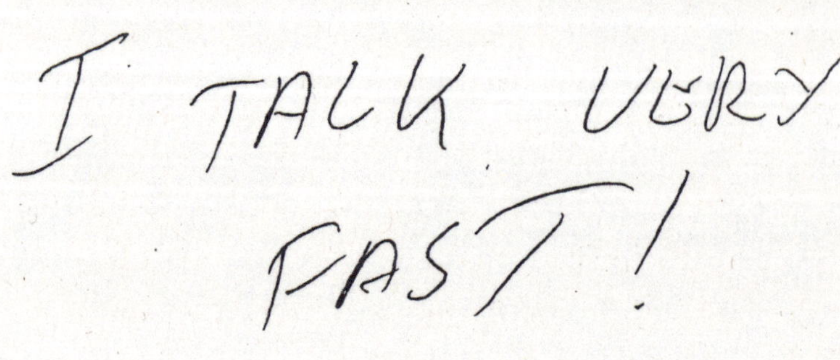

Something that we do not have a word for. The gray area between speech and writing is defined in part by the way inscribed speech retains traces of speech--by the way locution remains present. Writing, as an activity considered independent of speech, has evolved as a textual practice that has as a distinguishing feature an affinity with the genesis of printing--text on text, text in text, text from text. Writing does not retain traces of speech as much as it retains traces of its own origin: writing.

This gray area between speech and writing exists, in part, because our human nature is continuously challenged to mark its extremes. It's not, as Rousseau and other Enlightenment philosophers thought, our mere use of language that makes us human. Rather, it's our ability to keep using or recreating language is light of our physical subversions--muteness, deafness, and so on. In this sense, deafness is an enabling rather than disabling condition: it makes possible the sense of possibility--the sense that there are other ways to communicate, other ways to use language, other ways to be human. Yet, while deafness enables these communication exchanges, it does not ensure or guarantee that they will happen. They happen, like all communication exchanges, as part of a social compact. They happen because we make them happen.

So our subject is not really deafness. It is instead about how deafness configures communication. Mine. Yours. It's the contact that matters. The movement. The moment at which we are not quite ourselves because we behave a little differently by speaking and listening a little differently. You are not really speaking and you are not really writing, so how do you listen to what you are inscribing? Do you listen or do you read, or do you do what most people do: neither?

Get a big pie ex:
Two of the peices need to have peperoni

Not listen, not read, but <u>sense</u>. When speech verges on becoming writing it becomes, in an important way, conscious of the possibilities of writing. The space between a space--a space that discovers itself in the process of writing itself. Forced by necessity to be otherwise, the impulse is to speak in a way that acknowledges the paper upon which one is ~~writing speaking~~ drawing: words become images. In a sense, symbolic and conventionalized language undergoes regression by reverting to depiction, or pictographic writing, which Rousseau (in his essay *On the Origin of Language*) ascribes to passion--the articulation of needs and desires.

Like the gesture that supplements speech, the drawing that supplements writing is fundamental to communication. We use it (shall we say) instinctively, not entirely aware that we are doing so. At the next stage, when we become aware of what is happening, when drawing no longer supplements speech but becomes integrated into speech, we move on to a new strategy: the rebus. The rebus is important as a form of figuration for it both characterizes and constitutes the origin of writing. It is, shall we say, about the pleasure of making marks, of the movement from depiction to symbols without entirely abandoning the idea of drawing. The release of this pleasure is accompanied by the acquisition of pleasure--the pleasure of seeing one's speech and becoming acutely self-conscious of what one is seeing.

chocolate

ALISSA FRIEDMAN

AC PROJECT ROOM 558 BROOME STREET
NEW YORK NY 10013 TEL 212 226 7271

What have I just said? That this form of conversation is about the pleasure of making marks, and about the pleasure of seeing what one has drawn? Pleasure. The pleasure of using one's hand instead of one's mouth. The pleasure of seeing instead of hearing. The pleasure of discovering that there is such a thing as pleasure in the most banal and ordinary moments of our everyday lives.

Truth? What inevitably threatens an aesthetic of ordinariness is ordinariness itself--of being so unexceptional as to be pathetic. But perhaps that is actually something good, because the pathetic marks both a climax and a nadir about how we articulate our lives. It is a threshold: we can never be quite sure if it's us or it's them.

Us or them? You or me? Sometimes my hearing friends, forgetting that I am deaf, stand on their toes, cup their hand around the mouth, and whisper into my ear.

And I love it. The appeal, for me, is in the slippage of being not hearing on the one hand, and not deaf on the other. Of being in-between. Just as I forget that other people can hear. Sometimes I talk to them with my hands--the small gestures that say everything I want to say, yet say it unaloud. Why do we do this? Is it because we make over others into our own image--talk to them as we talk to ourselves?

Ordinariness again. The quotidian. For years and years the notes that people drew for me ended up in the trash. Perhaps this was necessary in order to prove their evanescence, and to prove that they were, at the least, speech-like. Yet I know some deaf people who save their conversations with hearing people for the same reason some people save their shopping receipts: proof.

Proof of a social transaction. Of the passage of speech. Of writing in a way that writing does not admit to. Of writing in a way that speech would not discover on its own. It has to be forced to act this way--forced by the necessity of difference--of being deaf, or dyslexic, or unworded.

Unworded? While walking about on the streets of New York I have met people who could write letters of the alphabet, but had (it seems) forgotten, or perhaps never learned, how to assemble them into words. You do not hear this in their speech. You cannot. And as they attempt to draw what they articulate so clearly, you realize that the space between speech and writing is a space filled with pain. Think of it: to be present in a world to which we have no access. To be there and not to be there. If you were to sit in class of deaf students learning English you could observe that one of their greatest struggles is with the first letter of the alpha-

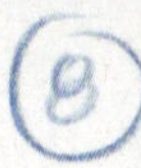

bet: 'a.' Imagine that: to stumble on the first letter of the alphabet, and to feel the bruise forever.

Perhaps this is a clue as to the nature of their struggle. As parts of speech, the articles of English (a-an-the) do not exist in American Sign Language. A part of speech: like a tongue, or an ear, a part of the mechanism of speech. It's only an idiom, of course, but so many of our linguistic idioms and metaphors have this intimate connection with the primacy of speech: they symbolize (rather than metonymize) language itself.

Closer now. Closer not to knowing what is here, but to feeling the immensity of the space between speech and writing. For those who are deaf, the effort to speak what one cannot hear involves exposing one's invisible sign of difference, just as, for others, the effort to write exposes theirs. The nasal sibilants of my speech reveal my difference. Your misspellings reveal yours. Your reluctance to ~~write~~ draw. And who are 'you?' A perpetually present presence. Always meeting each other when we least expect it.

But what is really happening when we meet? Language betrays us, that is true--but it is the same language that, in its fissures and unpredictable turns, makes so much else possible. Which is why mispronunciations, slips, and grammatical errors, rather than just being errors, are the very elements with which language is constructed: they exemplify the possibilities of the mind. This is the point at which play begins. 'Play.' It's a serious word. Perhaps, appropriately, the origin of our origins.

Nutmeg Biscotti
deep in choc.
$5.00 lb.

The beauty & the pleasure of fucking up.

the beauty and the pleasure of fucking up. –

This is the way we draw ourselves with language: each letter, each word, each pause marks of ourselves. Ordinariness. Like still-life painting, our everyday speech is a form rhophography, and as people write what they speak, they make a drawing that draws us from the inside as much as from the outside. A drawing that, coming off our fingers as it comes of our tongue is essentially unposed--an extemporaneous portrait. With each utterance, we draw a little more of ourselves. It's almost a little weird to think of inscribed conversations as a figurative art, but that's what they are: figurative. 'Representational,' even. Photographs of the speech act. Of ourselves. Click.

And then there's an inverse possibility: writing that is simply writing. Writing that makes no pretence to be speech. Writing that is not even the remnant of a conversation. Sometimes when I am in libraries, on subways, or walking in the street, I find a scrap of paper inscribed in a way that looks like a conversation, but isn't.

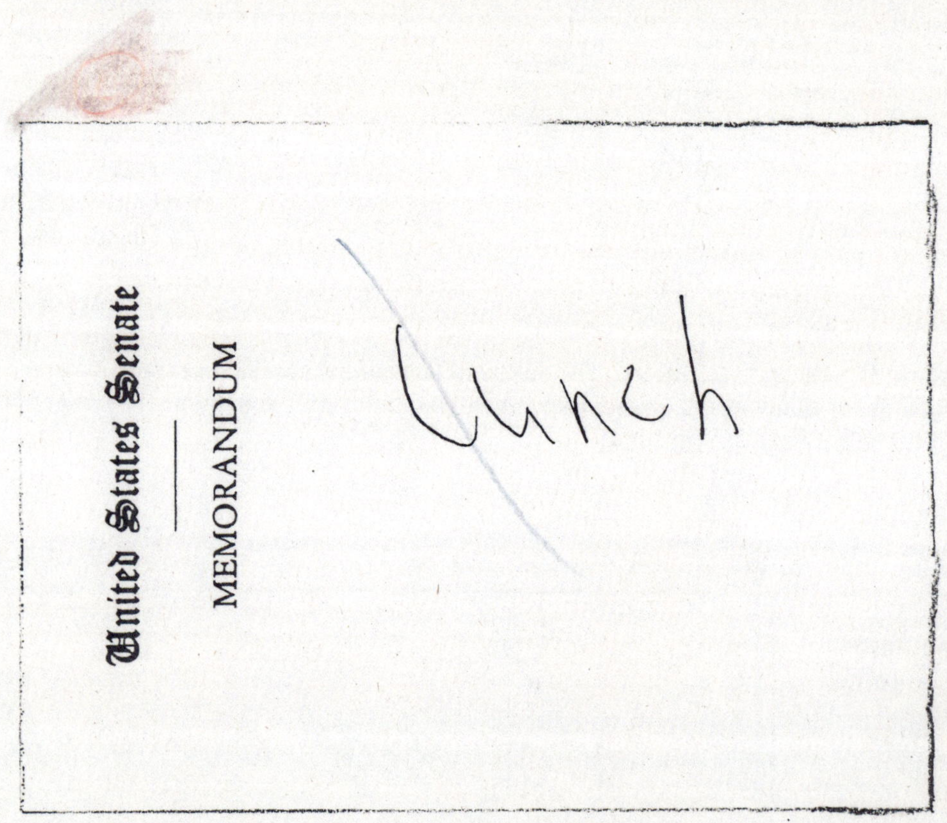

Yet how do I know? What makes an inscribed conversation different from other kinds of writing? Perhaps, instead, these found scraps are the conversations of another deaf person, or the conversations of hearing people, or the conversations of a single person. These too are written out of a manifest human need to communicate--

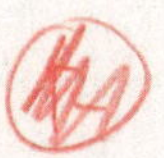

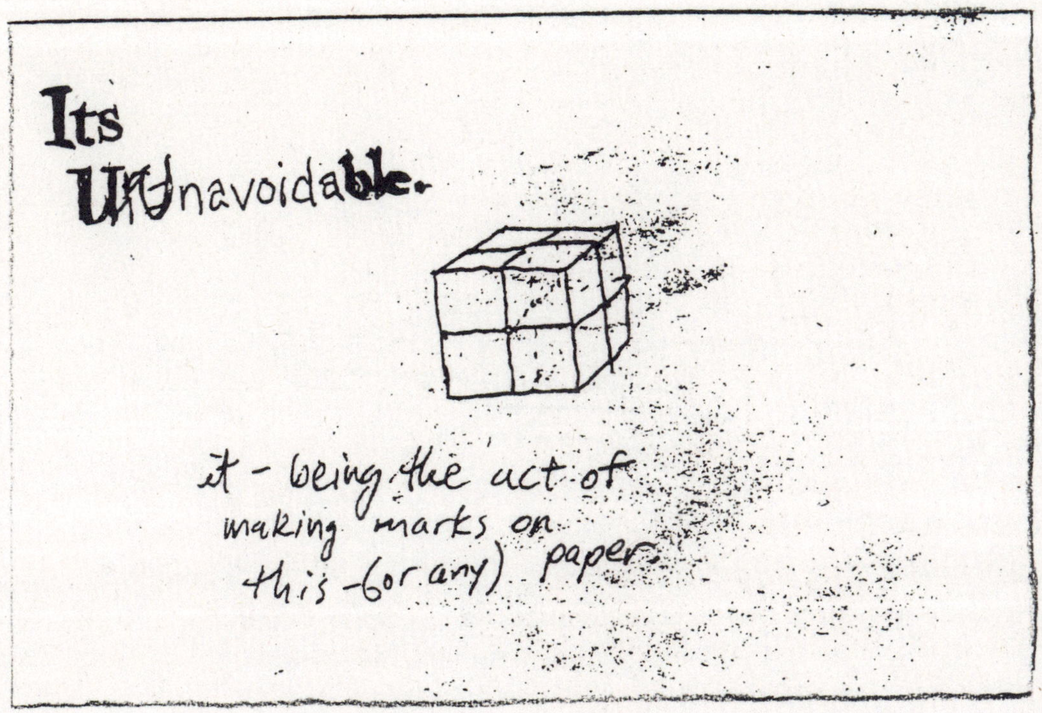

not with others, but with our selves. This partly explains our predisposition to write down ideas, make lists of things to do, and keep diaries. Writing preserves our thoughts, but even more than this it permits us the opportunity to step back from them, look at them, approach them, and engage ourselves in a--conversation--with them. Ultimately, we both respect and despise the inscribed word because of how it memorializes its own act of inscription. Unlike, say, the appeal of the evanescence of talking, and how this appeal cultivates certain genres of discourse suited to it: gossip and arguments, for example. Writing connotes a degree of premeditation--something implied when we say that we "sit down" to write. We talk standing up. Standing up, sitting down, on the phone, at meals, when driving, when drinking, when making love. What does it mean to ~~write draw~~ write when we're doing these things?

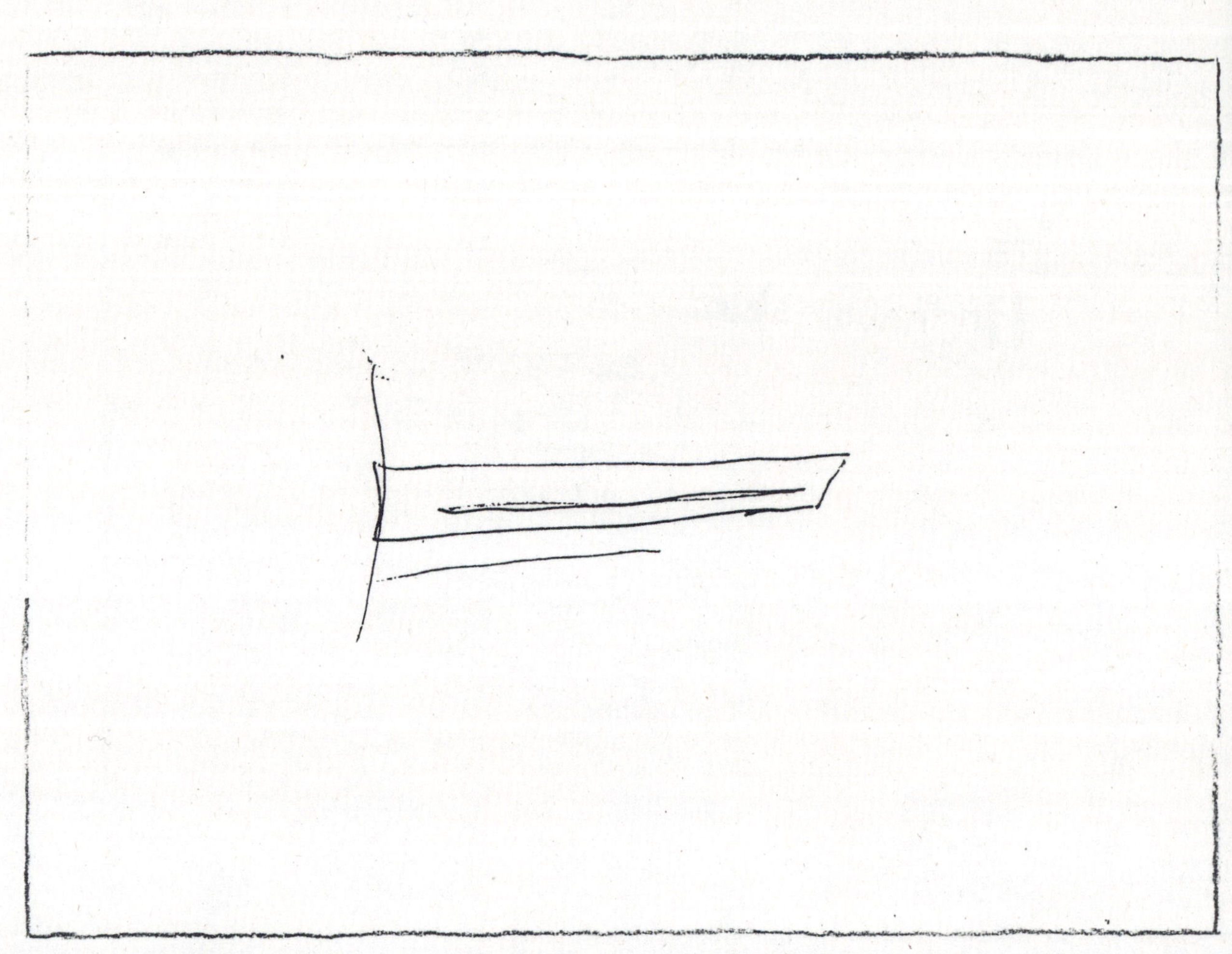

To write something that is not writing--is this what I mean to say? To draw speech, to draw figures of speech: it's not writing at all. It's speech that is distinguished by its very indistinguishability. A neurologist might acknowledge that writing can exist independently from writing: that such a thing as a non-verbal conversation is possible. Possible as a form of writing. Writing that is very definitely not writing. Which is what happens when I ask people to write down for me what they are saying, where they are saying, when they are saying.

What this means is that it is possible to engage a linguistic process and express it in a way that is other than writing. It is not so much the final, inscribed text that is so important (though it is), but the process of constructing it, or writing it, or drawing it, that constitutes the conversation. Classical literary theorists and iconologists use the term 'ekphrasis' to describe the verbal representation of visual representation. Ekphrasis is not just descriptive prose or poetry, but a conscious acknowledgment of the distinction between depiction and description. It is a paragone about two different kinds of representation: the verbal and the visual.

— Long pause —

When I gave her
a "look" for reading
our conversation
She said
'Oh please —
you were just
staring into
our conversation"

Don't be shocked —
its normal
between communicative
Mother/daughter —

Its part of being
a 'great' mother
withstanding torture, .

People sometimes ask me if I miss the experience of hearing--hearing music, hearing voices, hearing dogs barking. The answer is, I don't.

What I miss, instead, is overhearing. (R) Not just listening, but listening in. It's a perverse, yet logical desire. Perverse because the overtly voyeuristic aspect of eavesdropping involves the penetration of the privacy of others. Logical because it is precisely by engaging in this activity that we relate to the larger world in which we move--we learn things. Like looking--like 'stealing' a glance--there seems to be something fundamental about our desire to extract from the world of our experience a context that does not require our active participation. It's a form of passive involvement--to be there and to not be there. It is a form of desire that is always at the edge of being more than desire. Kleptomania, actually. The pleasure of stealing, and, ultimately, the embarrassment of getting caught. (L) — suburbs —

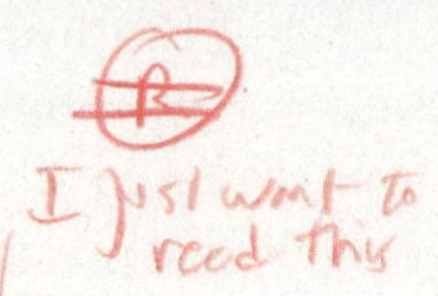

And then there are the ironies. One is that we often attempt to protect our own words and conversations from others, yet unhesitatingly make an effort to access *their* words and conversations. Linguists use the term 'audience design' to describe the ways in which we shape our conversations for the audience we are addressing (on the one hand) and the audience that may be overhearing us (on the other). Audience design involves a degree of self-consciousness that modulates the structure of our utterances and the strategies we employ to communicate to those whom we are addressing, and to evade those who we do not want to hear us.

I went to a Cafe
with David.
have you ever been
there?

You should go
there once.
got alot of
good material.
D. is a tremendous
adventuer.

So we erase our words. But how, having done this, do we erase our erasures? As we cross out our words we leave behind traces of our decision, traces of having said what we cannot completely unsay.

Imagine the possibility of tearing in half words that we speak. Imagine the possibility of lifting from the air strips of sentences so that we could fold them into a tight little wad, place the wad in an ashtray, and set it afire. Perhaps it is because we are aware that anything we say can be held against us that we try to reclaim, one way or another, the words that we say.

Whatever the reasons for this--the reasons are always ours alone--they do not seem to matter as much as the act itself--erasing, crossing out, tearing, and burning. Like speech and like writing, these gestures are the gestures of language. But now the word language is undergoing dislocation from the realm of formal linguistics. In our unending play with language we must face up to the consequences of this play--how it moves beyond the boundaries of 'codes' to what might be called the margins of speech.

14 (R) GOSSIP

It is a simple fact that when we write, we are vulnerable--our inscriptions will be read not just by those we intend to read them, but by others too. Read and misread; understood and misunderstood. It's almost inevitable. To put something 'in writing' is usually regarded as a way of protecting our intentions, but this approach is subject to the same vicissitudes as speech. The problem with language is that there's so much space in which to move--so many places to take our ideas, so many words to choose, so many sentences to construct--and in the midst of this endlessness, there are these tiny little finite differences among individual words that we misread and mishear: minimal pairs, homophones, and so on. We slip on semblance.

Bad curating.

I thought this said Bed Curtains

What is a great paradox here is knowing, as others get it wrong, that we too are getting it wrong. Throughout our lives we are turned into stories we did not tell. And we turn others into stories they did not tell.

Our little fictions.

Whether spoken or written, a conversation, removed from a site of conversation, is no longer a conversation. No longer is it speech. No longer is it the speaker's. The possibility of arranging the conversations as fictions is therefore the only possibility there is, because all speech, however reified, is no longer a locution. No longer do we possess our voices; they go through a process in which they are dispossessed and repossessed. Even when self-conscious of what we say, it is the saying that matters. There's nothing to worry about really. Lost in the space between, at play in the space between. Where? In between.

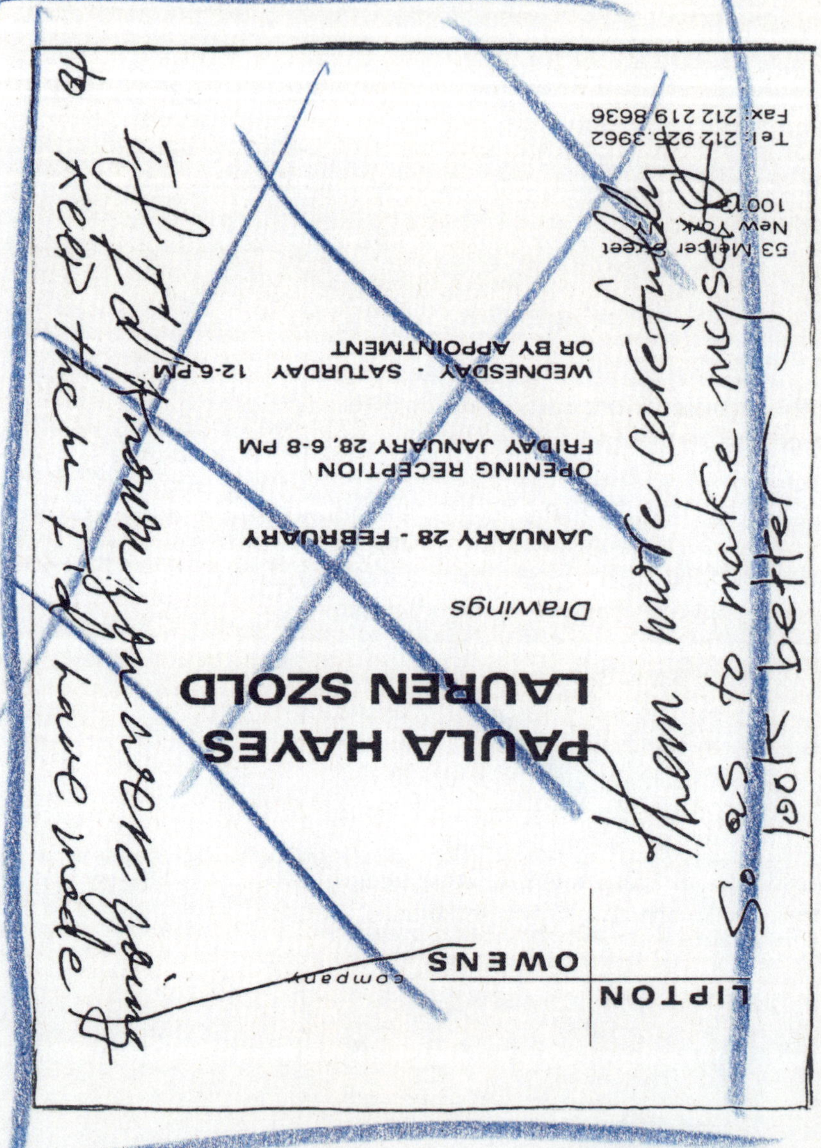

Fax to Marie Jeanne de Rooij, 1996

Manifesta 1 was developed as a pan-European biennial, with the first iteration held in Rotterdam in the spring and summer of 1996. The exhibition drew its artists from Europe, but somehow I was invited to participate by Andrew Renton, who organized a section of the exhibition devoted to artists whose work involved language. As part of the planning, I was asked how I might explain my intentions for the exhibition, and how they might relate to the idea of Europe.

19 April 1996

To: Marie Jeanne de Rooij
From: Joseph Grigely

Re: Manifesta

Dear Marie Jeanne,

Yesterday I received copies of your two faxes, which were forwarded to me in Michigan, where I am teaching until April 29th. I have been traveling extensively for the past three months, and so it sometimes takes a week or longer for faxes and mail to catch up to me; I apologize for the inconvenience that this has caused you.

Your second question is a good one, and the one I feel particularly obligated to respond to: What is my conception of Manifesta, and how might it relate to the idea of Europe?

My answer—and I hope you will pardon me for not being as comprehensive as I'd like to be—has a lot to do with how we conceive the notion of difference. I'm not a "European." The fact that I received in Europe part of my undergraduate education and all of my postgraduate education does not make me a European either. But inasmuch as Manifesta is intended to bring to question the complexity of a transnational conception of Europe, my presence might have something to bear on this subject. I'm not sure how to articulate this clearly, but it has something to do with the nature of communities best described as being diasporas—to be, as it were, of a culture that is perpetually in motion, a culture that has no homeland to which it can settle down. It is very much like this for deaf people, and about this subject there is a small story in David Wright's poetry. David was born in South Africa, became deaf at seven, and then was shipped off to England to attend Northampton School for the Deaf. In one of his poems he describes himself as being an "expatriate" in the region of his birth—a white man in a black country, a deaf man in a hearing country—how can it be otherwise? Like David, I too am deaf, and I too am an expatriate in my own country. When I am in a room with others, it makes no difference if they speak English or Dutch or Swahili—if they do not speak with me (as opposed to "to" me), I will not know the difference. It's always a little awkward when I travel, especially in Europe—I never know what language the people next to me are speaking unless someone tells me or unless I ask.

And it's almost a little ironic because, as a deaf person, I have always lived at the margins of communication, receiving, as it were, the bits and pieces of language consciously disseminated to me—the letters people send, the notes they write, the words or sentences they repeat five times in my effort to lipread them—an effort that usually ends up being unsuccessful. "Lipreading" is something of a misnomer. A more accurate word, I think, would be "lipmisreading." So the most effective thing for me to do is to ask people to write things down—. Of course, it's easier if there's a sign language interpreter around, but interpreters cost money, and not all of them are altogether skilled: A translation is, in the end, only as good as the translator. So usually I just ask people to write. Writing things down is convenient—it's cheap (pencils & paper are what I call "Luddite technology")—and it's something almost everyone can do. Whenever I'm talking in sign language with someone, people tend to keep a distance and treat us like aliens—which in a sense we are. But when people see someone writing things down they think—*hey, I can do that too*—and at that point the words flow.

And for me, this is the beauty of it all—to be, all at once, both present and absent, caught in the middle of a perpetual middle.

And so, when I am in Rotterdam, I hope to have the pleasure of conversing with people—. My intention is not to do an "exhibition" in the conventional sense, but to participate, as much as possible, in the exchange of words, and to share with others the things words ultimately represent in our everyday lives—.

Cordially,

Statement on *Portraits*, 1995–97

For two years, between 1995 and 1997, I produced a series of extemporaneous portraits of people while we were talking together. Instead of looking at people's eyes when they talk, I spend a lot of time looking at their hands, whether they are writing or using sign language. The images usually include some context: a hand or hands, a pen or pencil, the paper and words being written, or the table (when there is a table). I did not look through the lens when I took these photos; I simply aimed the camera in the general direction of the conversation as I did not want to disrupt the flow of the exchange taking place. The *Portraits* are unposed. They should perhaps be regarded less as objects and more as moments.

The *Portraits* were primarily printed as R-prints and C-prints in editions of three. A few black-and-white *Portraits* were printed as silver prints, a few others as Cibachromes. The scale is small: each one measures 8 by 12 centimeters (roughly 3 by 5 inches). In total, approximately forty portraits were produced.

The *Portraits* were first shown at AC Project Room in New York in May 1996. The exhibition announcement quoted from the fourteenth *Discourse* of English painter Sir Joshua Reynolds (who was himself deaf): "Every artist has some favourite part, on which he fixes his attention, and which he pursues with such eagerness, that it absorbs every other consideration." For me, this "favourite part" consists of people's hands.

Sometimes the *Portraits* were incorporated into larger installations. These installations varied: In some cases, the portraits were framed in contemporary desktop or bookcase "easel" frames; in other cases, they were tacked onto refrigerators with magnets, the refrigerator both a frame and a pedestal. Sometimes the *Portraits* were enlarged and pinned to the walls around a table covered with *Conversations*, which people were invited to pick up and read. This was the basis of the installation *Coffee and Conversations*, which was part of the 1997 Istanbul Biennial and was subsequently produced in various formats.

The *Portraits* have also played an important role in two publications that were presented as exhibitions, both curated by Hans Ulrich Obrist: *Point d'ironie*, no. 1, published in 1997; and *Addenda to Freud's "Psychopathology of Everyday Life": Portraits of Conversations*, printed in the newspaper *Der Standard* (Austria) in 1999. The latter project was organized by museum in progress and the Sigmund Freud Museum, Vienna.

THE FOURTEENTH DISCOURSE. 245

which is of greater consequence: whilst he is employed in the detail, the effect of the whole together is either forgotten or neglected. The likeness of a portrait, as I have formerly observed, consists more in preserving the general effect of the countenance than in the most minute finishing of the features, or any of the particular parts. Now Gainsborough's portraits were often little more, in regard to finishing, or determining the form of the features, than what generally attends a dead colour; but as he was always attentive to the general effect, or whole together, I have often imagined that this unfinished manner contributed even to that striking resemblance for which his portraits are so remarkable. Though this opinion may be considered as fanciful, yet I think a plausible reason may be given why such a mode of painting should have such an effect. It is presupposed that in this undetermined manner there is in the general effect enough to remind the spectator of the original; the imagination supplies the rest, and perhaps more satisfactorily to himself, if not more exactly, than the artist, with all his care, could possibly have done. At the same time it must be acknowledged there is one evil attending this mode; that if the portrait were seen previous to any knowledge of the original, different persons would form different ideas, and all would be disappointed at not finding the original correspond with their own conceptions; under the great latitude which indistinctness gives to the imagination to assume almost what character or form it pleases.

Every artist has some favourite part, on which he fixes his attention, and which he pursues with such eagerness, that it absorbs every other consideration; and he often falls into the opposite error of that which he would avoid, which is always ready to receive him. Now Gainsborough,

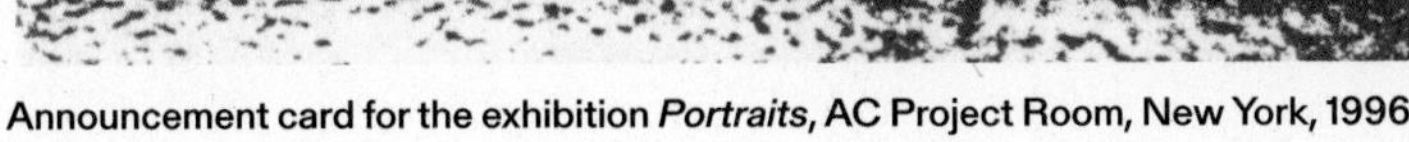

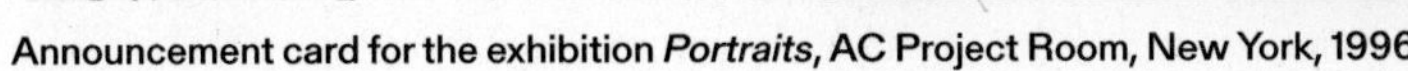

Announcement card for the exhibition *Portraits*, AC Project Room, New York, 1996

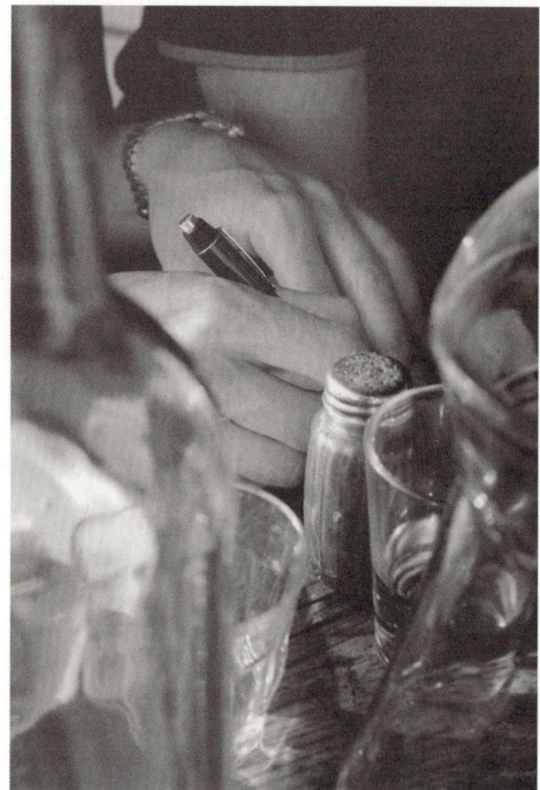

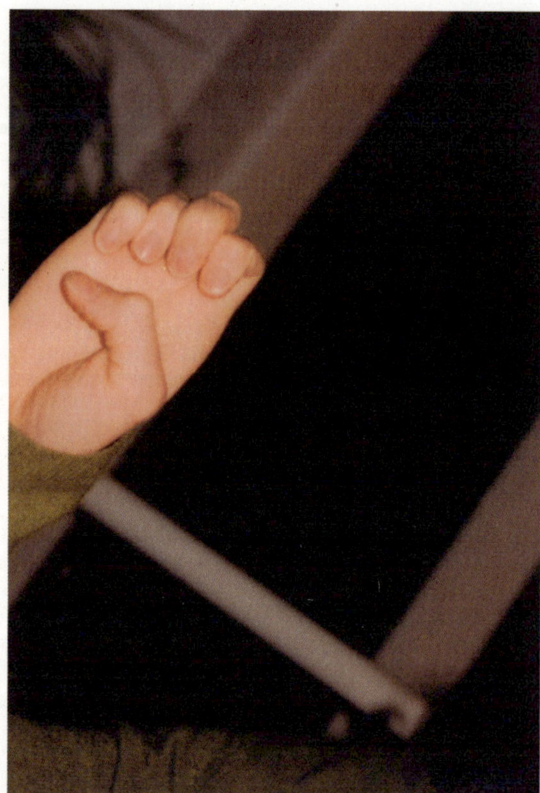

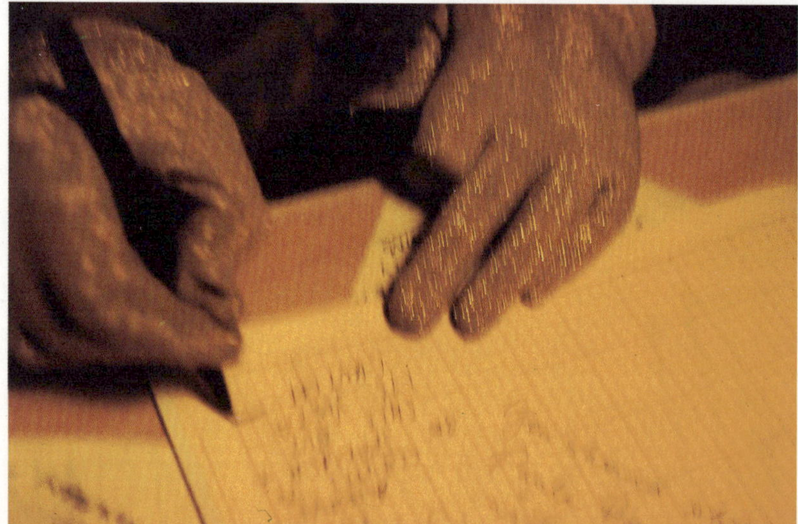

All works by Joseph Grigely. Clockwise from upper left: *Aletta De J. Rotterdam, June 1996*, 1997. Black-and-white silver print; *Amy V. Ghent, 29 January 1997*, 1997. R-print; *Jenny S. Ann Arbor, Michigan, 7 December 1995*, 1996. R-print

Palais Clam-Gallas
Währinger Str. 30, 1090 Wien, ☎ 319 65 03-41 oder 11, Fax: 310 76 90

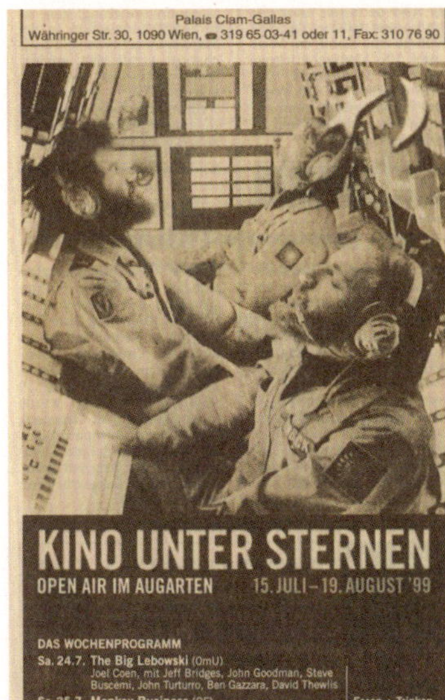

KINO UNTER STERNEN
OPEN AIR IM AUGARTEN 15. JULI – 19. AUGUST '99

DAS WOCHENPROGRAMM
Sa. 24.7. **The Big Lebowski** (OmU) Joel Coen, mit Jeff Bridges, John Goodman, Steve Buscemi, John Turturro, Ben Gazzara, David Thewlis
So. 25.7. **Monkey Business** (OF) Howard Hawks, mit Cary Grant, Ginger Rogers, Marilyn Monroe
Mo. 26.7. SPACE ODDITIES: **Dark Star** (DF) John Carpenter, mit Dre Pahich, Brian Narelle
Di. 27.7. **Lola Montez** (DF) Max Ophüls, mit Martine Carol, Peter Ustinov
Mi. 28.7. **Modern Times** (Stummfilm mit Musik) Charles Chaplin, mit Ch. Chaplin, Pauline Goddard
Do. 29.7. PREVIEW: **Dieu seul me voit** (OmU) Bruno Podalydès, m. D. Podalydès, Jeanne Balibar
Fr. 30.7. SPACE ODDITIES: **Der schweigende Stern** DEFA Kult Space Opera in „Totalvision"

Essen + Trinken ab 17 Uhr
Filmbeginn 21.30 Uhr
Kartenreservierung unter 350-46-32
www.kinountersternen.at
U2 U4 Schottenring
31 Gaußplatz

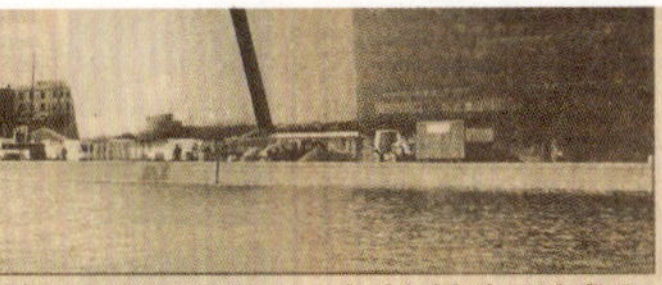

„Schwarzer Diamant": Fensterzeilen bündeln das Licht für Lesende, ohne Bücher zu gefährden. *Fotos: Schmidt,Hammer&Lassen*

zurück, um dort ein Filmprojekt zu realisieren.

Anschluß an Malmö

Im Jahr 2000 wird die acht Kilometer lange, zweistöckige „Øresund-Brücke" Kopenhagen mit dem schwedischen Malmö verbinden. Dann sollen auch die schwedischen Studenten vermehrt den „Schwarzen Diamanten" aufsuchen, um etwa die Origi- tete Atrium-Eingangshalle des „Schwarzen Diamanten" über eine breite Rolltreppe zum Hauptlesesaal und begutachtete die Verbindungsbrücke, über die man vom neuen zum alten Gebäude setzt: Klein-Metropolis. Was äußerlich für manche vielleicht einem Sarkophag ähneln mag (Nielsen: „Das ist Geschmackssache."), im Inneren ist es ein Ort der abenteuerlichen Muße.

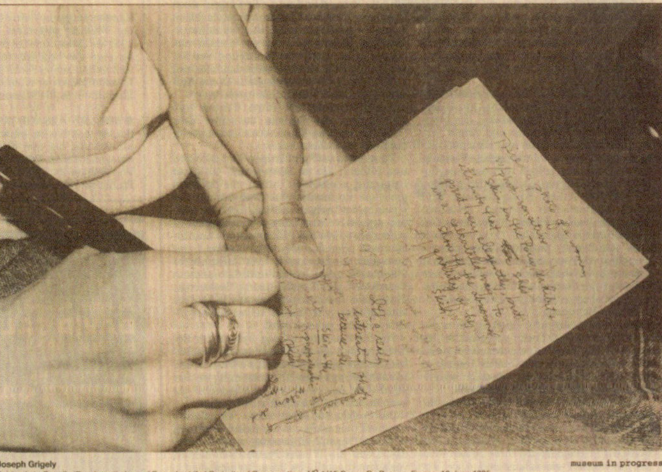

Joseph Grigely museum in progress
Addenda to Freud's 'Psychopathology of Everyday Life:' Portraits of Conversations Nº 1/15 Susan C., Beaune, France, 10 June 1995
in Kooperation mit dem Sigmund Freud-Museum Wien, ermöglicht durch **art-pool**

gelungen war. Vorbild für Österreich? „Schon", sagt Thomas Gangel, Generalsekretär des Schwimmverbands (VÖS), nur wären in Holland die Voraussetzungen andere. Schwimmen in den Niederlanden hat vor allem lange Tradition, also für Sponsoren höheren Wert, außerdem gibt es mehr als doppelt soviele Aktive wie in Österreich. Gangel: „Wenn uns ein Talent

Das 6:2, 6:3 brachte ihn schnurstracks ins Halbfinale der Generali Open. Und folgende Erkenntnis: „Ich kann wieder Winner schlagen."

Wer schon viel hat, möchte mehr, der 22jährige Koubek sieht seinem Semi gegen den Spanier Fernando Vicente (Samstag, ab 14.15 Uhr) eher gelassen entgegen. „Ein guter Mann, aber warum sollte ich ihn nicht schlagen." Vicente

bühel, es waren gleich zwei. Gilbert Schaller und der spätere Sieger Thomas Muster.

Koubek wird kommende Woche zumindest in den Top 50 aufscheinen, schon der Erfolg über Karol Kucera hat ihn dorthin befördert. Zum ersten Mal, sagte er selbst, habe er ein wichtiges Match ausschließlich im Kopf und mit einer für ihn untypischen Taktik gewonnen. „Natürlich schieße

schlecht, lediglich auf seine Doppelfehler konnte er sich verlassen. Koubek hingegen durfte endlich wieder drauf los hauen, zeigte Spielwitz (eingesprungene Rückhand), das Timing paßte, die Beinarbeit war perfekt. Und er übertauchte die kleinen Hänger. Als der Brasilianer im zweiten Satz den Plan änderte und hohe Bälle einstreute, erinnerte sich Koubek einfach an

gesellschaftliche Teil ist so gut wie und würdig abgeschlossen.

Die Generali Open gewinnen hingegen zusehends an Ernst. Speziell für Koubek. Ein allerletzter Scherz ist aber immer noch gegangen, das Endspiel beginnt am Sonntag nicht vor 16 Uhr, es ist auf drei Gewinnsätze angesetzt, kann also rund vier Stunden dauern. Irgendwann im Morgengrauen sollte der Interessierte, der ja nicht zwangsläufig Kitzbüheler sein muß, seine Heimat Wien, Graz, München oder Zürich erreicht haben. Und Koubek könnte es ganz schlimm erwischt haben, er spielt ab Montag das Turnier in Amsterdam.

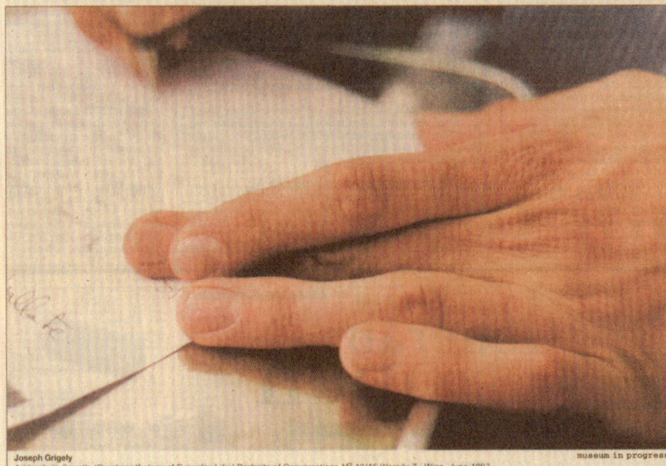

Joseph Grigely museum in progress
Addenda to Freud's 'Psychopathology of Everyday Life:' Portraits of Conversations Nº 12/15 Wassily Z., Wien, June 1997
in Kooperation mit dem Sigmund Freud-Museum Wien, ermöglicht durch **art-pool**

ERSTE DIVISION

Samstag: SV Wörgl – FC Kärnten (18.30), SV Braunau – WSG Wattens (19.30), Untersiebenbrunn – A. W. Mödling (19.30)
Steyr – Leoben 1:1 (0:1); Tore: 0:1 (27.) Guggi, 1:1 (47.) Ortner
Vienna – FCN St. Pölten 0:4 (0:2); Tore: 0:1 (3.) Metlitskij, 0:2 (37.) Nentwich, 0:3 (70.) Jasinski, 0:4 (72.) Kleer – Gelb-Rot: Gutlederer (Vienna/66./Foul)

A. W. Mödling	5	4	1	0	6: 0	13
DSV Leoben	6	4	1	1	7: 6	13
SV Wörgl	5	3	1	1	7: 4	10
FC Kärnten	5	2	2	1	6: 4	8
FCN St. Pölten	6	2	1	3	7: 5	7
WSG Wattens	5	2	1	2	9:11	7
Vienna	6	1	2	3	6: 9	5
SV Braunau	5	1	1	3	2: 4	4
Untersiebenbrunn	5	1	1	3	3: 6	4
Vorwärts Steyr	6	1	1	4	3: 7	4

SO GEHT'S WEITER

Dienstag, 3. August, max.BUNDESLIGA: SV Salzburg – SW Bregenz (19), Austria Lustenau – FC Tirol (19.30), Sturm Graz – SV Ried (19.30), LASK – GAK (20)

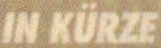

FUSSBALL

Mexiko/Confederations Cup, Gruppe A: Mexiko – Bolivien 1:0, Saudi Arabien – Ägypten 5:1

PFERDESPORT

Freudenau/Galoppen, SA (15), TIPS: 1 Nazanine, 2 Botschafter, 3 Velon, 4 R. St. John, 5 Albadou, 6 Hallplace, 7 Mukrin, 8 Trader
Baden/Traben, SO (14): 1 I. Mystere, 2 F. Lauderdale, 3 A. Excel, 4 Vuk, 5 L. Hochmoor, 6 C. Vip, 7 Nike S, 8 Cavern Club, 9 Shesterfield, 10 Kassandra, 11 Cl. Heat

RADSPORT

„Race across America", Stand nach 4528 von 4728 km: 1. Chew (USA), 2. Fasching (AUT) + 4 Min.

SCHWIMMEN

Istanbul/EM, HERREN, 50 m BRUST: 1. Warnecke (GER) 27,95, 2. Lisogor (UKR) 28,21, 3. Güttler (HUN) 28,29 – 200 m KRAUL: 1. Hoogenband (NED) 1:47,09, 2. Palmer (GBR) 1:48,01, 3. Rosolino (ITA) 1:48,27 – 1500 m KRAUL: 1. Snitko (UKR) 15:07,19, 2. Coman (ROM) 15:13,10, 3. Cros (FRA) 15:18,26 – 200m BRUST: 1. Perrot (FRA) 2:12,46, 2. Komornikow (RUS) 2:12,88, 3. Bernard (FRA) 2:12,96
DAMEN, 50 m BRUST: 1. Kovacs (HUN) 31,44, 2. Baker (GBR) 31,53, 3. Schäfer (GER) 32,22; 7. Lischka (AUT) 32,87
100 m RÜCKEN: 1. Völker (GER) 1:01,39, 2. Jivanevskaia (ESP) 1:01,98, 3. Maracineanu (FRA) 1:02,47 – 200 m LAGEN: 1. Klotschkowa (UKR) 2:14,02, 2. Caslaru (ROM) 2:15,12, 3. Klenz (GER) 2:16,95 – SPRINGEN, H., Synchron, 3 m: 1. Miranda/Marconi (ITA) 303,24 Pkte., 2. Mesch/Schlepps (GER) 299,79, 3. Ali/Shipman (GBR) 296,01

TENNIS

Kitzbühel, Generali Open, 535.000 Dollar, VIERTELFINALE: Koubek (AUT/15) – Meligeni (BRA/7) 6:2, 6:3, Vicente (ESP/13) – Lapentti (ECU/6) 6:7 (4/7), 6:1, 6:3, Kafelnikow (RUS/1) – Fromberg (AUS) 6:3, 6:7 (6/8), 6:3, A. Costa (ESP/5) – Ferrero (ESP) 3:6, 6:2, 6:3
Halbfinale, Samstag: Vicente – Koubek (14.15 live/ORF 1), Kafelnikow – A. Costa
DOPPEL, Viertelfinale: Melzer/Peya (AUT) – Goellner/Montana (GER/USA) 3:6, 6:2, 6:3

TISCHTENNIS

Linz, Benefiz, HERREN: Österreich – Ungarn All Star Team 6:3 Pkte.

ONLINE-STANDARD

Alle Ergebnisse und Berichte: http:// DerStandard.at/SportStandard

Joseph Grigely, *Addenda to Freud's "Psychopathology of Everyday Life": Portraits of Conversations*, published in *Der Standard*, Vienna, July 24–25, 1999 (top); July 31, 1999 (bottom)

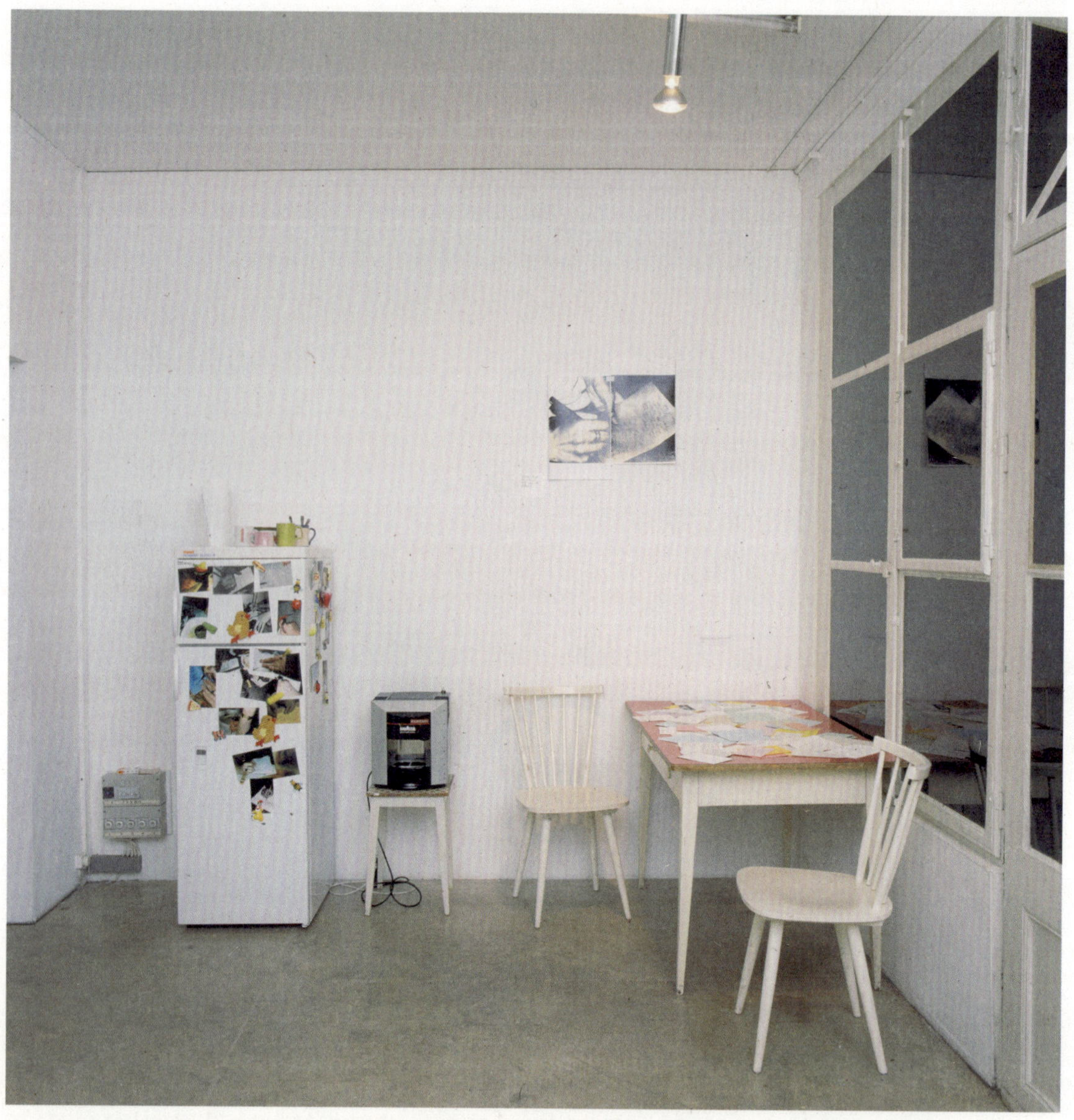

Joseph Grigely, *Coffee and Conversations*, 1997; Installation view, Galerie Francesca Pia, Bern, Switzerland, 1998

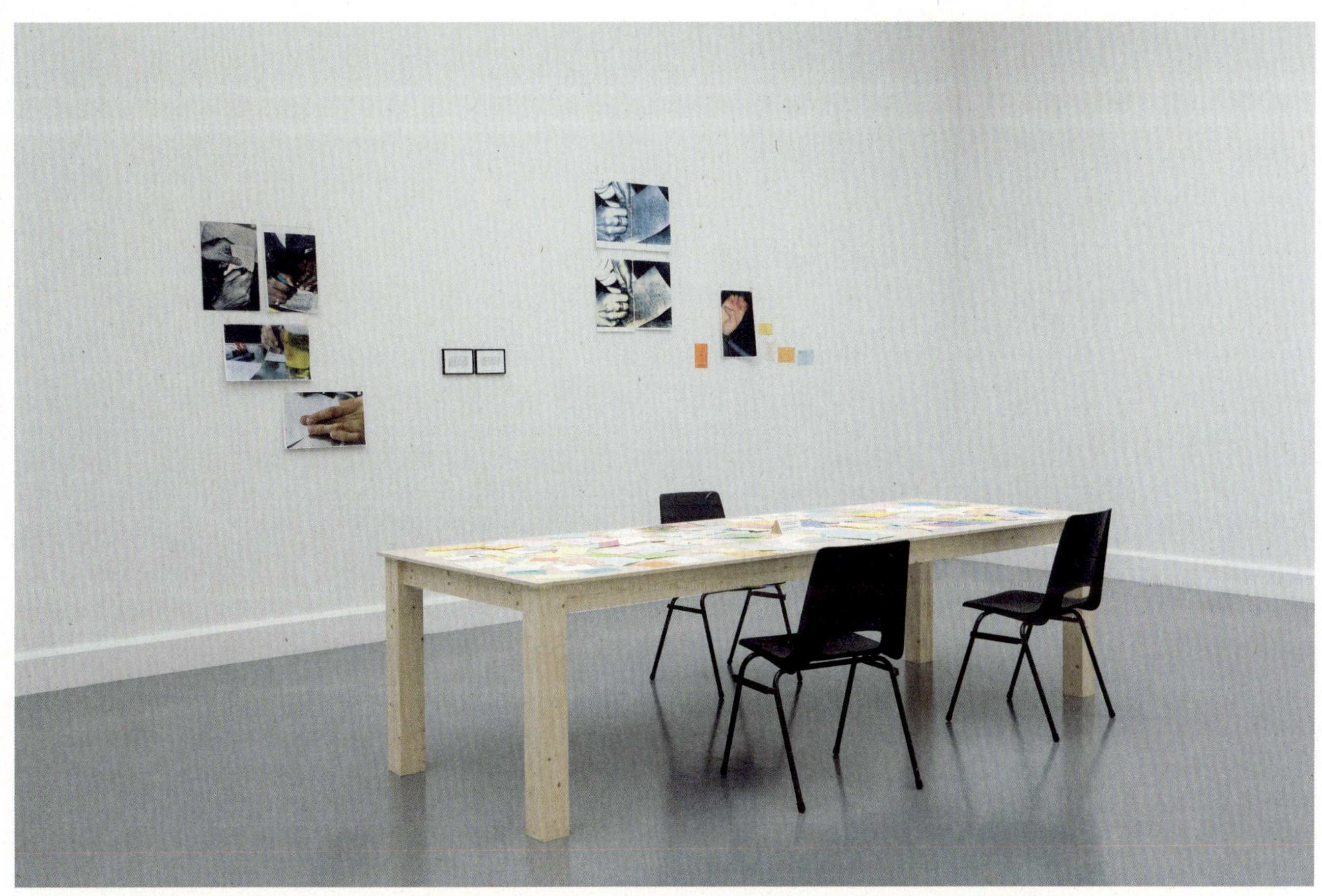

Joseph Grigely, *Listening*, 1997. Installation view, *EindhovenIstanbul*, Van Abbemuseum, Eindhoven, The Netherlands, 2005

Letter to Per Kirkeby, 1996

As part of the exhibition *NowHere* at the Louisiana Museum of Modern Art in Humlebaek, Denmark, in 1996, I wanted to do an installation that combined a suite of four abstract paintings by Per Kirkeby with a group of papers from my *Conversations with the Hearing*. Up to this point my work was primarily viewed as language art, and I wanted to direct attention to the way the grids of paper were also abstractions—and how language and abstraction could coexist. To my surprise, Kirkeby agreed to this, and the museum subsequently acquired the work.

7 May 1996

To: Per Kirkeby
From: Joseph Grigely

Dear Per Kirkeby,

I am an American artist, and between May and September I shall be participating in the exhibition *NowHere* at the Louisiana Museum in Humlebaek. I had an opportunity to visit the Museum in January, and found it very stimulating. I was especially engaged by your suite of six untitled paintings from 1983–4, and as part of my installation at Louisiana I would like to ask you for your permission to include four of them. (I originally tried to fax you this letter several weeks ago, but I was given the wrong fax number. I hope you will forgive this late, and, as a consequence, hasty request.)

My general intention at Louisiana is to create an installation that constitutes an intersection of discourses. The exhibition, like almost all exhibitions, will itself do this on a grand scale: a series of positionings, transpositionings, and juxtapositionings. The curators will play off each other, the artists will play off each other, the rooms will play off each other. And within each room will be the interplay of various modes and modalities of ideas and objects.

Most of my art consists of what I call *Conversations with the Hearing*. The *Conversations* themselves consist primarily of pieces of paper that are written upon by hearing people in the course of a conversation with me. Partly because I am totally deaf, written communication is the only practical and efficient way for me to communicate with people who do not know sign language: They write to me and I talk back. As we continue to talk, the words and the pages pile up. Although these words and pages are written, they are rather less like writing than they are like drawing, and I tend to think of them as abstractions almost—as drawings of speech. When the *Conversations* are exhibited, they are arranged in the form of fairly abstract grids, and then mounted to the wall using map pins. In the past year I have exhibited the *Conversations* at the Venice Biennale, ARC at the Musée d'Art Moderne de Paris, FRAC-Limoges, and the Anthony d'Offay Gallery in London.

At Louisiana my intention is this: In a semi-enclosed space I want to juxtapose on the walls four of the paintings from your untitled suite of six abstract paintings and a series of my *Conversations with the Hearing*. (I'd prefer to use all six, but the room in which I shall be doing the installation is too small for this.) The works would alternate on the wall—a painting here, a group of *Conversations* there, then a painting, then a *Conversation*—and in the middle of the installation would be a table covered with materials related to natural history, language, "abstraction," and papers produced in the course of putting together the installation.

My rationale is this: Historically, abstract painting has been seen as a refuge, or escape, from language—a site of ineffability. It's a fairly common belief, if not a myth, that abstraction is the furthest remove from language there is in art. This might also be said for deafness: Historically, deafness has been seen, like abstraction, as a refuge, or escape, from language—a condition best suited for "gestural" communication. Enlightenment thinkers like Condillac and Rousseau remarked that deafness is the furthest remove from language there is in life. By juxtaposing your paintings with my *Conversations*, my intention would be to bring all of these assumptions together without necessarily trying to resolve them. I hope to get people thinking about your abstract art as a representational art, and I want them to think about my representational *Conversations* as an abstract art—. I want them to think and to not think, to feel and to not feel—. Ideally, the juxtapositionings would help create a constant sense of movement between the various taxonomies that have become conventionalized discourse of art history and criticism. In this respect, my installation would be about the formlessness of form, and the form of formlessness.

I hope that you will find this proposition agreeable, and that you will consent to give your permission to display the paintings as I have described here. If you have any questions, please feel free to fax me here at Louisiana. Or you may also call my curator, Iwona Blazwick, and speak with her.

With thanks for your consideration, and with appreciation,

Sincerely yours,

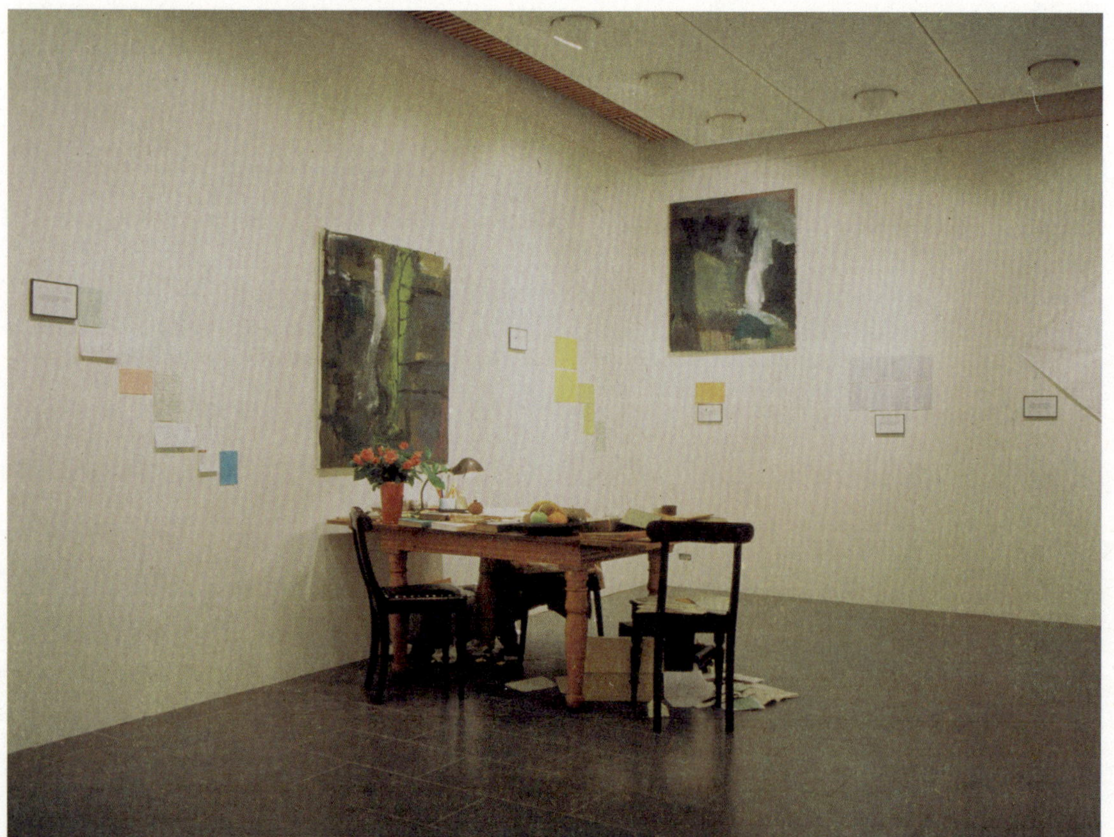

Joseph Grigely, *I Don't Really Know Why, But Maybe It's More Abstract This Way (with four untitled paintings by Per Kirkeby)*, 1996. Mixed media. Installation view, Louisiana Museum of Modern Art, Humlebaek, Denmark

Barbican Conversations, 1997

Occasionally, someone will feel offended by the content of the conversation notes in one of my works and express their indignation about the situation. Usually, the situation is manageable. But once, at the Barbican Centre in London, I did an exhibition that included conversation notes posted in a vitrine across from one of the theater stage bars; I also printed a number of conversations in brochures that were intentionally mixed in with the free programming handouts the Barbican distributed to visitors. Slowly but surely, the complaints—most about a ribald story that an acquaintance wrote on Barbican Centre stationery—reached the upper management offices. The curator was asked to explain herself, and, in turn, the curator asked me to explain myself, which I did. The exhibition was subsequently allowed to continue.

Barbican Centre

A guy is sitting at the bar telling the bartender how his wife left him because he was too kinky in bed. A woman at the end of the bar pipes in saying, "Wow, my husband just left me 'cause he said I was too kinky in bed." The guy says, "hey, since we got this in common, why not go back to your place?" So they do. At her place, she says "let me put something more comfortable on," and slips into the bedroom. She puts on the leather mask, chains, bustier, whips, the whole deal. She comes into the living room and the guy has his coat on, ready to go. She says "Hey, hey, buddy - where are you going -- we haven't even started yet?!" The guy says, "Lady, I just fucked your poodle and took a shit in your purse -- I'm ready to go!"

with compliments

CORPORATION OF LONDON

Silk Street London EC2Y 8DS Telephone 0171 638 4141 **Facsimile** 0171 920 9648 (main number)

Owned, funded and managed by the Corporation of London Managing Director John Tusa

Joseph Grigely, *Untitled Conversation (Barbican Bar)*, 1998. Ink on paper

03-FEB-98 17:10 P.01

Barbican Centre

facsimile

Date: 2 February 1998

To: Joseph Grigely — Fax: 0012017959466
Company: — Fax: 0013136681447

CC: Kathryn Standing

From: Ann Jones — Direct Telephone: 382 7033
E-Mail: — Direct Fax: 382 7037

RE: Barbican Conversations

Number of pages including cover sheet: 1

Joey — Here we go —

Dear Joseph,

People have expressed concern about some of the material incorporated in your leaflets and collages in the vitrines.

The concerns aired about the leaflets are that they should not be available to children because of the content and language used, what are your views on this?

We have received comments about the joke written on the Barbican Centre compliment slip, again concern about the text rather than the fact it is on a piece of Barbican Centre stationery.

Obviously we intend defending "Barbican Conversations" but would like to be as clear as possible about your reasons for the inclusion of material of a sexual nature and use of language that could be perceived as offensive.

I personally do not find any of the material offensive and am of the opinion that it is no worse than children are regularly subjected to in the media, however this is debatable. I think the joke on the Barbican Centre stationery is asking for trouble, not because of the joke but because it is associating the joke with a corporate image.

Tomorrow I have to have a meeting with the Managing Director and Divisional Directors to defend our project and reach a consistent line of justification so I would appreciate your immediate response to my fax.

Best wishes,

Ann

Ann Jones
HEAD OF VISUAL ARTS

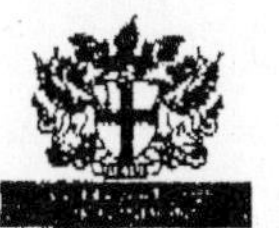

Silk Street London EC2Y 8DS Telephone 0171 638 4141 Facsimile 0171 920 9648 (main number)

805 Granger Street, Ann Arbor, Michigan 48104
Michigan fax +1.313.668.1447
111 First Street 6-5N, Jersey City, New Jersey 07302
NJ fax: +1.201.795.9466
email: jgrigely@umich.edu

Ann Arbor, 3rd February 1998

To: Ann Jones
Barbican fax 011.44.171.382.7037

Dear Ann,

I received your fax of February 2 a little while ago, and I'm very sorry to learn that you have received complaints about my installation at the Barbican, *Barbican Conversations*. It was not my intention to offend anyone--especially the Barbican, its staff, and its patrons--and I regret the work has caused such feelings. If you don't mind, I would like to explain a little about the origins of the project, and why certain 'conversations' that might be deemed offensive were included in the leaflets and vitrines.

While I have been deaf for over 30 years, it was only for the last eight years that I have asked people to write down for me the things that they are saying. At first I was quite surprised at what people wrote--but it became apparent over time that people communicated different things in different ways, and that writing involved a degree of intimacy--people, so I discovered, love to whisper on paper. I also discovered that people were very honest in writing things down--they'd say both boring and banal stuff right alongside unusual and revealing stuff--and this strange mixture helped me see more clearly how complex human communication is--and how beautiful, even disturbingly beautiful, it sometimes could be.

In the process of conceiving my commission with the Barbican Centre, I did not have preconceptions about what people would say in the course of having conversations with me; nor did I have preconceptions about what I would print in the leaflets or exhibit in the vitrines. My intention was simply to present an array of actual conversations with actual people--and present them in a way that is honest and forthright, and in a way that tells a story about human interaction. The people represented in the work range in age from 8 to 91. Some are close friends; some total strangers. As the press release says, the printed leaflets contain notes and exchanges written on whatever material was close to hand, and range from the poetic to the confessional.

That the work should baffle--surprise--and even disturb people--is in part what *Barbican Conversations* is all about. People say nice things, beautiful things, boring things, polite things, strange things, raunchy things, caring things--they say everything and anything, and they say these things in all kinds of places. Conversation has been for centuries a distinguished subject of English and Dutch art--particularly in the genre of work known as the "Conversation Piece." Hogarth, Stubbs, Gainsborough, and Dirck Hals (whose drawing "A Merry Company" is illustrated in one of my leaflets) all painted works whose focus is on the exchange of words between people. Conversation Pieces are distinguished by the fact that people are present, but their words are not. They are counterpoints to the scraps of paper that comprise my work, where the words are present, but the people who wrote them are not. Conversations Pieces are marked not by any stylistic idiom, but by their detail of incident--how they capture, like a snapshot, the traces of conversation in gestures and poses. The irony is that their conversations are never disclosed to us--and this sense of disclosure, of revealing the unrevealed, is precisely what my work is all about. Centered around the Barbican bars, the conversations in the leaflets and vitrines explore the differences between the perceived high culture of the theatre and orchestra with the bar's low-brow jokes and intimate conversations.

Of course, the meanings of the individual 'conversations' that are printed and displayed will not be immediately obvious--and I would be disappointed if they were. They are meant to perplex and intrigue, precisely because it is the goal of art like mine to encourage people to think about the world they live in--and learn to appreciate how it is constructed out of differences that we do not always share--different opinions, different thoughts, different ideas about what is 'normal.' The "conversations" that are printed in the leaflets and displayed in the vitrines represent a wide variety of different human voices. These voices permeate everyday life: we will, and do, hear them on television and in newspapers and in the conversations of people beside us. I would like to think that with this in mind, and with my own sense of care in mind, that the leaflets and vitrines might be looked at as opportunities to appreciate how people communicate, and why they communicate the things they do. I am not trying to offend anyone with my work. That some people *will* be offended is unavoidable, I think: and necessary too, for the process of sharing with people the experience of being deaf--and the intimate qualities of this experience--does not come without its own unique sense of enlightenment.

I regret that the joke that seems to trouble some people was written on Barbican stationary--this was unfortunate. It was, however, unavoidable: my conversations with people have always been written on whatever paper was at hand, and in this particular circumstance, it was a piece of Barbican Centre stationary. When I installed the paper in the vitrine, I had actually thought it would be appreciated that at least one "conversation" had a very definite sense of place to it. It was not my intention to attempt to discredit the Barbican--or even make a joke at it--by including this piece: it was included simply because it is a funny story--a little silly, a little raunchy--and in many ways, a typical bar story. It was intentional on my part that I located this "conversation" in the vitrine directly in front of the stalls floor bar: the story itself takes place at a bar. The fact that it is written on paper--written on Barbican stationary, in fact--reveals one of the important aspects of the entire project: about how written conversations are different from spoken ones. I am sympathetic to the fact that some people will not like to see a joke written on Barbican Centre stationary--but I am also saddened to think that such an incidental occurrence should be a cause for so much distress. In some ways, the formality of the stationary and the informality of the language of the "conversation" is a beautiful irony--one very similar to the irony on the exhibition announcement card. My work has always embraced such ironies, and makes an effort to show how the physical space of talking and the physical space of writing are very different kinds of spaces. My hope is that the directors of the Barbican Centre will appreciate the importance of this distinction and not feel intimidated by it.

Working on this project has been very important to me: it has extended, considerably, the range of human emotion in my work, and the range of emotions expressed towards it. This has been for me an enlightening and beautiful experience--not one I would willingly forego. I would be extremely disappointed if the project should be altered or changed at this point: it has as its most basic premise a desire to share with others the complexity of how we communicate with each other, and a very sincere hope that people will appreciate and respect this experience, even if it is not their own.

Sincerely,

Emails with Hans Ulrich Obrist, Molly Nesbit, and Rirkrit Tiravanija on My Proposals for *Utopia Station*, 2003

As part of the 2003 Venice Biennale, Hans Ulrich Obrist, Molly Nesbit, and Rirkrit Tiravanija organized a satellite exhibition, *Utopia Station*. One of the exhibition's goals was to create a physical platform for both visual media and performances. Leading up to the exhibition the organizers hosted symposia, including one at Vassar College in February 2003 where I gave a talk about the importance of architectural access titled "Pizza, Disability, and Difference." My original proposal asked the organizers to ensure the platform was wheelchair accessible, but I was told in reply that there were "some troubles we could have in relation to accommodating your idea."

In the end, the platform was not made accessible. When the project moved from Venice to Haus der Kunst in Munich, I repeated my request, but I was later informed by the head of the construction team that they were worried someone might trip on the wheelchair ramp, and so it was not built.

March 2003

HUO, Molly & Rirkrit:

I think I finally have a plan now. It has a lot to do with disability-related access issues. There's no real beginning point here—these issues keep coming up for me all the time, and in so many different ways. Sometimes it has to do with a lack of interpreters—for example, when I asked the Whitney for an interpreter for the opening for the 2000 Whitney Biennial, they said no—they said that since I had not written that into my budget, they couldn't do it. Which is interesting because my budget was $0.00—so it's not like I was asking for a lot. This sort of thing has happened many times. I stopped going to conferences in 1990 when the MLA insisted my interpreters (who I hired myself) also pay a registration fee. I always saw interpreting as my glass ceiling in academia and the art world—not just getting interpreters, but getting interpreters who could effectively translate postgraduate critical discourse. This is one reason why I am so grateful to Molly for having made the Vassar gathering work for me—and by extension, all of us.

But access issues have always been present for me and for others in the art world. I remember years ago—around 1993—I got in a tangle with someone about the Guerrilla Girls. She was arguing that such-and-such gallery represented so many men and so many women, and I said, yeah—people in wheelchairs can't even get inside the gallery to SEE the art—let alone be represented by the gallery. Getting inside the physical space of the gallery has always been a painful challenge to observe: One day I was doing the galleries in SoHo, and as I passed by Metro Pictures—this is back when they were on Greene Street—I saw someone in a wheelchair look through the glass door of the gallery. So I asked him if he wanted to go in, and he said yes, he hadn't been in a gallery before—. So another passerby and I helped get his electric wheelchair up a step into the gallery—and then I went in at the same time, and someone from the office came out, really upset about the wheelchair—I'm not sure what the exact words were, but I know it was something about the wheelchair tires marking the floor, or maybe marking the floor—but it was just bizarre seeing that the people in the gallery were upset by having someone in a wheelchair inside. A lot of galleries in New York, even those newly renovated in Chelsea, remain inaccessible.

For years, I've kept this out of my art. Angry art isn't my thing. I did however write an essay on disability in the early 1990s—the "Postcards to Sophie Calle"—where I tried to develop some kind of theory of disability. But generally, I've tried to construct a body of work that is essentially about communication, and the ways the human imagination can create linguistic and paralinguistic interfaces. It's not really grandiose as technology: pencils and papers. But it's grandiose as a cognitive act: The brain, as a malleable machine for the generation of social discourse, will do whatever is necessary to make that discourse happen.

Now with this subject for Venice being Utopia, I've found myself readdressing a long and dystopic history of inaccessibility. There have been so many times when I have wanted to be "present" for something, but have not been able to do this because of obstacles—people saying no to my request for interpreters, a dean once asking me to teach a course without an interpreter because it would make for more "direct contact" with the students—ad infinitum, ad nauseam. And I'm reluctant even now to discuss this in detail, because it is such a weighty political & personal subject, and it makes people so uncomfortable—just as it makes people uncomfortable to be around those who are physically disabled. I think it's interesting that the disabled often come across as being more than a little pathetic—but there are reasons: The way access laws in the US are written, there is this condescending notion that society has to "accommodate" the disabled—as if access was a monodirectional thing. As if access was only "for" the disabled. You don't hear advocates for diversity telling us about how having disabled people around is good for culture. Instead you have neo-eugenicists telling us how genetic engineering will ameliorate disability, or philosophers like Peter Singer telling us that parents should have the right to kill disabled babies—that infanticide is OK if a baby is born with a severe handicap.

Anyhow, after reflecting on this subject for some time, I've decided that my project for Venice would be devoted to absence, and to making absence a presence. Here are my projects:

1) For the poster: Coated white paper with no image and no text. One small Biennial logo, as Ariane [Beyn] specified.

2) Catalogue: Just my name. No images. A blank page.

3) For the exhibition: Nothing.

I know, you will say: This has been done before (such as Robert Barry's empty galleries in the 1960s, and Laurie Parsons's "nothing" show at Lorence-Monk around 1990). They both had a conceptual and formal basis, but not a political one. This one is political—.

This also alleviates the need for me to beg for money to produce a project or to go to Venice—I'm really tired of having to ask—and have people say in reply, "It's difficult to get funding for American artists." (As if I don't know?) This is a very tiresome subject for me. Especially when people think, "Oh he shows a lot, so he must have enough money to finance projects." If only. If.

Anyhow—I'm sorry it's not a splashy or pretty or otherwise engaging project. Most people will probably dislike it—oversimplify it, reduce it, shrug at it. To be honest with you, I really don't care.

Joseph

March 27, 2003

Dear Joseph,

I am back now from ten days in Europe, now dealing with all the email piled up, and here's your new plan, which is a beautiful solution to a situation full of obstacles.

But still, whenever I see a pizza, I see you.

Amitiés,
Molly

April 16, 2003

Dear Molly, Hans Ulrich, and Rirkrit,

I very much regret and apologize for the frustration we are all experiencing with this seemingly innocuous project—it wasn't meant this way. When I gave my Vassar talk about disability and Civil Rights, I did so with the explicit intention to bring art to politics, not bring politics to art. The political dimension of engaging issues of disability in the context of Venice, or the art world more generally, is very alienating—people just don't want to be told how to arrange their physical and material lives. Yet, since the assigned subject was Utopia, it would be hypocritical of me to present a project about disability access and not also request—even demand—that the architecture of our project be accessible. Yet, I don't like meddling in other people's projects. This is one of the reasons I have avoided making what could be construed as didactic art—. The trouble with disability as a social and political construct is that no one wants to be accused of being uncaring. Most disability-related discrimination is unique as a form of patronization or paternalization—people mean well, but access is about independence that comes from changes that recognize the lack of a homogeneous body to define a sense of the normal. In the world of disability, normal is what is not.

So my disability-related work will stay within the realm of American jurisprudence. I will keep it out of the art world. And I am very sorry that what I have said about this has disconcerted so many people.

I have decided to make a small emendation to my Venice poster—. As I said a little while ago, the blank poster was not very much liked among the people with whom I shared the project; and Elena [Filipovic]'s recent email asking if I might like to add a text of some kind—something that might explain, in so many words, what this was all about—also suggested a little too much ambiguity.

I have attached a file of a revised poster. The revised poster has a text of four words in the middle, printed in black:

Wish you were Here

The poster itself remains a blank white space. "Here" is necessarily an abstract space—one both real and not.

Ariane [Beyn], I will send printing specs to you in a separate message.

For the exhibition, what I'd like to do is make a Super 8 film of the phrase "Wish you were Here" using a handheld camera, degrade the film stock, then do a digital transfer to DVD. I imagine a 3-minute loop. For projection, I'd like to project the film on a home-movie screen (about 1.5m wide).

I'm not sure if I can do this in time for the exhibition—it depends mostly on finances, and whether I can get the transfers done in time for the exhibition. I won't be able to work on this until late May, so it's pretty much an iffy situation. But I will try.

With best wishes, and with thanks for your patience,

Joseph

Proposal for *White Noise* (1999), and a Proposal for a Two-Room Version at the Massachusetts Museum of Contemporary Art (2023)

White Noise was exhibited in *Voilà: Le Monde dans la tête* at the Musée d'Art Moderne de Paris (2000); in *Joseph Grigely: White Noise* at the Whitney Museum of American Art (2001); in *Erre* at the Centre Pompidou-Metz (2011); and, in its two-room incarnation, in *Joseph Grigely: In What Way Wham? (White Noise and Other Works, 1996–2023)* at the Massachusetts Museum of Contemporary Art (2023).

In 1999, Hans Ulrich Obrist invited me to contribute an installation for an exhibition called *Voilà: Le Monde dans la tête* at the Musée d'Art Moderne de Paris. After ten years of collecting and archiving conversation notes, I felt I had a sufficiently large accumulation to realize an installation I had imagined years earlier. The original proposal called for an elliptical room 20 meters long and 4 meters high, filled floor to ceiling with conversations on white paper. This would have required nearly seven thousand conversation papers. For practical reasons, both architectural and archival, the room size was reduced to 8 meters in length. In subsequent installations at the Whitney Museum of American Art (2001) and the Centre Pompidou-Metz (2011), the same dimensions were used. For the 2023 installation at MASS MoCA, two interconnected rooms were built: a monochrome room, where all the conversations were written on white paper, and a slightly smaller polychrome room, where all the conversations were on colored paper. The polychrome room required thirty years of collecting conversations before I had a sufficient quantity to create the work.

Both the original 1999 proposal and the revised 2023 proposal are printed here.

1999 Proposal

Note from Hans Ulrich Obrist: *Some other issue is a project which we prepare for the Museum in Paris for 2000. It has to do with encyclopedia and is about "infinite and unfinished" archives. I told my colleagues about your unrealized project of having all your text in a chapel-like space with ladders which you had told me about whilst we had dinner in Antwerpen. If you can send me some lines by email on this project that would be great, as I can propose it concretely in the next meeting we have in Paris.*

To: Hans Ulrich Obrist
From: Joseph Grigely
Subject: Proposal for *White Noise*

Dear Hans Ulrich,

I am sending to you a proposal for the exhibition on the "infinite and unfinished"—a work entitled *White Noise*.

Proposal: *White Noise*

"White noise" is a term used by audiologists to describe a noise that occupies a wide bandwidth of discursive frequencies. Like the color white—which contains all colors of the spectrum—white noise contains a full spectrum of frequencies. Essentially, white noise is an audio blur: Its primary distinction is that it lacks continuity, cohesion, and intelligibility.

What is the visual equivalent of white noise?

In my work as an artist, I typically explore conversations—the paths they take, the shapes and colors they have, and the stories they tell in the process of being retold. Partly because I am totally deaf, written communication is the only practical and efficient way for me to communicate with people who do not know sign language: They write to me and I talk back. As we continue to talk, the words and the papers pile up—over days, over weeks, over months, and over years, the archive continues to grow as I continue to converse. Ultimately, this archive constitutes the raw material of my art: the scraps of paper on which hearing people have written notes, names, or phrases in order to "converse" with me. I then use these scraps of conversations to build wall pieces and tabletop tableaux that all take as their subject matter the ineluctable differences between speech and writing and reading and listening.

In *White Noise*, my intention is to present an archive of "Conversations" inscribed on white paper. Ideally, the work would be installed in a large room approximately 20 meters long by 12 meters wide by 4 meters high. The "Conversations" would be attached to the walls from the floor to the ceiling—allowing a bit of space (about 2–3 cm) between each piece of paper. Some of the papers would be very small—about 2 cm square—some would be very large—up to 1 m × 1.5 m (these are usually paper tablecloths from restaurants). To fill a room from floor to ceiling with "Conversations" like these would require approximately 6,656 inscribed pieces of paper.

The "Conversations" chosen for the installation would be randomly selected from my archive. They would be installed in such a way as to present formal grids (square and rectangular pieces of white paper on white walls). The "Conversations" themselves, being haphazard and discursive—as most human conversations are—would lack continuity and cohesiveness. Attached to the wall, they are simply a collection of fragments of conversations: statements, questions, unfinished utterances, erasures. In a sense, the installation could also be seen as a form of still-life drawing. Like flowers in vases and fruit in baskets, language is a conventionalized aspect of domestic settings. Through its omnipresence, it defines our sense of the quotidian. Yet, its inescapable escapability reminds us how inured we are to the evanescence of speech. Imagine how different it would be if every word we spoke took on a material presence. Imagine if every word we spoke occupied space and place. Think of the possibilities here: Scraps of language lying on the counter. Drawers full of sentences. Peelings of words in the sink. Imagine dustbins filled with words—the ordinary words of our ordinary lives—the things all of us say. Imagine huge piles of them. This is a special kind of still life: a still life of ordinary language and everyday speech.

The installation would include two or three aluminum library ladders on wheels so that visitors to the exhibition would have access to all the "Conversations."

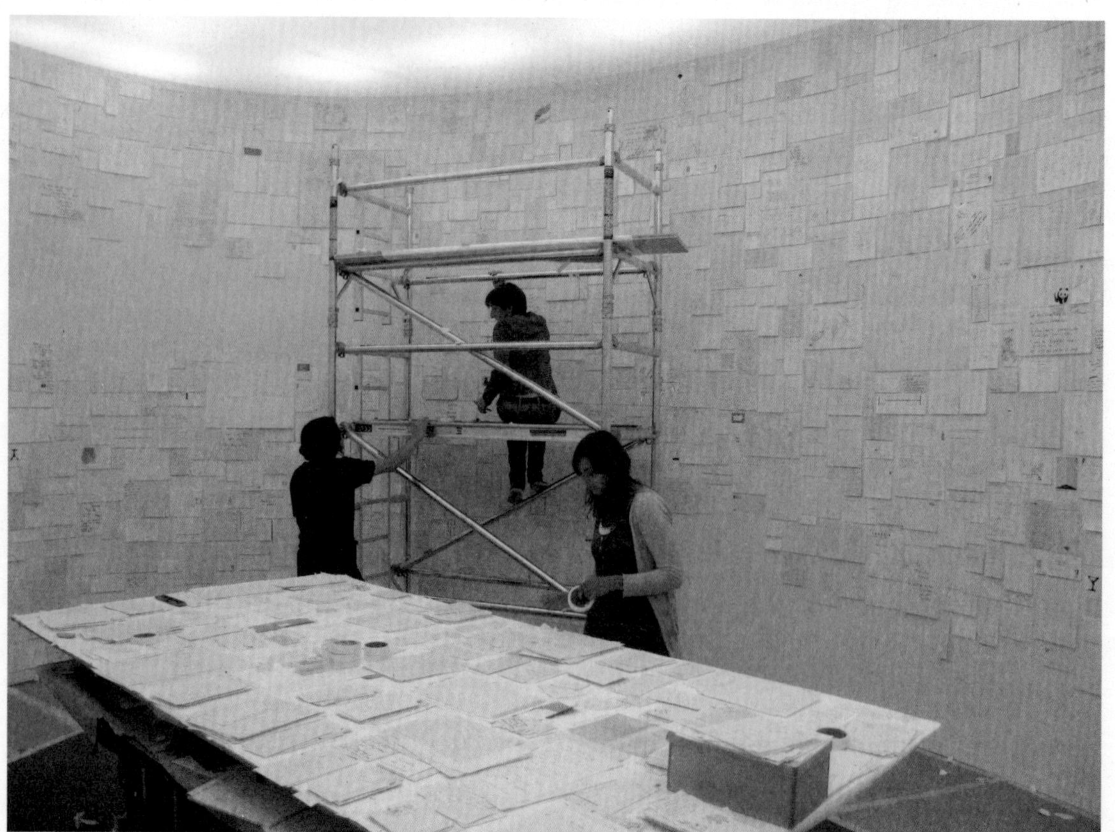

Installation (in progress) of *White Noise*, 2000. Centre Pompidou-Metz, France, 2011

2023 Proposal for MASS MoCA

Joseph Grigely
White Noise
2000/2023
Ink and pencil on paper, pins
Two connected oval rooms, each 26′ 6″ × 19′ 6″ × 12′ 6″ (variable)

Exhibition History:

Voilà: Le Monde dans la tête, Musée d'Art Moderne de Paris, 2000 (catalogue)
Joseph Grigely: White Noise, Whitney Museum of American Art, 2001 (catalogue)
Erre, Centre Pompidou-Metz, 2011 (catalogue)

"White noise" is a term used by audiologists to describe a noise that occupies a wide bandwidth of discursive frequencies. Like the color white—which contains all colors of the spectrum—white noise contains a full spectrum of frequencies. Essentially, white noise is an audio blur: Its primary distinction is that it lacks continuity, cohesion, and intelligibility.

White Noise was originally presented as an oval room, roughly 27′ long, 20′ wide, and 12′ high, filled floor to ceiling with conversations written on white paper. The "Conversations" chosen for the installation are deliberately selected from an archive of approximately 20,000 papers. They are installed in such a way as to present formal grids (square and rectangular pieces of white paper on white walls). The "Conversations" themselves, being haphazard and fragmented—as most human conversations are—lack continuity and cohesiveness. Attached to the wall, they constitute a collection of fragments of conversations: statements, questions, unfinished utterances, erasures—a visual form of white noise. The entire room contains approximately 2,700 sheets of paper.

The installation was first realized at the Musée d'Art Moderne de Paris in 2000, and was later exhibited at the Whitney Museum of American Art (2001) and the Centre Pompidou-Metz, France (2011).

The MASS MoCA proposal expands on this project, adding a second room, slightly smaller in size than the first room; but the conversations in this room, instead of being written on white paper, are all written on multicolored papers. The two rooms are designated as the Monochrome Room (white papers) and the Polychrome Room (colored papers). Both rooms would be connected at the single point where they touch each other. It has taken me thirty years to build up the archive of conversations on colored papers. Such paper is less common in the paper stream of daily life, and comes from limited sources: Post-its, cut-up watercolor drawings, index cards, and colored copy papers. When the papers are installed, they are positioned in relation to each other in consideration of various elements: the size and shape of the paper, the verbal content of the conversation, and how the inscription is written. The room with multicolored papers adds a consideration for color relations (in an Albers-like sense) to the placement of the papers.

Room Construction:

When *White Noise* was first installed at the Musée d'Art Moderne de Paris in 2000, the room had the following dimensions:

Length: 8 m (approx. 26.5′)
Width: 6 m (approx. 19.5′)
Height: 4.1 m (approx. 13.5′)

The installations at the Whitney Museum in 2001 and the Centre Pompidou in 2011 roughly followed the same dimensions, although the height was 12′ 6″. These dimensions can be adapted ± 5% without materially affecting the number of "Conversations" used.

The Whitney schematics for the construction of the room are as follows:

The rooms are constructed using 1/4″ "high-flex" drywall. The walls should have smooth contours. To save installation time, the rooms can be fabricated off-site, dismantled, and then reconstructed on-site.

The exterior can either be exposed (which would require finishing the exterior surfaces), or buried into walls. I prefer that both rooms be finished externally, if possible—they would in this case become sculptures also. But I also realize the technical requirements to make two freestanding oval rooms are challenging.

Each room should have only one external entrance, positioned at (approximately) a 45-degree angle from any of the quadrants of the room. The size of the entranceway should be governed by existing legal requirements, and should be large enough to accommodate a wheelchair. The height should also be governed by existing construction codes. A passageway should also be constructed between the two rooms—the position being decided by the logistics of the installation venue, possible columns, and other considerations.

The entire top of each room should be covered with stretched white muslin (or a similar fabric; the Pompidou used a slightly opaque polyester film, which worked very well).

A baseboard approximately 1/8″ thick and 3″ high should be installed around the bottom perimeter of the rooms.

Both rooms should be painted with a flat, slightly off-white paint. The color of the ceiling muslin should be similar to the paint. The baseboard should also be painted.

When *White Noise* was first installed at the Musée d'Art Moderne de Paris, natural lighting was used. The museum's skylight was covered with UV-protective film, and this created an environment of variegated lighting which I consider ideal for the installation. In the absence of natural lighting, bounced lighting should be used. The illumination levels should be kept relatively low, for conservation reasons.

Installation Process:

The installation process involves a crew of 4–5 people, including one supervisor for each room (myself and an assistant who has worked on the project previously). While the papers are organized by sections, the installation differs from my other large wall works in that no template is used. The process requires very deliberate consideration for paper placement, and the installation team works closely together on this. A team can complete each room in 8–10 days. The papers are first attached to the walls using 3M Low Tack Paper Tape 3051, stock #021200-86009. After this is done, the papers are attached to the walls using Moore brand #102 white map tacks; the room with colored papers uses Moore brand #107 black map tacks.

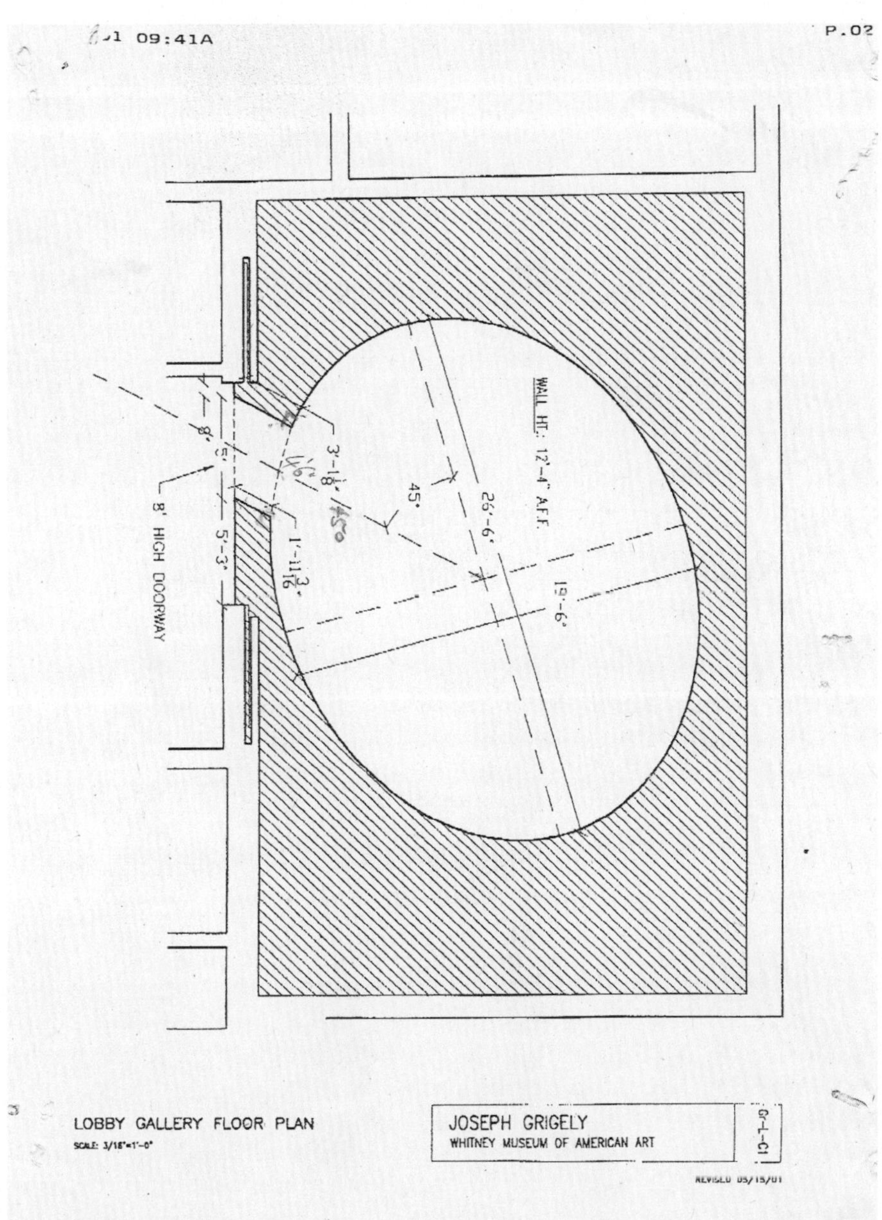

Floor plan for *White Noise*, Whitney Museum of American Art, New York, 2001

The Moore company went out of business in 2020. While I have inventoried a large number of pins for the installation, I may need to obtain additional/backup pins on the secondary market.

Materials:

The work is shipped in three crates: one for the white papers, one for the multicolored papers, and one for the oversize papers. Each crate contains a series of archival clamshell and drop-top boxes containing labeled envelopes and folders. Inside the envelopes and folders can be found the "Conversation" papers, which make up the entire installation of *White Noise*. Each box and folder are marked in such a way as to designate a particular wall area where they are to be

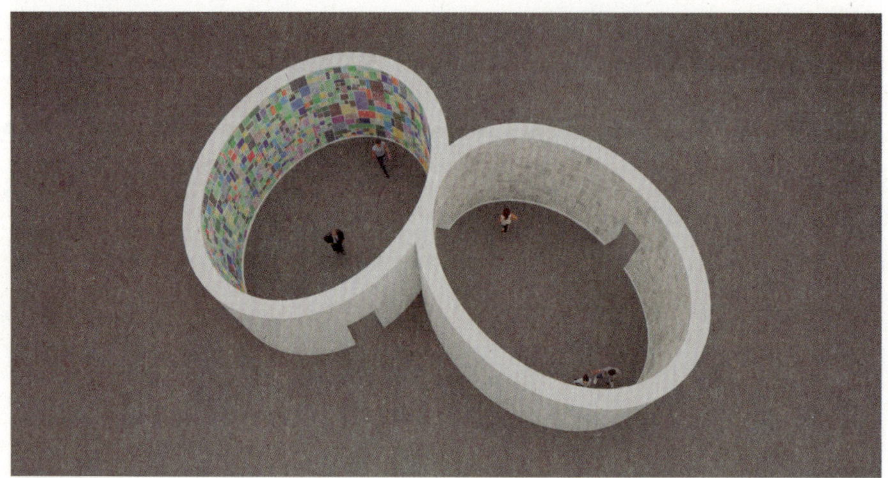

Prudence Cuming, 3-D rendering for *White Noise (monochrome)* and *White Noise (polychrome)*

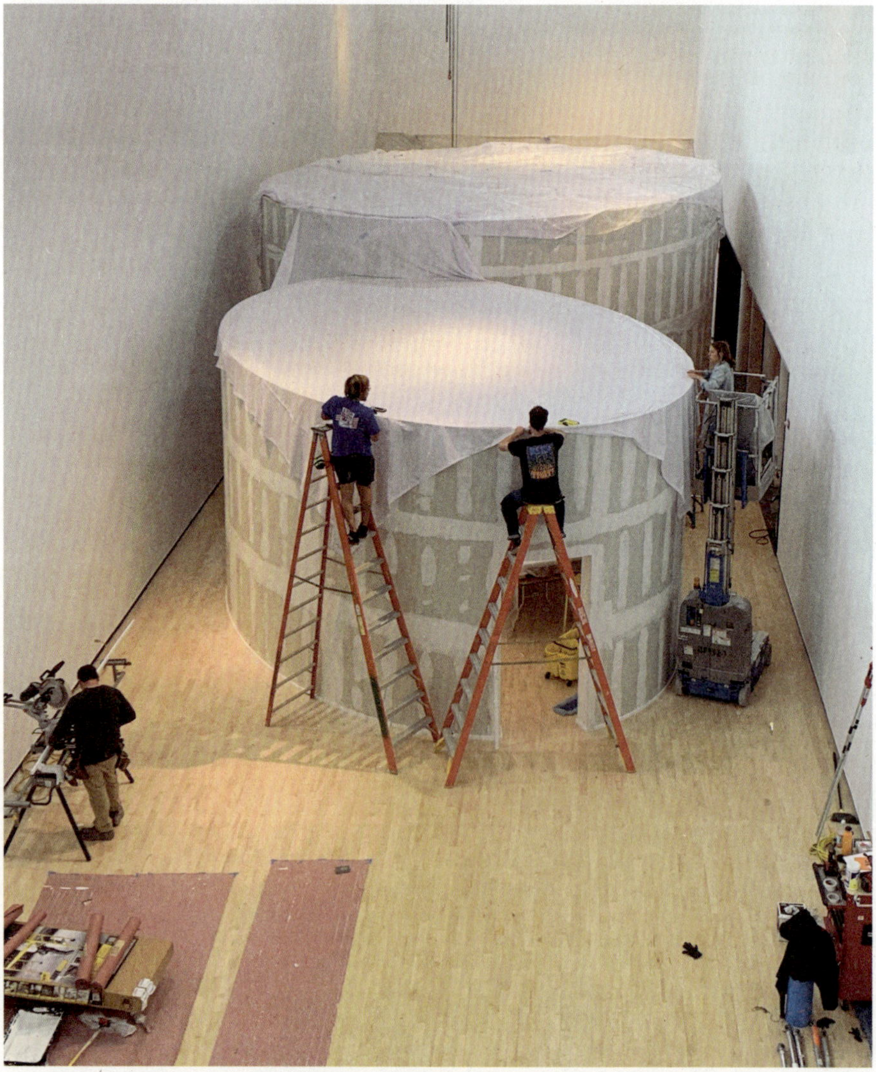

Construction of *White Noise (monochrome)*, 2000, and *White Noise (polychrome)*, 2023. Massachusetts Museum of Contemporary Art, 2023

mounted. The boxes contain approximately 20–30% more papers than will be required for the installation, so the installation team has latitude for specific placements.

Additional Materials Necessary for the Installation:

1) Clean butcher paper for the perimeter floor of the gallery.
2) A large table, or tables, providing a combined surface area of approximately 10′ × 4′. The table should be covered with white butcher paper. Ideally the table should be about 4′ high, to reduce the amount of bending installers must do.
3) Stepladders and scaffolding.
4) Protective thumb and finger cots for installing the map pins.

Prior to Installation:

The rooms should be cleaned and vacuumed. A 4-foot-wide strip of butcher paper should be placed on the floor around the perimeter of each room—this will protect the "Conversation" papers that might fall during the installation process. During the installation, the workers should remove their shoes and work in socks or slippers.

Installation Process:

The papers should be handled with extreme care.

Hands should be washed and dried before handling the papers (cotton gloves are not used because they do not allow one to hold the papers carefully and consequently cause more damage).

The rooms are divided into four quadrants, and each quadrant has four levels (or sections), each about 3′ high. These should be marked out using a laser level.

The installation should begin by installing the largest papers first.

The installation of the papers that fill the room should begin at mid-level, although—given restraints of installation time—it is possible to work on different levels in different quadrants simultaneously. Ideally:

1) Level 2 should be installed first
2) Level 3 should be installed second
3) Level 4 should be installed third
4) Level 1 should be installed fourth

Each quadrant/level has a selected set of "Conversations" that can be found in the archival folders, each marked for a respective level and/or quadrant.

Please refer to the installation photographs to get a general idea of the way the papers should be spaced. In general, most of the papers are spaced 1 cm apart. Each paper is initially attached to the wall using a piece of low-tack tape (larger papers will require two pieces of tape). Do not use any other kind of tape except the tape supplied. The use of low-tack tape permits easy and safe repositioning of the papers. A few papers, because of their weight, may need to be pinned up during the installation process. In general, though, the tape is used until the installation is complete, at which point the papers are pinned and the tape is removed.

There is no template for positioning the papers. I will instruct the installation crew on the process of choosing papers based on their color, size, and verbal narrative.

As the process of installing proceeds, it is important to check to make sure that the spacing of the papers is relatively even throughout the room.

Level 4 (top of room) should stop about 6 cm from the actual top.
Level 1 (bottom of room) should stop at the top of the baseboard.

When the entire installation is complete, check the spacing one last time—then proceed to secure the papers to the wall with Moore map pins. Do not use any other kind of pins except those supplied. Use two pins for each paper, in the upper right and left corners, approximately 1/4″ diagonally from the corner of the paper. If a paper already has holes, use these holes; do not make new holes in the paper unless necessary (e.g., an existing hole is torn through).

Remove low-tack tape, being careful not to tear papers.

NB: Sometimes you will need to remove a pin for one reason or another. It is important to use extreme care when removing the pins (and during de-installation). DO NOT EXCESSIVELY WIGGLE PINS as this will cause the holes to enlarge and the papers to tear. If the head of a pin comes off, simply slide the paper over and off the metal protrusion. After the paper has been removed, the protrusion may be pulled from the wall with pliers and discarded.

Furniture:

Ideally, each room should be furnished with a single rectangular bench made from unpainted wood—a Donald Judd sort of bench, approximately 6′ × 2′ would be ideal. I am open to other possible seating structures.

Security:

1) At ARC the Musée d'Art Moderne, Paris, the Whitney, and the Pompidou, we did not use a physical stanchion; instead, a strip of tape (white at ARC and the Pompidou; friction tape at the Whitney) was placed on the floor 40 cm from the wall. The tape effectively deterred people from getting too close. If greater security is desired, a low-level (1 foot high?) stanchion can be built, following the museum's usual guidelines for stanchions. If this is done, it is important to preserve the elliptical shape of the room by making the stanchion elliptical as well.

2) It is necessary to have a security guard in the room at all times. At ARC, the Whitney, and the Pompidou, the number of people in the room at one time was limited to 5–7 people. This helped maintain a degree of austerity in the atmosphere, and also made it easier for the guard to monitor the room.

Proposal for *St. Cecilia*, 2007

Presented at the Contemporary Museum, Baltimore (2007); Orange County Museum of Art (2007); Frances Young Tang Teaching Museum and Art Gallery at Skidmore College (2008); and the Museum of Contemporary Art Chicago (2008–9).

In 2007, Ian Berry, of the Frances Young Tang Teaching Museum and Art Gallery at Skidmore College, and Irene Hofmann, of the Contemporary Museum, Baltimore, co-organized a traveling exhibition of work I had made over the previous decade. In the process of preparing for the show, titled *St. Cecilia*, I was invited to submit a proposal for a newly commissioned film project. My original proposal included three possible options; in the end, we focused on a film that explored the way lipreading is comically ineffective as a mode of communication. The project involved rewriting the lyrics of three traditional Christmas songs so that, on the lips, they look correct—but when heard, they constitute a series of illogical misunderstandings. Based on lipreading tests given to about sixty people of a variety of backgrounds and ages, I made an archive for each line of the song and then edited the compositions line by line—which was a slow process because it involved mixing and recombining phrases, words, and morphemes in a way that resulted in a meaningful kind of meaninglessness. When the lyrics were finished, they were sent to the Baltimore Choral Arts Society and set to the original music. We then filmed the chorus performing the lyrics. Audio editing was done by Lou Mallozzi at Experimental Sound Studio in Chicago, and film editing was done at the Wexner Center for the Arts in Columbus, Ohio.

Background to *St. Cecilia*

Between the ages five and ten, the only art I knew intimately was music: I played the clarinet in the school orchestra, and music of various kinds was omnipresent in our distinctly suburban household. A large, credenza-sized stereo was the main piece of furniture in our living room, and on it my mother played an array of her favorite selections. It was an eclectic mix, from classical music to Bing Crosby to traditional Christmas carols. Without us quite realizing it at that time, music marked itself as being a necessary component of our everyday life.

All of this changed for me in 1967, when, at the age of ten, I fell down a hill while playing a game of King on the Mountain with some neighborhood friends. This incident left me totally deaf. I stopped playing the clarinet, but the music did not stop playing in my head. The absolute silence of the external world permitted me the freedom to play and replay the various performances I had heard over the years. Sometimes these performances were recorded, sometimes they were live concerts, and sometimes they were from television—background music, commercials, and even, as embarrassing as this may seem, the theme song from *Gilligan's Island*. When you become deaf suddenly, you don't have a choice about what you are privileged to remember. Even now, after forty years of being deaf, I constantly replay and remake these compositions and songs.

One of the more unusual discoveries about being deaf is the fact I have continued to be intrigued by the process of watching music performances. Even in the absence of hearing an orchestra or a choir or a rock band, the visual nature of the performance permits one to "hear" the sound as a fiction: When you watch the bows of the violins, or the conductor, or the mouths of a choir, or the wrenched-up faces of rockers, implied sounds come together in an ineffable way. It's a weird mix of disparities: the silly and the serious, the meaningful and the meaningless. This difference between how sound looks and how sound sounds is in many ways both the theme of my life as a deaf person and the theme of my work as an artist.

St. Cecilia

Lipreading is a difficult art, and the experience is essentially a subjective one. Linguists generally acknowledge that no more than 30–40 percent of the sounds of speech can be identified by visual observation. This is because many speech sounds are not produced by the lips alone, but through unvoiced articulatory processes. Additionally, the degrees of nuance and subtlety that are involved create numerous opportunities for error and misunderstanding. Many words and phrases that are pronounced differently look alike on the lips—for example, when you say "vacuum," it looks like you are saying "fuck you." In this regard, lipreading is a flawed process, less about reading than about the inevitability of misreading—what I call "lipmisreading."

The production of *St. Cecilia* involved rewriting the lyrics of three traditional Christmas songs—"Silent Night" (1818), "Jolly Old St. Nicholas" (1881), and "My Favorite Things" (1959)—so that, on the lips, they look correct, but when heard, they constitute a series of illogical misunderstandings. I created a lipreading test that involved scrambling the lines and throwing in a dummy song, so people couldn't guess too easily what they were lipreading—and then my partner, Amy Vogel, would give the lipreading tests to people. The tests usually involved two songs at a time, and Amy would speak—without speaking aloud—each line three times. This process took about a year.

Here is one example of the way the songs were composed:

Original version:	Rewritten version:
1. Jolly old Saint Nicholas,	1. Check close those lucky legs
2. Lean your ear this way!	2. Lips and hair are white
3. Don't you tell a single soul	3. Don't foretell a seafood dog
4. What I'm going to say;	4. When I'm going to die
5. Christmas Eve is coming soon;	5. Reevy Stevens coughs up blue
6. Now, you dear old man,	6. Now you see our mind
7. Whisper what you'll bring to me;	7. Whisper waterworks for me
8. Tell me if you can.	8. Tell me if you lied
9. When the clock is striking twelve,	9. What the clock is trying to tock
10. When I'm fast asleep,	10. When I'm forced to slip
11. Down the chimney broad and black,	11. Tell the chippers brown and black
12. With your pack you'll creep;	12. The weatherman is ripped
13. All the stockings you will find	13. All the socks flippin'-fly
14. Hanging in a row;	14. Hanging in the road
15. Mine will be the shortest one,	15. My woman read the story once
16. You'll be sure to know.	16. You'll be sure to know
17. Johnny wants a pair of skates;	17. Johnny was a bastard child
18. Susy wants a dolly;	18. Doosie wants a collie
19. Nellie wants a storybook;	19. Nellie wants a storybook
20. She thinks dolls are folly;	20. She thinks dogs are falling
21. As for me, my little brain	21. Ask for me my little bride
22. Isn't very bright;	22. In a flowerpot
23. Choose for me, old Santa Claus,	23. Do for me hotel lots
24. What you think is right.	24. When it's thick it's fried

The songs were sung by thirty members of the Baltimore Choral Arts Society at the Brown Memorial Park Avenue Presbyterian Church in Baltimore. Tom Hall conducted the performance, which took place in January 2007. The filming involved three video cameras and one Super 8 camera shooting both B&W and Ektachrome film stocks. Editing took place over a three-week period at the Wexner, and the film premiered at Baltimore's Contemporary Museum in May 2007.

The film's basic premise involves questioning the assumptions we make about what we hear and what we see—and how linguistic communication is constantly subverted by subtle nuances that transcend language itself.

Installation Logistics

The film is a two-channel projection installation. The screen size can be adapted from 16 feet wide to 23 feet wide.

Audio is provided by two audio spotlights, a technology recently developed at MIT which allows one to project sound in a discrete and circumscribed space. The audio spotlights are installed from the ceiling, slightly in front of the projectors. Each projects audio from separate tracks—the left audio spotlight projects the audio from the "correct" song. The right audio spotlight projects audio from the rewritten version of the song. This way, viewers can move back and forth between the different audios. The space between is filled with a low murmur, so that there is also a third level of audio: that of no distinct audio at all. This brings the viewers into the position of seeing sound with the sound turned off—one of the underlying goals of the project.

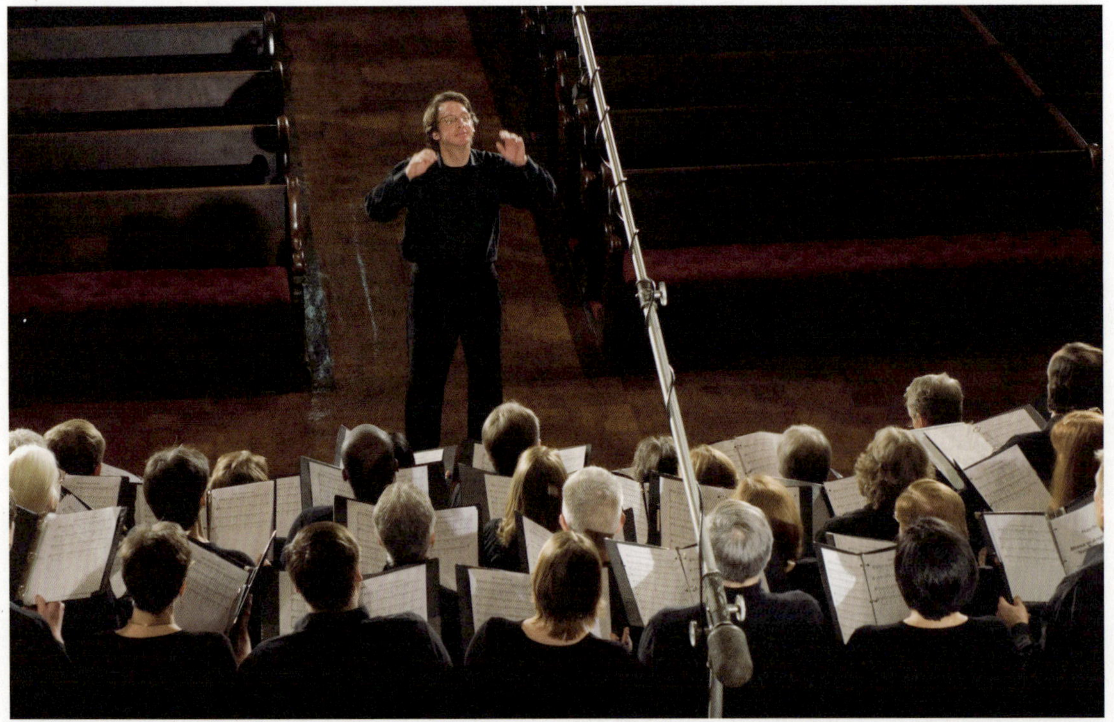

Still from Joseph Grigely, *St. Cecilia*, 2007. Two-channel video installation

The Czar is Afraid of Everything

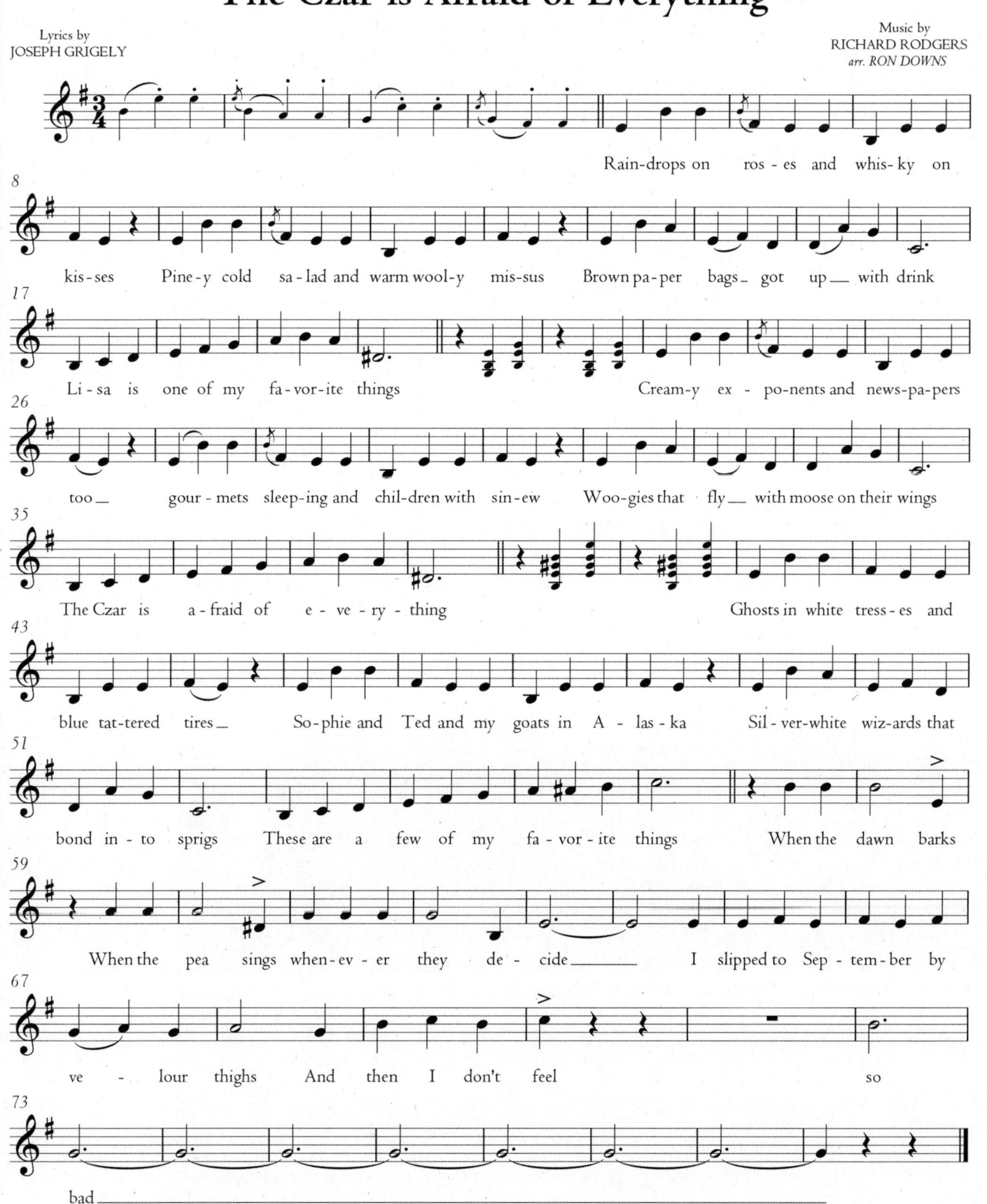

Sheet music from Joseph Grigely, *St. Cecilia*, 2012. Digital pigment print

Letters, Statements, Proposals, Incidents

Part 2, Access

Draft of a Letter to the President and Trustees of Saint Anselm College, 1992

15 January 1992

Dear President and Trustees,

What follows is a story about why one St. Anselm's graduate has not repaid his undergraduate loan. It is probably not like most defaulter's stories, but it is, I believe, a story worth telling.

I graduated from St. Anselm's magna cum laude in 1978. After a year spent volunteering on a research project developing speech and hearing aids at the University of Washington, I went to graduate school at Oxford University where I received a doctorate in English literature in 1984. I taught at Gallaudet College (in Washington, D.C.) for two years before going to Stanford University, where I was Andrew W. Mellon Postdoctoral Fellow in English between 1985-7. I returned to Gallaudet, received early tenure in 1990, and I was recently awarded an NEH Fellowship for College Teachers for 1992-3.

To these basic facts I should perhaps add one more: I am deaf.

This footnote does not concern most aspects of my life; but in educational matters, where education involves sharing and sharing involves discourse, it is a crucial consideration. In order to have access to this discourse and in order to have access to the education I was paying to receive, I requested (at the beginning of my senior year) permission to study American Sign Language, and I also requested sign language interpreters for my classes. Having transferred to St. Anselm's from Rochester Institute of Technology and the National Technical Institute for the Deaf, I was sufficiently familiar with sign language to realize that to really benefit from attending classes--and St. Anselm's had mandatory class attendance at that time--interpreters would be crucial. But both of my requests were turned down.

I was shocked--numb even--for, while this refusal was legal in 1977, it was only marginally legal; the Rehabilitation Act of 1973 left a loophole through which an institution receiving federal funds had no obligation to make all of its programs accessible. But this has since changed, and what St. Anselm's did in 1977 would be illegal today: both the Civil Rights Restoration Act of 1989 and the Americans with Disabilities Act of 1990 mandate access of precisely the kind I desired and was denied.

When I left St. Anselm's I realized that the effort disabled people must put into the struggle for accessibility often consumes more energy the cause for which they seek access. And it is unbearably degrading to have to explain and justify our requests for access: one is made to feel like a child. But how far can a young person go in a struggle for equality? I, for one, wanted to spend my energy getting an education, not fighting just to get into the classroom. That is why, in the end, I went to Oxford for graduate school: no classrooms, no stigma. But I would have liked to have gone to Oxford because I wanted to; not because St. Anselm's had convinced me that I had no other choice.

After Oxford came Gallaudet College (now University)--America's oldest college for the Deaf--where I began teaching English literature. And after Gallaudet came Stanford where, with a sign language interpreter in the classroom, I taught graduate and undergraduate courses in literature. It worked great--it worked precisely as it <u>could</u> have worked at St. Anselm's, had St. Anselm's the moral courage to allow it to happen.

Which brings us back to the loan which remained unpaid through all of this--a loan which is, like my St. Anselm's degree, a symbol of a certain painful experience. And like all painful experiences, it was not immediately clear to me what was happening when it was happening--it took time. And time took its toll.

I acknowledge that I owe a formal debt and that the obligation to repay it is formal too: on paper, the numbers of finance are impervious to feelings about what constitutes just behavior. Or to put it another way: my debt to St. Anselm's is merely financial; but St. Anselm's debt to the disabled is something else. And while St. Anselm's cannot repay the portion of this debt it owes to me, it may perhaps do so to others. Should you proceed to deposit the enclosed check for the amount of my outstanding loan ($2,536.35), I would like to request of you--I would prefer to dare you--to use the money to establish a scholarship fund for disabled students attending St. Anselm's.

There is no denying that St. Anselm's College has had a profound influence on me--but an influence that is largely of a disconcerting kind. It is by repaying this debt and returning my degree to the College that I wish to confront this experience, share it with you, and ask that steps be taken to ensure that it does not happen again.

Sincerely yours,

Joseph Grigely, D.Phil.
Associate Professor

Request for a Sign Language Interpreter for the Opening of the 2000 Whitney Biennial, and an Email from Amy Vogel to Andrea Miller-Keller, 2000

During the installation of the 2000 Whitney Biennial, I asked the exhibition manager if the Whitney would provide a sign language interpreter for the opening. I was informed this was not possible because the exhibition was over budget. Unsatisfied with this response, I wrote to the museum's director, Maxwell Anderson, and he replied that I should take up the issue with my curator, not him. My curator, Andrea Miller-Keller, in turn, was unwilling, or perhaps unable, to do anything about the situation—and this led my girlfriend (and later wife), Amy Vogel, to write to the curator about the situation. Amy's email is printed here, along with my original request and the Whitney's reply. In the end, the Whitney did not provide an interpreter.

'VHITNEY.ORG,3/13/00 8:04 PM,RE: new news 1

342

284

From: r@WHITNEY.ORG
To: jgrigely@umich.edu
Subject: RE: new news
Date: Mon, 13 Mar 2000 20:04:06 -0500
MIME-Version: 1.0
Status:

Hi Joseph:
Tomorrow at 3 p.m. is fine for you to drop by the museum. If you still have your Biennial ID, just come right to the 4th floor.

We really can't pay for a sign language interpreter for you. I'm really sorry to say. At this point, I'm extremely over budget for the entire exhibition as it is.

Looking forward to seeing you tomorrow.

-----Original Message-----
From: Joseph Grigely [mailto:jgrigely@umich.edu]
Sent: Monday, March 13, 2000 1548
To: :@WHITNEY.ORG
Subject: new news

Hi, Maura--

I hope everything is going smoothly--I'm very much looking forward to seeing the show.

I have two questions:

1) Can I stop by tomorrow afternoon (Tuesday, around 3) so I can check out the storyline drafts against the wall piece?

2) I'd like to ask if the Whitney would provide a sign language interpreter for the opening on the 21st. I know it's late for such a request--but I just emailed Debbie Swamback (who has interpreted for me before and who coordinates interpreters at Columbia)--and she said she'd be available.
Can we swing this?
Her email address is swamback@exchange.tc.columbia.edu.

See you tomorrow, I hope--

best,
Joseph

Dear Andrea—

I have had to beg Joseph to allow him to let me contact you. It is something I HAD to do for fear I would explode if asked to keep quiet.

Let me start by saying I know Joseph can be a pain. He lets nothing slide by and is slow to compromise. I have learned he has to [do this] with his work or, by the very nature of it, its "casualness" would get the better of it. With no gallerist, he has also had to be his own voice of complaint. He wanted what was promised to him—what he stipulated was the "minimum" he needed. Maura has done her best to please everyone and is obviously overworked, overextended, overwrought. Joseph did not want to have to burden Maura with the interpreter issue, and by all accounts it is absurd that it is her responsibility. She is tired—this has been a lot of work for her. Joseph had been apologetic about his request for an interpreter. This should not be.

Andrea, I don't know how I can possibly explain how totally demeaned Joseph feels. It of course is not only the Whitney but a constant and continued life of struggle for the basic things we take for granted. I had a deaf and disabled sister. I have lived with Joseph now for four years. I can tell you, if any woman, or minority, was treated half the way the disabled are, there would be riots in the street.

Joseph and I never go to lectures, not even at the university where he is a tenured professor. We never attend conferences. No interpreters. Last fall he was in the book *CREAM*—they had a symposium with most of the curators, and I sat and scribbled what notes I could because they would not get an interpreter. Recently the MLA (Modern Language Association) asked Joseph to give a lecture based on his book *Textualterity*, a great honor. He said no. Ten years ago, after struggling for years, he left the MLA because of the interpreter issue.

Faculty at the University of MI complained the first year Joseph was there because he did not attend more meetings. The first year the only reason he did not attend meetings was because there were no interpreters. What do you think they think he should have done? Just sit there watching their mouths move? I told him he should go and sit and play solitaire. We attended last year's graduation and a student got up to speak, and as I reentered the courtyard I heard the student talking about Joseph and what a profound difference in his life and education he made. It was a lengthy and beautiful speech and it depressed me to no end, for I knew Joseph was just sitting there not having any idea what was being said, because there was no interpreter.

Andrea, I am sorry to go on and on, but truthfully this isn't a quarter, a fraction, a tidbit of what I have experienced with him—in four years, and he's been deaf for thirty-three years. Maura should not have had to deal with this, this is the Whitney's responsibility, there should be someone responsible for equal access for all disabled. Perhaps Joseph should have said something earlier—why didn't he? Probably because, as I have witnessed, this often excludes him from things. "Oh we love and want Joseph"—OK, but I'll need an interpreter. And that is that. Too much fear? Too much money? So the best way he has learned to succeed in life is to keep to himself and make the deafness as secondhand as possible—an afterthought. Interpreting should not be a part of his "budget"—his accessibility to the director, the curators, and other artists is not his art. It is his humanity.

One question. What do you think Joseph should do the night of the opening if Max Anderson is speaking? Congratulating artists, perhaps speaking of our First Amendment rights as they connect with Hans Haacke's piece. Do you think Max will write it [down] for him? Will you?

Is it my responsibility? Or, what mostly happens and makes everyone the happiest, should he just sit there smiling? Andrea, can you imagine how degrading it is?

I will end this now though I could go on and on. I, and Joseph, KNOW it is not a just world, and mostly for our own sanity we both stay quiet. But Andrea, even if there were problems with money and time—though Joseph would contact and arrange for his own interpreter—what is so utterly hurtful is that people would say they were "disappointed" in him for asking for an interpreter. Why? Because it is too much of a pain? Because he has demanded a lot for his work, he cannot ask for this? I cannot accept the fact that because too many walls had to come up and down, and too many lights had to be changed, that Joseph should be made to look demanding and selfish to ask for an interpreter to an important event.

I know Joseph is terribly upset, for many reasons, but also for the damage he feels this has inevitably caused [in] his relationship with you. I do not want to make things worse but I could not not say anything.

Years ago Joseph left Gallaudet University. He wanted to be defined by his mind and work and self and not the deafness. He wants friends that he likes because of their ideas, personalities, not because they necessarily can or cannot hear.

I have thought a lot about how I would live my life as a deaf person and I know, unfortunately, that I would surround myself with other deaf people. It's easier. I would feel more human.

In the end Joseph will get an interpreter. The Whitney may or may not pay for it. I'll hope our evening isn't spent discussing this instead of the art and other stuff—who is with who, where are we going for drinks? So I guess what this long email is all about, and all I can ask, is for you to please try to separate all the demands you have as a curator, everyone's desperate and pressing needs, and try to understand this for what it is. Someone asking to experience an important moment in its fullest. To not burden friends. To be seen for who and what he is, not for the deafness.

Sincerely,
Amy

Diversity for All, 2003

Over the years I have written several opinion pieces about disability and sent these to *The New York Times*. The *Times* tends to take a fairly liberal approach to civil rights, but has a curiously guarded position in relation to disability. In the process of writing op-eds to address some of these issues, I have tried to consider the space between legal and moral justice, and to find a tone that takes into account a more general audience. While op-eds are essentially rhetorical documents, they try to do something that art also does: put into the space of public opinion a situation, and let the public sort it out. None of the op-eds I submitted to the *Times* were published.

Joseph Grigely
'Diversity for All'
June 2003

For many people there was a great sigh of relief this week when the Supreme Court affirmed the Constitutional legitimacy of affirmative action as part of the process of assessing comparative merit among college applicatants. In an effort to be circumspect and respectful of the many minorities that make up our nation, the Court required that race be considered in a "flexible, non-mechanical way." The Court agreed with Justice Powell's opinion in the Bakke case 25 years ago that the value of a diverse student body in schools across America is a legitimate Federal interest. The question now is: what exactly do we mean by 'diversity?'

When Congress passed the Civil Rights Act of 1964, it did not really do so with consideration of a comprehensive idea of 'diversity' in mind. Instead, Congress intended to undo the wrongs of America's unenviable past by creating a body of laws that offered discrimination protection to communities defined by race, gender, religion, and national origin. For various reasons Congress did not at this time address disability or sexual orientation. If this was debatable then, it's a different debate today: we have to think more broadly than Congress did in 1964.

The situation for disabled people is particularly challenging. When the Civil Rights Act was passed in 1964, disabled people had only limited federal and state protections, and virtually none in private industry. In 1990 the Americans with Disabilities Act (ADA) was adopted, with the promise of bringing fundamental civil rights to the disabled. But ADA has turned out to be far less than it was intended to be. As the Supreme Court decided in several recent decisions, disabled people therefore do not have protection of the Fourteenth Amendment's equal-protection clause. Justice Rehnquist stated that, in passing ADA, Congress had not proven that states regularly and repeatedly engaged in "irrational" employment discrimination against the disabled. In Alabama v Garrett, which was decided by a 5-4 vote, Rehnquist wrote: "the Fourteenth Amendment does not require the States to make special accommodations for the disabled, so long as their actions toward such individuals are rational. They could hardheadedly—and perhaps hardheartedly—hold to job-qualification requirements which do not make allowance for the disabled. If special accommodations for the disabled are to be required, they have to come from positive law and not through the Equal Protection Clause."

The problem here can be found in Rehnquist's implication that "special accommodations" are special, and therefore a privilege not granted to others. Justice Scalia commented during the oral arguments of Tennessee v Lane that an inaccessible polling place is not evidence of discrimantion; it's simply evidence that the state did not go out of its way to "help" disabled people. In so many ways, ADA simply maintains the paternalistic principles of charitable behavior that characterize the ways disabled people have been treated historically. As the legal philosopher Martha Minow has written, "law has failed to resolve the meaning of equality for people defined as different by society."[1]

The history of oppression in America is a vast history, and an unfinished one as well: discriminatory behavior will constantly reinvent itself. For this reason, anti-discrimination statutes will always have an important place in our civic infrastructure, but they will not by themselves change the behavior of the populace. Nor will they makes us more receptive to the possibilities of diversity. The history of social change in America would seem to bear this out: the workers' movement, the suffrage movement, and the Civil Rights movement, effectively combined a groundswell of visible public activism alongside meaningful cultural productivity as part of the process of educating the public psyche. In other words: change does not come alone from new statutes; it comes from redistributing into everyday life new ways of thinking. It is difficult to imagine the workers' movement being successful the way it was without Upton Sinclair's novel, *The Jungle*. It is hard to imagine the Civil Rights movement without the novels of Richard Wright and Ralph Ellison, or the essays of W.E.B. Dubois. The challenge is not to create an alternative cultural model, but rather to insert within the authority of 'mainstream' culture an alternative consciousness that shows the ways disability is, like other human differences, a fundamental state of being.

Disability is arbitrary and unpredictable. Despite the great progress that science has made in eliminating disabling illnesses, and despite the great hopes that people have for genomic research, it's a fact that accidents happen. Sooner or later, in one way or another, temporarily or permanently, most of us are affected by a disabling condition. It's not always the tragedy it seems. It's simply another way of being human, another way of getting on with things, another way of exploring the possibilities of life. It enables people to examine the world from from unusual angles. It's something to embrace, not something to fear.

Conclusion:

Those who are disabled neither require nor want "special" treatment; we simply want equal access, not just to libraries & schools & museums and courtrooms; we also want equal access to being counted as part of the definition of diversity.

[1] Making All the Difference, 9.

Letter to the Dean of Faculty at the School of the Art Institute of Chicago Regarding Access Issues, 2007

For the forty years I have taught in higher education, not one of the schools where I was employed had a coordinator for managing access requests by disabled faculty and staff. Nor were any of the faculty or administrative staff provided with training in disability resources and accommodations as they relate to the Americans with Disabilities Act. Everything was a DIY operation, where I was constantly tasked with self-advocacy, explaining what is needed and why. It was an exhausting process. In this letter to the dean of faculty at the School of the Art Institute of Chicago, I attempted to explain the situation in detail and clarify why it would be helpful to have an institutional coordinator for disability and disability advocacy. Eighteen years later, SAIC still does not have an administrative position that provides leadership for disabled faculty and staff.

November 4, 2007

Dear Lisa,

As promised, I am sharing with you my thoughts about various ways we can work to make SAIC a more inclusive community. I'm sorry that my resignation from the Tenure Review Board seemed so sudden—but there was nothing sudden about the events that precipitated my decision. They've been building up slowly through the semester while working with the Tenure Review Board. On at least two occasions, the candidates presenting lectures did not bring copies of their papers for me and the interpreters, as requested, and offered what I felt were unacceptable excuses; on another occasion, we had a new interpreter, one of many we've had this semester, who was clearly unqualified to interpret for us; on several occasions, the lighting in the screening room could not be adjusted properly for interpreting—either the extension cord was missing, or the interpreting light itself was missing; on one occasion I had to interrupt the deliberations of the committee to remind the committee members that I can't participate in a meaningful way unless as individuals they raise their hands prior to speaking so I know who is speaking, and that they remember that because of the interpreter I am 4–5 seconds behind everyone; finally, at the candidate's lecture last Wednesday, while the technician was trying to set up lighting for the interpreters and left the room to get an extension cord, the introduction to the talk began—leaving me in the dark about what was being said. This is an extremely humiliating experience—to be there and not to be there. And so I left the room, not just because of this, but also to avoid further interruption of the candidate's lecture when the technician returned.

These experiences illustrate the following four problems I think we need to address:

1) The SAIC community does not really know how to work with interpreters. Most people mean well, they just don't have the experience or the guidelines to know what to do. On Wednesday afternoon, for example, the lecture introductions should not have begun until the interpreting light was in place.

2) The arrangements for illuminating interpreters in SAIC classrooms and lecture theatres is piecemeal and improvised, and puts an unfair burden on both the deaf person and the technicians to find last-moment solutions that invariably prove disruptive to everyone—and so in the end the deaf person gets blamed for the disruption.

3) Our interpreting arrangements through the Chicago Hearing Society are similarly piecemeal—we've had five or six different interpreters this semester alone, at least two clearly unqualified. The problem with this is that everything said in classes and meetings and lectures gets pulled down to the level of the interpreters. Interpreting that is incommensurate with the intellectual level of the discourse being exchanged is, literally, a disabling rather than enabling situation.

4) We do not have at SAIC a dedicated staff member whose responsibility is to advocate for access issues on behalf of disabled faculty. While we do have a Disability and Learning Resource Center for disabled students, faculty have to do their own advocacy in a DIY fashion—which burdens them with the task of educating their colleagues and staff about communications and access protocol. This is very awkward, not just because of the time it takes, but because of the emotional energy it takes. In the past, when requesting interpreters from other departments & programs (including the museum), I have sometimes found myself having to justify my request, and repeat it, and it's really just so tiring, it's more productive for me to just stay in my studio and make art.

Here are some solutions to these concerns that I'd like to propose:

1) Interpreting protocol. Because we also have deaf students at SAIC, and because the presence of interpreters and CART [Communication Access Realtime Translation] transcribers is a way of life here, the SAIC community needs to be made aware of proper protocol in the process of working together. Normally at the start of the semester I explain this protocol to my students, and it is very effective. I'd like to suggest that SAIC prepare and distribute to the SAIC community a memorandum on communications access protocols. Like sexual harassment, communications access is a legal obligation, and because of this it's important to stress that the process of making it effective and meaningful applies to everyone. The document need not be legalistic, but rather a set of helpful guidelines written in a way that considers the uniqueness of our institution and its resources. I've seen no preexisting guidelines that do this well—but perhaps the SAIC DLRC could prepare a draft, which I'd be happy to review prior to distribution.

2) Lighting and illumination. Two issues here: A) Lecture and screening rooms, including MacLean 1307 and the Columbus lecture hall, need to have permanent interpreting spotlights installed. Ideally, one on each side of the lecture hall, and each with remote adjustment controls. (As an aside, the Rubloff [Auditorium] is well-equipped in this regard, the technicians there have always been able to illuminate the interpreters in a way that minimizes shadow throw.) B) Classrooms, especially rooms used for art history and any "smart" classrooms, need lighting reassessment. None of the art history/VCS [Visual and Critical Studies] classrooms have blackboard lights to illuminate the blackboards when lights are off for projections. I found blackboard lights very useful when I was teaching at Michigan—I could write names on the boards that everyone could see clearly, and the residual lighting was sufficient for interpreters. Three years ago I asked the staff involved with classroom management to improve the lighting in the two rooms I use most often, because even at the highest settings the rooms were still dim. Their efforts resulted in marginal, but insufficient improvement. This is important to me because watching interpreters for a three-hour-long seminar of critical discourse is exhausting enough, and doubly so if the lighting is not adequate. Right now it is not.

3) Interpreting quality. For the past five years we've been contracting for interpreters on an as-needed basis through the Chicago Hearing Society. This means when we need an interpreter for a meeting or a guest lecture, Shay or Teena in the VCS office will email CHS and request an interpreter. Sometimes we get a regular interpreter who is good (Michael Albert), sometimes we get someone who is acceptable, sometimes we get someone unqualified, and sometimes we get nobody (as has happened several times). Good interpreters who can handle the kind of critical discourse we engage in are rare and in high demand. After several interpreting disasters early in my tenure at SAIC, George Roeder agreed that we needed to work towards arranging for a setup similar to what I had in Michigan: a staff interpreter. A staff interpreter would be someone hired for approximately twenty hours per week, who would be familiar with arts discourse, and also read assigned readings to be familiar with specific names, theories, and diction related to my work at SAIC. After George died and I went on sabbatical, it was discussed that this would be enacted when I returned from sabbatical—and for my part I was explicit to my colleagues in VCS that I would not take on administrative duties until we had a staff interpreter. Shay and I completed the job description last spring, but for various reasons not explained to me, the advertising and interviewing have been held up—I think it's all in the hands of HR now, but thus far I haven't been contacted by HR with any update. I thus entered the fall semester as Director of the Graduate Program in VCS and as a member of the Tenure Review Board without the interpreting arrangement we really need to make it work properly. Additionally, the many different interpreters we have had has made it hard on my students—they need to be able to trust the interpreters, and when a different person with different signing

skills shows up, it throws them off. It throws me off too. The solution to all of this is to find out what has happened to the job posting I prepared—interview candidates—and make a hire of the staff interpreter, who would work as a team with Michael Albert, and therefore provide the kind of consistent, quality interpreting we need.

4) Disability access advocate. While disabled students at SAIC can turn to the DLRC to advocate for their needs, disabled faculty have no one to provide this support. Either they ask their administrative assistants or their Chairs (neither of whom are skilled as professional disability advocates) or they do it themselves DIY-style. Either way, it is wearying for the people involved. It also creates a demoralizing situation, because the more I have to advocate for my own needs, the more friction it creates among colleagues, and the more I withdraw from being a public presence at SAIC. Because of this, SAIC needs to have a professional access advocate working on behalf of disabled faculty and staff. This person can be a resource for various kinds of advocacy, both on an internal level and also on an external level—for example, when attending a conference in LA and the organizers give me a hassle about interpreters (this kind of thing happens often), the Disability Access Advocate could get on the phone and start advocating on my—and SAIC's—behalf.

I realize some of these proposals might require administrative discussion before they are made real—but I hope in the meantime you will consider these proposals as a sincere effort to make SAIC a more inclusive environment for all of its members.

Sincerely,

Joseph

Email to Tony Karman and Stephanie Cristello Regarding Access at Expo Chicago Art Fair, 2019

August 26, 2019

Dear Tony and Stephanie,

I am looking forward to this year's Art Expo, and appreciate your continued effort to bring the best in international contemporary art to Chicago.

But I do have an important concern: Oddly (to me) the Expo Chicago website provides no information on access and accommodations for visitors with disabilities. The Visit page has information on parking, but no information on parking for disabled visitors, or where wheelchair drop-offs should take place. The page on Programs, where talks and panels are listed, has no information on making sign language interpreter requests. The Contacts page has no information on who to contact regarding access issues. It's not clear where visitors who use chairs are to access the fair, as the main access point is usually reached by escalator. In short, there is no information whatsoever on access issues—which for me is not the kind of thoroughness and thoughtfulness that is historically part of the Art Expo experience. Can you please address this issue?

Two years ago, some of my students in my disability class started a conversation on access at Art Expo, and some of their comments (from my notes and their emails) are as follows:

"The architecture of EXPO also posed problems for accessibility. Many of the partitioned galleries had tight spaces…without consideration that such narrow spaces create even more difficulties of mobility for individuals in wheelchairs."

"In total, I saw 3 people in wheelchairs. One of them was in the restroom at the same time I was. When she needed to wash her hands, the sink was too high for her and she decided to keep her hands dirty."

"Even the short films that were shown lacked subtitles, thus singling out the Deaf community from understanding what was occurring. All in all, it was evident that during the events curation, the topic of accessibility to those with disabilities was unfortunately not thought of even once."

Surely Expo Chicago can do better than this? I'm sorry I have to be the messenger in this case I hate having to do this—but it's very frustrating seeing this degree of neglect for such a large public event that I frequently participate in.

Some suggestions:

1) Appoint an accessibility coordinator for the Fair—someone who has oversight of all forms of disability-related access. If you need help doing this, an organization like Access Living might be able to provide some guidance, and perhaps even a "review" of the Expo's access issues in order to prepare better for next year.

2) Create an access page for the website, providing all basic information on access and accommodations, along with contact information for making accommodations requests. For example, it's not clear who I am to contact to request sign language interpreters for some of the panel discussions on Saturday and Sunday. I am sure I am not the only deaf person in Chicago who would like to participate.

3) Provide for all the participating galleries a checklist on making their booths more accessible for visitors with disabilities—spacing between floor-mounted works and walls, heights for labels, transcripts/captions for videos, and so on.

4) VIP events with partner institutions should have some kind of contact liaison through Art Expo so people with access issues do not have to run around trying to figure out who to contact at events that are co-sponsored by Expo.

Perhaps you already do some of this, only it's not apparent? In any case, it would help greatly to make access issues more legible as part of the public experience of participating in the Fair.

Sincerely,

Joseph

Joseph Grigely
Professor
Visual & Critical Studies
The School of the Art Institute of Chicago

Cripping the World, an Email to My Students, 2020

When the Covid pandemic in the spring of 2020 resulted in a shift from in-person classes to remote classes taught online, the academic community was deeply unsettled by the experience. My students, many of whom lived alone, no longer had access to the structures of their daily education—particularly the resources of their studios. To address their frustrations, I wrote them an email explaining the situation from the perspective of disability.

Dear Class,

I've heard from a few of you about how challenging it is getting back into your studio work and your research, and I am seeing this play out at my own home in different ways: I'm tying a lot of trout flies, my partner (after being sick and quarantined) is baking a lot, and my daughter is playing Switch-stuff with her friends via phone. In a way, though, we're all working, even if it's not what we "should" be working on.

Let me explain a little more about this.

My personal opinion about what's happening now—which is based on fifty-three years of intimate experience with the subject as a disabled person—is this: The world's been cripped. In disability theory we use this phrase to describe inversals of abledness. The habits of biological normalcy of the global body have been thrown into disarray, in a way similar to what happens when individual bodies become disabled. All it takes is a blink, and in a moment, nothing is as it was.

If you read carefully between the lines of public discourse, you will find many people with disabilities are saying: *Now the world will feel what we feel. Now the world will experience life as we experience it.* This involves an inability to move freely or access information with ease; isolation; frustration with institutional procedures and practices; and a very special kind of anger that one's plans have been disrupted. You feel robbed of fairness and justice.

So the frustration and anger that some are feeling, and that is coming out into the open in different ways, is not unexpected. We can't change what is happening around us, as far as the pandemic itself is concerned. We can only change how we relate to it, and how we assimilate the circumstances, and realign ourselves in relation to those circumstances.

The online/distance learning component of our class is, practically speaking, merely a way of keeping in touch: It doesn't replace being in a room together, or in a studio together, and it's not meant to. Enabling technologies do not displace, supplant, or replace the original functions of human engagement; they simply supplement those functions (what pedagogical authorities euphemistically call "enrichment learning"). The goal (for me) of distance learning is to habilitate (as opposed to rehabilitate) ourselves to these new circumstances. People with disabilities do this every day, negotiating, like electricity, a path of least resistance.

The first step in managing things is to be kind to yourself. It's OK to put aside all your big goals and plans if you feel you need to. You can come back to them later. Or maybe they'll change—this all takes time. What's important is to find things to do from which you derive some satisfaction—and these things will vary for each of us. Day after day after day, the ennui can be frustrating; but then I think of On Kawara, painting one date painting after another. The thing is not to worry about the expectations of others; not to worry about what the world thinks. Do what feels right for you, on your own terms.

It feels a little strange and proselytizing saying all this stuff—so take it for whatever it's worth, or not. But I feel I have to say something. In the world of disability, the notion of "overcoming" is a problematic construction: It assumes that one must overcome circumstances to move on. But it's not overcoming that matters: It's *inter*coming, working with the situation, reshaping and realigning yourself as you go. Be creative doing it. Be persistent. Listen to yourself, and what your mind and body tell you. And—dare I say it?—try to have fun too.

Those are my thoughts anyhow. They may not parallel what you are hearing from others, or even what you are hearing from your own inner recesses; but I want to give you the space to reorient your ways of working, if not your work itself. As Edgar says at the end of *King Lear*, when acknowledging the tragedy that has unfolded: "The weight of this sad time we must obey / Speak what we feel, not what we ought to say."

See you all next week in our Zoom Room.

Joseph

Inventory of Apologies, 2020

Originally published in *VoCA Journal*, December 7, 2020.

One consequence of the pandemic is that it forced many arts institutions to move their public programs—including talks, roundtable discussions, webinars, and video art projects—to digital platforms.

In the process of doing so, many neglected to consider that deaf people cannot access this material without captioning, and that effective captioning is a good institutional practice, in addition to being a mandate of the Americans with Disabilities Act (in the US) and the Equality Act (in the UK).

Of the fifty or so online events I attended during the first six months of the pandemic, only two of them provided captions without asking, and without hassle. It was very frustrating to write back and forth with institutions and get an array of excuses and apologies, and in many cases little meaningful progress.

I originally posted some of the apologies on Instagram, and *VoCA Journal*, published by the nonprofit arts organization Voices in Contemporary Art, offered to publish them shortly afterward. The initial list contained approximately fifty apologies. I removed the names of the individuals and institutions. They include large and small cultural and political institutions, both public and private, all of whom were, based on their replies, quite aware of their obligations. A fair number of institutions did not reply at all to concerns about disability-related access and deserve their own list. Since the original list was published in December 2020, the number of apologies I have received has more than doubled. I no longer collect them.

Joseph—our apologies, as it's a live event and we don't have closed caption capabilities.

Unfortunately no captions for this program. But we hope so soon for a future event!

I apologize that this happened today and I will ensure this does not happen again. I hope you can join us for the next talk.

Unfortunately this session is not being captioned…I apologize for any difficulty this may cause.

Unfortunately, no captioning has been organized for today's panel.

It is a real shame that we could not figure out the technology to have the captioning stream from Zoom to YouTube on this new platform we worked on with the developers, though we tried through many tests and it seems not to be working consistently.

I am sorry we did not (and found ourselves unable to) provide closed captioning from the get-go. It was a serious oversight on our behalf and I wish we had been better.

Unfortunately, our Zoom plan does not allow for closed captioning and transcriptions of webinars. I also spoke with Zoom, who confirmed that was not a feature our plan supported. I have told them that they should include accessibility options for every account by default, and they said they would pass along that feedback to their team. I apologize that it does not provide a solution for us currently.

I flagged this for our ITS department…I am hoping the solution is up and available moving forward. The events on Thursday and Friday are also in English and our hope is to have this solved by then.

On behalf of our entire team producing today's Dialogues program, I apologize greatly for the lack of closed caption. That was not our intention, and I can assure you the recorded video, which will be available by next week, will have the closed caption. I will personally email you a copy of that link as soon as it is available. I am grateful that you reached out to us so quickly and I can assure you we will correct that issue.

Unfortunately, our digital Festival is not fully accessible. It will be broadcasted on YouTube where you can find automated subtitles. We are aware that this is not sufficient in making the program fully inclusive and we will work on improving that aspect.

We recognize that we fell well short of our goal in this instance and that we need to do better. ADA compliance is something we take seriously, and although we have yet to schedule any more online events, I can assure you that our next one will be compliant.

Sorry all, that was really insensitive of me to post without captions previously please forgive.

I'm truly sorry. I will ask them to make sure the recording is captioned, though I know that's no substitute for watching it as [it is] happening.

I completely understand the need for this and apologize we did not figure this out earlier.

We appreciate your feedback and are sorry for any accessibility challenges you or others have experienced.

We sincerely apologize for falling short on inclusivity in our digital programs and we are working to correct this as soon as possible.

I assure you we are on fixing this permanently given our new normal, but I am so sorry that we had to hear this from you / the frustration that it caused.

We apologize for the delay in getting back to you. This is an on-going process, but all of our new videos will be captioned. We are also working to ensure our past videos will be captioned as well.

I was involved with planning the event and because of my own ability privilege it did not occur to me that having a transcript after the event is not sufficient... I have been part of many programs at other institutions that offer live captioning so I know it is very doable. Thank you for sharing this with me and I'm sorry for the lack of care.

I do apologize for any inconvenience this has caused. I have escalated this issue to our help desk team, a ticket was created to have captions placed for the video.

I apologize about the captioning. It's up and running now.

I'm sorry for the delayed reply. The office has been very busy due to finals and wrapping up the semester with last minute duties. Unfortunately, video captioning all the videos will most likely not be dealt with until next semester. We want to give it the proper time it demands and therefore I'm sorry to inform you that we will not be able to meet your requests.

In fact, we very much regret that we are currently unable to realize the project in another way. It is a great concern of ours to make our programs in both the physical and digital space gradually less barrier-free [*sic*] and more inclusive. We should have specified the details in our announcement and apologize for this. Cultural inclusion is important to us!

We truly appreciate your message. It seems the captions in these videos were not enabled on the front end. I deeply apologize for the error and they should now appear.

We send the episode as soon as it is finalized (so last night) to our transcriber, who usually turns it around to us within two days. So the transcript will be up by tomorrow (copy edited by me, so I guarantee it!). I'm sorry it is not sooner, and I'm going to work on how to guarantee it gets up the same day as publication.

Many thanks again for raising this and no need to be gracious on your part, we are playing catch up with this and are behind on many fronts!

Again, I am sincerely sorry you had difficulty using our services. I am also sincerely sorry that our customer service team chose to argue with you instead of helping you, which is what they should have done in the first place.

Again, I apologize for this and will contact the individuals working on social media videos.

I am sorry for my ableist oversight. It was/is fucked up and I will do better.

Deeply sorry I didn't realize [the tech people and event organizers] were that dumb which was my mistake.

Despite our plans to make closed captioning available during the livestream, we experienced a technical challenge that affected the caption functionality. We are committed to providing equitable access to our content and sincerely apologize that your experience was impacted in this way.

Apologies for the inconvenience.

Again, I apologize for our complete oversight.

We are trying to find a solution to this, Joseph.

I am deeply sorry for the experience you had at our program last week. I also want to apologize for the fact that you did not hear back from us promptly in response to your first email.

While I wish you didn't have to, thank you, sincerely, for taking the time to explain my privilege to me. I promise we will do better.

While we are grateful to you and others for keeping us accountable, we know that the work to provide equitable access to all our audiences lies with us. We are committed to learning and doing better.

I understand that an apology will only go so far and know that you have heard many of them from the School. We nonetheless remain sincerely sorry that we failed you and other members of our community.

Joseph—we still haven't solved it—so sorry.

A Generic Email Template on the Proactive Benefits of Online Captions, 2020

During the pandemic, many institutions used AI captioning on their platforms. While the quality of speech recognition has improved much over the past decade, AI captioning remains unreliable and rife with errors—producing what I call "craptions." To explain the situation in more detail from the perspective of a deaf viewer, and to emphasize the relevance of captions for a larger audience, especially those who speak English as a second language, I prepared a generic letter that I sent to more than a dozen museums, galleries, and art schools.

Dear XYZ,

I am writing to you because we have worked together before in one way or another—on an exhibition, or a publication, or another related art project. As curators, museum administrators, and gallerists, you play an important role disseminating culture, and making programming platforms accessible for everyone.

I want to bring attention to a very important kind of institutional access: open captions for deaf and hard-of-hearing people on videos and other online programming. As Covid-19 has forced many arts institutions to shift public programs to digital platforms—talks, roundtable discussions, webinars, video art projects—it is important to remember that deaf people cannot access this material without captioning, and that effective captioning is a good institutional practice, in addition to being a mandate of the Americans with Disabilities Act (in the US) and the Equality Act (in the UK). While different countries have different requirements, the real issue here is not a legal one—it's a moral one: doing the right thing. If art is going to be a critical part of our social and political moment, and if diversity is to encompass the intersectional enfolding of race and disability, it needs to be accessible for everybody.

Thus, I am writing to ask you to recognize the importance of, and to implement, real-time captions for your online public programming, whether it is hosted by your own website, by Zoom, or by YouTube. And because Instagram Live does not host real-time captions, I want to ask you NOT to use this platform for live programming (just as you would not work with institutions that violate statutes related to race and gender discrimination), as it is in violation of the ADA, and your participation in it amounts to complicity. We all have to support each other in the quest for meaningful change for all marginalized people.

Real-time captioning, to be effective, requires a human captionist. Third-party captionists are readily available: Some companies are VERY good at this stuff and can streamline the process for you. There are also volunteer groups that provide captioning support for low-income institutions, and there are captioning grants too. I urge caution when using automatic speech recognition (ASR) programs like Otter or YouTube: They are not very accurate, at best getting 85–90 percent of stereotypical speech correct, and expecting the deaf person to figure out the rest.

That's not effective access: Imagine a wheelchair ramp for ten steps that goes up only nine steps and leaves the person in the chair to figure out how to get over the last step. National, regional, and racial accents result in much lower success rates, because the algorithms are based on "normal" white male speech. (The error rate for Black speakers is twice the rate for white speakers. See: https://arstechnica.com/science/2020/03/speech-recognition-algorithms-may-also-have-racial-bias/.) Additionally, ASR programs are very poor at recognizing art-world names, whether of people or institutions. Effective captioning requires care, especially as it relates to your institutional mission. It's not going to work well for anyone if it's treated merely as an afterthought.

It's important to note that live captioning is a vital part of the process. Captioning done after the fact does not allow deaf people to participate in real time—which is a separate-but-equal kind of situation. I am often told: "We're sorry we didn't caption the presentation, we will have captions on the archived video, please check back in with us in one or two weeks." This is deeply offensive, the kind of differential treatment that *Brown v. Board of Education* was meant to eliminate over fifty years ago. Only with real-time captioning can deaf people truly participate in an event and ask questions like others. Access is not a one-way process: If it allows disabled people access to the event, it also allows others access to people with disabilities, who can contribute to the conversations taking place.

Another institutional benefit of live captioning is that, at the end of the event, you have a transcript, which will require only minor corrections (usually to names) to make it a complete and accurate record—which is useful in so many ways as part of your institutional archive.

I should also state that this is not just about being deaf or hearing: It's also about sharing information. We live in a world of many languages, and making English more accessible through the use of captions is part of the reality of living in a global information economy. Additionally, studies have shown that captioning benefits all children, regardless of their ability to hear or not: Literacy and learning outcomes both improve when captions are used. While most deaf people know how to enable closed captions, hearing people often don't (consider younger audiences, international audiences, and elderly audiences)—so open captions make your message more . . . open.

I also realize that for some institutions the cost of live captioning can become an unreasonable financial burden. But costs can be managed. Many institutions require people to register for online events using a third-party vendor like Eventbrite. But this registration process never (in my experience) includes a means by which someone can request a reasonable accommodation. It's an enormous hassle to navigate websites to find out who to contact. If the process of event registration incorporated accommodation requests, institutions would be able to channel resources to these requests, and would also have a consolidated record of them for reporting and tax purposes—because, if your institution pays taxes, there are deductions available for disability-related accommodations. At the School of the Art Institute of Chicago, every event announcement, whether a wall poster or a digital poster or an email event blast, includes a contact email address for making accommodation requests that is routed to a central authority responsible for implementing these requests. This is a good practice to follow.

Of the fifty or so online events I attended this spring and early summer, only one of them provided captions without asking. It was very frustrating to write back and forth with institutions about access issues. And with so much that's gone awry in our world right now, people often put disability access at the bottom of their list of cares. It shouldn't be this way. Access is a metaphor for inclusion. As institutions address their own history of racial exclusion, among other things, providing access to linguistic information is one way of making sure this effort has a measurable outcome.

So I am asking you to make this kind of care a priority for your institution. Moreover, I am asking you to emphasize this kind of care to your colleagues at other institutions, with other curators or museum directors or gallerists or artists—because ensuring equitable access to art is central to making it meaningful.

Sincerely,
Joseph

Paragraph X, 2021

Of the many contracts I have signed, both for exhibitions and public lectures, there is rarely any mention of the host institution's legal obligations with respect to disability. When the pandemic initiated a rush to move public programming online, the issue became more complicated, as an international audience was implicitly invited to participate. Every country has different access statutes, and it seemed to me a timely opportunity for all contracts—not just those involving disabled artists or speakers—to have a disability-access rider to focus attention on global participation. Many disabled artists have their own riders for their own needs; with *Paragraph X*, I was thinking of a larger scope, beyond my needs. I wanted to consider the needs of those individuals whose participation was otherwise unexpected or unplanned for, and the importance of having institutional mechanisms in place to meet those needs. This is the purpose of *Paragraph X*.

A colleague asked me why I did not make the rider more radical, and my response was that if any arts institution followed current legal mandates, they would be doing something far more radical than they've ever done before as far as disability access is concerned.

Joseph Grigely
Paragraph X
2021

X. All public events, both online and in person, should be accessible to people with disabilities, and follow the national accessibility statutes of the host institution(s). Additionally, provisions for access should be clearly stated in promotional advertising for events, and the advertising should include a contact person to whom inquiries about access can be directed. When documentation of the event is posted online, this material should also be effectively accessible.

Letter to the Editor of *Artforum*, 2021 (unpublished)

Dear Editor,

In your May issue, in a feature titled "Close-Up: Indifference and Repetition," David Rimanelli shares a few words about Dean Sameshima's *Outlaw* (2003). As Rimanelli writes, the work consists of "a group of seventeen photos of a cute, presumably gay guy demonstrating the American Sign Language (ASL) gestures for, oh, let's see: *mutual masturbation*, *climax*, *gay*, *blow job*, *erection*, *ejaculation*, *well-hung*, *group sex*, *testicles*, etc." Deriving from a 1990s issue of a gay porn magazine, *IN TOUCH For Men*, Rimanelli describes the images as being "objectively sourced."

Do I laugh or do I cry?

The images might be objective; the language isn't—you can't be objective about a language you don't know, and all Rimanelli can do is ogle at the gay guy presumably making this sign or that sign, and needing an English caption to tell which is which. It's classic cultural appropriation, and ASL has a history of being exploited by artists who have no idea about the language they are working with. Adrienne Rich, Orlan, and Martin Wong are among the many appropriators who have maligned ASL in an effort to achieve some heightened effect. Wong's *Traffic Signs for the Hearing Impaired* are especially glaring: In one case he attempted to make a traffic sign that said "School for Deaf" in both English and the ASL alphabet. But he misspelled the fingerspelled version, mistaking the letter *f* for the number 6, so the signs actually read "School 6or Dea6."

If Sameshima had learned some ASL because he wanted to fuck someone who is deaf, he'd at least have meaningful intent on the agenda—there are few better ways to learn a language than in the sack. But to use ASL just as a visual prop, to turn dicks and balls into metaphors, removes the language from its place as language qua language in the world of the Deaf. If Rimanelli really wanted to give us a "close-up" of the place of ASL in the gay world, he could have gone a lot deeper into his subject by going inside that world. The world of MFA programs might cover a lot of queer history, as Rimanelli acknowledges, but it totally sucks at surveying disability history, or granting disability a place at the table of diversity alongside race and gender. Likewise, the art world is doing a pretty lousy job when it comes to linguistic access in the form of ASL interpreters and captions, and as a result those of us who are Deaf are going to feel possessive about ASL: It's at the very core of our being, with a long history of tragedy behind it, and not something to be toyed with. If you're going to use someone else's language in your art, especially the language of an oppressed minority, either make an effort to learn it or STFU.

Joseph Grigely

Ableism in Language, 2021

A proposal sent to the *The New York Times*.

Editor, Op-Eds
The New York Times Company
620 Eighth Avenue
New York, NY 10018

I am attaching for your consideration a graphic op-ed on the subject of ableism in the titles of articles from the editorial pages of *The New York Times*. The op-ed has two parts: a visual graphic of collaged titles from the *Times*, and a caption of approximately 150 words. The titles are screenshots from the *Times*' website, and scans from my own collection of hard copies, covering a period from the 1980s–present. Most are from the past decade. The dates are not all visible in the graphic; however, all can be confirmed by using a title search on the *Times*' website.

Over the past few decades, the editorial pages of *The New York Times* have undergone many changes that have helped make the paper a more diverse reading experience—especially in terms of the range of editorial voices. But one thing that has not changed since the 1980s is the paper's use of deafness and blindness as pejorative metaphors to connote ignorance and a lack of attention. The *Times* is widely regarded as a barometer of linguistic permissiveness, and the ongoing use of outworn figures of speech reflects a casual disregard for the place of disability in everyday life. When the Americans with Disabilities Act was passed thirty years ago, many who are disabled thought we would see the end of such language. How wrong we were. Inclusion is not just about things like wheelchair ramps and interpreters for the deaf; it's also about how people are represented with the words we use, especially the words used in daily newspapers like *The New York Times*.

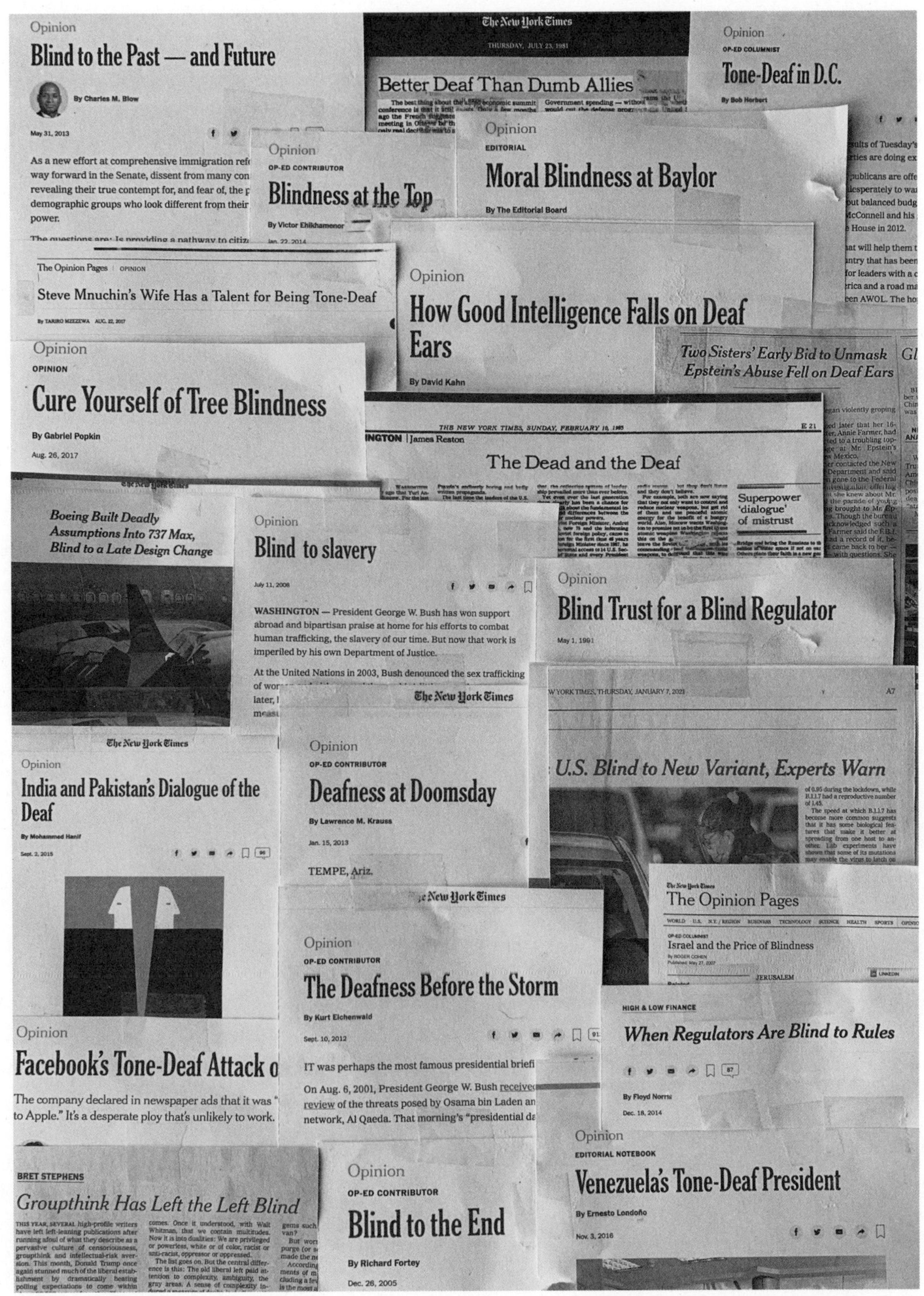

Opinion

Blind to the Past — and Future

By Charles M. Blow

May 31, 2013

As a new effort at comprehensive immigration ref… way forward in the Senate, dissent from many con… revealing their true contempt for, and fear of, the p… demographic groups who look different from their… power.

The New York Times

THURSDAY, JULY 23, 1981

Better Deaf Than Dumb Allies

Opinion

OP-ED COLUMNIST

Tone-Deaf in D.C.

By Bob Herbert

Opinion

OP-ED CONTRIBUTOR

Blindness at the Top

By Victor Ehikhamenor

Opinion

EDITORIAL

Moral Blindness at Baylor

By The Editorial Board

The Opinion Pages | OPINION

Steve Mnuchin's Wife Has a Talent for Being Tone-Deaf

By TARIRO MZEZEWA AUG. 22, 2017

Opinion

How Good Intelligence Falls on Deaf Ears

By David Kahn

Two Sisters' Early Bid to Unmask Epstein's Abuse Fell on Deaf Ears

Opinion

OPINION

Cure Yourself of Tree Blindness

By Gabriel Popkin

Aug. 26, 2017

THE NEW YORK TIMES, SUNDAY, FEBRUARY 10, 1985

James Reston

The Dead and the Deaf

Superpower 'dialogue' of mistrust

The New York Times

Boeing Built Deadly Assumptions Into 737 Max, Blind to a Late Design Change

Opinion

Blind to slavery

July 11, 2008

WASHINGTON — President George W. Bush has won support abroad and bipartisan praise at home for his efforts to combat human trafficking, the slavery of our time. But now that work is imperiled by his own Department of Justice.

At the United Nations in 2003, Bush denounced the sex trafficking…

Opinion

Blind Trust for a Blind Regulator

May 1, 1991

THE NEW YORK TIMES, THURSDAY, JANUARY 7, 2021 A7

U.S. Blind to New Variant, Experts Warn

The New York Times

Opinion

India and Pakistan's Dialogue of the Deaf

By Mohammed Hanif

Sept. 2, 2015

The New York Times

Opinion

OP-ED CONTRIBUTOR

Deafness at Doomsday

By Lawrence M. Krauss

Jan. 15, 2013

TEMPE, Ariz.

The New York Times

The Opinion Pages

OP-ED COLUMNIST

Israel and the Price of Blindness

By ROGER COHEN

JERUSALEM

The New York Times

Opinion

OP-ED CONTRIBUTOR

The Deafness Before the Storm

By Kurt Eichenwald

Sept. 10, 2012

IT was perhaps the most famous presidential briefi…

On Aug. 6, 2001, President George W. Bush received… review of the threats posed by Osama bin Laden an… network, Al Qaeda. That morning's "presidential da…

HIGH & LOW FINANCE

When Regulators Are Blind to Rules

By Floyd Norris

Dec. 18, 2014

Opinion

Facebook's Tone-Deaf Attack o…

The company declared in newspaper ads that it was "… to Apple." It's a desperate ploy that's unlikely to work.

BRET STEPHENS

Groupthink Has Left the Left Blind

Opinion

OP-ED CONTRIBUTOR

Blind to the End

By Richard Fortey

Dec. 26, 2005

Opinion

EDITORIAL NOTEBOOK

Venezuela's Tone-Deaf President

By Ernesto Londoño

Nov. 3, 2016

Advocacy

In one of his essays, the Russian filmmaker Andrey Tarkovsky wrote: "The artist has no right to an idea to which he is not socially committed, or the realisation of which could involve a dichotomy between his professional activity and the rest of his life. In our personal lives we perform actions, as honourable or dishonourable people. We accept that an honourable action may bring pressure down on us, or even bring us into conflict with our milieu." I have always felt reassured by this remark—that doing the right thing, whatever it might be, for whomever we might be, comes with risk. And that we cannot easily separate what we do professionally as an artist and what we do personally as a citizen—they are imbricated activities. But the dilemma of being an artist is that galleries and museums are not always the best venues in which to pursue social change, as the force of political persuasion arguably has more weight in other places—particularly within the three branches of our government. Tarkovsky didn't have the liberty to engage with the space of public opinion and law in his life as a Soviet citizen, so his art had to do the heavy lifting. But for myself, I have found that the voices of disability justice and advocacy are more effective in such spaces—and that, at times, effective advocacy requires taking actions such as filing lawsuits.

Up to a certain point, disability advocacy usually involves persuasion—trying to explain to institutions how access considerations are not just about disabled people, but about the institution more generally, and how the institution, not just the disabled individual, is the beneficiary of efficient accessibility. But sometimes the message does not get through. Or sometimes it just doesn't reach the right people—those who have the capacity to change things. One dilemma in making a complaint of any kind is that the optics are self-defeating: No one likes a complainer. As I wrote earlier, in the introduction to this book, attention often shifts from the basis of the complaint to the person making the complaint.

When institutions fail to respond to complaints in a meaningful way, it sometimes becomes necessary to take a path that involves filing a formal legal motion—either directly, with the institution, or (depending on the nature of the alleged violation) with the Department of Justice, which is tasked with overseeing the Americans with Disabilities Act. Other government branches, such as the Equal Employment Opportunity Commission and state/city commissions on human rights, also have enforcement programs that apply to different aspects of the ADA. Legal complaints are time-consuming to file. They also require learning the language of another discipline. But sometimes they are the only way to get an institution to pay the necessary attention to the gravity of a situation. Every year the Department of Justice receives thousands of Title III complaints (which cover access to public institutions), but they pursue lawsuits in response to only a small number of these. Others are referred to mediation, and yet others, despite having legal merit, are not pursued because of limited resources within the DOJ. In such instances, complainants are given the option of filing their own private lawsuits.

Correspondence With, and Concerning, the Modern Language Association, 1985–90

In 1985, I began a two-year Mellon Post-doctoral Fellowship in the English department at Stanford. A routine professional obligation was to attend, and present papers, at the annual convention of the Modern Language Association. At this time the MLA was the largest organization in the US devoted to the humanities, and the annual convention drew roughly ten thousand registrants. In 1984, the first year I planned to attend, the organizers refused to provide sign language interpreters. The following year, when I was at Stanford and had a paper accepted to the convention, the MLA again responded to my request for interpreting by saying "It is not possible." At this point, a number of my colleagues at Stanford jumped into the fray, and for several years the MLA stumbled through the process of learning how to make itself accessible as a professional organization. By 1990, however, the process had taken its toll on me, and I resigned from the MLA.

STANFORD UNIVERSITY
STANFORD, CALIFORNIA 94305

[DE]PARTMENT OF ENGLISH

13 November 1985

Dear Ann Hull,

For the second consecutive year I note that the Convention Program (p. 871) advises people "who need any special assistance" at the convention to contact the MLA, and for the second consecutive year I am asking the MLA to provide American Sign Language (ASL) interpreting services for selected sessions at the 1985 Chicago convention.

Although I have not yet identified each session I would like to attend, a rough time estimate would include two sessions on Friday, four on Saturday, four on Sunday, and perhaps one on Monday. I therefore suggest that you try to secure, for these sessions, the concurrent services of two RID-certified interpreters* whose backgrounds and interests are compatible with concerns of the MLA.

At last year's convention in Washington, the MLA categorically refused to provide ASL interpreting services, and I am hoping that this unfortunate situation will not be repeated. If the MLA again feels it cannot, or should not, provide such services, I shall be grateful to receive a detailed explanation. I further request that you inform me of the position of your commitment by December 5th so that, should the worst occur, I will have sufficient time to make alternative ~~xg~~ arrangements.

Sincerely,

Joseph Grigely, D.Phil.
Andrew W. Mellon Fellow in Eglish

* Registry of Interpreters for the Deaf

Ms. Ann Hull
Director of Convention Programmes
Modern Language Association, N.Y., N.Y.

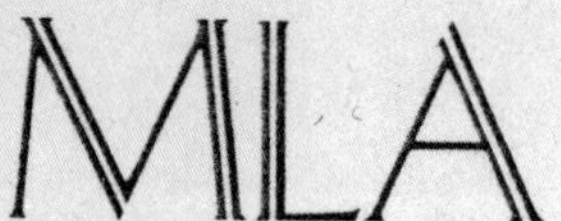

MODERN LANGUAGE ASSOCIATION OF AMERICA 62 FIFTH AVENUE. NEW YORK, NEW YORK 10011 (212) 741-5588

Telephone (212) 741-5587

6 December 1985

Mr. Joseph Grigely
Department of English
Stanford University
Stanford, CA 94305

Dear Mr. Grigely:

Thank you for your letter of 13 November. In the interest of being as helpful to you as we can, we have looked into various options and their consequences.

I would like to pose two alternatives for your consideration. If someone is accompanying you, we can supply that person with a complimentary badge. Or, if you think it would be useful, we can have a convention aide meet you at the entrance to any meeting room in order to make certain you have a front row seat. Please let me know if either of these possibilities interests you, and if you choose the latter option, the program numbers of the meetings you will attend. Unfortunately, it is not possible for us to provide American Sign Language interpreting services for convention sessions.

In addition as you may know, the names and affiliations of all convention participants are listed in the convention program. You might want to write and request copies of papers from participants in any programs you attend.

I hope you enjoy the 1985 convention's lively and enriching program. Please let me know if I may be of any further service to you.

Very truly yours,

Ann Hull

Ann Hull
Director of Convention Programs

AH:jr

L.BRAGG

Fax Transmission
total: 7 pages

To: Lois Bragg
English Department

From: Joseph Grigely

Re: MLA

Hi, Lo--

Here's a year-by-year breakdown on my relationship with the MLA. I'm also sending along a copy of the letter I sent to Phyllis Franklin when I resigned from the MLA in December 1990. I hope this information helps; thanks for asking, and thanks for taking the time and trouble to go to San Diego.

1984--First request for interpreters. English Showalter was Executive Director at this time. Refused to provide interpreters without stating a reason.

1985--Second request for interpreters. Phyllis Franklin was the new Executive Director, and Ann Hull was director of the convention. Hull replied to my request that while the MLA couldn't provide interpreters, the Association could provide an aide who would meet me at the door of the meeting rooms and escort me to a front-row seat (!). I was at Stanford at this time under a Mellon post-doctoral fellowship, and my Department Chair (Al Gelpi) and an MLA Executive Committee Member (Mary Louise Pratt) engaged others to pressure the MLA on the subject. A few days before the convention, Phyllis Franklin sent me an express mail letter saying that I could bring my own interpreter and that the MLA woould pay costs up to a certain amount ($200 I think, but the letter is filed away and I don't have access to it just now).

1986--Third request for interpreters, and the MLA agreed to obtain them for pre-selected sessions. It turned out to be a disaster as the MLA did not contract to obtain certified interpreters, and in the middle of the first talk during the first session the interpreter gave up because she couldn't handle the either the linguistic register or the subject matter.

1987, 1988, 1989--During these years I made my own arrangements for interpreters and the MLA paid. It was a time-consuming process, but at least the interpreting quality was good. During this period I presented several papers related to ASL and ASL literature (see list, below).

1990--A new convention director, Maribeth Krauss, replaced Ann Hull. Krauss wanted to know over one month in advance the specific sessions I would attend, and demanded that my interpreter pay a registration fee. Since neither of these conditions applied to other convention participants, I resigned in a letter of December 10, 1990 and did not attend the convention.

L. BRAGG

Papers:

1985 "A Social Theory of Language Evolution in American Sign Language" (with Diane Brentari)

1986 "Texts, Oral Texts, and Metatexts"

1987 "Ethnicity, American Sign Language, and the Deaf"

1988 "American Sign Language Poetry and Medium-Governed Restrictions on Iconicity"
"Textualterity: Paralogical Investigations into Texts and Textual Alterity"

1989 "Languages of Art or Metaphors of Language?"
"Deconstructing Visual Iconicity"
Organized (with Diane Brentari) an ASL poetry reading; moderated discussion after the reading

1990 Organized two special sessions: "Language in Art: Theoretical Issues" and "Language in Art"

L. BRAGG

Lois— When i transferred files to print This out, The computer (a new one) reformatted everything.— I've printed in in an unreconstructed format.— Joe,

10 December 1990

email: jgrigely@gallua.bitnet

Dear Phyllis Franklin,

I have delayed responding to your letter of October 15th to Diane Brentari, a copy of which you were good enough to send me, largely because the matter of sign language interpreters involves particular consideration and care that cannot be offered in an immediate reply. What follows represents the culmination of several TDD conversations with Diane about the contents of your letter, a personal visit to do the same, and discussions about the matter with a number of deaf and hearing colleagues at Gallaudet. Although the voice that follows is essentially my own, my concerns are in a larger sense those of both Deaf and hearing colleagues in the profession. I hope it is not too presumptuous of me to ask you to read this letter with particular care. It is considerably longer than I would wish it to be, but the necessity of this length, like the necessity of its contents, is unavoidable.

The exchanges of communication which have taken place in the past autumn--your letter of October 15th to Diane Brentari, Diane's letter to you of October1st, your telephone conversation with Diane in late September, and Stacy Courtney's telephone call to Diane shortly beforehand--all indicate that certain problems related to interpreting assignments and MLA policies remain largely unresolved, perhaps suggesting a need to address the issues in a more coherent and concerted manner than has been done in the past. This letter will, I hope, address both principal and tangential issues arising from these recent communications. If I understand your letter of October 15th correctly, you do not object to Diane Brentari serving as my full-time interpreter; rather, because Diane is an MLA member, and had paid registration fees to attend the convention in the past, you assert that you find it difficult to justify waiving her registration fee this year--even though she will be functioning, as she explained, as a full-time interpreter. As a consequence you are implicitly offering me two choices: either to pay the registration fee for my interpreter, or to advise the MLA convention office in advance which specific sessions I would like to attend so that passes for the interpreter can be issued for those sessions. In the first case I am being asked, in effect, to pay an additional registration fee for my ears; in the second case my access to the convention is being limited to specific sessions--essentially defeating the purpose of a full-time interpreter, which is to provide spontaneous and unfettered communication whenever the need arises--whether in a meeting room, the hallway, or on the shuttle bus. I am certain that you do not intend your suggestions to be understood in such negative terms; it is merely a bare, naked reality that these implications should be as they are. For now, however, I would like to backtrack briefly to clarify an important misunderstanding that apparently led you to present these options.

My concern is your analogy that if Diane Brentari had registered for previous conventions which she attended as my interpreter, then she should certainly register again. A bit of history here might help explain precisely why, and on what terms, Diane registered in the past. The first of the conventions which I attended was the

1984 convention in Washington, D.C. The MLA, then under English Showalter, refused (without explanation) to provide an interpreters. As a colleague at Gallaudet who was then teaching ESL to deaf students, Diane volunteered to interpret for me and, as I recall, subsequently registered for the convention because she was not offered a badge as my interpreter. We did not protest these decisions at that time but rather decided to give the MLA a second chance the following year. You will recall that my written request for interpreters was thereupon denied in 1985, and only after a defensive exchange of letters and the intervention of a number of colleagues was the decision reversed.

After the 1984 convention, however, and prior to the 1985 experience, Diane and I engaged another kind of response: we sent off a jointly authored paper on phono-morphological change in ASL to Alan Walker Read, who--much to his credit--accepted it for the 1985 convention. Recognizing that the source of our problems was largely rooted in ignorance, not maliciousness, our intention was to begin a program of education by presenting papers on ASL. Over the next four years Diane and I presented eleven additional papers (and organized an ASL poetry reading) that had as their locus either ASL or its theoretical implications--and we did this, as I suggested, not because we specifically wanted to, but because the state of gross ignorance about ASL, the Deaf community, and ASL literature in the profession left us with no choice. I am, by training and desire, a scholar of nineteenth-century British literature. I am, by fate and necessity, a shaman of ASL politics. I doubt that I, or any other Deaf scholar, has a choice: how can we participate in our chosen fields if we must continually, repeatedly, for almost every audience, explain the needs of our participation--and then meet with resistance and skepticism? I shall return to this question in a moment; it bothers me just now only because it is continually bothering me--a point which, when given thought, is not so redundant as it seems to be.

A brief summary now: in the five years between the 1985 convention in Chicago and the 1989 convention in Washington, Diane (as you note in your letter) paid registration fees. But she did so not (as your letter states) in the capacity as my interpreter, but (as your letter does not state) as a participating member of those conventions, having presented papers at each of them. In other words: she was fulfilling a moral obligation to the MLA--and we have done this at other conventions where we have both been participants. I cannot recall any occasion in which my interpreter was forced to register, nor has my access to the interpreter been restricted by architectural geography; either of these restraints would in effect amount to inequitable access. For the 1990 convention Diane and I have closed the circle on the effort initiated by the 1984 convention: neither of us, as a matter of choice, is presenting a paper (although I am scheduled to chair a special session). Diane, as she explained to you, would be functioning fully in the capacity as my interpreter and reverting to the role interpreters traditionally provide: that of a communication facilitator, not just for the deaf person, but for the hearing as well. Her continued membership in the MLA bespeaks her familiarity with the discourse of the profession, and thus reinforces her ability to provide the quality interpretation that the convention requires. In your letter you remark that you "cannot see how the situation at the 1990 convention differs from previous meetings"; I hope you can now.

Of course the situation is probably more complex, given, as you say, the current MLA policy that all Association members must register for conventions they attend. Hence I understand your concern that having an unregistered MLA member walking around at the convention might establish some kind of precedence. Sometimes, however, precedence is a necessary precursor of humane understanding, even when history shows us that people are made uncomfortable or disconcerted by such acts.

Might it be that there is something wrong not with my request but with the policy that you are, as you say, "supposed to implement"? Very rarely is discrimination willful or malicious; it rather arises out of a combination of ignorance and fear --an unwillingness to enjoin a human evaluation of a human issue. Perhaps then the MLA might wish to look more closely at this registration policy as it applies to interpreters. Perhaps--dare I say it?--the MLA might even recruit (as nonpaying members of the Association) highly qualified sign language interpreters so as to ensure the availability of interpreters familiar with the terminology and topics of the profession. This would indeed establish precedence--precedence of the kind that would make a great number of organizations both respect and envy the MLA.

I'm reaching the tangents now: the various issues which are inextricable from the fundamental concerns of this letter. Consider a small fact about interpreters: the discourse being interpreted is, in the end, only as good as the interpreter--not the speaker. No interpreter can improve a bad talk, but a bad or mediocre interpreter can quite destroy a good one. Perhaps this doesn't need saying. Yet at the 1986 MLA convention in New York--the first (and only) year I have entrusted the MLA to obtain interpreters on its own--the interpreters were so incompetent in relation to the critical discourse of the papers that ten minutes into the first session on the first night I had to ask my interpreter to stop wasting her energy and, leaving behind me Marjorie Perloff and Donald Kuspit, went looking for Jack Daniel and Johnny Walker. To say that I was angry is to use a euphemism. Yet the general unavailability of highly qualified interpreters strikes me an issue somehow relevant to the fact that (to my knowledge) the number of deaf PhDs in English can be counted on one hand--all of us, I am both proud and sorry to say, ensconced and ghettoized at Gallaudet. The reasons for this are most certainly complex; but chief among these reasons is interpreters--their availability, their skills, their knowledge of our discipline. I would like to hope that some day the MLA might recognize there is something wrong with these numbers; that something can be done; that something <u>will</u> be done. Neither I nor my colleagues at Gallaudet can do this alone. In the undefined political canon of the profession we are not a certified minority but an uncertified minority, an asterisk in the domain of alterity. Unlike women, unlike African-Americans, the Deaf simply do not have the numbers to assert themselves as a political force or a physical presence. For most of us this is not even our goal; we simply want to do what everyone else does: participate. The availability of good interpreters helps, but in the long run this alone is not a panacea; more fundamental problems besiege the human consciousness and our ways of thinking about the Other. Even at the MLA convention I am regularly asked how ASL can effectively translate English critical discourse. A question like this does not assert prejudice, but rather the sense of doubt which underlies prejudice. Normally such questions do not bother me too much. But when such a question comes between myself and a job, or between one of my deaf colleagues and a job, then I become more than just bothered. One of my greatest hopes is to some day attend an MLA convention and not be reminded I am a deaf person.

I am optimistic enough to believe that there may be solutions to many of these problems. However, for the past five years the correspondence that we have exchanged about interpreting and related matters would suggest that these issues cannot be resolved on a local level between myself and the MLA; it is time, I think, to consider the idea of 'access' on a more global level. I therefore request that the MLA establish a commission to investigate the needs of the disabled in the profession: a commission (or Ad Hoc Committee) composed of disabled members of the profession, professionals in the field of disability resource services, and MLA officers, which would be entrusted with the task of carefully examining the situation of disabled people involved in fields of language and literature. Such a commission is long overdue: we have in this manner served many minority groups in the profession, and, given the recent passage of the Americans with Disabilities Act of 1990, it would seem particularly advantageous that the MLA take up this challenge to gather statistics on the representation of disabled people in the profession and make recommendations based on this information. In connection with this I also request that the MLA appoint a Special-Interest Delegate representing the Disabled in the Profession. I hope you will consider these requests with the earnest seriousness that they deserve.

A transition now; my main points behind me, I wish to move to a more personal level. Are you ready? I am, to put it mildly, mentally exhausted and demoralized by the sort of resistance the MLA has put up this year in handling my interpreting arrangements. When I sent off my convention registration forms and indicated that Diane Brentari would be my interpreter, I expected this would be a perfunctory matter, as no doubt it should be. If there was to be a problem with the arrangements, I fully expected the MLA to contact the author of those arrangements--me. It is therefore particularly disconcerting that Stacy Courtney telephoned Diane Brentari at U.C. Davis in late September to say that there was a problem with Diane's registration. Why was not this matter immediately brought to my attention? Is it because it is less troublesome to contact a hearing person on the telephone? Does the MLA have a TDD of its own, and experience using it? I do not presume to know the answers here. I do however feel ostracized by the pattern of communication that took place.

For some sad reason I am not surprised by what has occurred. The turnaround that marked the 1985 MLA convention might be described as having inaugurated a five-year period of increasing consciousness about ASL-related issues: the language, its literature, and its speech community. All of this change occurred with the help of hearing colleagues, and--here I am grateful to you--with the help of the MLA. Yet the events that have led to this letter somehow seem to evince the presence of deeper problems which we have not yet addressed, except in a reflexive manner. I doubt that we have any fundamental differences between us; or that the MLA would consciously discriminate in any way. But there remain a great number of misunderstandings--misunderstandings that affect a larger, intertextual conception of deafness and ASL. I find it particularly depressing--I think that's the word I want here--to acknowledge this reality. And I am sufficiently discouraged--again, the right word--by this reality. My own efforts, as I said earlier, cannot enact or sustain the kinds of changes that yet need to occur. Given this situation, and given the conditions you have presented for my interpreter at the 1990 convention--conditions which I cannot as a matter of principle accept--I am resigning from the MLA and will not participate in the Chicago convention.

This is a painful decision for me. Yet is is a necessary decision, for the events of the last five years, though a sign of progress, are a sign of insufficient progress. I am at a point where writing letters like this is becoming a traumatic ritual. My academic career is beginning to take on the apparition of a defense of my right to equality in the profession, consuming, in the process, both desire and energy. This is not what I envisioned the public dimension of an academic career to be about, and it is not what I wish it to continue to be. Had the problems with my interpreter this year not occurred I would not be entreated to make this decision. Should the MLA appoint, as I described, a Commission on the Disabled in the Profession, I would be willing to reconsider my position. As it stands now, however, the issues which remain cannot be resolved by myself or the MLA, but only through the collective voice of all those concerned. For the sake of the profession I hope that you agree.

L.BRAGG

Very truly yours,

Joseph Grigely
Assistant Professor

xc: Diane Brentari
Houston Baker, Jr.
Nancy Kensicki

Grigely v. Union Station Redevelopment Corp., et al., 1993–95

One day in the 1990s, while I was waiting for a shuttle bus to take me from Union Station in Washington, DC, to my teaching job at Gallaudet University, I was feeling dizzy—I had Ménière's disease—so I lay down on a bench inside the station and closed my eyes. This helped mitigate the vertigo. A few moments later I was pulled upright by three policemen. I explained I was deaf, and had vertigo, and was waiting for a shuttle bus, and appreciated their attention but did not need any help, thank you.

But as I tried to lie down again, three more officers came, and they surrounded me—one grabbed one arm, another grabbed another arm, and they pulled me off the bench. Then two more officers grabbed my legs and proceeded to carry me outside. But in the process, they dropped me and dragged my face along the marble floor. Another officer trotted behind them with my briefcase and computer and threw them into the gutter.

This was my reward for lying down on the bench and failing to follow their oral commands to sit upright.

During the subsequent depositions, one of the officers said in reply to the question of why they did not write after I told them I was deaf: "We tried to, but he wouldn't let us." When asked how I stopped them from writing, they shrugged. As if I could.

My lawsuit was settled without going to trial. Nonetheless, the settlement agreement was onerous to put together and involved agreements with three different companies involved in the incident. For three years after the event every policeman and security officer working in Union Station had to undergo in-person disability sensitivity training. Notably, the settlement agreement permits me to write about the incident—what happened, how it played out, and what might be learned from the experience. The financial details, however, are protected by a nondisclosure agreement.

PLAINTIFF'S CONFIDENTIAL STATEMENT

Grigely v. Union Station Redevelopment Corp., et al.
(Civil Action Number 1:94CV02622)

STATEMENT OF THE FACTS

The plaintiff, Dr. Joseph Grigely, is profoundly deaf and has Delayed Endolymphatic Hydrops/Meniere's Syndrome, a disorder of the inner ear which causes episodes of severe dizziness, vertigo, nausea, and vomiting. Below is a brief summary of the incident which gave rise to this action.

On the morning of December 7, 1993, Dr. Grigely was sitting on a backless bench in Union Station waiting for the Gallaudet University shuttle bus. While waiting, he experienced the onset of an attack of Meniere's Syndrome which forced him to lay back on the bench and close his eyes. When he opened his eyes a short while later, he saw three security officers, one of whom was an Amtrak officer, standing closely around him. He sat up and verbally explained to the officers that he was deaf and that he was experiencing dizziness due to Meniere's Syndrome. He told them that he would be all right in a few minutes, that the Gallaudet shuttle bus would arrive to pick him up, and that he did not need any help. He then laid back down on the bench and closed his eyes. Shortly thereafter, he opened his eyes once again and saw six officers standing around him. He sat up and again explained his situation. This time he communicated in sign language as well as orally.

When he tried to lie back a third time, two of the officers grabbed him by the arms and pulled him up from the bench onto his feet, at which point he fell to his knees. The officers dragged him on his knees across the station floor. One of the officers pulled harder than the other and Dr. Grigely fell forward, striking his face on the floor. Two of the other officers then grabbed his legs and helped the first two officers carry him bodily out of the station. The officers dropped him on a bench outside of the station and he fell off the narrow bench onto the ground. Another officer came behind the others and threw Dr. Grigely's briefcase and computer down on the ground next to him.

After staying on the ground for a moment in order to orient himself, Dr. Grigely picked up his briefcase and computer and went back inside. He then approached the officers and requested, in spoken English, to see their identification and produced a manila envelope for them to write upon. The Burns officers, who were not wearing any identification, refused his request and walked away. The Amtrak officer, who did have an identification badge, wrote on the envelope: "I work for Amtrak--Those people work for LaSalle Company". He then agreed to take Dr. Grigely to the security office where an Amtrak employee paged a security supervisor who wrote down the names of the officers involved.

DISCUSSION OF THE LEGAL ISSUES

A. Civil Rights Claims

Dr. Grigely has brought civil rights claims under 42 U.S.C. § 1983, the Americans with Disabilities Act, § 504 of the Rehabilitation Act, and the D.C. Human Rights Act. The § 1983 claims are based on the fact that the defendants, as state actors, created and implemented policies which deprived Dr. Grigely of rights secured by the Fourth Amendment to the Constitution of the United States and federal law.

The Americans with Disabilities Act, § 504 of the Rehabilitation Act, and the D.C. Human Rights Act each have their own requirements. However, the same basic violations underlie all of Dr. Grigely's claims under these statutes: (1) indiscriminate application of a "no reclining" policy which prohibits individuals from reclining on benches in Union Station, and (2) ineffective communication.

1. Indiscriminate Application

Central to this case is defendants' policy that prohibits reclining on benches in Union Station and the fact that this policy is applied uniformly, regardless of the discriminatory impact that it may have on individuals with disabilities. As noted above, at the time of the incident, Dr. Grigely was suffering from an attack of Meniere's syndrome. The dizziness from this attack forced him to recline on the bench, and because he reclined, he was physically removed from Union Station. Thus, it was Dr. Grigely's disability which ultimately caused his violation of defendants' policy and his subsequent removal from the station. By indiscriminately applying a "no reclining" policy without taking into account its discriminatory impact on persons with disabilities, the defendants violated Dr. Grigely's civil rights.

2. Ineffective Communication

There are no signs in Union Station indicating the existence of the "no reclining" policy. Therefore, the only way patrons are made aware of this policy is if they happen to lay back on a bench and are told by security guards to sit up. While this manner of notification may be sufficient for hearing individuals, it is clearly deficient for deaf individuals unless the security guards are trained to communicate with deaf people through the use of sign language, writing, or some other means. In Dr. Grigely's situation none of these means was used. Thus, the manner in which the defendants publicize their policy discriminates against individuals who are deaf, since they are unable to comply with a policy they do not know exists. This is especially significant in light of the fact that Union Station is the closest Metro station serving Gallaudet, and hundreds of deaf students, faculty, and staff go to Union Station every day, not only to use the Metro and the Amtrak trains, but also to patronize the restaurants, shops, and movie theaters within the station.

In addition, the failure of the defendants to provide for adequate communication with deaf people is a violation of civil rights law. Deaf patrons seeking directions or physical assistance in Union Station are unable to communicate with the security guards who work there due to the defendants failure to establish effective methods of communication. In Dr. Grigely's case, this failure to provide communication resulted in his bodily removal from the station.

B. Tort Claims

The security guards employed by defendant Burns committed assault and battery, false arrest and imprisonment, and intentional infliction of emotional distress against Dr. Grigely. Under the principles of respondeat superior and agency, defendants Burns and LaSalle are responsible for the actions of their employees and contractors in the furtherance of their ends and goals.

STATUS OF DISCOVERY

Plaintiff has responded to the interrogatories and request for production of documents submitted by Union Station Redevelopment Corporation, Union Station Venture Limited, and LaSalle Partners. Rule 26(a)(1) initial disclosures are not complete. Further discovery will be necessary.

SIGNIFICANCE OF THE CASE/OUTCOME SOUGHT

See attached letter from Dr. Grigely.

111 First Street 6-5N, Jersey City, New Jersey 07302
4 May 1995

To: Doug, Laura, Malini, & Brian
IPR

From: Joseph Grigely

Re: A statement of sorts

Well, here it is.

In asking me to describe "the significance of the case" in a way that feels comfortable, I have written about my feelings and reflections in the form of a letter to all of you--though the letter is in fact written to myself as a way of sorting out my thoughts, and it is written with the understanding that others are overhearing me--not just the mediator, but anyone. Initially I thought I could use this to serve as the basis for an article that uses an epistolary format, but I realize this won't do now--not in its present form--but perhaps it might, with considerably more time, be worked into something.

Since the mediator gives no indication about what form she wants us to present the "statement", I'd like to keep the epistolary format for this part of the position paper--assuming you feel this is a decent idea. In any case, feel free to edit and revise in a way that you feel is appropriate. Comments and suggestions for revisions at my end are very welcome.

The desired "outcome" in my letter is very general in a way that addresses both remediation and an assurance that such an incident does not happen again. If you feel that it is necessary to be very specific here, then we should cite what we cited during your previous meeting with the defendant's attorneys. If anything we should reiterate those initial settlement terms in order to convey both the consistency of our position and how serious we are about what happened.

I'm sorry this took so long to write--it's really just a rough draft and not the sort of thing I'd like to prepare. But it's something--a couple of good sentences here are worth salvaging, I think, and if I could get by with three of them, I would.

I'll be in the studio for a little while now--so feel free to call.

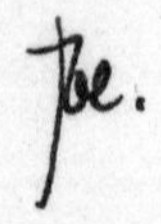

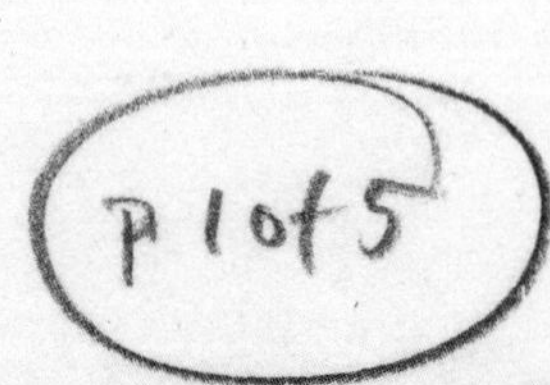

3 May 1995
Jersey City, New Jersey

Dear Doug, Laura, Brian, and Malini--

I'm addressing all of you here, but I'm really writing this letter to myself--writing this letter to explain to myself, and to whomever might overhear it, why I have filed this lawsuit named Grigely v. Union Station Redevelopment Corporation et al. It seems strange seeing my name at one end of this: Grigely *versus* . . . . It's not like me, yet out of necessity, out of a strange and bewildering necessity, it is indeed me. I've never filed a lawsuit before. But this one I just had to do. It wasn't a choice. It was an obligation.

As you might surmise, this is not an easy letter to write. Part of the difficulty lies in the ineffability of the experience of what happened to me on December 7, 1993--of being dragged and carried out of Union Station in Washington by security personnel for no reason other than the fact I was deaf and was experiencing dizziness from a condition known as Meniere's Syndrome. It's still very hard for me to speak about it, let alone write about it. And when I search for answers for how this might have happened--a search that has taken me through the history of the disabled and the history of the Civil Rights movement--I find myself finding answers that are almost as traumatic as the experience itself.

I've been deaf--totally deaf, according to Dr. Arthur Boothroyd, one of the country's leading audiologists--for 28 of my 38 years. It's really true: I can't hear anything--not birds, not buses. Luckily and unluckily, I still remember how to speak. It sounds a little strange when I do--it's a slightly hoarse, slightly gutteral voice. Sometimes a little nasal too. One of my hearing students told me recently that it sounds more European than it sounds "deaf"--whatever that is. I'm not ashamed of it, though--weird or not, it's me. It's the way I come--sort of a package deal. Being deaf bothered me a little at the beginning, but after a while I got used to it, and after a while longer I got to like it. A few years ago I got to the point of loving my deafness--got to the point of realizing that I was actually lucky--lucky!--to have this special take on the world--to see the world without hearing it, and to hear it by seeing it. And it's really nice too, this privilege (for that is what it must be) to exist in this strange space of betweeness: between hearing and seeing, between deafness and muteness, between speech and writing, between English and American Sign Language. In recent years I have tried to share this experience with others in my work as a professional artist (my recent and forthcoming exhibitions include shows at AC Project Room in New York, Washington Project for the Arts in D.C., the Venice Biennale in Italy, and the Museum of Modern Art in Paris), and as a university professor with transdisciplinary teaching and research interests (I'm a tenured associate professor in the English Department at Gallaudet, where my students are all deaf, but I have also taught at Stanford University--where I was a Mellon Postdoctoral Fellow--and at the University of Michigan, where I was recently a visiting associate professor in the Department of the History of Art). I *like* being deaf, precisely because being deaf has taught me how special the experience can be. It's been a remarkably fortuitous and beautiful 28 years.

It's been ugly too. Really ugly. When you're disabled, you learn what discrimination is really fast. You learn a lot of things, actually. You learn to act dumb, you learn to be pathetic, you learn to shut up and accept, with kind words, the benevolence of others. You learn to wait too--disabled people spend a lot of time waiting. We waited 27 years for the Americans With Disabilities Act to grant us some of the same dignities granted to others under the Civil Rights Act of 1964. There is an irony here, but I am not sure what it is, or to whom it belongs.

Anyhow, the ugliness--I'm trying to digress, trying to avoid recalling the parts of my life I don't want to recall, the parts that are almost too surreal to be real--though they are not. I had interpreters denied to me throughout my schooling at hearing institutions (which is why I went to Europe for graduate school--we didn't have any classes); I've had job interviews end when the subject of sign language interpreters came up; I've had my Meniere's Syndrome parodied--parodied!--in the Harvard Lampoon (in 1987); and I have had a museum guard at the Metropolitan Museum of Art in New York strike me hard on the shoulder and berate me because, while sitting on the floor as I gazed at one of Jacques Louis David's mesmerizing paintings, I did not get up onto my feet when he told me to do so. It just didn't occur to him that some people in this country are deaf, and to be deaf is not a cliché for ignorance: it means someone can't hear. It seems so redundant, but it's not--it actually makes me wonder how many times someone has said to me: "hey, what's the matter, you deaf or something?" People really have a hard time accepting the fact that some of us are, in fact, really, genuinely, unhearing. And then when they realize that we are actually deaf, their skepticism is replaced with stereotypes. This part of my life was always harder on my hearing girfriend than on me. It was she who had to hear people ask her if her boyfriend "lived in a home" (a doctor once asked this), or if her boyfriend "knew how to read" (she was often asked this).

What's clear from this history is that disabled people are expected to act disabled--to bear visible, and not just ontological, signs of our disability--to wear our difference like a sign around our neck that says: "DISABLED". The crux of the matter, it seems to me, is how contemporary American society places the burden of proving one's disability on the disabled person. We have to prove, and prove by showing, and show continuously to everyone who doubts us, that we are "disabled." Those who must prove their gender or their racial or ethnic determination do not, it seems to me, face the same conditions when seeking differential treatment--or equal access--to which they are entitled by law.

I say this because disability is a vicarious condition. Those employed at the sites of publicly-financed transportation--token clerks, conductors, and, of course, transit officers--have, therefore, a special responsibility of being sensitive to the different ways in which disabilities are manifest, whether those disabilities are visible or not. Given that Federal transit laws define the disabled as a particular category of clients to which Amtrak has legal responsibilities, and given the fact that Union Station itself bears related obligations in terms of access under the Americans with Disabilities Act, it strikes me as remarkably negligent that my removal from Union Station was done in such an aggressive and humiliating way. Once, when I was in London at Paddington Station and had a similar state of dizziness that led to vertigo, a transit officer brought me blankets and stayed with me until I was well enough to continue on my way. My experience in Union Station was not just different--it was different in a bizarre and hauntingly painful way.

The most ironic aspect of this incident is to be betrayed by people whose job is to enforce the law and to protect citizens seeking protection of the law--which is precisely what I sought to do by twice telling the security officers that I was deaf, that I had Meniere's Syndrome, and that I was dizzy because of it.

This leads to a double irony. By having spoken to the officers in English--and thereby 'passing' as an able-bodied person--my disability was denied to me at the very moment it was significant to me. At one moment I was a body without a definition; at the next, a definition without a body. As I said a moment ago, our society is a society that stereotypes the disabled to the point we are expected to 'look' and 'act' disabled and become, as it were, emblems of pathos. Again, another irony: we are expected to possess visible signs denoting our difference, a direct contradiction to the very idea of equal access, which theoretically functions to remove traces of stigma.

This emphasis on stereotyping is important, in part because it unreasonably puts, as I remarked earlier, the burden of proving one's disability on the disabled person. It is not that this is simply a pervasive social phenomenon that I find troubling, but the fact that it regularly happens when dealing with transit authorities. Two examples are relevant to this consideration. First, my Washington Metro Area Transit Card required audiology examinations and a doctor's certification to obtain, yet it generally is not accepted by NYC subway token clerks, even though the ID clearly denotes that I am a person with a disability. Second (and more significant, I believe), was a 1992 "audit" of users of half-fare transit passes in NYC. The New York Times' account of the audit, reported on February 6, 1992 (section B3), contains the following paragraph:

> The auditors found additional evidence that the half-fare passes were being used by *people who did not appear to qualify* for them. They*watched* 46 token booths in 39 subway stations around the city, as well as 11 bus stops, for 30 to 60 minutes each. They counted 131 people entering the subway and buses using half-fare paeses for the disabled; only 17 of the people, or 13 percent, had *an obvious disability* that would have entitled them to the pass, the audit determined.
> (emphasis mine)

What is nothing short of incredible in such instances as these is that, having already medically proven our disability in order to obtain a document verifying it, disabled people face the additional burden of providing visible proof of our disability: we are judged, as the audit says, on the basis of whether we "appear" to be disabled or not. Thus transit officials--who have considerable and significant contact with the disabled--continue to stereotype us and judge us on the basis of their own arbitrary criteria.

It is precisely such arbitrary and reckless conduct on the part of the officers and administering institutions that directly and indirectly participated in my egregious and humiliating ejection from Union Station that has prompted this lawsuit. The turning point for me occurred when a representative for the LaSalle agency, Hugo Quispe, told my Dean at Gallaudet that I had left Union Station under my own power, thereby again discrediting me in a way that impinges on both my personal and professional reputation.

Of course, I'm angry--angry, hurt, and scared. And I'm all of these things because the continual denials on the part of the defendants that they forcibly removed me suggests the ease with which this sort of thing is likely to happen again--and again and again. You know how it is that people in the state of California live in fear of what they call 'The Big One'--an earthquake of incomprehensibly large proportions. I too now live in fear of the disabled person's idea of 'The Big One'--an incident of incomprehensibly large proportions that does more than put my dignity at risk, but my life as well. What happened at Union Station on December 7, 1993 has made me realize that my deafness is socially dangerous, and that the arbitrary decisions of security guards will decide, for themselves, whether I am deaf or not, or whether I have Meniere's Syndrome or not. What they need to learn--and this is what I hope this suit will communicate--is that those who are disabled do not have choices about what they hear, what they see, or where they place their bodies: these decisions are made by our bodies alone, and it is with these bodies that we must live and take in the pleasure of being human beings.

How can I bring a letter like this to an end? For myself there can be no end to the trauma of my experience, but I would like to hope that for other disabled people there will be no beginning of such an experience--that what happened to me will not happen again, either in Union Station or anywhere that Amtrak, the LaSalle Company, and Burns Security maintain their presence and interaction with disabled citizens. I know this sounds hopeful, perhaps even grandoise, but it shouldn't be. Disabled people should not have to live hoping for our dignity; we should not have to live feeling that the privileges granted to others are for us something grandoise. If it is for this purpose that the Americans with Disabilities Act exists, I would like to see a resolution that communicates to everyone--the defendants, myself, and anyone whom might be affected by it--that the ADA was not written, passed, and enacted in vain.

Sincerely yours,

Joe.

Joseph Grigely

ADA Complaint Against the Chicago Police Department, 2009

1327 West Washington Blvd. #2D, Chicago, Illinois 60607
24 November 2009

US Department of Justice
Civil Rights Division
950 Pennsylvania Ave. NW
Disability Rights-NYAV
Washington, DC 20530

I am writing to file a complaint of disability discrimination under Title II of the Americans with Disabilities Act of 1990, 42 U.S.C. § 12132

Complainant:
Joseph Grigely
1327 West Washington Blvd. #2D
Chicago, Illinois 60607
(no telephone, I am deaf)

Respondent:
City of Chicago Police
Officer #12743
Chicago Police District Station 12
100 South Racine Ave.
Chicago, Illinois 60607

Date of incident: Tuesday 24 November, 2009 9–9:30am

Description:
At 9am on Tuesday 24 November 2009, I was out walking my dog along West Adams Street. At the intersection of West Adams and Throop Street, my dog and I attempted to cross the street. However the crosswalk was blocked by an automobile with two adults—a woman driver and a male passenger. This is a crosswalk to an elementary school at this location—the Mark Skinner West Elementary School. I asked the male, who was outside the car, to please move the car because it was blocking a crosswalk. The man replied with a belligerent gesture of his hands and face—I felt very threatened—and I stepped back. Using my texting phone I took a picture of the car and the man, and another one of the license plate as it drove away.

I was shaken up by the incident because the crosswalks are so important in this area—there are signs indicating that deaf and blind pedestrians are in the area. Blocking the crosswalks creates a very dangerous situation for pedestrians and children in the area.

I then walked with my dog to the 12th station precinct with the intent to file a report. I went into the station and addressed an officer at the counter. I told him I was deaf, and what happened, and that I felt threatened and wanted to file a report. I showed him the two photographs (attached) of the car blocking the crosswalk and the license.

The officer, who wore badge number 12743, said something to me. So I restated I was totally deaf and asked him to write what he said. He wrote:

"What did he say to you...word for word?" (copy attached)

What did he
Say to YOU...
Word for word?

Sir because
we do not know
What was Said
we are not
able to write you
a report.

Sorry
#12743

(312)

I explained that I was deaf—I do not know what he said—but that his gestures and facial expressions were threatening, and he made no immediate effort to move the car. It was only when I pulled out my text phone to take a picture that he got into his car and left.

The officer consulted two other officers and came back and wrote to me:

“Sir because we do not know what was said we are not able to write a report. Sorry”
(copy attached)

Despite the fact that I reiterated that the photo showed a clear violation of the driving laws of the state of Illinois, the officer refused my request to write and file a report.

A person can be threatened, and made to feel threatened, without the presence of words. By denying my request to file a report, the officer discriminated against me on the basis of my disability, since no deaf person can ever know what was said to them “word for word.” Under this rubric, no deaf person can file a complaint. By requiring knowledge of “what was said” the officer discounted the visual evidence and further discriminated by making such evidence secondary to verbal evidence. The officer’s argument is one that implies by analogy that one must hear a threat to know a threat exists. This is discrimination under Title II of the Americans with Disabilities Act.

I am therefore requesting that the DOJ investigate this complaint; that the Chicago Police Department be required to reassess all policies and procedures for implicit discrimination against disabled people and undergo disability sensitivity training.

I submit under the penalty of perjury that the above account is true and correct.

Joseph Grigely

United States of America v. GPH Management, LLC, 1996–2011

The backstory to *United States of America v. GPH Management, LLC,* is as follows: In May 1996 I did a project with AC Project Room as part of the Gramercy International Art Fair (now The Armory Show), which was held in the guest rooms of the Gramercy Park Hotel in New York City. At one point I needed to make a phone call, so I went to the reception desk to ask for a TDD (telecommunications device for the deaf) so I could make the call. This was six years after the Americans with Disabilities Act had been passed, so the hotel was required to have a TDD. But they didn't. When I asked the manager why, he wrote in reply: "No one has ever asked before." It was plausible. So, I let it go and had someone else make the call for me. But I saved the manager's business card and the conversation note.

Eight years later, in 2004, I was staying at the hotel as a guest and needed to make a call. The manager was pleasant, but said the hotel did not have a TDD. When I pointed out that they had not had one eight years earlier, and surely they knew by now—fourteen years after the ADA had been passed—that they were obligated to have one, she shrugged.

When I got back to Chicago, I wrote a letter about the situation to the New York City Commission on Human Rights and the United States Department of Justice, and an investigation ensued. The DOJ found dozens of violations of the ADA by the Gramercy Park Hotel—not just a lack of a TDD. The hotel tried to explain the situation by saying that it was an old hotel, and that it was scheduled to be renovated, and that the renovation would take full cognizance of the ADA. The Department of Justice agreed to pause their investigation to allow the hotel renovations to take place.

When the renovations were completed, six years later, the DOJ went back and found numerous new violations in the hotel. A suit was filed on September 7, 2011. Seven days later, recognizing their failure, but, at the same time, not admitting to it, the Gramercy Park Hotel signed a consent decree. Together, the complaint and the consent decree demonstrate the intricate level of legal detail that is central to the ADA and its enforcement. The entire process, from the first incident to the signing of the consent decree, took fifteen years.

Joseph Grigely
1327 W. Washington Blvd #2D, Chicago, Illinois 60607
jgrigely@artic.edu

Date: June 10, 2004

United States Department of Justice
Civil Rights Division
950 Pennsylvania Avenue NW
Disability Rights Section NYAV
Washington, DC 20530

Office of the NY State Attorney General
Civil Rights Bureau
120 Broadway, 23rd Floor
New York
NY 10271

New York City Commission on Human Rights
Law Enforcement Bureau
40 Rector Street—9th floor
New York
NY 10006

I am writing to file a formal complaint alleging discrimination on the basis of disability by the Gramercy Park Hotel in New York City. The facts of my case are outlined below.

1) I stayed at the Gramercy Park Hotel on the nights of May 14, 15, and 16, 2004. The Hotel is located at 2 Lexington Avenue, New York, NY 10010. My Reservation was made online (reservation number 107343811).

2) I am profoundly deaf: when communicating I speak for myself, and ask other people to write down on paper what they are saying. I also speak using sign language.

3) The day after checking in, I asked the counter staff if they would bring to my room a Tele-device-for the deaf (TDD/TTY) so I could make a telephone call. I also asked that appropriate visual signaling equipment (fire alarm light, door knocker light) be installed in my room.

4) The desk staff replied they would look for the equipment. They kept me waiting for over an hour before acknowledging they did not have the equipment necessary to meet my access needs. They were polite throughout the process. The switchboard operator, Celia, called a supervisor who indicated that if I called an outside operator, the operator who had a TDD could make the call for me (Addendum A). I explained to Celia that this would not work, as I needed a TDD to make the call: that I could not use a regular telephone without a TDD to facilitate its use. Cecilia then indicated there was nothing we could do until the next day, when I should talk with the manager, Rosario Bianchi (whose card she gave me) or a supervisor named Sharon.

5) The next day I spoke with Sharon. When I asked her if they had located a TDD, she wrote in reply "We do not have a machine." (Addendum B) I asked if she was aware this was an explicit violation of Title III of the Americans with Disabilities Act, and she acknowledged she did.

6) Sharon offered no apology. I subsequently paid my bill on Monday 17th May and returned to Chicago. A copy of my Credit Card bill is attached as Addendum C.

7) This is not the first time the Gramercy Park Hotel has refused to accommodate my disability. In May 1996 I was a participating artist in an event at the hotel known as the Gramercy Art Fair. During the event I needed to make a telephone call, and requested from the front desk a TDD to do so. The desk staff member directed me to the General Manager, Mr. Thomas O'Brien. Mr. O'Brien said they did not have a TDD at the hotel. When I asked Mr. O'Brien why this was the case, more than five years after the passage of the Americans with Disabilities Act, Mr. O'Brien wrote in reply "No one has ever asked before." (Addendum D). I saved Mr. O'Brien's card and note out of habit.

Under the penalty of perjury I submit that these facts are true to the best of my knowledge.

My struggle for access at the Gramercy Park Hotel has been a very humiliating experience. I can understand how and why the hotel did not have a TDD in 1996. But by 2004 this should have been corrected. The Hotel has exhibited willful and egregious disregard for the law in not accommodating my disability. And this disregard, in light of my communications with Mr. O'Brien, is ostentatious.

I am requesting that all three of the above named agencies: the DOJ, the NY State Attorney General, and the NYC Human Rights Commission initiate a joint suit against the Hotel on the basis of violating Title III of ADA and applicable NY State Laws. I respectfully request that the suit seek compliance as well as punititive damages. The Gramercy Park Hotel is a well-known hotel with a vast international array of clients and guests. Fourteen years after the passage of ADA, it continues to flout the law, embarrass and inconvenience disabled guests like me, and symbolize not a great hotel in a great city, but a shameful hotel in a carefree city. This should not have happened, and it should not happen again.

Sincerely,

Joseph Grigely

MR. GRIGLEY,

I CALLED SUPERVISOR. SHE SAYS IF YOU CALL OUTSIDE OPERATOR (9-0) SHE WILL BE ABLE TO MAKE CALL FOR YOU. THEY HAVE SPECIAL MACHINES.

DOES THIS MAKE SENSE?

CELIA

WE DO NOT
have A
MACHINE

GRAMERCY I

GRAMERCY PARK HOTEL

ROSARIO BIANCHI
Front Office Manager

GRAMERCY PARK HOTEL
2 LEXINGTON AVENUE NEW YORK, NEW YORK 10010
(212) 475-4320 FAX (212) 505-0535
DIRECT (212) 201-2172
rosario.bianchi@ianschragerhotels.com

NO ONE
HAS EVER
ASKED BEFORE

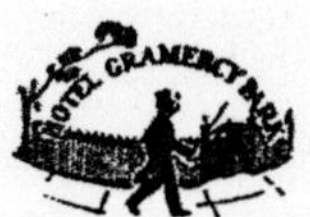

1-800-221-4083

THOMAS J. O'BRIEN

GENERAL MANAGER

GRAMERCY PARK HOTEL
2 LEXINGTON AVENUE AT 21ST STREET
NEW YORK, N.Y. 10010

212-475-4320
FAX 212-505-0535

Add. C

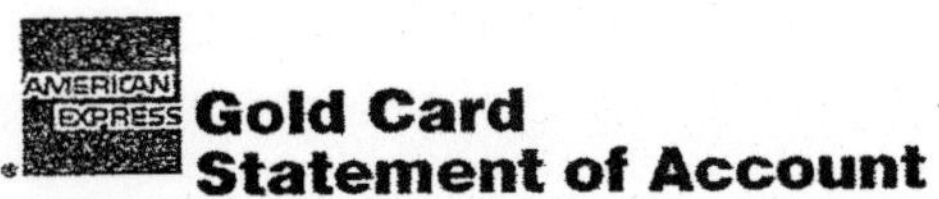

Gold Card Statement of Account

Earn points on all of your purchases, everywhere you use the Card.
Visit www.americanexpress.com/rewards.

Prepared For
JOSEPH C GRIGELY JR

Account Number
[redacted]

Closing Date
06/04/04

Previous Balance $	Payment Activity $	New Activity $ Inc. Adjustments	New Balance $
1,504.99	-1,504.99	+1,256.23	1,256.23

Please Pay By 06/19/04

Please refer to page 3 for important information regarding your account

Your membership will be renewed next month. Please refer to the Renewal Notice on page 3

Contact us at www.americanexpress.com or call Customer Service at 1-800-327-2177.

You Are Eligible For Gold Card Events
With American Express® Gold Card Events, you have access to some of the best seats, to some of the hottest events nationwide. Want to be among the first to find out about the biggest Broadway hits, your favorite artist's upcoming tour or sporting and family events? Visit us at **www.americanexpress.com/gce** to sign up for your weekly e-mail. Entertainment news right to your inbox!

For a complete listing of events, visit us at **www.americanexpress.com/gce** or call **1-800-448-TIKS**. Terms and Conditions apply.

Activity

* Indicates posting date

		Amount $
05/06/04*	Payment Received - Thank You	-415.10
05/22/04*	Payment Received - Thank You	-1,089.89
Total of Payment Activity		**-1,504.99**

Due in Full Activity for JOSEPH C GRIGELY JR
Card [redacted]

		Amount $
05/06/04	PEARL ART & CRAFT #6CHICAGO IL ART SUPPLIES/ACC	100.30
05/06/04	ART STORE #600 CHICAGO IL GLASS PAINT WALLPAP	130.94
05/17/04	GRAMERCY PARK HOTEL NEW YORK NY Arrival Date 05/14/04 Departure Date 05/17/04 No of Nights 3 00000000	941.37
05/10/04	PAYPAL 8304 *MEMBER 402 935 7733 CA PROFESSIONAL SERVICE	1.95

Continued on Page 3

Please fold on the perforation below, detach and return with your payment

Joseph Grigely
1327 West Washington Blvd. #2D, Chicago, Illinois 60607
September 18, 2005

Raymond Wayne
Assistant Managing Attorney
Law Enforcement Bureau
New York City Commission on Human Rights
40 Rector Street, 9th Floor
New York, New York 10006

Re: Joseph Grigely v. Gramercy Park Hotel, Rosario Bianchi
Complaint No. M-P-D-05-1016411

Dear Mr. Wayne:

This letter constitutes a rebuttal to statements and claims made by the Respondents Gramercy Park Hotel and Rosario Bianchi in the above-referenced Complaint. This rebuttal addresses the Respondent's request to dismiss the Complaint (dated June 17, 2005) as well as allegations and claims made by the Respondent as part of the Verified Answer Respondent made to the Complaint (also dated June 17, 2005).

Request to dismiss. Complainant respectfully requests that the Commission continue with its investigation, for the reasons outlined below:

1) Respondent claims that by proceeding with its investigation that "the Commission will be duplicating the efforts of the United States Attorney for the Southern District of New York." This is not entirely correct. The Department of Justice investigation has a singular focus of investigating whether the Gramercy Park Hotel has been in compliance with federal law, specifically the Americans with Disabilities Act of 1990 (ADA).

The Commission on Human Rights in turn has a stated responsibility to investigate the Hotel's compliance with Title 8 of the Administrative Code of the City of New York, otherwise known as "The New York City Human Rights Law."

The Hotel's obligations under ADA and Title 8 are therefore not identical. Furthermore, should the Hotel be found in violation of each respective code, remedial action for each respective code is different.

2) It is important for the Commission to proceed in its investigation because the outcome of the investigation has a bearing on the stated mission of the Commission, which focuses on mutual understanding, respect, and equality of treatment for "all persons in the City of New York" (§ 8-105 Functions). This mission includes informing both the Mayor and Council of investigation outcomes, and issuing "reports of investigations and research designed to promote good will and minimize or eliminate prejudice, intolerance, bigotry, discrimination and disorder occasioned thereby" (§ 8-105 Powers and duties). Thus, in proceeding with its investigation, the Commission will fulfill an obligation to the people of New York, which is very different than the DOJ investigation.

3) Respondent asserts that the owners of the Gramercy Park Hotel took over operational control of the hotel in April 2004, with "the express intent of shutting the facility and conducting renovations…but also remained open as a hotel." Since the Hotel remained open for the purpose of business, and since the Hotel, as a place of public accommodation, engaged in a monetary transaction with me, the Hotel remained subject to all extant City, State, and Federal laws. The fact that the Hotel was closed for renovations after the discrimination occurred in no way absolves the Hotel from the responsibilities it had towards its paying guests while it was open, or the responsibility for damage incurred as the result of its failure to submit to City, State, and Federal laws.

4) Respondent states in a letter dated June 17, 2005, that the Gramercy Park Hotel is now undergoing renovations, and that it "will not re-open until the hotel is fully compliant with the disabilities laws." This is promising. But two questions remain: 1) Who will investigate compliance? 2) If the hotel is not "fully compliant" when it re-opens (the definitions of "fully compliant" and "re-open" need to be given), what punitive measures might be instituted as recourse to compliance? Additionally, "compliance" is not simply a matter of hiring an astute and accomplished designer, although I must here applaud this move on the part of the Respondent; compliance also involves the everyday responsibilities and actions of the hotel staff, and the ways they communicate and interact with disabled people. For this reason, no definition of compliance will be satisfactory without also including provisions for disability-sensitivity training for the Hotel staff, with the training consisting of an independent training facilitator giving face-to-face training.

5) Respondent, in a letter dated March 21st and addressed to John Cronan of the US Department of Justice, claims "by Mr. Grigely's admission, another method to accommodate him was found at that time (see attachment ¶ 7)." This is emphatically not true. Paragraph 7 refers to my statement in my Complaint wherein I cite a note written to me by a Hotel employee named Celia, who, after the desk staff could not provide me with a TDD, wrote: "I called supervisor. She says if you call outside operator (9-0) she will be able to make call for you. They have special machines." What Celia did not understand then, and what the Respondent still does not understand, is that it is impossible for a deaf person to call an outside operator—or anyone—without having a TDD to make the call. Thus, no accommodation of my hearing disability in any form actually took place, and Respondent misrepresents this matter by claiming otherwise.

6) Respondent, in its Answer to the Complaint, denies "each and every allegation" of discrimination with respect to Section 8 107.4(a) of the Administrative Code of the City of New York, and therefore requests "dismissing the Complaint in its entirety." This Answer is dated June 17, 2005. Four months earlier, in a letter to the Respondent's attorneys, the US Department of Justice concluded that there was "no reason to doubt the veracity of [the] allegations," and, in relation to the Complaint, "concluded that the Hotel is not in compliance with ADA." (John P. Cronan to Banks Brown, Esq. February 24, 2005). Since the Hotel continues to deny that discrimination occurred, despite overwhelming evidence to the contrary, the Commission should continue its investigation.

Respondent's Answer

In the process of proceeding with the Investigation, the following section addresses claims made in the Respondent's Verified Answer, dated June 17, 2005:

1) In paragraphs 6, 7, and 8 Respondent insinuates that I have the capacity to make telephone calls. "Grigley (sic) made telephone calls from his guest room" (6), "Grigley (sic) made

telephone calls from his guest room" (7), "Grigley (sic) made telephone calls from his guest room" (8). Furthermore, in paragraph 4, Respondent claims "Grigley (sic) made his reservation through a toll-free telephone call." Respondent offers no proof that I actually made these calls. My reservation was in fact made online, and confirmation made through a telephone call by a hearing person calling on my behalf because the hotel did not possess a TDD/TTY number. Additionally, the calls that the Respondent claims I made from the room to a toll-free number were, I recall, data calls placed to my internet service provider via my computer for the purpose of checking e-mail. I am physiologically incapable of hearing human speech on a telephone. By claiming I made telephone calls on the phone, Respondent insinuates that my claim of discrimination is unwarranted, if not also false. This is insulting, if not also malicious, in its attempt to discredit the veracity of my Complaint.

2) Respondent in paragraph 4 claims that I did not request accommodation upon my arrival. This is a moot point. Neither Section 8-107.4(a) of the Administrative Code of the City of New York nor ADA specify that access to public places be accomplished through prior arrangement. A hotel, in particular, is a place for transient guests, and as such has the obligation to respond to transient situations. Respondent displayed in the reception area a sign indicating it had visual signaling equipment available on request; I made a request for this equipment; Respondent then asserted it in fact did not possess this equipment, and after a night and morning wait, still could not produce the equipment. While a TDD might be regarded as an ancillary device, the lack of emergency signaling lights and a door knocker light created a manifestly hazardous situation that threatened both my health and safety.

3) Respondent claims in paragraphs 6, 7, and 8 that it "shared a TDD kit (complete with visual equipment and equipment to allow a hearing-impaired guest to make a telephone call) with a sister facility in Manhattan." Respondent offers no proof of this; neither proof of purchase of the equipment, proof of joint ownership of the equipment, or proof of the "sister facility." Even if the Hotel did in fact "share" this equipment, it failed to make the equipment available to me, and therefore failed to provide me with a legally obligated service while simultaneously charging me $941.37 for my stay. The cost of a visual signaling kit is even less than the sum of money the Gramercy Park Hotel charged me. It was clearly not an unreasonable burden on the hotel to possess its own visual signaling kit.

4) Respondent claims in paragraphs 5, 6, and 7 that it has "no record" of communications respectively outlined in my Complaint. The record of these communications, written by Gramercy Park Hotel employees on Gramercy Park Hotel stationery and other stationery provided by the hotel, constitutes evidence whose authenticity the DOJ has stated it has "no reason to doubt" (John P. Cronan to Banks Brown, Esq. February 24, 2005). Both the authenticity and authorship of the documents can be demonstrated by simple paleographic analysis.

Conclusion

Since hotels are a fundamental part of New York City's civic, social, and economic infrastructure, the outcome of my complaint has broad implications for more than just the Gramercy Park Hotel—it has implications for every disabled person staying as a guest at any hotel in the city. As § 8-126 of Title 8 states, Civil penalties may be imposed by the Commission for unlawful discriminatory practices in order "to vindicate the public interest." As I stated in my original Complaint of June 10, 2004, the Gramercy Park Hotel not only flouted ADA for 14 years (since passage; 12 years since implementation was required), but did so, in my case, on two verifiable occasions. The evidence of discrimination is incontrovertible. The DOJ, for its own part, has found numerous violations of ADA in its own on-site investigation of the Hotel. Yet the Gramercy Park Hotel, through its Answer to my complaint, denies these findings and fails to acknowledge culpability. For these reasons, I respectfully request the Commission on Human Rights to continue its investigation. Furthermore, because the Gramercy Park Hotel has exhibited both a cavalier disregard for the law, and egregious disregard for the welfare of disabled people, I request the Commission to seek the greatest Civil penalty possible under law in order to vindicate public interest.

Sincerely,

Joseph Grigely

Joseph Grigely
1327 West Washington Blvd. #2D, Chicago, Illinois 60607
November 12, 2005

Michael J. Garcia
US Attorney for the Southern District of New York
United States Attorney's Office
86 Chambers Street
New York, New York 10007

Re: ADA Complaint Against the Gramercy Park Hotel

Dear Mr. Garcia:

Thank you for your letter of October 12th. I appreciate the opportunity to respond to the DOJ investigation of ADA-related discrimination by the Gramercy Park Hotel.

As your letter indicated, I have in my possession a letter from Banks Brown, Esq., attorney for the Hotel, dated March 21, 2005, and addressed to Mr. John Cronan of the US Department of Justice. Attorney Brown's letter contains several inaccurate and/or misleading statements. A copy of this letter was provided to me by the New York City Commission on Human Rights, which is conducting its own investigation into allegations of discrimination by the Hotel in relation to The New York City Human Rights Law. Specifically, the attorneys for the Hotel submitted Mr. Brown's letter to the Commission as evidence that it did not discriminate against me during my stay at the Hotel in May 2004. In the sections that follow, I have outlined specific inaccurate and inconsistent statements in Mr. Brown's letter, as well as other issues that I believe to be of salient nature.

1) Mr. Brown asserts that the owners of the Gramercy Park Hotel took over operational control of the hotel in April 2004, at which point "serious planning for the renovations then commenced." Since the Hotel remained open for the purpose of business, and since the Hotel, as a place of public accommodation, engaged in a monetary transaction with me, the Hotel remained subject to all extant Federal laws. The fact that the Hotel was closed for renovations after the discrimination occurred in no way absolves the Hotel from the responsibilities it had towards its paying guests while it was open, or the responsibility for damage incurred as the result of its failure to submit to Federal laws.

2) Mr. Brown claims "by Mr. Grigely's admission, another method to accommodate him was found at that time (see attachment ¶ 7)." This is emphatically not true. Paragraph 7 refers to my statement in my Complaint wherein I cite a note written to me by a Hotel employee named Celia, who, after the desk staff could not provide me with a TDD, wrote: "I called supervisor. She says if you call outside operator (9-0) she will be able to make call for you. They have special machines." What Celia did not understand then, and what the Respondent still does not understand, is that it is impossible for a deaf person to call an outside operator—or anyone—without having a TDD to make the call. The hotel did not furnish me with a TDD, as requested. The hotel did not furnish me with a door knocking light, as requested. The hotel did not furnish my room with emergency signaling equipment, as requested. Thus, no accommodation of my hearing disability in *any* form actually took place, and Mr. Brown grossly misrepresents this matter by claiming otherwise.

3) Mr. Brown states that the owners of the hotel, Morgans Hotel Group Management, "apologizes for his [Mr. Grigely's] inconvenience." The discrimination that happened to me at the hotel was not an "inconvenience." It was an explicit violation of my civil rights as a disabled person. Civil rights laws protect all of us from the act of discrimination, regardless of the rationale of the respondent. Mr. Brown reduces ADA to a consumer's complaint of inconvenience, and therefore shows that the true meaning of ADA as a civil rights law is not being reflected in his response to the DOJ. To reiterate: I was not simply inconvenienced during my visit to the Gramercy Park Hotel in May 2004; the hotel engaged in a monetary transaction with me, and violated my civil rights by failing to provide reasonable accommodation of my disability, and did so by subverting a law that had been in effect for over a decade. The hotel's actions do not fall under the purview of rational basis review; the cost of the accommodation was insignificant in relation to the size and operating budget of the hotel.

4) The Hotel, in its Answer to the Complaint being investigated by the New York City Commission on Human Rights, denies "each and every allegation" of discrimination with respect to Section 8-107.4(a) of the Administrative Code of the City of New York, and therefore requests "dismissing the Complaint in its entirety." This Answer is dated June 17, 2005. Four months earlier the US Department of Justice concluded that there was "no reason to doubt the veracity of [the] allegations [of discrimination]" and further concluded that "the Hotel is not in compliance with ADA." (John P. Cronan to Banks Brown, Esq. February 24, 2005). The hotel is therefore continuing to deny that discrimination occurred, despite DOJ conclusions to the contrary.

With respect to remedial action:

5) Mr. Brown states that the Gramercy Park Hotel is now undergoing renovations, and that the owners had hired an ADA specialist to oversee the adaptation [of] the hotel, and that "the renovation will take full cognizance of ADA." While this statement is promising, Mr. Brown's failure to understand that ADA is as much about human actions as it is about physical structures leaves me doubtful that this gesture assuages the situation. 1) Who will investigate compliance? 2) If the hotel is not "fully compliant" when it re-opens (the definitions of "fully compliant" and "re-open" need to be given), what punitive measures might be instituted as recourse to compliance? Additionally, "compliance" is not simply a matter of hiring an astute and accomplished designer; compliance also involves the everyday responsibilities and actions of the hotel staff, and the ways they communicate and interact with disabled people. For this reason, no definition of compliance will be satisfactory without also including provisions for disability-sensitivity training for the Hotel staff, with the training consisting of an independent training facilitator giving face-to-face training.

The facts of Mr. Brown's letter, as well as the tone, provide compelling evidence that the Hotel has failed to directly acknowledge that I was discriminated against, and further failed to acknowledge the seriousness of this discrimination. This is a case about civil rights, not consumer laws. For this reason, I urge the DOJ to prosecute the Hotel to the fullest extent possible under law.

Sincerely,

Joseph Grigely

JUDGE SWEET

COPY

PREET BHARARA
United States Attorney
Southern District of New York
By: BRIAN M. FELDMAN
Assistant United States Attorney
86 Chambers Street, 3rd Floor
New York, New York 10007
Telephone No. (212) 637-2777
Facsimile No. (212) 637-2717
Brian.Feldman@usdoj.gov

11 CIV 6238

UNITED STATES DISTRICT COURT
SOUTHERN DISTRICT OF NEW YORK

UNITED STATES OF AMERICA,

Plaintiff,

-against-

GPH MANAGEMENT, LLC, as owner of THE GRAMERCY PARK HOTEL, and RFR HOTEL GROUP, LLC, as operator of THE GRAMERCY PARK HOTEL,

Defendants.

ECF CASE

COMPLAINT

11 Civ. ___________

Plaintiff United States of America (the "United States"), by its attorney Preet Bharara, the United States Attorney for the Southern District of New York, alleges as follows:

Preliminary Statement

1. The United States brings this civil action to redress discrimination on the basis of disability in violation of Title III of the Americans with Disabilities Act of 1990 ("ADA"), 42 U.S.C. §§ 12181 *et seq.*, and its implementing regulation, 28 C.F.R. Part 36. As set forth more fully below, the defendants operate a hotel in New York City, The Gramercy Park Hotel (the "Hotel"), which is not in compliance with the ADA.

Jurisdiction and Venue

2. This Court has jurisdiction over this action pursuant to 42 U.S.C. § 12188(b)(1)(B) and 28 U.S.C. §§ 1331 and 1345.

3. Venue lies in this District pursuant to 28 U.S.C. § 1391(b). The acts of discrimination alleged in this complaint occurred in this District, and the property that is the subject of this action is situated in this District.

The Parties

4. Plaintiff is the United States of America.

5. Defendant GPH Management LLC is a New York limited liability company located in Manhattan, which owns the Gramercy Park Hotel, a hotel in New York City. Defendant RFR Hotel Group LLC is a Delaware limited liability company, which operates the Gramercy Park Hotel. Defendants are a "public accommodation" within the meaning of Title III of the ADA because they own and/or operate the Gramercy Park Hotel, which is a place of public accommodation. See 42 U.S.C. §§ 12181(7)(A), 12182(a); 28 C.F.R. § 36.104.

Factual Background

6. The Gramercy Park Hotel is a hotel located at 2 Lexington Avenue, New York, New York 10010. The Gramercy Park Hotel is a "place of public accommodation" within the meaning of Title III of the ADA because its operations affect commerce and, among other things, it is "an inn, hotel, motel, or other place of lodging." 42 U.S.C. § 12181(7)(A); see 28 C.F.R. § 36.104

7. A complaint was filed with the United States Department of Justice by a former guest of the Gramercy Park Hotel, alleging that the Hotel had discriminated against him on the

basis of his disability. The complainant described himself as "profoundly deaf," explaining that he requires written text or sign language to communicate. The complainant specifically alleged that during his first stay at the Hotel, he requested a Telephone Device for the Deaf ("TDD"). The complainant was told by the Hotel's general manager, in writing, that the Hotel did not possess this device because no one had asked for one in the past. The complainant further alleged that during a second stay at the Hotel, he again requested a TDD, as well as additional visual notification equipment, such as a fire alarm light and a door knocker light, for his room. It took the hotel staff an hour to inform the complainant that they did not possess the requested visual notification equipment, and it was not until the next day that a supervisor admitted, again in writing, that the Hotel did not possess a TDD. The complainant additionally alleged that the supervisor acknowledged that the Hotel's failure to provide the requested device violated the ADA.

8. In response to this complaint, the United States Attorney's Office for the Southern District of New York (the "United States Attorney") informed Defendants that it would be conducting an investigation into whether the Gramercy Park Hotel was in compliance with the ADA and its implementing regulations.

9. In response, Defendants advised the United States Attorney that it was about to commence planned renovations of the facilities. Defendants represented that when the Hotel opened its doors to the public, after approximately fourteen months, it would be in full compliance with the ADA.

10. The United States Attorney then conducted an initial, on-site inspection of the Gramercy Park Hotel to determine the extent of its non-compliance with the ADA and its implementing regulations.

11. Having observed several violations in its inspection, the United States Attorney informed Defendants that the Gramercy Park Hotel was operating in violation of the ADA.

12. In the course of a series of discussions between Defendants and the United States Attorney, Defendants represented to the United States Attorney that the planned renovations would bring the Hotel into compliance with the ADA.

13. On January 29, 2009, after the last of the Gramercy Park Hotel's renovations had been completed, the United States Attorney again conducted an inspection of the building. This investigation revealed not only that the Gramercy Park Hotel's renovations had failed to correct the original ADA violations detected in the initial United States Attorney inspection, but that the renovations had actually led to additional ADA violations.

14. Numerous architectural barriers at the Gramercy Park Hotel prevent or restrict access to the Gramercy Park Hotel by individuals with disabilities. 42 U.S.C. § 12182(b)(2)(A); 28 C.F.R. § 36.304. The Gramercy Park Hotel's services, features, elements, and spaces are not readily accessible to, or usable by, individuals with disabilities, as specified by the Regulations promulgated under the ADA. *See* ADA Standards for Accessible Design, 28 C.F.R. Part 36, App. D (the " 1991 Standards"). The Gramercy Park Hotel has failed to engage in readily achievable barrier removal, *see* 28 C.F.R. § 36.304; failed, in the course of making alterations, to ensure that the altered portions of the facility are readily accessible to the maximum extent feasible, *see* 28 C.F.R. § 36.402; and failed to ensure that the paths of travel to altered areas are readily accessible to the maximum extent feasible, *see* 28 C.F.R. § 36.403.

15. Barriers to access that exist within the Gramercy Park Hotel include, but are not limited to, the following:

A. <u>Guest Rooms</u>

i. The Gramercy Park Hotel has provided an insufficient number of accessible guestrooms for persons with hearing and speech impairments. The Gramercy Park Hotel has a total of 185 guestrooms, and under the Standards, is required to have no fewer than 14 rooms meeting the requirements of accessibility for such persons as set out in section 9.1.3 of the Standards, *see* Standards §§ 9.1.2, 9.1.3, 9.2.2(8). The Hotel may alternatively satisfy this requirement by providing no less than 14 portable kits that meet the "equivalent facilitation" requirement of section 9.3.2 of the Standards. The Gramercy Park Hotel has provided no rooms that meet these requirements, and provides only one portable kit that meets the "equivalent facilitation" alternative requirement.

ii. The Gramercy Park Hotel has left the best rooms in the house inaccessible to persons with disabilities. Accessible guest rooms must be dispersed among the various classes of sleeping accommodations, taking into consideration room size, cost, amenities, and number of beds to ensure guests with disabilities are provided with the same range of options as other guests at the Hotel. *See* Standards § 9.1.4. The Gramercy Park Hotel makes only two types of rooms accessible to persons with disabilities. The Hotel fails to offer other types of accessible rooms, including the best rooms in the house, such as the Gramercy Suites and the Penthouse Suites.

iii. The designated accessible King Loft rooms are not in compliance with the Standards. Specifically:

1. Door signage for the rooms does not have a "non-glare finish" and "characters and symbols [that] contrast with their background," as required by sections 4.1.3(16)(a) and 4.30.5 of the Standards.

2. Maneuvering clearance on the latch side of the entry door for a forward pull approach is only 17 inches. Clearance is required to be 18 inches. *See* Standards §§ 9.2.2(3), 4.13.6, Fig. 25(a).

3. Thermostat controls are located 59 inches above the finished floor. The maximum allowable height is 54 inches. *See* Standards §§ 9.2.2(5), 4.27.3, 4.2.6, and Fig. 6.

4. Storage spaces in the rooms do not comply with the Standards. The closet rod is 67 inches above the finished floor, whereas the Standards require that it be no more than 54 inches above the finished floor. *See* Standards §§ 9.2.2(4), 4.25.3, 4.2.6, Fig. 6, Fig. 38(b). Furthermore, the armoire door provided requires tight pinching to operate, whereas the Standards prohibit door hardware that requires tight pinching to operate. *See* Standards §§ 4.25.4, 4.27.4.

5. One full bathroom is not accessible within each unit as required by section 9.2.2(6)(e) of the Standards.

A. The threshold in the rooms is three-quarters of an inch high, whereas the Standards require that a threshold be no higher than one half inch. *See* Standards §§ 4.1.3(7)(b), 4.13.8, 4.5.2.

B. The toilet clear space is only 54 inches deep, whereas the Standards require the clear space to be at least 56 inches deep. *See* Standards §§ 9.2.2(6)(e), 4.23.4, 4.16.2, Fig. 28.

C. The roll-in showers and bathtubs lack a fixed, folding seat, as required by Standards §§ 9.1.2, 9.2.2(6)(e), 4.23.8, 4.20.3, 4.21.3, Fig. 33, Fig. 34, Fig. 57(a).

D. The low back-wall grab bar is eleven inches above the tub rim, whereas the Standards require that it be exactly nine inches above the tub rim. *See* Standards §§ 9.2.2(6)(e), 4.23.8, 4.20.4, Fig. 34.

iv. The single designated accessible one-bedroom suite is not in compliance with the Standards. Specifically:

1. Door signage for the room does not have a "non-glare finish" and "characters and symbols [that] contrast with their background," as required by sections 4.1.3(16)(a) and 4.30.5 of the Standards.

2. Maneuvering clearance on the latch side of the entry door for a forward pull approach is only 12 inches, but is required to be at least 18 inches. *See* Standards §§ 9.2.2(3), 4.13.6, Fig. 25(a).

3. The maneuvering space in between the bed and the window wall is only 34.5 inches, whereas the Standards require there to be a maneuvering space of at least 36 inches in width connecting all spaces and surrounding both sides of the bed. *See* Standards §§ 9.2.2(1).

4. Storage space in the rooms does not comply with the Standards. The closet rod is 67 inches above the finished floor, whereas the Standards require that it be no more than 54 inches above the finished floor. *See* Standards §§ 9.2.2(4), 4.25.3, 4.2.6, Fig. 6, Fig. 38(b). Furthermore, the armoire door provided also requires tight pinching to operate, whereas the Standards prohibit door hardware that requires tight pinching to operate. *See* Standards §§ 4.25.4, 4.27.4.

5. Thermostat controls are located 60 inches above the finished floor. The maximum height permitted by the Standards is 54 inches. *See* Standards §§ 9.2.2(5), 4.27.3, 4.2.6, Fig. 6.

6. The roll-in shower does not comport with certain guidelines. *See* Standards §§ 9.1.2, 9.2.2(6)(e), 4.23.8.

A. The entrance to the shower is only 34 inches wide, whereas the Standards require that it be at least 36 inches wide. *See* Standards § 4.21.2, Fig. 57(b).

B. The roll-in shower has a curb that is two inches high, which is prohibited by the Standards. *See* Standards § 4.21.3, Fig. 57(b).

C. The roll-in shower lacks a fixed, folding seat, as required by Standards §§ 9.1.2, 9.2.2(6)(e), 4.23.8, 4.20.3, 4.21.3, Fig. 33, Fig. 34, Fig. 57(a).

D. The toilet grab bar is mounted only 52 inches from the rear wall, whereas the Standards require that it be mounted a minimum of 54 inches from the rear wall. *See* Standards §§ 9.1.2, 9.2.2(6)(e), 4.16.4, 4.23.4, Fig. 29(b).

B. <u>Hotel Entrances</u>

i. The Hotel lacks signage near its inaccessible entrances, marked with the International Symbol of Accessibility, indicating the route to a designated accessible entrance, whereas such signage is required by sections 4.1.2(7)(c), 4.1.6(1)(h), and 4.30.7 of the Standards.

ii. The force required to open the interior vestibule door of the Hotel is 20 lbs, whereas the maximum allowable force prescribed by the

Standards is 5 lbs. *See* Standards §§ 4.1.3(7)(a), 4.13.11(b).

C. Lobby Level Facilities

i. Two of the four unisex toilet rooms in the lobby level are not accessible, as the pictogram on the toilet signage is not accompanied by the equivalent verbal description below the pictogram, as mandated by the Standards. *See* Standards, §§ 4.1.3(16)(a), 4.30.4.

ii. Telephone counters are not accessible. Specifically:

1. Typical lobby telephone counters, which have a clear floor space that is 32 inches wide, are located in an alcove that is 28 inches deep, whereas the Standards provide that a counter with a 32-inch wide clear floor space must be located in an alcove with a maximum depth of 24 inches. *See* Standards §§ 4.1.3(18), 4.32.2, 4.2.4, Fig. 4.

2. Knee space provided under the typical telephone counter is 12 inches, whereas the Standards provide that it be at least 19 inches. *See* Standards §§ 4.1.3(18), 4.32.3, Fig. 45.

3. The typical counter top is 36 inches above the finished floor, whereas the Standards require that the counter top be between 28 and 34 inches above the finished floor. *See* Standards §§ 4.1.3(18), 4.32.4.

iii. There are an insufficient number of accessible telephones in the lobby. There must be at least one public telephone that is "hearing aid compatible." *See* Standards §§ 9.1.1, 4.1.3(17)(a), 4.31.5(1). The Gramercy Park Hotel has provided no such telephones.

iv. Lobby telephones are not equipped with sufficient volume controls. There must be at least one public telephone with a volume control "capable of a minimum of 12 dbA and a maximum of 18 dbA above normal." *See* Standards §§ 4.1.3(17)(b), 4.31.5(2), 4.30.7. The Gramercy Park Hotel has provided no telephones with such volume controls.

D. **Second Floor Amenities**

i. Drinking fountains provided in the Hotel Aerospace Fitness Center and AeroSpa are not accessible to those who have trouble bending or stooping in violation of section 4.1.3(10)(a) of the Standards.

ii. The spa toilet room and shower are not accessible. Specifically:

1. The spa toilet room threshold is three-quarters of an inch high, whereas the Standards require that it be no greater than one half inch. *See* Standards §§ 4.13(7)(b), 4.13.8, 4.5.2.

2. The spa toilet room's centerline is 19 inches from the wall, whereas the Standards require that it be exactly 18 inches from the wall. *See* Standards §§ 4.1.3(11), 4.22.4, 4.16.2, Fig. 28.

3. The spa toilet room rear grab bar is only 32 inches long, whereas the Standards require that it be 36 inches long. *See*

Standards §§ 4.13(11), 4.22.4, 4.16.4, Fig. 29.

4. The spa shower door requires tight pinching to operate, whereas the Standards mandate that door hardware must not require tight pinching to operate. *See* Standards §§ 4.1.3(11), 4.23.8, 4.1.3(7)(b), 4.13.9.

5. The spa shower partition is located within the shower clear floor space, whereas the Standards require a clear floor space adjacent to the roll-in shower that is 36 inches wide by 60 inches deep. *See* Standards §§ 4.1.3(11), 4.23.8, 4.21.2, Fig. 35(b).

6. The spa shower has a 36-inch long grab bar on the back shower wall, which does not cover the length of the wall, whereas the Standards require the bar to cover the full length of the shower walls. *See* Standards §§ 4.1.3(11), 4.23.8, 4.21.4, Fig. 37(b).

iii. At least one storage space in areas of public access must comply with the Standards' guidelines. *See* Standards § 4.1.3(12)(a). The closet space in the Park Room East conference room does not meet these standards. Specifically, it has a closet shelf that is 69 inches above the finished floor and a closet rod that is 64 inches above the finished floor, whereas the Standards require that such items be at most 54 inches above the finished floor. *See* Standards §§

4.1.3(12)(a), 4.2.6, 4.25.3, Fig. 6, Fig. 38(a),(b).

iv. The unisex toilet rooms have a lavatory support located in the toilet clear space, whereas the Standards require toilet clear floor space that is a minimum of 48 inches wide. *See* Standards §§ 4.1.3(11), 4.22.4, 4.16.2, Fig. 28.

v. The unisex toilet rooms' rear grab bars are only 24 inches long, whereas the Standards require they be at least 36 inches long. *See* Standards §§ 4.1.3(11), 4.22.4, 4.16.4, Fig. 29.

vi. The unisex toilet rooms' sign pictogram is not accompanied by the equivalent verbal description below the pictogram as required by the Standards. *See* Standards §§ 4.1.3(16)(a), 4.30.4.

E. <u>Guest Room Corridors</u>

i. The room number signs in the guest room corridors have neither a "non-glare finish" nor "characters and symbols [that] contrast with their background," as required by the Standards. *See* Standards §§ 4.1.3(16)(a), 4.30.5.

ii. The guest room corridor fire extinguisher cabinet protrudes five and one half inches from the corridor wall and is mounted 44 inches above the finished floor to the leading edge, whereas the Standards require that objects projecting from their wall with their leading edges between 27 and 80 inches should protrude no more than four inches into a corridor. *See* Standards §§ 4.1.3(2), 4.4.1.

F. <u>Roof Club & Gardens</u>

i. The roof club and gardens are not connected to the building by at least one accessible route in violation of the Standards. *See* Standards § 4.1.3(1).

ii. The route from the roof club meeting and reception rooms to the gardens is via a six-inch riser, whereas the Standards require that any level change greater than one half inch have a curb ramp, ramp, elevator, or platform lift. *See* Standards § 4.3.8.

iii. The counter in the reception room projects nine inches from the wall and is mounted 40.5 inches above the finished floor to the leading edge, whereas the Standards direct that objects projecting from the wall with leading edges between 27 and 80 inches should protrude no more than four inches into circulation paths. *See* Standards §§ 4.1.3(2), 4.4.1.

iv. The men's and women's toilet rooms lack the directional signage indicating the route to the designated accessible toilet rooms required by the Standards. *See* Standards §§ 4.1.6(3)(e)(iii), 4.30.7.

v. The unisex toilet room provided does not have either a 60-inch diameter turning space or a T-shaped turning space, as required by the Standards. *See* Standards §§ 4.1.3(11), 4.2.3, 4.22.3, Fig. 3.

vi. The toilet centerline in the unisex toilet room is 19.75 inches from the wall, whereas the Standards require it be exactly 18 inches from the side wall. *See* Standards §§ 4.1.3(11), 4.16.2, 4.22.4, Fig. 28.

16. It would be readily achievable for Defendants to remove some or all of the barriers to access. Moreover, Defendants could have feasibly made some or all of the altered areas accessible during renovations.

17. Defendants have failed to remove some or all of the barriers to access. Despite recent renovations to some or all of the areas containing these barriers to access, Defendants failed to make the altered portions of the Hotel readily accessible to maximum extent feasible and failed to ensure that the paths of travel to the altered areas were readily accessible to the maximum extent feasible.

Claim for Relief

18. Plaintiff repeats and realleges the allegations set forth in Paragraphs 1 through 17 of this Complaint as if fully set forth in this paragraph.

19. The ADA Standards for Accessible Design, 28 C.F.R. Part 36, App. D, provides the standards for determining whether a public accommodation is accessible in compliance with the ADA.

20. Numerous violations of the ADA Standards for Accessible Design exist within the Gramercy Park Hotel that prevent or restrict access to the Gramercy Park Hotel by individuals with disabilities. The Gramercy Park Hotel's services, features, elements and spaces are not readily accessible to, or usable by, individuals with disabilities, as specified by the Regulations promulgated under the ADA. *See* Standards for Accessible Design, 28 C.F.R. Part 36, App. A.

21. By failing to remove barriers to access, and by failing to bring the Gramercy Park Hotel into compliance with the Standards where it is readily achievable to do so, Defendants

have discriminated against individuals with disabilities in violation of sections 302(a) and 302(b)(2)(A)(iv) of the ADA, 42 U.S.C. § 12182(a), (b)(2)(A)(iv), and in violation of 28 C.F.R. § 36.304.

22. Defendants' failure to remove barriers to access, and Defendants' failure to bring the Gramercy Park Hotel into compliance with the Standards where it is readily achievable to do so, constitutes a pattern or practice of discrimination within the meaning of 42 U.S.C. § 12188(b)(1)(B)(i) and 28 C.F.R. § 503(a).

23. Defendants' failure, in the course of making alterations, to ensure that the altered portions of the facility are readily accessible to the maximum extent feasible, *see* 28 C.F.R. § 36.402; and failure to ensure that the paths of travel to, and the restrooms, telephones, and drinking fountains serving, altered primary function areas are readily accessible to the maximum extent feasible, *see* 28 C.F.R. § 36.403, constitutes a pattern or practice of discrimination within the meaning of 42 U.S.C. § 12188(b)(1)(B)(i) and 28 C.F.R. § 503(a).

24. Defendants' failure to remove barriers to access, and Defendants' failure to bring the Gramercy Park Hotel into compliance with the Standards where it is readily achievable to do so, constitutes unlawful discrimination that raises an issue of general public importance within the meaning of 42 U.S.C. § 12188(b)(1)(B)(ii) and 28 C.F.R. § 36.503(b).

25. Defendants acted willfully and with reckless disregard for the rights of individuals with disabilities by engaging in the conduct described above, including by falsely promising the United States Attorney that the Gramercy Park Hotel would remove barriers to access during the renovation of the Hotel, and by engaging in renovation that both failed to remove barriers to access and created new barriers to access.

Prayer for Relief

WHEREFORE, the United States of America prays that this Court enter judgment:

A. Declaring that Defendants have violated Title III of the ADA and its implementing Regulations;

B. Ordering Defendants to remove all violations of Title III of the ADA, including, but not limited to, the violations set forth above;

C. Awarding monetary damages to the aggrieved complainant to compensate him for the discrimination he received as authorized by 42 U.S.C. § 12188(b)(2)(B); 28 C.F.R. § 36.504(a)(2);

D. Assessing a civil penalty against Defendants as authorized by 42 U.S.C. § 12188(b)(2)(C); 28 C.F.R. § 36.504(a)(3), in an amount sufficient to vindicate the public interest; and

E. Granting such other relief as the interests of justice may require.

Dated: New York, New York
September 2, 2011

ERIC H. HOLDER
Attorney General

By: [signature]
THOMAS E. PEREZ
Assistant Attorney General
Civil Rights Division

PREET BHARARA
United States Attorney for the
Southern District of New York

By: [signature]
BRIAN M. FELDMAN
Assistant United States Attorney
86 Chambers Street, 3rd Fl.
New York, New York 10007
Tel.: (212) 637-2777
Fax: (212) 637-2717

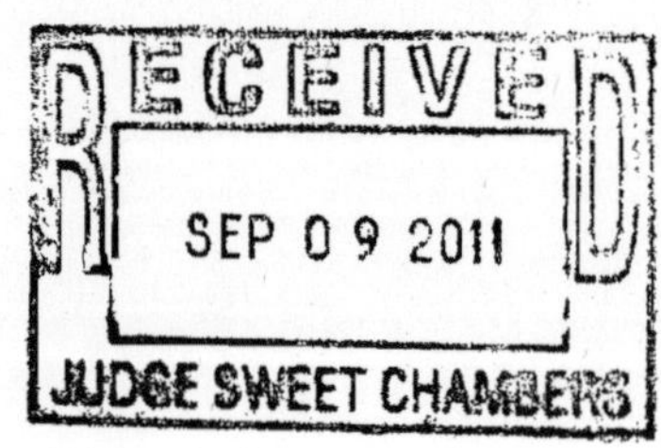

UNITED STATES DISTRICT COURT
SOUTHERN DISTRICT OF NEW YORK

UNITED STATES OF AMERICA,

Plaintiff,

-against-

GPH MANAGEMENT, LLC, as owner of THE GRAMERCY PARK HOTEL, and RFR HOTEL GROUP, LLC, as operator of THE GRAMERCY PARK HOTEL,

Defendants.

CONSENT DECREE

11 Civ. 6238

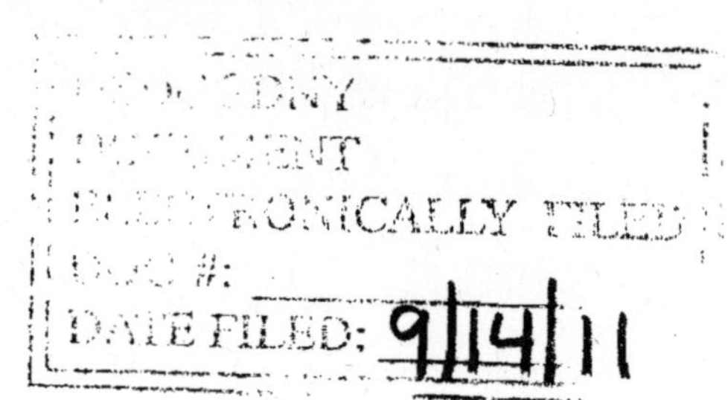

WHEREAS, Plaintiff United States of America (the "Government") commenced this action to enforce the Americans with Disabilities Act of 1990 (the "ADA") against Defendants GPH Management, LLC ("GPH Management"), and RFR Hotel Group, LLC (the "RFR Hotel Group") (collectively, "Defendants"), pursuant to 42 U.S.C. § 12188(b)(1)(B), with respect to the Gramercy Park Hotel, a hotel located at 2 Lexington Avenue, New York, New York 10010 (the "Hotel");

WHEREAS, the complaint alleges that Defendants and/or their predecessors violated Title III of the ADA, 42 U.S.C. §§ 12181-89, and the Department of Justice's implementing regulations, 28 C.F.R. Pt. 36, by, among other things, failing to make alterations in such a manner that, to the maximum extent feasible, the altered portions of the Hotel are readily accessible to and usable by individuals with disabilities; failing to remove architectural barriers to access where it is readily achievable to do so; failing to use readily achievable alternatives to barrier removal where barrier removal is not readily achievable; and by failing to reasonably modify policies, practices, and procedures to make the goods and services offered at the Hotel accessible to individuals with disabilities;

WHEREAS, the commencement of this action by the Government follows an investigation by the United States Department of Justice into a complaint filed by an individual (the "Aggrieved Party") who alleged that the Hotel violated the ADA by failing to accommodate his needs as a hearing impaired guest during visits to the Hotel in May 1996 and May 2004;

WHEREAS, following notification of the Government's investigation, Defendants and/or their predecessors substantially modified and altered the Hotel;

WHEREAS, the Government alleges that such alterations were not made in a manner that, to the maximum extent feasible, the altered portions of the Hotel were readily accessible to and usable by individuals with disabilities;

WHEREAS, Defendants have represented that the RFR Hotel Group was not the managing partner of GPH Management at the time such modifications and alterations were made, and that the RFR Hotel Group did not oversee those modifications and alterations;

WHEREAS, Defendants deny liability for any violation of Title III of the ADA with respect to the Hotel, and have consented to the entry of this Consent Decree without trial or adjudication of any issues of fact or law and without this Consent Decree constituting an admission by Defendants with respect to any such issue of fact or law; and

WHEREAS, the Government and Defendants agree that settlement of these matters without further litigation is in the public interest and that the entry of this Consent Decree is the most appropriate means of resolving these matters;

NOW, THEREFORE, IT IS ORDERED, ADJUDGED AND DECREED as follows:

I. JURISDICTION AND VENUE

1. This Court has jurisdiction over this action pursuant to 42 U.S.C. § 12188(b)(1)(B) and 42 U.S.C. §§ 1331 and 1345.

2. Venue lies in the Southern District of New York pursuant to 28 U.S.C. § 1391(b) because the Hotel is located within this District and the acts of discrimination alleged in the complaint in this case occurred in this District.

II. APPLICATION AND PARTIES BOUND

3. This Consent Decree shall be binding on Defendants, their agents, and their employees. This Consent Decree shall also be binding on all of Defendants' successors, and as well as any person or entity carrying on the same or similar use of the Hotel. Defendants must promptly notify, in writing, all successors, as well as any other persons or entities carrying on the same or similar use of the Hotel, of the existence of this Consent Decree and its contents.

4. The Hotel is a place of public accommodation within the meaning of 42 U.S.C. § 12181(7) because, among other things, it is "an inn, hotel, motel, or other place of lodging." 42 U.S.C. § 12181(7)(A); *see* 28 C.F.R. § 36.104.

5. Defendants are governed by Title III of the ADA because, as owners and managers of the Hotel, they operate the Hotel, a place of public accommodation. *See* 42 U.S.C. § 12182(a); 28 C.F.R. § 36.104.

III. FACILITIES COVERED BY THIS CONSENT DECREE

6. Except as expressly excluded from this Consent Decree, this Consent Decree shall apply to all public use and common areas within the Hotel, including, but not limited to, the

public entrance to the Hotel, the guest registration desk, the lobby, the public telephones, the public restrooms, the elevators, the units, sleeping rooms, and suites, and all routes into and within the Hotel connecting all such areas. This Consent Decree shall not apply to the private park called Gramercy Park located between Gramercy Park South, Gramercy Park North, Gramercy Park West, and Gramercy Park East.

7. This Consent Decree shall not absolve Defendants or any other person or entity from liability for any violation or potential violation of the ADA concerning any facility or establishment within the Hotel not expressly included within the coverage of this Consent Decree. Nothing in this Consent Decree shall preclude the Government from commencing or continuing any investigation with respect to any facility or establishment not expressly included within the coverage of this Consent Decree, including but not limited to Gramercy Park, and nothing in this Consent Decree shall preclude the Government from commencing a civil action against any person or entity with respect to any facility or establishment of the Hotel not expressly included in this Consent Decree's coverage.

IV. GENERAL INJUNCTIVE RELIEF

8. Defendants shall not discriminate against individuals on the basis of disability in the full and equal enjoyment of the goods, services, facilities, privileges, advantages, or accommodations of the Hotel.

9. Defendants shall provide individuals with disabilities an equal opportunity to benefit from the goods, services, facilities, privileges, advantages, and accommodations of the Hotel.

V. DESIGNATED ACCESSIBLE GUEST ROOMS

10. The Hotel currently provides eight (8) rooms designated as accessible to persons with mobility impairments (the "Current Eight Designated Mobility Accessible Guest Rooms"), seven (7) of which are Loft Rooms with King Sized Beds, and one (1) of which is a One Bedroom Suite. All of the Current Eight Designated Mobility Accessible Guest Rooms are also designated as accessible to persons with hearing and speech impairments. In addition, the Hotel currently provides six (6) additional rooms that are also designated as accessible to persons with hearing and speech impairments (the "Six Additional Rooms"), each of which is a Loft Room with a King Sized Bed.

11. Defendants shall ensure that, within fifteen (15) months after the date of entry of this Consent Decree, or such later date as the parties may agree to in writing, the Hotel will substitute the following two rooms as designated accessible rooms for any two of the Current Eight Designated Mobility Accessible Guest Rooms: (a) one of the custom luxury suites marketed, as of March 7, 2011, as a "Deluxe Gramercy Suite"; and (b) one of the custom luxury penthouse suites marketed, as of March 7, 2011, as a "Penthouse Suite" (the "Designated Accessible Penthouse Suite"). As a result, the eight (8) rooms designated as accessible to persons with mobility impairments shall be six (6) Loft Rooms with King Sized Beds (the "Final Designated Mobility Accessible Loft Rooms"), one (1) Deluxe Gramercy Suite, and one (1) Penthouse Suite (collectively, the "Final Eight Mobility Accessible Guest Rooms").

12. Defendants shall ensure that the Final Eight Mobility Accessible Guest Rooms comply with the 1991 ADA Accessibility Guidelines for Buildings and Facilities, 28 C.F.R. Pt. 36, App. A (the "Standards"), for designated accessible rooms; provided, however, that, in lieu

of bringing the Designated Accessible Penthouse Suite into compliance with the mobility accessibility provisions of the Standards, the Hotel may bring into compliance with the mobility accessibility provisions of the Standards the One Bedroom Park Suite adjoining the Designated Accessible Penthouse Suite, including the doorway between the adjoining One Bedroom Park Suite and the Designated Accessible Penthouse Suite, so that a guest with a disability who reserves the Designated Accessible Penthouse Suite would be provided, at no additional cost, with a reservation of both the Designated Accessible Penthouse Suite and the adjoining One Bedroom Park Suite; and, if the Hotel so modifies the adjoining One Bedroom Park Suite, the Defendants shall have no obligation to modify any aspect of the Designated Accessible Penthouse Suite to comply with the mobility accessibility provisions of the Standards, except for its obligation to modify the doorway between the One Bedroom Park Suite and the Designated Accessible Penthouse Suite to ensure compliance with the mobility accessibility provisions of the Standards.

13. Defendants shall ensure that the Final Eight Mobility Accessible Guest Rooms, the Six Additional Rooms, and at least five other rooms (which are to be modified within eleven (11) months of entry of this Consent Decree, or such other date as the parties may agree to in writing) are accessible to persons with hearing and speech impairments by providing visual alarms, notification devices, and a TDD machine for each room, in accordance with Sections 9.1 and 9.3 of Standards and 28 C.F.R. § 36.303(c)-(d).

14. If the Hotel maintains portable kits to satisfy their obligations set forth in the preceding paragraph, then Defendants shall: (A) in each of the rooms listed in the preceding paragraph, provide an accessible, conspicuously labeled electrical outlet for portable visual

alarm devices that are connected to the Hotel's alarm systems, and provide an unobstructed electrical outlet within four feet of an unobstructed telephone connection for power to a free standing TDD; (B) train all appropriate Hotel reservations, check-in, and front desk staff regarding the room designations, their features and equipment, and the location of the kits; (C) maintain visual alarms, notification devices, and TDD machines in good working condition, by, among other things, acquiring appropriate contracts for service, maintenance, and proper repair of the telephone; and (D) install signs at the registration desk informing persons who are deaf, hard of hearing, or who have speech impairments of the availability of the TDD at the registration desk and in the guest rooms equipped for persons who are deaf, hard of hearing, or who have speech impairments.

VI. REMOVAL OF BARRIERS

15. Defendants shall comply with their obligations to remove barriers under the ADA and pursuant to paragraphs 8 and 9 of this Consent Decree by removing barriers to access to and within the Hotel in the manner set forth below:

A. Lobby Telephone(s)

16. Within six months of the entry of this Consent Decree, or such other date as the parties agree to in writing, Defendants shall ensure that there is at least one telephone in the Hotel lobby that is hearing aid compatible, in accordance with Sections 9.1.1, 4.1.3(17)(a), and 4.31.5(1) of the Standards, and which is equipped with volume control capable of a minimum of 12 dbA and a maximum of 18 dbA above normal.

17. If Defendants provide any additional telephones in the Hotel lobby, at least one other telephone, in addition to the one hearing aid compatible telephone required by the

preceding paragraph, shall be equipped with volume control capable of a minimum of 12 dbA and a maximum of 18 dbA above normal.

B. The Designated Accessible Loft Rooms

18. Within eleven (11) months of the entry of this Consent Decree, or such other date as the parties agree to in writing, Defendants shall modify the Final Designated Mobility Accessible Loft Rooms as follows:

a. Defendants shall provide room number signs with a non-glare finish and characters and symbols that contrast with their background;

b. Defendants shall provide a minimum maneuvering clearance of 18 inches on the latch side of the entry door for a forward pull approach;

c. Defendants shall lower the thermostats so that they are no higher than 54 inches above the floor;

d. Defendants shall ensure that closet rods are provided that are no higher than 54 inches above the floor;

e. Defendants shall replace the hardware on the armoire door with hardware that does not require tight pinching to operate;

f. Defendants shall modify the thresholds within bathrooms so that they are no higher than half an inch and beveled with a slope no greater than 1:2;

g. Defendants shall provide at least 56 inches of clear space around the toilet, in accordance with Sections 9.2.2(6)(e), 4.23.4, 4.16.2, and Figure 28 of the Standards.

h. Defendants shall provide fixed, folding seats in roll-in showers and bathtubs; and

i. Defendants shall modify roll-in showers to provide a depth of at least 30 inches;

j. Defendants shall adjust the low back wall grab bar to exactly nine inches above the tub rim.

C. Non-Designated Accessible Guest Room Doorways

19. Within fifteen (15) months of the entry of this Consent Decree, or such other date as the parties agree to in writing, Defendants shall ensure that the following doors and doorways have a minimum clear opening of 32 inches: (1) all doors and doorways into and within all Hotel guest rooms, to the extent that the frames of such doors and doorways have been altered since January 26, 1992, and (2) all other Hotel doors or doorways required to be accessible by Section 4.1 of the Standards.

D. Hotel Entrance

20. Within six (6) months of the entry of this Consent Decree, or such other date as the parties agree to in writing, Defendants shall provide, at the Hotel's main entrance, directional signage indicating the route to the nearest accessible entrance. Such signage must be identified with the International Symbol of Accessibility.

21. Within six (6) months of the entry of this Consent Decree, or such other date as the parties agree to in writing, Defendants shall adjust the Hotel's main inside entrance door, so that no more than 5 lbs of force is required to open the door.

E. Lobby Level Facilities

22. Within fifteen (15) months of the entry of this Consent Decree, or such other date as the parties agree to in writing, Defendants shall modify the Hotel's lobby level facilities as follows:

a. Defendants shall ensure that four common use toilet rooms are accessible;

b. Defendants shall modify the toilet room signage to provide an equivalent text description below the pictograms;

c. To the extent that Defendants provide any telephones in the lobby, they shall do so in compliance with the Standards.

F. Second Floor Facilities

23. Defendants' current redesign of the Hotel's second floor facilities (which Defendants currently estimate as fifteen (15) months from entry of the Consent Decree) shall ensure that the Hotel's second floor facilities are in full compliance with the Standards. In any event, no later than two years following entry of the Consent Decree, or such other date as the parties agree to in writing, Defendants shall modify the Hotel's second floor facilities, to the extent any such facilities remain, as follows:

a. The water fountain must be a hi-lo water fountain;

b. Defendants shall modify the threshold within the Spa Toilet Room so that it is no higher than half an inch and beveled with a slope no greater than 1:2;

c. Defendants shall modify the toilet centerline within the Spa Toilet Room so that it is 18 inches from the wall;

d. Defendants shall replace the 32-inch grab bar in the Spa Toilet Room with a 36-inch grab bar;

e. Defendants shall replace the Spa Shower Room door with hardware that does not require tight grasping, tight pinching, or twisting of the wrist to operate;

f. Defendants shall provide a clear floor space adjacent to the roll-in shower that is 36 inches wide by 60 inches deep, and which is not obstructed in any way by the shower partition;

g. Defendants shall provide a grab bar along the entire length of the back shower wall;

h. Defendants shall lower the height of the closet shelves and closet rods within the storage space in the Park Room East so that they are no greater than 54 inches above the floor;

i. Defendants shall provide a minimum of 48 inches in width of clear floor space in the Unisex Toilet Rooms that is not obstructed by the lavatory support;

j. Defendants shall replace the 24-inch long rear grab bars in the Unisex Toilet Rooms with 36-inch long rear grab bars; and

k. Defendants shall modify the toilet room signage to provide an equivalent text description below the pictograms.

G. Guest Room Corridors

24. Within six (6) months of the entry of this Consent Decree, or such other date as the parties agree to in writing, Defendants shall modify the Hotel guest room corridors as follows:

a. Defendants shall provide room number signs with a non-glare finish and characters and symbols that contrast with their background; and

b. Defendants shall provide cane detectable barriers below the alarm control devices, in accordance with Section 4.4 and Figure 8 of the Standards.

H. Roof Club and Gardens

25. Defendants' current redesign of the Hotel's roof top facilities (which Defendants currently estimate as fifteen (15) months from entry of the Consent Decree) shall ensure that the Hotel's roof top facilities are in full compliance with the Standards. In any event, no later than two years following entry of the Consent Decree, or such other date as the parties agree to in writing, Defendants shall modify the Hotel's roof top facilities, to the extent any such facilities remain, as follows:

a. Defendants shall provide a curb ramp, ramp, or platform lift, in accordance with Section 4.3.8 of the Standards, for the route between the Roof Club Meeting and Reception Rooms and the Gardens;

b. Defendants shall provide a cane detectable barrier below the reception room counter, in accordance with Section 4.4 and Figure 8 of the Standards;

c. Defendants shall provide directional signage indicating the route to the accessible toilet room;

d. Defendants shall provide, in the Unisex Toilet Room, either a 60-inch diameter turning space or a T-shaped turning space, as required by the Standards; and

e. Defendants shall modify the position of the toilet in relation to the side wall within the Unisex Toilet Room, so that the toilet centerline is 18 inches from the side wall.

VII. POLICIES AND PROCEDURES

26. Defendants shall implement and enforce a written policy with regard to the ADA compliance at the Hotel. The Hotel's policy shall specify that accessible rooms may be rented to persons who do not have the corresponding disabilities only if all non-accessible rooms in the same class in the Hotel are occupied or reserved. In addition, the Hotel's policy shall specify that persons with disabilities may reserve accessible rooms in the same manner that guests may reserve other rooms. The Hotel shall enforce these policies with respect to all reservation practices under its control. As for reservations taken by entities not controlled by the Hotel, including internet booking engines, the Hotel shall satisfy its obligations under this paragraph by providing such entities with a copy of the Hotel's written policy.

27. Defendants shall ensure that, if a person with a disability requests a room at the Hotel in an advertised or otherwise available price range in which there are no accessible rooms available, that person must be given an accessible guest room in the next higher price range in which an accessible guest room is available. The more expensive guest room must be rented at the price of the room originally requested by the person with a disability.

28. Defendants shall ensure that the Hotel implements and enforces a written policy requiring that it will relocate persons without disabilities who occupy accessible rooms to other rooms in the event that other rooms of the same class become available and a person with a corresponding disability requests an accessible room, and no other accessible rooms are available. This policy shall not apply to the Penthouse, as it is the only room of its class.

29. In addition to the specific requirements set forth in the Consent Decree, Defendants agree to ensure that all accessible features within the Hotel are maintained in operable working condition, within the meaning of 28 C.F.R. § 36.211.

30. Defendants shall implement and enforce a written policy, providing that the Hotel will welcome persons with disabilities accompanied by service animals, as required by 42 U.S.C. § 12182(b)(2)(A)(iii), and 28 C.F.R. §§ 36.201 and 36.302 (2011).

VIII. TRAINING

31. Defendants shall ensure that all staff members at the Hotel are trained in all ADA issues relevant to the Hotel, including, but not limited to: (1) the location and type of accessible guest rooms; (2) accessible features within each accessible room; (3) the location and use of accessible equipment, such as TDD machines, visual alarms, and notification devices; (4) all Hotel reservations polices and other policies regarding visitors with disabilities or accessible features; (5) the Hotel's service animal policy; and (6) all other requirements of this Consent Decree.

32. Defendants agree to take measures to ensure that employees of the Hotel comply with the obligations in the Consent Decree and shall use all of their powers to do so, including, but not limited to, using personnel actions, reprimands, or terminations of employment, to

address instances where an employee violates, or causes a failure to comply with, this Consent Decree.

IX. DAMAGES AND CIVIL PENALTIES

33. Defendants shall pay ten thousand dollars ($10,000.00) in full and final settlement and satisfaction of any and all claims brought by the Government for monetary damages on behalf of the Aggrieved Party identified in Defendants' letter to the Government, dated March 21, 2005. Payment shall be made within thirty (30) days after the date of entry of this Consent Decree by check payable to the name of the Aggrieved Party. Such check shall be delivered to the following address:

United States Attorney's Office
Southern District of New York
86 Chambers Street, 3rd Floor
New York, NY 10007
Attention: Chief, Civil Rights Unit

34. Defendants shall pay twenty thousand dollars ($20,000.00) in full and final settlement and satisfaction of any and all claims asserted by the Government in this action for civil penalties. Payment shall be made within thirty (30) days after the date of entry of this Consent Decree by check payable to the United States Department of Justice. Such check shall be delivered to the address specified in the preceding paragraph.

X. CERTIFICATION

35. One (1) month after the expiration of each of the various time frames specified in this Consent Decree, Defendants shall submit to the Government a certification, under penalty of perjury, stating that they have complied with all obligations of this Consent Decree that are required to be satisfied or completed at that time.

XI. RIGHT TO REVIEW COMPLIANCE

36. The Government may review compliance with this Consent Decree at any time. Upon reasonable advance notice to Defendants (through undersigned counsel), Defendants shall permit the Government and any person acting on its behalf unlimited access to the Hotel to review compliance with the ADA and this Consent Decree, provided that such access does not interfere with the comfort, privacy or safety of the guests at the Hotel, or unreasonably interfere with the management and operation of the Hotel. If the Government believes that Defendants have violated this Consent Decree or are otherwise not in full compliance with the ADA, the Government will notify Defendants in writing and seek to resolve the matter amicably before applying to the Court for relief. Failure by the Government to enforce any provision or deadline of this Consent Decree shall not be construed as a waiver of its right to enforce other provisions or deadlines of this Consent Decree.

XII. ALTERATIONS

37. Defendants agree that any alteration to the Hotel shall comply with the Standards to the maximum extent feasible, pursuant to 28 C.F.R. § 36.402. Defendants further acknowledge and agree that if an alteration affects or could affect the usability of or access to an area of the Hotel that contains a primary function, that alteration shall be made so as to ensure that, to the maximum extent feasible, the path of travel to the altered area and the restrooms, telephones, and drinking fountain serving the altered area are readily accessible to and usable by individuals with disabilities, including individuals who use wheelchairs, unless the cost and scope of such alterations is disproportionate to the cost of the overall alteration. In addition to the written notifications required herein, Defendants shall, on each anniversary date of this

Consent Decree, provide a written report to counsel for the United States of any alterations to the Hotel during the term of this Consent Decree commenced during the preceding calendar year and shall, in that notification, specify the steps taken to ensure that the alterations comply with the Standards to the maximum extent feasible.

XIII. VIOLATION OF THIS CONSENT DECREE

38. A violation of this Consent Decree shall be deemed a subsequent violation of the ADA under 42 U.S.C. § 12188(b)(2)(C); 28 C.F.R. § 36.404(a)(3).

XIV. MODIFICATION

39. There shall be no modification of this Consent Decree without the written consent of the Government and Defendants and the approval of the Court; provided, however, that the parties may agree in writing to extend the time frames specified in this Consent Decree (with the exception of the time frame specified in Part XVI).

XV. ENTIRE AGREEMENT

40. This Consent Decree represents the entire agreement between the Government and Defendants. No prior agreements, oral representations or statements shall be considered part of this Consent Decree.

XVI. RETENTION OF JURISDICTION

41. This Court shall retain jurisdiction of this action for a period of three (3) years from the date of the certification required by paragraph 35 of this Consent Decree to enforce or modify the provisions of this Consent Decree, to resolve any dispute that arises under this Consent Decree, and to entertain any application and issue any orders (including, without

limitation, orders directing the modification of policies, practices, and procedures, and orders requiring the removal of barriers to access) as may be necessary or appropriate for the effectuation of its terms. The parties shall discuss and attempt to negotiate a resolution of any dispute relating to the interpretation or enforcement of this Consent Decree before bringing the matter to the Court's attention for resolution.

XVII. EXECUTION OF CONSENT DECREE

42. This Consent Decree may be executed in counterparts, each of which shall be an original and shall constitute one and the same instrument.

XVIII. COSTS AND ATTORNEYS' FEES

43. All parties shall bear their own costs and attorneys' fees in this action.

THE PARTIES HEREBY CONSENT to entry of the foregoing Consent Decree:

Dated: New York, New York
September 2, 2011

PREET BHARARA
United States Attorney for the
Southern District of New York
Attorney for the United States of America

By: ______________________
BRIAN M. FELDMAN
Assistant United States Attorney
86 Chambers Street, 3rd Floor
New York, New York 10007
Telephone No. (212) 637-2777
Facsimile No. (212) 637-2717
Brian.Feldman@usdoj.gov

Dated: New York, New York
September 8, 2011

McDERMOTT WILL & EMERY
Attorneys for Defendants GPH Management LLC, and RFR Hotel Group LLC

By: ______________________
BANKS BROWN
340 Madison Avenue
New York, New York 10173-1922
Telephone No. (212) 547-5488
Facsimile No. (212) 547-5444
Bbrown@mwe.com

JUDGMENT IS HEREBY ENTERED in accordance with the foregoing Consent Decree.

Dated: New York, New York
9/14, 2011

UNITED STATES DISTRICT JUDGE

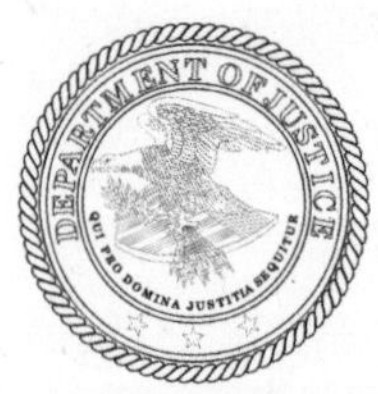

United States Attorney
Southern District of New York

FOR IMMEDIATE RELEASE
SEPTEMBER 15, 2011

CONTACT: U.S. ATTORNEY'S OFFICE
ELLEN DAVIS, CARLY SULLIVAN,
JERIKA RICHARDSON
PUBLIC INFORMATION OFFICE
(212) 637-2600

MANHATTAN U.S. ATTORNEY SETTLES CIVIL RIGHTS LAWSUIT AGAINST GRAMERCY PARK HOTEL

PREET BHARARA, the United States Attorney for the Southern District of New York, announced that the United States has filed, and simultaneously settled, a federal civil rights lawsuit alleging that the owners and operators of the GRAMERCY PARK HOTEL, a historic, luxury hotel in Manhattan, discriminated against persons with disabilities and repeatedly violated the Americans with Disabilities Act of 1990 ("ADA"). As part of the settlement, the hotel owner, GPH MANAGEMENT, LLC, and operator, RFR HOTEL GROUP, LLC, agreed to remove barriers that impeded the accessibility of the hotel, to change hotel policies to benefit persons with disabilities, and to pay penalties. The settlement agreement, in the form of a consent decree, was approved late yesterday by U.S. District Judge ROBERT W. SWEET.

Manhattan U.S. Attorney PREET BHARARA stated: "New York City hosts millions of visitors each year, and it is essential that our hotels are open and accessible to all. This agreement helps ensure that individuals with disabilities will have the same access to hotel accommodations that are enjoyed by others."

According to the Complaint filed September 7, 2011, in Manhattan federal court:

The GRAMERCY PARK HOTEL, located at 2 Lexington Avenue in Manhattan, repeatedly violated the ADA and discriminated against persons with disabilities by refusing to accommodate the needs of a guest with a hearing impairment, failing to remove barriers to access, and renovating the hotel in violation of the ADA.

On two separate occasions, a hotel guest, who described himself as "profoundly deaf," was denied communications devices that the hotel was required to maintain under federal law. The Complaint also alleges that the hotel contains numerous barriers to access, including the design and layout of the entrances, interiors, and bathrooms of the guest rooms the Hotel itself

and lobby, the Hotel's spa, andthe Hotel's roof club and
In addition, the best rooms in the hotel, including the penthouse and Gramercy Suites, are inaccessible to persons with disabilities.

According to the Complaint, the owners and operators of the GRAMERCY PARK HOTEL represented to the United States that a planned renovation of the hotel would address any ADA violations. However, the renovation failed to correct ADA violations at the hotel and created additional barriers to access.

In the consent decree, the owner and operator of the hotel agreed to, among other things:

- Retrofit luxury suites to ensure that guests with disabilities can rent and access the best rooms in the hotel, including by providing access to the penthouse;

- Maintain sufficient equipment for the benefit of hard of hearing and visually impaired guests; and

- Retrofit the lobby, entrance, ADA designated guest rooms, hotel facilities, roof, and gardens to comply with the ADA.

As part of the consent decree, the GRAMERCY PARK HOTEL agreed to adopt policies accommodating guests with disabilities, pay $10,000 to compensate a victim of the alleged discrimination, and pay a $20,000 civil penalty to the Government.

The case is being handled by the Office's Civil Rights Unit. Assistant U.S. Attorney DAVID J. KENNEDY is in charge of the case.

11-275 ###

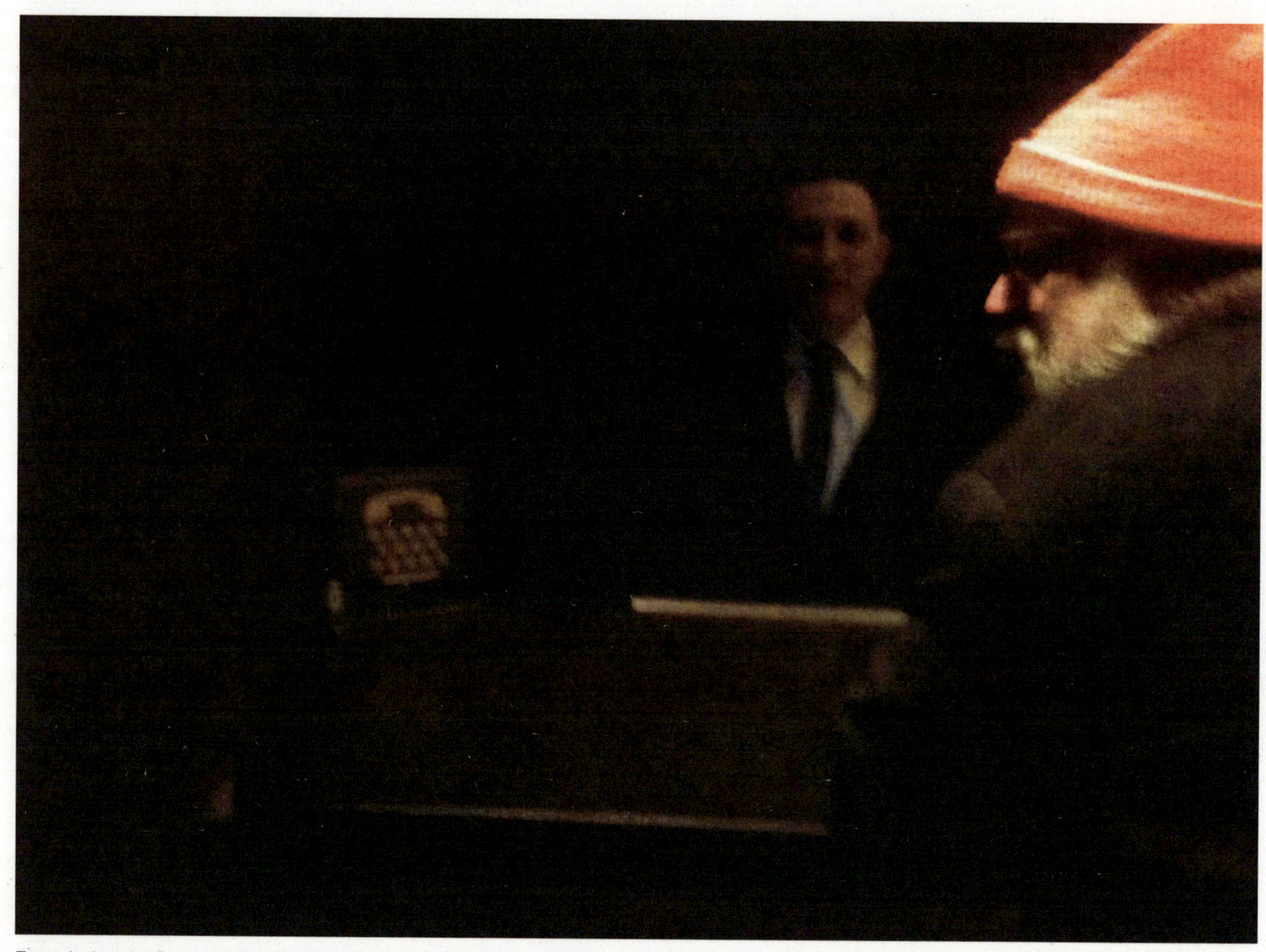

Front desk at the Gramercy Park Hotel, during the pe-opening party of the 2014 Whitney Biennial, March 3, 2014. Photo: Ben Kinmont

Joseph Grigely
1327 West Washington Blvd. #2D, Chicago, Illinois 60607
October 20, 2011

Brian Feldman
Harter Secrest & Emery LLP
1600 Bausch & Lomb Place
Rochester, New York 14606

Dear Brian,

I want to thank you for bringing to a productive conclusion the case of USA v. Gramercy Park Hotel. The outcome was some time in coming, from the first gesture of discrimination on the part of GPH in 1996, to the Consent Decree in 2011, 15 years is a long time.

But worth waiting for.

As you always told me, and as I gradually came to understand, the office of the Attorney General represents the United States of America, not me personally; but since the USA is not likely to notice the outcome of this case, much less thank you for it, I want to personally express to you my appreciation for your work. Thank you.

Sincerely,

Joseph Grigely

ADA Complaint Against Various Graduate Schools Requiring Voice Telephone Numbers as Part of the Process of Submitting Letters of Recommendation, 2011

As a college professor, I typically spend time writing letters of recommendation for undergraduate students who are applying to graduate school. Although it seems onerous, it's actually very satisfying, in part because I've been lucky to have so many smart, imaginative, and caring students over the years. Writing recommendations for them is actually a pleasure.

What's often not a pleasure is when I try to submit the recommendation and get an auto-notice saying that I need to include a phone number or the recommendation cannot be sent. The entire process assumes that everyone writing a recommendation is hearing—as if there are no deaf people in higher education. The situation is not very different from long-standing examples of institutional discrimination: It presumes homogenous bodies are the only bodies that write recommendation letters. While the issue might on its surface appear like just another form of glitchy bureaucracy, it's exactly this type of stereotyping that makes it so troubling. Whenever I fill out an automated form—for a recommendation letter, for a plane ticket—I am constantly reminded that I am deaf and that my deafness does not fit into paradigms of normalcy.

Joseph Grigely
Department of Visual & Critical Studies
The School of the Art Institute of Chicago
112 South Michigan Avenue
Chicago Illinois 60603

15 December 2011

U.S. Department of Justice
950 Pennsylvania Avenue, NW
Civil Rights Division
Disability Rights - NYAVE
Washington, D.C. 20530

I am writing to file a Title III complaint of discrimination against the graduate schools and the companies that manage their application process, cited below. My complaint is based on the fact that the process of submitting graduate school application recommendations for the students requires a telephone number, and that the online process required for recommendations only accepts numbers. In a numbers-only field, one cannot write down "TDD" or cannot write down "no phone I am deaf--please use email to contact." More problematic is that the process will not permit a recommender to submit the recommendation for a student UNLESS a voice phone number is given. A recommendation without a voice number flagged as being "incomplete." Therefore, unless one provides a voice number, one cannot submit a recommendation, and this discriminates against recommenders who are deaf or cannot use a phone.

Between November 26 and December 15, I attempted to submit recommendations on behalf of two of my students to the following schools: New York University, Steinhardt School of Culture, Education, and Human Development; Emory University, Laney Graduate School; and Harvard University, the Graduate School of Arts and Sciences. The process of managing the submission of recommendations was through two online admissions service providers: Embark and ApplyWEB. ApplyWEB is a unit of Collegenet.com, which claims over 1300 college and University clients. Embark.com is, according to its website, "a leading provider of online services to help students and schools through the college and graduate admissions process." Both have a large-scale presence in managing the college admissions applications of thousands of schools in the US.

Because each application required a voice number in the form of number only, the systems rejected the submission of my letters of recommendation. Therefore, this complaint names not just Harvard, NYU, and Emory, but also Embark and ApplyWEB.

In each case, I attempted to seek an immediate solution by contacting both the schools involved, and the online service providers. Their responses varied. None of the online service providers offered a constructive response, as one said to me in an email: "the school has created the form with phone number as required field. If you have questions regarding this decision, I would suggest following up directly with the school."

At Emory, the Assistant Dean of Operations, Ulf Nilsson, suggested that I submit my application by using "a fake phone number". This was also suggested by the Customer Service at ApplyWEB.com. It seems ironic that in the matter of submitting a statement based on a factual assessment of my students, I was asked by the institutions to lie in order to submit the assessment. In the end, after several exchanges with Emory's ADA office, the phone field was changed from numbers to permit letters, but it was still only 10 digits long, so I could not write "TDD" with my phone number. They truly do not know what a TDD is at Emory, it seems. So as it is, their process remains inaccessible. Given that Emory has not been particularly accommodating of Title III (as in Barker v. Emory University), I feel there is a question of persistent and repeated discriminatory practices to be addressed here.

At NYU's Steinhardt School I contacted the Graduate Admissions office (but received no reply); I also wrote to the ADA officer, who replied saying they would work on it. I was told to email my letter to the admissions office, which had the adversive affect of breaching the confidentiality of the application process, and singling out unfairly the student for whom I was writing the recommendation.

At Harvard, I emailed the Dean (no reply as of yet). Because the deadline was so short, and not wishing to jeopardize the application of my student, I was forced to put down a false phone number (999-999-9999) in order to submit the letter of recommendation.

In summary: Harvard, Emory, and NYU's Steinhardt school have a process of submitting recommendations that discriminates against deaf people and people who cannot use a phone under Title III of ADA, and this discrimination is both facilitated and condoned by the companies the schools employ to manage the admissions process, Embark and ApplyWEB.

I suggested to all three schools they can do what the University of Chicago does: make the required phone number an "open field" with sufficient character space so one can write down a "TDD" and a TDD number, or write down "no phone, I am deaf--please use email to contact." None of the schools cited in this complaint has implemented this suggestion.

As a deaf person, I find it hard enough, in the matter of everyday life, to negotiate the world of the hearing. When I find discriminatory obstacles like these, I generally make an effort to fix them as politely as I can. But it seems institutions do not want to believe a deaf person, acting as an individual, might be right about something like this--and it's insulting and tiring to be ignored or dismissed. These are not "glitches" (as Emory said to me)--these are clear evidence of a pattern of discrimination that is being committed more than 20 years after the signing of ADA. I therefore encourage the DOJ to expand the reach of the case of National Federation of the Blind v. Law School Admission Council to include the admissions process for graduate schools in the arts & sciences, including, and particularly, the process of submitting letters of recommendation.

Sincerely,

Joseph Grigely, D. Phil.
Professor & Chair
Department of Visual & Critical Studies
The School of the Art Institute of Chicago

Graduate School of Arts and Sciences Dean's Office
Harvard University
1350 Massachusetts Avenue
Holyoke Center 350
Cambridge, MA 02138-3654
telephone: 617-495-1814
facsimile: 617-495-2928
gsaf@fas.harvard.edu

New York University
Steinhardt School of Culture, Education, and Human Development
Office of Graduate Admissions
82 Washington Square East, 3rd Floor
New York, NY 10003
Phone: 212 998 5030
Fax: 212 995 4328
steinhardt.gradadmissions@nyu.edu

Laney Graduate School
Emory University
209 Administration Building
Mailstop 1000-001-1AF
201 Dowman Drive
Atlanta, GA 30322
Phone: 404-727-6028
Fax: 404-727-4990
gradschool-1@listserv.cc.emory.edu

Embark Corporation
1 Embarcadero Center, Suite 500
San Francisco, CA 94111
Phone: 415.773.2858

ApplyWEB
CollegeNET, Inc.
805 SW Broadway
Suite 1600
Portland, OR 97205
tel: 503.973.5200

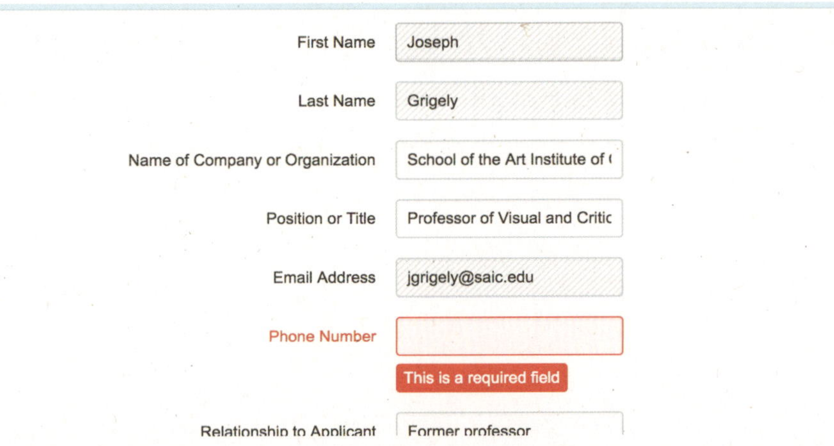

First Name Joseph
Last Name Grigely
Name of Company or Organization School of the Art Institute of (
Position or Title Professor of Visual and Critic
Email Address jgrigely@saic.edu
Phone Number
This is a required field
Relationship to Applicant Former professor

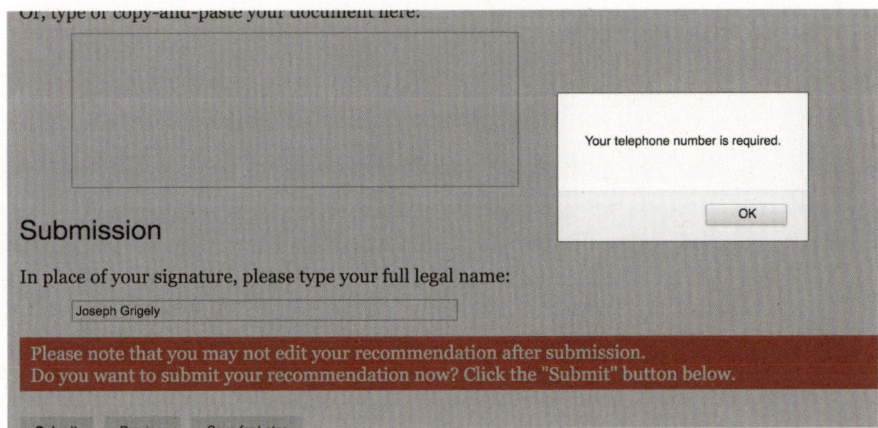

Or, type or copy-and-paste your document here:

Your telephone number is required.
OK

Submission

In place of your signature, please type your full legal name:

Joseph Grigely

Please note that you may not edit your recommendation after submission.
Do you want to submit your recommendation now? Click the "Submit" button below.

Country*
United States

Phone Number*

Email*
jgrigely@artic.edu

Recommendation

TO THE RECOMMENDER: We would appreciate your opinion of this candida
support from) UCLA. The University is particularly interested in an evaluation
achievement. Explicit descriptions of academic strengths and weaknesses a
character, integrity or motivation are also appreciated, if pertinent. The expe
Rankings should be related to other students in the same class or academic
share the contents of this form with the candidate.

Intellectual Ability*
Outstanding

Research Aptitude and Potential *

Screenshots made during the process of submitting online references for students' graduate-school applications

Redacted Nondisclosure Agreement, undated

A nondisclosure agreement, or NDA, summarizes the conditions of a legal settlement by outlining a brief history of the complaint, and the terms under which the two parties agree to bring the complaint to a conclusion. NDAs typically include language stating that there is no admission of liability or guilt; that the two parties essentially agree to end the dispute to cap the cost of ongoing litigation. The dilemma for the plaintiffs is that institutions have larger financial and legal resources than individuals do; so individual plaintiffs are placed in a position of limited leverage. Once they sign an NDA, they cannot speak or write about what occurred without putting themselves at legal risk for breaching the agreement—and, in turn at risk of liability and retaliation.

I also dislike NDAs because they do not serve any useful social purpose for establishing a history of discrimination; they bury that history. While an NDA might include mitigating measures, individual plaintiffs continue to carry the burden of the situation that gave rise to the individual suit, and institutions have the freedom to carry on as if nothing had happened. For this reason, when possible, I try to channel disability discrimination suits through the Department of Justice, where they become a matter of public record. But this is not always possible; the DOJ is either overwhelmed with requests for support, or under administrative directives not to pursue various ADA and Section 504 protections; and one of the few recourses left is a private lawsuit.

Confidential; for settlement purposes only

CONFIDENTIAL SETTLEMENT AGREEMENT AND GENERAL RELEASE

This Confidential Settlement Agreement and General Release ("Agreement") is entered into by and between Joseph Grigely,

WHEREAS, the Parties acknowledge that Grigely has raised certain claims and allegations arising from including but not limited to allegations of disability discrimination, failure to accommodate, retaliation, and emotional distress under the Americans with Disabilities Act, as memorialized in correspondence between the Parties.

now desire to finally resolve, compromise, and settle all claims and disputes arising from

1.

B.

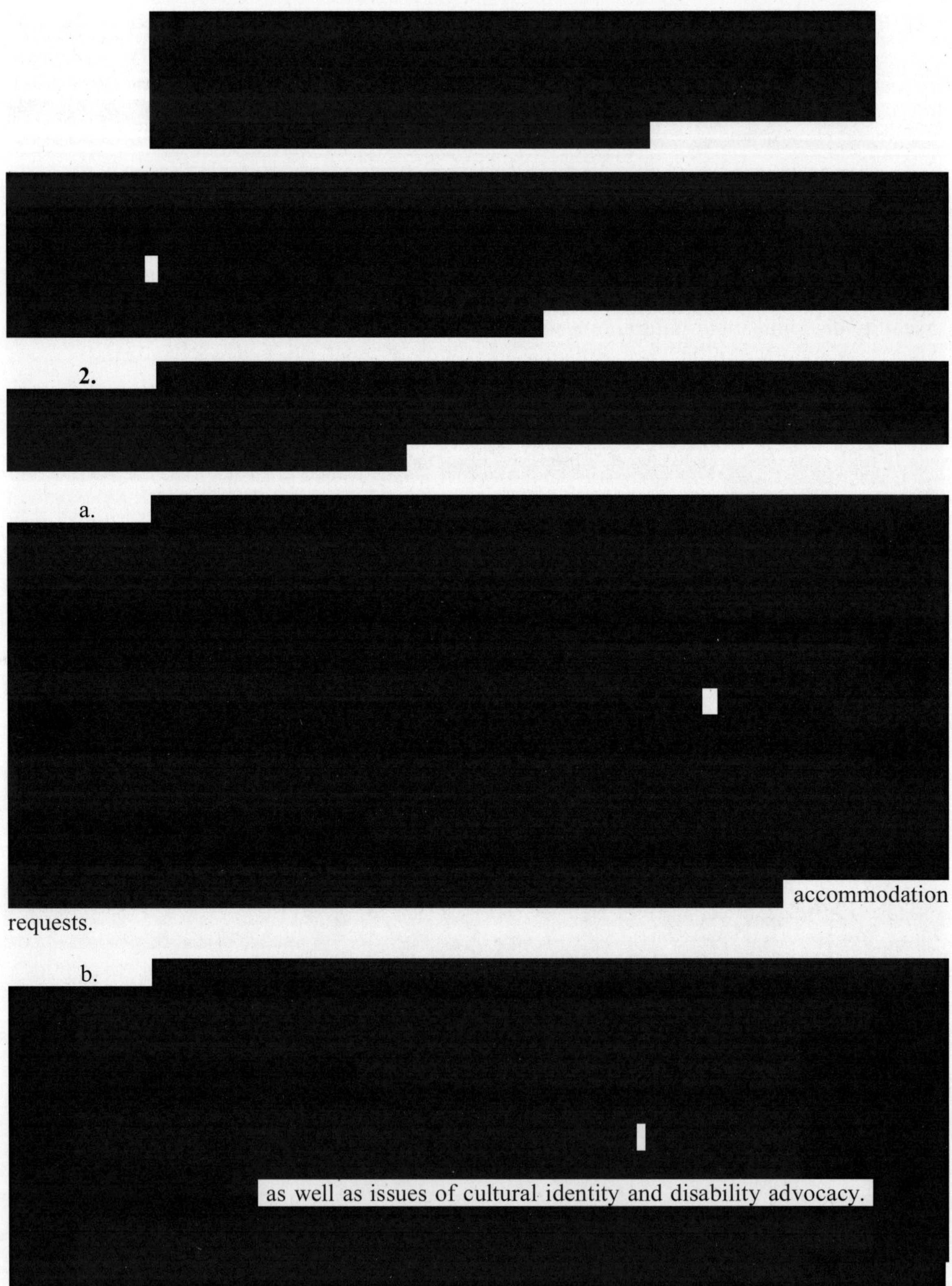

2.

a.

accommodation requests.

b.

as well as issues of cultural identity and disability advocacy.

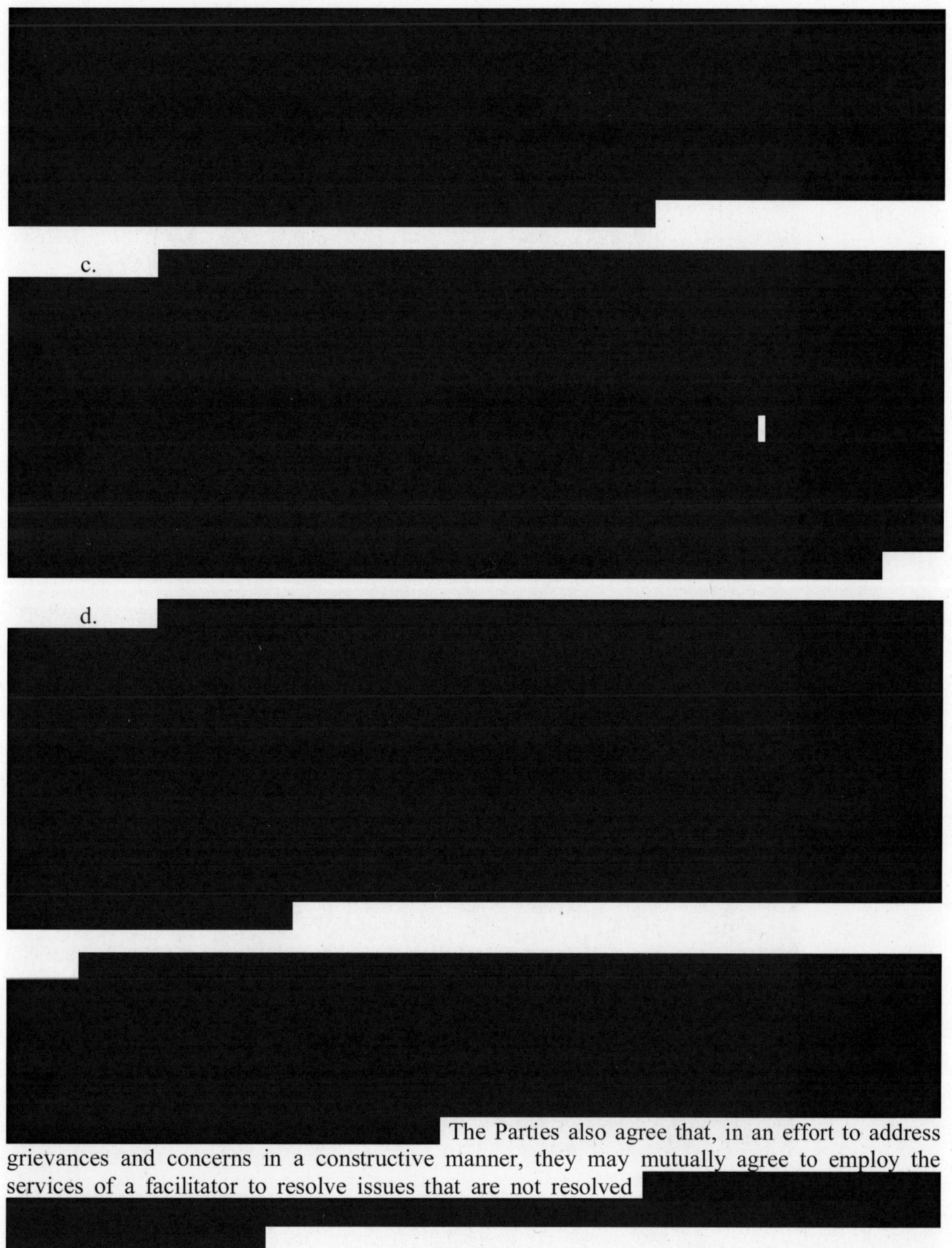

c.

d.

The Parties also agree that, in an effort to address grievances and concerns in a constructive manner, they may mutually agree to employ the services of a facilitator to resolve issues that are not resolved

e.

(ii)

(iii)

g.

(i)

(ii)

h.

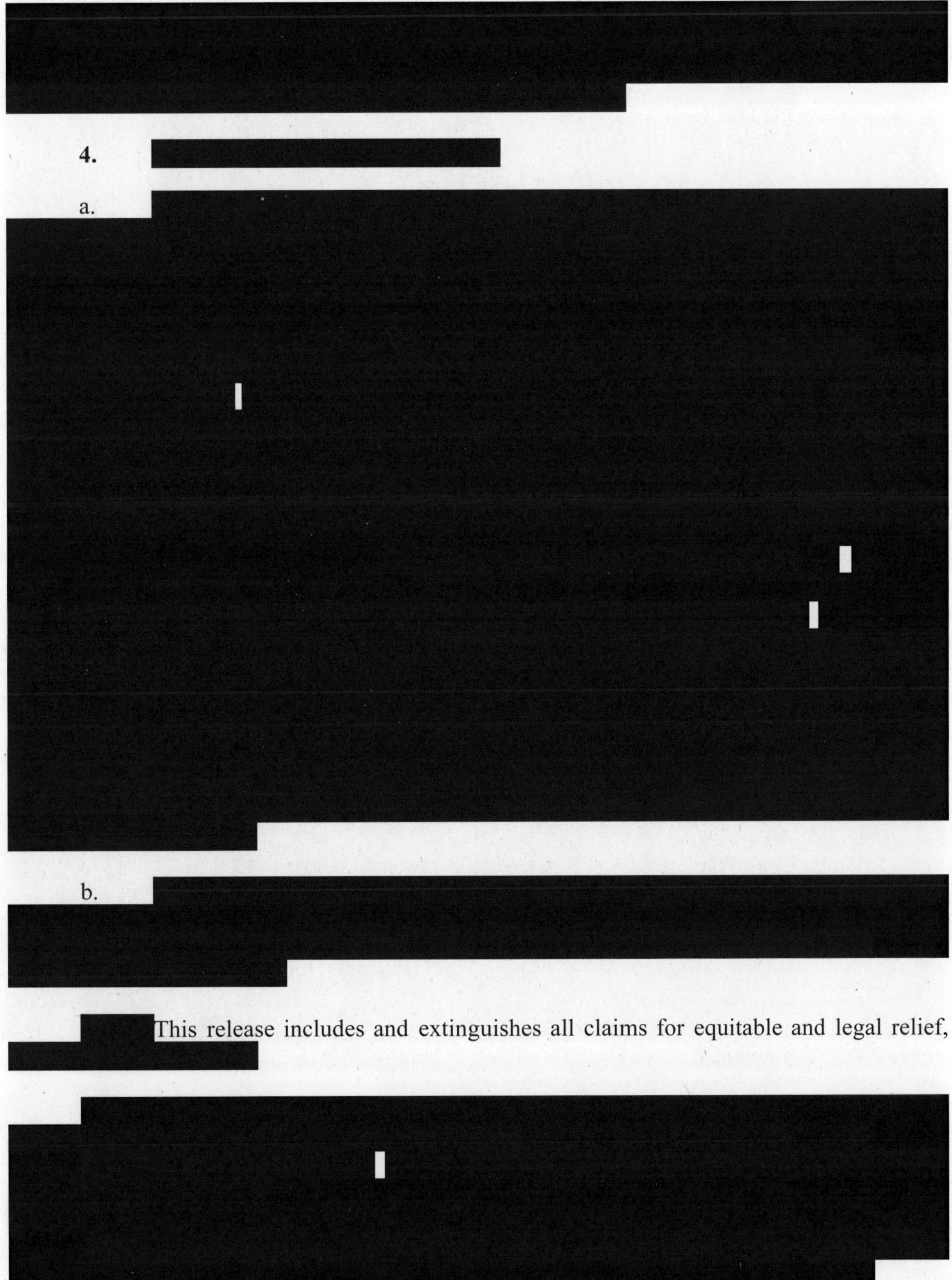

4.

a.

b.

This release includes and extinguishes all claims for equitable and legal relief,

Nothing in this Paragraph constitutes a waiver of Grigely's right to financial recovery from any action for breach of this Agreement.

5.

6.

a.

Grigely shall respond only by stating that "the matter has been resolved."

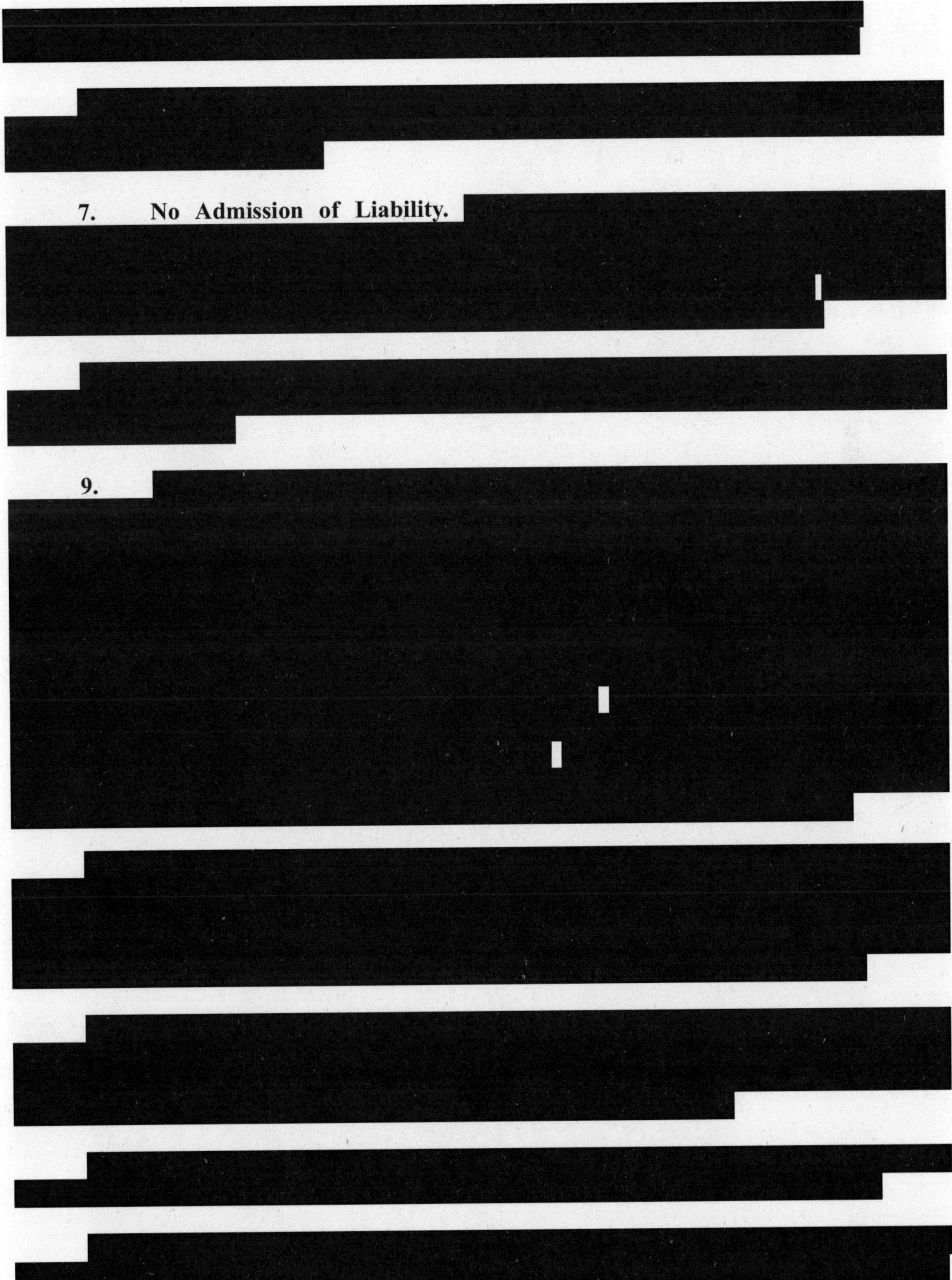

7. No Admission of Liability.

9.

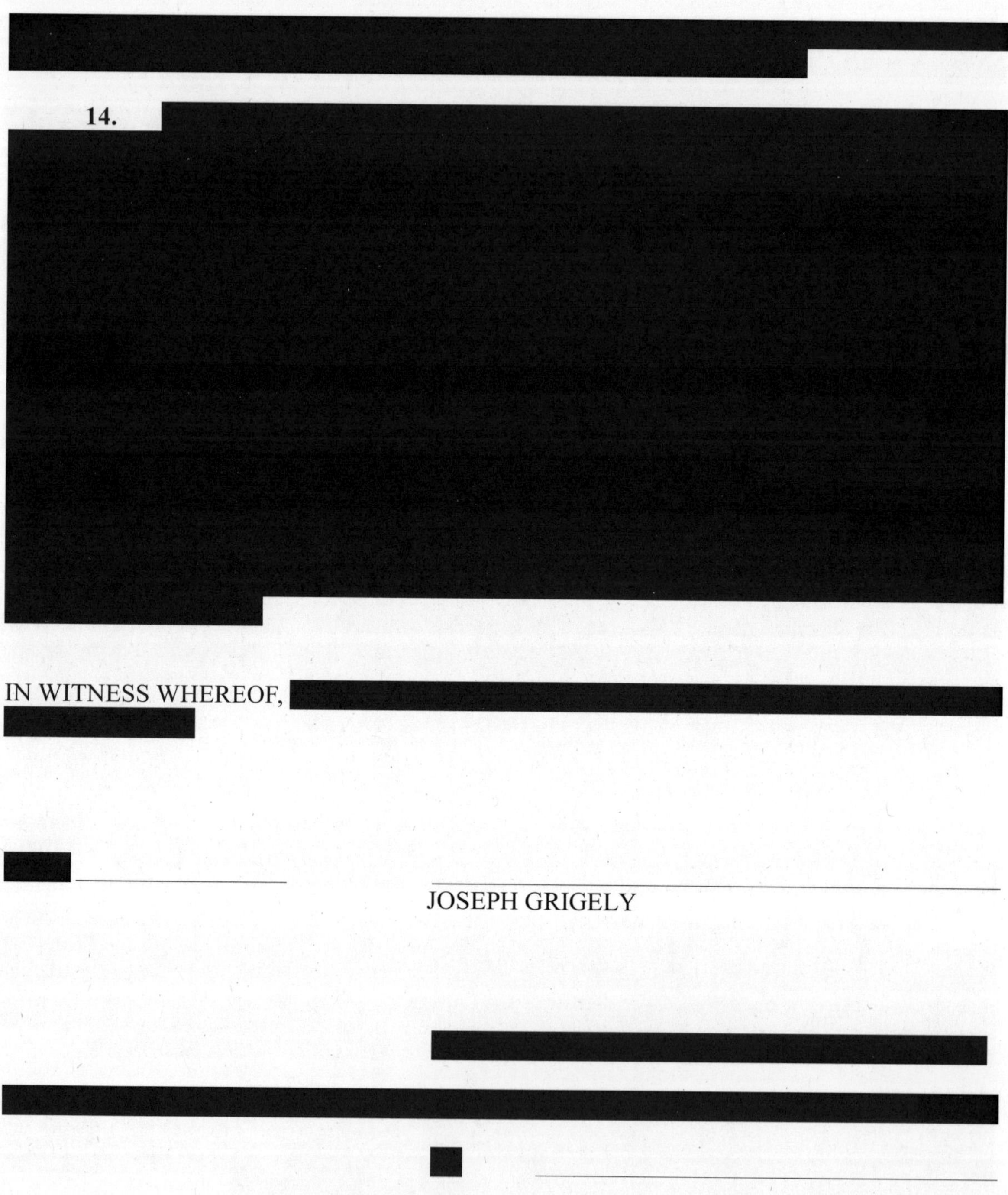

14.

IN WITNESS WHEREOF,

JOSEPH GRIGELY

Ah × DAhr (plus $1) = RP/S: A Formula for Commensurate Payment for Disability Advocacy, 2024

Disability discrimination is not easy to summarize when one tries to equate dignity with dollars. What constitutes a reasonable payment that fairly values the time and energy disabled people spend advocating for access? Sometimes they can spend years—even decades—advocating for change. Disability activists often remark that advocacy is like an unpaid second job. Or maybe it's really a first job—but in any case, it's generally unpaid.

So I have come up with a formula for payment:

Ah × DAhr (plus $1) = RP/S

Where Ah = Advocacy hours (number of hours spent explaining disability and access to institutions); DAhr = Defense Attorney's hourly rate (which is charged to defend institutions against access lawsuits) plus $1; and RP/S = Reasonable Payment/Settlement.

The idea is that time spent advocating for access is worth more than what is spent defending institutions from the responsibility of providing access—and adding $1 to whatever the defense attorneys are being paid (often several hundred dollars per hour) guarantees that the fight for access is worth more than the fight against it. Most disability lawsuits are, in the end, symbolic, in the sense that what is won is usually far less than what is desired, or what might be regarded as meaningfully commensurate to the energy expended, or the harm caused.

Part of the problem is that cases under the Americans with Disabilities Act are limited in a way that civil rights cases are not. ADA cases have a maximum payout of $300,000. When a jury awarded an aggrieved neurodivergent employee $13 million in a disability discrimination case in 2000, a judge reduced the total payout to $300,000, because that's the limit permissible under the ADA. In another case from 2021, when a jury awarded $125 million to a claimant under the ADA, it too was reduced to $300,000. In this respect, the ADA is a bit of a farce.

But that doesn't mean we can't start moving the ground around us—and invoicing institutions at the regular rate of Ah × DAhr (plus $1) whenever we are tasked with providing them personal expertise and knowledge about disability and access. Send them invoices! Making art about changing the world is easy; actually changing the world is a lot harder.

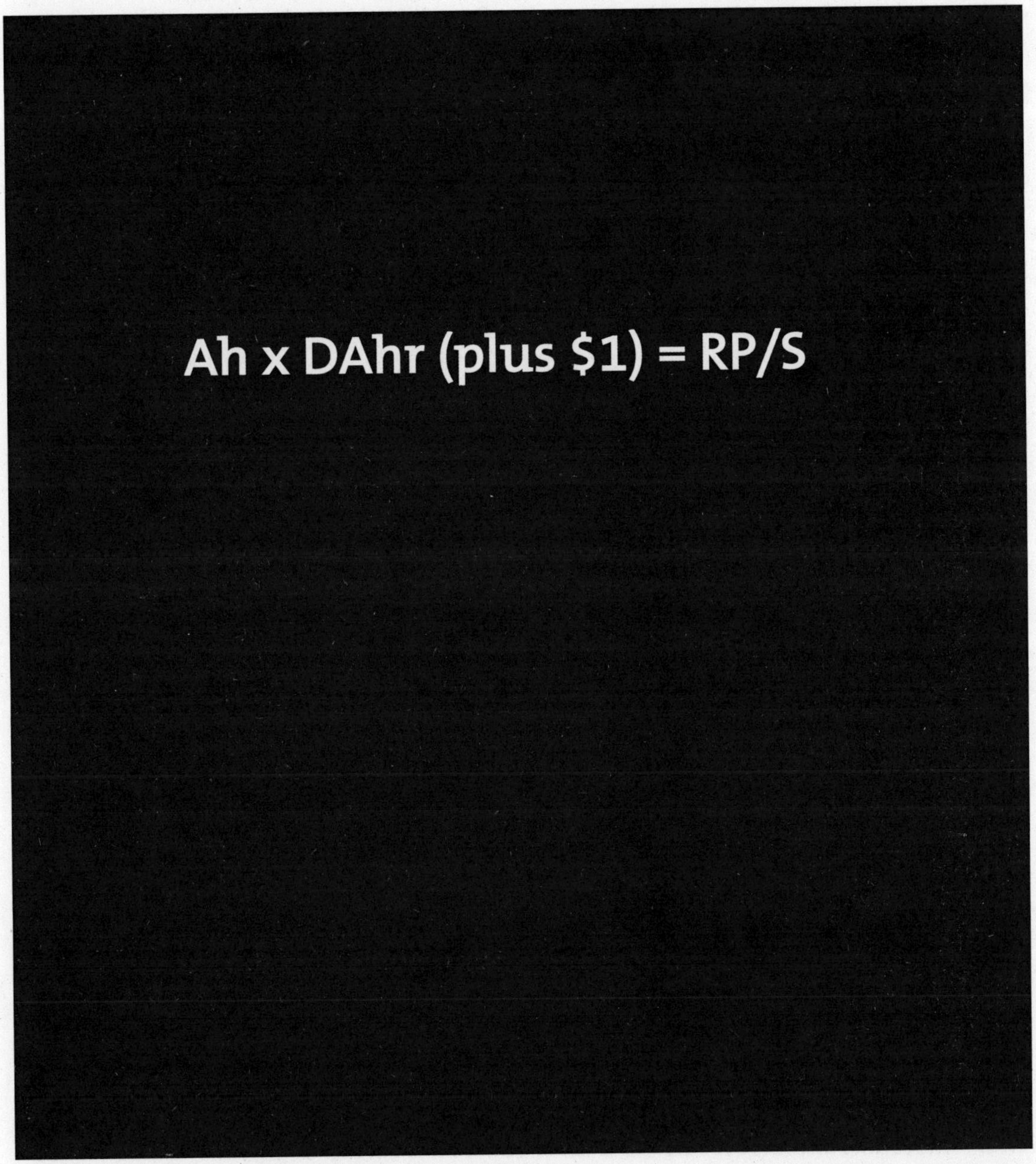

Ah x DAhr (plus \$1) = RP/S

Joseph Grigely, *Ah × DAhr (plus \$1) = RP/S*, 2024. Mixed media

Otherhow: Essays and Documents on Art and Disability 1985–2024

ISBN: 979-8-9910367-1-9

Editor: James Hoff
Editorial Assistance: Ryan Haley and Sam Korman
Designer: Siiri Tännler
Copy Editor: Allison Dubinsky

Primary Information
232 3rd Street, #A113
Brooklyn, NY 11215
www.primaryinformation.org

Printed at Conti Tipocolor, Italy

This book is made possible, in part, with lead support from The Stolbun Family and The Stolbun Collection. Major support is provided by Leah and Andrew Witkin.

Primary Information is a 501(c)(3) non-profit organization founded in 2006 to publish artists' books and writings. The organization's programming advances the often-intertwined relationship between artists' books and arts' activism, creating a platform for historically marginalized artistic communities and practices. The organization receives generous support through grants from the Michael Asher Foundation, Galerie Buchholz, the Patrick and Aimee Butler Family Foundation, The Cowles Charitable Trust, Empty Gallery, The Ford Foundation, The Fox Aarons Foundation, the Helen Frankenthaler Foundation, Furthermore: a program of the J. M. Kaplan Fund, the Graham Foundation for Advanced Studies in the Fine Arts, Greene Naftali, the Greenwich Collection Ltd, the John W. and Clara C. Higgins Foundation, Metabolic Studio, the Mellon Foundation, the New York City Department of Cultural Affairs in partnership with the City Council, the New York State Council on the Arts with the support of the Office of the Governor and the New York State Legislature, the Orbit Fund, the Robert Rauschenberg Foundation, the Stichting Egress Foundation, VIA Art Fund, The Jacques Louis Vidal Charitable Fund, Wagner Foundation, The Andy Warhol Foundation for the Visual Arts, the Wilhelm Family Foundation, and individuals worldwide. Primary Information receives support from the Arison Arts Foundation, The Willem de Kooning Foundation, the Marian Goodman Foundation, the Henry Luce Foundation, the Mellon Foundation, and Teiger Foundation through the Coalition of Small Arts NYC.

Backpiece: Joseph Grigely, *Deaf Child Signs*, 2023. Digital print